Lizensierte Ausgabe für den ADAC Verlag
mit freundlicher Genehmigung der
Automobile Association Developments Limited.

Titelbild: Stonehenge, Wiltshire (britainonview/Martin Brent)

1. Auflage
© Automobile Association Developments Limited

Revised version of the atlas formerly known as *Complete Atlas of Britain*.

Published by AA Publishing (a trading name of Automobile Association
Developments Limited, whose registered office is Fanum House, Basing
View, Basingstoke, Hampshire RG21 4EA, UK. Registered number
1878835).

Mapping produced by the Cartography Department of The Automobile
Association. This atlas has been compiled and produced from the
Automaps database utilising electronic and computer technology
(A02878).

Die abgebildete Kartographie der Innenstadt Londons (Central London)
in diesem Atlas wurde hergestellt von der Abteilung Kartographie der
Automobile Association. Die Schuladressdaten wurden zur Verfügung
gestellt von Education Direct. Die Daten für die Einbahnstraßen wurden
bereit gestellt von ©Tele Atlas N.V. The Post Office ist eine geschützte
Handelsmarke der Post Office Ltd in Großbritannien und anderen
Ländern. Die Informationen zu den Tankstellen wurden zur Verfügung
gestellt von Johnsons. Die Daten zu den Grenzen der Londoner City-
Mautgebührenzone (London Congestion Charging Zone) wurden bereit
gestellt von Transport for London.

ISBN-10: 0 7495 4908 4ISBN-13: 978 0 7495 4908 4

A CIP catalogue record for this book is available from The British Library.

Printed in Italy by Canale & C. S.P.A., Torino

A&E hospitals derived from data supplied by Johnsons.

Information on National Parks in England provided by The Countryside
Agency.

Information on National Nature Reserves in England provided by English
Nature.

Information on National Parks, National Scenic Areas and National
Nature Reserves in Scotland provided by Scottish Natural Heritage.

Information on National Parks and National Nature Reserves in Wales
provided by The Countryside Council for Wales.

Information on Forest Parks provided by the Forestry Commission.

The RSPB sites shown are a selection chosen by the Royal Society for
the Protection of Birds.

National Trust properties shown are a selection of those open to the
public as indicated in the handbooks of the National Trust and the
National Trust for Scotland.

Tyne and Wear metro symbol © Nexus.

RoadPilot® Information on fixed speed camera locations provided by RoadPilot © Copyright RoadPilot® Driving
Technology.

Großbritannien
Great Britain

Inhaltsverzeichnis

Speed camera locations

Speed camera locations provided in association with RoadPilot Ltd

RoadPilot is the developer of one
of the largest and most accurate
databases of speed camera
locations in the UK and Europe*. It
has provided the speed camera
formation in this atlas. RoadPilot is
the UK's pioneer and market leader
in GPS (Global Positioning System)
road safety technologies.

MicroGo (pictured right) is
RoadPilot's latest in-car speed
camera location system. It improves
road safety by alerting you to the
location of accident black spots,

fixed and mobile camera sites.
RoadPilot's MicroGo does not jam
police lasers and is therefore
completely legal. RoadPilot's
database of fixed camera locations
has been compiled with the full
co-operation of regional police
forces and the Safety Camera
Partnerships.

For more information on RoadPilot's
GPS road safety products, please
visit **www.roadpilot.com**
or telephone 0870 240 1701

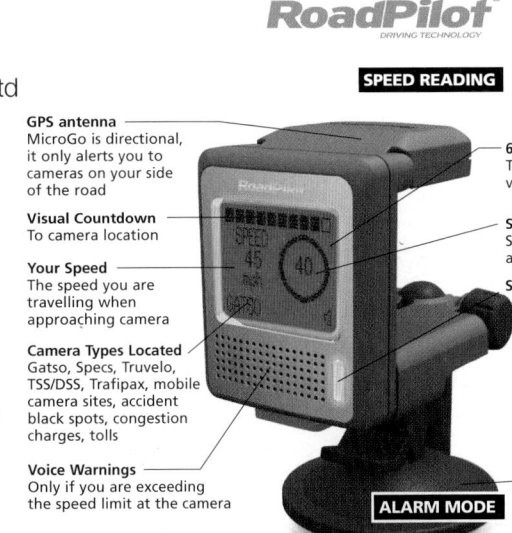

GPS antenna
MicroGo is directional,
it only alerts you to
cameras on your side
of the road

Visual Countdown
To camera location

Your Speed
The speed you are
travelling when
approaching camera

Camera Types Located
Gatso, Specs, Truvelo,
TSS/DSS, Trafipax, mobile
camera sites, accident
black spots, congestion
charges, tolls

Voice Warnings
Only if you are exceeding
the speed limit at the camera

64 Colour Options
To match your
vehicle's illumination

Speed Limit at Camera
Screen turns red as
additional visual alert

Single Button Operation
...for easy access
to speed display,
camera warning,
rescue me location,
trip computer,
compass heading,
congestion charge,
max speed alarm,
date and time

Plug and Go
Easy to move from
vehicle to vehicle

*European database included

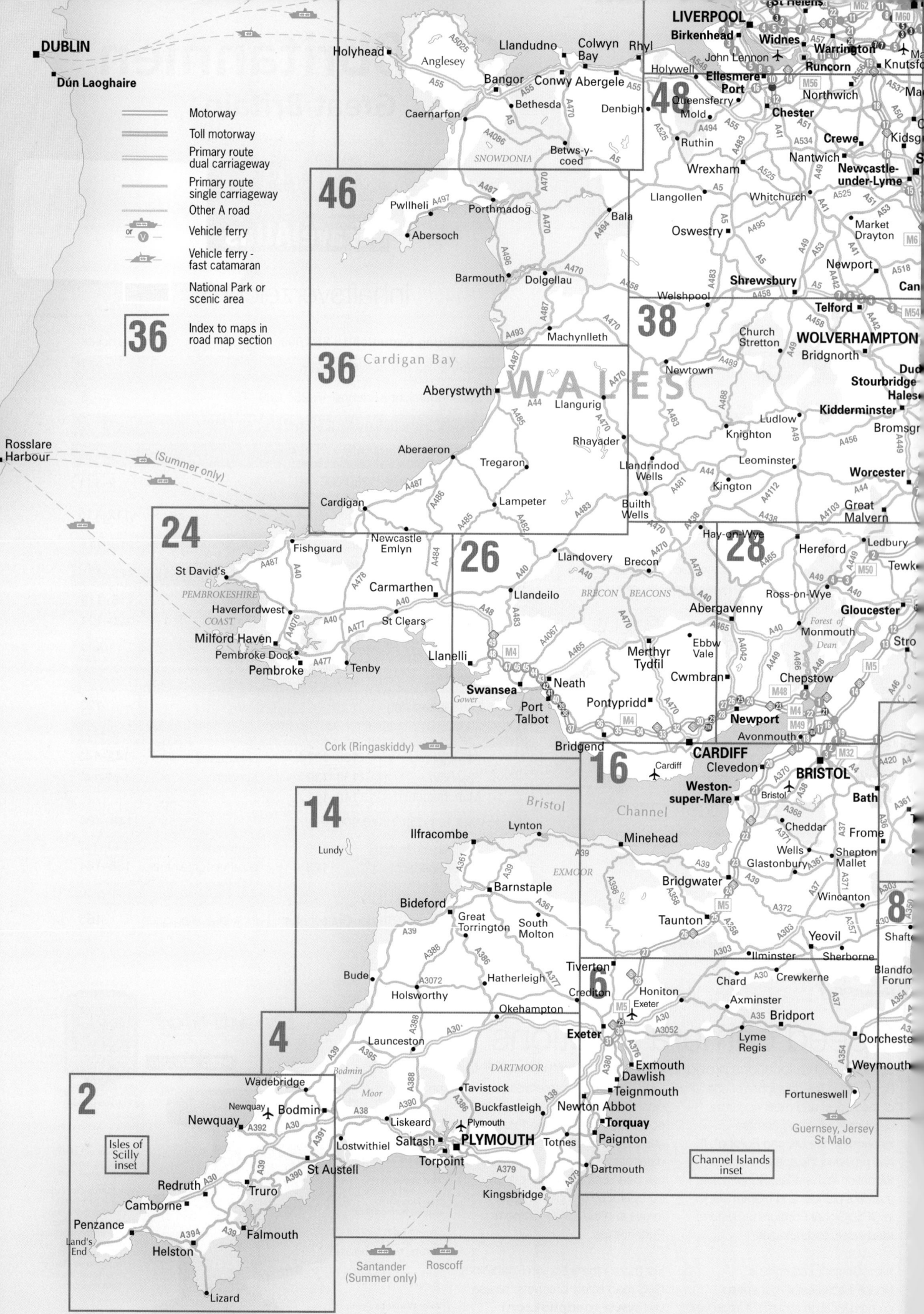

DUBLIN
Dún Laoghaire

	Motorway
	Toll motorway
	Primary route dual carriageway
	Primary route single carriageway
	Other A road
or V	Vehicle ferry
	Vehicle ferry - fast catamaran
	National Park or scenic area
36	Index to maps in road map section

Rosslare Harbour

(Summer only)

Cork (Ringaskiddy)

Santander (Summer only)   Roscoff

Guernsey, Jersey St Malo

Channel Islands inset

Isles of Scilly inset

LIVERPOOL
Birkenhead   Widnes   Warrington   Knutsfo
Runcorn
John Lennon
Ellesmere Port   Northwich
Queensferry   Mold
Chester   Crewe   Kidsg
Ruthin   Nantwich
Wrexham   Newcastle-under-Lyme
Llangollen   Market Drayton
Oswestry   Newport   Can
Shrewsbury   Telford
Welshpool
Church Stretton   WOLVERHAMPTON
Bridgnorth
Newtown   Stourbridge
Hales
Ludlow   Kidderminster   Bromsgr
Knighton   Worcester
Leominster
Llandrindod Wells   Kington   Great Malvern
Builth Wells   Hay-on-Wye   Hereford   Ledbury   Tewk
Ross-on-Wye   Gloucester   Stro
Abergavenny   Forest of Monmouth Dean   Chepstow
Merthyr Tydfil   Ebbw Vale   Cwmbran   Newport   Avonmouth
Pontypridd   CARDIFF   Clevedon   BRISTOL   Bath
Bridgend   Cardiff   Weston-super-Mare   Bristol   Cheddar   Frome
Swansea   Neath   Minehead   Wells   Shepton Mallet
Port Talbot   Bridgwater   Glastonbury   Wincanton
Taunton   Yeovil   Shafte
Ilminster   Sherborne   Blandfo Forum
Tiverton   Crewkerne   Bridport   Dorcheste
Crediton   Chard   Axminster   Lyme Regis   Weymouth
Exeter   Honiton   Fortuneswell
Exmouth   Dawlish   A3052
Exeter   Teignmouth
Newton Abbot   Torquay
Paignton
Dartmouth

WALES
Cardigan Bay
Aberystwyth   Llangurig
Aberaeron   Rhayader
Tregaron
Lampeter
Cardigan   Newcastle Emlyn
Fishguard   Carmarthen
St David's   Haverfordwest   St Clears
PEMBROKESHIRE COAST
Milford Haven   Llandovery   Brecon
Pembroke Dock   Llandeilo   BRECON BEACONS
Pembroke   Tenby   Llanelli
Gower

Holyhead   Anglesey   Llandudno   Colwyn Bay   Rhyl
Bangor   Conwy   Abergele   Holywell
Caernarfon   Bethesda   Denbigh
SNOWDONIA   Betws-y-coed
Pwllheli   Porthmadog
Abersoch   Bala
Barmouth   Dolgellau
Machynlleth

48
46
36
38
28
24
26
16
14
8
4
6
2

Bristol Channel

EXMOOR
Lynton
Ilfracombe
Lundy
Barnstaple
Bideford   South Molton
Great Torrington
Bude   Hatherleigh
Holsworthy   Okehampton
DARTMOOR
Launceston   Tavistock   Buckfastleigh
Wadebridge   Bodmin   Liskeard   Plymouth   Totnes
Newquay   Lostwithiel   Saltash   PLYMOUTH   Kingsbridge
St Austell   Torpoint
Redruth   Truro
Camborne   St Austell
Penzance   Falmouth
Land's End   Helston
Lizard

Route planner

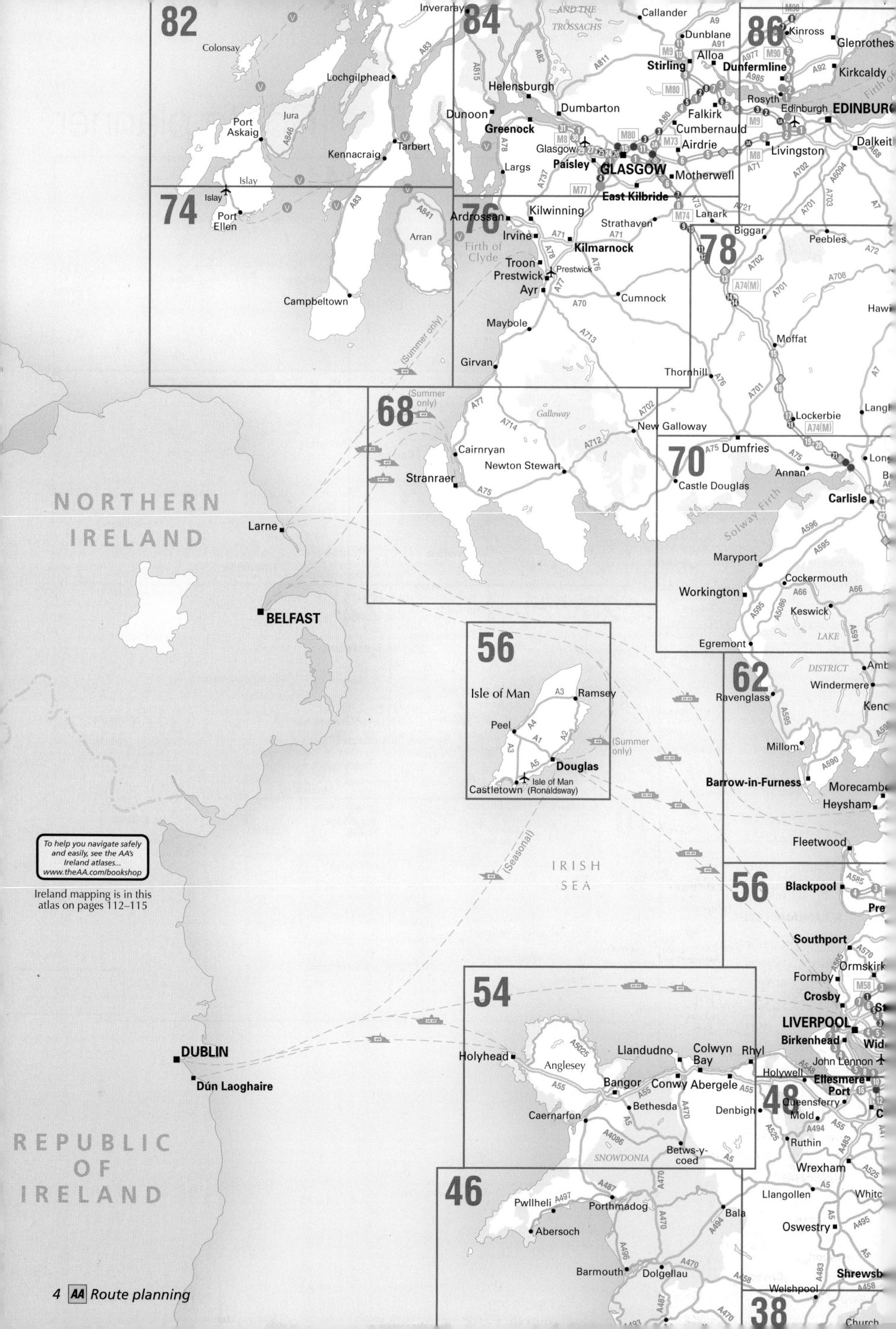

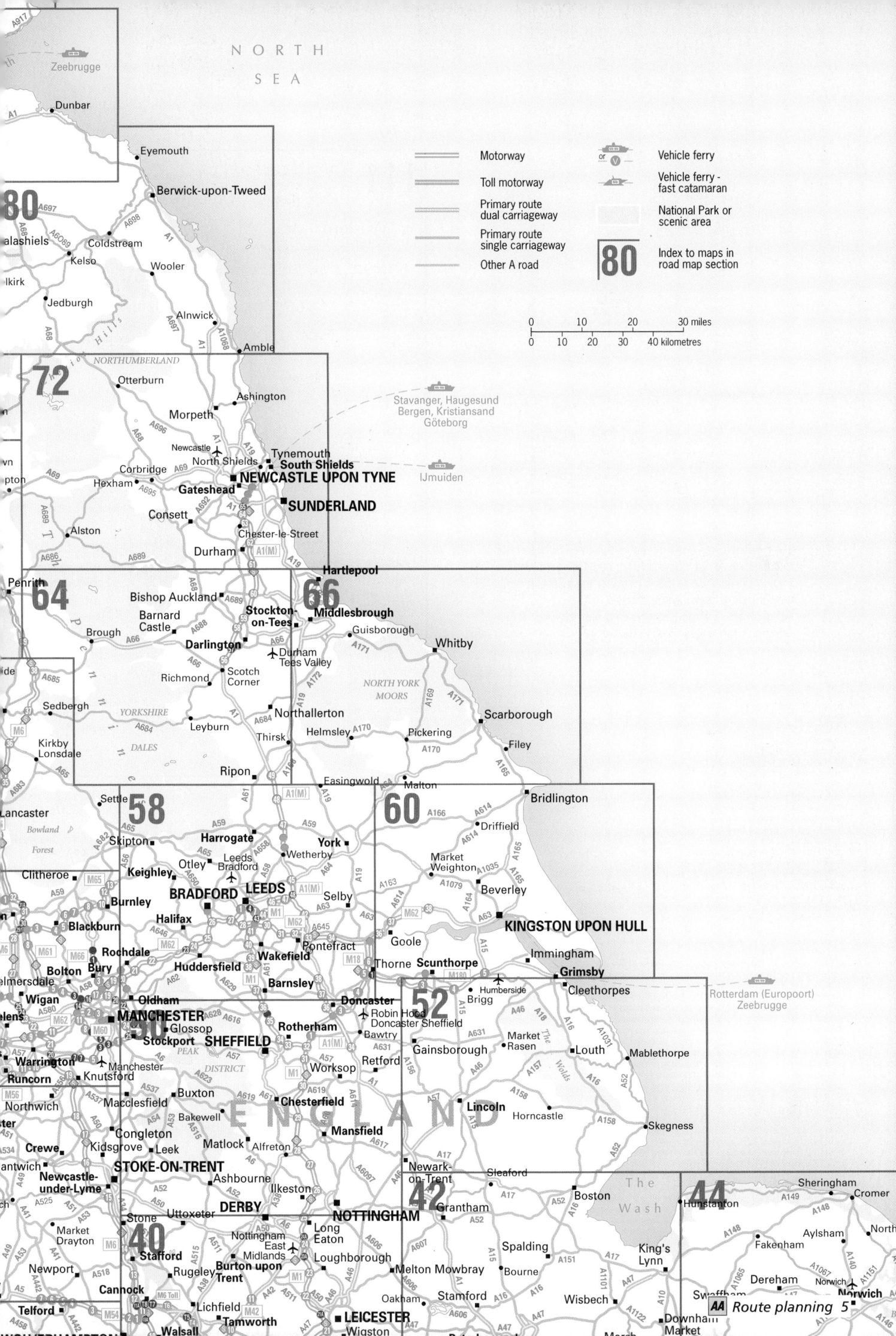

NORTH SEA

Motorway
Toll motorway
Primary route dual carriageway
Primary route single carriageway
Other A road

Vehicle ferry
Vehicle ferry - fast catamaran
National Park or scenic area

80 Index to maps in road map section

| 0 | 10 | 20 | 30 miles |
| 0 | 10 | 20 | 30 | 40 kilometres |

Zeebrugge
Dunbar
Eyemouth
Berwick-upon-Tweed

80
alashiels
Coldstream
Kelso
Wooler
lkirk
Jedburgh
Alnwick
Amble

72
NORTHUMBERLAND
Otterburn
Ashington
Morpeth
Newcastle
North Shields
Tynemouth
South Shields
Corbridge
NEWCASTLE UPON TYNE
Hexham
Gateshead
Consett
SUNDERLAND
Alston
Chester-le-Street
Durham

Stavanger, Haugesund
Bergen, Kristiansand
Göteborg

IJmuiden

Penrith
64
Bishop Auckland
Barnard Castle
Brough
Stockton-on-Tees
66
Hartlepool
Middlesbrough
Guisborough
Whitby
Darlington
Durham Tees Valley
Richmond
Scotch Corner
NORTH YORK MOORS
Sedbergh
YORKSHIRE
Leyburn
Northallerton
Scarborough
Kirkby Lonsdale
DALES
Thirsk
Helmsley
Pickering
Filey
Ripon
Easingwold
Malton

Settle
58
Skipton
Harrogate
60
Bridlington
Lancaster
Keighley
Otley
Wetherby
Driffield
Bowland Forest
BRADFORD
Leeds Bradford
York
Market Weighton
Clitheroe
Burnley
Halifax
LEEDS
Selby
Beverley
Blackburn
Huddersfield
Wakefield
Goole
KINGSTON UPON HULL
Bolton
Bury
Barnsley
Thorne
Scunthorpe
Immingham
Wigan
Oldham
Doncaster
52
Grimsby
MANCHESTER
Glossop
Rotherham
Robin Hood Doncaster Sheffield
Cleethorpes
Warrington
Stockport
SHEFFIELD
Bawtry
Humberside
Brigg
Runcorn
Knutsford
Manchester
PEAK DISTRICT
Worksop
Retford
Gainsborough
Market Rasen
Louth
Mablethorpe
Northwich
Macclesfield
Buxton
Chesterfield
ENGLAND
Crewe
Congleton
Bakewell
Matlock
Mansfield
Lincoln
Horncastle
Skegness
Newcastle-under-Lyme
Kidsgrove
Leek
Alfreton
Newark-on-Trent
Market Drayton
STOKE-ON-TRENT
Ashbourne
Ilkeston
42
The Wash
44
Sheringham
Cromer
Newport
40
Uttoxeter
DERBY
NOTTINGHAM
Grantham
Sleaford
Boston
Hunstanton
Aylsham
Telford
Stafford
Stone
Rugeley
Burton upon Trent
Long Eaton
Nottingham East Midlands
Loughborough
Melton Mowbray
Spalding
Bourne
King's Lynn
Fakenham
Dereham
Norwich
Cannock
Lichfield
Stamford
Wisbech
Swaffham
Downham Market
Walsall
Tamworth
LEICESTER
Oakham
Wigston

AA Route planning 5

Wick
Inverness
Aberdeen
Fort William
Perth
Edinburgh
Glasgow
Newcastle upon Tyne
Stranraer
Carlisle
Middlesbrough
Kendal
York
Preston
Leeds
Kingston upon Hull
Holyhead
Liverpool
Manchester
Sheffield
Stoke-on-Trent
Lincoln
Nottingham
Shrewsbury
Norwich
Aberystwyth
Birmingham
Peterborough
Northampton
Hereford
Cambridge
Gloucester
Carmarthen
Cardiff
Oxford
LONDON
Bristol
Barnstaple
Guildford
Maidstone
Salisbury
Taunton
Southampton
Dover
Exeter
Brighton
Dorchester
Portsmouth
Penzance
Plymouth

The mileage chart shows distances in miles between two towns along AA-recommended routes. Using motorways and other main roads this is normally the fastest route, though not necessarily the shortest.
For example, the road distance between Norwich and Southampton is 204 miles (328 km)

	Aberdeen	Aberystwyth	Barnstaple	Birmingham	Brighton	Bristol	Cambridge	Cardiff	Carlisle	Carmarthen	Dorchester	Dover	Edinburgh	Exeter	Fort William	Glasgow	Gloucester	Guildford	Hereford	Holyhead	Hull	Inverness	Kendal	Leeds	Lincoln	Liverpool	Maidstone	Manchester	Middlesbrough	Newcastle	Northampton	Norwich	Nottingham	Oxford	Penzance	Perth	Peterborough	Plymouth	Portsmouth	Preston	Salisbury	Sheffield	Shrewsbury	Southampton	Stoke-on-Trent	Stranraer	Taunton	Wick	York
Aberystwyth	472
Barnstaple	608	214
Birmingham	436	124	180
Brighton	613	288	210	171
Bristol	518	130	100	90	169
Cambridge	463	215	267	97	120	170
Cardiff	537	111	128	109	202	44	203
Carlisle	236	236	371	199	376	281	256	300
Carmarthen	520	48	190	172	264	107	266	68	284
Dorchester	600	206	94	172	119	62	184	120	364	182
Dover	587	326	272	208	82	205	124	239	381	301	200
Edinburgh	126	336	471	299	476	381	333	400	100	386	463	458
Exeter	593	198	44	165	178	84	259	113	356	175	57	248	455
Fort William	156	435	570	398	576	480	456	499	199	485	562	580	137	554
Glasgow	150	332	467	295	472	377	353	396	96	382	459	477	47	451	102
Gloucester	484	113	126	56	155	36	150	63	248	125	118	192	346	110	445	343
Guildford	571	224	175	128	44	106	96	139	335	201	97	97	433	150	532	430	99
Hereford	487	79	144	59	189	54	153	59	250	85	136	225	349	129	448	346	34	133
Holyhead	464	102	339	167	345	249	259	202	228	150	331	369	326	323	425	323	215	302	156
Hull	376	227	320	139	258	230	138	250	170	311	312	262	247	304	367	266	196	239	198	218
Inverness	106	496	631	459	637	541	517	561	260	546	623	641	157	616	66	176	507	595	510	488	430
Kendal	283	189	324	153	330	234	251	254	47	240	316	354	145	309	245	143	200	288	203	181	164	307
Leeds	329	173	301	120	262	211	146	230	123	224	293	271	200	285	321	219	177	220	179	165	59	383	110
Lincoln	388	199	275	98	216	185	95	205	182	267	246	220	258	260	379	277	151	173	154	204	44	441	176	74
Liverpool	362	110	272	101	278	182	193	202	126	158	264	302	224	257	324	222	148	236	151	102	128	386	79	74	139
Maidstone	545	284	234	166	50	167	82	200	339	262	161	41	416	209	537	435	153	58	186	327	220	599	313	231	178	261
Manchester	357	134	261	89	266	171	160	190	120	184	253	290	219	245	318	216	136	224	139	125	97	380	74	44	85	34	248
Middlesbrough	276	244	357	176	318	267	197	286	95	294	349	322	146	341	283	190	232	276	235	235	89	308	84	64	122	145	280	114
Newcastle	235	275	388	207	349	298	229	317	60	325	380	353	106	372	242	153	264	307	266	266	142	267	102	95	154	176	311	145	39
Northampton	486	174	212	56	133	115	56	162	249	224	159	155	348	196	447	345	79	90	111	217	152	509	203	136	94	151	113	139	189	220
Norwich	488	278	329	160	168	233	63	266	282	328	241	172	359	313	480	378	212	160	215	321	147	542	276	174	103	240	130	185	223	254	118
Nottingham	395	162	232	51	193	142	86	161	189	223	224	210	266	216	387	285	107	151	110	178	93	449	164	77	39	112	168	71	130	161	64	119
Oxford	510	160	170	68	109	73	82	107	274	169	115	146	373	154	472	370	48	67	81	242	190	534	228	174	132	176	107	164	227	258	44	146	102
Penzance	702	308	108	274	287	193	368	222	466	284	167	357	564	109	663	562	220	259	238	434	415	726	419	403	370	367	318	356	451	482	326	433	326	265
Perth	86	388	523	351	529	433	378	453	152	438	515	503	42	507	102	64	399	486	401	379	291	114	199	245	303	278	461	275	192	150	400	404	310	426	617
Peterborough	435	204	263	86	158	173	37	193	229	255	204	162	306	248	427	325	139	115	142	225	110	489	223	121	51	159	120	132	170	201	45	78	58	86	357	351
Plymouth	633	239	62	205	218	124	299	153	397	215	98	288	495	44	594	493	151	190	169	365	346	657	350	334	301	298	249	287	382	413	257	364	257	196	78	544	288
Portsmouth	596	244	162	154	53	125	137	158	360	220	73	141	458	132	558	456	118	45	152	328	276	620	314	260	215	262	102	250	313	344	130	204	188	85	241	508	157	172
Preston	326	146	281	110	287	191	209	211	89	197	273	311	188	266	287	185	157	245	160	138	122	349	43	69	134	36	269	35	103	139	159	235	121	184	375	237	180	306	270
Salisbury	549	184	118	121	90	52	145	98	313	160	39	160	411	93	511	409	72	62	105	281	261	573	267	244	202	215	121	203	298	329	115	212	173	70	203	461	165	134	44	223
Sheffield	397	166	272	91	233	182	122	201	161	263	264	247	236	256	359	257	148	191	150	157	66	421	115	38	47	79	205	39	100	131	104	148	45	142	366	309	93	297	228	73	212
Shrewsbury	417	75	220	48	226	130	140	111	181	110	212	250	279	205	379	277	96	184	52	105	162	441	135	119	124	65	208	71	190	221	98	203	87	123	314	329	129	245	209	92	161	88
Southampton	578	225	142	135	66	106	136	140	342	201	53	152	440	111	539	437	100	49	133	309	258	601	295	241	199	243	113	232	294	325	111	204	169	67	221	489	157	152	20	252	23	209	191
Stoke-on-Trent	392	112	220	48	226	130	140	150	156	211	212	250	254	205	353	251	96	184	99	123	129	415	109	93	91	57	208	46	164	195	98	172	54	123	314	303	99	245	209	66	161	50	38	191
Stranraer	235	342	477	305	482	387	363	406	106	392	469	487	132	461	181	86	352	440	355	333	276	261	153	229	288	232	445	229	201	163	354	388	295	380	571	149	333	502	466	195	418	267	287	447	261
Taunton	560	165	50	132	160	51	226	80	323	142	45	224	422	34	521	419	77	126	96	291	272	583	277	261	228	225	185	213	309	340	183	291	184	123	144	471	215	75	114	234	70	224	172	94	172	429
Wick	207	597	732	560	738	642	618	662	361	647	724	742	258	716	166	277	608	695	610	588	531	104	408	484	543	487	700	484	409	367	609	644	550	635	826	215	589	757	721	451	673	523	542	702	516	362	684
York	323	201	314	133	275	224	154	243	116	251	306	279	193	298	314	212	189	233	192	192	38	376	91	24	79	102	237	71	51	89	146	180	87	184	408	239	125	339	269	96	254	57	146	251	120	223	265	477
LONDON	550	239	216	121	54	120	59	153	314	215	125	78	413	200	512	410	102	31	136	282	186	574	268	201	143	216	39	204	254	285	68	118	129	56	310	462	86	241	75	225	85	169	163	77	161	420	167	675	211

Norwich - Southampton = 204 miles

1 mile = 1.6 kilometres

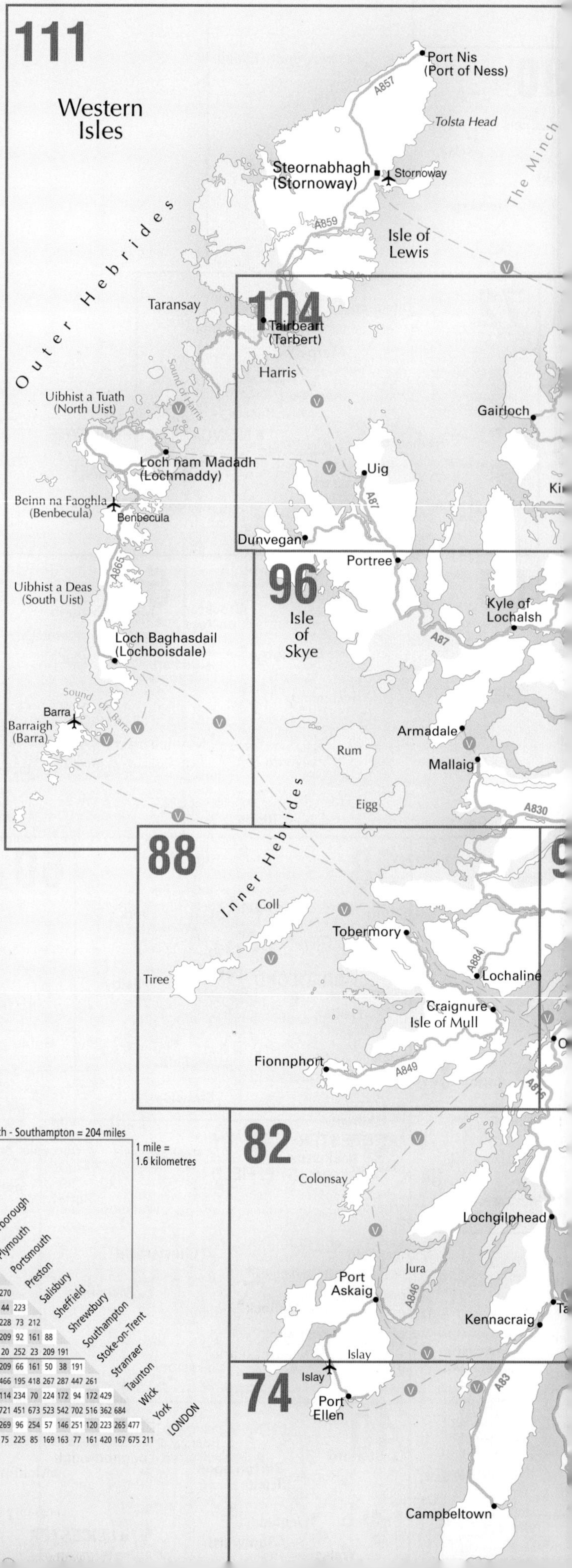

111
Western Isles
Port Nis (Port of Ness)
A857
Tolsta Head
The Minch
Steornabhagh (Stornoway)
Stornoway
A859
Isle of Lewis
Outer Hebrides
Taransay
104
Tairbeart (Tarbert)
Harris
Sound of Harris
Gairloch
Uibhist a Tuath (North Uist)
Loch nam Madadh (Lochmaddy)
Uig
A87
Beinn na Faoghla (Benbecula)
Benbecula
Dunvegan
Portree
A865
Uibhist a Deas (South Uist)
96
Isle of Skye
Kyle of Lochalsh
A87
Loch Baghasdail (Lochboisdale)
Sound of Barra
Barra
Barraigh (Barra)
Armadale
Rum
Mallaig
Inner Hebrides
Eigg
A830
88
Coll
Tobermory
Tiree
A884
Lochaline
Craignure
Isle of Mull
Fionnphort
A849
82
Colonsay
Lochgilphead
Jura
Port Askaig
A846
Kennacraig
Islay
74
Islay
Port Ellen
A83
Campbeltown

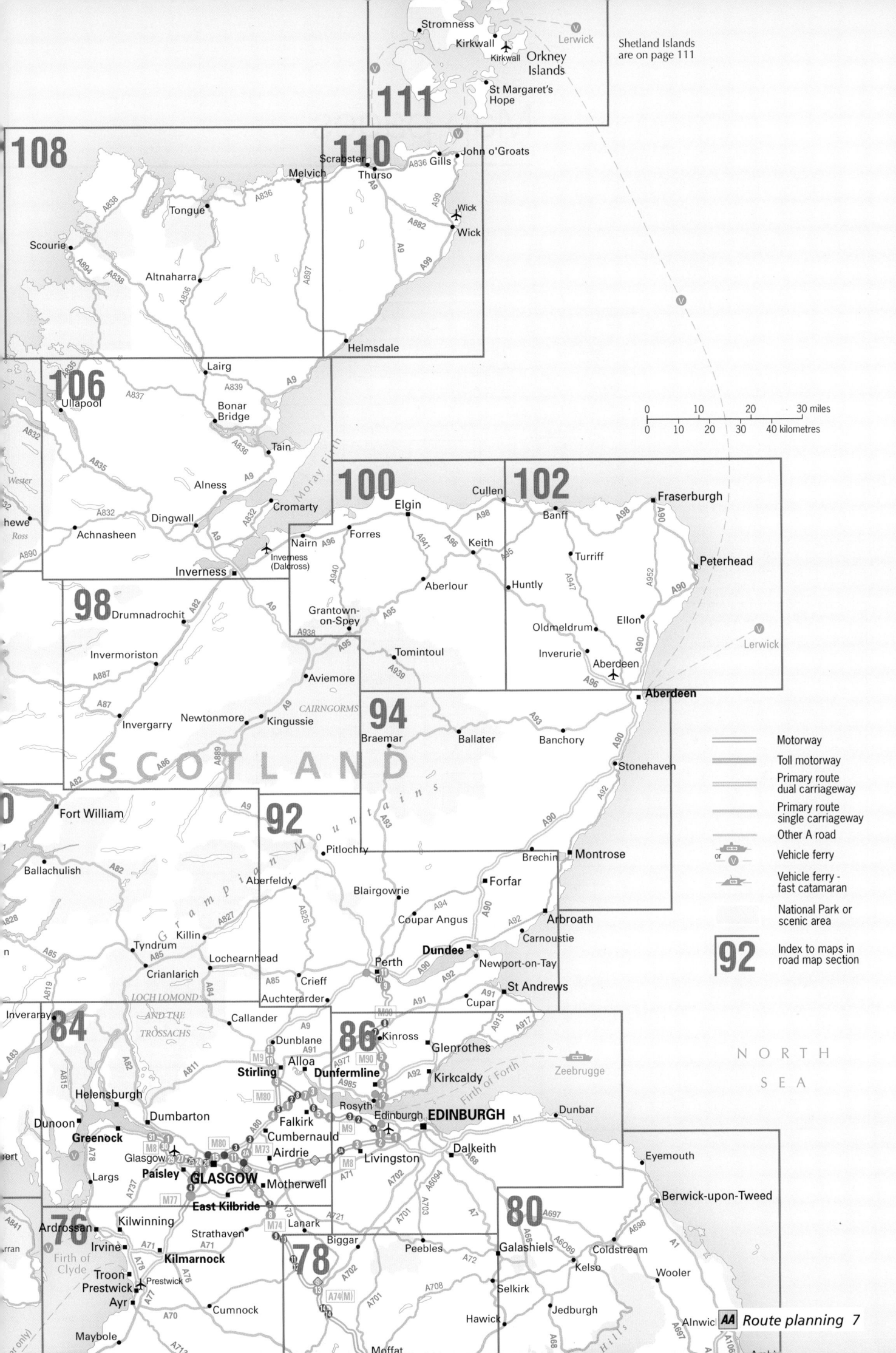

Shetland Islands are on page 111

111 Orkney Islands
Stromness · Kirkwall · Kirkwall · St Margaret's Hope · Lerwick

108
Scourie · Tongue · Altnaharra
A838 · A836 · A894 · A838 · A837

110
Scrabster · Melvich · Thurso · Gills · John o'Groats · A836 · A9 · A882 · A99 · Wick · Wick · A9 · A99 · Helmsdale

Wester · Ross · hewe

106
Ullapool · Lairg · A839 · Bonar Bridge · A837 · A836 · Tain · A832 · A835 · Alness · A9 · Cromarty · Achnasheen · Dingwall · A832 · A832 · A890 · Inverness · Nairn · A96 · Forres · Inverness (Dalcross)

0 10 20 30 miles
0 10 20 30 40 kilometres

100
Elgin · Cullen · A98 · Keith · A941 · A96 · Aberlour · Grantown-on-Spey · A95 · A938 · A95 · A939 · Tomintoul

102
Banff · A98 · Fraserburgh · A90 · Turriff · A95 · A947 · Huntly · A952 · Peterhead · Oldmeldrum · A90 · Ellon · Inverurie · A96 · Aberdeen · Aberdeen · Lerwick

98
Drumnadrochit · A82 · Invermoriston · A887 · A9 · A87 · Invergarry · A889 · Newtonmore · Kingussie · A86 · Aviemore · CAIRNGORMS

S C O T L A N D

94
Braemar · Ballater · Banchory · A93 · A90 · Stonehaven · A92

Fort William · A9 · A82 · A828 · Ballachulish · A85 · A82

92
Pitlochry · A9 · Aberfeldy · A827 · Blairgowrie · A826 · Coupar Angus · A94 · Forfar · A90 · Brechin · Montrose · Arbroath · Carnoustie · A92

Tyndrum · Killin · A85 · Crianlarich · Lochearnhead · A84 · A85 · Crieff · Perth · Dundee · Newport-on-Tay · A90 · A92 · St Andrews · A91 · Cupar · A915 · A917

Inveraray · A819 · LOCH LOMOND AND THE TROSSACHS · Callander · Auchterarder · A9 · Kinross

84
Helensburgh · A815 · A82 · Dumbarton · Dunoon · Greenock · A78 · Largs · A737 · Paisley · GLASGOW · M77 · East Kilbride

86
Dunblane · A91 · Alloa · Stirling · M9 · M80 · Dunfermline · A985 · Rosyth · Falkirk · Cumbernauld · M73 · Airdrie · M9 · Livingston · Edinburgh · EDINBURGH · A1 · Dunbar · Glenrothes · Kirkcaldy · A92 · Firth of Forth · Zeebrugge · Motherwell · A71 · Dalkeith

N O R T H
S E A

76
Ardrossan · Kilwinning · Irvine · A71 · A78 · Troon · Prestwick · Prestwick · Ayr · A77 · A76 · Cumnock · A70 · Maybole · A713 · Firth of Clyde

Strathaven · Lanark · M74 · Biggar · A721 · Peebles · A702 · A701 · A703 · A6094 · A702 · A72 · Galashiels · Selkirk · A708 · Hawick · Moffat

78
A74(M)

80
Eyemouth · Berwick-upon-Tweed · A1 · Coldstream · A697 · Kelso · Wooler · Jedburgh · A68 · Alnwick · A6089

Kilmarnock

Motorway
Toll motorway
Primary route dual carriageway
Primary route single carriageway
Other A road
or V **Vehicle ferry**
Vehicle ferry - fast catamaran
National Park or scenic area
92 **Index to maps in road map section**

Map pages

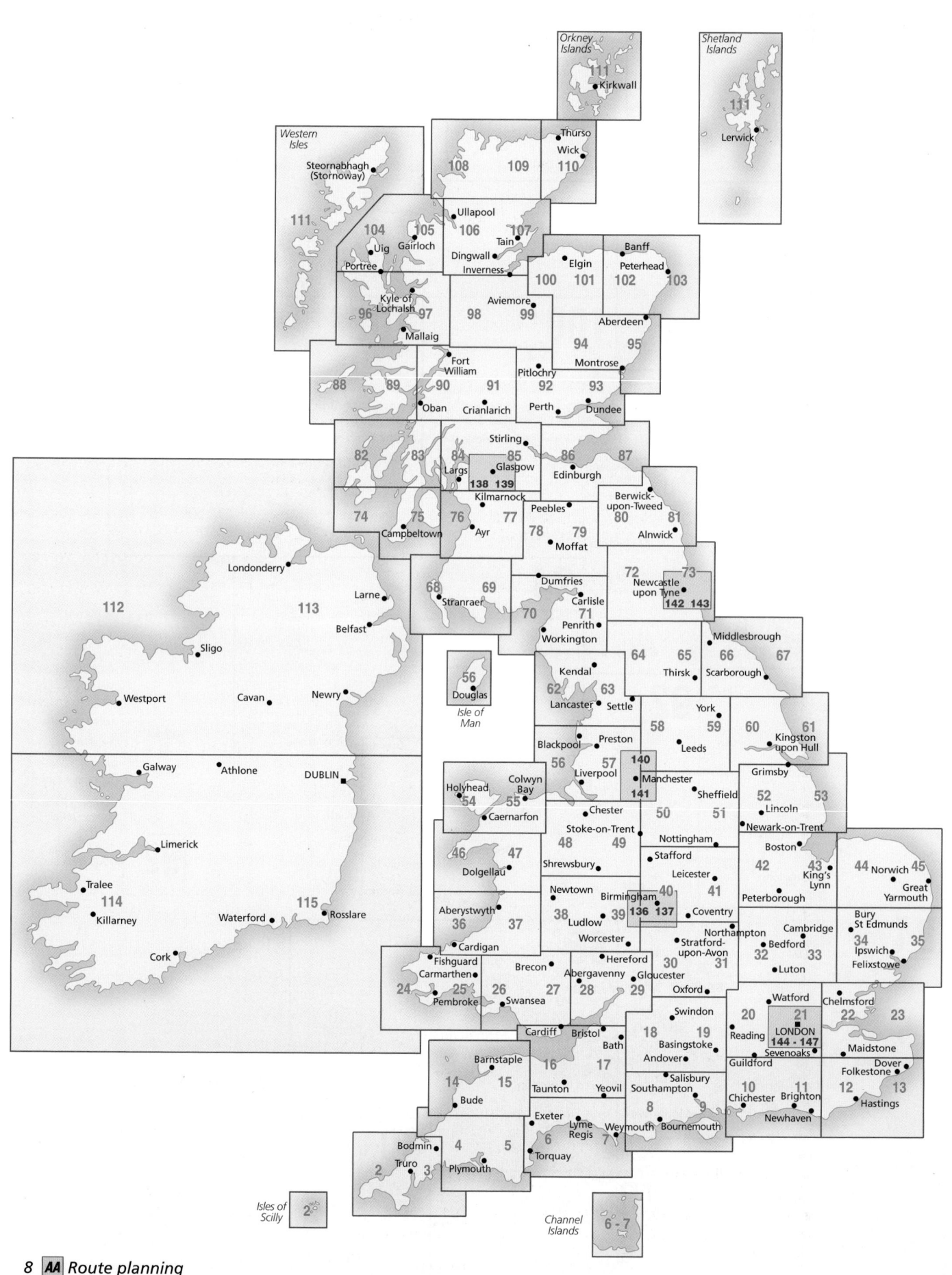

Road map symbols

Motoring information

M4	Motorway with number	BATH	Primary route destination	Toll	Road toll
Toll	Toll motorway with toll station	A1123	Other A road single/dual carriageway	5	Distance in miles between symbols
	Motorway junction with and without number	B2070	B road single/dual carriageway	or V	Vehicle ferry
3	Restricted motorway junctions		Minor road more than 4 metres wide, less than 4 metres wide		Vehicle ferry - fast catamaran
S Fleet	Motorway service area		Roundabout		Railway line/in tunnel
	Motorway and junction under construction		Interchange/junction	—o—x—	Railway station and level crossing
A3	Primary route single/dual carriageway		Narrow primary/other A/B road with passing places (Scotland)	++++++++	Tourist railway
	Primary route junction with and without number		Road under construction	(A) (H) (F)	Airport, heliport, international freight terminal
3	Restricted primary route junctions	F=======	Road tunnel	H	24-hour Accident & Emergency hospital
S Grantham North	Primary route service area		Steep gradient (arrows point downhill)	*	Major shopping centre

Speed camera site (fixed location)	
Section of road with two or more fixed speed cameras	
P·R	Park and Ride (at least 6 days per week)
	City, town, village or other built-up area
628 ▲	Spot height in metres
348 Rannoch Moor	Pass
	Sandy beach
	National boundary
	County, administrative boundary
23	Page continuation number

Touring information

Places of interest are also shown on town plans. Before visiting check opening times, to avoid disappointment.

	Tourist Information Centre		Agricultural showground		Roman antiquity		Air show venue
	Tourist Information Centre (seasonal)		Theme park		Prehistoric monument		Ski slope – natural
	Visitor or heritage centre		Farm or animal centre	1066	Battle site with year		Ski slope – artificial
	Abbey, cathedral or priory		Zoological or wildlife collection		Steam centre (railway)	NT	National Trust property
	Ruined abbey, cathedral or priory		Bird collection		Cave	NTS	National Trust for Scotland property
	Castle		Aquarium		Windmill	★	Other place of interest
	Historic house or building	RSPB	RSPB site		Monument		Boxed symbols indicate attractions within urban areas
	Museum or art gallery		National Nature Reserves (England, Scotland, Wales)		Golf course		National Park
	Industrial interest		Local nature reserve		County cricket ground		National Scenic Area (Scotland)
	Aqueduct or viaduct	·············	Forest drive		Rugby Union national stadium		Forest Park
	Garden	– – – – –	National trail		International athletics stadium		Heritage coast
	Arboretum		Viewpoint		Horse racing		
	Vineyard		Picnic site		Show jumping/equestrian circuit		
	Country park		Hill-fort		Motor-racing circuit		

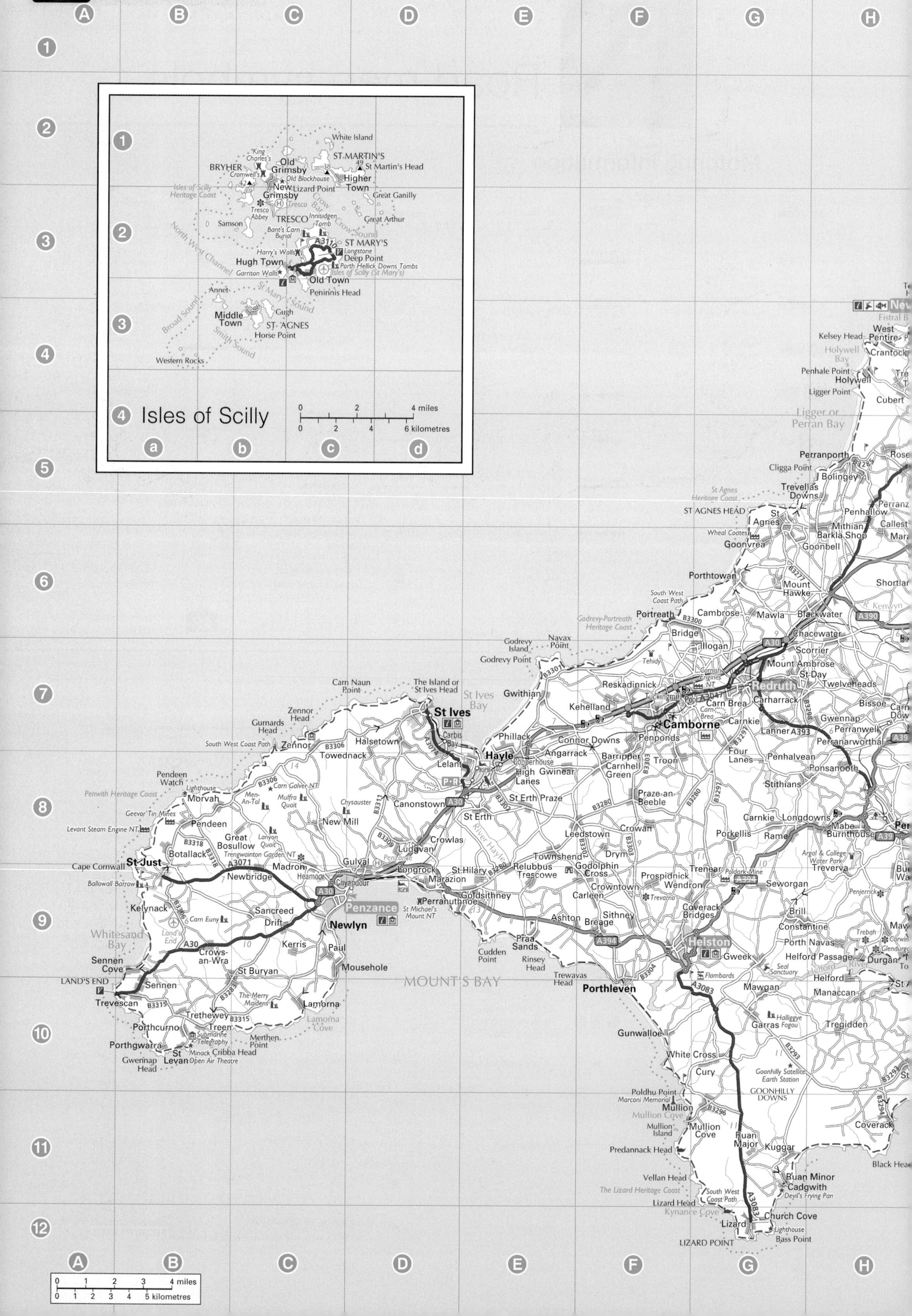

A   B   C   D   E   F   G   H

1

2

Isles of Scilly

Inset map

1

White Island
ST. MARTIN'S
'King Charles's
Old
Grimsby
St Martin's Head
BRYHER
Cromwell's
Lizard Point
Old Blockhouse
Higher Town
New Grimsby
Great Ganilly
Tresco Abbey
TRESCO
Innisidgen Tomb
Great Arthur
Samson
Bant's Carn Burial
ST MARY'S
Harry's Walls
Longstone
Deep Point
Hugh Town
Porth Hellick Downs Tombs
Garrison Walls
Isles of Scilly (St Mary's)
Old Town
Annet
Peninnis Head
St Mary's Sound
Middle Town
Gugh
ST. AGNES
Horse Point
Broad Sound
Smith Sound
Western Rocks

North West Channel

Crow Sound

2

3

4 Isles of Scilly

0   2   4 miles
0   2   4   6 kilometres

a   b   c   d

5

Newquay
Fistral B
Kelsey Head
West Pentire
Holywell Bay
Crantock
Penhale Point
Holywell
Ligger Point
Cubert
Ligger or Perran Bay

Perranporth
Cligga Point
Bolingey
Rose
Trevellas Downs
Perranzabuloe
Perranwell
Penhallow
St Agnes Heritage Coast
ST AGNES HEAD
St Agnes
Mithian
Callestick
Wheal Coates
Barkla Shop
Mara
Goonvrea
Goonbell

6

Porthtowan
Mount Hawke
Shortlan
South West Coast Path
Portreath
Cambrose
Mawla
Blackwater
Godrevy-Portreath Heritage Coast
Bridge
B3300
Illogan
Chacewater
A390
A30
Scorrier
Godrevy Island
Navax Point
Tehidy
Mount Ambrose
St Day
Twelveheads
Godrevy Point
Reskadinnick
Cornish Engines NT
Tuckingmill Pool
Carn Brea
Redruth
Bissoe
Carn Dow

7

Carn Naun Point
The Island or St Ives Head
St Ives Bay
Gwithian
Kehelland
Carn Brea
Carharrack
Gwennap
Zennor Head
St Ives
Carbis Bay
Phillack
Camborne
Carnkie
Perranarworthal
A393
A39
Gurnards Head
Halsetown
Lelant
Connor Downs
Penponds
Lanner
South West Coast Path
Zennor
B3306
Towednack
Hayle
Angarrack
Barripper
Troon
Four Lanes
Penhalvean
Ponsanooth

8

Pendeen Watch
B3306
Carn Galver NT
High Gwinear Lanes
St Erth Praze
B3280
Praze-an-Beeble
Stithians
Lighthouse
Men-An-Tol
Mulfra Quoit
Canonstown
A30
Carnkie
Longdowns
Mabe
Per
Morvah
Chysauster
St Erth
Crowan
Porkellis
Rame
Burnthouse
A39
Geevor Tin Mines
Pendeen
New Mill
Leedstown
Drym
Levant Steam Engine NT.
Great Bosullow
Lanyon Quoit
Ludgvan
Townshend
Godolphin Cross
Prospidnick
Trenear
Argal & College Water Park
Treverva
Botallack
B3318
Trengwainton Garden NT
Relubbus
Trescowe
Poldark Mine
Cape Cornwall
St Just
Madron
Gulval
Crowlas
St Hilary
Crowntown
Wendron
A394
Seworgan
Ballswall Barrow
A3071
Newbridge
Heamoor
Longrock
St Michael's Mount NT
Carleen
Penjerrick

9

Kelynack
Sancreed
Drift
Chyandour
Marazion
Ashton
Sithney
Breage
Coverack Bridges
Constantine
Brill
Maw
Whitesand Bay
Carn Euny
Penzance
Perranuthnoe
Helston
Porth Navas
Trebah
Corwi
Sennen Cove
Crows-an-Wra
Newlyn
Praa Sands
Gweek
Helford Passage
Durgan
To
LAND'S END
A30
Kerris
Paul
Cudden Point
Rinsey Head
A3083
Seal Sanctuary
Helford
Trevescan
Sennen
B3315
St Buryan
Mousehole
Trewavas Head
Mawgan
Manaccan
St A

10

Porthcurno
Treen
B3315
The Merry Maidens
Lamorna
MOUNT'S BAY
Porthleven
Garras
Halliggye Fogou
Tregidden
Porthgwarra
St Levan
Submarine Telegraphy
Merthen Point
Lamorna Cove
Gunwalloe
White Cross
Goonhilly Satellite Earth Station
Gwennap Head
Minack Open Air Theatre
Cribba Head
Cury
GOONHILLY DOWNS
B3293
St

11

Poldhu Point
Marconi Memorial
Mullion
B3296
Ruan Major
Coverack
Vellan Head
Mullion Cove
Kuggar
Predannack Head
Mullion Island
Ruan Minor
Cadgwith
Black Head
The Lizard Heritage Coast
Devil's Frying Pan

12

Lizard Head
South West Coast Path
Kynance Cove
A3083
Church Cove
Lizard
Lighthouse
Bass Point
LIZARD POINT

A   B   C   D   E   F   G   H

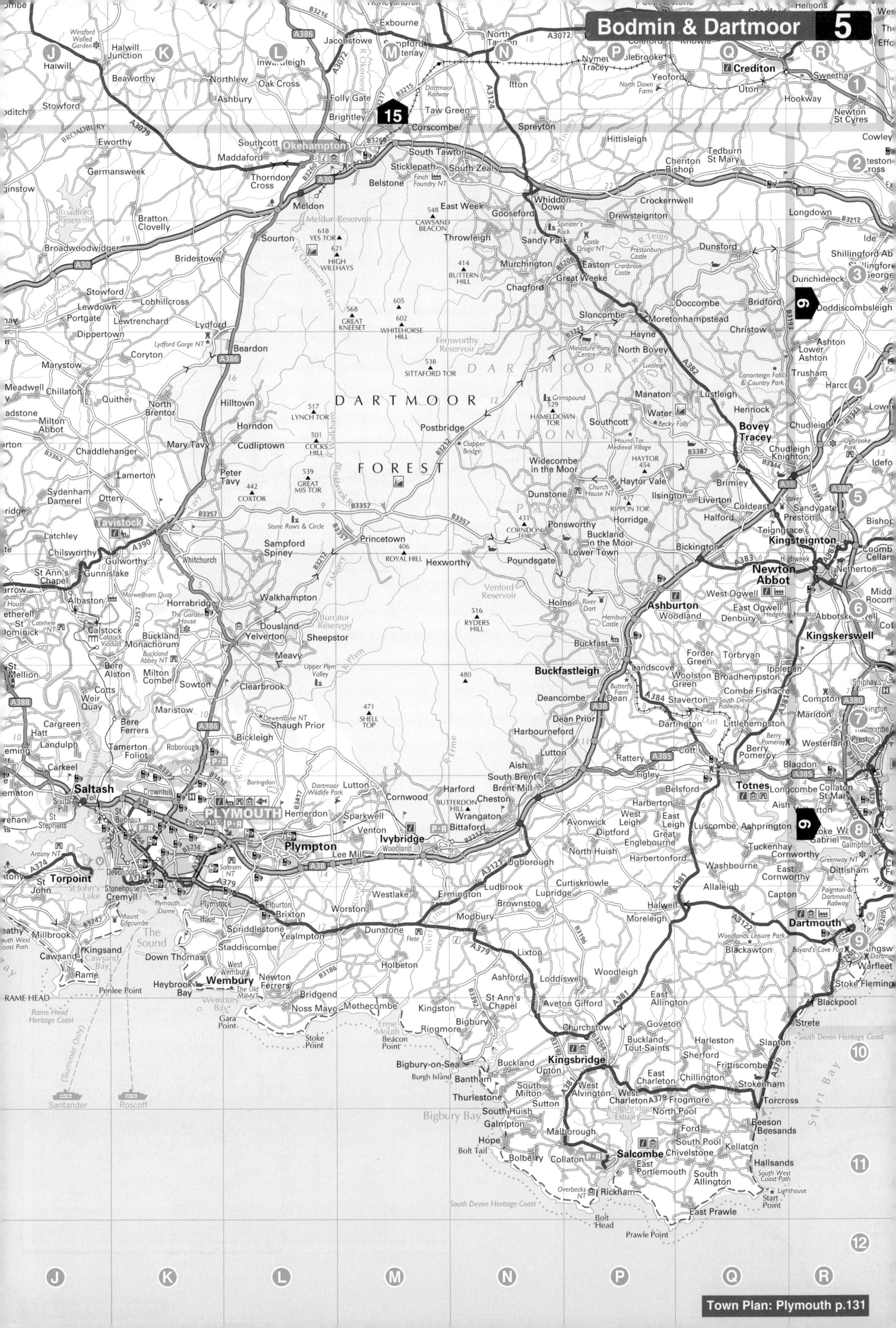

Weymouth Harbour

Jersey

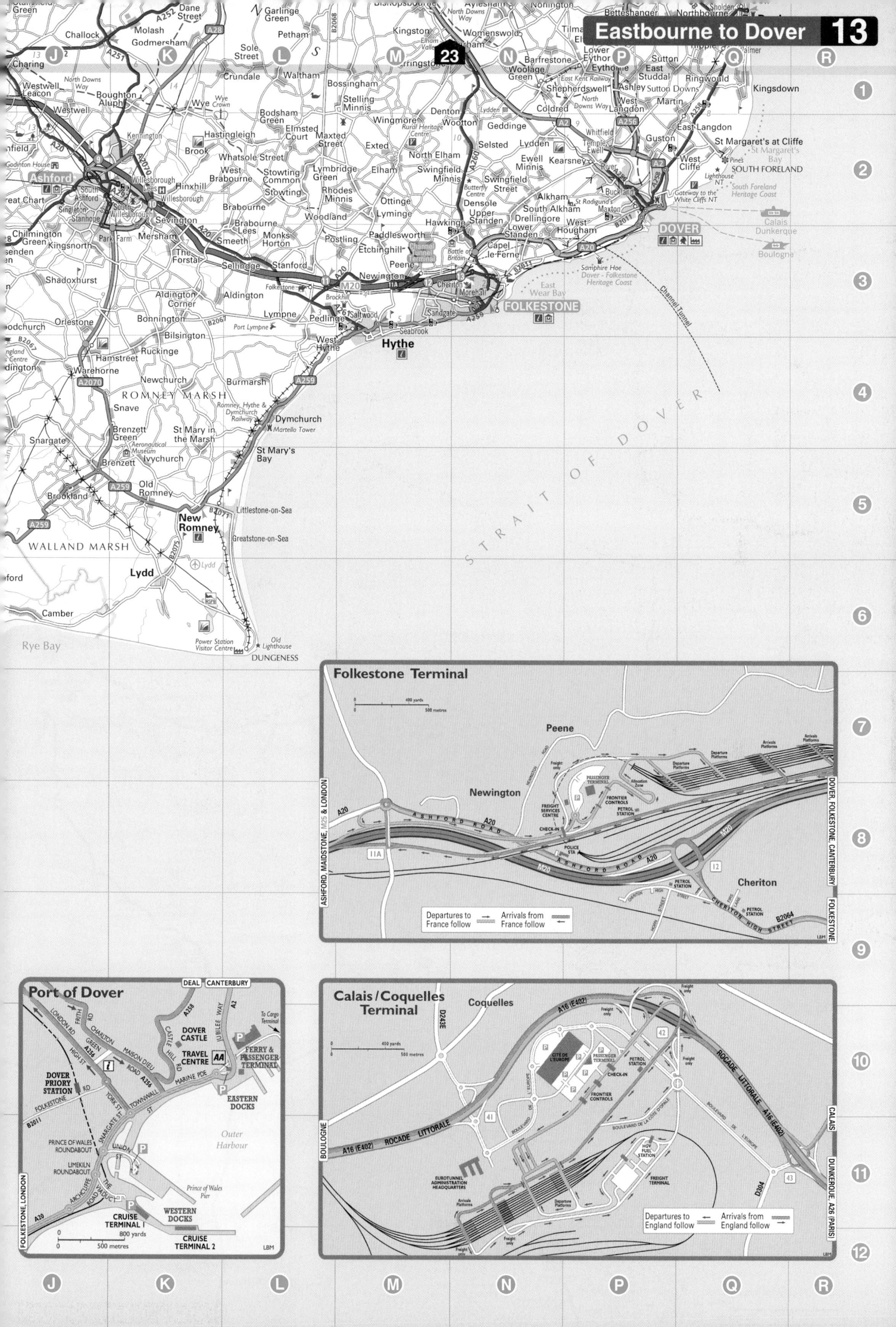

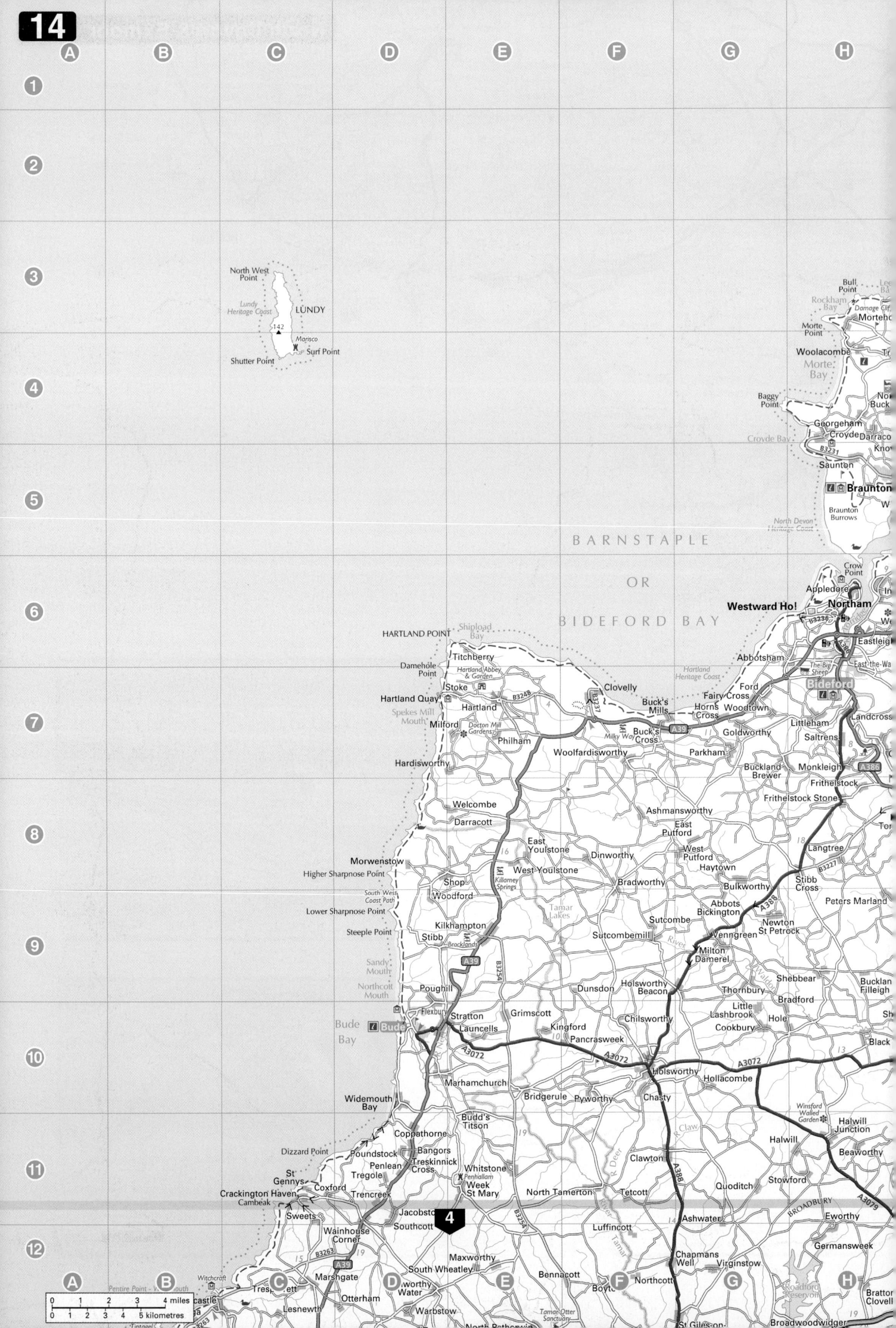

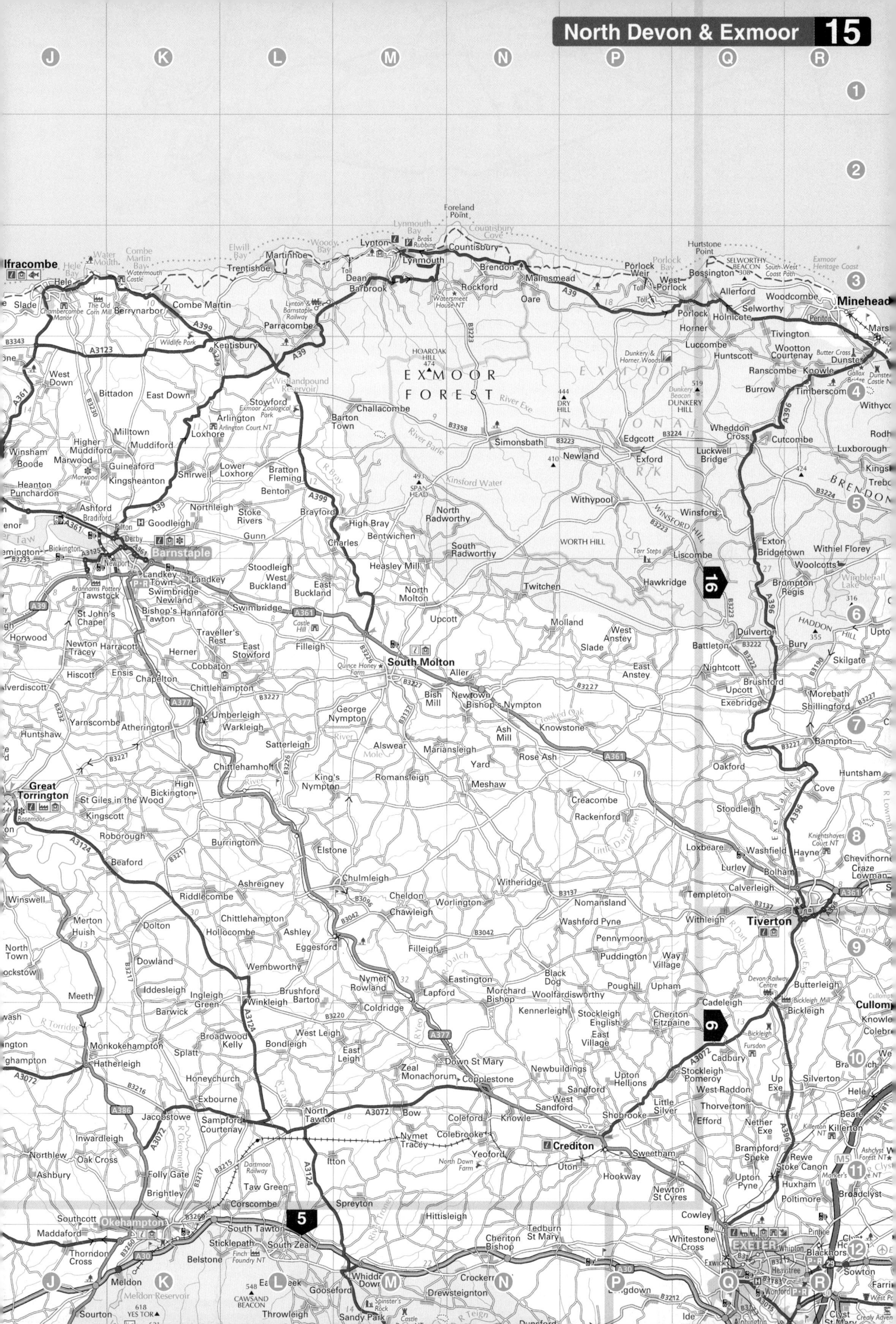

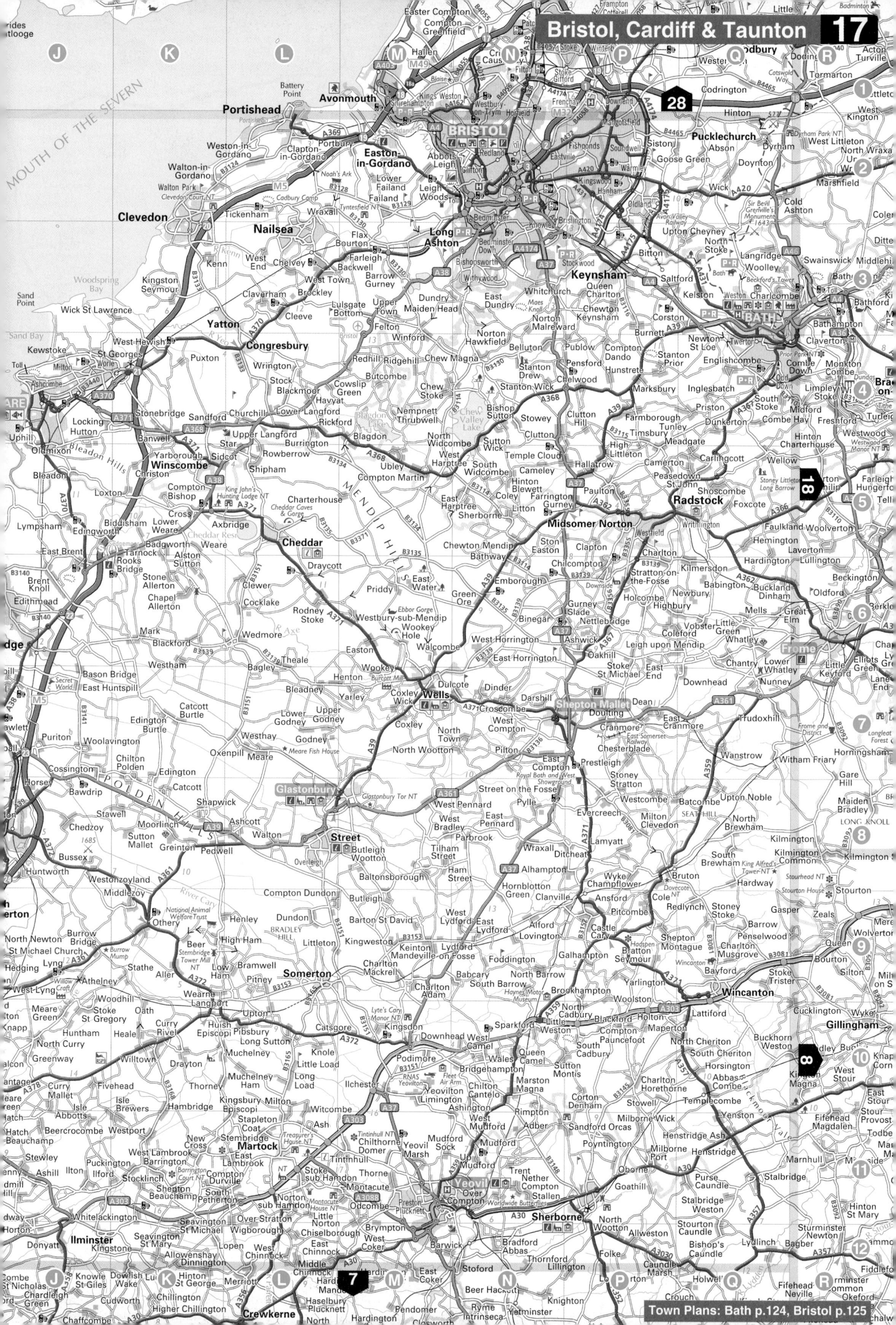

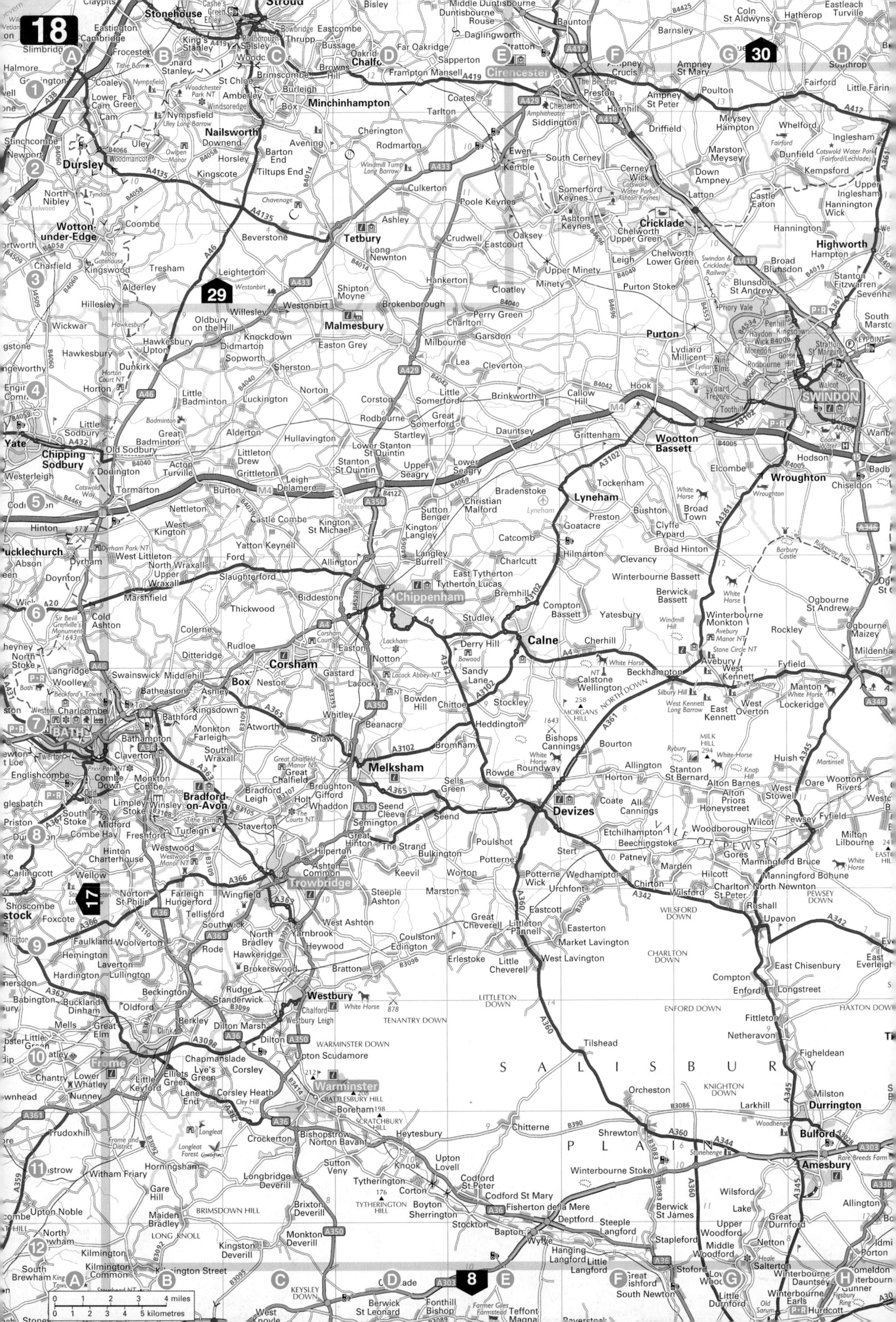

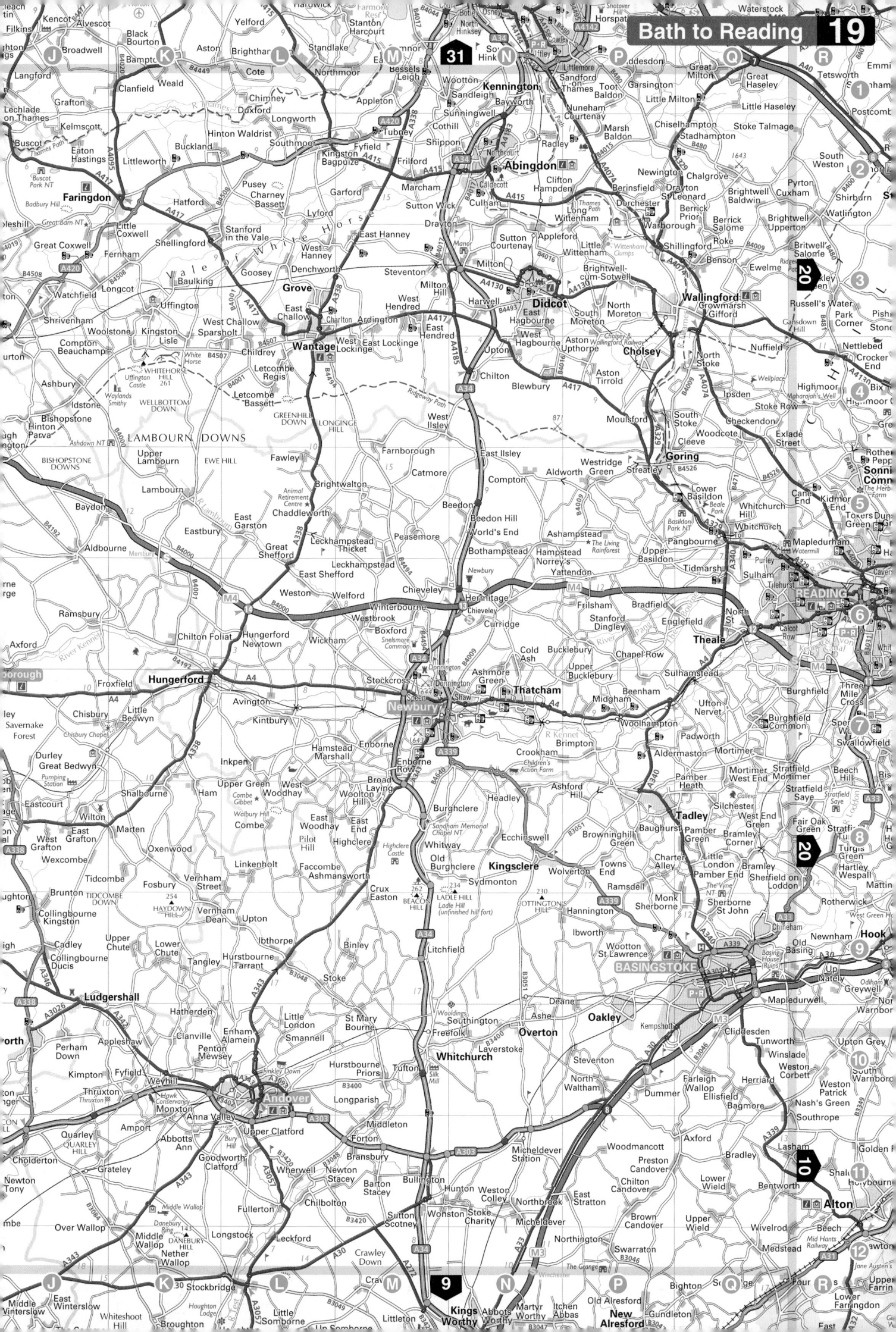

Ramsgate

BROADSTAIRS

MARGATE

MARGATE RD

CANTERBURY, DOVER

CHATHAM STREET

CHATHAM HOUSE GRAMMAR SCHOOL

SCHOOL

RAMSGATE SPORTS CENTRE

ALMSHOUSES

LIBRARY
FIRE STA
SCHOOL

DSS

GRANVILLE THEATRE & CINEMA

BANDSTAND

DC OFFICES

LIFT

OBELISK
GROSVENOR CASINO

MARITIME MUSEUM

STEAM TUG 'CERVIA'

ARGYLE SHOPPING CENTRE

MASTHEAD

Marina

Inner Harbour

MEDICAL CENTRE

TENNIS COURTS

MOTOR MUSEUM

ST AUGUSTINE'S ABBEY

SCHOOL

RAMSGATE MODEL VILLAGE

RAMSGATE NEW PORT FREIGHT FERRY TERMINAL

(Terminal Access Road)

0   200 metres

LBM

Colne Point

MERSEA ISLAND

Cudmore Grove

East Mersea

West Mersea

Shinglehead Point

Sales Point

Bradwell Waterside
Bradwell-on-Sea

Lawrence Bay

Tillingham

Dengie

Asheldham

Southminster

Holliwell Point

Foulness Point

Burnham-on-Crouch

Wallasea Island

Courtsend

Churchend

FOULNESS ISLAND

Minster

Warden Point

Eastchurch

Leysdown-on-Sea

ISLE OF SHEPPEY

Isle of Harty

The Swale

Shell Ness

Whitstable

Whitstable Bay

Tankerton

Seasalter

Seaselife

Chestfield

South Street

Swalecliffe

Herne Bay

Hampton

Beltinge

Reculver

Bishopstone

Greenhill

Broomfield

Herne

St Nicholas at Wade

Boyden Gate

Sarre

Chislet

Wildwood

Westgate on Sea

Birchington

MARGATE

Westbrook

Cliftonville
Northdown

Kingsgate

NORTH FORELAND

Foreness Point

Lighthouse

Garlinge

Salmestone Grange

Lydden

Westwood

ISLE OF THANET

Acol

Kent International

Broadstairs

Dumpton

Hereson

St Peter's

Ramsgate

Faversham

Oare

Broom Street

Graveney

Goodnestone

Yorkletts
Highstreet

Dargate

Druidstone

Tyler Hill

Broad Oak

Hoath

Upstreet

West Stourmouth

East Stourmouth

Westmarsh

Pegwell Bay

Oostende

Richborough

Sandwich Bay

Lewson Street

Painter's Forstal

Ospringe

Preston

Hernhill

Staplestreet

Dunkirk

Blean

Rough Common

Upper Harbledown

Hales Place

Sturry

Fordwich

Littlebourne

Wickhambreaux

Seaton

Ickham

Preston

Elmstone

Cop Street

Hoaden

Ash

Durlock

Wingham

Marshborough

Woodnesborough

Sandwich

Royal St George's

North Street

Sheldwich

Hogben's Hill

Selling

Old Wives Lees

Overland

South Street

Harbledown

Thanington

Chartham Hatch

Canterbury

Bekesbourne

Patrixbourne

Bramling

Staple

Goodnestone

Eastry

Statenborough

Ham

Hacklinge

Finglesham

Eastling

Badlesmere

Shottenden

Chilham

Dane Street

Shalmsford Street

Nackington

Chartham

Street End

Bridge

Lower Hardres

Bishopsbourne

Higham Park

Adisham

Aylesham

Nonington

Chillenden

Ratling

Betteshanger

Northbourne

Great Mongeham

Upper

Ripple

The Downs

Deal

Challock

Molash

Godmersham

Garlinge Green

Petham

Kingston

Elham Valley

Barham

Womenswold

Tilmanstone

Elvington

Lower Eythorne

Sutton

East Studdal

Leaveland

Charing

A252

Sole Street

Derringstone

Barfrestone

Woolage Green

Shepherdswell

North Langdon

West Langdon

Martin

Kingsdown

Walmer

Crundale

Waltham

Bossingham

Stelling Minnis

Denton

Coldred

Sutton Downs

Ringwould

Westwell

Leacon

Boughton Aluph

Wye

Crown

Bodsham Green

Wingmore

Lydden

East Kent Railway

North Downs Way

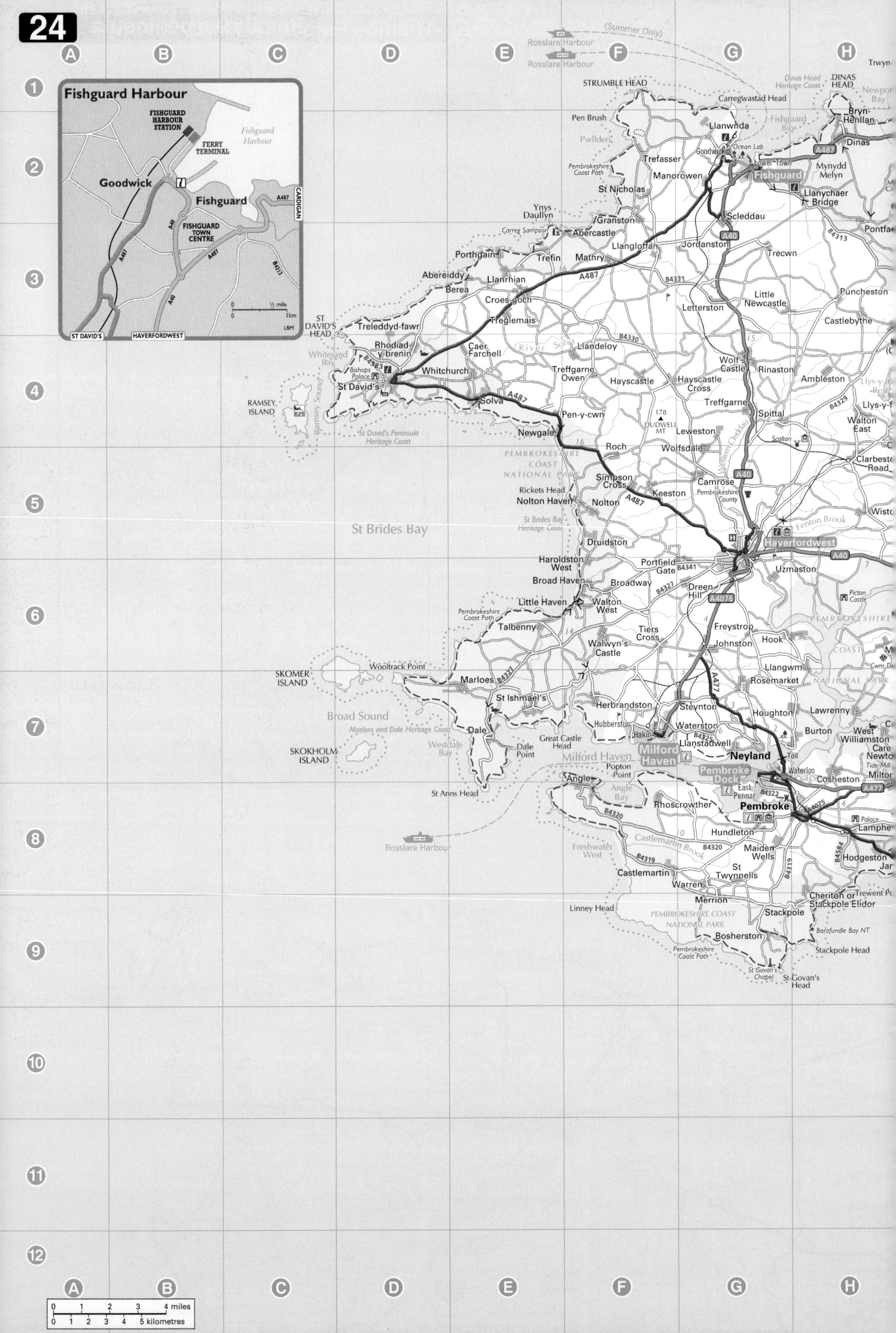

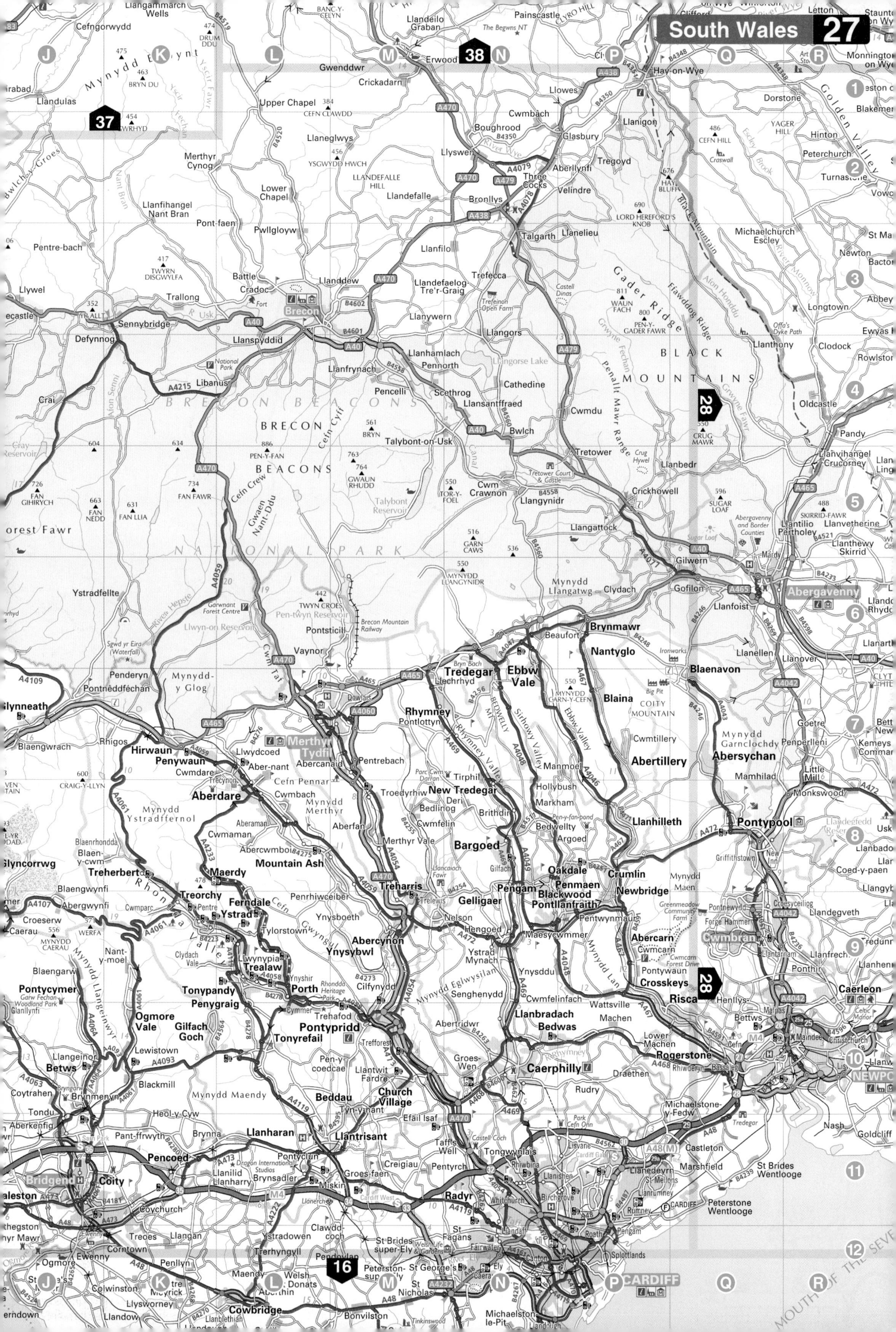

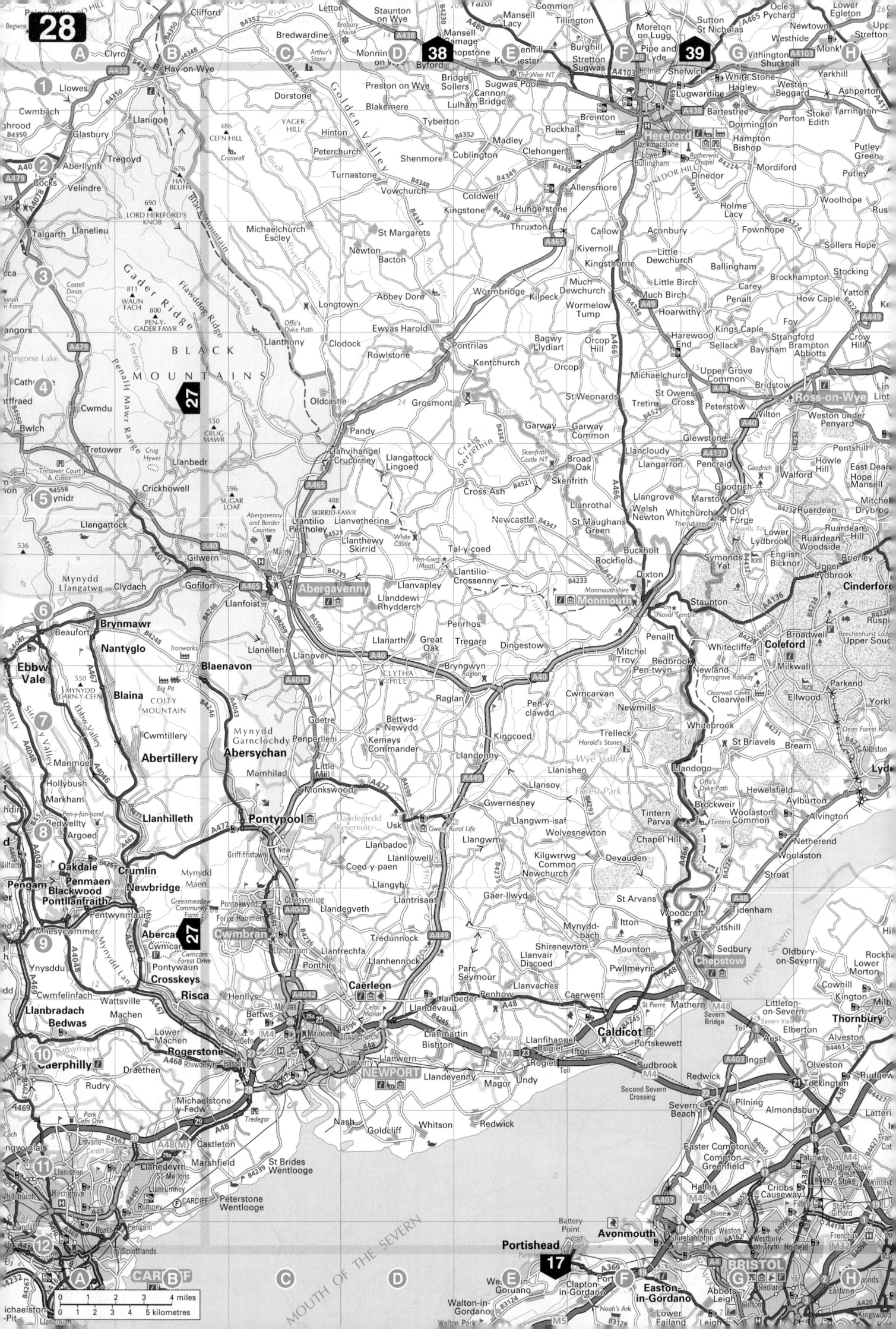

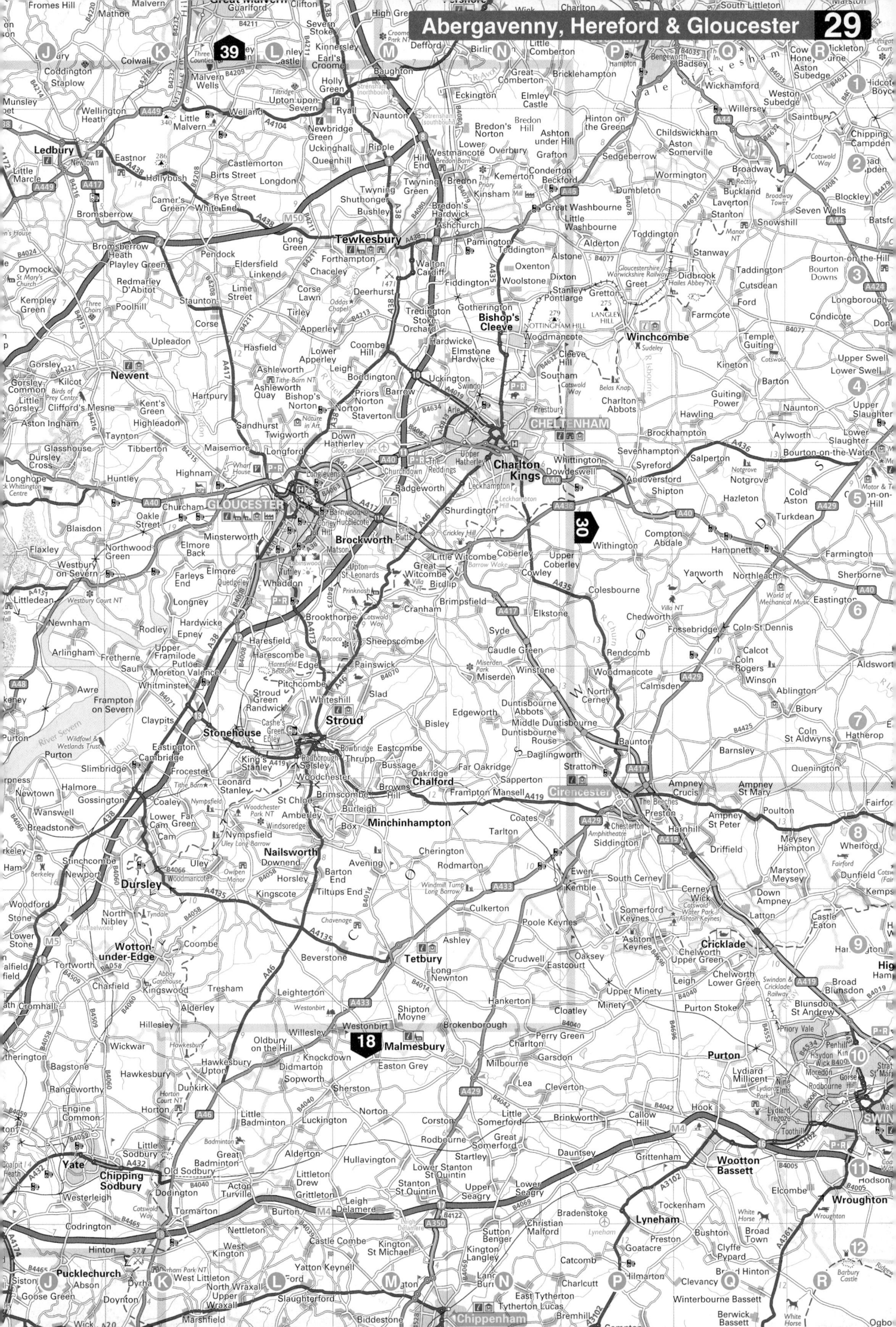

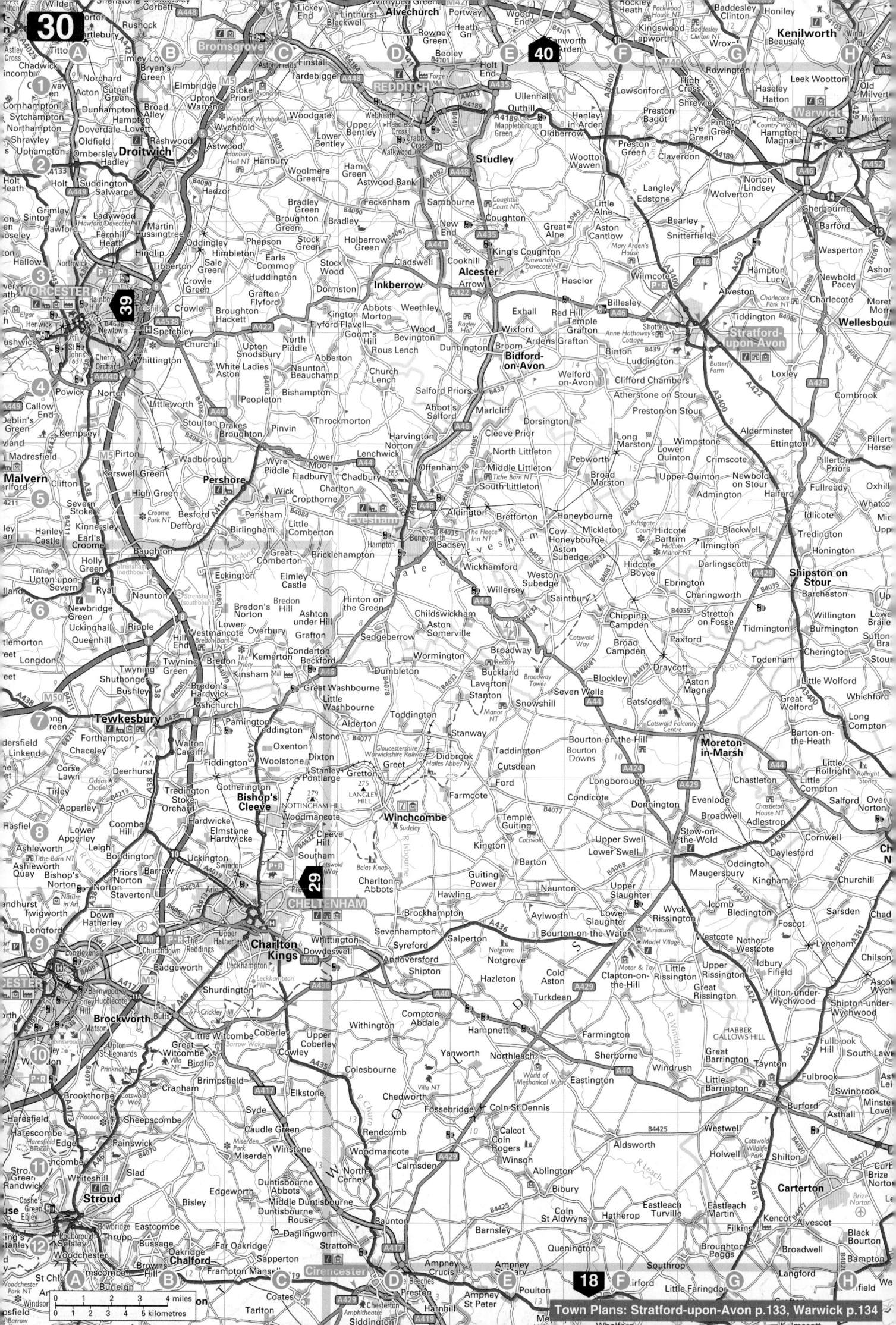

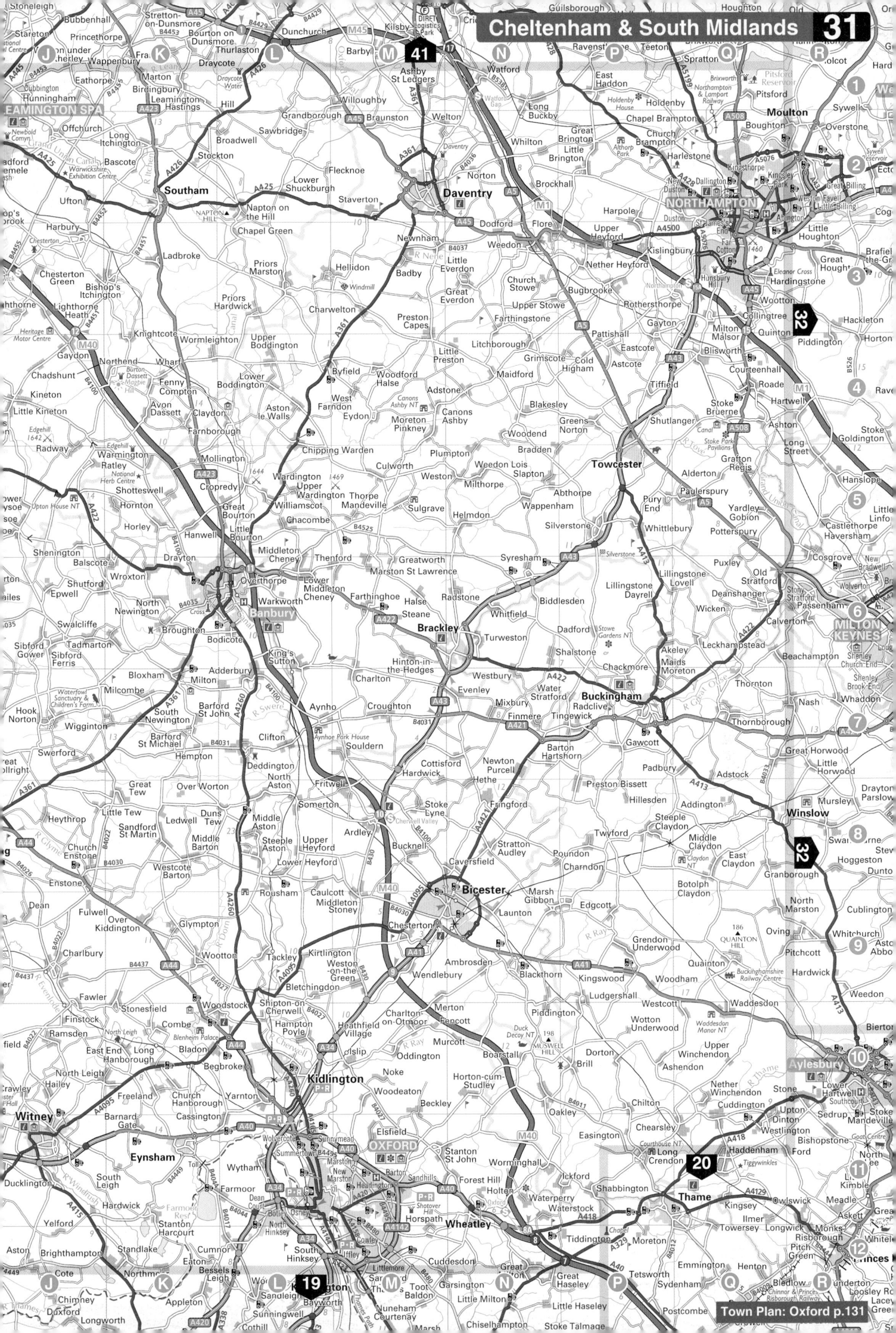

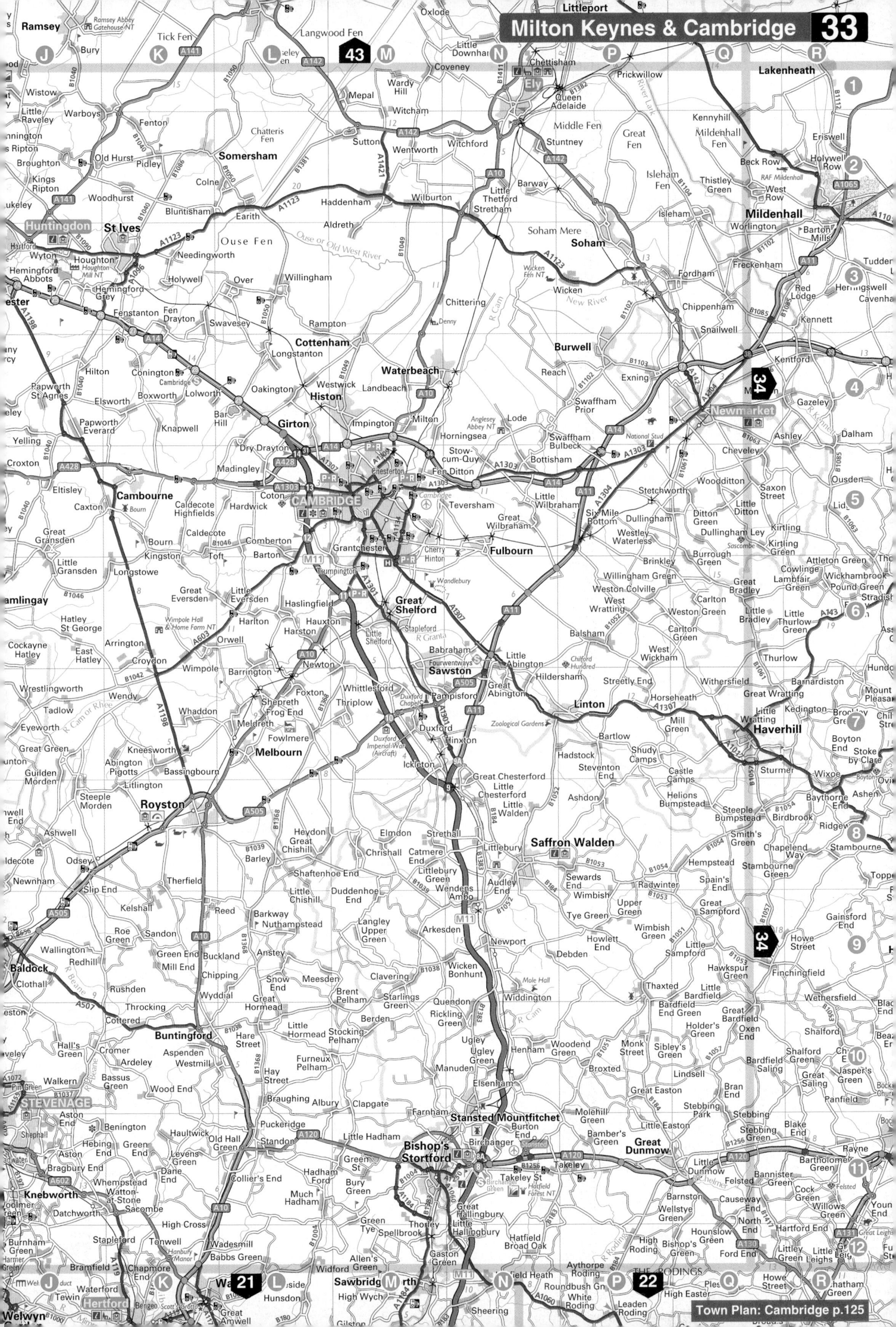

Suffolk Heritage Coast

Covehithe
South Cove
Sole Bay
Southwold
Walberswick

Dunwich

Minsmere RSPB
Westleton
Eastbridge
Leiston
Thorpe Ness
Thorpeness
Aldringham
Coldfair Green
Friston
Knodishall
Saxmundham
Sternfield
Snape Street
High Street
Aldeburgh
The Maltings
Iken
Sudbourne
Aldeburgh Bay
Orford
Orford Ness
Orfordness-Havergate
Suffolk Heritage Coast

Gissing
Tivetshall St Mary
Pulham Market
Pulham St Mary
Starston
Homersfield
Ilketshall St Margaret
Corner
Redisham
Street
Wortwell
St Margaret South Elmham
Rumburgh
Brampton
Stoven
Wrentham
Shimpling
Dickleburgh
Needham
Rushall
Harleston
Mendham
Weybread
Withersdale Street
St Cross South Elmham
St James South Elmham
Spexhall
Wissett
Westhall
Uggeshall
Wangford
Reydon
Diss
Billingford
Hoxne
Weybread Street
Metfield
Fressingfield
Wingfield
Linstead Parva
Cheditson
Holton
Blyford
Wenhaston
Blythburgh
Lighthouse
Scole
Stuston
Brome
Oakley
Brome Street
Cross Street
Heckfield Green
Denham
Stradbroke
Ashfield Green
Huntingfield
Walpole
Thorington
Bramfield
Blackheath
Halesworth
Cookley
Cratfield
Heveningham

Eye
Braiseworth
Redlingfield Green
Athelington
Wilby
Horham
Wootten Green
Brundish Street
Ubbeston Green
Peasenhall
Sibton
Darsham
Westleton
Stoke Ash
Occold
Redlingfield
Brundish
Crown Corner
Worlingworth
Badingham
Yoxford
Middleton
Middleton Moor
Thorndon
Bedingfield Southolt
Fingal Street
Tannington
Bruisyard
Bruisyard Street
Rendham
Theberton
Thwaite
Rishangles
Bedingfield Street
Shop Street
Bedfield
Saxtead Little Green
Dennington
Cransford
Kelsale
Carlton
Eastbridge
Wetheringsett
Kenton
Monk Soham
Saxtead
Saxtead Green
Post Mill
Shawsgate
Swefling
Great Glemham
Benhall Street
Benhall Green
Saxmundham
Mickfield
Winston
Ashfield
Earl Soham
Framlingham
North Green
Stratford St Andrew
Sternfield
Knodishall
Mill Green
Debenham
Cretingham
Brandeston
Parham
Friday Street
Friston
Wetherup Street
Crowfield
Pettaugh
Framsden
Kettleburgh
Hacheston
Farnham
Snape
Stonham Aspal
Suffolk Owl Sanctuary
Helmingham
Helmingham Hall
Monewden
Letheringham
Easton
Marlesford
Little Glemham
Gosbeck
Otley
Charsfield
Wickham Market
Blaxhall
Ashbocking
Ashbocking Green
Clopton Corner
Dallinghoo
Debach
Pettistree
Campsea Ash
Tunstall
Swilland
Grundisburgh
Clopton
Bredfield
Rendlesham
Chillesford
Barham
Henley
Witnesham
Burgh
Ufford
Eyke
Bromeswell
Butley
Claydon
Akenham
Tuddenham
Hasketon
Melton
Great Bealings
Sutton Hoo NT
Woodbridge
Capel St Andrew
Westerfield
Playford
Martlesham
Boyton
Castle Hill
Kesgrave
Martlesham Heath
Sutton
Waldringfield
IPSWICH
Suffolk
Brightwell
Shottisham
Hollesley
Chantry
Newbourne
Hemley
Belstead
Wherstead
Nacton
Bucklesham
Alderton
Hollesley Bay
Freston
Levington
Kirton
Falkenham
Woolverstone
Trimley
Tattingstone White Horse
Tattingstone
Holbrook
Chelmondiston
Walton
Old Felixstowe
Stutton
Shotley
Felixstowe
Erwarton
Shotley Street
Harkstead
Shotley Gate
The Redoubt
Holbrook Bay
International Ferry Terminal
Bath Side
Landguard Fort
Mistley
Wrabness
Upper Dovercourt
Dovercourt Harbour
Landguard Point
New Mistley
Bradfield
Ramsey
Harwich
Horsleycross Street
Wix
Bradfield Heath
Little Oakley
Hoek van Holland
Goose Green
Great Oakley
Hoek van Holland Esbjerg
Tendring Heath
Stones Green
Horsey Island
Pennyhole Bay
Little Bentley
Tendring Green
Goose Green
Kirby le Soken
The Naze
Tendring
Thorpe Green
Thorpe-le-Soken
Kirby Cross
Walton on the Naze
Weeley
Weeley Heath
Cook's Green
Great Holland
Frinton-on-Sea
Little Clacton
Holland-on-Sea
Jaywick
CLACTON-ON-SEA

Harwich International Port

River Stour
HARWICH INTERNATIONAL PORT STATION (PASSENGER FERRY TERMINAL)
CAR FERRY TERMINAL
EAST DOCK RD
INTERNATIONAL FREIGHT ENTRANCE
WEST DOCK RD
PETROL STATION
Parkeston
PARKESTON ROUNDABOUT
ST NICHOLAS ROUNDABOUT
PATRICKS JUNCTION
HARWICH
Premier Travel Inn
IPSWICH, COLCHESTER
A120
DOVERCOURT BYPASS
PARKESTON ROAD
MAIN ROAD
B1352
MAIN ROAD
B1414
FRONKS ROAD
B1352
½ mile
1 km
LBM

36

A B C D E F G H

1

2
C A R D I G A N

B A Y

3

4

5

6

Llar

Llansantffraid

Llanon

7
Aberarth

Aberaeron

8
New Quay

Ceredigion Heritage Coast
Llanina
Llwyncelyn
A482

Maen-y-groes
Llanerchaeron NT

Cwmtydu
Cross
Inn
Gilfachrheda
Llanarth
Oakford

Nanternis
A486
B4342

A4339

Caerwedros 7
A487
Dihewyd
Aerc
Ynys-Lochtyn
Ystra

Llwyndafydd
Mydroilyn

Pontgarreg
B4321
Temp

Llangranog
B4334
Plwmp
B4338

Penbryn
9
Pentregat
A486
Gorsgoch

Aberporth
Sarnau
15
Talgarreg
311

Cardigan
Island
Felinwynt-Rainforest
& Butterfly Centre
Traethsaith
Brynhoffnant
Cwrt-newydd
B4459
324

Cardigan Island
Coastal Farm Park
Mwnt
Clettwr Fawr
B4338

Y Ferwig
Tremain
Blaenannerch
Tan-y-groes
Pontshaen
Cwmsychbant

Penparc
A487
Glynarthen
Rhydlewis
Ffostrasol
12
A475

Poppit
Sands
Blaenporth
B4571
Maesllyn
Prengwyn
Llanwenog
Drefach

Pembrokeshire
Coast-Path
Beulah
Bettws
Evan
Hawen
Troedyraur
Penrhiw-pal
Tre-groes
Rhydowen
Llanybydder

10
St Dogmaels Moylgrove
Heritage Coast
St-Dogmaelsh
B4546
B4548
Llechryd
Ponthirwaun
Brongest
Croes-lan
258
Rock Mill Woollen
& Water Mill
Capel
Dewi

Geibwr Bay
Welsh
Wildlife Centre
A484
Llandygwydd
12
Llandysul
A485

Moylgrove
Pen-y-
bryn
A487
Afon Teifi
NVY SIDE
Cwm-
cou
Landyfriog
15
Teifi
Valley
Railway
Penrhiwllan
Llandysul
Llanfihangel-
ar-arth
Trwyn-y-bwa
Cilgerran
Abercych
Cenarth
Adpar
Henllan
Llangeler
Pontwelly
Llanllwni
NAS
EAD
Newport
A478
Rhoshill
Pen-rhiw
B4332
Newcastle
Emlyn
A484
Drefach
B4336

Bryn-
Henllan
A4571
Nevern
Felindre
Farchog
Newchapel
Felindre
Pentre-cwrt
Dinas
Newport
B4582
Castell
Henllys
Eglwyswrw
Boncath
25
Cwmhiraeth
Glynteg
23
Mynydd
Llanllwhi

311
Pentre
Ifan
Crosswell
Blaenffos
Capel Iwan
Cwmpengraig
Pencader
New Inn
369
Gwe

12
MYNYDD
CAREGOG
Brynberian
Bwlch-y-groes
335
362
Rhos
257
314
358

Penlo
PEMBROKESHIRE COAST
Cry
ch
al
Gwyddgrug

A B C D E F G H

Pontf
Tegryn
B4333
20
A484

SELI
Hermon

NATIONAL PARK

0 1 2 3 4 miles
0 1 2 3 4 5 kilometres

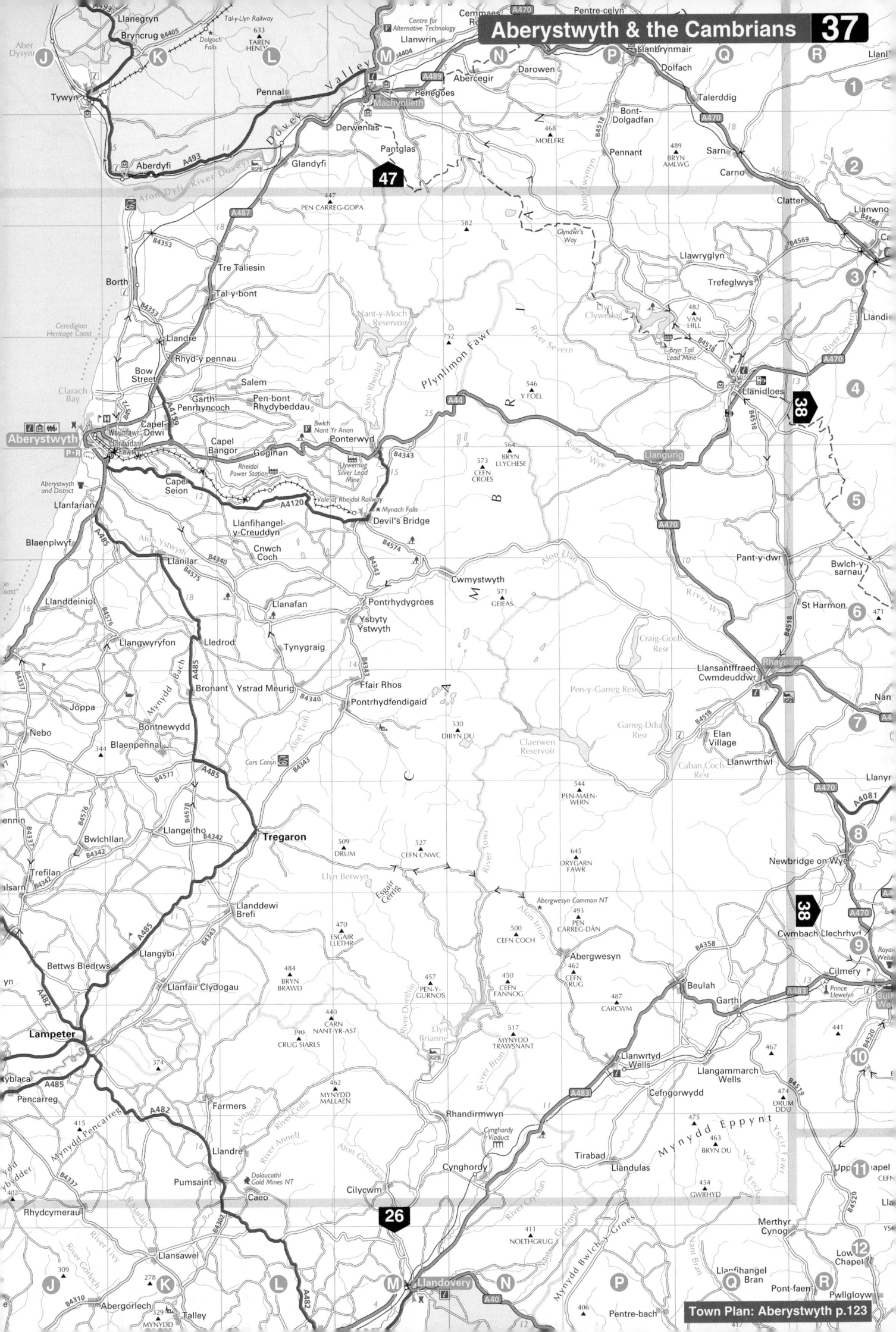

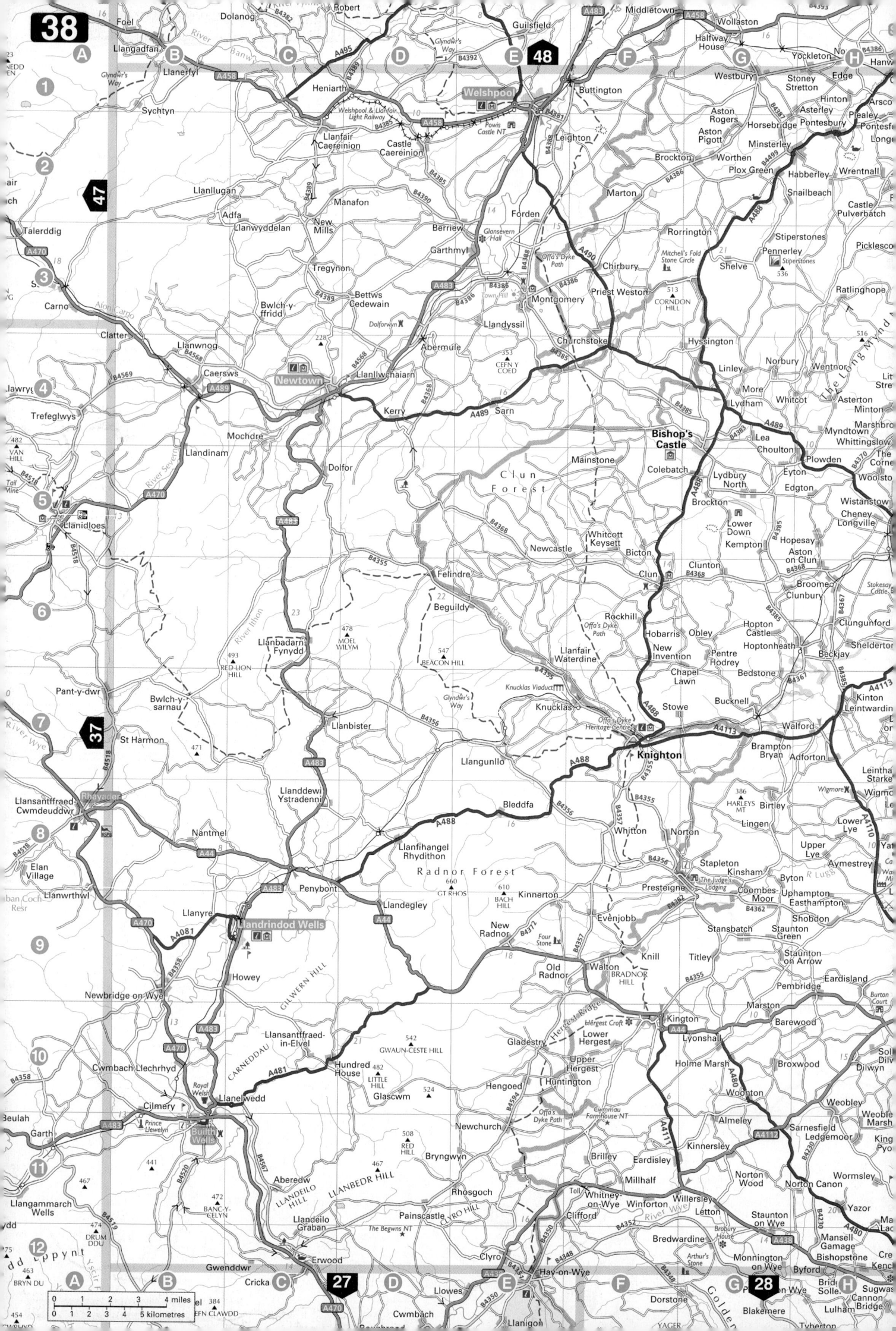

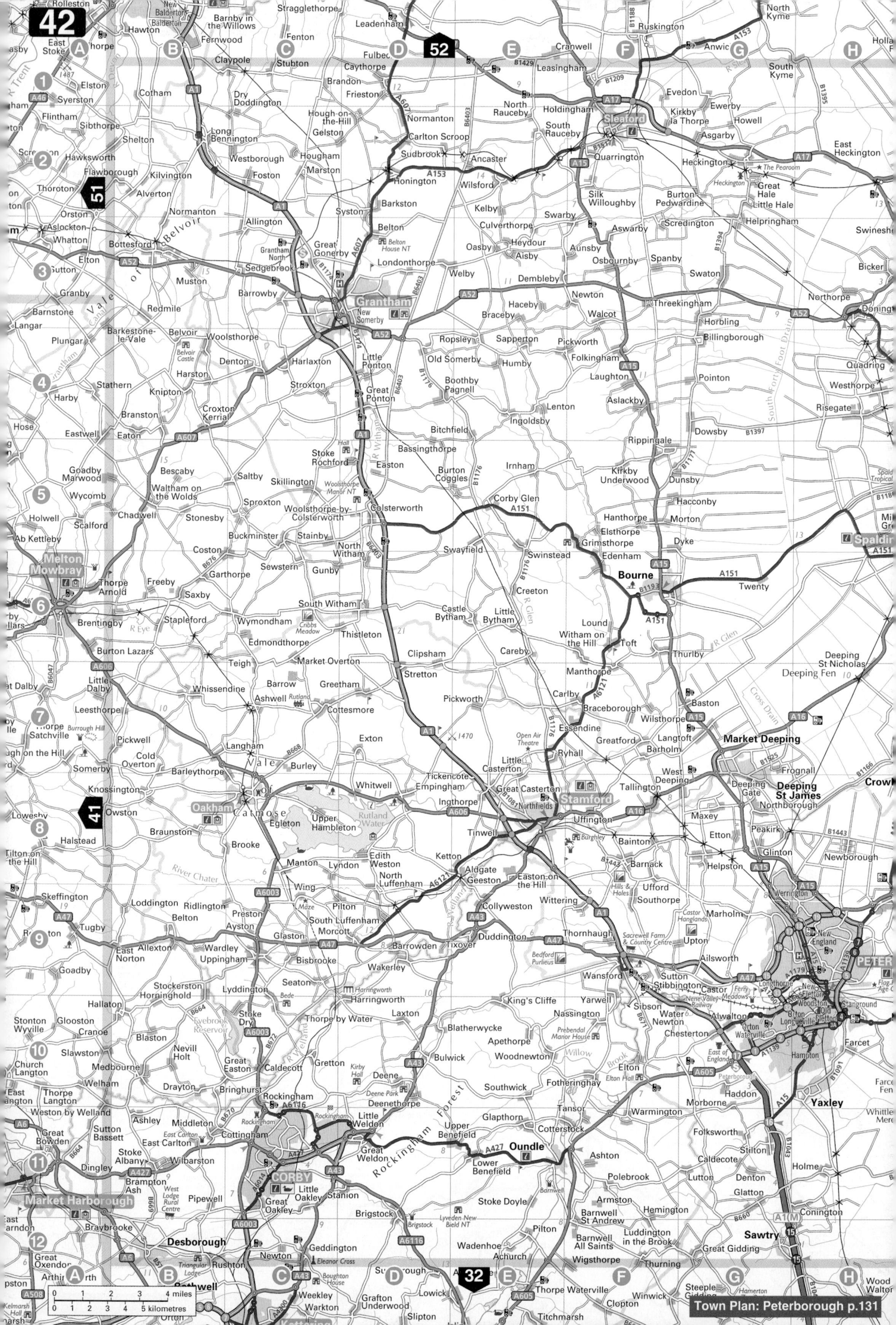

A　B　C　D　E　F　G　H

1

2

54

3

4

5

6

7

8

9

10

11

12

A　B　C　D　E　F　G　H

CAERNARFON BAY

CARDIGAN

BAY

Llanwnda
Rhostryf
Llandwrog
Carmel
Glynllifon
Penygroes
Talysarn
Pontlyfni
Llanllyfni
Nebo
Clynnog-fawr
Nasareth
Pant Glas
522
Y GYRN-DDU
Trefor
Garn-Dolben Dolb
Tre'r Ceiri
Llanaelhaearn
Bryncir
564
YR EIFL
20
Llithfaen
Trwyn y Grolech
Pistyll
St Cybi's Well
Llangybi
Pentre
Carreg Ddu
Porth Nefyn
Nefyn
Morfa Nefyn
Edern
Bodfuan
Y Ffor
B4354
Llanystumdwy
Chwilog
Llannor
Abererch
Pennarth Fawr
Criccieth
Porth Ysgaden
Tudweiliog
Llandudwen
Efailnewydd
Pen-ychain
Tremadog Bay
Porth Colman
Dinas
371
Carn Fadrun
Llaniestyn
Rhyd-y-clafdy
B4415
Bryn-mawr
Pen-y-graig
Meyllteyrn
Penrhos
Pwllheli
Llangwnnadl
Sarn
Botwnnog
Llanbedrog
Bryncroes
Porthor
Rhoshirwaun
Trwyn Llanbedrog
Llangian
St Tudwal's Road
Plas-Yn-Rhiw NT
Y Rhiw
Llanengan
Abersoch
Aberdaron
Llanfaelrhys
Bwlchtocyn
Marchros
St Tudwal's Island East
Aberdaron Bay
Porth Ysgo
Porth Neigwl
Porth Geiriad
St Tudwal's Island West
Lleyn Heritage Coast
St Mary's
BARDSEY ISLAND
Bardsey Sound

LLEYN

PENINSULA

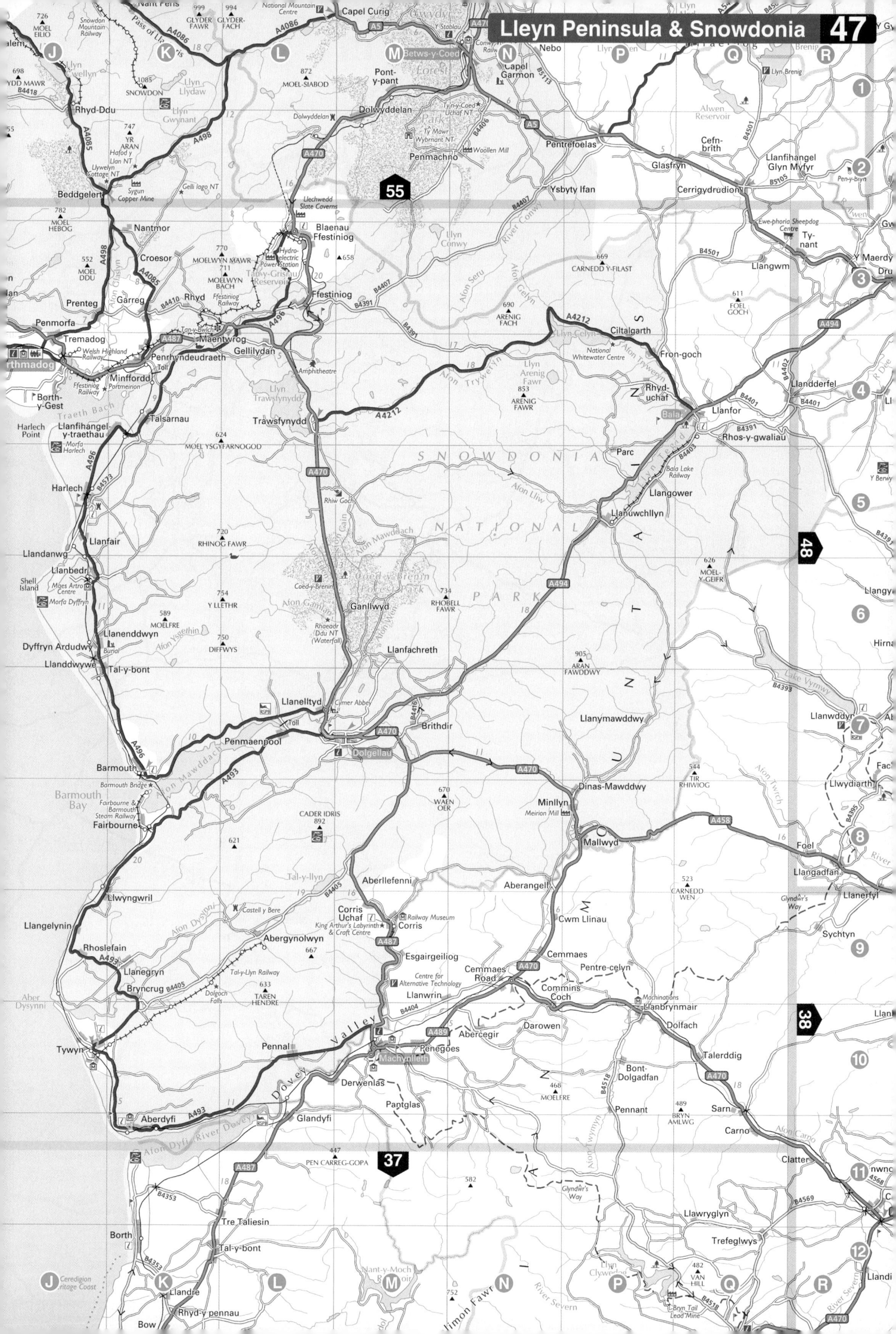

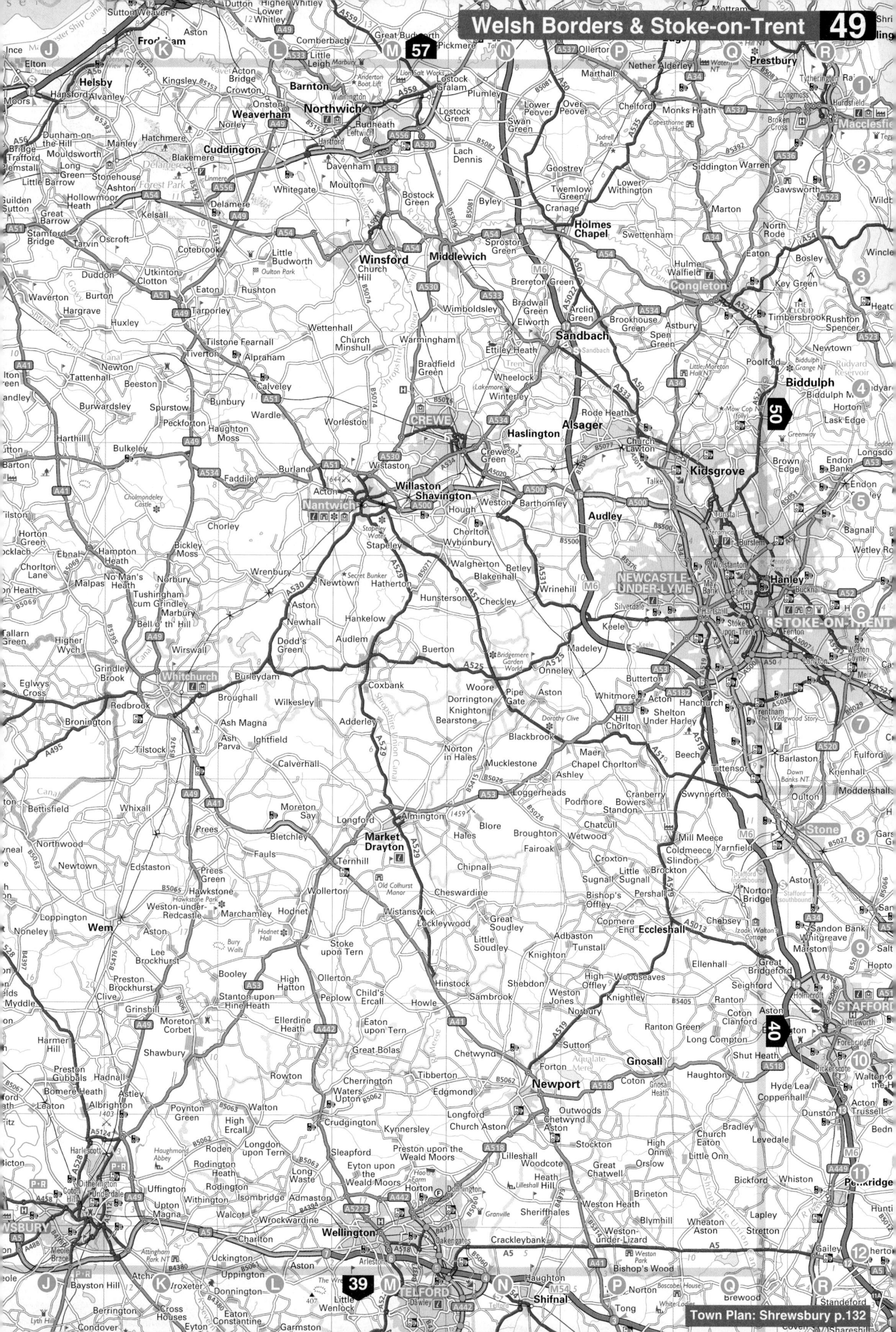

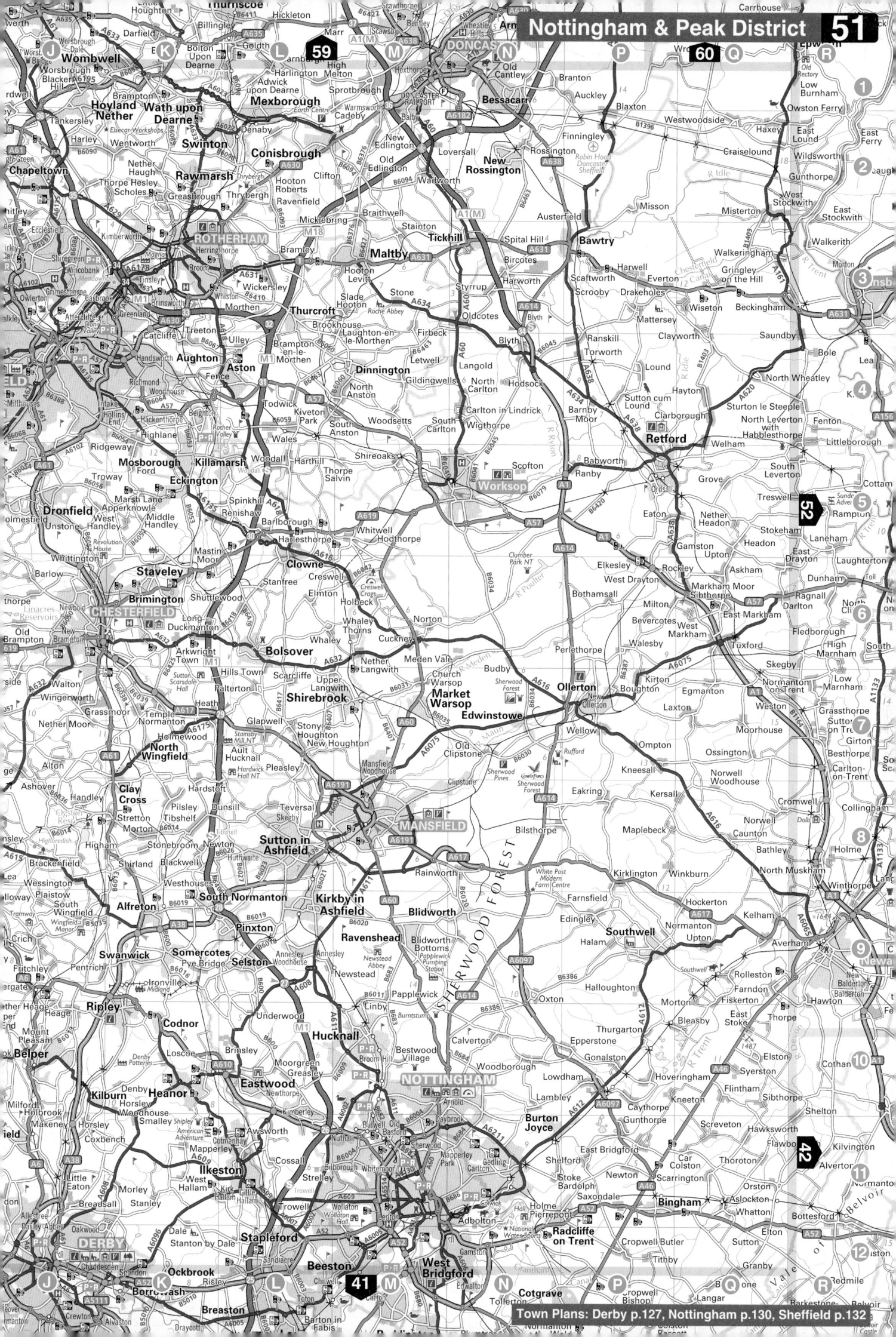

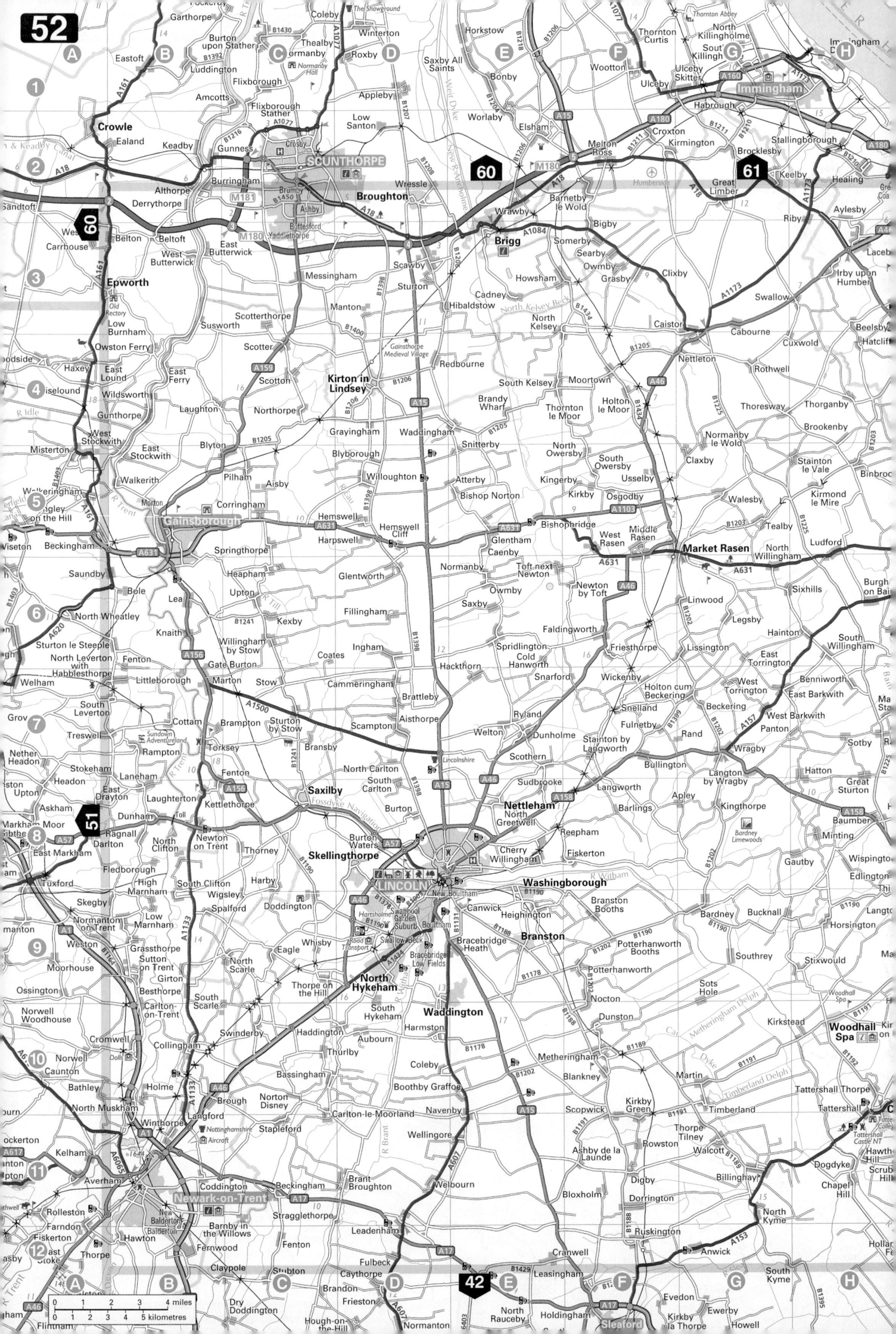

Skeffling
B1445 Easington
Kilnsea
Spurn Heritage Coast

J K L M N P Q R

SPURN HEAD
Spurn Heritage Coast

61

Rotterdam (Europoort)
Zeebrugge

GRIMSBY
West Marsh
Old Clee
Cleethorpes
Nunsthorpe
Scartho
Thrunscoe
The Jungle
Pleasure Island
Humberston

New Waltham
Holton le Clay
Waltham Windmill
Brigsley
Ashby cum Fenby
Grainsby
Waithe
North Thoresby
dale
Tetney
North Cotes
Marsh Chapel
Wold Newton
Fulstow
Grainthorpe
North Somercotes
Ludborough
Lincolnshire Wolds Railway
Conisholme
North Ormsby
Covenham St Bartholomew
Covenham St Mary
Saltfleet
Utterby
Yarburgh
Fotherby
Little Grimsby
Alvingham
North Cockerington
Saltfleetby St Clement
Kelstern
A631
South Elkington
South Cockerington
Saltfleetby All Saints
Welton le Wold
Grimoldby
Saltfleetby St Peter
Theddlethorpe St Helen
A157
Louth
Manby
Theddlethorpe All Saints
Hallington
Little Carlton
Raithby
Legbourne
Great Carlton
Withcall
North Reston
Mablethorpe
Tathwell
Little Cawthorpe
Gayton le Marsh
Trusthorpe
Haugham
South Reston
Withern
Sutton on Sea
Cadwell Park
Muckton
Authorpe
Maltby le Marsh
Sandilands
Asterby
Maidenwell
Burwell
Belleau
Beesby
Scamblesby
Saleby
Markby
Oxcombe
White Pit
Swaby
Watermill & Wildfowl Gardens
Huttoft
Ketsby
Aby
Bilsby
Thurlby
South Thoresby
Belchford
South Ormsby
Alford
Anderby Creek
Far Thorpe
Driby
Rigsby
Anderby
Fulletby
Tetford
Well
Farlesthorpe
Mumby
Salmonby
Brinkhill
Ulceby
Cumberworth
Chapel Point
West Ashby
Somersby
Sutterby
Willoughby
Hogsthorpe
Chapel St Leonards
Horncastle
Harrington
Bag Enderby
Langton
Sloothby
Ashby Puerorum
Skendleby
Habertoft
Addlethorpe
Greetham
Aswardby
Sausthorpe
Partney
Welton le Marsh
Fantasy Island
High Toynton
Hagworthingham
Scremby
Ingoldmells
Mareham on the Hill
Snipe Dales
Raithby
Candlesby
Orby
Ingoldmells Point
Hameringham
Mavis Enderby
Spilsby
Ashby by Partney
Gunby
Asgarby
Hundleby
Monksthorpe
Burgh le Marsh
Hareby
Halton Holegate
Great Steeping
Bratoft
Moorby
Old Bolingbroke
Toynton All Saints
Northcote
Wood Enderby
Miningsby
Bolingbroke
Irby in the Marsh
Skegness
East Kirkby
East Keal
Little Steeping
Firsby
Revesby
Keal Cotes
Croft
Battle of Britain Memorial Flight
Lincolnshire Aviation
Stickford
Fendike Corner
Thorpe St Peter
Tumby Woodside
New Bolingbroke
New Leake
Wainfleet All Saints
New York
New Stickney
Eastville
Wainfleet St Mary
Gibraltar Point
East Fen
Friskney
West Fen Northlands
Leake Common Side
Gipsey Bridge
Frithville
Sibsey Trader
Sibsey
Wrangle
Fishtoft Drove
Old Leake
Anton's Gowt
Hill Dyke
Leverton
Benington

J K L M N P Q R

43

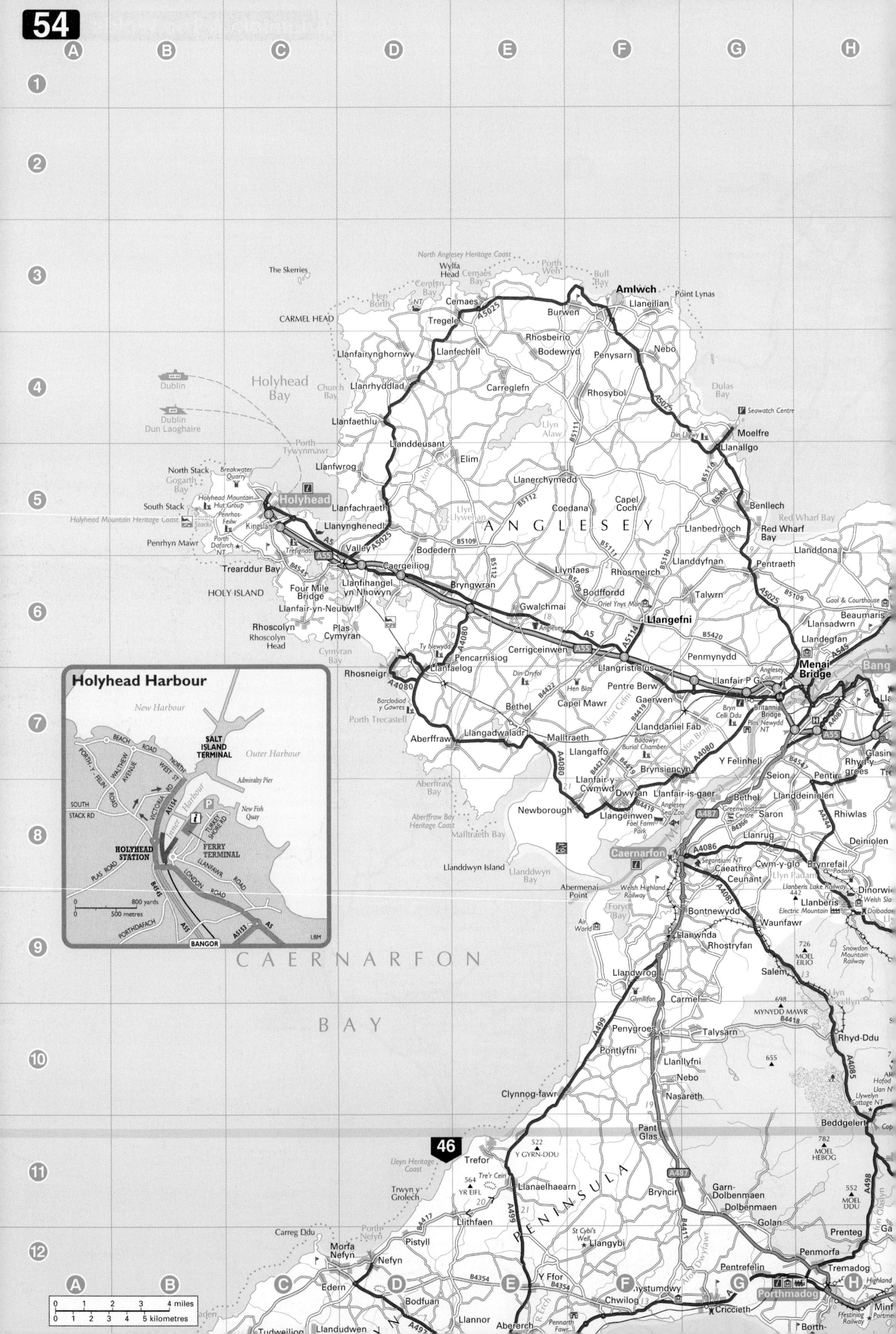

Holyhead Harbour

New Harbour

SALT ISLAND TERMINAL

Outer Harbour

Admiralty Pier

New Fish Quay

BEACH ROAD

PORTH-Y-FELIN ROAD

WALTHEW AVENUE

NORTH

WEST ST

VICTORIA RD

SOUTH STACK RD

PLAS ROAD

A5154

TURKEY SHORE RD

HOLYHEAD STATION

FERRY TERMINAL

LLANFAWR ROAD

LONDON ROAD

B5545

PORTHDAFARCH

A55

A5153

A5

BANGOR

LBM

800 yards

500 metres

CAERNARFON

BAY

Dublin
Dublin Dun Laoghaire

Holyhead Bay

The Skerries

CARMEL HEAD

North Anglesey Heritage Coast

Wylfa Head

Porth Wen

Bull Bay

Amlwch

Point Lynas

Cemlyn Bay

Hen Borth

NT

Cemaes

Cemaes Bay

A5025

Burwen

Llaneilian

Tregele

Rhosbeirio

Bodewryd

Nebo

Llanfairynghornwy

Llanfechell

Penysarn

Church Bay

Llanrhyddlad

Carreglefn

Rhosybol

Dulas Bay

Llanfaethlu

Seawatch Centre

Llyn Alaw

B5111

Din Llogw

Moelfre

Llanddeusant

Llanallgo

Llanfwrog

Elim

A5025

B5110

Llanerchymedd

Capel Coch

Benllech

North Stack
Gogarth Bay

Breakwater Quarry

Holyhead

Holyhead Mountain Hut Group

Llanfachraeth

Red Wharf Bay

ANGLESEY

South Stack

Holyhead Mountain Heritage Coast

Penrhos-Feilw

Llyn Llywenan

Coedana

B5112

Llanynghenedl

Llanddyfnan

Red Wharf Bay

Penrhyn Mawr

Porth Dafarch NT

Kingsland

Trefignath

A5

Valley

A5025

Bodedern

B5109

Llynfaes

Rhosmeirch

Llanddona

Trearddur Bay

A5

Caergeiliog

Bodffordd

Talwrn

Pentraeth

A5543

Llanfihangel yn Nhowyn

Bryngwran

B5112

Oriel Ynys Mon

B5420

Gaol & Courthouse

HOLY ISLAND

Four Mile Bridge

Gwalchmai

Llangefni

A5

Beaumaris

Llanfair-yn-Neubwll

A55

B5109

Llansadwrn

Rhoscolyn

Plas Cymyran

Cerrigceinwen

A5114

Penmynydd

Llandegfan

Rhoscolyn Head

A4080

Llangristiolus

Llanfair P G

Menai Bridge

Cymyran Bay

Llanfaelog

Din-Dryfol

Pentre Berw

A55

Anglesey Column

Bang

Rhosneigr

A4080

Hen Blas

B4422

Gaerwen

Britannia Bridge

Barclodiad y Gawres

Bethel

Capel Mawr

A4419

Bryn Celli Ddu

Plas Newydd NT

A487

Porth Trecastell

Malltraeth

B4421

Bodowyr Burial Chamber

Llanddaniel Fab

A55

Aberffraw

Llangaffo

Brynsiencyn

Y Felinheli

B4547

Rhyd-y-grees

Llangadwaladr

A4080

Llanfair-y-Cwmwd

A4080

Anglesey Sea Zoo

Seion

Pentir

Aberffraw Bay

Dwyran

Llanfair-is-gaer

Bethel

Llanddeiniolen

Aberffraw Bay Heritage Coast

Newborough

Llangeinwen

Foel Farm Park

A487

Greenwood Centre

Saron

Rhiwlas

Malltraeth Bay

A4086

Deiniolen

Llanddwyn Island

Llanddwyn Bay

Abermenai Point

Caernarfon

Segontium NT

Caeathro

Cwm-y-glo

Brynrefail

Llanrug

Llanberis Lake Railway

Dinorwig

Welsh Slate

Ceunant

Llyn Padarn

Electric Mountain

Llanberis

Dolbadarn

Welsh Highland Railway

442

Foryd Bay

Bontnewydd

A4086

Waunfawr

Snowdon Mountain Railway

Air World

726
MOEL EILIO

Llanwnda

Rhostryfan

Salem

13

Llyn Cwellyn

Glynllifon

Carmel

698

MYNYDD MAWR

B4418

A4085

Penygroes

Talysarn

655

Rhyd-Ddu

A499

Pontllyfni

Llanllyfni

Nebo

Nasareth

Snowdon Mountain Railway

Clynnog-fawr

19

Pant Glas

Beddgelert

46

Lleyn Heritage Coast

Trefor

522
Y GYRN-DDU

A487

782
MOEL HEBOG

Trwyn y Grolech

564
Tre'r Ceiri
YR EIFL

207

Llanaelhaearn

Bryncir

Garn-Dolbenmaen

552
MOEL DDU

Carreg Ddu

Porth Nefyn

B4417

Llithfaen

A499

21

PENINSULA

Dolbenmaen

Golan

Prenteg

Morfa Nefyn

Pistyll

St Cybi's Well

Llangybi

B4411

Penmorfa

Tremadog

Gar

Nefyn

Y Ffor

B4354

Pentrefelin

Edern

B4354

Porthmadog

Bodfuan

Chwilog

Pennarth Fawr

Criccieth

Ffestiniog Railway

Llannor

Tudweiliog

Llandudwen

A497

Abererch

Afon Erch

Afon Dwyfor

Highland

Borth-

0 1 2 3 4 miles
0 1 2 3 4 5 kilometres

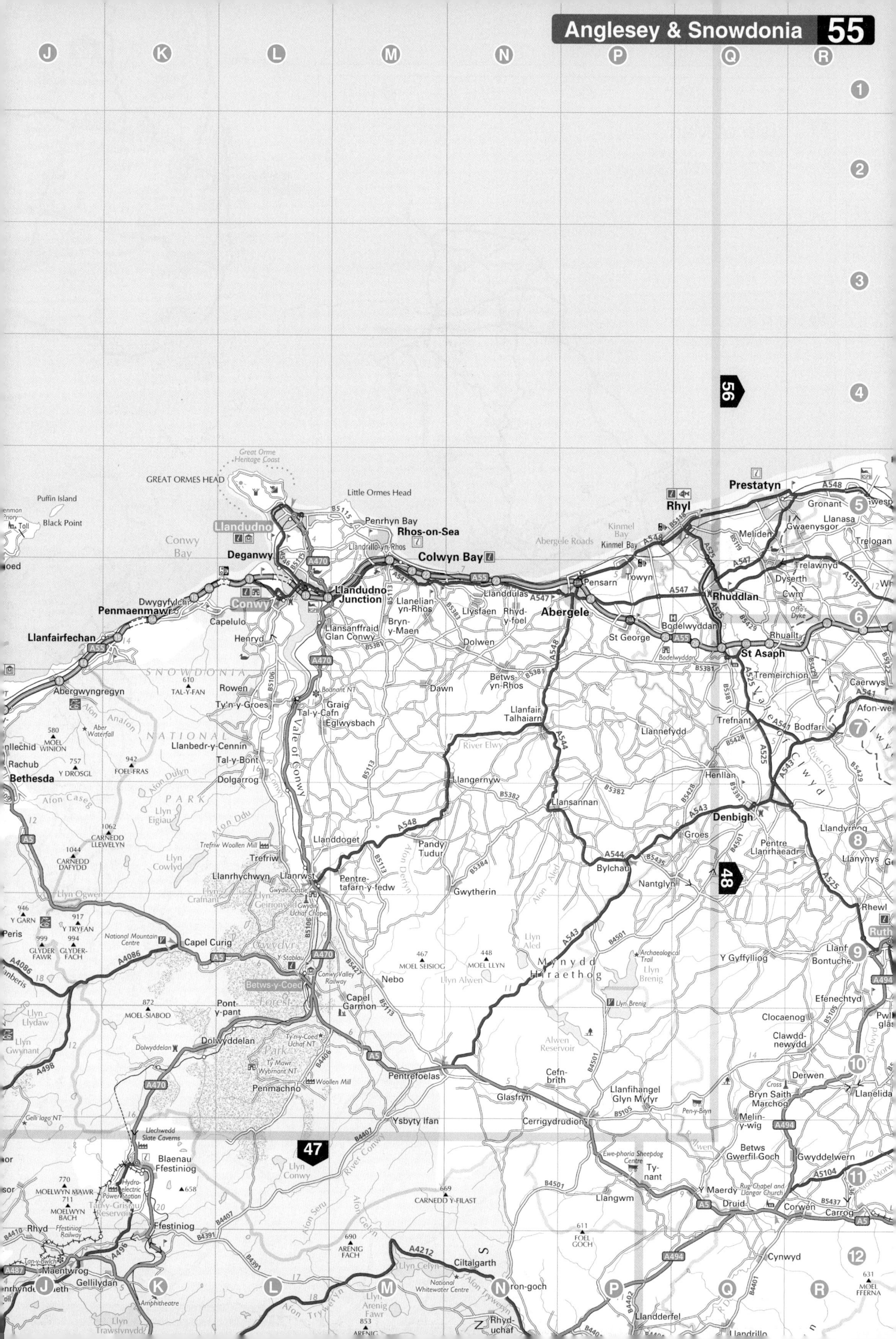

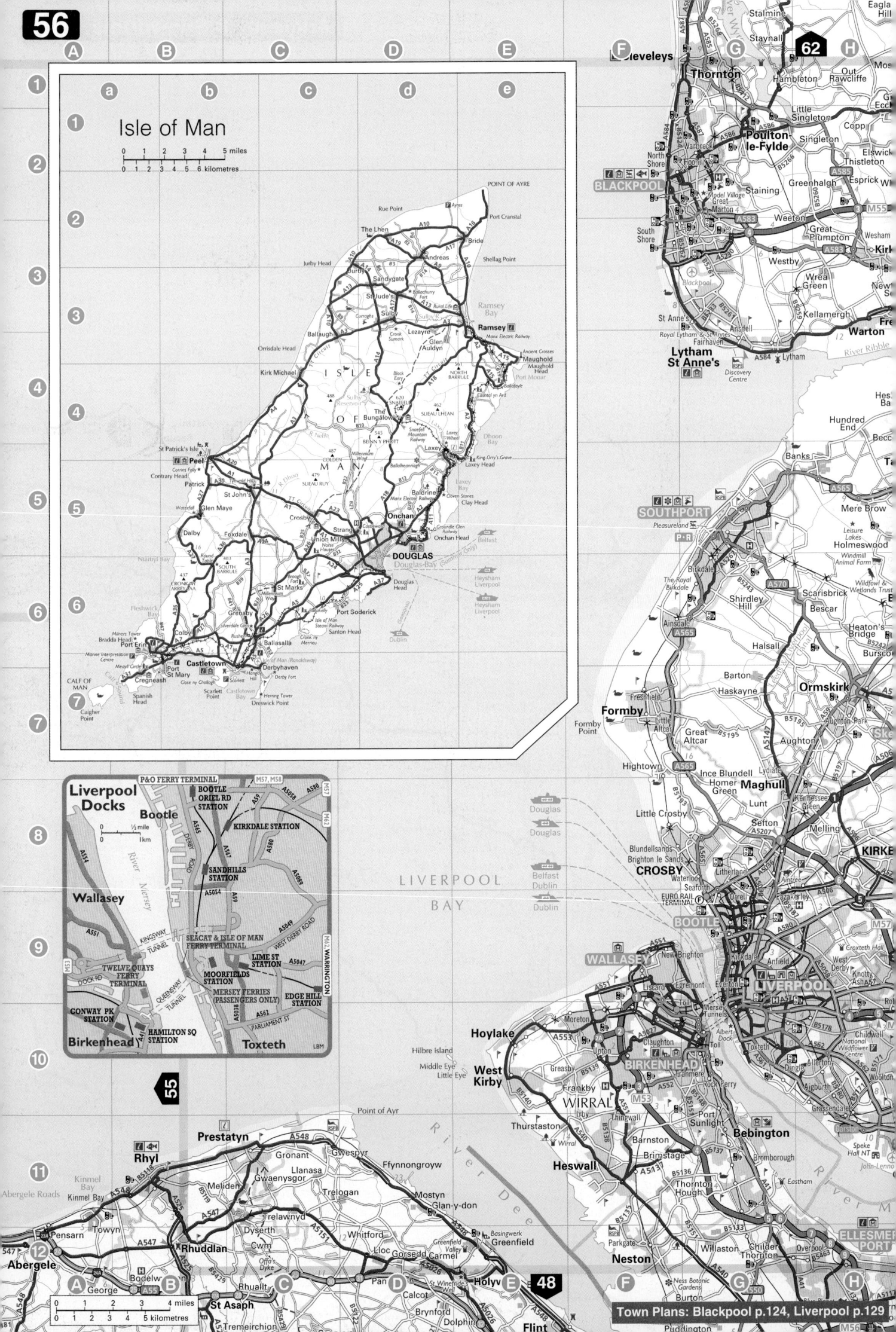

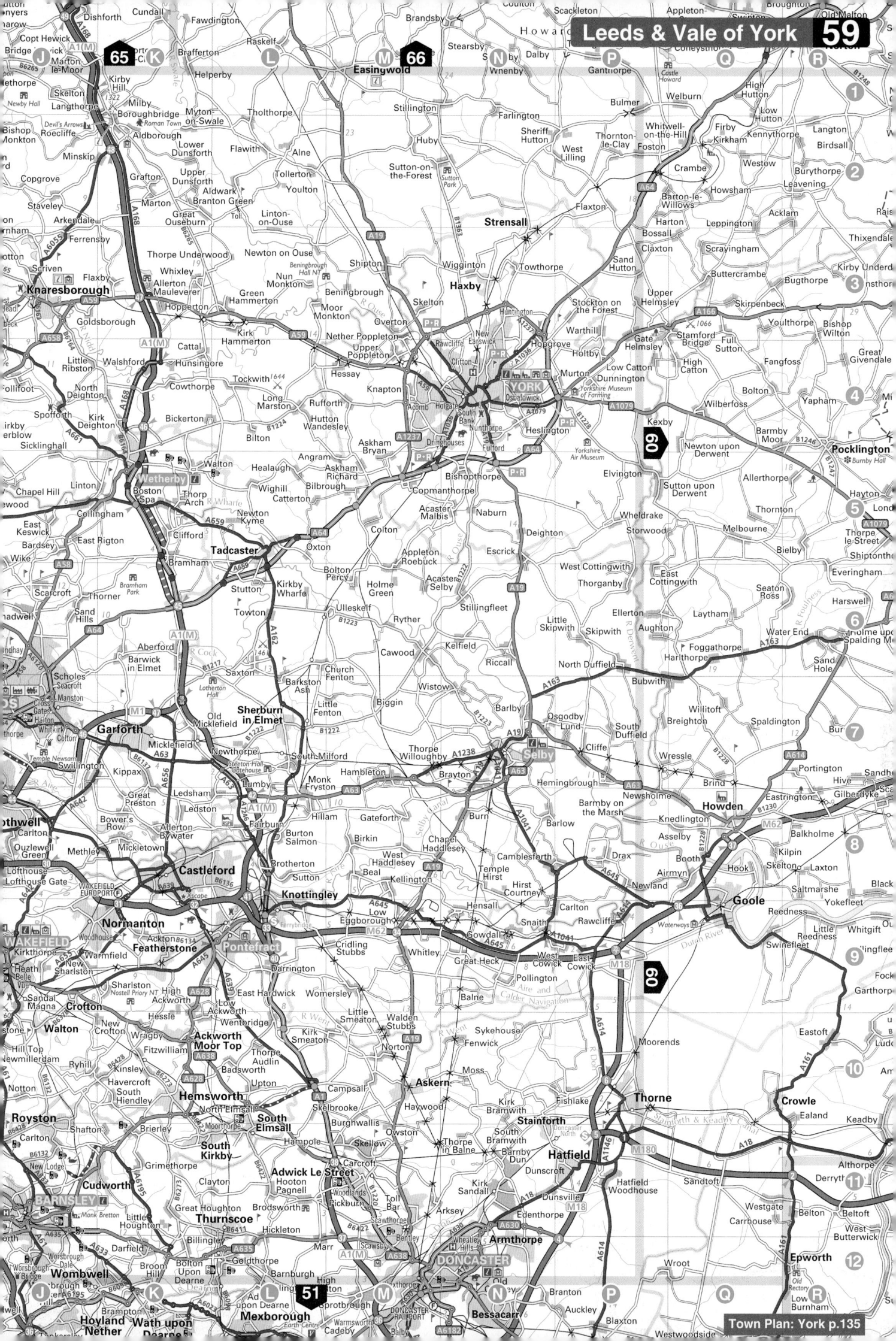

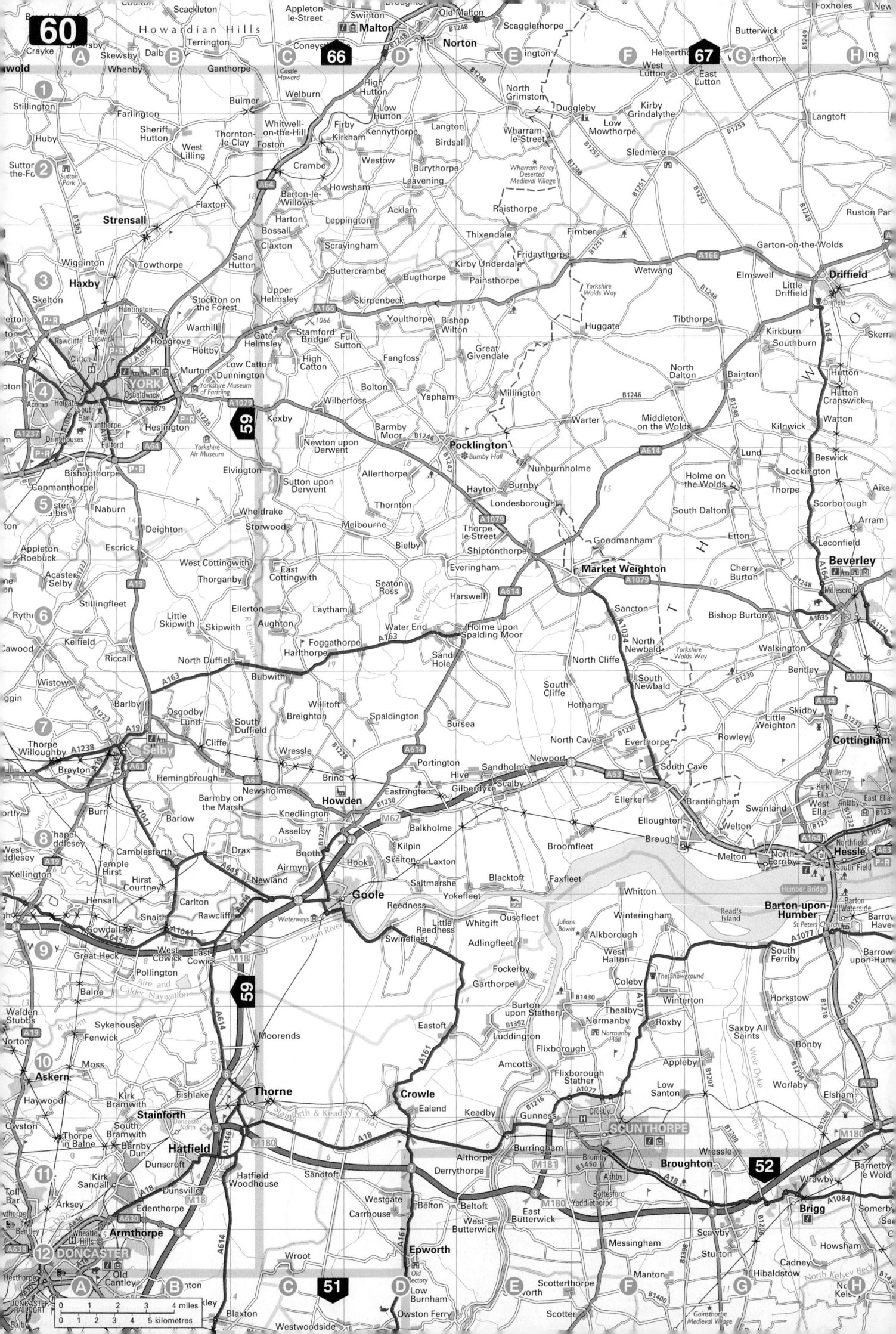

J K 67 L M N P Q R

1
2
3
4
5
6
7
8
9
10
11
12

Burton Fleming
Grindale
A165
Buckton
Bempton
B1229
North Landing
Selwicks Bay
Lighthouse
FLAMBOROUGH HEAD

J
dston
A1253
Monolith
Boynton
Bessingby
Carnaby
Haisthorpe
Thornholme
on Agnes
S
ham
horpe
D
rpe
Fraisthorpe
Gransmoor
Great Kelk
Lissett
Gembling
sford
Cruckley Animal Farm
Foston on the Wolds
Beeford
North odingham
A165
Dunnington

K
Sewerby
B1255
B259
Flamborough

L
Bridlington
Hilderthorpe

M
Bondville Miniature Village
BRIDLINGTON BAY

Barmston
B1242
15
Ulrome
Skipsea

Atwick

North Frodingham

Brandesburton
Nunkeeling
Bewholme
B1242
Honeysuckle Farm
Hornsea Mere
Hornsea

Leven
B1244
Seaton
Catwick
Sigglesthorne
Goxhill
Rolston
Mappleton
Mappleton Sands
Routh
A39
Long Riston
B1243
Little Hatfield
Rise
Great Hatfield
B1242
Great Cowden
Arnold
H
O
Skirlaugh
New Ellerby
Withernwick
insey
Wawne
Old Ellerby
Marton
West Newton
Aldbrough
earne
nswell
Swine
13
A165
L
D
E
Burton Constable Hall
Flinton
B1238
B1242
Garton
17
Coniston
Ganstead
Wyton
Sproatley
Humbleton
Hilston
A1033
Bransholme
B1237
Sutton on Hull
A165
Bilton
B1238
Lelley
B1240
Owstwick
Tunstall
Stoneferry
A1079
R
Marfleet
A1033
Preston
Elstronwick
B1239
Burton Pidsea
Roos
Rimswell
B1242
Owthorne
KINGSTON UPON HULL
International Ferry Terminal
Hedon
Burstwick
Halsham
B1362
Withernsea
Paull
Fort Paull
Thorngumbald
Keyingham
A1033
16
Ottringham
E
S
S
Winestead
Hollym
4
A1033
Holmpton
New Holland
Patrington
B1206
Goxhill
Patrington Haven
Welwick
Weeton
B1445
Easington
East Halton
Skeffling
Thornton Abbey
Thornton Curtis
North Killingholme
Immingham Dock
South Killingholme
14
Spurn Heritage Coast
Ulceby Skitter
A160
A1171
Kilnsea
Ulceby
Immingham
Habrough
15
A180
Croxton
Kirmington
B1211
B1210
Stallingborough
A180
10
Brocklesby
B1210
Spurn Heritage Coast
SPURN HEAD
Humberside
A18
Great Limber
Keelby
Healing
West Marsh
B1210
GRIMSBY
52
12
Riby
Aylesby
Great Coates
B1136
A46
A16
Nunsthorpe
Old Clee
Cleethorpes
Thrunscoe
Rotterdam (Europoort) Zeebrugge
53
Clixby
Bradley
Scartho
A1098
The Jungle
Pleasure Island
Laceby
B1203
Irby upon Humber
A1031
Humberston
Cabourne
Swallow
7
Waltham
Waltham Windmill
New Waltham
Holton le Clay
RSPB
rnoldby Beck
Beelsby
Brigsley
Ashby cum Fenby
Tetney
North Cotes
Cuxwold
Hatcliffe
Waithe
B1205
Nettleton

RIVER HUMBER

J K L M N P Q R

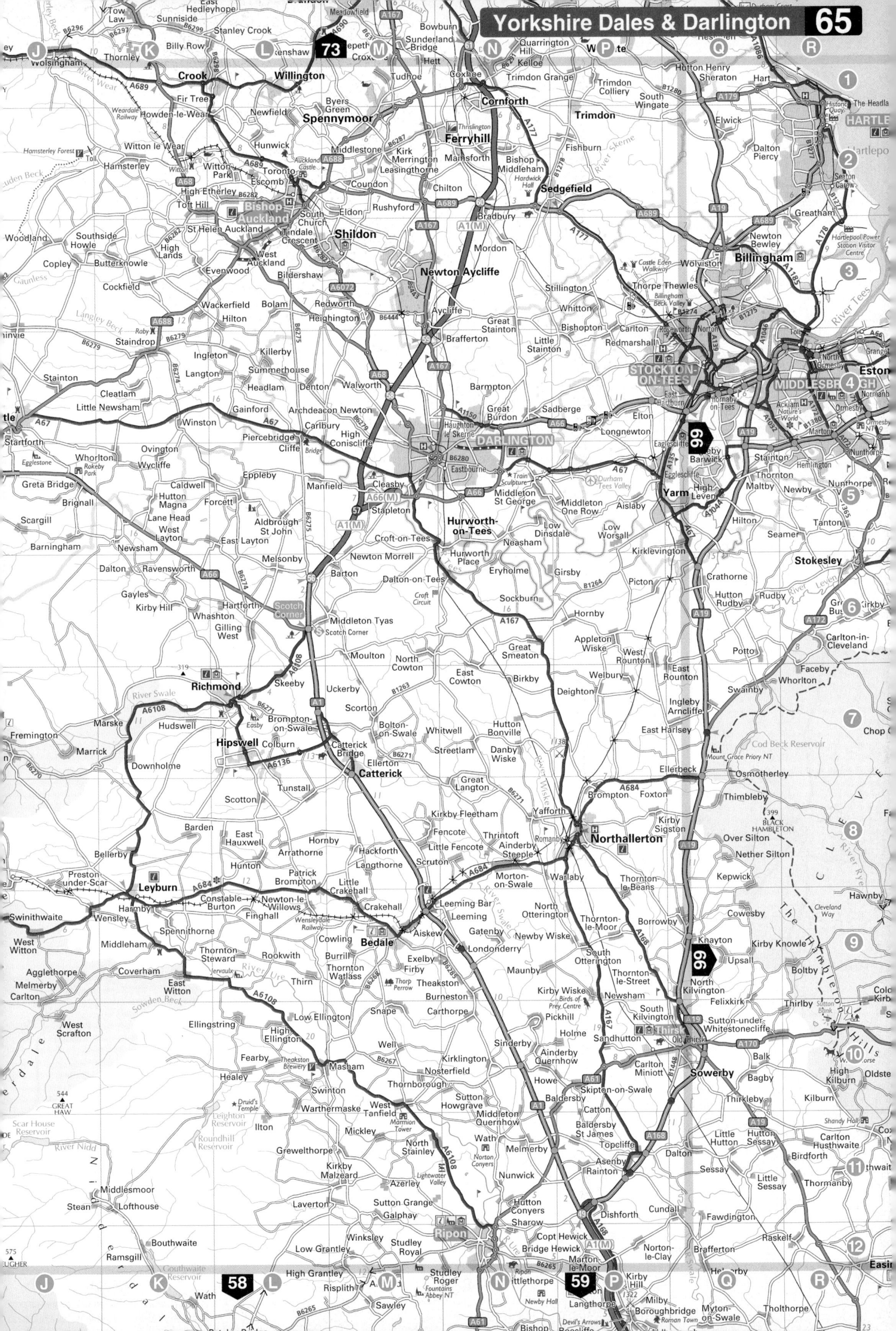

Scarborough

WHITBY

North Bay

ALEXANDRA BOWLS CENTRE

HOLLYWOOD PLAZA

COLUMBUS RAVINE

Cricket Ground

MARINE DRIVE

CASTLE

ROMAN SIGNAL STATION

ANNE BRONTE'S GRAVE

ST PETER'S (RC)

ST MARY'S

FIRE STA

YMCA TH

METH CENTRAL HALL

SCHOOL

COVERED MKT

EASTBOROUGH

LUNA PARK

RNLI

HARBOUR OFFICE

FISH QUAY

BRUNSWICK SHOPPING CENTRE

LIBRARY

TOWN HALL

FUTURIST CINEMA & THEATRE

MAG & LAW CTS

CLINIC

POL STA

STEPHEN JOSEPH TH

LIGHTHOUSE & YACHT CLUB

OLYMPIA LEISURE (SUPERBOWL)

South Bay

PICKERING, MALTON

FALSGRAVE

A64

FILEY

SCARBOROUGH STATION SUPERSTORE

YORKSHIRE COAST COLLEGE

RADIO YORK

ART GALLERY

WOOD END MUSEUM OF NATURAL HIST

ROTUNDA MUS

THE SPA COMPLEX

NORTH WAY

VALLEY BRIDGE RD

0   200 metres

LBM

North Yorkshire and Cleveland Heritage Coast

dsborough
Overdale Wyke
Lythe
Sandsend Wyke
nsley
Newholm
Whitby
Saltwick Bay
Ruswarp
Briggswath
Stainsacre
Aislaby
Sneaton
High Hawsker
Sleights
Ugglebarnby
Iburndale
smont
Ness Point or North Cheek
Robin Hood's Bay
Fylingthorpe
Robin Hood's Bay
Old Peak or South Cheek
Ravenscar
292
Staintondale
Shire Horse Centre
Hayburn Wyke
Harwood Dale
Cloughton Wyke
Cloughton
Bridestones (Rock Formation)
Bickley
Broxa
Silpho
Cromer Point
Burniston
Dalby Forest Drive
Langdale End
Hackness
Suffield
Cleveland Way
Lockton
239
Scalby
North Riding Forest Park
Scarborough
Dalby Forest
Falsgrave
Hatherleigh Deep Sea Trawler
Oliver's Mount
West Ayton
East Ayton
Eastfield
Cayton Bay
Sawdon
Irton
Osgodby
The Wyke
Wilton
Ebberston
Ruston
Hutton Buscel
Seamer
Crossgates
Allerston
Snainton
Wykeham
Cayton
Filey Brigg
Brompton
Lebberston
Filey
Gristhorpe
Yedingham
Willerby
Folkton
Muston
Filey Bay
Flixton
Staxton
Sherburn
Ganton
Yorkshire Wolds Way
Hunmanby
West Knapton
Knapton
East Heslerton
Potter Brompton
Fordon
Reighton
mpston
West Heslerton
Speeton
Flamborough Head Heritage Coast
Thornwick Bay
Thorpe Bassett
Wintringham
Foxholes
Wold Newton
Buckton
Bempton
North Landing
Selwicks Bay
cagglethorpe
ettrington
Butterwick
Burton Fleming
Grindale
Flamborough
FLAMBOROUGH HEAD
Helperthorpe
Weaverthorpe
Thwing
Lighthouse
North Grimston
Duggleby
West Lutton
East Lutton
Langtoft
Rudston
Monolith
Boynton
Bridlington
BRIDLINGTON
Kirby Grindalythe
Low
Bessingby

60

61

Girvan
Dounepark
Woodland
Pinminnoch
C
A
Barr
GR HILL
Pinmore
Balligmorrie
Lendalfoot
Muck Water
Bennane Head
Colmonell
Pinwherry
River Stinchar
B734
Dusk River
B734
B7044
Heronsford
Water of Tig
Barrhill
Ballantrae
Feoch Burn
Lochton
437
BENERAIRD
321
CARLOCK HILL
305
BENBRAKE HILL
Loch Maberry
387
ALTIMEG HILL
Glen App
Southern Upland Way
Milleur Point
Lady Bay
Currarie Port
Glenwhilly
Laggangairn Standing Stones
Corsewall Point
Larne
(Summer Only)
Larne
Barnhills
Portencalzie
17
Main Water of Luce
271
ARTFIELD FELL
Belfast
Kirkcolm
Cairnryan
Penwhirn Reservoir
B738
Black Burn
Belfast
Loch Connell
Ervie
B738
A718
Braid Fell
Cross Water of Luce
New Luce
Loch Ron
Low Barbeth
Low Salchrie
Loch Ryan
B7043
Black Loch
Tarff Water
Knocknain
Leswalt
Castle Kennedy
194
CRAIG FELL
Balgracie
Castle of St John
Innermessan
A751
Chlenry
A77
Auchnotteroch
Stranraer
Aird
Castle Kennedy
Glenluce Abbey NTS
A75
Portslogan
A716
A75
Dernaglar
Broadsea Bay
B738
10
Glenwhan
Dunragit
Glenluce
Whitecrook
Black Head
Lochans
Kildrochet House
Pilanton Burn
B7077
Ringdoo Point
Milton
A747
Castle Loch
181
CAIRN PAT
8
14
Stairhaven
Portpatrick
A77
A716
B7084
19
Auchenmalg
Mochrum Loch
Stoneykirk
North Milmain
18
Mull of Sinniness
Auchenmalg Bay
B7042
Cairngarroch
Sandhead
Chapel Finian (ruin)
Money Head
Kirkmadrine
A747
High Ardwell
Ardwell House
Ardwell
L U C E   B A Y
Ardwell Bay
Chapel Rossan
Drumbreddon
Balgowan
Logan
Port Logan Bay
B7065
A716
Port Logan
Garrochtrie
Clanyard Bay
Kilstay
Laggantalluch Head
Kirkmaiden
Drummore
Barncorkrie
High Drummore
Killiness Point
Drumnaglaur
Maryport
B7041
Cardryne
Cardrain
West Cairngaan
RSPB
MULL OF GALLOWAY

Stranraer Ferry Port

Loch Ryan

KIRKCOLM
GIRVAN
A718
B7257
CAR FERRY TERMINAL
STRANRAER STATION
NEWTON STEWART
A77
A75
GARRICK HOSPITAL
A716
DRUMMORE
LBM

0   ½ mile
0   1 km

---

0   1   2   3   4 miles
0 1 2 3 4 5 kilometres

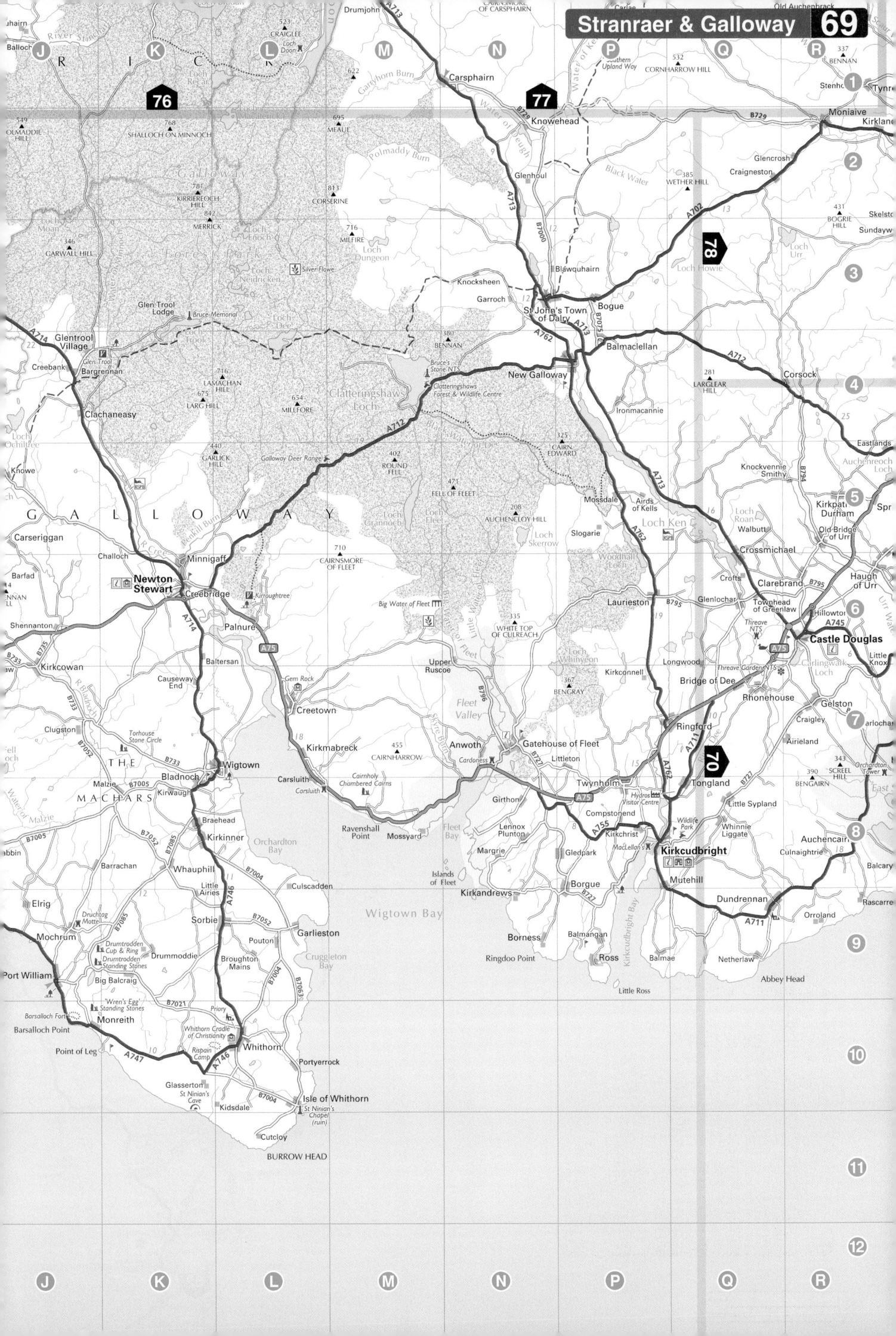

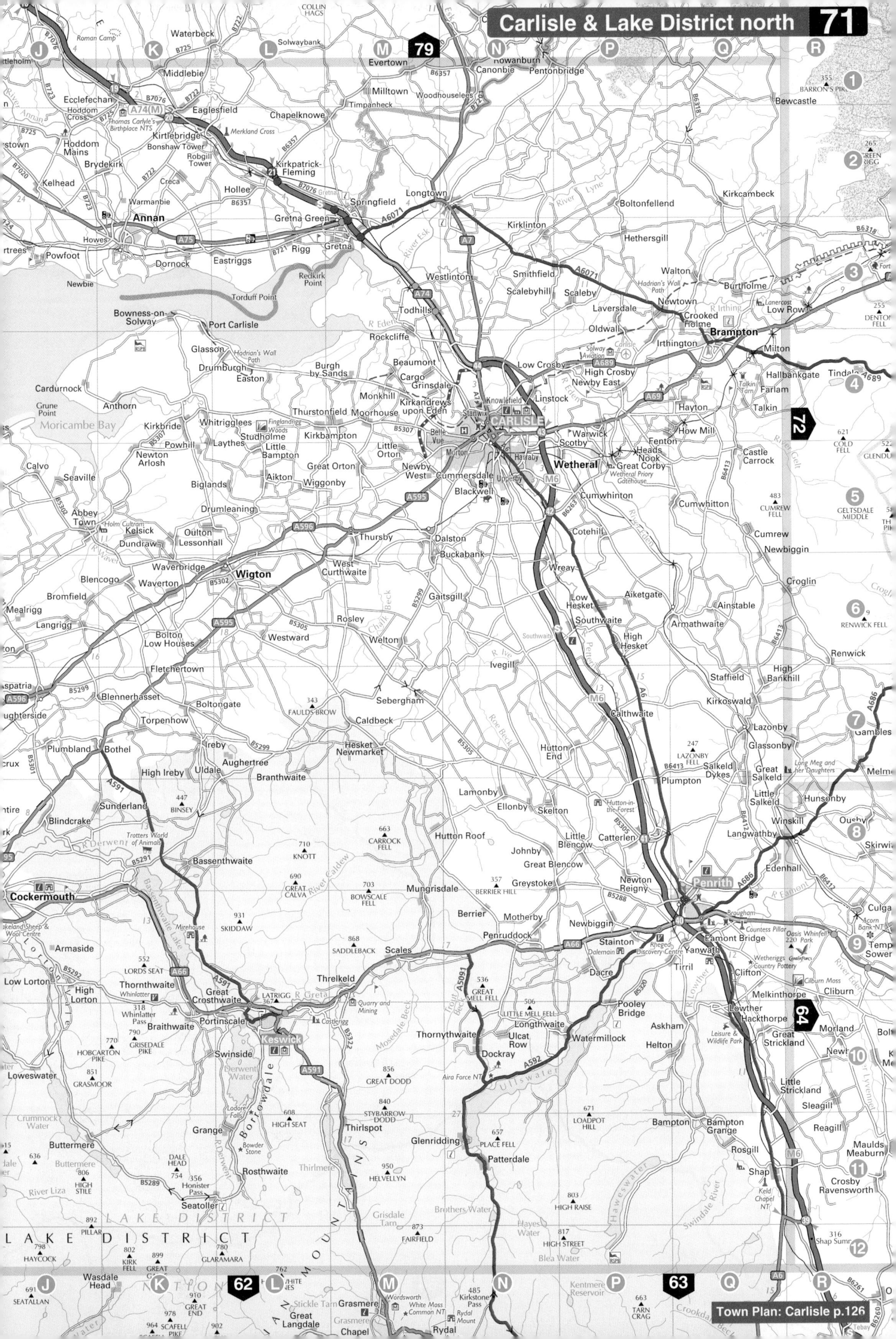

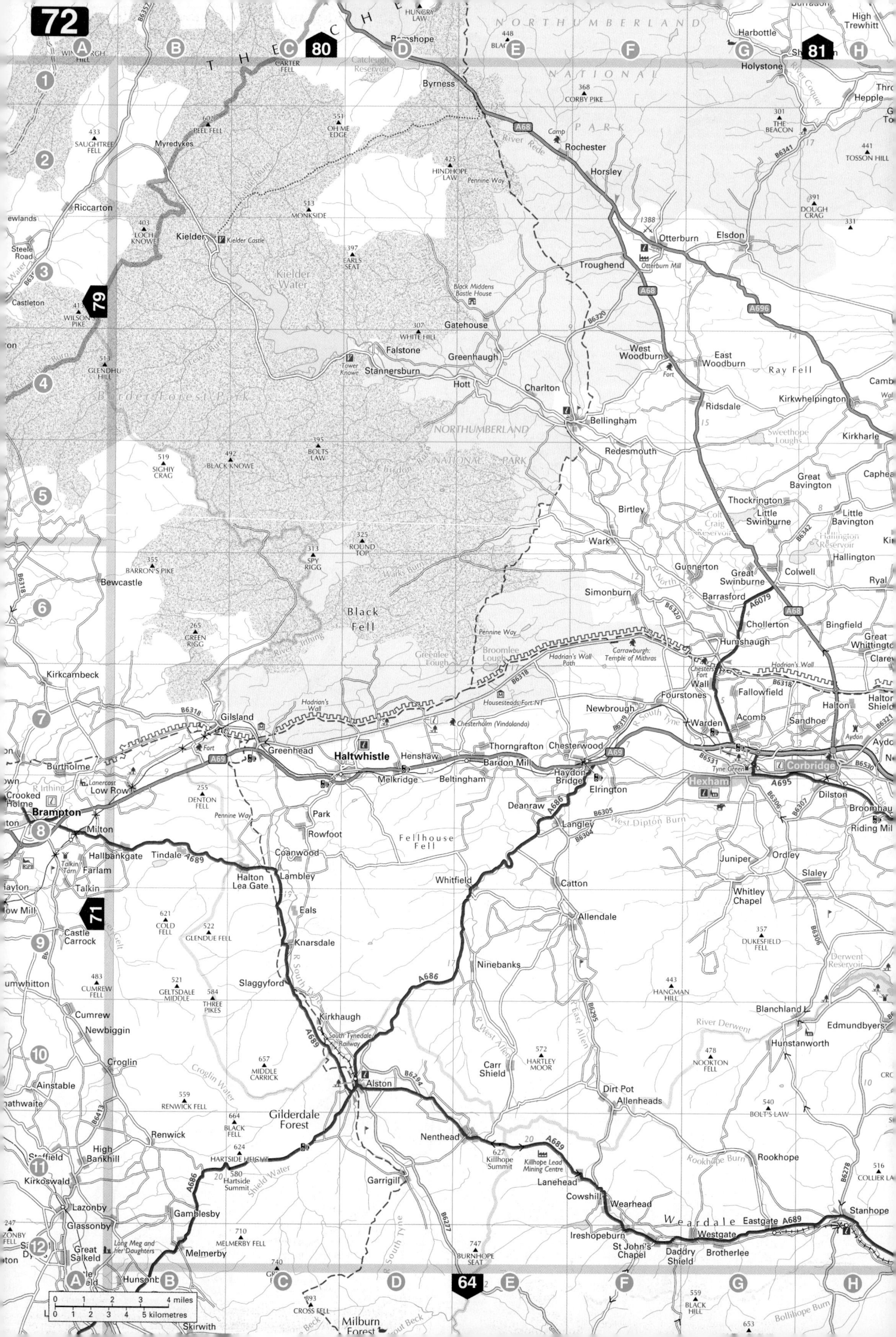

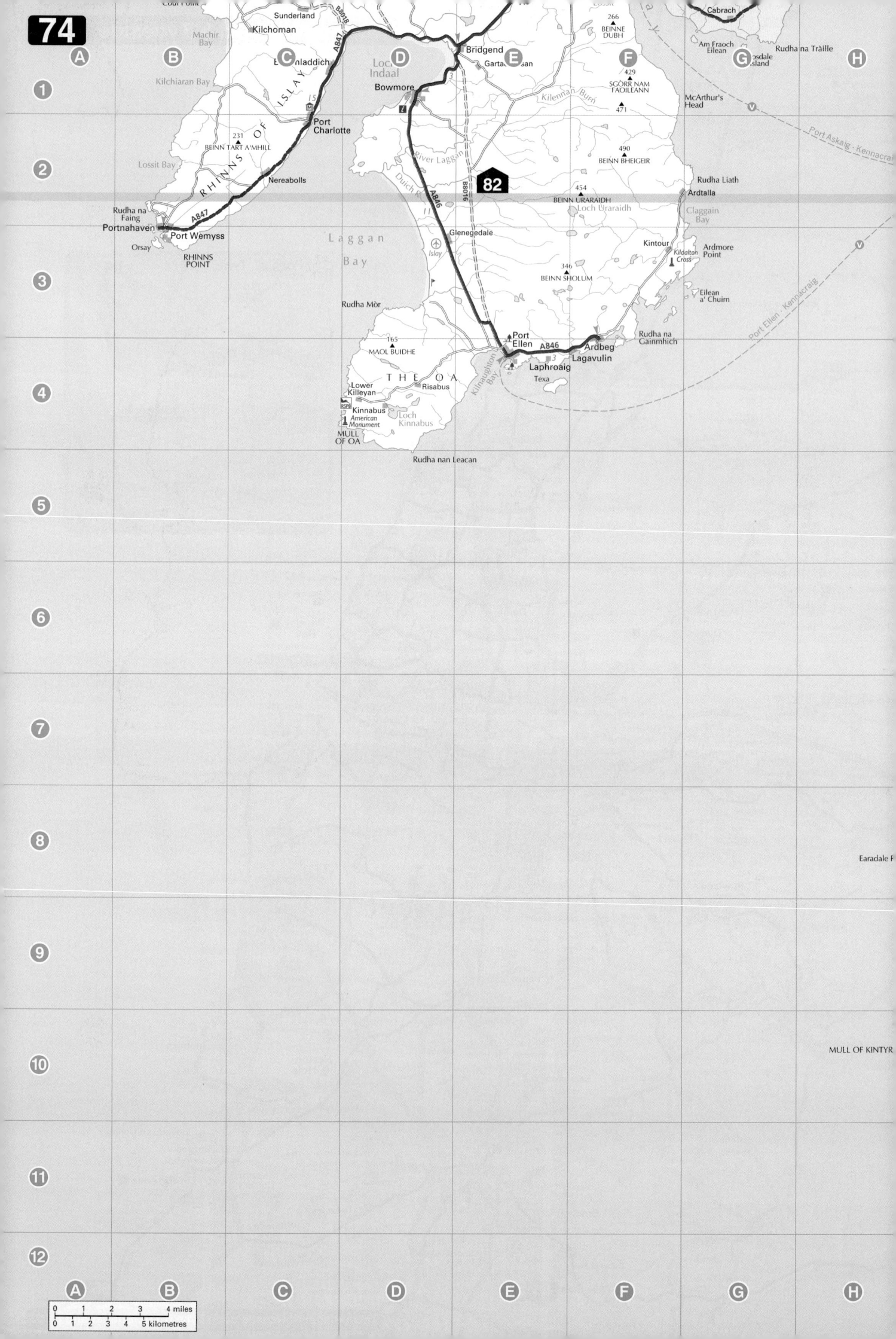

82

Sunderland
Kilchoman
Kilchiaran Bay
Machir
Bay
Coul Point
B8018
A847
Bridgend
Gartac...san
Loc...
Indaal
Bowmore
BEINNE
DUBH
266
Am Fraoch
Eilean
Rudha na Tràille
...sdale
...land
429
SGORR NAM
FAOILEANN
McArthur's
Head
Port Askaig · Kennacrai...
Kilennan Burn
471
E...nladdich
Port
Charlotte
231
BEINN TART A'MHILL
Lossit Bay
RHINNS OF ISLAY
Nereabolls
490
BEINN BHEIGEIR
454
BEINN URARAIDH
Loch Uraraidh
Rudha Liath
Ardtalla
Claggain
Bay
Rudha na
Faing
Portnahaven
Port Wemyss
Orsay
RHINNS
POINT
A847
River Laggan
Duich R...
A846
B8016
Glenegedale
Laggan
Bay
Islay
Kintour
Kildalton
Cross
Ardmore
Point
346
BEINN SHOLUM
Eilean
a' Chuirn
Port Ellen · Kennacraig
Rudha Mòr
165
MAOL BUIDHE
THE OA
Risabus
Lower
Killeyan
RSPB
Kinnabus
American
Monument
Loch
Kinnabus
MULL
OF OA
Port
Ellen
Kilnaughton Bay
3
Laphroaig
Texa
Ardbeg
Lagavulin
Rudha na
Gainmhich
Rudha nan Leacan

Earadale ...

MULL OF KINTYR...

0   1   2   3   4 miles
0   1   2   3   4   5 kilometres

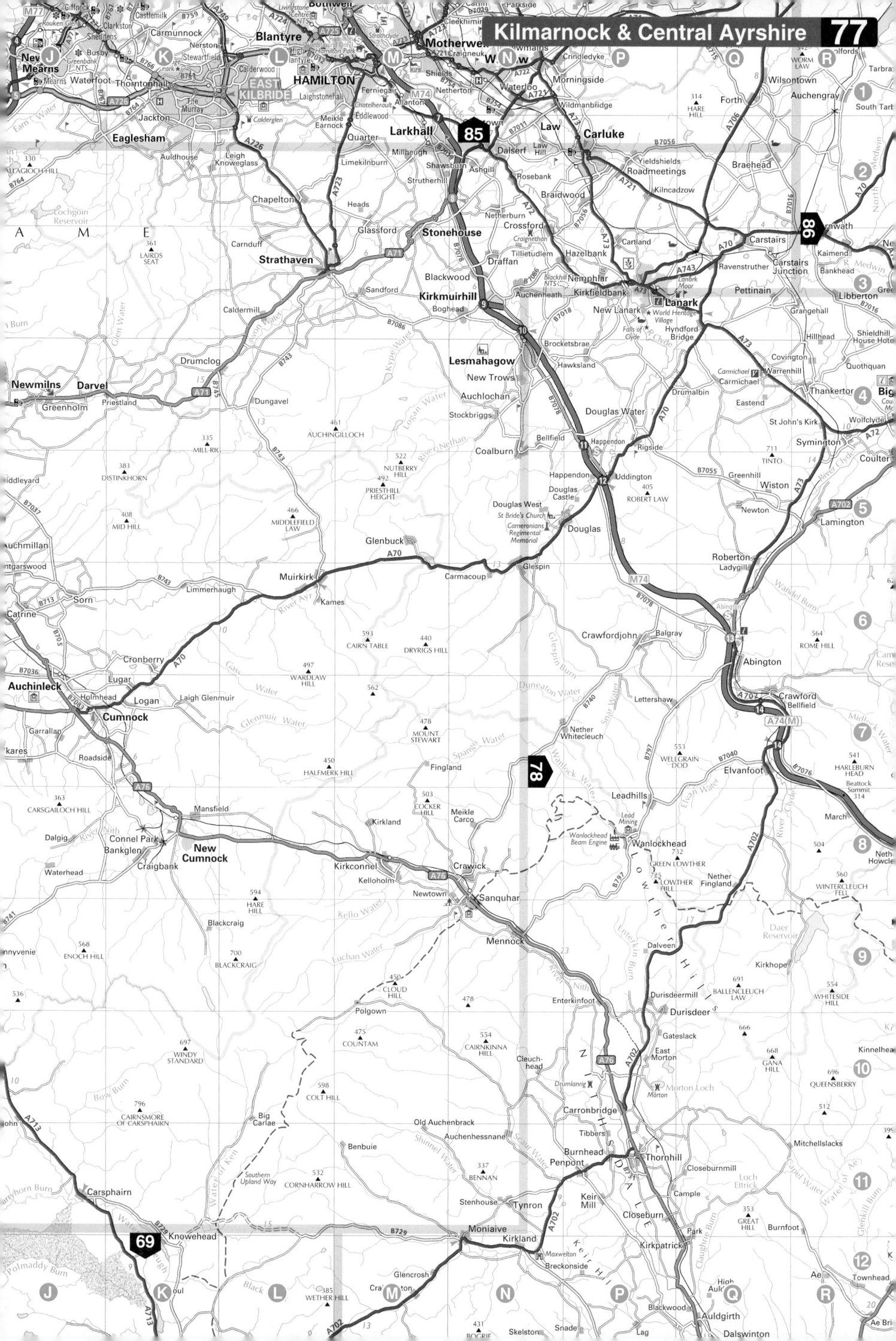

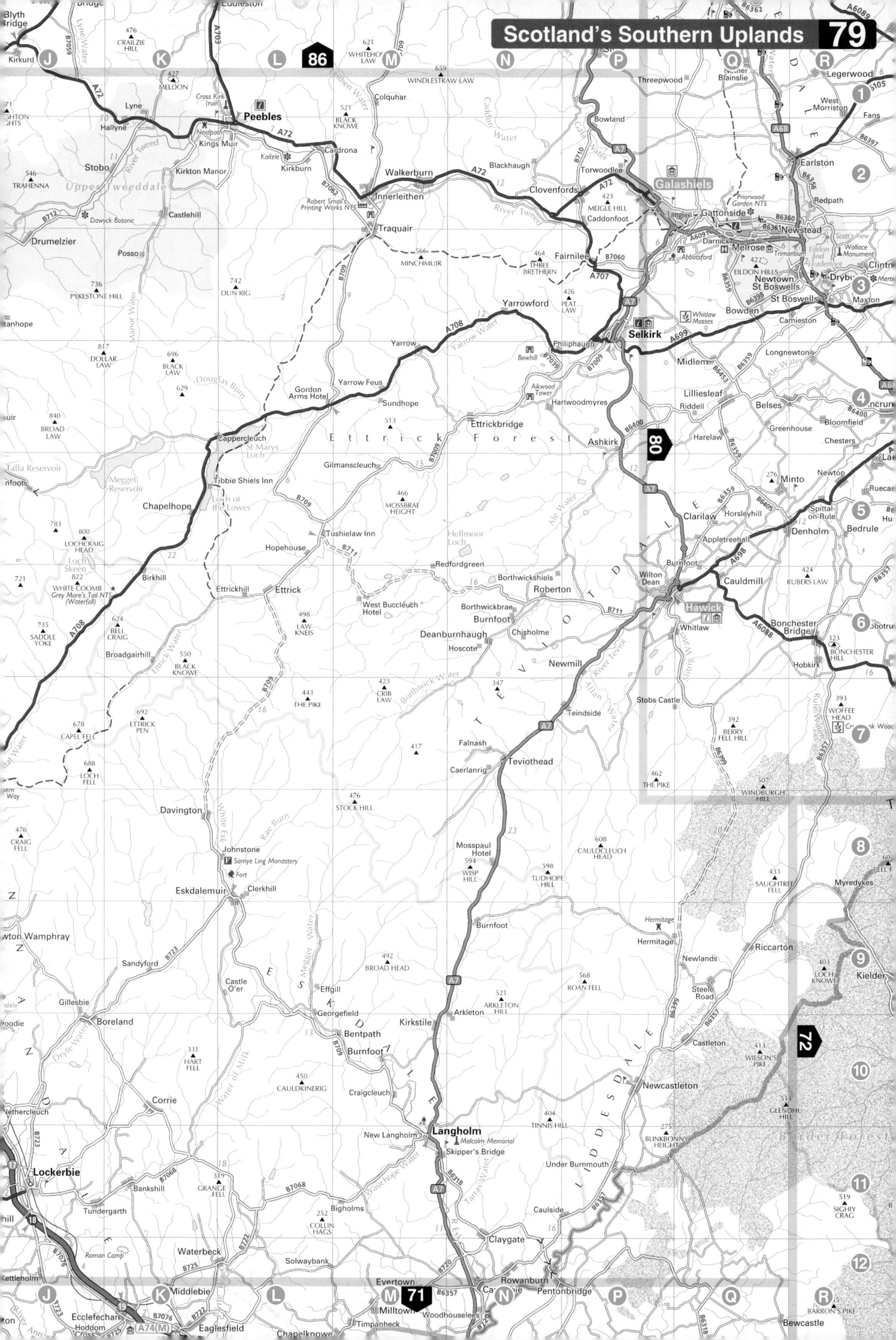

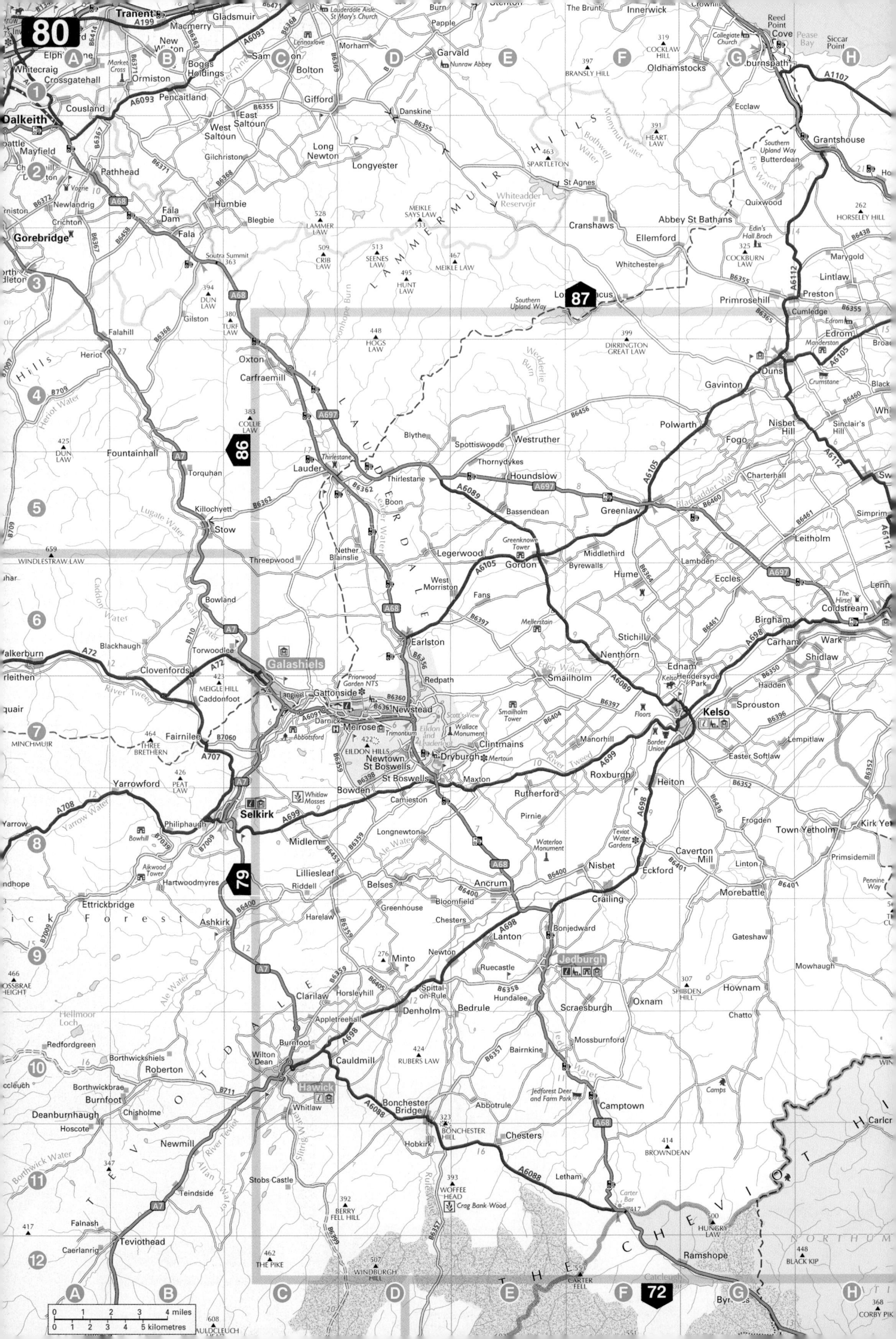

J   K   L   M   N   P   Q   R

1
2
3
4
5
6
7
8
9
10
11
12

St Abb's Head
ST ABB'S HEAD
Coldingham Loch
St Abbs
Coldingham Bay
Coldingham
B6438
A1107
22
Cairncross
Eyemouth
B6355
Burnmouth
Ayton
A1
Preston
Lamberton
encrow
B6437
B6355
Foulden
Marshall Meadows Bay
North Northumberland Heritage Coast
Edington
Whiteadder Water
1333
Hutton
Tithe Barn
Allanton
A6105
Berwick-upon-Tweed
side bridge
Paxton
Town Ramparts
Barracks
B6460
Paxton
B6461
Tweedmouth
Spital
Hilton
Horndean
Horncliffe
Huds Head
B6461
Ladykirk
Murton
Scremerston
Norham
Thornton
A698
A1
Upsettlington
River Tweed
B6470
A697
Cheswick
Ancroft
Haggerston
CAUSEWAY FLOODED AT HIGH TIDE
Cornhill-on-Tweed
B6354
Beal
HOLY ISLAND
Etal
Duddo
Bowsden
Holy Island
Etal
B6525
Lindisfarne NT
Heatherslaw Light Railway
Heatherslaw Corn Mill
Lindisfarne Priory
Castle Point
The Lady Waterford Hall
B6353
Guile Point
Branxton
Lowick
Fenwick
Longstone Lighthouse
1513
Crookham
Ford
Buckton
FARNE ISLANDS
NT
Staple Sound
North Northumberland Heritage Coast
Howtel
A697
St Cuthbert's Cave NT
Inner Sound
Milfield
B6352
Fenton
B6525
Belford
B1342
Bamburgh
Thornington
Nesbit
Budle Bay
Bamburgh
B1340
Lanton
Doddington
B6349
Yeavering
Coupland
B1341
Seahouses
Kirknewton
B6351
Lucker
North Sunderland
YEAVERING BELL
362
Akeld
B6348
Warenford
Beadnell
Hethpool
Wooler
Chatton
A1
Chathill
Swinhoe
Beadnell Bay
Ros Castle NT
Newstead
Tughall
Newtown
Chillingham Wild Cattle Park
Ellingham
NORTHUMBERLAND
525
Preston
Brunton
Newton-by-the-Sea
PRESTON HILL
Preston Pele Tower
Christon Bank
Embleton
NATIONAL PARK
Ilderton
267
North Charlton
Falloden
Embleton Bay
SCHIL
CATERAN HILL
Old Bewick
Dunstanburgh NT
816
Ditchburn
South Charlton
THE CHEVIOT
B6346
Dunstan
New Bewick
Eglingham
Rock
Craster
Rennington
Stamford
Hartside
Branton
Beanley
Howick Hall
Howick
Ingram
Powburn
B6341
Cullernose Point
Fawdon
Glanton
Longhoughton
Prendwick
River Aln
Denwick
Boulmer
Bolton
Alnwick
Seaton Point
616
Whittingham
Lesbury
CUSHAT LAW
334
COCHRANE PIKE
Great Ryle
A1
Alnmouth
Barrow Burn
Alnham
A1068
Alnmouth Bay
500
Netherton
Edlingham
ILLHOPE LAW
319
Shilbottle
LONG CRAG
305
Burradon
High Trewhitt
260
GLANTLEES HILL
Newton-on-the-Moor
A697
Warkworth Castle & Hermitage
Warkworth
Alwinton
Sharperton
Snitter
Cragside House NT
Harbottle
Holystone
Hepple
Thropton
Rothbury
73
Guyzance
Gloster Hill
Amble
Coquet Island
Longframlington
Felton
Togston
High Buxley
River Coquet
Whitton
Newtown
Broomhill
Great Tosson
East Thirston
South
301

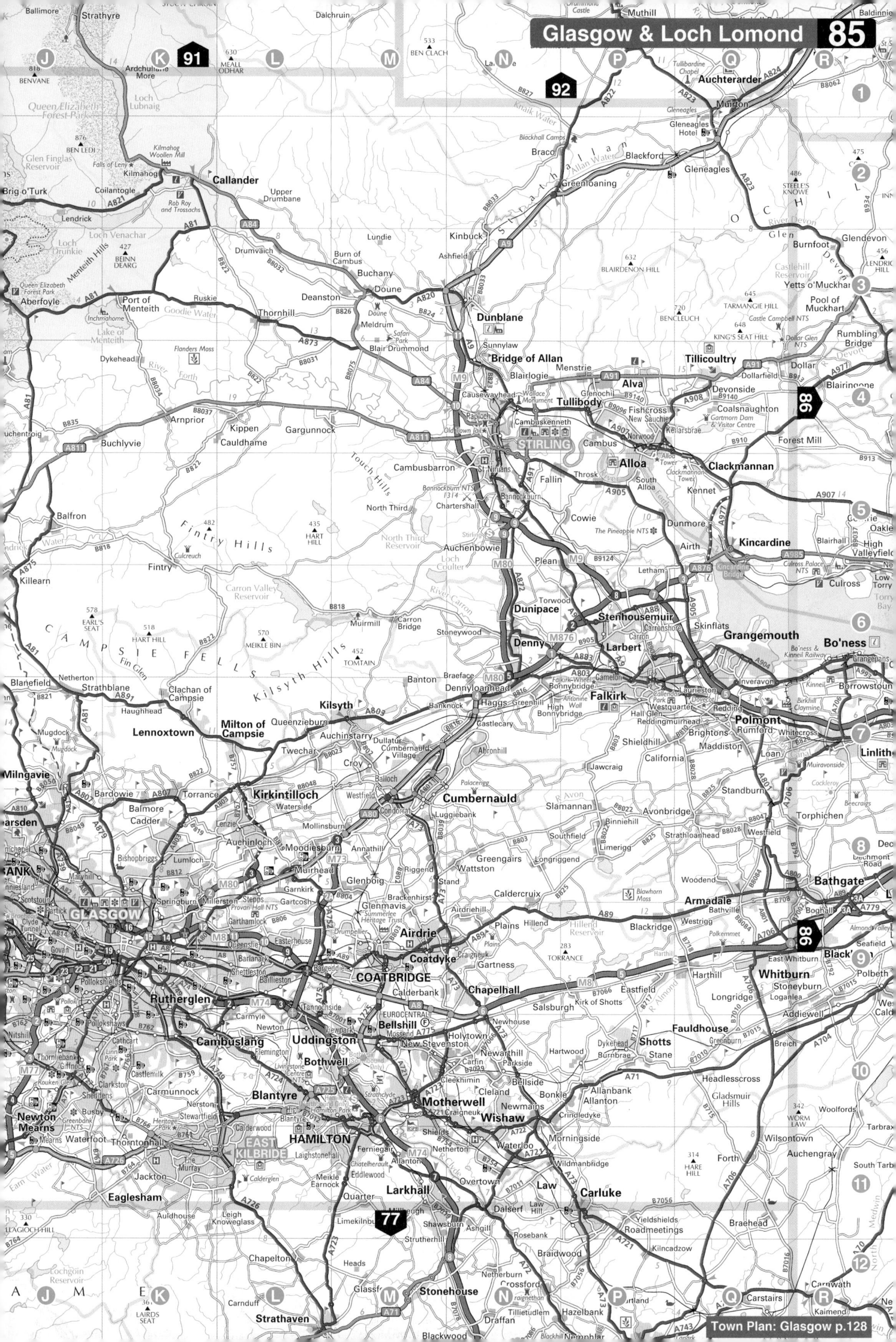

Rosyth Harbour

DUNFERMLINE
KINCARDINE BRIDGE
PERTH
ROSYTH STATION
A823(M)
M90
A985
A921
Rosyth
INVERKEITHING STATION
Inverkeithing
HM NAVAL BASE
ROSYTH EUROPARC
CAR FERRY TERMINAL
B980
B981
A90
NORTH QUEENSFERRY STATION
EDINBURGH
LBM
½ mile
1 km

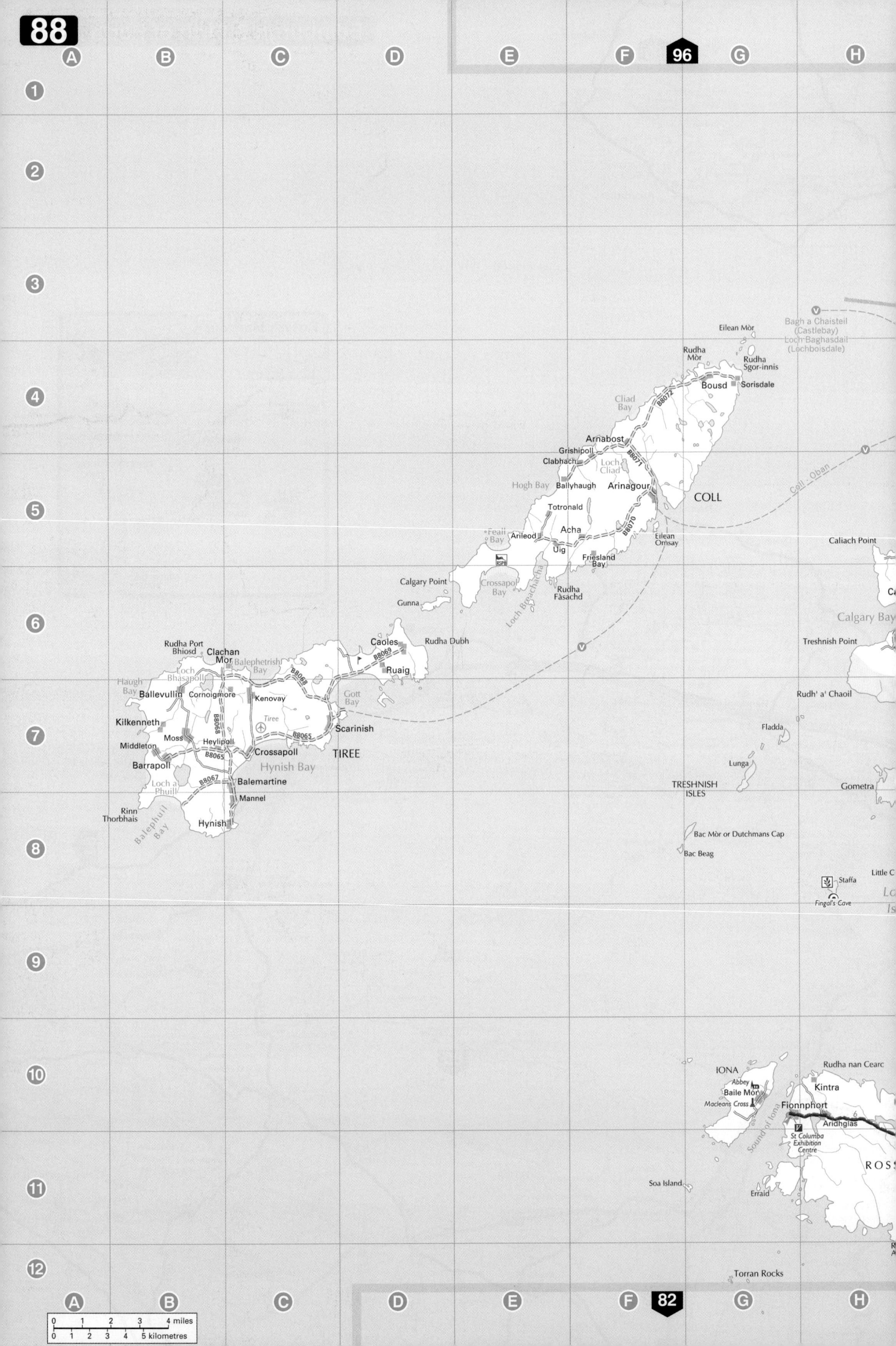

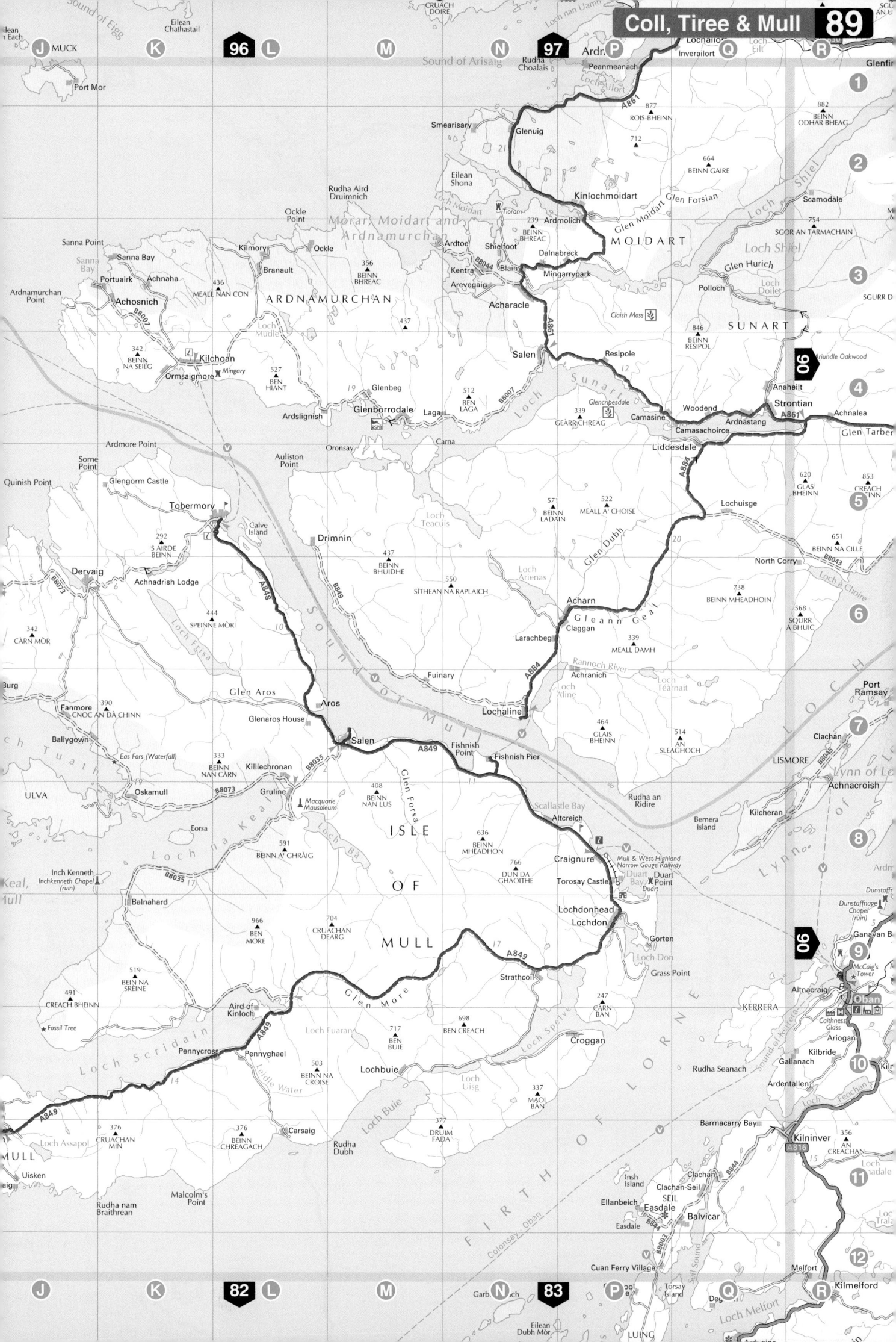

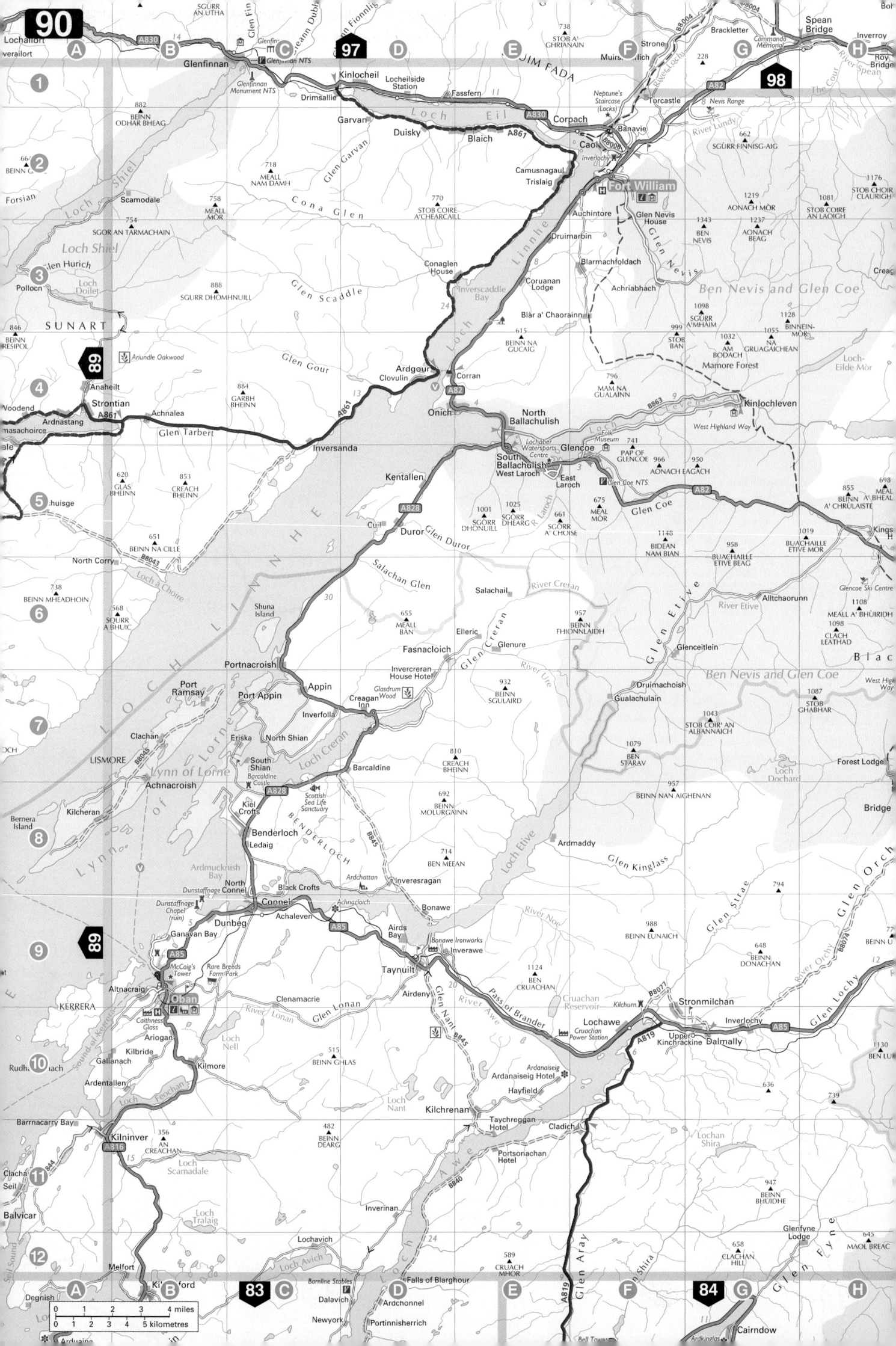

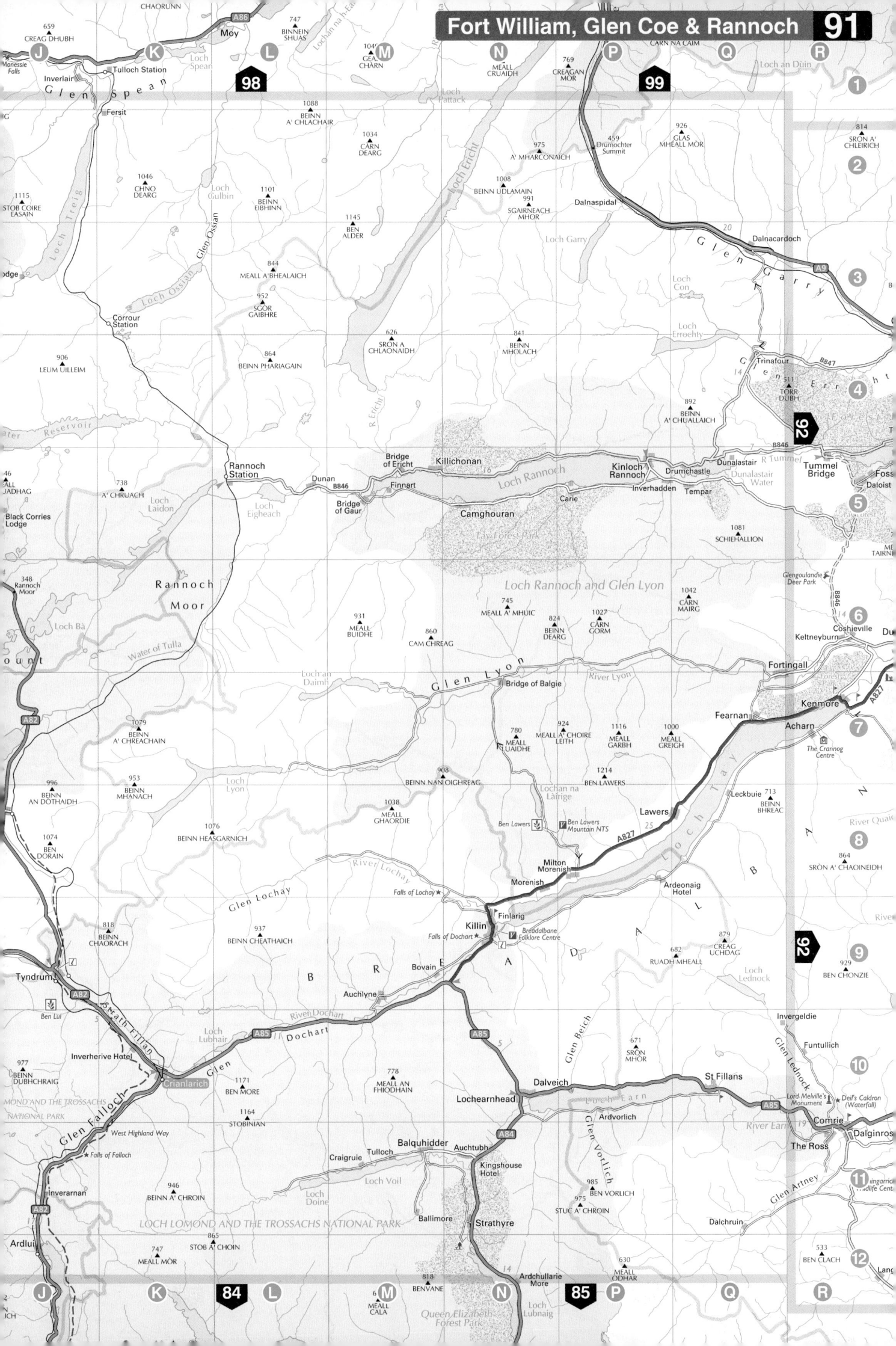

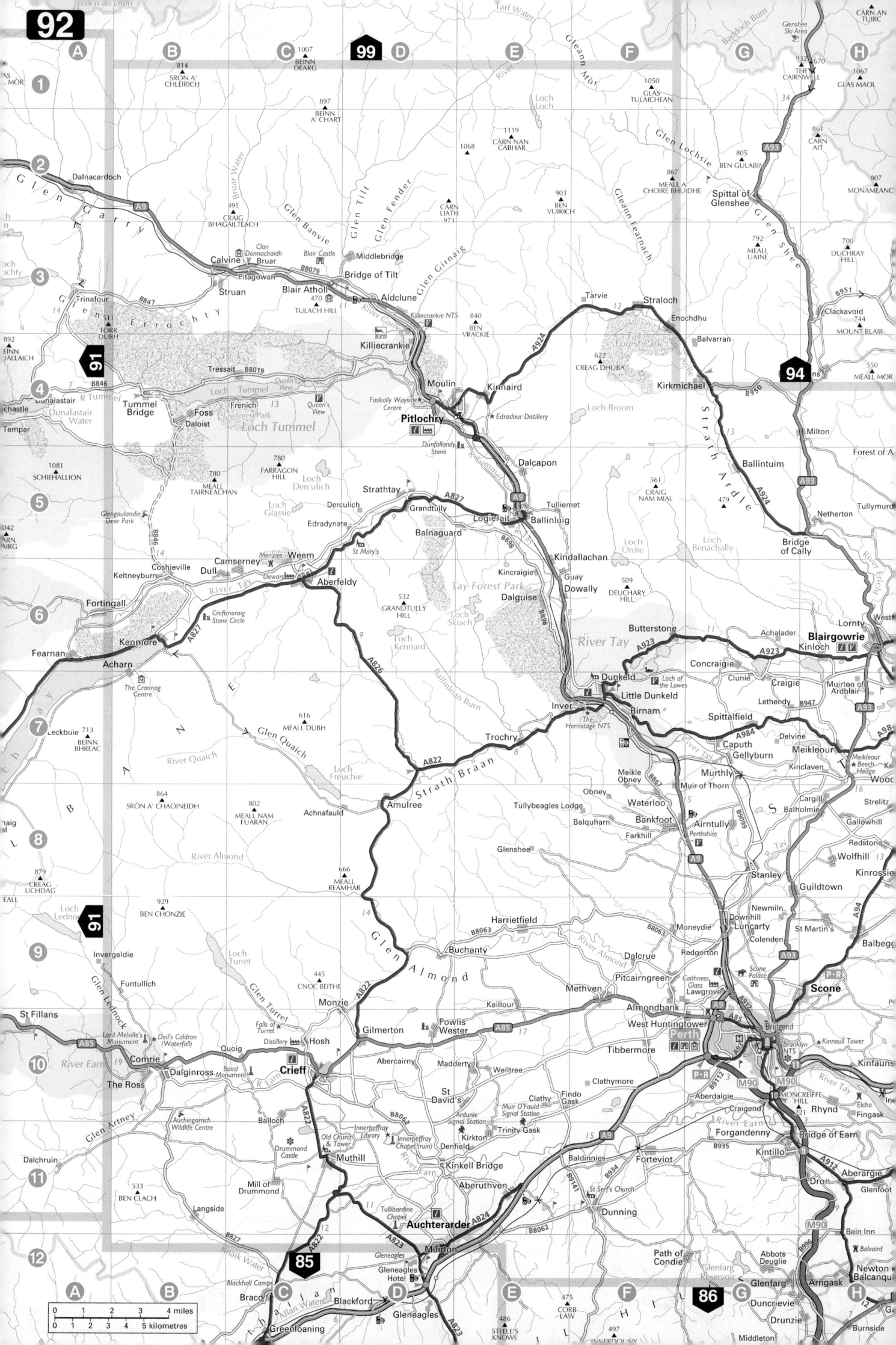

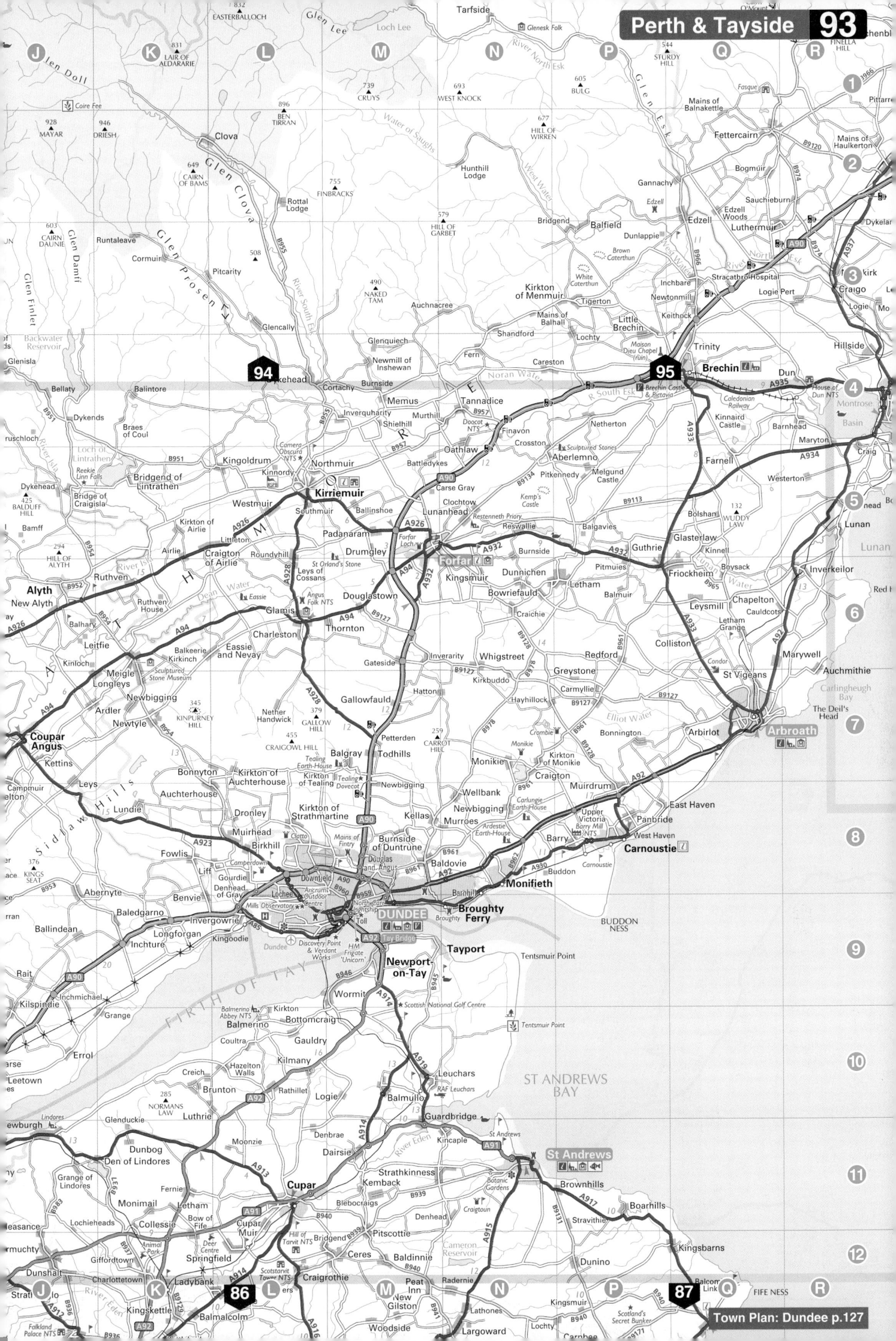

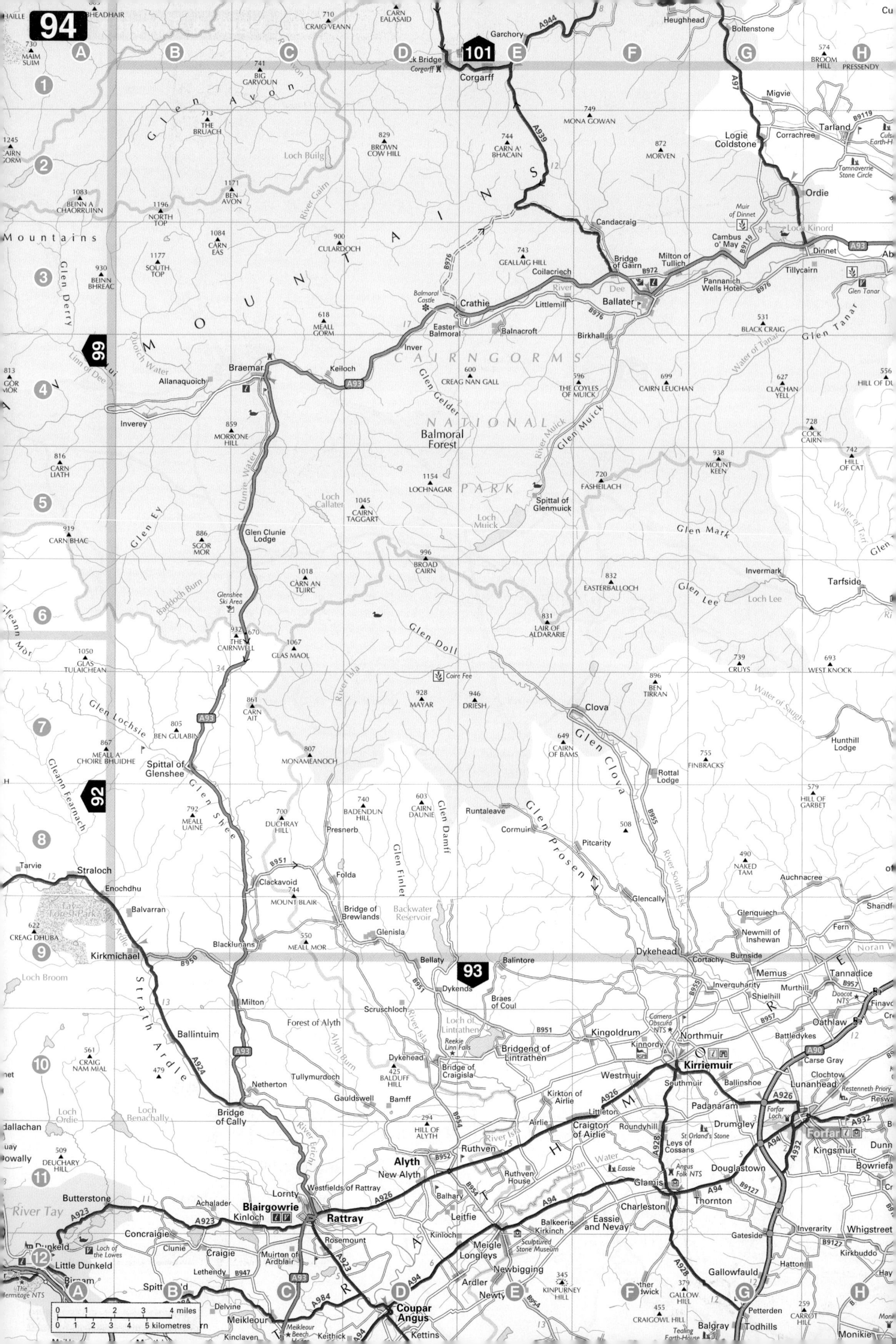

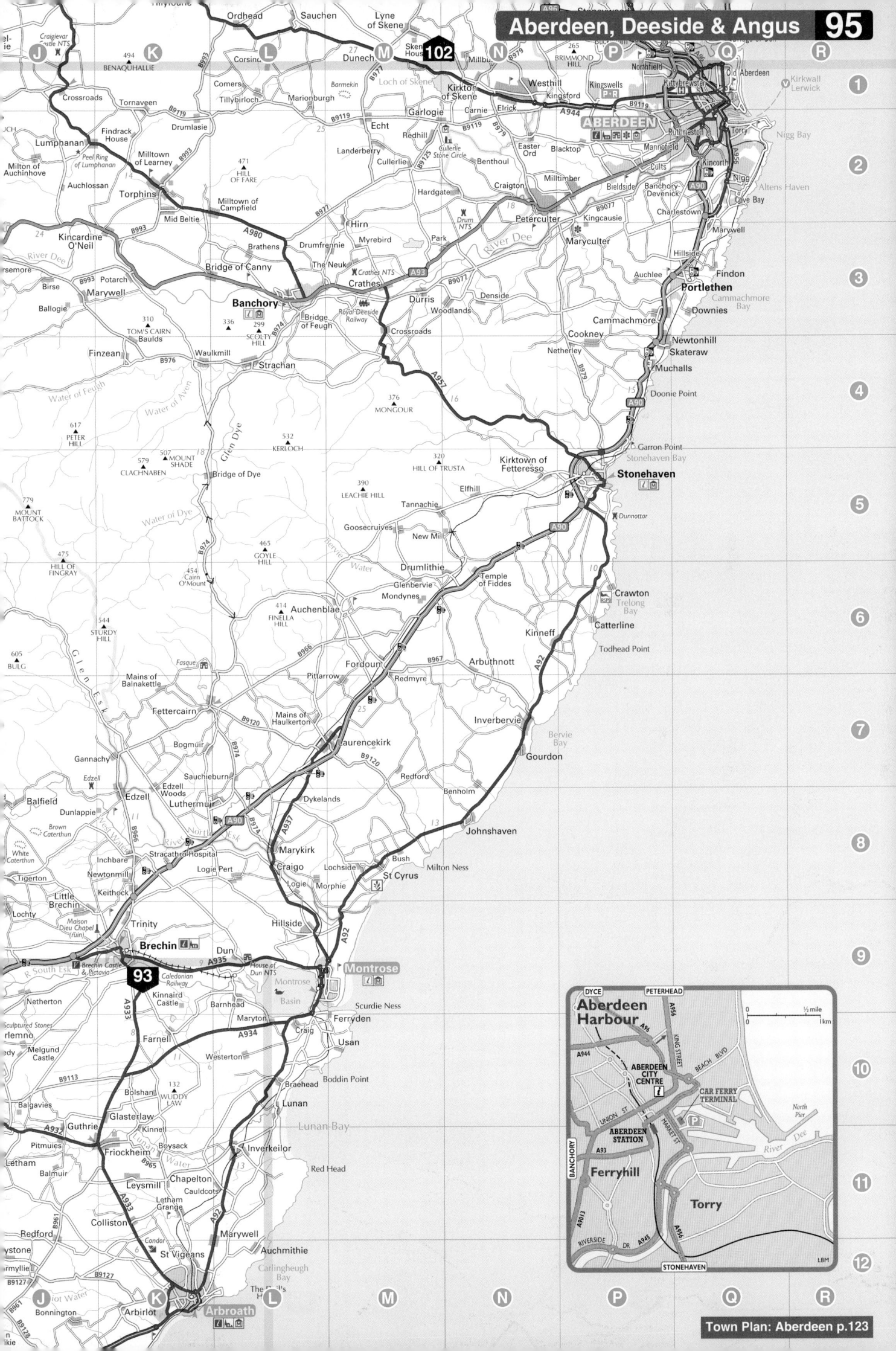

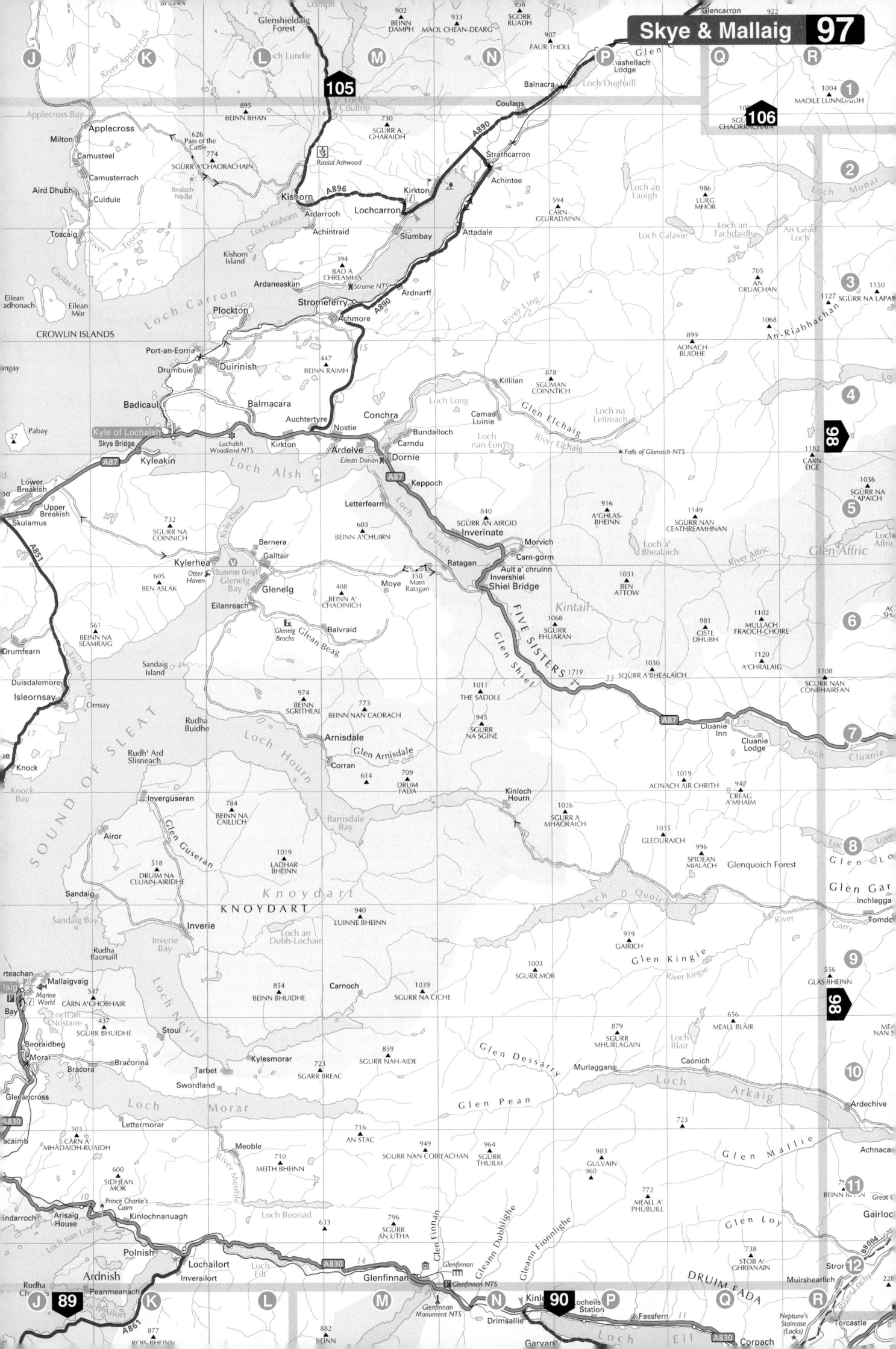

J K L M N P Q R

Glencarron 922

105 106

MAOILE LUNNDAIDH 1004 1

SGÙRR A' CHAORACHAIN

Glenshieldaig Forest Loch Lundie 902 933 958 SGORR RUADH 907 FAUR THOLL Glen Balnacra Nashellach Lodge Loch Dughaill

River Applecross River Lair

Applecross Bay 895 BEINN BHAN 730 SGURR A GHARAIDH Coulags A890 Loch an Laoigh

Applecross 626 Pass of the Cattle 774 SGÙRR A'CHAORACHAIN Rassal Ashwood Strathcarron 594 CÀRN GEURADAINN 986 LURG MHÓR 705 AN CRUACHAN 1150

Milton Camusteel Camusterrach Bealach-Na-Ba Kirkton Achintee 1127 SGÙRR NA LAPAICH

Aird Dhubh Culduie Kishorn A896 Lochcarron Loch an Tachdaidh An Gead Loch

Loch Kishorn Ardarroch Slumbay Loch Calavie 1068 An-Riabhachan

Kishorn Island Achintraid Attadale 899 AONACH BUIDHE

394 BAD A CHREAMHA Strome NTS River Ling

CROWLIN ISLANDS Ardaneaskan Ardnarff 878 SGUMAN COINNTICH

Loch Carron Stromeferry A890 Killilan

ongay Plockton Achmore Loch Long Glen Elchaig Loch na Leitreach 1182

Eilean adhonach Eilean Mòr 15 Camas Luinie CARN EIGE

Port-an-Eorna Beinn Raimh 447 Loch nan Eun Falls of Glomach NTS

Drumbuie Duirinish Conchra Bundalloch River Elchaig 86 1036 SGÙRR NA SPAICH

27 Pabay Badicaul Balmacara Auchtertyre Nostie Carndu 5

Kyle of Lochalsh Skye Bridge Lochalsh Woodland NTS Kirkton Ardelve Dornie Keppoch 840 SGÙRR AN AIRGID 916 A'GHLAS-BHEINN 1149 SGÙRR NAN CEATHREAMHNAN Glen Affric

Skye Bridge Eilean Donan A87 Letterfearn Loch Duich Loch a' Bhealaich River Affric

A87 Kyleakin 732 SGÙRR NA COINNICH 603 BEINN A'CHUIRN Inverinate Morvich 1031 BEN ATTOW

Lower Breakish Carn-gorm Kintail

Upper Breakish Kyle Rhea Bernera Galltair Ratagan Ault a' chruinn 1102 MULLACH FRAOCH-CHOIRE

Skulamus A851 Kylerhea 605 BEN ASLAK Summer Only 350 Mam Ratagan Invershiel 1068 SGÙRR FHUARAN 981 CISTE DHUBH 1120 A'CHRALAIG 6

Otter Haven Glenelg Bay Moye Shiel Bridge FIVE SISTERS 1108 SGÙRR NAN CONBHAIREAN

Drumfearn 561 BEINN NA SEAMRAIG Glenelg 408 BEINN A' CHAOINICH Glen Shiel 1030 SGÙRR A'BHEALAICH 33

Eilanreach Balvraid 1719 SGÙRR A'BHEALAICH A87 Cluanie Inn

Duisdalemore Gleann Beag Glenelg Brochs 974 BEINN SGRITHEAL 773 BEINN NAN CAORACH 1011 THE SADDLE Cluanie Lodge 7

Isleornsay Ornsay Rudha Buidhe 945 SGÙRR NA SGINE Loch Cluanie

17 Rudh' Ard Slisneach Arnisdale Glen Arnisdale 1019 AONACH AIR CHRITH 947 CREAG A'MHAIM

Knock Corran 614 709 DRUM FADA Kinloch Hourn 1026 SGÙRR A MHAORAICH 8

Knock Bay Inverguseran 784 BEINN NA CAILLICH Barrisdale Bay 1035 GLEOURAICH 996 SPIDEAN MIALACH Glenquoich Forest

SOUND OF SLEAT Airor 518 DRUM NA CLUAIN-AIRIDHE 1019 LADHAR BHEINN Glen Quoich Glen Garry

Sandaig Glen Guseran KNOYDART Knoydart Loch Quoich Inchlaggan

Sandaig Bay Inverie 940 LUINNE BHEINN 919 GAIRICH River Garry Tomdo

rteachan Rudha Raonuill Inverie Bay Loch an Dubh-Lochain 1003 SGURR MÓR Glen Kingie River Kingie 556 GLAS BHEINN 9

Mallaigvaig 547 CÀRN A'GHOBHAIR 854 BEINN BHUIDHE Carnoch 1039 SGURR NA CICHE 88

laig Marine World 437 SGÙRR BHUIDHE 879 SGÙRR MHURLAGAIN 656 MEALL BLÀIR

Bay Loch an Nostaire Stoul Loch Nevis Glen Dessarry Loch Blair MEALL NAN S

Beoraidbeg Bracara Kylesmorar 859 SGURR NAH-AIDE Murlaggan Caonich 10

Morar Bracorina Tarbet 723 SGARR BREAC Loch Arkaig Ardechive

Glenancross Swordland Glen Pean 723 Achnaca

A830 Lettermorar Loch Morar 716 AN STAC Glen Mallie

acaimb 503 CÀRN A' MHÀDAIDH-RUAIDH Meoble 949 SGURR NAN COIREACHAN 964 SGURR THUILM 983 GULVAIN 960 Glen Loy

600 SIDHEAN MÓR 710 MEITH BHEINN 772 MEALL A' PHÙBUILL 7 BEINN B 11

indarroch Prince Charlie's Cairn Kinlochnanuagh Loch Beoriad 633 796 SGÙRR AN UTHA 738 STOB A' GHRIANAIN Gairlo

Arisaig House Polnish Glen Finnan Glenfinnan DRUM FADA River Lochy 12

Ardnish Peanmeanach Lochailort Inverailort Glenfinnan NTS Glenfinnan Glenfinnan Monument NTS Kinlo Lochails Station Muirshearlich 228

89 A830 14 Kinlo Fassfern Neptune's Staircase (Locks) Stro

Rudha Ch... J 89 K L M N 90 P Q R

877 ROIS-BHEINN 882 BEINN A861 Drimsallie Locheils Station Torcastle A830 Garvan Loch Eil Corpach

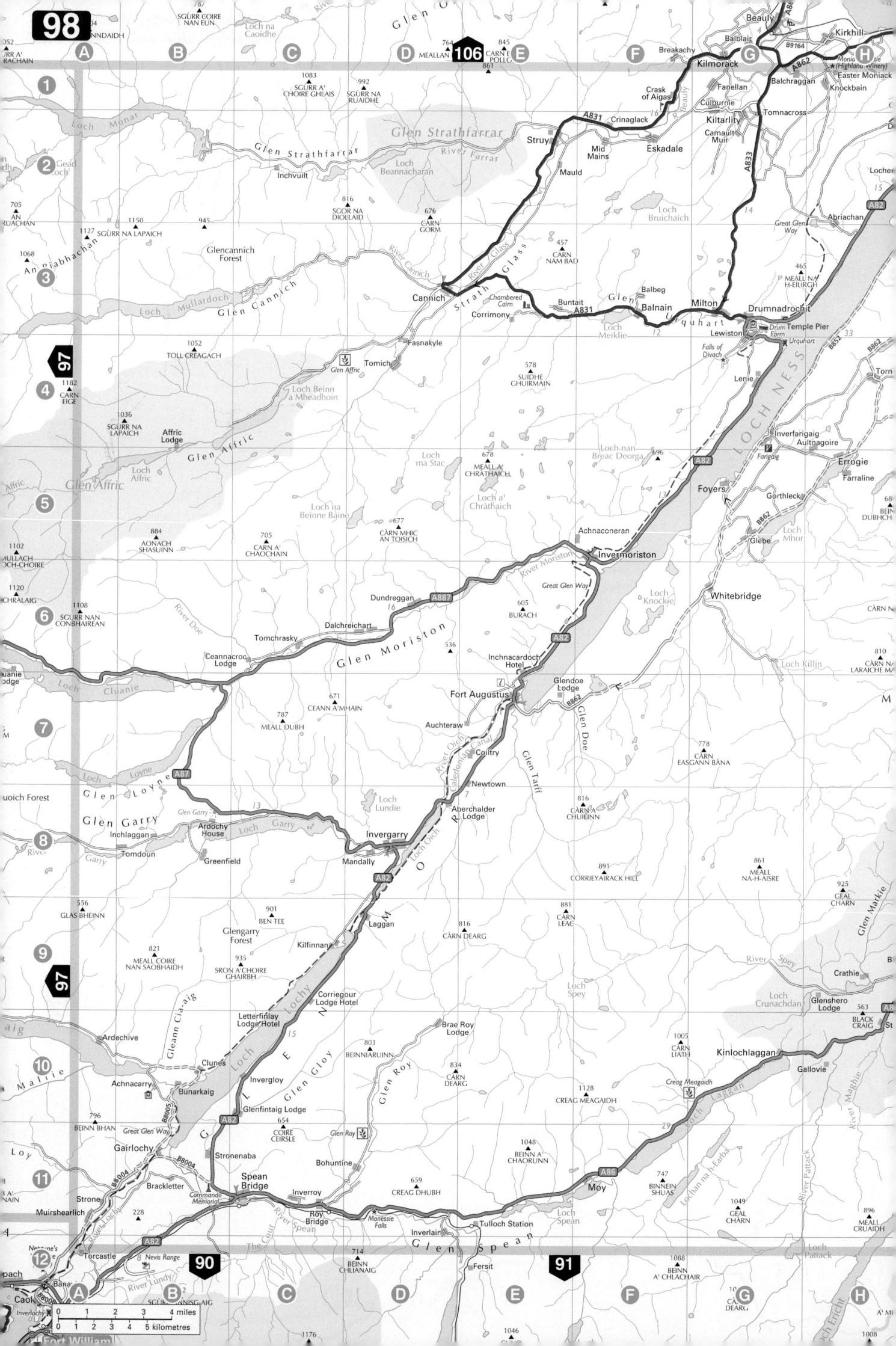

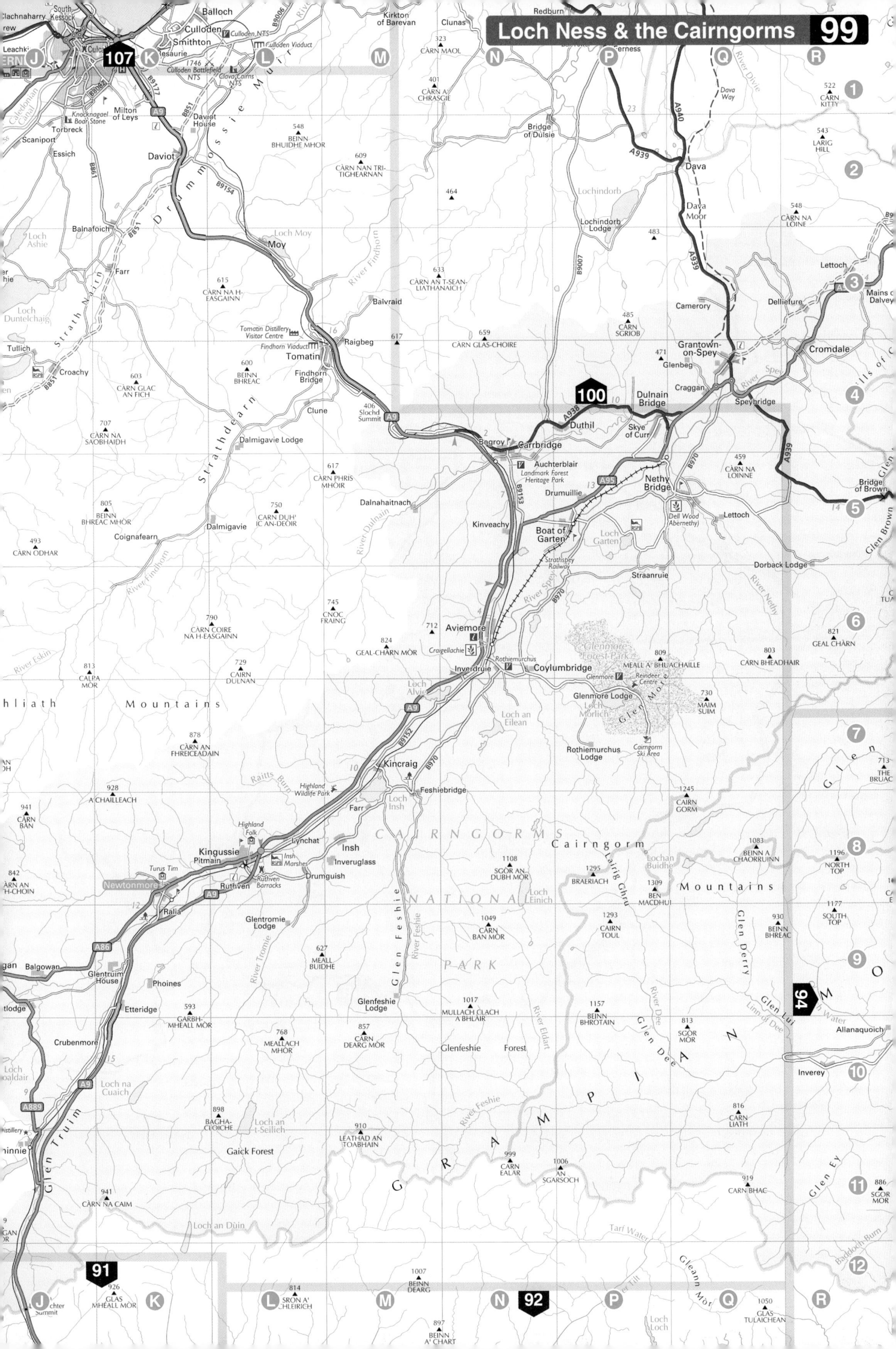

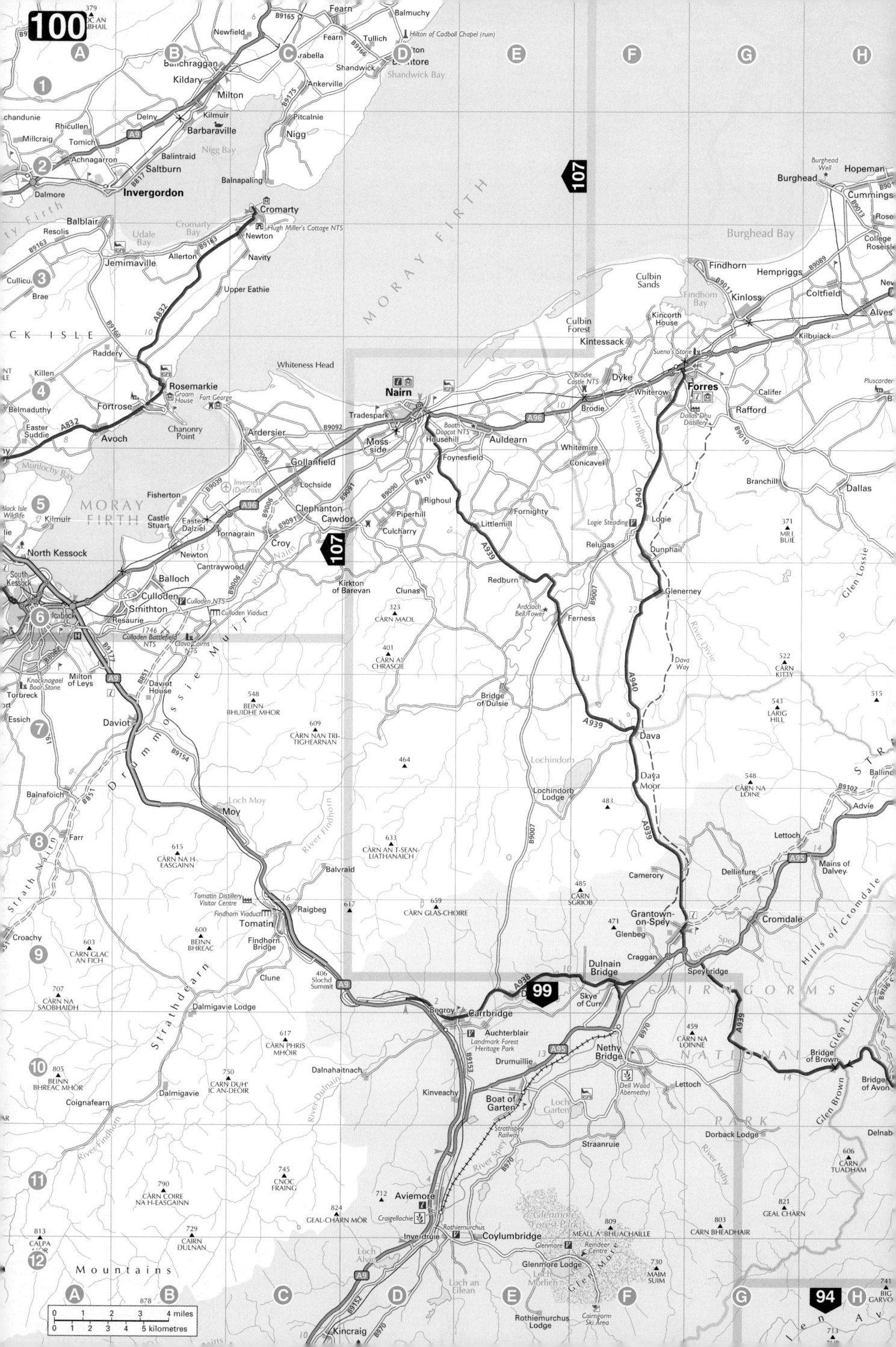

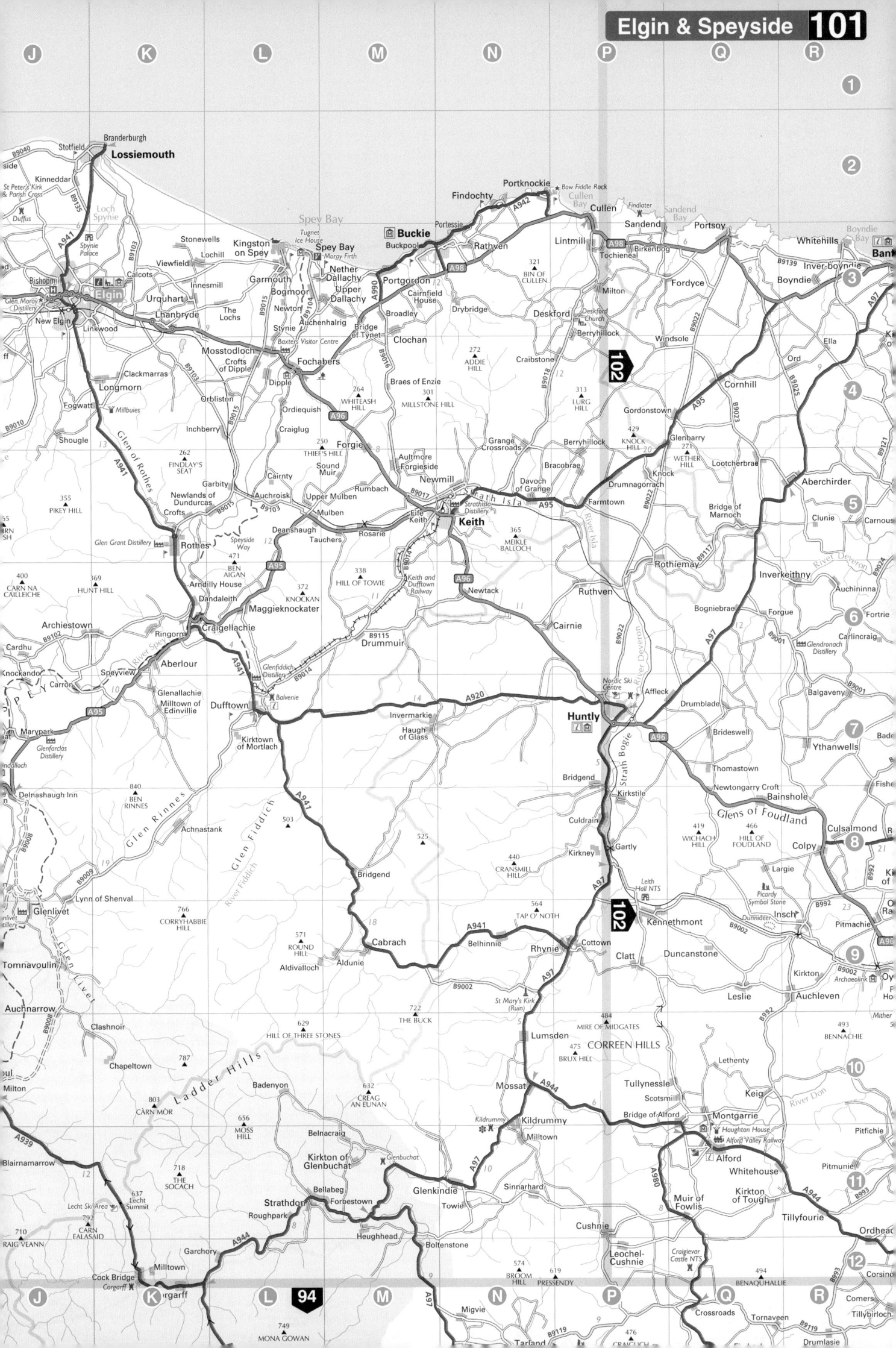

J K L M N P Q R

1
2
3
4
5
6
7
8
9
10
11
12

Rosehearty
Pittulie
Sandhaven
Lighthouse
Kinnaird Head
Craigiefold
Peathill
Percyhorner
Kirktown
Fraserburgh
Coburby
Mid Ardlaw
Pitblae
A90
Fraserburgh Bay
Moggie's Hoosie
Cairnbulg
Inverallochy
Whitelinks Bay
Boyndlie
B9031
A98
B9032
Memsie
Rathen
St Combs
Memsie Cairn
A981
Newburgh
Crofts of Savoch
Lonmay
Rattray Head
234 WAUGHTON HILL
A952
Crimond
Loch of Strathbeg
B9093
Strichen
New Leeds
Blackhill
18
B9093
Leys
Backfolds
Kirktown
St Fergus
Denhead
A90
Fetterangus
Rora
Deer Abbey
Maud
Dunshillock
Aden
Mintlaw
Longside
Inverugie
Buchanhaven
Peterhead
B9106
A950
B9029
Old Deer
Inverquhomery
A950
A981
Blackhill of Clackriach
B9029
Peterhead Bay
Drymuir
Stuartfield
Millbreck
Nether Kinmundy
Hillhead of Cocklaw
Burnhaven
A948
Bulwark
B9028
Buchan Ness
Nethermuir
Kinnadie
Clola
Little Dens
Boddam
Knaven
B9030
Blackhill
Stirling
Auchnagatt
Kinknockie
Lendrum Terrace
Inkhorn
Longhaven
Coldwells
A952
Bullers of Buchan
A948
Hatton
A90
Auchiries
North Haven
Arthrath
Muirtack
Slains
Cruden Bay
Bogbrae
Chapel Hill
Bay of Cruden
Ythanbank
Birness
Whinnyfold
The Skares
B9005
Auchedly
Artrochie
Kinharrachie
Ythsie
Ellon
Esslemont
A920
Kirkton of Logie Buchan
Kirktown of Slains
Collieston
Pitmedden
Logierieve
Forvie
Housieside
B9000
B9000
Udny Station
A90
Newburgh
Culterculllen
Foveran
A975
Delfrigs
Causeyend
Newmachar
B979
Balmedie
Whitecairns
Belhelvie
Balmedie
B977
B977
B999
Potterton
B977
Blackdog
Parkhill House
B999
Dyce
B997
Denmore
Kirkwall Lerwick
A90
Bridge of Don
Bankhead
95
Northfield
B9119
DEEN

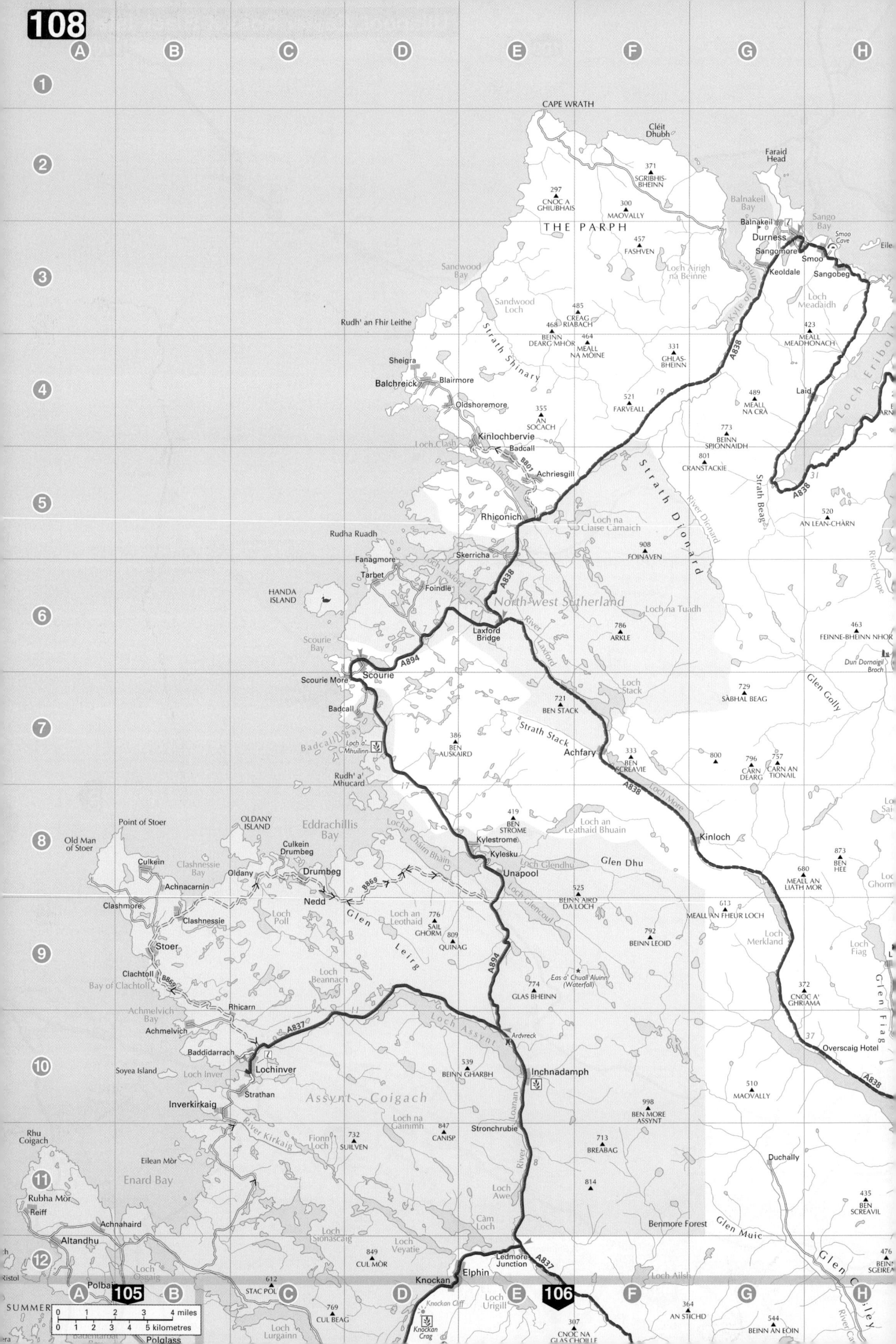

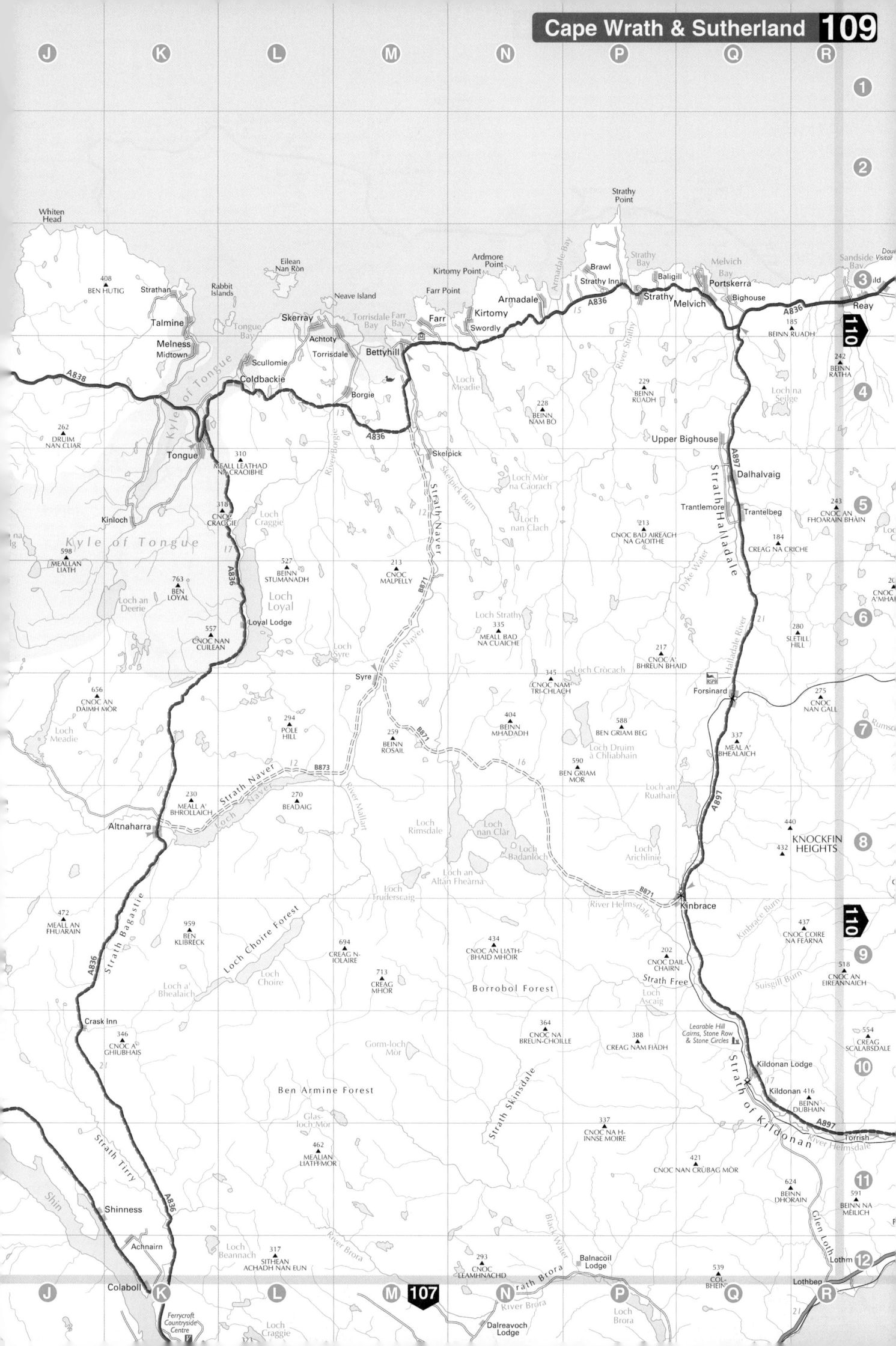

Whiten Head

408
BEN HUTIG
Strathan
Rabbit Islands
Eilean Nan Ròn
Neave Island

Strathy Point

Ardmore Point
Kirtomy Point

Brawl
Strathy Inn
Strathy Bay
Baligill
Melvich Bay
Melvich
Portskerra
Bighouse

A836
Reay
Sandside Bay
Douglas Visitor

Talmine
Skerray
Torrisdale Bay
Farr Bay
Farr Point
Armadale
Kirtomy
Swordly
Farr

A836
Strathy
185
BEINN RUADH

Melness
Midtown
Achtoty
Torrisdale
Scullomie
Bettyhill
15

242
BEINN RATHA

Coldbackie
Borgie

Loch Meadie
229
BEINN RUADH

Upper Bighouse
Loch na Seilge

262
DRUIM NAN CLIAR

13
A836
228
BEINN NAM BÒ

Strath Halladale
A897
Dalhalvaig

Tongue
310
MEALL LEATHAD NA CRAOIBHE
Skelpick
Trantlemore
Trantelbeg
243
CNOC AN FHOARAIN BHÀIN

318
CNOC CRAGGIE
Loch Craggie
Loch Mòr na Caorach
213
CNOC BAD AIREACH NA GAOITHE
184
CREAG NA CRICHE

Kinloch
Kyle of Tongue
598
MEALLAN LIATH

527
BEINN STUMANADH
213
CNOC MALPELLY
Loch nan Clach
20
CNOC A'MHAI

763
BEN LOYAL
Loch Loyal
Strath Naver
335
MEALL BAD NA CUAICHE
280
SLETILL HILL

557
CNOC NAN CUILEAN
Loyal Lodge
Loch Syre
345
CNOC NAM TRI-CHLACH
217
CNOC A' BHREUN BHAID
Loch Cròcach

A836
Syre
RSPB
Forsinard
275
CNOC NAN GALL

656
CNOC AN DAIMH MÒR
294
POLE HILL
404
BEINN MHADADH
588
BEN GRIAM BEG
337
MEAL A' BHEALAICH
Rumsc

Loch Meadie
259
BEINN ROSAIL
B871
Loch Druim à Chliabhain
590
BEN GRIAM MOR
A897

230
MEALL A' BHROLLAICH
270
BEADAIG
Strath Naver
12
B873
River Maillart
Loch Rimsdale
Loch nan Clàr
Loch Badanloch
Loch an Ruathair
440

Altnaharra
Loch Naver
Loch an Altàn Fheàrna
432
KNOCKFIN HEIGHTS

472
MEALL AN FHUARAIN
Loch Truderscaig
B871
River Helmsdale
Kinbrace

959
BEN KLIBRECK
Loch Choire Forest
694
CREAG N-IOLAIRE
434
CNOC AN LIATH-BHAID MHÒIR
437
CNOC NA COIRE NA FEARNA

Crask Inn
713
CREAG MHÒR
Borrobol Forest
202
CNOC DAIL-CHAIRN
Strath Free
518
CNOC AN EIREANNAICH

346
CNOC A' GHIUBHAIS
Loch a' Bhealaich
Loch Choire
Gorm-loch Mòr
364
CNOC NA BREUN-CHOILLE
388
CREAG NAM FIÀDH
Learable Hill Cairns, Stone Row & Stone Circles
Loch Ascaig
554
CREAG SCALABSDALE

Ben Armine Forest
Strath Skinsdale
Kildonan Lodge
Strath of Kildonan

Strath Tirry
462
MEALLAN LIATH-MOR
337
CNOC NA H-INNSE MOIRE
Kildonan
416
BEINN DUBHAIN
A897

Shin
Shinness
421
CNOC NAN CRÙBAG MÒR
Torrish
River Helmsdale

624
BEINN DHORAIN
591
BEINN NA MÈILICH

Achnairn
317
SITHEAN ACHADH NAN EUN
River Brora
293
CNOC LEAMHNACHD
Balnacoil Lodge
539
COL-BHEIN
Glen Loth
Lothm

Loch Beannach
Colaboll
A838
A836
B871
110
110
107

Ferrycroft Countryside Centre
Loch Craggie
rath Brora
Dalreavoch Lodge
Loch Brora
Lothbeg

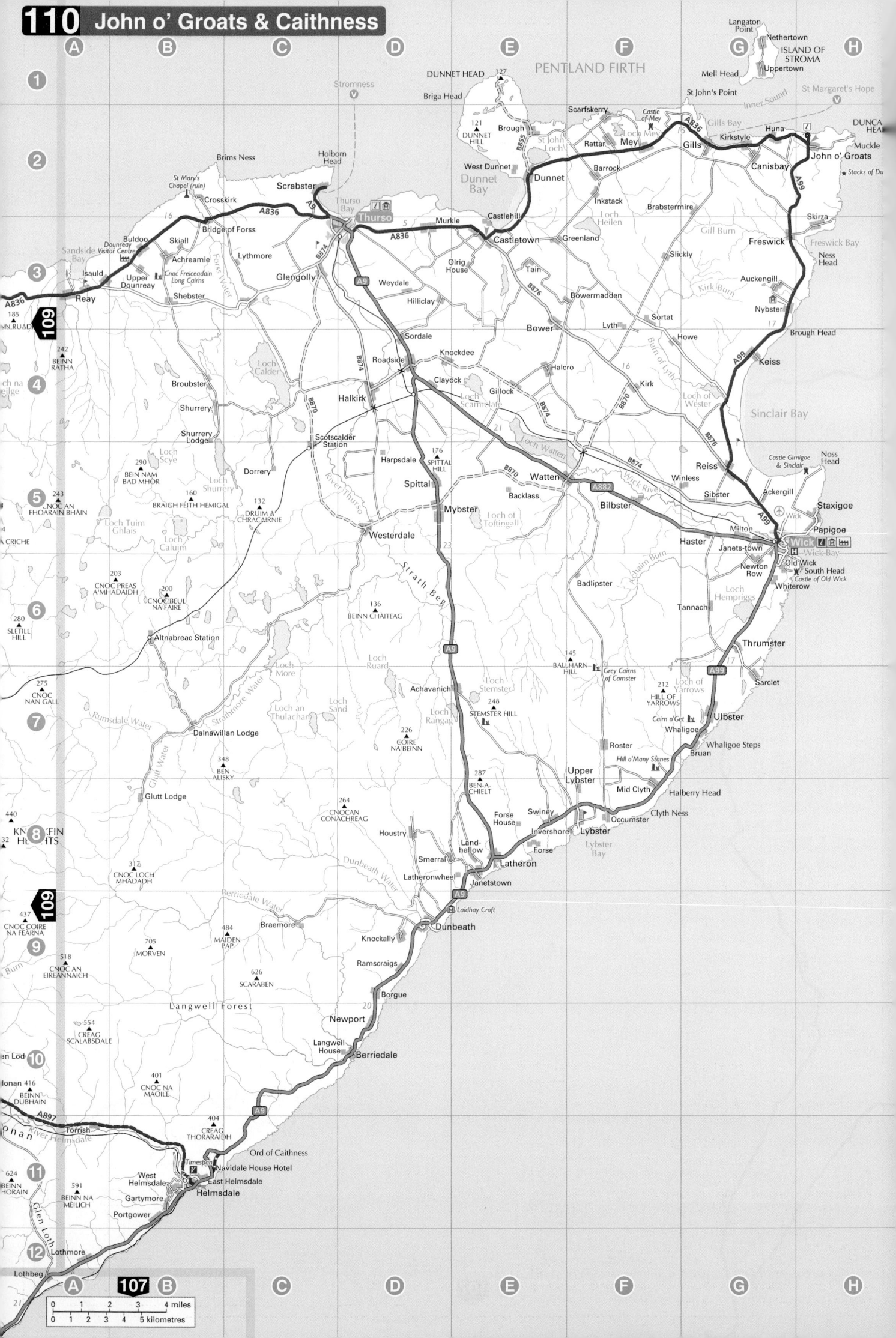

ISLAND OF STROMA

PENTLAND FIRTH

Langaton Point
Netherton
Mell Head
Uppertown

DUNNET HEAD
Briga Head
St John's Point
Gills Bay
Stacks of Du

DUNCA HEAD
Muckle
John o' Groats
St Margaret's Hope

121
DUNNET HILL
Brough
Scarfskerry
Castle of Mey
Gills
Kirkstyle
Huna
Canisbay

St John's Loch
Mey
Rattar

West Dunnet
Dunnet
Barrock

Dunnet Bay
Castlehill
Greenland
Inkstack
Brabstermire
Skirza

Scrabster
Holborn Head
Thurso Bay
Thurso
Murkle
Castletown
Tain
Slickly
Freswick
Freswick Bay

Brims Ness

St Mary's Chapel (ruin)
Crosskirk
A836
Bridge of Forss
Lythmore
Glengolly
Weydale
Hilliclay
Olrig House
Bower
Bowermadden
Lyth
Sortat
Howe
Ness Head
Auckengill
Nybster
Brough Head

16
Skiall
Achreamie
Cnoc Freiceadain Long Cairns
Shebster
Sordale
Roadside
Knockdee
Clayock
Halcro
Kirk
Keiss

Buldoo
Dounreay Visitor Centre
Upper Dounreay
Halkirk
Gillock
B876
Loch of Wester
Sinclair Bay

Sandside Bay
Isauld
Reay
109
185
NN RUAD
242
BEINN RATHA
Broubster
Loch Calder
Scotscalder Station
Loch Scarmclate
Reiss

ch na eilge
Shurrery
Harpsdale
Watten
Winless
Ackergill
Castle Girnigoe & Sinclair
Noss Head

290
BEINN NAM BAD MHOR
Shurrery Lodge
176
SPITTAL HILL
Spittal
A882
Bilbster
Sibster
Staxigoe
Papigoe

243
CNOC AN FHOARAIN BHÀIN
Loch Scye
Dorrery
Mybster
Backlass
Haster
Wick
Old Wick

160
BRAIGH FEITH HEMIGAL
132
DRUIM A' CHRACAIRNIE
Westerdale
Loch of Toftingall
Milton
Janets-town
Newton Row
South Head
Castle of Old Wick
Whiterow

Loch Tuim Ghlais
Loch Caluim
Loch Ruard
Loch Sand
Badlipster
Loch Hempriggs
Tannach
Thrumster

203
CNOC PREAS A'MHADAIDH
200
CNOC BEUL NA FAIRE
Loch More
Loch an Thulachan
Achavanich
Loch Stemster
248
STEMSTER HILL
145
BALLHARN HILL
212
HILL OF YARROWS
Loch of Yarrows
Sarclet

280
SLETILL HILL
Altnabreac Station
Loch Rangag
Grey Cairns of Camster
Cairn o' Get
Ulbster

275
CNOC NAN GALL
Rumsdale Water
136
BEINN CHÀITEAG
226
COIRE NA BEINN
287
BEN-A-CHIELT
Whaligoe
Whaligoe Steps

Dalnawillan Lodge
Strathmore Water
Houstry
Roster
Hill o' Many Stanes
Bruan

348
BEN ALISKY
Upper Lybster
Mid Clyth
Clyth Ness

Glutt Water
264
CNOCAN CONACHREAG
Forse House
Swiney
Halberry Head

Glutt Lodge
Smerral
Land-hallow
Invershore
Lybster
Occumster

440
312
CNOC LOCH MHADADH
Latheronwheel
Forse
Lybster Bay
Latheron

KNO KFIN H TS
32
Berriedale Water
Latheron
Janetstown
A9
Laidhay Croft

109
437
CNOC COIRE NA FEARNA
Dunbeath Water
Dunbeath

Burn
518
CNOC AN EIREANNAICH
705
MORVEN
484
MAIDEN PAP
626
SCARABEN
Knockally
Ramscraigs
Borgue

Langwell Forest
Newport
Langwell House
Berriedale

554
CREAG SCALABSDALE
401
CNOC NA MAOILE
20

an Lod
onan 416
BEINN DUBHAIN
A897
Torrish
River Helmsdale
404
CREAG THORARAIDH
A9
Ord of Caithness
Navidale House Hotel

onan
Glen Loth
624
BEINN HORAIN
591
BEINN NA MÈILICH
West Helmsdale
East Helmsdale
Helmsdale
Gartymore
Portgower
Timespan

Lothmore
Lothbeg
21
107

0 1 2 3 4 miles
0 1 2 3 4 5 kilometres

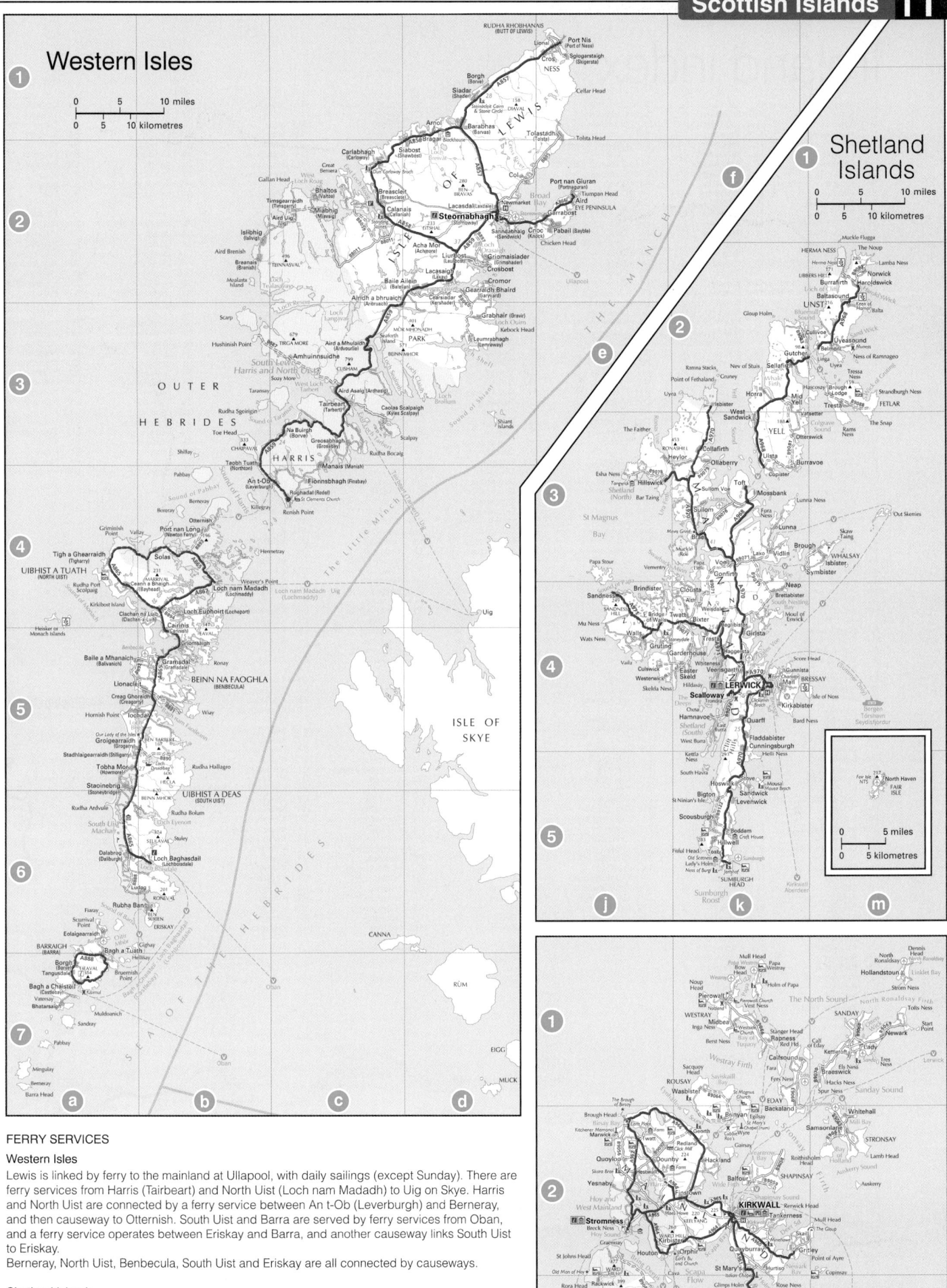

Western Isles

0   5   10 miles
0   5   10 kilometres

Shetland Islands

0   5   10 miles
0   5   10 kilometres

Orkney Islands

0   5   10 miles
0   5   10 kilometres

FERRY SERVICES

Western Isles

Lewis is linked by ferry to the mainland at Ullapool, with daily sailings (except Sunday). There are ferry services from Harris (Tairbeart) and North Uist (Loch nam Madadh) to Uig on Skye. Harris and North Uist are connected by a ferry service between An t-Ob (Leverburgh) and Berneray, and then causeway to Otternish. South Uist and Barra are served by ferry services from Oban, and a ferry service operates between Eriskay and Barra, and another causeway links South Uist to Eriskay.

Berneray, North Uist, Benbecula, South Uist and Eriskay are all connected by causeways.

Shetland Islands

The main service is from Aberdeen on the mainland to the island port of Lerwick. A service from Kirkwall (Orkney) to Lerwick is also available. During the summer months there are also services linking Shetland with Norway, the Faroe Islands and Iceland. Shetland Islands Council operates an inter-island car ferry service.

Orkney Islands

The main service is from Scrabster on the Caithness coast to the island port of Stromness and there is a further service from Gills (Caithness) to St Margaret's Hope on South Ronaldsay.

A service from Aberdeen to Kirkwall provides a link to Shetland at Lerwick. Inter-island car ferry services are also operated (advance reservations recommended).

Ireland index

114

0   10   20 miles
0 10   20   30 kilometres

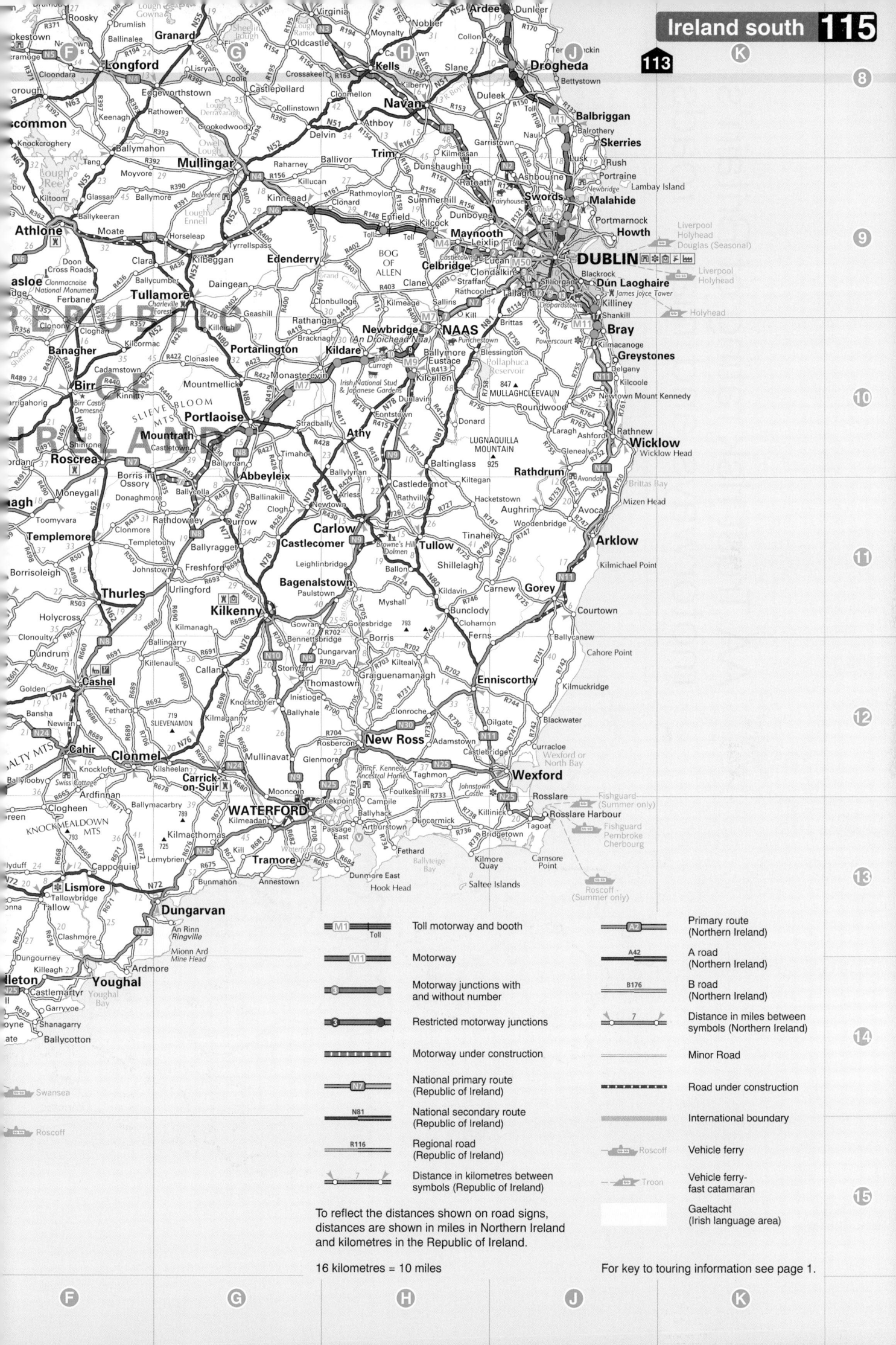

To reflect the distances shown on road signs, distances are shown in miles in Northern Ireland and kilometres in the Republic of Ireland.

16 kilometres = 10 miles

For key to touring information see page 1.

AA Trust risk rating of Britain's motorways and major roads

Research led by The AA Motoring Trust as part of the European Road Assessment Programme (EuroRAP) shows that the risk of death or serious injury on a single carriageway road is typically far higher than on a motorway.

This map shows the statistical risk of death or serious injury occurring on Britain's motorways and major roads for 2002-2004. The risk is calculated by comparing the frequency of death and serious injury on every stretch of road with how much traffic each road is carrying. For example, if there are 20 collisions involving death or serious injury on a stretch of road 5 miles long that carries 10,000 vehicles a day, then the risk is 10 times higher than if the road section has the same number of collisions but carries 100,000 vehicles.

Some of the roads shown have had improvements made to them recently, but during the survey period the risk of a fatal or serious injury collision on the black road sections was more than 10 times higher than on the safest (green) roads.

For more information on the statistical background to this research, visit the EuroRAP website at www.eurorap.org. For further road safety information, see www.aatrust.com. For navigation purposes please refer to the road maps in the main section of this atlas.

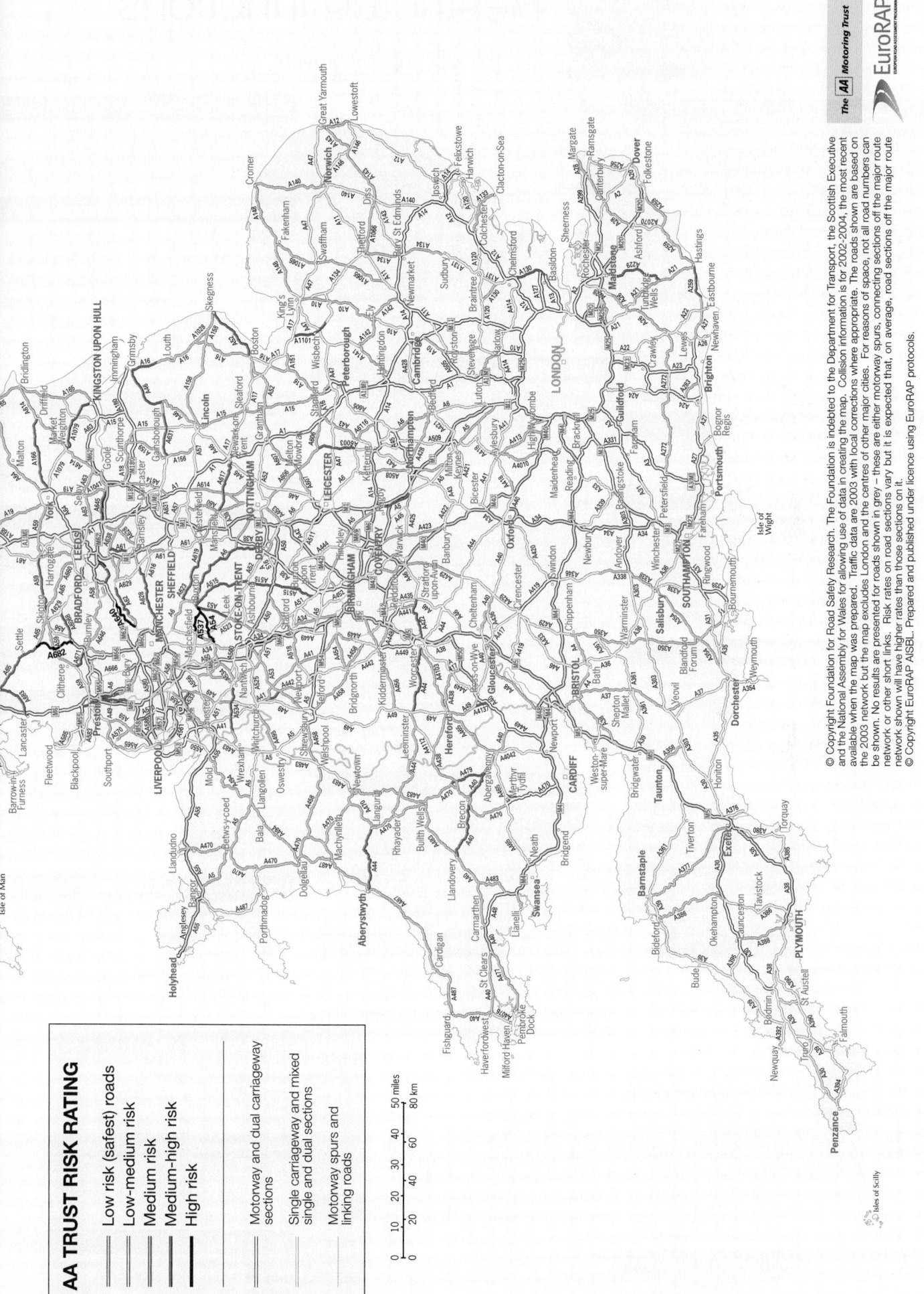

AA TRUST RISK RATING

═══ Low risk (safest) roads
═══ Low–medium risk
═══ Medium risk
═══ Medium–high risk
═══ High risk

═══ Motorway and dual carriageway sections
─── Single carriageway and mixed single and dual sections
─── Motorway spurs and linking roads

Restricted junctions

Motorway and Primary Route junctions which have access or exit restrictions are shown thus 3 , 56 on the map pages.

M1 London - Leeds

Junction	Northbound	Southbound
2	Access only from A1 (*northbound*)	Exit only to A1 (*southbound*)
4	Access only from A41 (*northbound*)	Exit only to A41 (*southbound*)
6A	Access only from M25 (no link from A405)	Exit only to M25 (no link from A405)
7	Access only from M10	Exit only to M10
17	Exit only to M45	Access only from M45
19	Exit only to northbound M6	Access only from M6
21A	Exit only to A46	Access only from A46
23A	Access only from A42	Exit only to A42
24A	Access only from A50	Exit only to A50
35A	Exit only to A616	Access only from A616
43	Exit only to M621	Access only from M621
48	Exit only to A1(M) (*northbound*)	Access only from A1(M) (*southbound*)

M2 Rochester - Faversham

Junction	Westbound	Eastbound
1	Exit only to A289 (*eastbound*)	Access only from A289 (*westbound*)

M3 Sunbury - Southampton

Junction	Southwestbound	Northeastbound
8	Exit only to A303	Access only from A303
10	Access only from Winchester & A31	Exit only to Winchester & A31
13	Access only to M27 (westbound) & A33	No restriction
14	Exit only to M27 (eastbound) & A33	Access only

M4 London - South Wales

Junction	Westbound	Eastbound
1	Access only from A4 (*westbound*)	Exit only to A4 (*eastbound*)
4A	No exit to A4 (*westbound*)	No restriction
21	Exit only to M48	Access only from M48
23	Access only from M48	Exit only to M48
25	Exit only to B4596	Access only from B4596
25A	Exit only to A4042	Access only from A4042
29	Exit only to A48(M)	Access only from A48(M)
38	Exit only to A48	No restriction
39	Access only from A48	No access/exit
42	Staggered junction; follow signs - exit only to A483	Staggered junction; follow signs - access only from A483

M5 Birmingham - Exeter

Junction	Southwestbound	Northeastbound
10	Exit only to A4019	Access only from A4019
11A	Exit only to A417 (*eastbound*)	Access only from A417 (*westbound*)
18A	Access only from M49	Exit only to M49
29	Access only from A30 (*westbound*)	No restriction

M6 Toll Motorway

Junction	Northbound	Southbound
T1	Access only	No access or exit
T2	No access or exit	Exit only
T3	Staggered junction; follow signs - access only from A38	Staggered junction; follow signs - no restriction
T5	Access only from A5127 (*southbound*)	Exit only to A5148 (*northbound*)
T7	Exit only	Access only
T8	Exit only	Access only

M6 Rugby - Carlisle

Junction	Northbound	Southbound
3A	Exit only	Access only
4	No access from M42 (*southbound*). No exit to M42 (*northbound*)	No access from M42 (*southbound*). No exit to M42
4A	Access only from M42 (*southbound*)	Exit only to M42
5	Exit only to A452	Access only from A452
10A	Exit only to M54	Access only from M54
11A	Access only	Exit only
20A (with M56)	No restriction	No access from M56 (*westbound*)
20	Access only from A50	No restriction
24	Access only from A58	Exit only to A58
25	Exit only	Access only
29	No direct access, use adjacent slip road to jct 29A	No direct exit, use adjacent slip road from jct 29A
29A	No direct exit, use adjacent slip road from jct 29	No direct access, use adjacent slip road to jct 29
30	Access only from M61	Exit only to M61
31A	Exit only	Access only

M8 Edinburgh - Bishopton

Junction	Westbound	Eastbound
8	No access from M73 (*southbound*) or from A8 (*eastbound*) & A89	No exit to M73 (*northbound*) or to A8 (*westbound*) & A89
9	Access only	Exit only
13	Access only from M80 (*southbound*)	Exit only to M80 (*northbound*)
14	Access only	Exit only
16	Exit only to A804	Access only from A879
17	Exit only to A82	No restriction
18	Access only from A82 (*eastbound*)	Exit only to A814
19	No access from A814 (westbound)	Exit only to A814 (*westbound*)
20	Exit only	Access only
21	Access only	Exit only to A8
22	Exit only to M77 (*southbound*)	Access only from M77 (*northbound*)
23	Exit only to B768	Access only from B768
25	No access or exit from or to A8	No access or exit from or to A8
25A	Exit only	Access only
28	Exit only	Access only
28A	Exit only to A737	Access only from A737

M9 Edinburgh - Dunblane

Junction	Northwestbound	Southeastbound
1A	Exit only to A8000	Access only from A8000
2	Access only	Exit only
3	Exit only	Access only
6	Access only from A904	Exit only to A905
8	Exit only to M876 (*southwestbound*)	Access only from M876 (*northeastbound*)

M10 St Albans - M1

Junction	Northwestbound	Southeastbound
with M1 (jct 7)	Exit only to M1 (*northbound*)	Access only from M1 (*southbound*)

M11 London - Cambridge

Junction	Northbound	Southbound
4	Access only from A406	Exit only to A406
5	Exit only to A1168	Access only from A1168
9	Exit only to A11	Access only from A11
13	Exit only to A1303	Access only from A1303
14	Exit only to A14 (*eastbound*)	Access only from A14

M20 Swanley - Folkestone

Junction	Southeastbound	Northwestbound
2	Staggered junction; follow signs - exit only to A227	Staggered junction; follow signs - access only from A227
3	Access only from M26 (*eastbound*)	Exit only to M26 (*westbound*)
5	For access follow signs - exit only to A20	Access only from A20
6	For exit follow signs	No restriction
11A	Exit only	Access only

M23 Hooley - Crawley

Junction	Southbound	Northbound
7	Access only from A23 (*southbound*)	Exit only to A23 (*northbound*)
10A	Exit only to B2036	Access only from B2036

M25 London Orbital Motorway

Junction	Clockwise	Anticlockwise
1B	No direct access, use slip road to Jct 2. Exit only to A296	Access only from A296. No exit - use jct 2
5	No exit to M26	No access from M26
19	Exit only to A41	Access only from A41
21	Access only from M1 (*southbound*). Exit only to M1 (*northbound*)	Access only from M1 (*southbound*). Exit only to M1 (*northbound*)
31	No exit (use slip road via jct 30)	For access follow signs

M26 Sevenoaks - Wrotham

Junction	Eastbound	Westbound
with M25 (jct 5)	Access only from anticlockwise M25 (*eastbound*)	Exit only to clockwise M25 (*westbound*)
with M20 (jct 3)	Exit only to M20 (*southeastbound*)	Access only from M20 (*northwestbound*)

M27 Cadnam - Portsmouth

Junction	Eastbound	Westbound
4	Staggered junction; follow signs - access only from M3 (*southbound*). Exit only to M3 (*northbound*)	Staggered junction; follow signs - access only from M3 (*southbound*). Exit only to M3 (*northbound*)
10	Access only from A32	Exit only to A32
12	Staggered junction; follow signs - access only from M275 (*northbound*)	Staggered junction; follow signs - exit only to M275 (*southbound*)

M40 London - Birmingham

Junction	Northwestbound	Southeastbound
3	Exit only to A40	Access only from A40
7	Exit only to A329	Access only from A329
8	Exit only to A40	Access only from A40
13	Exit only to A452	Access only from A452
14	Access only from A452	Exit only to A452
16	Access only from A3400	Exit only to A3400

M42 Bromsgrove - Measham

Junction	Northeastbound	Southwestbound
1	Access only from A38	Exit only to A38
7	Exit only to M6 (*northwestbound*)	Access only from M6 (*northwestbound*)
7A	Exit only to M6 (*southeastbound*)	No access or exit
8	Access only from M6 (*southeastbound*)	Exit only to M6 (*northwestbound*)

M45 Coventry - M1

Junction	Eastbound	Westbound
unnumbered (Dunchurch)	Exit only to A45 & B4429	Access only from A45 & B4429
with M1 (jct 17)	Exit only to M1 (*southbound*)	Access only from M1 (*northbound*)

M53 Mersey Tunnel - Chester

Junction	Southeastbound	Northwestbound
11	Access only from M56 (*westbound*). Exit only to M56 (*eastbound*)	Access only from M56 (*westbound*). Exit only to M56 (*eastbound*)

M54 Telford

Junction	Westbound	Eastbound
with M6 (jct 10A)	Access only from M6 (*northbound*)	Exit only to M6 (*soutbound*)

M56 North Cheshire

Junction	Westbound	Eastbound
1	Access only from M60 (*westbound*)	Exit only to M60 (*eastbound*) & A34 (*northbound*)
2	Exit only to A560	Access only from A560
3	Access only from A5103	Exit only to A5103 & A560
4	Exit only	Access only
9	Exit to M6 (*southbound*) via A50 interchange	Access from M6 (*northbound*) via A50 interchange
15	Exit only to M53	Access only from M53

M57 Liverpool Outer Ring Road

Junction	Northwestbound	Southeastbound
3	Access only from A526	Exit only to A526
5	Access only from A580 (*westbound*)	Exit only to A580

M58 Liverpool - Wigan

Junction	Eastbound	Westbound
1	Access only	Exit Only

M60 Manchester Orbital

Junction	Clockwise	Anticlockwise
2	Access only from A560	Exit only to A560
3	No access from M56	Access only from A34 (*northbound*)
4	Access only from A34 (*northbound*). Exit only to M56	Access only from M56 (*eastbound*). Exit only to A34 (*southbound*)
5	Access and exit only from and to A5103	Access and exit only from and to A5103 (*southbound*)
7	No direct access, use slip road to jct 8. Exit only to A56	Access only from A56. No exit - use jct 8
14	Access from A580 (*eastbound*)	Exit only to A580 (*westbound*)
16	Access only from A666	Exit only to A666
20	Exit only to A664	Access only from A664
22	No restriction	Exit only to A62
25	Exit only to A6017	No restriction
26	No restriction	No access or exit
27	Access only from A626	Exit only to A626

M61 Manchester - Preston

Junction	Northwestbound	Southeastbound
3	No access or exit	Exit only to A666
with M6 (jct 30)	Exit only to M6 (*northbound*)	Access only from M6 (*southbound*)

M62 Liverpool - Kingston upon Hull

Junction	Eastbound	Westbound
23	Exit only to A640	Access only from A640

M65 Preston - Colne

Junction	Northeastbound	Southwestbound
1	Access and exit to M6 only	Access and exit to M6 only
9	Exit only to A679	Access only from A679
11	Access only	Exit only

M66 Bury

Junction	Southbound	Northbound
with A56	Access only from A56 (*southbound*)	Exit only to A56 (*northbound*)
1	Access only from A56	Exit only to A56

M67 Hyde Bypass

Junction	Eastbound	Westbound
1	Exit only to A6017	Access only from A6017
2	Access only	Exit only to A57
3	No restriction	Exit only to A627

M69 Coventry - Leicester

Junction	Northbound	Southbound
2	Access only from B4669	Exit only to B4669

M73 East of Glasgow

Junction	Northbound	Southbound
2	No access from or exit to A89. No access from M8 (*eastbound*).	No access from or exit to A89. No exit to M8 (*westbound*).
3	Exit only to A80 (*northeastbound*)	Access only from A80 (*southwestbound*)

M74 and A74(M) Glasgow - Gretna

Junction	Southbound	Northbound
2	Access only from A763	Exit only to A763
3	Exit only	Access only
7	Exit only to A72	Access only from A72
9	Exit only to B7078	No access or exit
10	Access only from B7078	No restrictions
11	Exit only to B7078	Access only from B7078
12	Access only from A70	Exit only to A70
18	Access only from B723	Exit only to B723
21	Exit only to B6357	Access only from B6357
with B7076	Access only	Exit only
Gretna Green	Exit only	Access only
with A75	Access only from A75	Exit only to A75
with A6071	Exit only to A74 (*southbound*)	Access only from A74 (*northbound*)

M77 South of Glasgow

Junction	Southbound	Northbound
with M8 (jct 22)	No access from M8 (*eastbound*)	No exit to M8 (*westbound*)
4	Exit only	Access only
with A77	Exit only to A77 (*southbound*)	Access only from A77 (*northbound*)

M80 Stepps Bypass

Junction	Northeastbound	Southwestbound
1	Access only	No restriction
3	Exit only	Access only

M80 Bonnybridge - Stirling

Junction	Northbound	Southbound
5	Exit only to M876 (*northeastbound*)	Access only from M876 (*southwestbound*)

M90 Forth Road Bridge - Perth

Junction	Northbound	Southbound
2a	Exit only to A92 (*eastbound*)	Access only from A92 (*westbound*)
7	Access only from A91	Exit only to A91
8	Exit only to A91	Access only from A91
10	No access from A912. No exit to A912 (*southbound*)	No access from A912 (*northbound*). No exit to A912

M180 Doncaster - Grimsby

Junction	Eastbound	Westbound
1	Exit only A18	Access only from A18

M606 Bradford Spur

Junction	Northbound	Southbound
2	Exit only	No restriction

M621 Leeds - M1

Junction	Clockwise	Anticlockwise
2a	Access only	Exit only
4	Exit only	No restriction
5	Access only	Exit only
6	Exit only	Access only
with M1 (jct 43)	Exit only to M1 (*southbound*)	Access only from M1 (*northbound*)

M876 Bonnybridge - Kincardine Bridge

Junction	Northeastbound	Southwestbound
with M80 (jct 5)	Access only from M80 (*northbound*)	Exit only to M80 (*southbound*)
2	Exit only to A9	Access only from A9
with M9 (jct 8)	Exit only to M9 (*eastbound*)	Access only from M9 (*westbound*)

A1(M) South Mimms - Baldock

Junction	Northbound	Southbound
2	Exit only to A1001	Access only from A1001
3	No restriction	Exit only to A414
5	Access only	No access or exit

A1(M) East of Leeds

Junction	Northbound	Southbound
44	Access only from M1 (*northbound*)	Exit only to M1 (*southbound*)

A1(M) Scotch Corner - Newcastle upon Tyne

Junction	Northbound	Southbound
57	Exit only to A66(M) (*eastbound*)	Access only from A66(M) (*westbound*)
65	No access Exit only to A194(M) & A1 (*northbound*)	No exit Access only from A194(M) and A1 (*southbound*)

A3(M) Horndean - Havant

Junction	Southbound	Northbound
1	Exit only to A3	Access only from A3
4	Access only	Exit only

A48(M) Cardiff Spur

Junction	Westbound	Eastbound
29	Access only from M4 (*westbound*)	Exit only to M4 (*eastbound*)
29a	Exit only to A48 (*westbound*)	Access only from A48 (*eastbound*)

A66(M) Darlington Spur

Junction	Eastbound	Westbound
with A1(M) (jct 57)	Access only from A1(M) (*northbound*)	Exit only to A1(M) (*southbound*)

A194(M) Newcastle upon Tyne

Junction	Northbound	Southbound
with A1(M) (jct 65)	Access only from A1(M) (*northbound*)	Exit only to A1(M) (*southbound*)

A12 M25 - Ipswich

Junction	Northeastbound	Southwestbound
13	Access only from B1002	No restriction
14	Exit only	Access only
20a	Exit only to B1137	Access only from B1137
20b	Access only B1137	Exit only to B1137
21	No restriction	Access only from B1389
23	Exit only to B1024	Access only from B1024
24	Access only from B1024	Exit only from B1024
27	Exit only to A113	Access only from A113
unnumbered (with A120)	Exit only A120	Access only from A120
29	Access only from A120 and A1232	Exit only to A120 and A1232
unnumbered	Access only	No restriction

A14 M1 - Felixstowe

Junction	Eastbound	Westbound
With M1/M6 (jct19)	Access only from M6 and M1 (*southbound*)	Exit only to M6 and M1 (*northbound*)
4	Access only from B669	Exit only to B669
31	Access only from A428 & M11. Exit only to A1307	Exit only to A428 & M11. Access only from A1307
34	Exit only to B1047	Access only from B1047
unnumbered	No access from or exit to A1303	Access only from A1303
36	Access only from A11	Exit only to A11
38	Exit only to A11	Access only from A11
39	Access only from B1506	Exit only to B1506
49	Exit only to A1308	Access only from A1308
61	Exit only to A154	Access only from A154

A55 Holyhead - Chester

Junction	Eastbound	Westbound
8a	Access only from A5	Exit only to A5
23a	Exit only	Access only
24a	No access or exit	Exit only
33a	No access from or exit to B5126	Exit only to B5126
33b	Access only from A494	Exit only to A494
35a (west)	Exit only A5104	Access only from A5104
35b (east)	Access only from A5104	Exit only to A5104

M25 London orbital motorway

Refer also to atlas pages 20–21

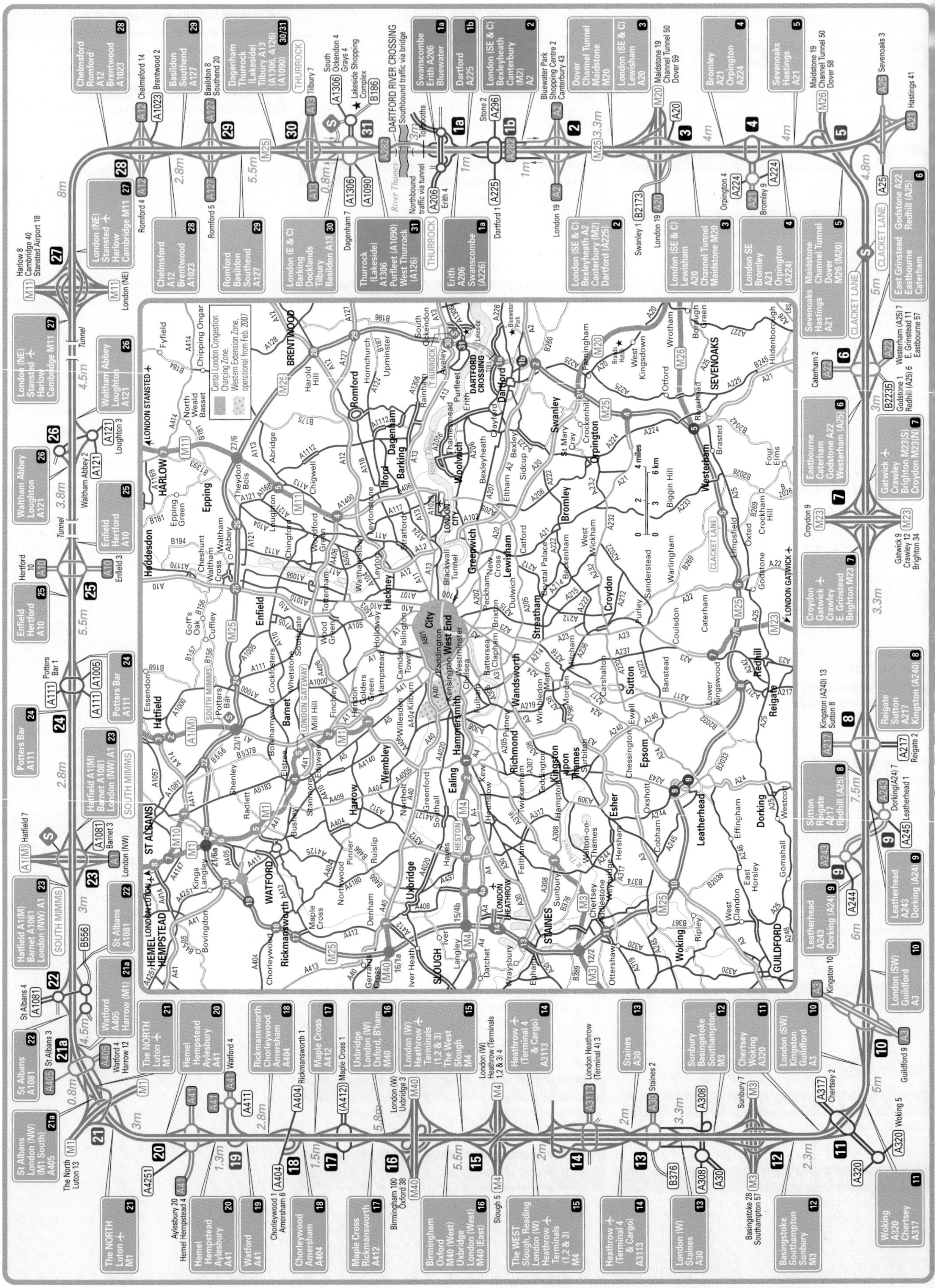

M6 Toll motorway

Refer also to atlas page 40

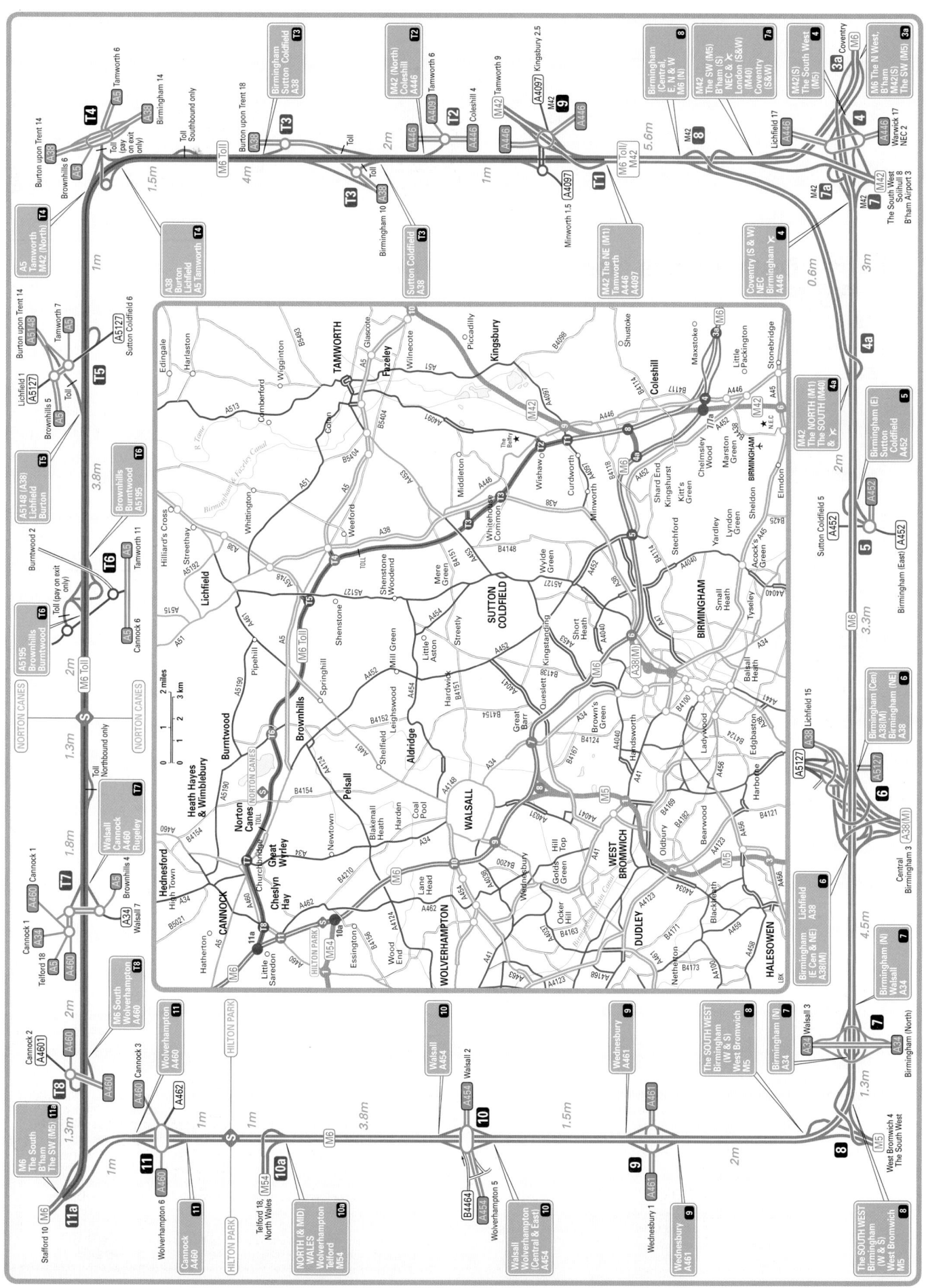

Street map symbols

Town plans

M8 Motorway with number	B road	Restricted road/ pedestrians only	← One-way street	**H** 24-hour Accident & Emergency hospital	**i** Tourist Information Centre
Primary road	Other road	**COLLEGE** Building of interest	**P** Car park	Toilet, with facilities for the less able	Light rapid transit system (with station)
A road	**6 3** Numbered junction	Park or open space	**P+** Park and Ride (at least 6 days per week)	Shopmobility	† Church/chapel

District maps (see pages 136–147) For key to touring information see page 1

M60 Motorway with number	Unclassified road single/dual	● Railway station	**H H** 24-hour Accident & Emergency, hospital
M6 Toll M6 Toll motorway (Birmingham district)	Road under construction	○ Light rapid transit system station	**Crem** Crematorium
Primary route single/dual	Restricted road	⊖ ⊖ London Underground station (LRT)	Central London Congestion Charging Zone
Other A road single/dual	Railway line/in tunnel	⊖ Railway station/LRT interchange	Western Extension to the Charging Zone (operational from February 2007)
B road single/dual	++++++ Tourist railway	⊖ Docklands Light Railway (DLR) station	Charge free routes through the Charging Zone

Central London street map (see pages 148–157)

Primary route single/dual	Railway line	**PO** Post Office	Theatre or performing arts centre
Other A road single/dual	← One-way street	**H** 24-hour Accident & Emergency hospital	Cinema
B road single/dual	⇄ Railway station	Public library	AA inspected restaurant
Unclassified road single/dual	**LC** Level crossing	Historic house or building	**i** Tourist Information Centre (open all year)
Road under construction	⊖ London Underground station (LRT)	**Wakehurst Place NT** National Trust property	Park or open space
Road tunnel	⊖ Docklands Light Railway (DLR) station	Building of interest	Woodland
Minor/private road (access may be restricted)	**P** Car park	Cathedral	Cemetery
Track or footpath	Petrol station open 24-hours/not 24-hour (main suppliers only)	† Church/chapel	Central London Congestion Charging Zone boundary, includi the western extension (due operational February 2007)
Pedestrian street	Toilet, with facilities for the less able	**M** Museum or art gallery	Charge free routes through the Charging Zone

Royal Parks (opening and closing times for traffic)

Green Park	Constitution Hill: closed Sundays, 8.00 am–dusk
Hyde Park	Open 5.00 am–midnight
Regent's Park	Open 5.00 am–midnight
St James's Park	The Mall: closed Sundays, 8.00 am–dusk

Traffic regulations in the City of London include security checkpoints and restrict the number of entry and exit points.

Note: Oxford Street is closed to through-traffic (except buses & taxis) 7.00 am–7.00 pm Monday–Saturday. Restricted parts of Frith Street/Old Compton Street are closed to vehicles 12.00 noon–1.00 am daily.

Central London Congestion Charging Zone

Introduced in 2003 and extended westwards to include most of Chelsea, Kensington and Westminster (due operational February 2007), the charge for driving or parking in the Central London area is £8 per vehicle per day. The zone operates between 7.00 am and 6.30 pm (6.00 pm from February 2007) Monday to Friday only. There are two charge free routes through the charging zone: the A40 (Westway) and the A5/A4202/A302/A202 (Edgware Road - Park Lane -Grosvenor Place - Vauxhall Bridge Road). There is currently no charge on weekends and public holidays.

For up-to-date information on the status of the zone, exemptions, discounts and how to pay, telephone 0845 900 1234 (020 7649 9121 for minicom users), visit *www.cclondon.com* or write to Congestion Charging London, P.O. Box 2985, Coventry, CV7 8ZR.

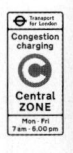

Town plans

Town plan contents

Central London

Aberdeen
Aberystwyth

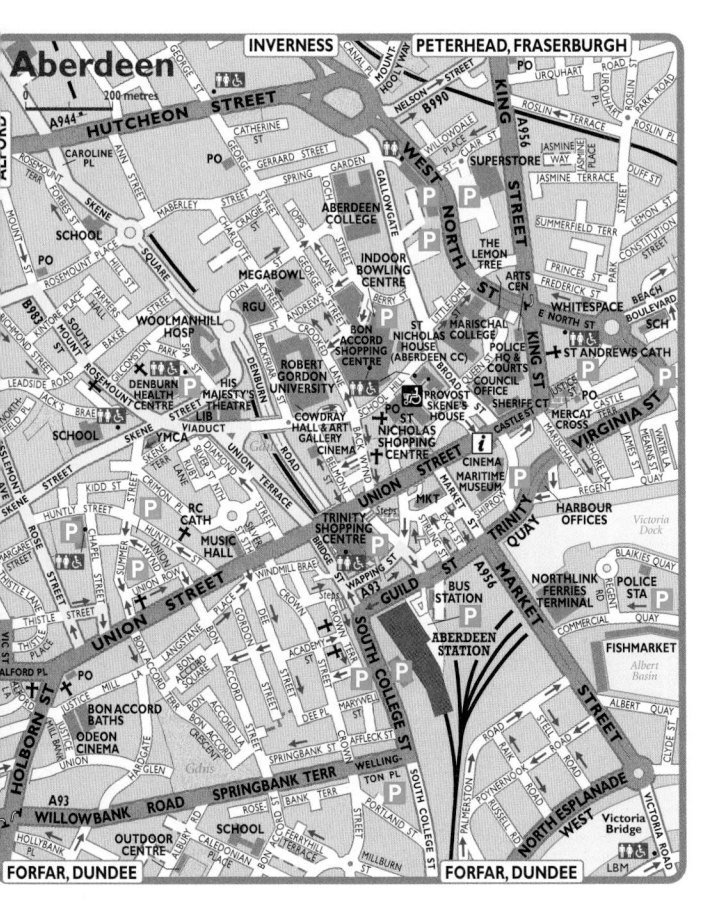

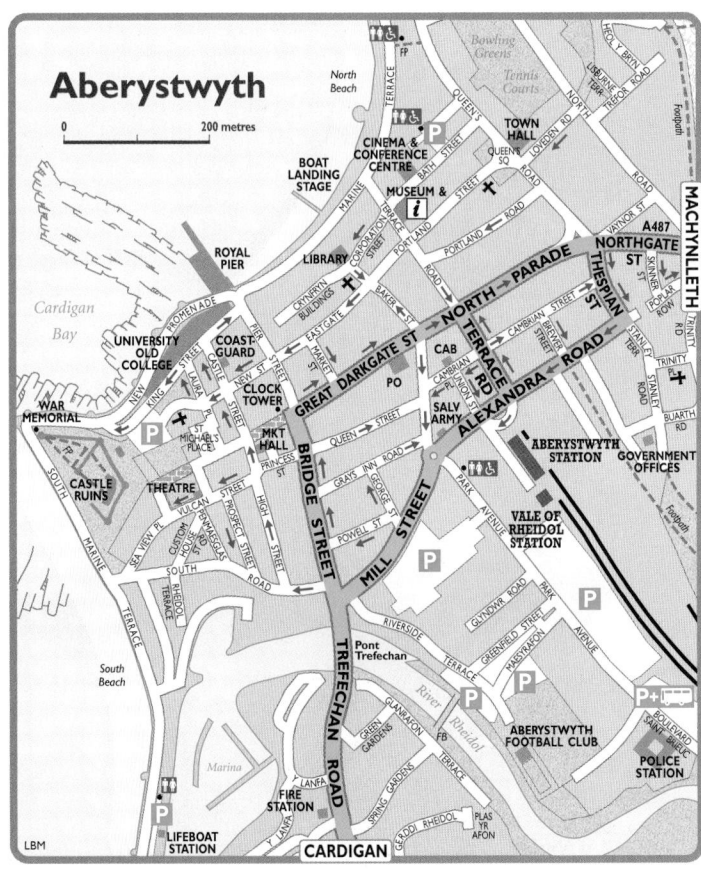

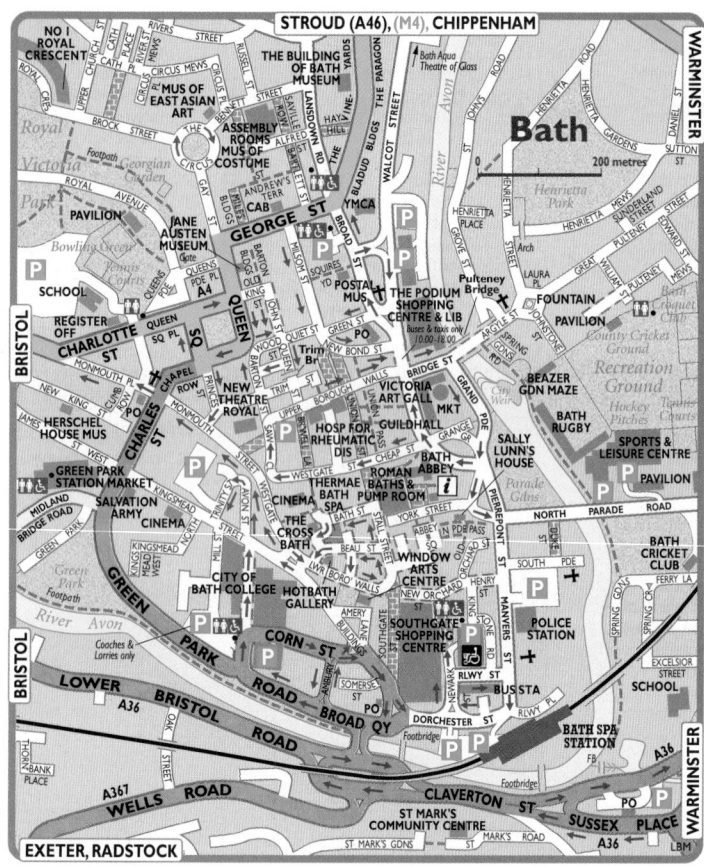

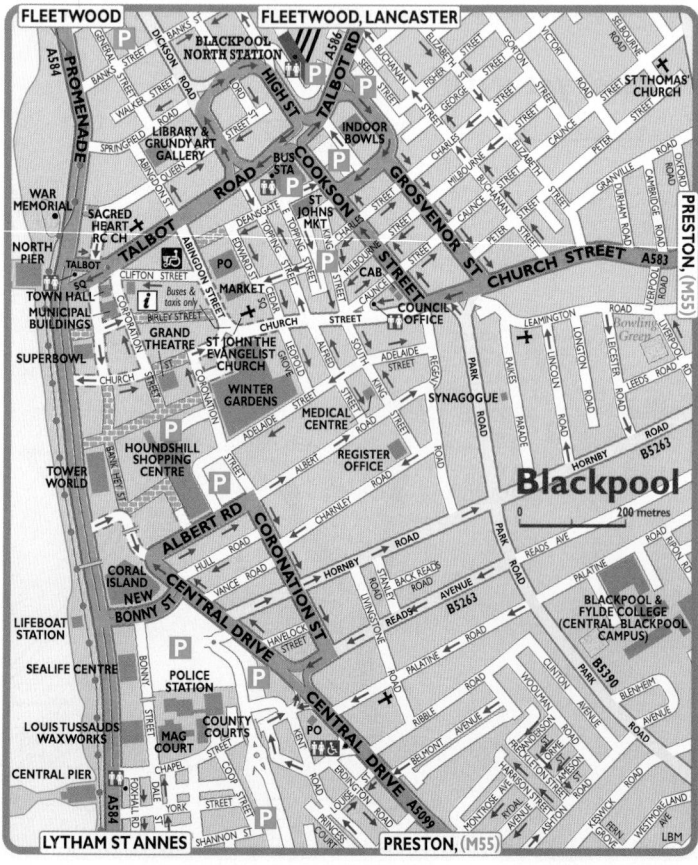

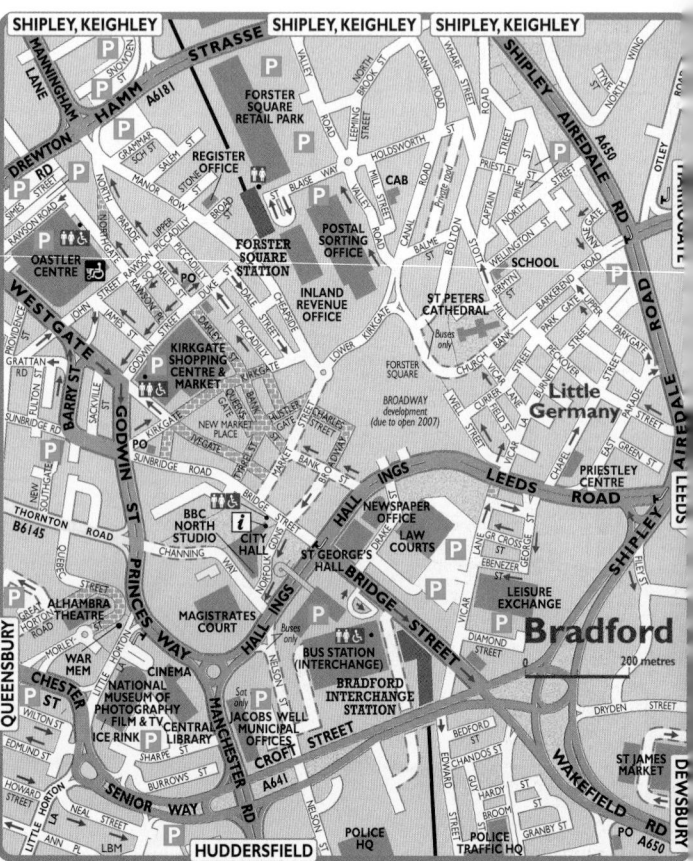

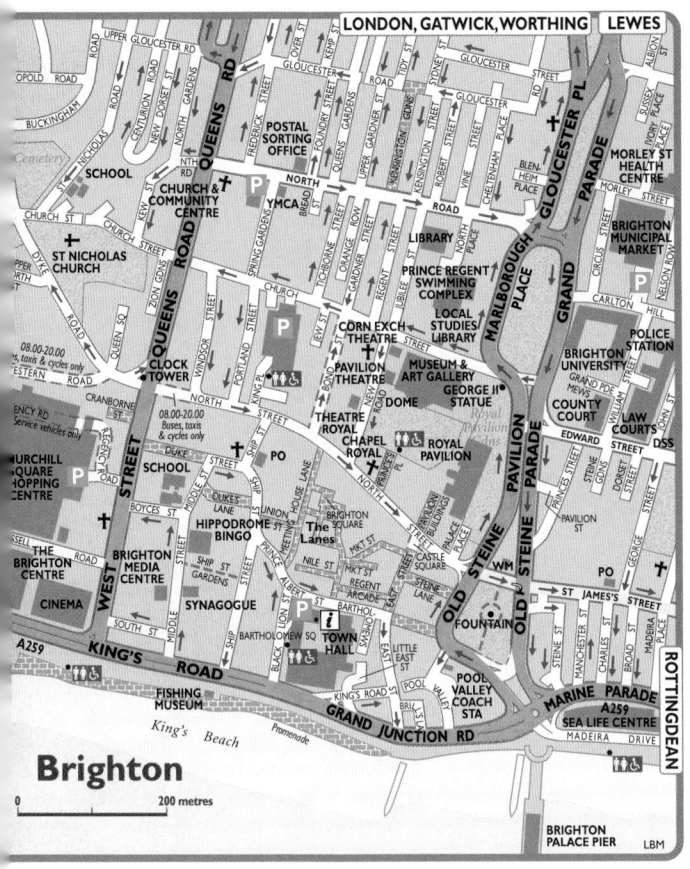

Brighton

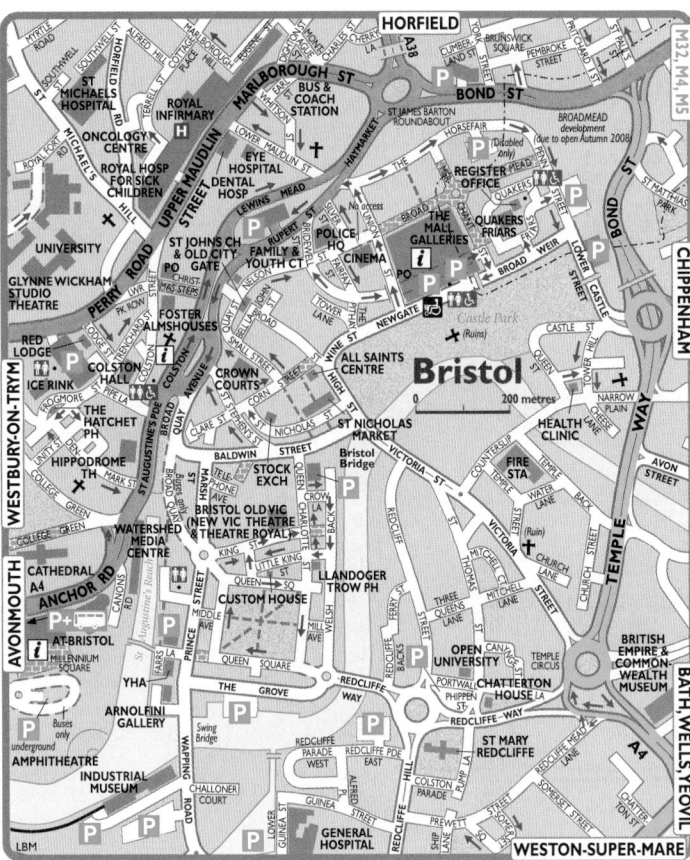

Bristol

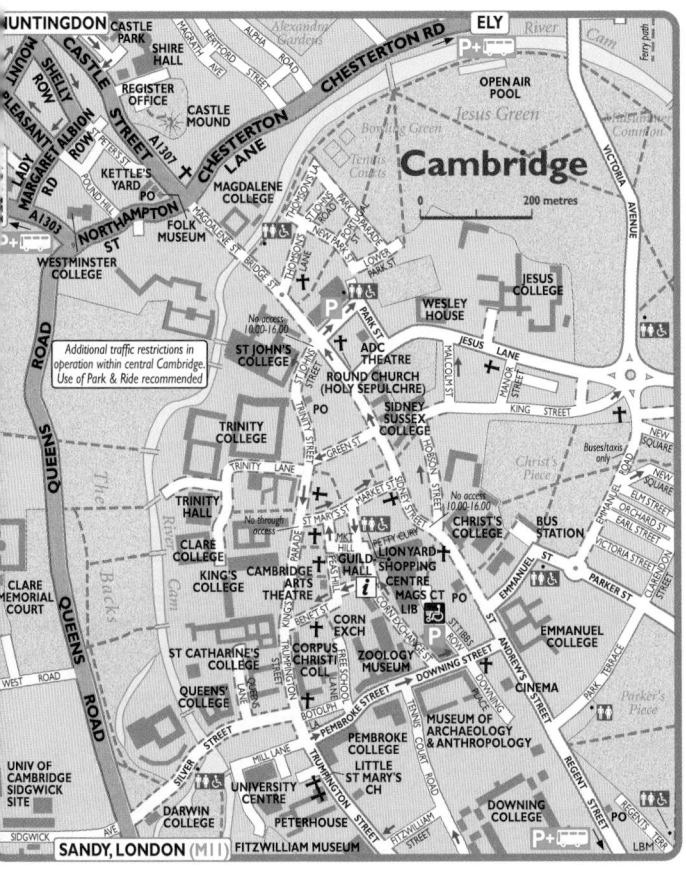

Cambridge

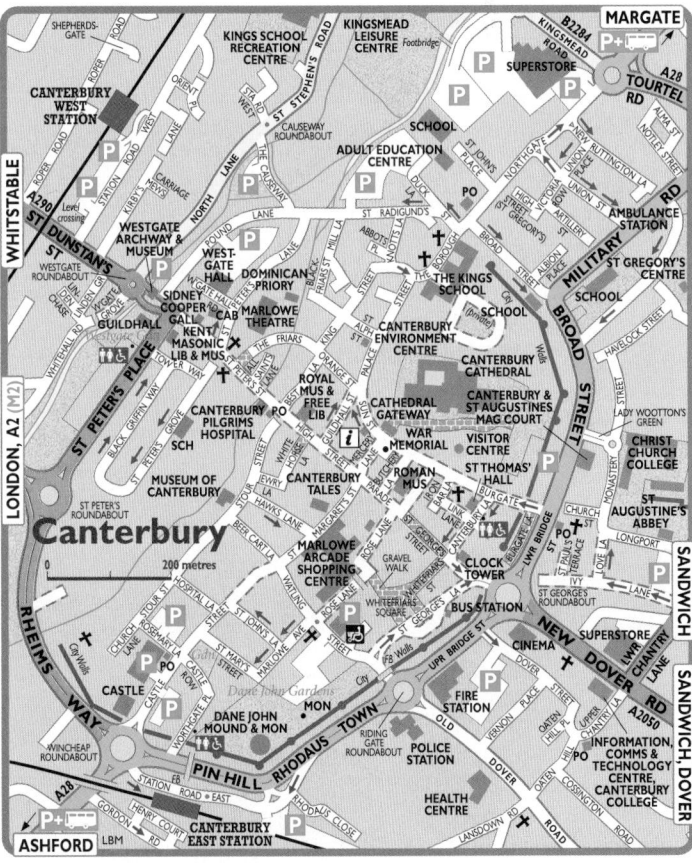

Canterbury

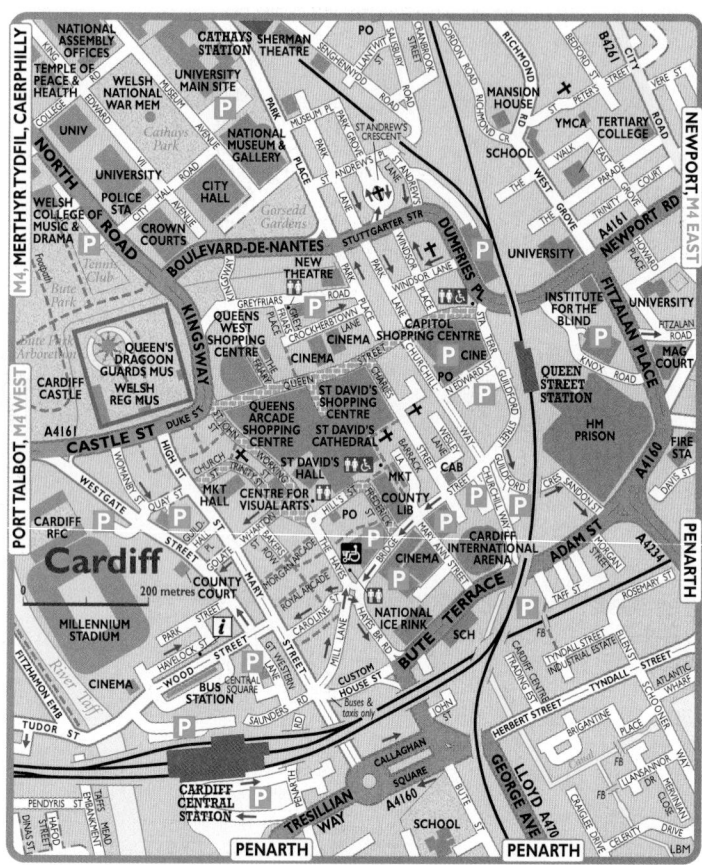

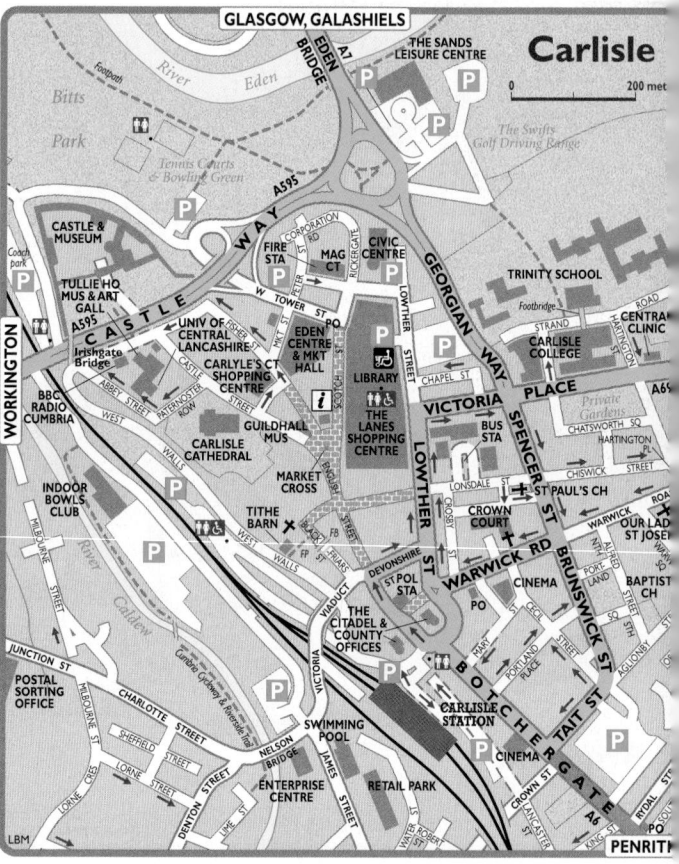

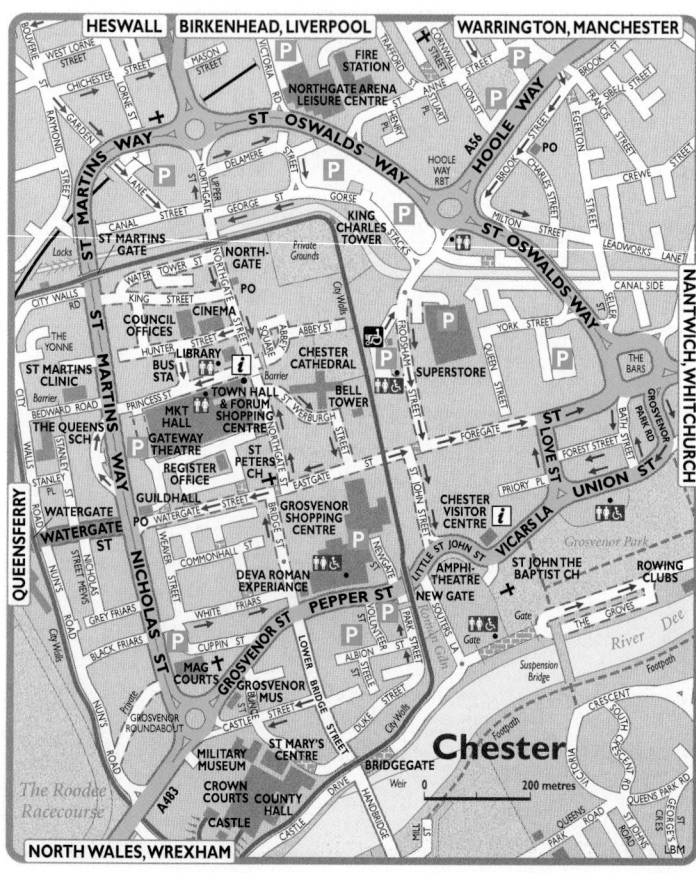

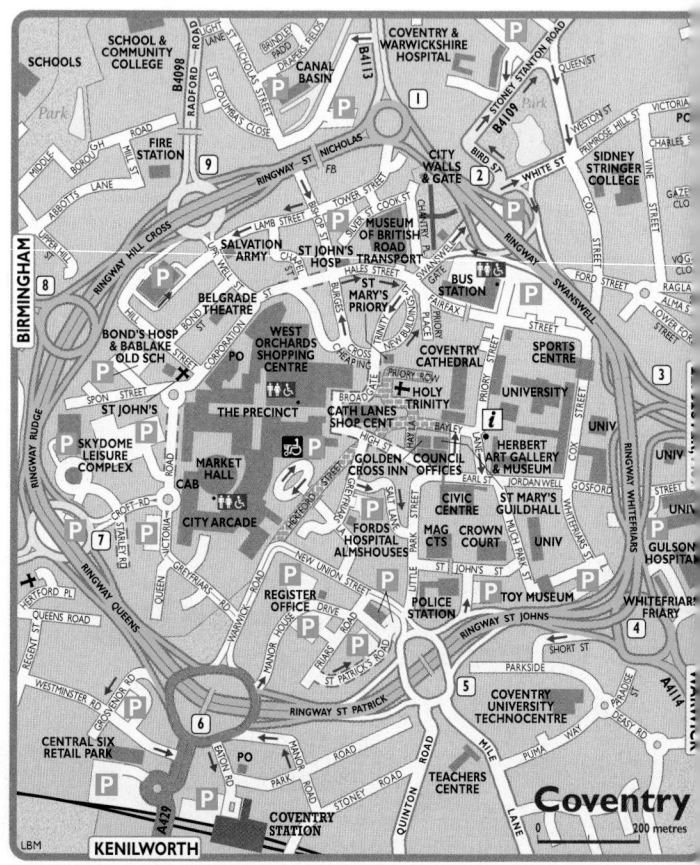

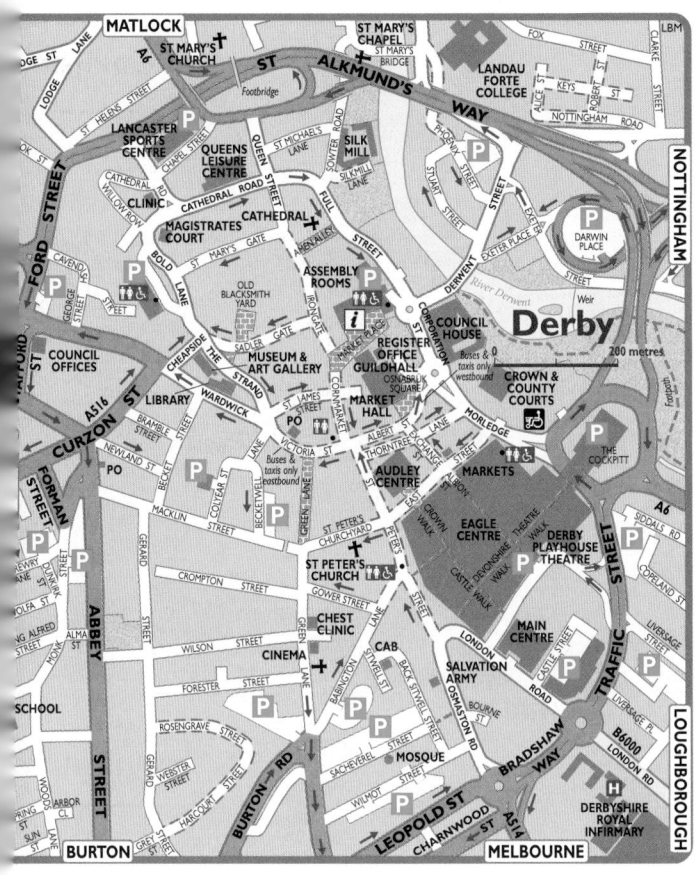

Derby

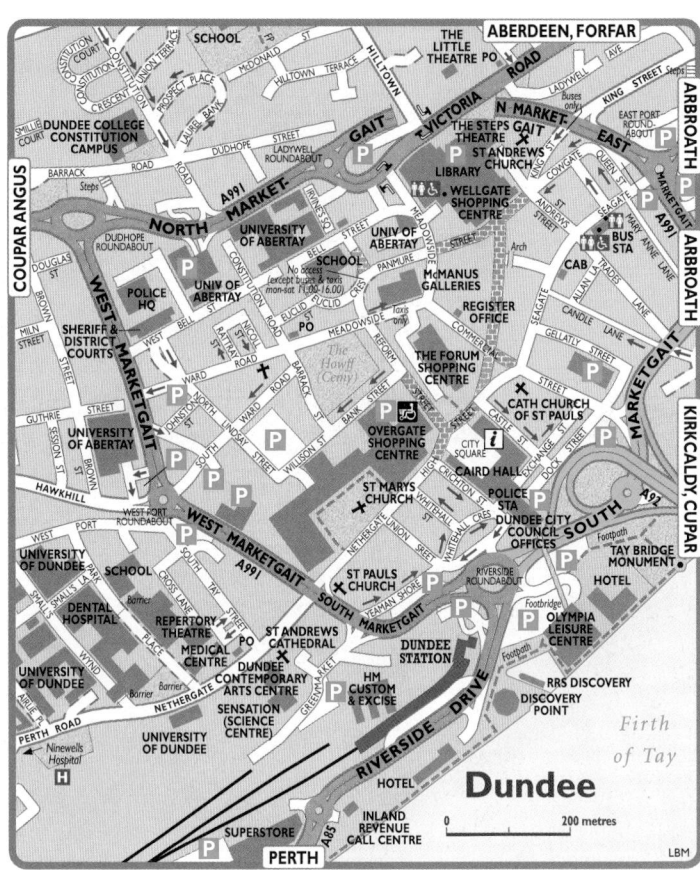

Dundee

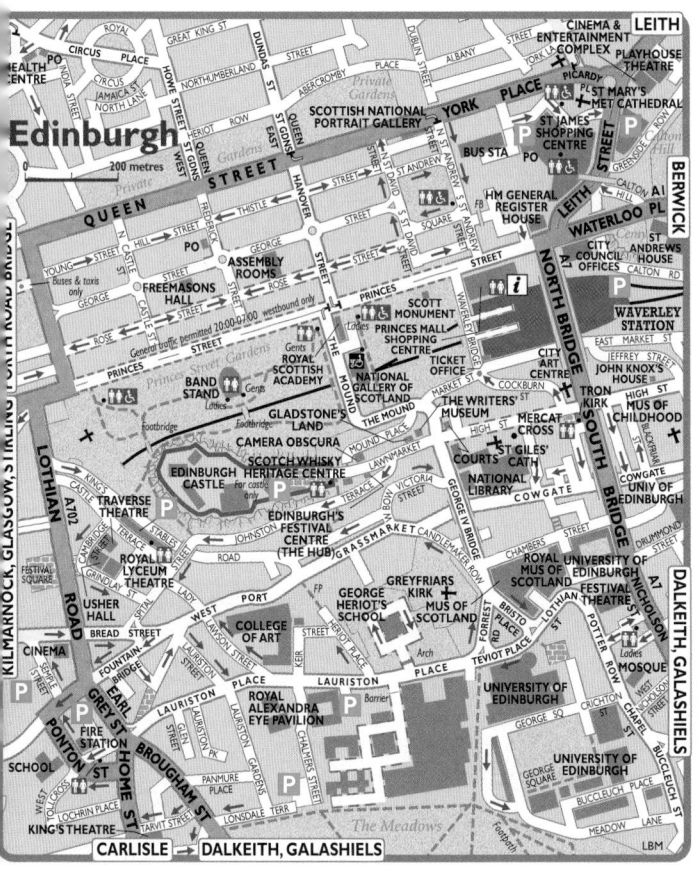

Edinburgh

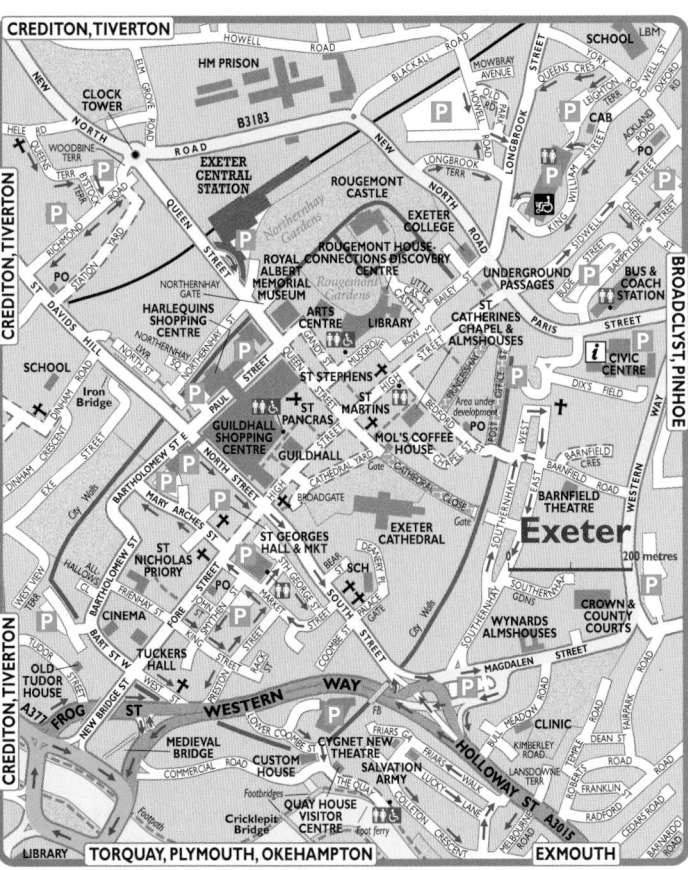

Exeter

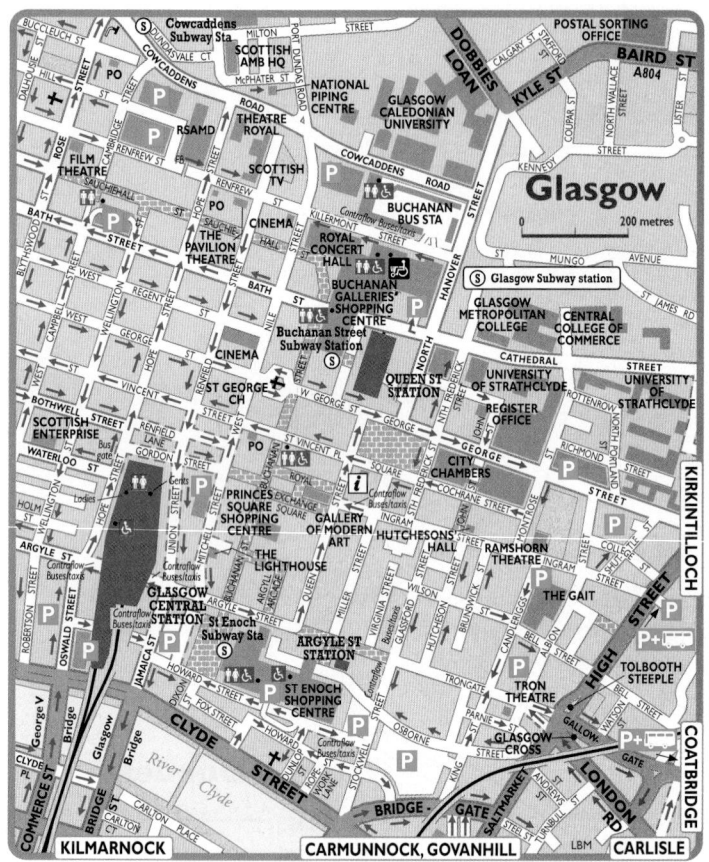

Glasgow

Ipswich

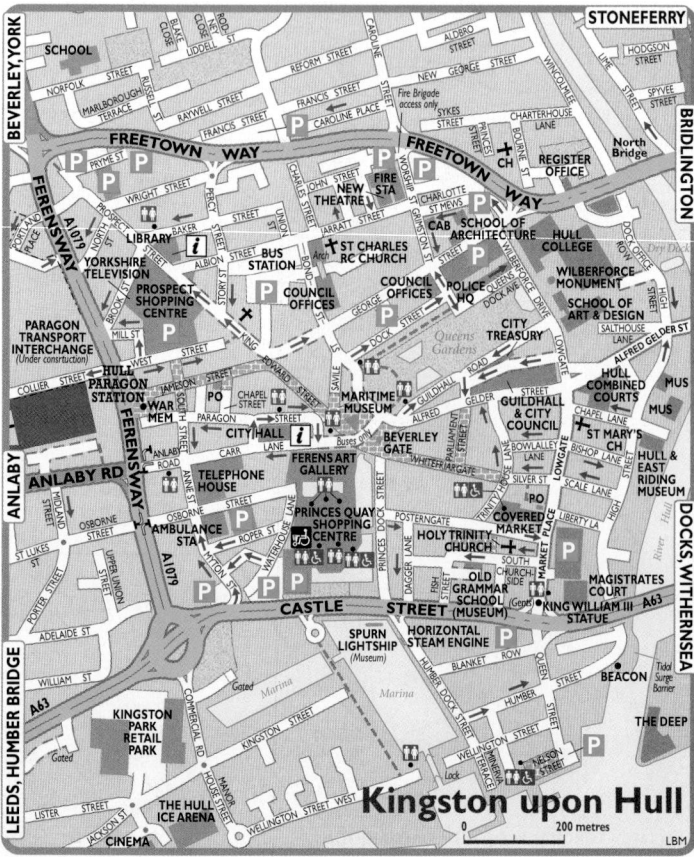

Kingston upon Hull

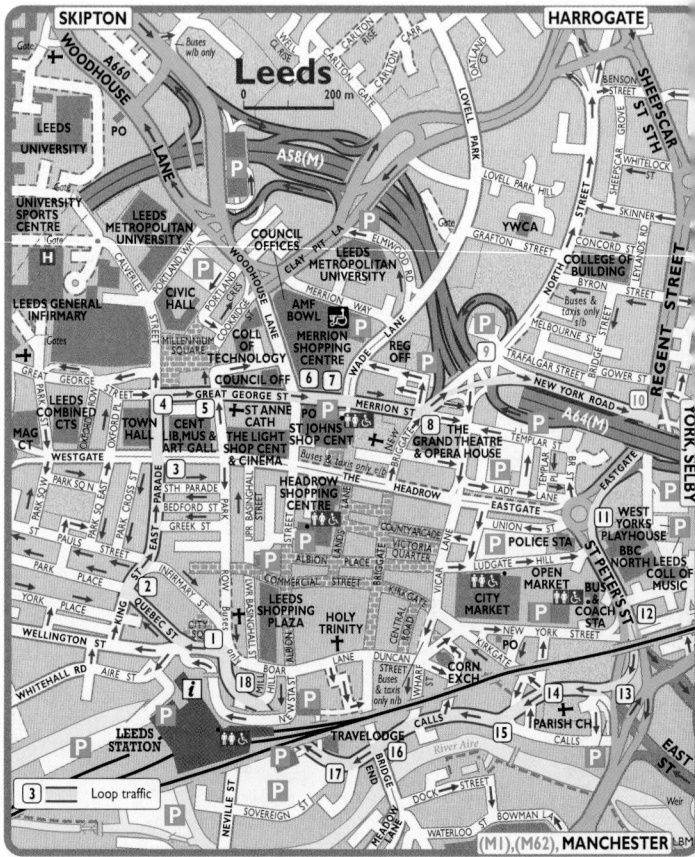

Leeds

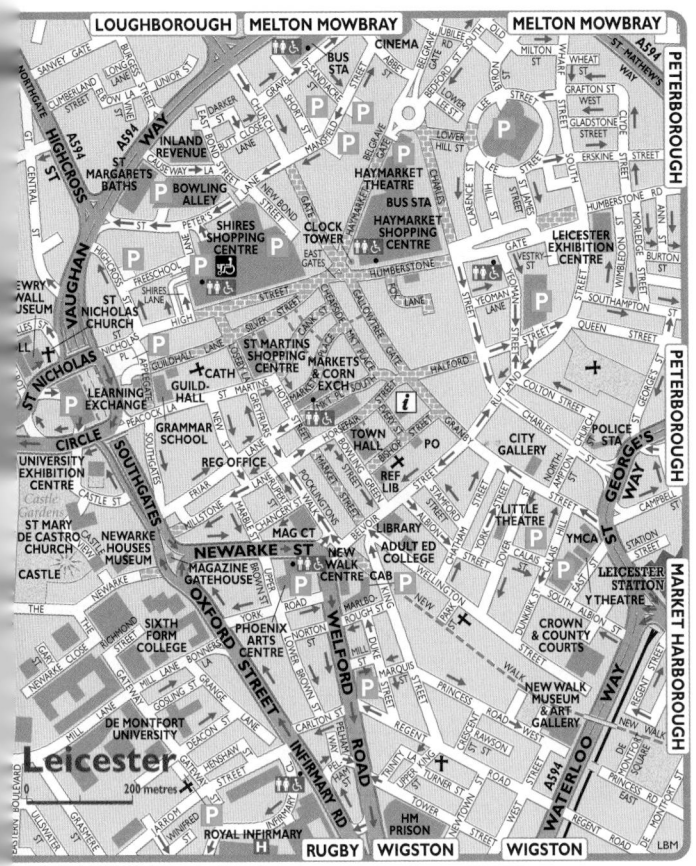

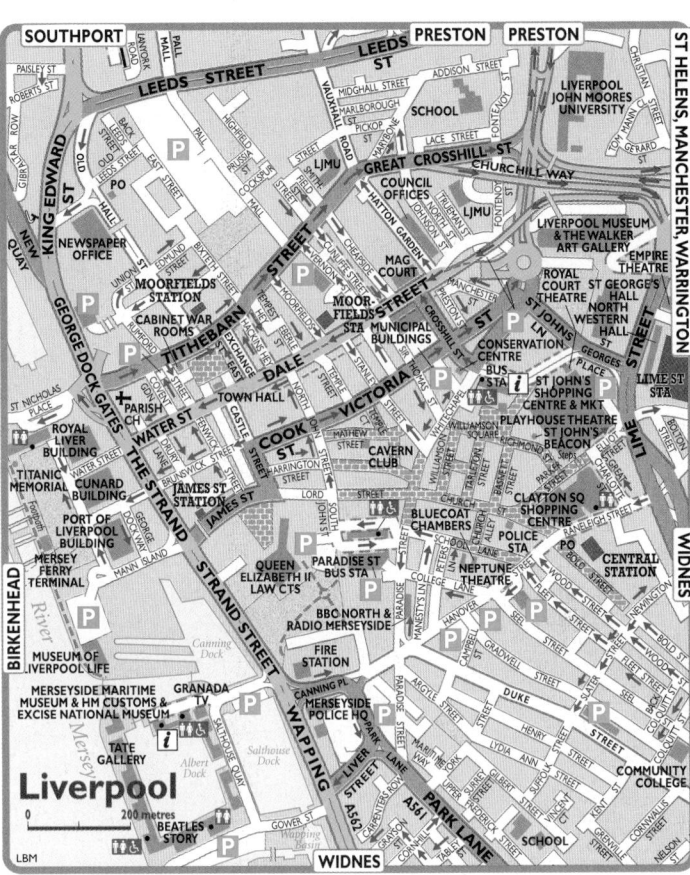

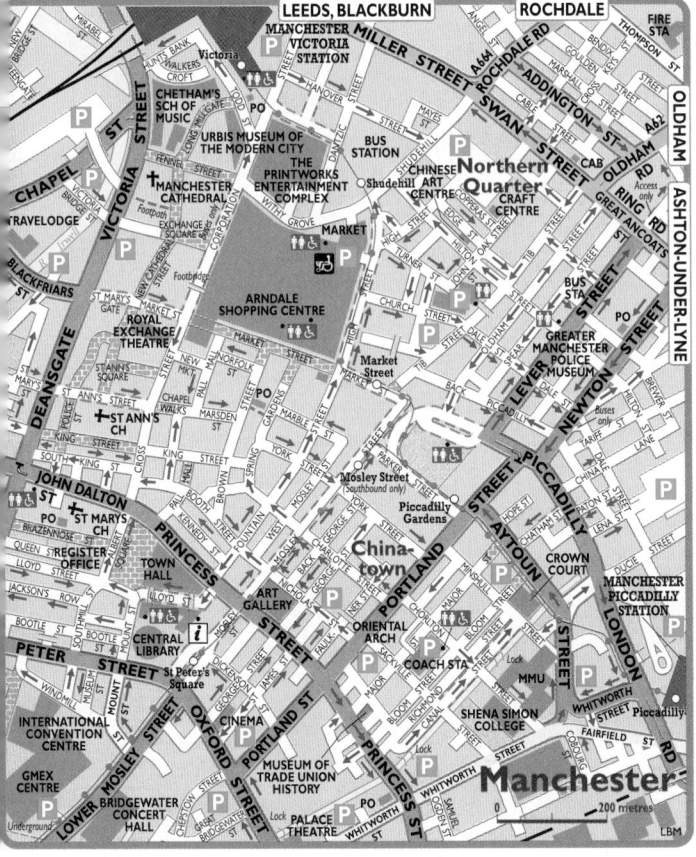

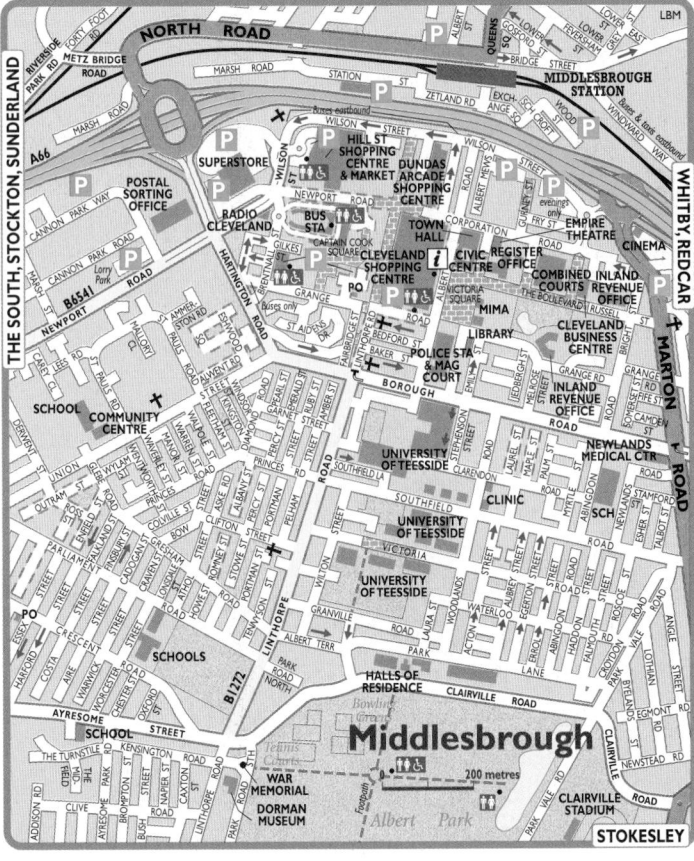

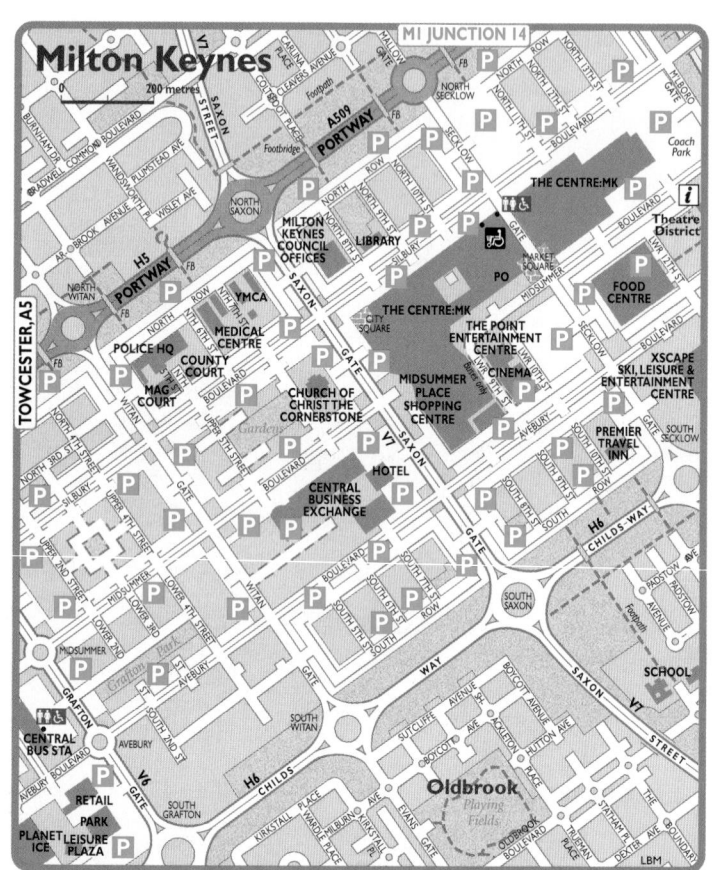

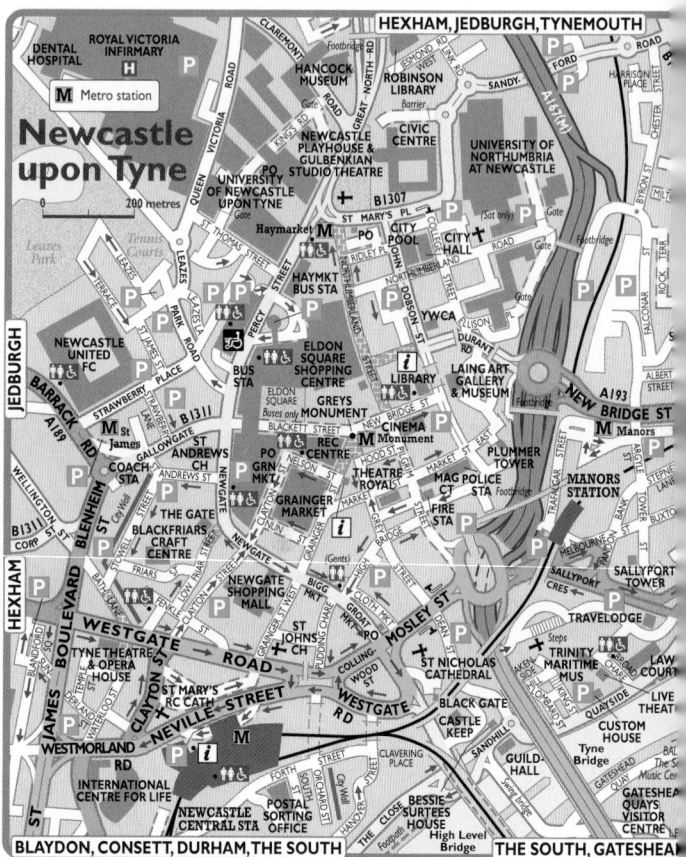

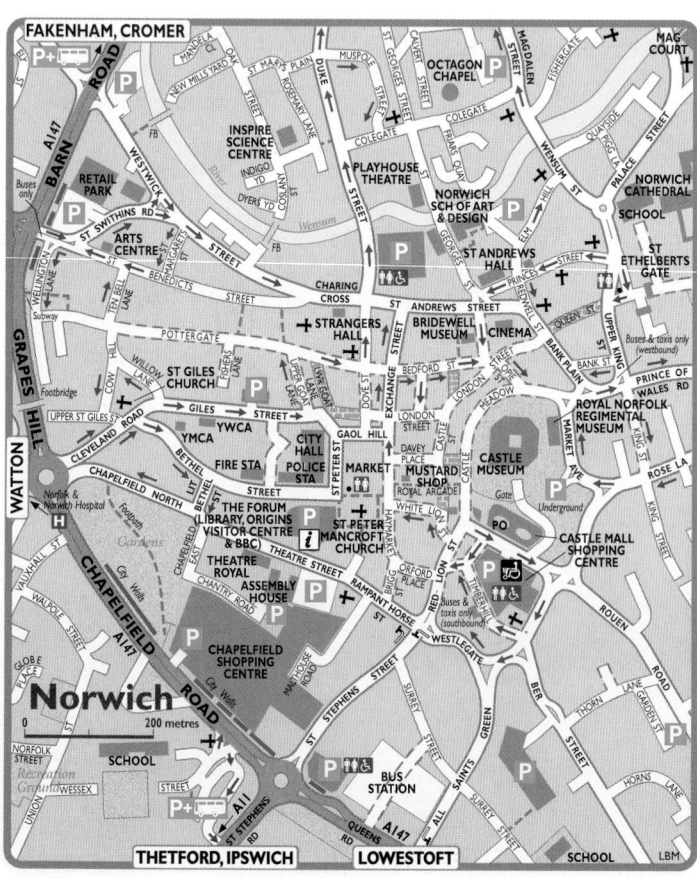

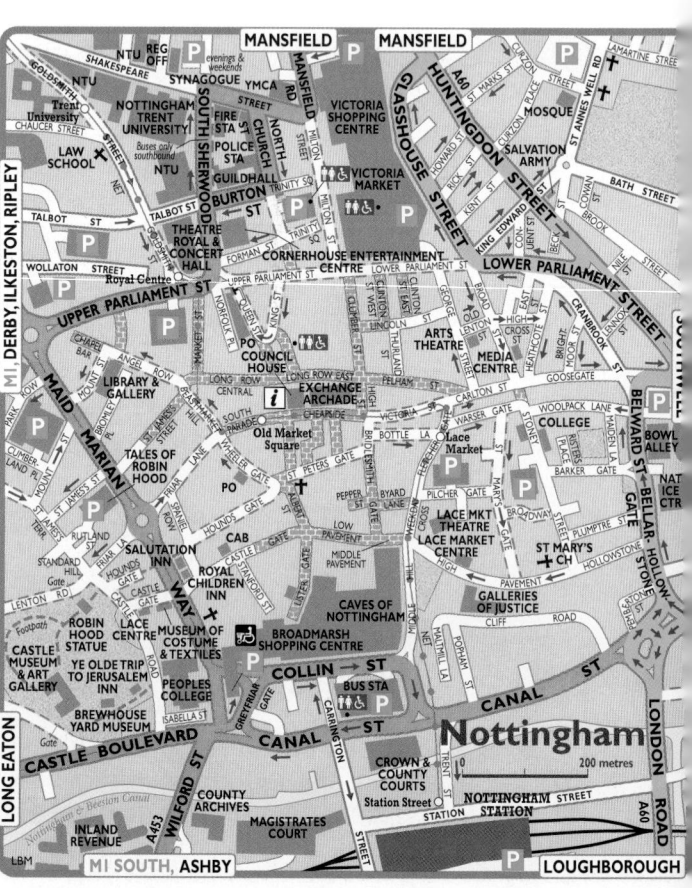

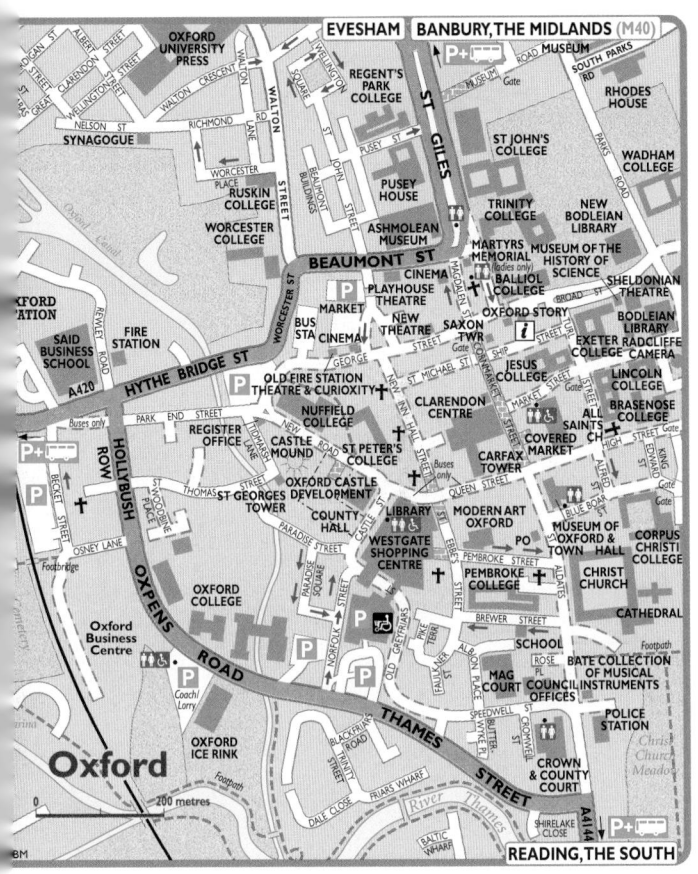

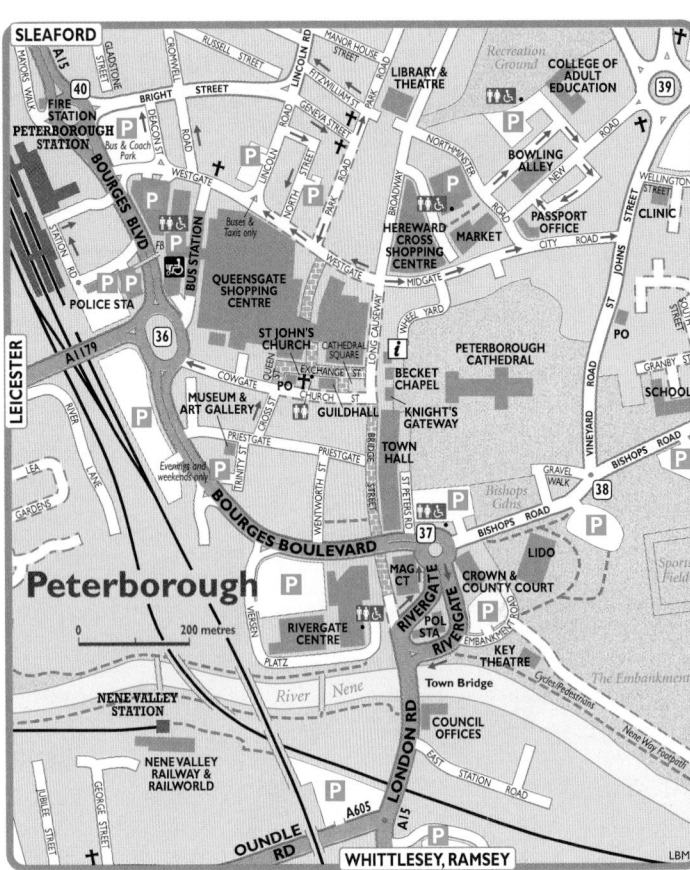

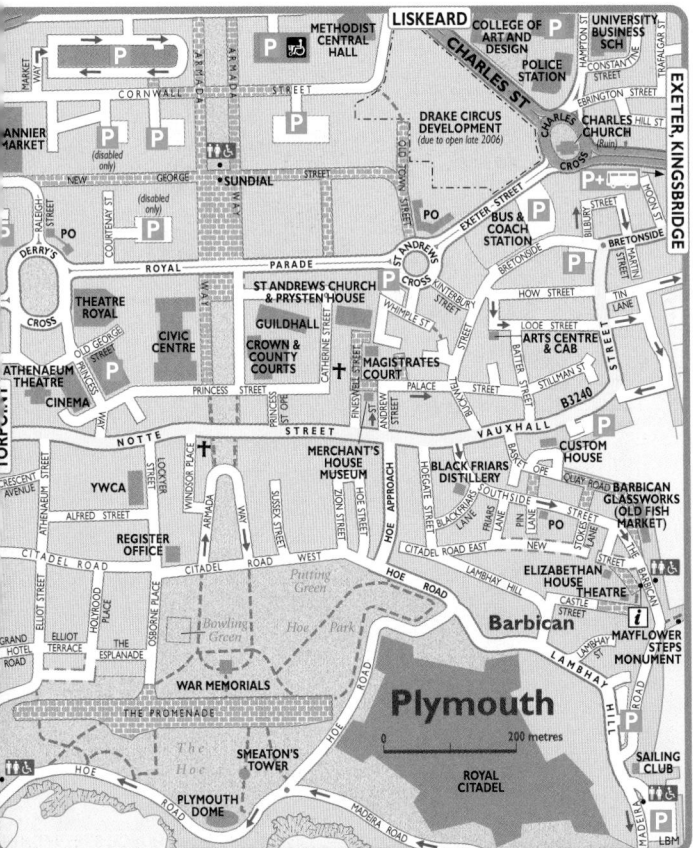

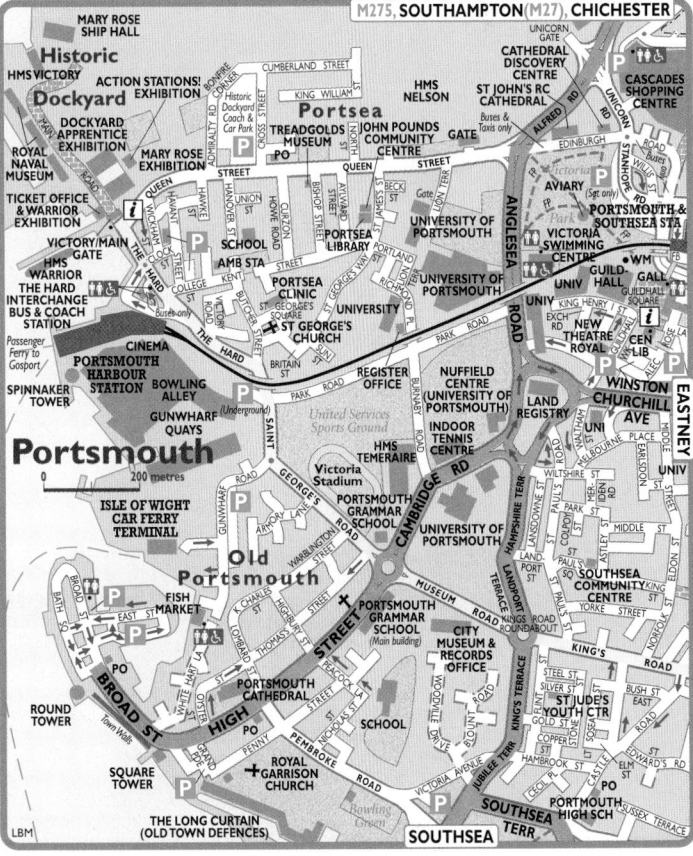

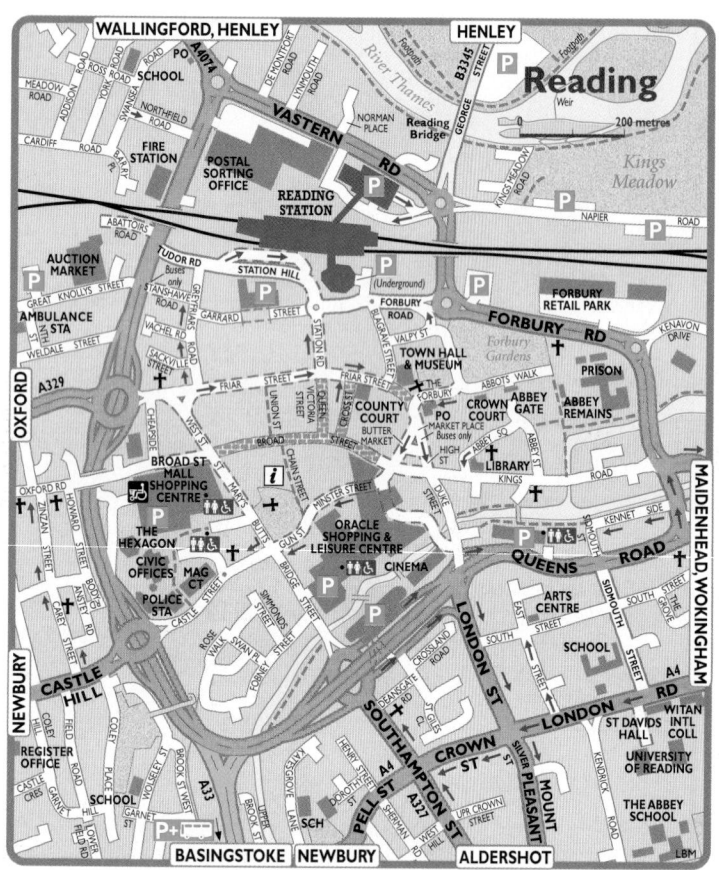

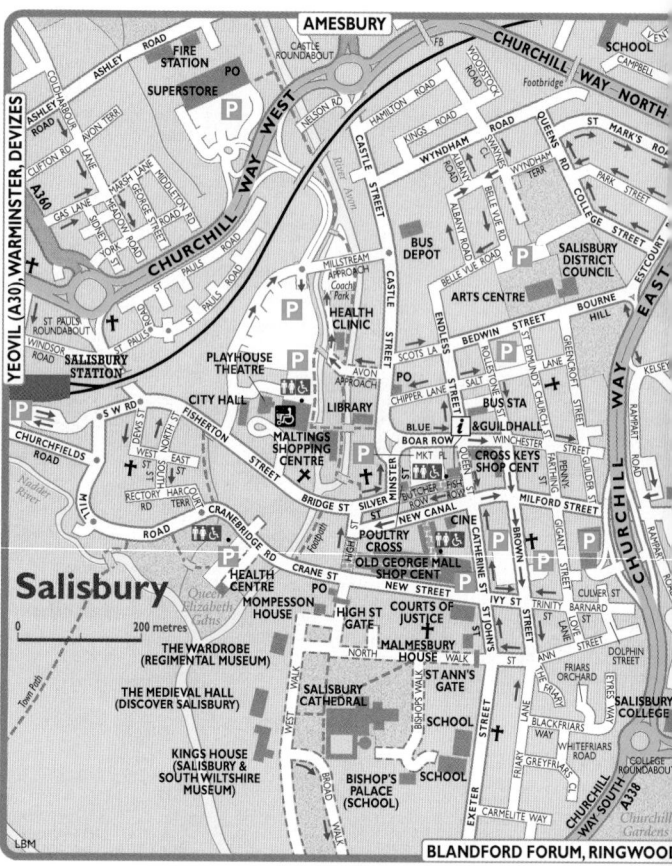

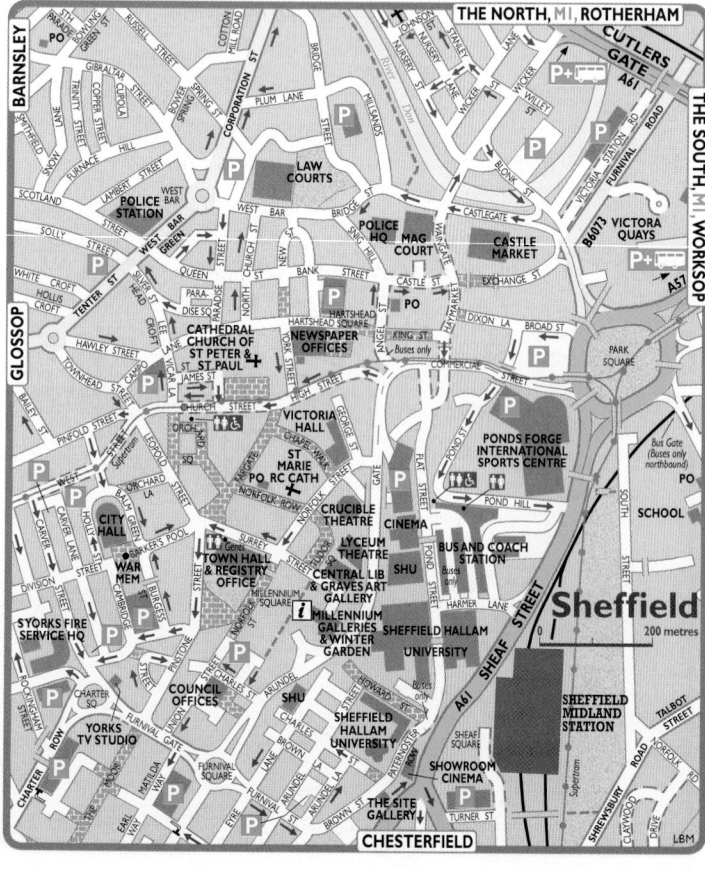

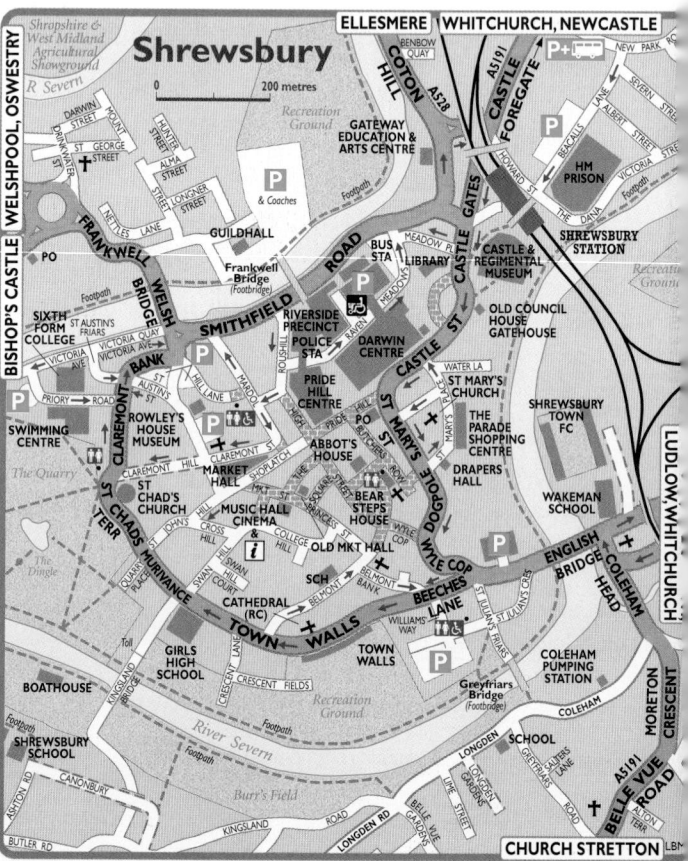

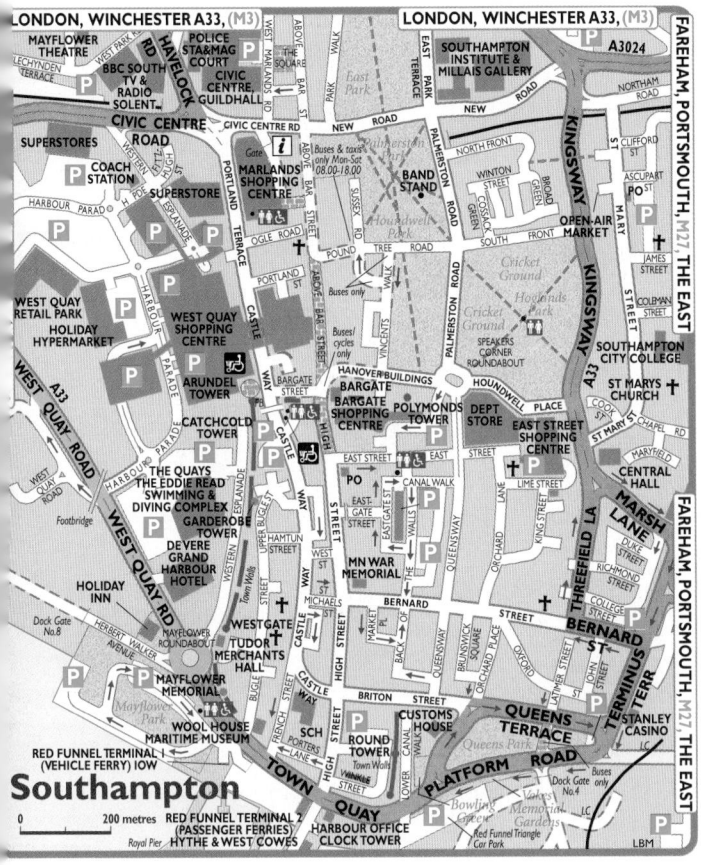

Southampton

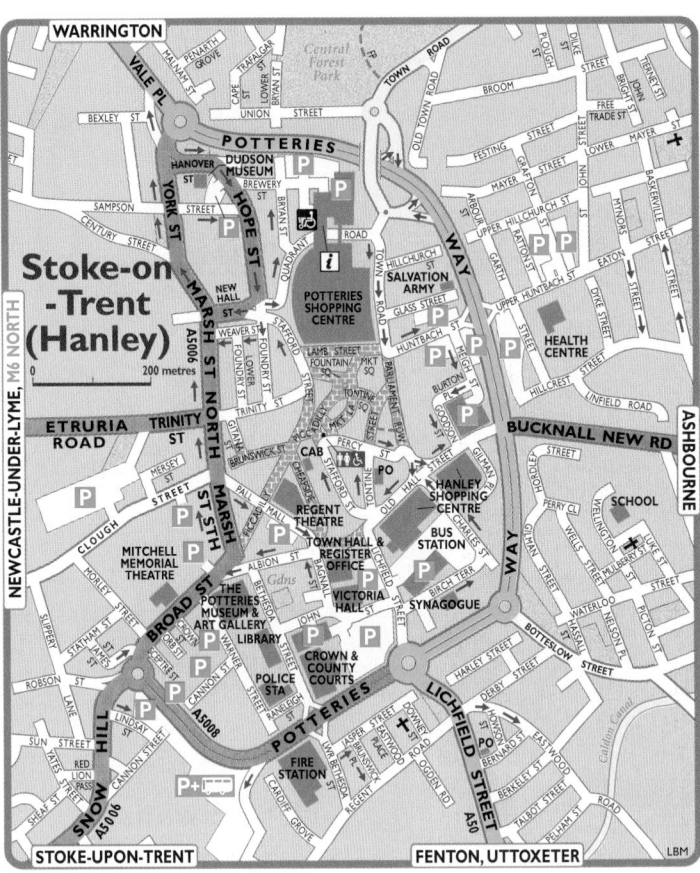

Stoke-on-Trent (Hanley)

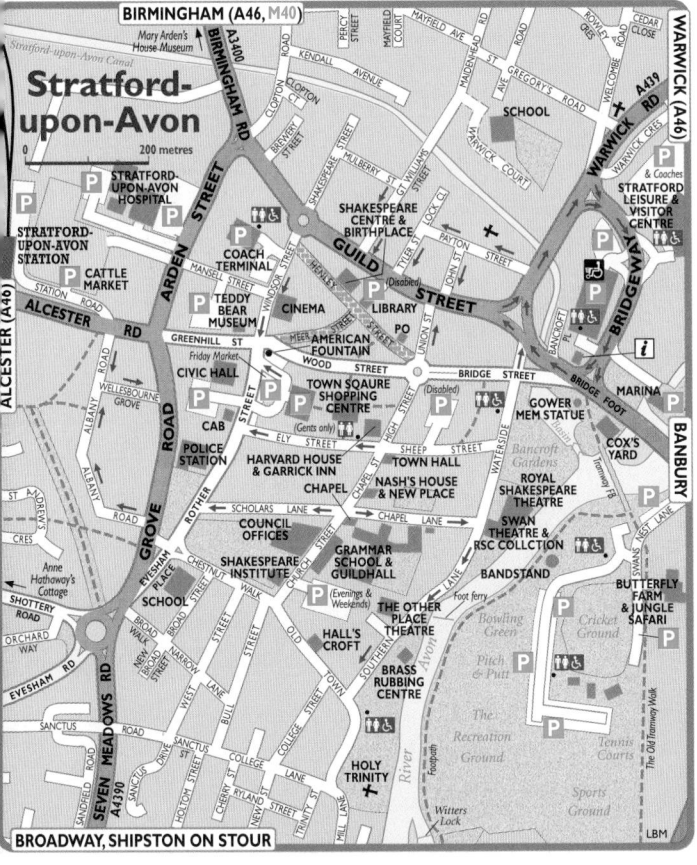

Stratford-upon-Avon

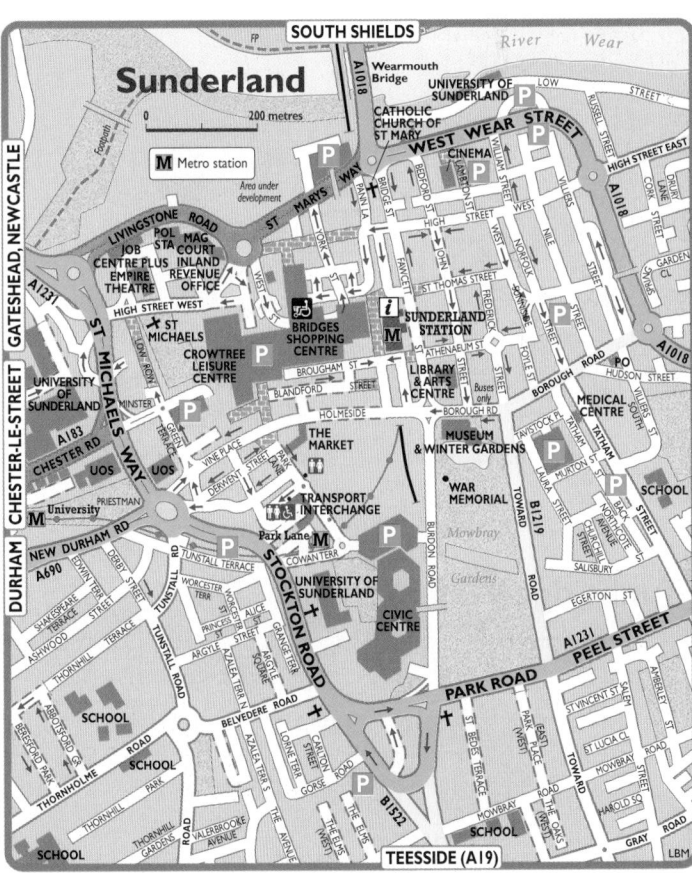

Sunderland

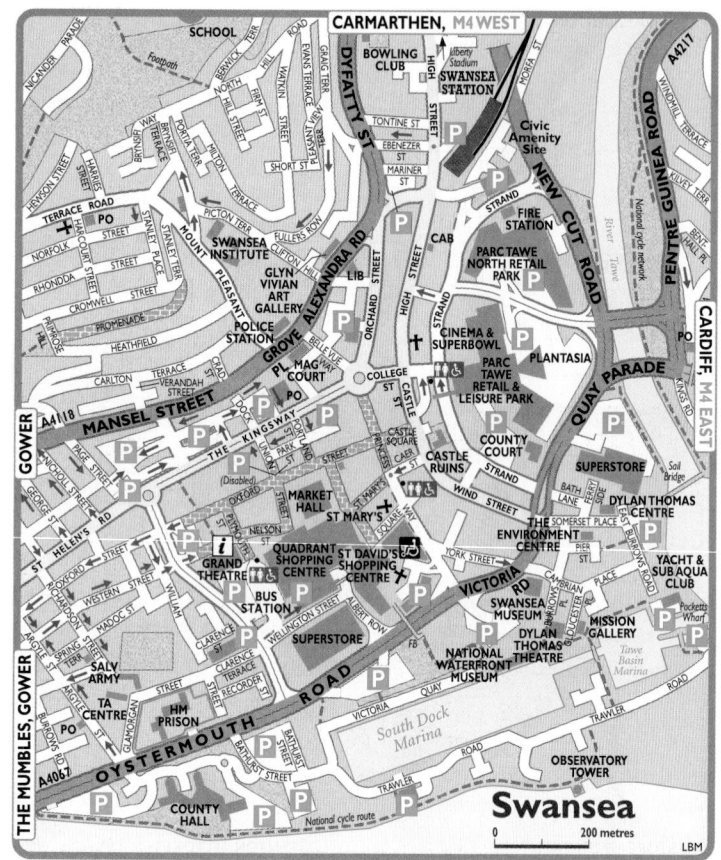

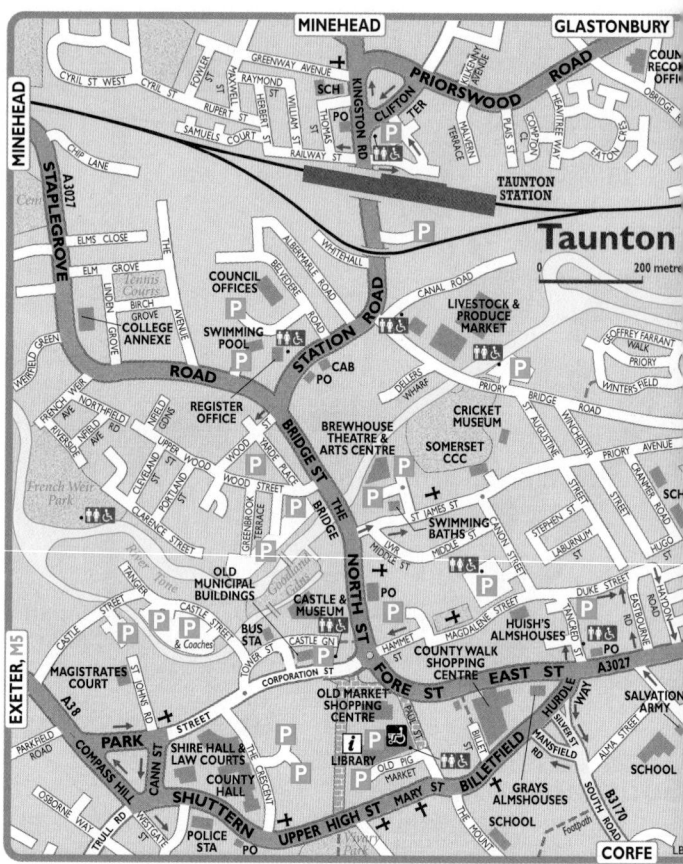

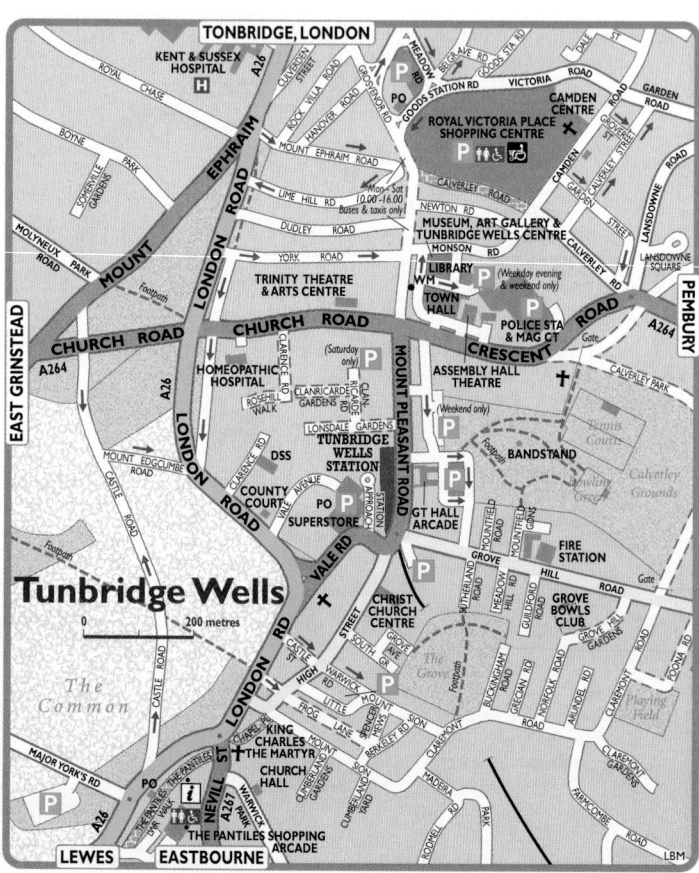

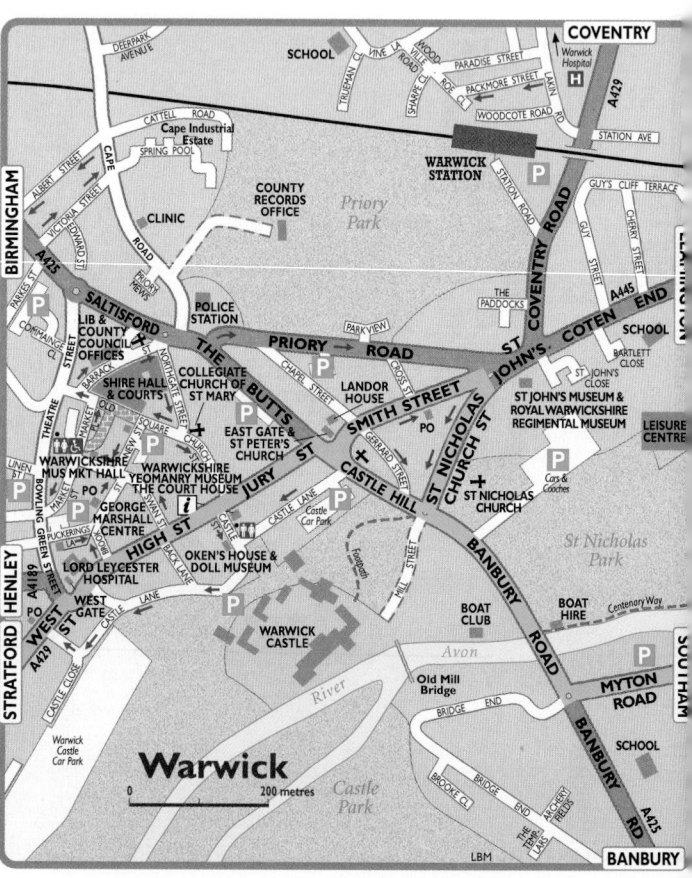

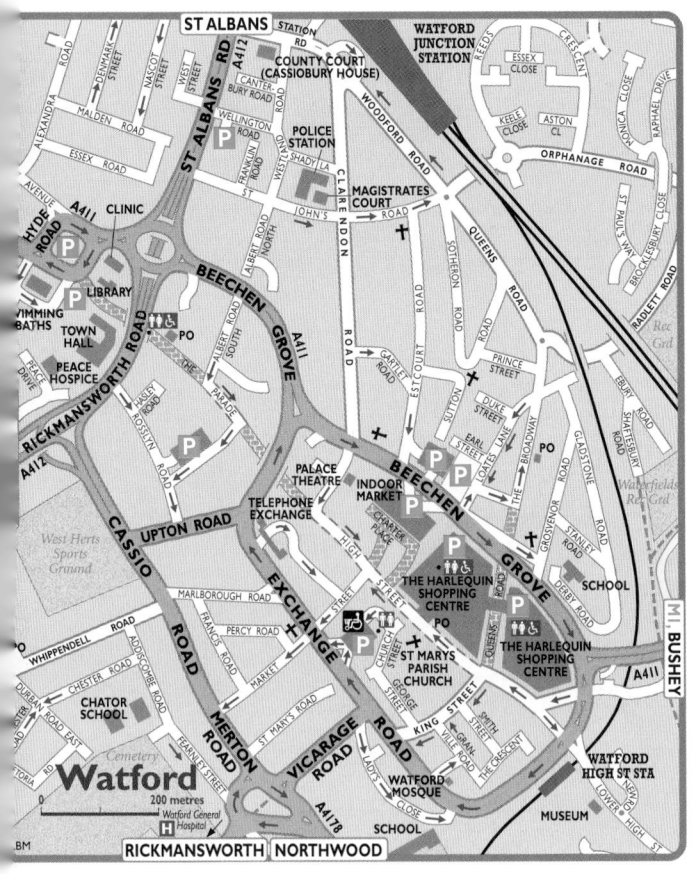

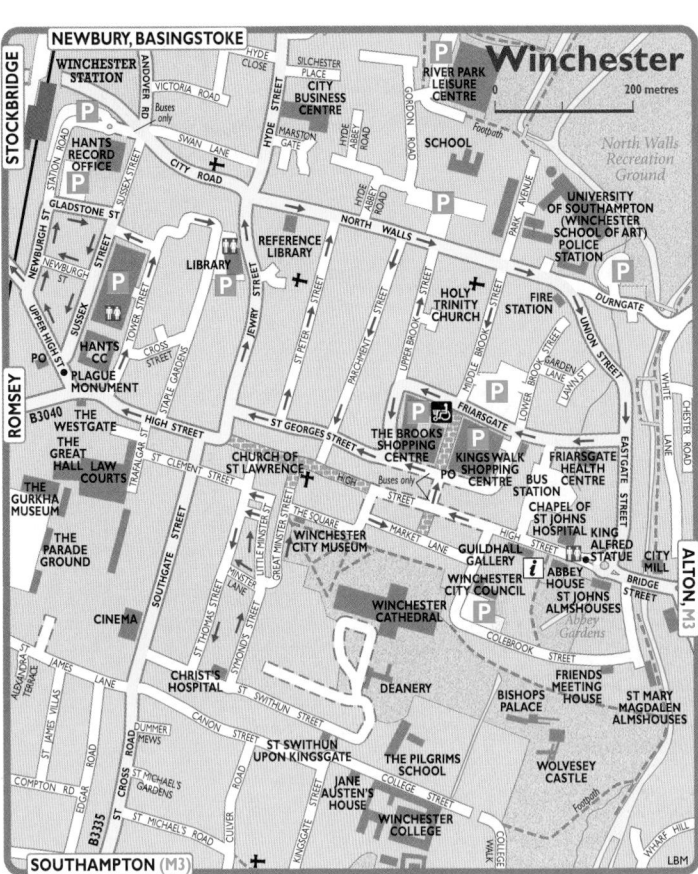

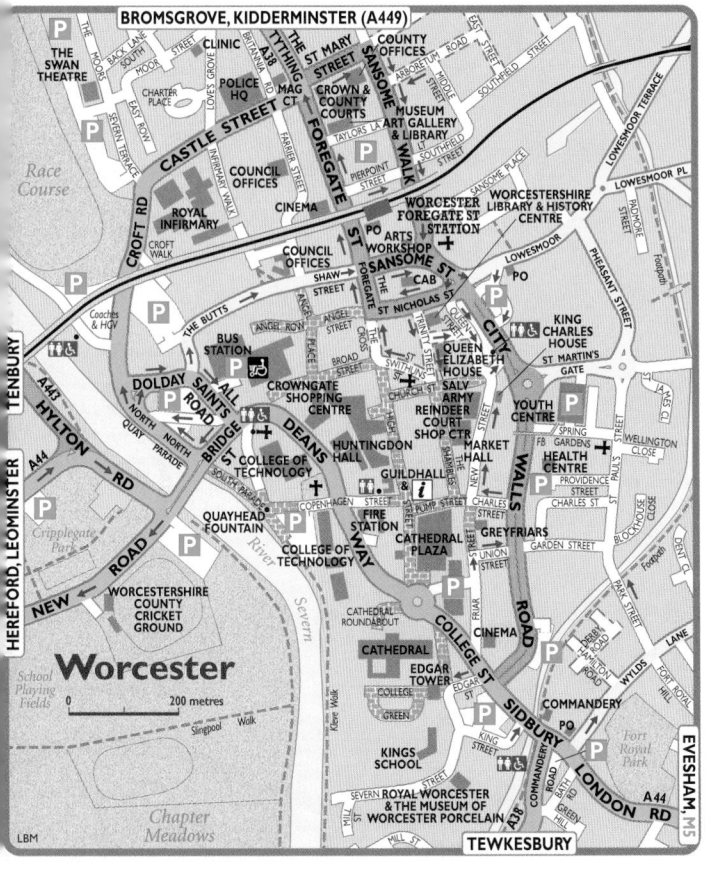

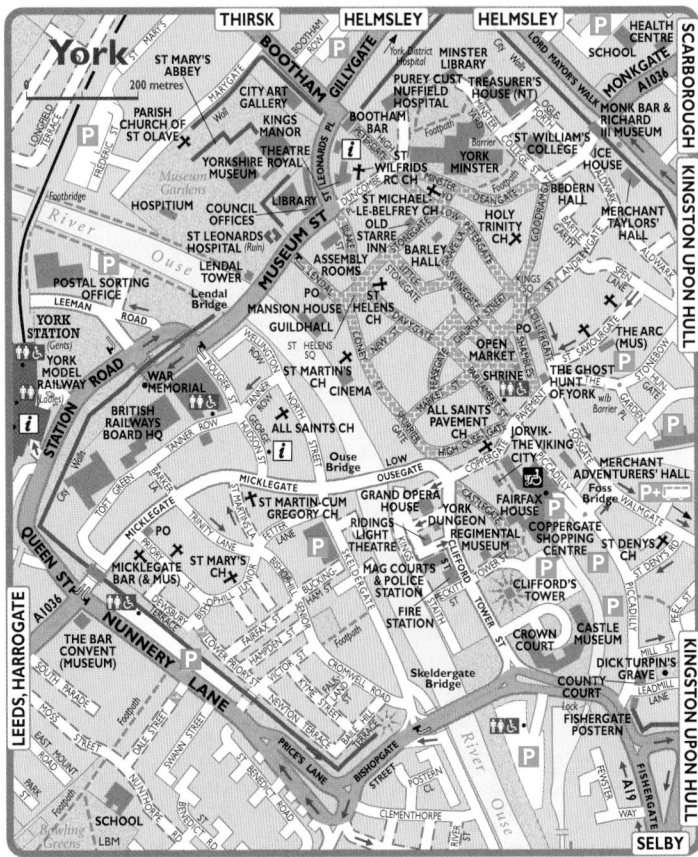

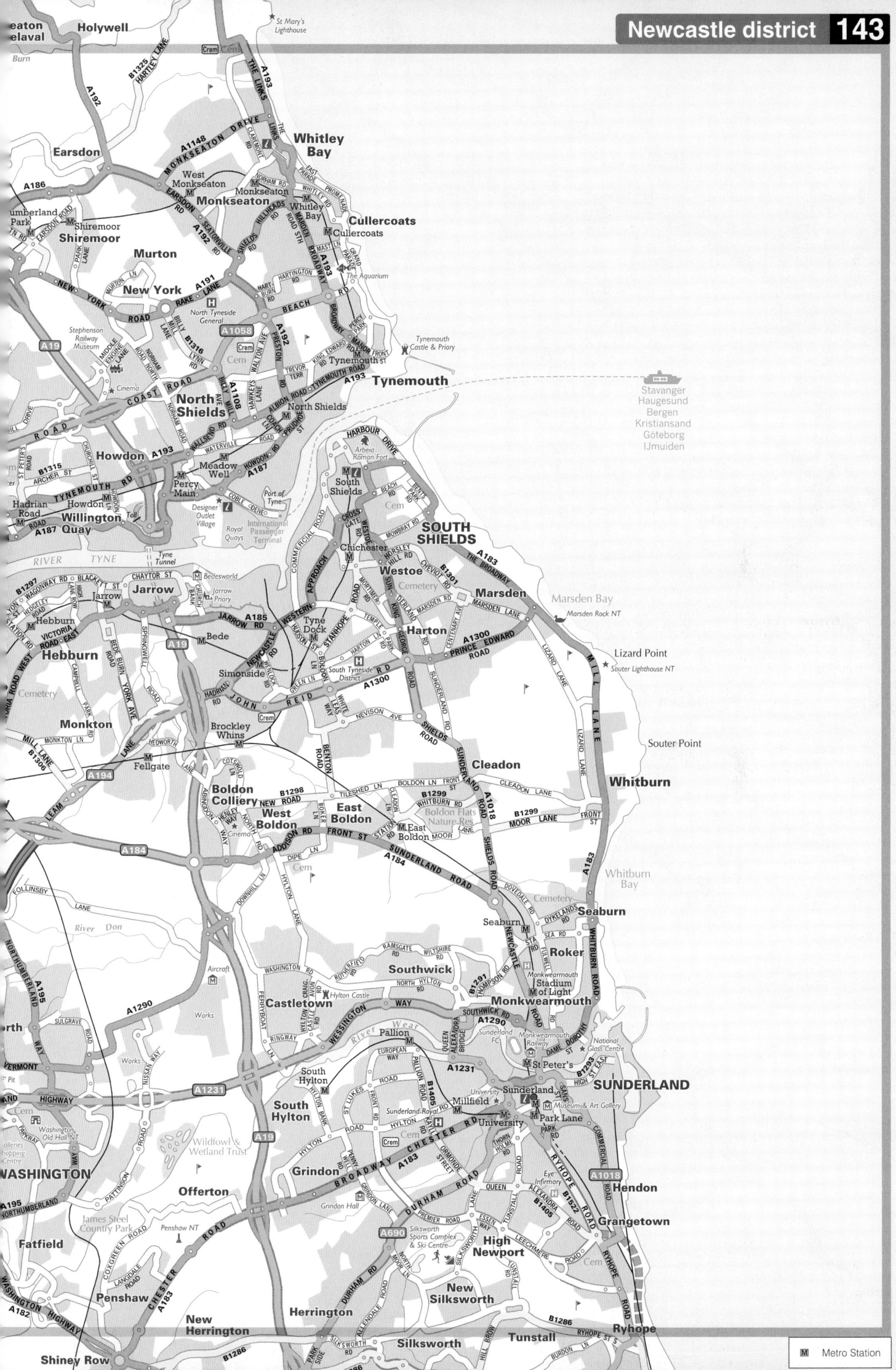

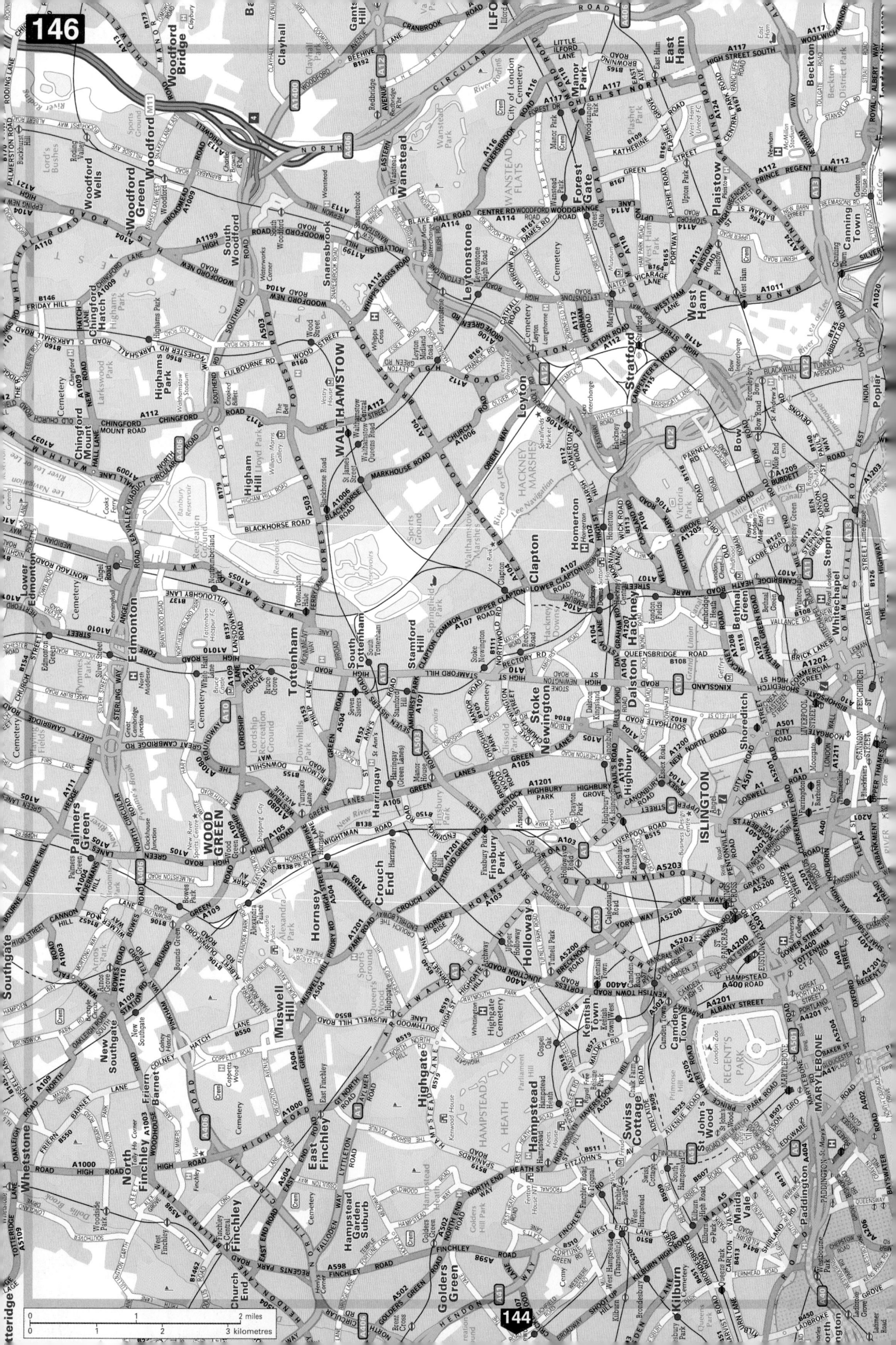

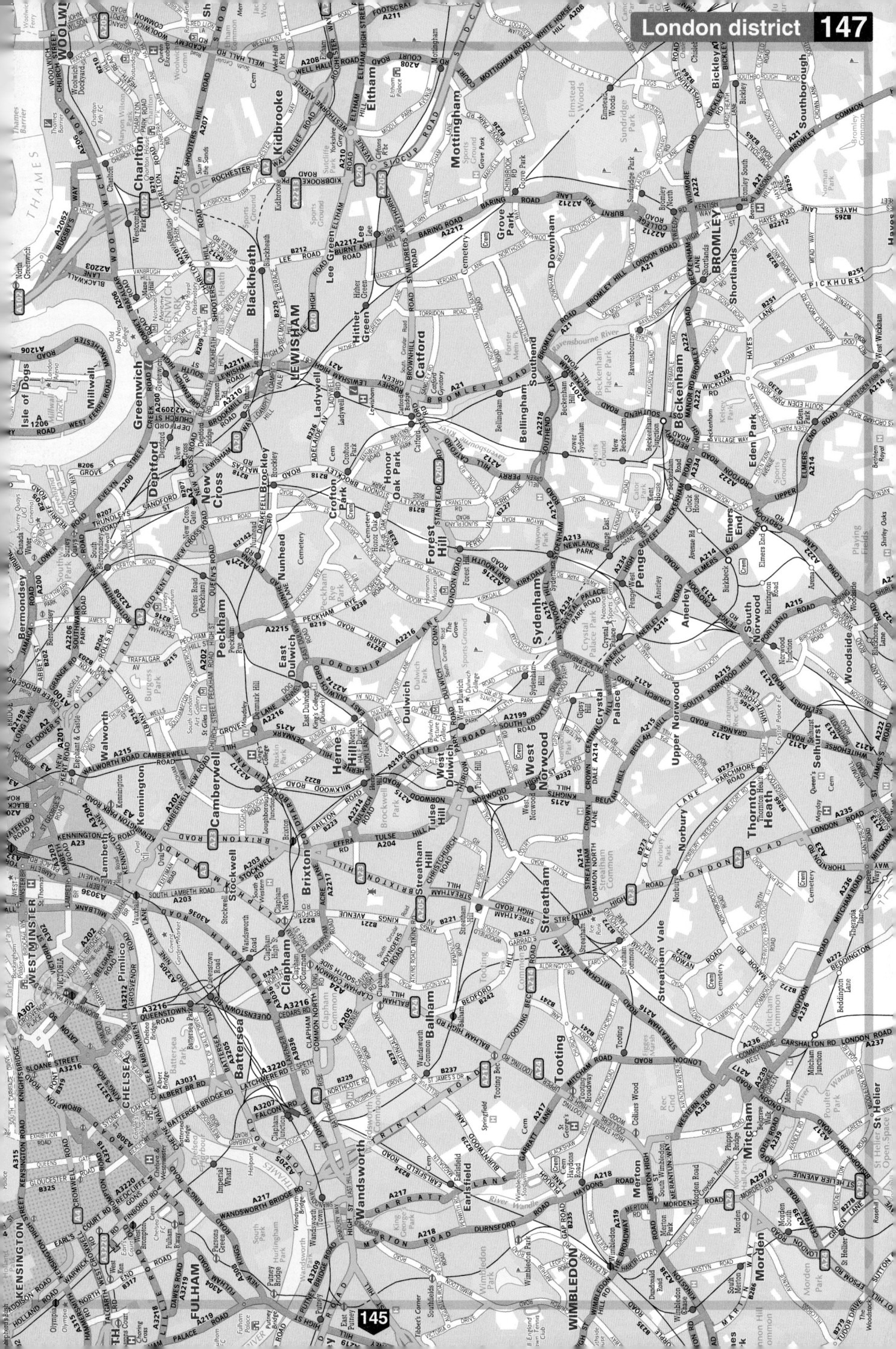

Central London street index

In the index, street names are listed in alphabetical order and written in full, but may be abbreviated on the map. Each entry is followed by its Postcode District and each street name is preceded by the page number and the grid reference to the square in which the name is found. Names are asterisked (*) in the index where there is insufficient space to show them on the map.

Burne Street - Dunster Court 159

148 F4 Burne Street NW1
153 G7 Burnsall Street SW3
157 J5 Burnside Close SE16
156 F2 Buross Street * E1
156 D4 Burr Close E1W
155 H1 Burrell Street SE1
155 H2 Burrows Mews SE1
156 A6 Bursar Street * SE1
156 E3 Burslem Street E1
155 L7 Burton Grove SE17
153 K5 Burton Mews SW1W
150 C3 Burton Place WC1H
150 C3 Burton Street WC1H
156 F3 Burwell Close E1
149 G6 Burwood Place W2
157 J5 Bury Close SE16
156 A2 Bury Court EC3A
150 D5 Bury Place WC1A
156 A3 Bury Street EC3A
154 A1 Bury Street SW1Y
152 F6 Bury Walk SW3
156 A8 Bushbaby Close SE1
151 L7 Bush Lane EC4R
157 J3 Butcher Row E14
152 E5 Bute Street SW7
156 A5 Butlers & Colonial Wharf SE1
156 E7 Butterfield Close SE16
151 M2 Buttesland Street N1
157 L6 Byefield Close SE16
157 J5 Byelands Close SE16
157 K6 Byfield Close SE16
150 B4 Byng Place WC1E
156 A3 Byward Street EC3R
157 K5 Bywater Place SE16
153 G6 Bywater Street SW3
149 M5 Bywell Place * W1W

C

148 F5 Cabbell Street NW1
156 C4 Cable Street EC3N
156 C8 Cadbury Way SE16
155 K7 Cadiz Street SE17
153 H6 Cadogan Gardens SW3
153 H5 Cadogan Gate SW1X
153 J4 Cadogan Lane SW1X
153 J4 Cadogan Place SW1X
153 H5 Cadogan Square SW1X
153 G6 Cadogan Street SW3
151 K3 Cahill Street * EC1Y
150 D1 Caledonia Street N1
152 F6 Cale Street SW3
152 D4 Callendar Road SW7
157 M2 Callingham Close E14
152 D8 Callow Street SW3
150 E3 Calthorpe Street WC1X
157 L8 Calypso Way SE16
150 C7 Cambridge Circus W1D
148 A1 Cambridge Gardens NW6
149 L3 Cambridge Gate NW1
149 L3 Cambridge Gate Mews NW1
152 C3 Cambridge Place * W8
148 A2 Cambridge Road NW6
148 F6 Cambridge Square W2
153 L6 Cambridge Street SW1V
149 L2 Cambridge Terrace NW1
149 L2 Cambridge Terrace Mews * NW1
157 K2 Camdenhurst Street E14
152 D8 Camera Place SW10
156 F2 Cameron Place E1
156 A2 Camomile Street EC3A
152 A2 Campden Grove W8
152 A3 Campden Hill Road W8
152 A2 Campden House Close W8
152 A2 Campden House Terrace * W8
156 C3 Camperdown Street E1
157 G7 Canada Estate SE16
157 H7 Canada Street SE16
155 L8 Canal Street SE5
149 M5 Candover Street * W1W
152 C4 Canning Passage * W8
152 C4 Canning Place W8
152 C3 Canning Place Mews * W8
157 M4 Cannon Drive E14
151 J6 Cannon Street EC4M
156 E3 Cannon Street Road E1
157 G6 Canon Beck Road SE16
156 B8 Canon Murnane Road SE16
154 D3 Canon Row SW1A
155 J6 Canterbury Place SE17
155 J1 Canvey Street SE1
153 J3 Capener's Close SW1X
156 E5 Cape Yard E1W
148 F3 Capland Street NW8
157 K5 Capstan Way SE16
157 L2 Carbis Road E14
149 L4 Carburton Street W1W
154 F7 Cardigan Street SE11
155 L4 Cardinal Bourne Street * SE1
150 A2 Cardington Street NW1
151 J6 Carey Lane EC2V
154 B6 Carey Place SW1P
150 F6 Carey Street WC2A
156 B3 Carlisle Avenue EC3N
154 F4 Carlisle Lane SE1
153 M5 Carlisle Place SW1P
150 B6 Carlisle Street W1F
149 K7 Carlos Place W1K
154 B2 Carlton Gardens SW1Y
148 C1 Carlton Hill NW8
154 B1 Carlton House Terrace SW1Y
154 B1 Carlton Street SW1Y
153 H4 Carlton Tower Place SW1X
148 B1 Carlton Vale W9
152 F7 Carlyle Square SW3
152 A3 Carmel Court W8
151 G7 Carmelite Street EC4Y
150 A7 Carnaby Street W1B
148 B8 Caroline Close W2
148 B7 Caroline Place W2
148 B8 Caroline Place Mews * W2
157 J3 Caroline Street E1
153 J6 Caroline Terrace SW1W
149 K7 Carpenter Street W1K
153 L2 Carrington Street W1J
157 K2 Carr Street E14
154 B3 Carteret Street SW1H
151 H6 Carter Lane EC4V
155 K7 Carter Place SE17
155 J7 Carter Street SE17
151 J4 Carthusian Street EC1M
150 D8 Carting Lane WC2R
150 C3 Cartwright Gardens WC1H
156 C4 Cartwright Street EC3N
148 F2 Casey Close NW8
156 D1 Casson Street E1
148 B3 Castellain Road W9
151 H7 Castle Baynard Street EC4V
155 H5 Castlebrook Close SE11
151 L6 Castle Court * EC3V
154 A4 Castle Lane SW1E
156 E1 Castlemaine Street E1
149 G6 Castlereagh Street W1H
155 H1 Castle Yard * SE1
155 L6 Catesby Street SE17
157 F7 Cathay Street SE16
152 C8 Cathcart Road SW10
155 L1 Cathedral Street SE1
151 G3 Catherine Griffiths Court EC1R
153 M4 Catherine Place SW1E
150 E7 Catherine Street * WC2B
156 A1 Catherine Wheel Alley EC2M
153 M2 Catherine Wheel Yard SW1A
149 G5 Cato Street W1H
150 E5 Catton Street WC1B
154 B6 Causton Street SW1P
152 D7 Cavaye Place SW10
156 F1 Cavell Street E1
148 E1 Cavendish Avenue NW8
148 E2 Cavendish Close NW8
149 L5 Cavendish Mews North W1B
149 L5 Cavendish Mews South * W1W
149 L6 Cavendish Place W1G
149 L6 Cavendish Square W1G
151 L1 Cavendish Street N1
153 G8 Caversham Street SW3
154 B4 Caxton Street SW1H
156 A6 Cayenne Court SE1
151 K2 Cayton Street EC1V
150 C7 Cecil Court WC2H
148 B5 Celbridge Mews W2
154 F4 Centaur Street SE1
151 J3 Central Street EC1V
148 B7 Cervantes Court W2
151 G1 Chadwell Street EC1R
154 B4 Chadwick Street SW1P
149 H3 Chagford Street NW1
150 B2 Chalton Street NW1
156 D6 Chambers Street SE16
156 C3 Chamber Street E1
155 H1 Chancel Street SE1
150 F5 Chancery Lane WC2A
156 F5 Chandler Street E1W
150 D8 Chandos Place WC2N
149 L5 Chandos Street W1G
152 B4 Chantry Square W8
155 K2 Chapel Court SE1
149 L6 Chapel Place W1G
148 B7 Chapel Side W2
148 F5 Chapel Street NW1
153 K3 Chapel Street SW1X
155 G3 Chaplin Close SE1
156 E3 Chapman Street E1
155 J7 Chapter Road SE17
154 B6 Chapter Street SW1P
154 C1 Charing Cross * WC2N
150 C7 Charing Cross Road WC2H
153 G7 Charles II Place SW3
154 B1 Charles II Street SW1Y
148 F1 Charles Lane NW8
150 A2 Charles Place * NW1
151 M2 Charles Square N1
151 M2 Charles Square Estate N1
153 L1 Charles Street W1J
155 K6 Charleston Street SE17
150 A4 Charlotte Mews W1T
150 A5 Charlotte Place W1T
151 M2 Charlotte Road N1
150 A4 Charlotte Street W1T
154 A6 Charlwood Place SW1V
153 M7 Charlwood Street SW1V
151 J4 Charterhouse Buildings EC1M
151 H4 Charterhouse Mews EC1M
151 G5 Charterhouse Street EC1N
151 L2 Chart Street N1
157 K2 Chaseley Street E14
155 L5 Chatham Street SE17
151 K6 Cheapside EC2V
153 K8 Chelsea Bridge SW3
153 J6 Chelsea Bridge Road SW1W
153 G8 Chelsea Embankment SW3
152 F7 Chelsea Manor Gardens SW3
152 F7 Chelsea Manor Street SW3
152 E8 Chelsea Park Gardens SW3
152 F7 Chelsea Square SW3
153 H6 Cheltenham Terrace SW3
150 B4 Chenies Mews WC1E
150 B4 Chenies Street W1T
152 A4 Cheniston Gardens W8
148 A6 Chepstow Corner * W2
148 A6 Chepstow Place W2
148 A6 Chepstow Road W2
151 K4 Chequer Street EC1Y
151 L1 Cherbury Street N1
156 F7 Cherry Garden Street SE16
151 K4 Cherry Tree Walk EC1Y
153 J4 Chesham Close * SW1X
153 J4 Chesham Mews SW1X
153 J4 Chesham Place SW1X
153 J4 Chesham Street SW1X
153 K3 Chester Close SW1X
149 L2 Chester Close North NW1
149 L2 Chester Close South NW1
153 K1 Chesterfield Gardens * W1J
149 K8 Chesterfield Hill W1J
153 K1 Chesterfield Street W1J
149 L2 Chester Gate NW1
153 K4 Chester Mews SW1X
149 L1 Chester Place NW1
149 K2 Chester Road NW1
153 J6 Chester Row SW1W
153 K5 Chester Square SW1W
153 K4 Chester Square Mews * SW1W
153 K4 Chester Street SW1X
149 L2 Chester Terrace NW1
155 G6 Chester Way SE11
155 L4 Chettle Close SE1
152 F4 Cheval Place SW7
153 G8 Cheyne Gardens SW3
153 G8 Cheyne Mews SW3
153 G8 Cheyne Place SW3
152 F8 Cheyne Row SW3
152 F8 Cheyne Walk SW3
154 E2 Chicheley Street SE1
148 C5 Chichester Road W2
154 A7 Chichester Street SW1V
156 D1 Chicksand Estate E1
156 C1 Chicksand Street E1
156 E4 Chigwell Hill E1
152 A6 Child's Mews * SW5
152 A6 Child's Place SW5
152 A5 Child's Street SW5
152 A5 Child's Walk * SW5
149 J5 Chiltern Street W1U
148 D6 Chilworth Mews W2
148 D6 Chilworth Street W2
157 H8 China Hall Mews SE16
151 L4 Chiswell Street EC1Y
150 A4 Chitty Street W1T
153 H7 Christchurch Street SW3
153 H8 Christchurch Terrace * SW3
156 E2 Christian Street E1
151 M3 Christina Street EC2A
150 C2 Christopher Place * NW1
151 M4 Christopher Street EC2A
157 J2 Chudleigh Street E1
155 M8 Chumleigh Street SE5
153 M7 Churchill Gardens SW1V
153 L7 Churchill Gardens Road SW1V
148 C7 Church Street W2
148 E4 Church Street Estate NW8
150 B2 Churchway NW1
155 H6 Churchyard Row SE11
154 A6 Churton Place SW1V
154 A6 Churton Street SW1V
156 F5 Cinnamon Street E1W
149 G5 Circus Mews * W1H
151 L5 Circus Place * EC2M
148 E1 Circus Road NW8
148 A4 Cirencester Street W2
154 E6 Citadel Place SE11
151 J1 City Garden Row N1
151 H1 City Road EC1V
155 M3 City Walk SE1
153 H5 Clabon Mews SW1X
157 G7 Clack Street SE16
148 A7 Clanricarde Gardens W2
151 G1 Claremont Close N1
151 G1 Claremont Square N1
149 L2 Clarence Gardens NW1
149 H3 Clarence Gate NW1
150 C1 Clarence Passage * NW1
149 H3 Clarence Terrace NW1
148 F7 Clarendon Close * W2
148 D4 Clarendon Gardens W9
148 F7 Clarendon Gate W2
148 F7 Clarendon Mews W2
148 F7 Clarendon Place W2
153 L7 Clarendon Street SW1V
148 D3 Clarendon Terrace W9
152 D6 Clareville Grove SW7
152 D6 Clareville Street SW7
153 L1 Clarges Mews W1J
153 L1 Clarges Street W1J
149 K5 Clarkes Mews W1G
149 M1 Clarkson Row NW1
156 F2 Clark Street E1
154 A7 Claverton Street SW1V
156 F5 Clave Street E1W
149 H5 Clay Street W1U
154 F8 Clayton Street SE11
157 H2 Clearbrook Way E1
148 B4 Clearwell Drive W9
155 G7 Cleaver Square SE11
155 G7 Cleaver Street SE11
156 F5 Clegg Street E1W
157 L2 Clemence Street E14
150 F6 Clements Inn WC2A
151 L7 Clement's Lane EC4N
156 E8 Clement's Road SE16
155 K2 Clennam Street * SE1
149 H6 Clenston Mews W1H
151 M3 Clere Place EC2A
151 M3 Clere Street EC2A
151 G3 Clerkenwell Close EC1R
151 G4 Clerkenwell Green EC1R
150 F4 Clerkenwell Road EC1R
148 C6 Cleveland Gardens W2
149 M4 Cleveland Mews W1T
154 A1 Cleveland Place SW1Y
154 A2 Cleveland Row SW1A
148 C7 Cleveland Square W2
149 L3 Cleveland Street NW1
148 D6 Cleveland Terrace W2
157 G1 Clichy Estate E1
149 M7 Clifford Street W1S
148 C4 Clifton Gardens W9
148 E7 Clifton Place W2
157 G6 Clifton Place SE16
148 D3 Clifton Road W9
151 M4 Clifton Street EC2A
148 C4 Clifton Villas W9
155 L1 Clink Street SE1
157 H6 Clipper Close SE16
149 M4 Clipstone Mews W1W
149 L4 Clipstone Street W1W
153 J5 Cliveden Place SW1W
151 K7 Cloak Lane EC4R
151 J5 Cloth Court EC1A
151 J5 Cloth Fair EC1A
156 B2 Clothier Street EC3A
151 J4 Cloth Street EC1A
157 G2 Clovelly Way E1
153 H8 Clover Mews SW3
151 M1 Clunbury Street N1
156 A7 Cluny Estate SE1
156 A7 Cluny Place SE1
150 B1 Clyde Court NW1
149 L7 Coach & Horses Yard W1S
156 B2 Cobb Street E1
150 A2 Cobourg Street NW1
154 A5 Coburg Close SW1P
157 G3 Coburg Dwellings E1
148 E1 Cochrane Mews NW8
148 E1 Cochrane Street NW8
151 H5 Cock Lane EC1A
154 C1 Cockspur Court SW1Y
154 C1 Cockspur Street SW1Y
156 E5 Codling Close * E1W
155 G1 Coin Street SE1
156 D2 Coke Street E1
152 C6 Colbeck Mews SW5
156 C2 Colchester Street E1
150 F3 Coldbath Square EC1R
151 H1 Colebrooke Row N1
152 B7 Coleherne Mews SW10
152 B7 Coleherne Road SW10
151 L6 Coleman Street EC2R
155 K3 Cole Street SE1
150 F3 Coley Street WC1X
156 C2 College East * E1
151 K7 College Hill * EC4R
154 D4 College Mews SW1P
151 K7 College Street * EC4R
156 E8 Collett Road SE16
150 E1 Collier Street N1
152 C6 Collingham Gardens SW5
152 B5 Collingham Place SW5
152 B5 Collingham Road SW5
155 J3 Collinson Street SE1
155 J3 Collinson Walk SE1
155 H4 Colnbrook Street SE1
155 H1 Colombo Street SE1
150 D4 Colonnade WC1N
149 L3 Colosseum Terrace NW1
150 B5 Colville Place W1T
155 K6 Colworth Grove SE17
157 K3 Commercial Road E14
156 C2 Commercial Road E1
156 B1 Commercial Street E1
157 J1 Commodore Street E1
149 L2 Compton Close NW1
151 H3 Compton Passage EC1V
150 D3 Compton Place WC1H
151 H3 Compton Street EC1V
155 M6 Comus Place SE17
156 D3 Conant Mews E1
154 F2 Concert Hall Approach SE1
157 K2 Conder Street E14
150 C7 Conduit Court * WC2E
148 E6 Conduit Mews W2
148 E6 Conduit Passage W2
148 E6 Conduit Place W2
149 L7 Conduit Street W1S
155 M5 Congreve Street SE17
149 G6 Coniston Court * W2
148 F6 Connaught Close W2
149 G7 Connaught Place W2
149 G6 Connaught Square W2
148 F6 Connaught Street W2
155 G2 Cons Street * SE1
153 L3 Constitution Hill SW1A
155 K6 Content Street SE17
149 M4 Conway Mews W1T
149 M4 Conway Street W1T
155 H8 Cook's Road SE17
151 J1 Coombs Street N1
155 G3 Cooper Close SE1
150 C1 Coopers Lane NW1
156 B3 Cooper's Row EC3N
152 E7 Copenhagen Gardens SW3
157 L3 Copenhagen Place E14
152 A4 Cope Place W8
155 J8 Copley Close SE17
155 J2 Copperfield Street SE1
156 B6 Copper Row SE1
151 L6 Copthall Avenue EC2R
150 C5 Coptic Street WC1A
155 G3 Coral Street SE1
150 C3 Coram Street WC1H
156 C1 Corbet Place E1
156 E5 Cork Square E1W
149 M7 Cork Street W1S
149 M7 Cork Street Mews W1S
148 F5 Corlett Street W2
151 M6 Cornhill EC3V
152 C5 Cornwall Gardens SW7
152 B5 Cornwall Gardens Walk SW7
152 C5 Cornwall Mews South SW7
152 B4 Cornwall Mews West * SW7
154 F1 Cornwall Road SE1
156 F3 Cornwall Street E1
149 H3 Cornwall Terrace NW1
149 H4 Cornwall Terrace Mews NW1
157 G2 Cornwood Drive E1
151 M2 Coronet Street N1
151 G3 Corporation Row EC1R
151 L2 Corsham Street N1
150 D4 Cosmo Place WC1B
154 F4 Cosser Street SE1
149 G4 Cosway Street NW1
155 K6 Cotham Street SE17
152 F4 Cottage Place SW7
155 G4 Cottesloe Mews SE1
152 B4 Cottesmore Gardens W8
155 G6 Cottington Street SE11
155 G6 Cotton Gardens Estate SE11
155 M1 Cottons Centre SE1
153 H6 Coulson Street SW3
155 M1 Counter Street SE1
155 K5 County Street SE1
154 F7 Courtenay Square SE11
154 F6 Courtenay Street SE11
152 B6 Courtfield Gardens SW5
152 C6 Courtfield Mews * SW7
152 C5 Courtfield Road SW7
156 E1 Court Street E1
151 K7 Cousin Lane EC4R
150 D7 Covent Garden WC2E
150 D7 Covent Garden Piazza WC2E
150 B8 Coventry Street W1J
156 D1 Coverley Close * E1
151 H4 Cowcross Street EC1M
154 C4 Cowley Street SW1P
151 L3 Cowper Street EC1Y
156 B7 Coxson Way SE1
154 C1 Craig's Court SW1A
155 L5 Crail Row SE17
149 J5 Cramer Street W1U
155 J6 Crampton Street SE17
150 C7 Cranbourn Street WC2H
151 G6 Crane Court EC4A
157 J3 Cranford Street E1W
150 A1 Cranleigh Street NW1
152 E7 Cranley Gardens SW3
152 D6 Cranley Mews SW7
152 E6 Cranley Place SW7
151 L1 Cranston Estate N1
151 L2 Cranwood Street EC1V
148 D7 Craven Hill W2
148 C7 Craven Hill Gardens W2
148 D7 Craven Hill Mews W2
148 D7 Craven Road W2
154 D1 Craven Street WC2N
148 D7 Craven Terrace W2
151 G3 Crawford Passage EC1R
149 G5 Crawford Place W2
149 H5 Crawford Street W1H
156 B3 Creechurch Lane EC3A
156 B3 Creechurch Place * EC3A
151 H6 Creed Lane EC4V
156 B4 Crescent EC3N
152 F5 Crescent Place SW3
151 J3 Crescent Row EC1Y
152 C6 Cresswell Gardens * SW5
152 C6 Cresswell Place SW5
157 G1 Cressy Houses * E1
150 D1 Crestfield Street NW1
156 B8 Crimscott Street SE1
151 K4 Cripplegate Street * EC2Y
156 F2 Crispin Street E1
156 D4 Crofts Street E1
156 C4 Croft Street E1
148 C7 Cromarty Villas * W2
150 D2 Cromer Street WC1H
148 D4 Crompton Street W2
152 E5 Cromwell Gardens SW7
152 E5 Cromwell Mews * SW7
152 E5 Cromwell Place SW7
152 D5 Cromwell Road SW7
151 M1 Crondall Street N1
148 D2 Cropthorne Court NW8
155 L3 Crosby Row SE1
149 K5 Cross Keys Close W1U
155 M5 Crosslet Street SE17
156 B3 Crosswall EC3N
156 E3 Crowder Street E1
150 D6 Crown Court WC2B
151 G7 Crown Office Row EC4Y
154 A1 Crown Passage SW1Y
151 M4 Crown Place EC2A
156 A6 Crucifix Lane SE1
150 F1 Cruickshank Street WC1X
156 B3 Crutched Friars EC3R
157 M6 Cuba Street E14
150 E2 Cubitt Street WC1X
153 H6 Culford Gardens SW3
157 G7 Culling Road SE16
156 A3 Cullum Street EC3M
149 J8 Culross Street W1K
148 F1 Culworth Street NW8
150 F2 Cumberland Gardens WC1X
149 K1 Cumberland Gate NW1
149 H7 Cumberland Gate W1H
149 L2 Cumberland Market NW1
155 G7 Cumberland Mews SE11
149 L2 Cumberland Place NW1
153 L6 Cumberland Street SW1V
149 K1 Cumberland Terrace NW1
149 L1 Cumberland Terrace Mews NW1
150 E1 Cumming Street N1
153 K6 Cundy Street SW1W
148 E3 Cunningham Place NW8
154 C6 Cureton Street SW1P
156 C6 Curlew Street SE1
150 F6 Cursitor Street EC4A
151 M4 Curtain Road EC2A
153 K2 Curzon Place W1K
153 L1 Curzon Street W1J
157 L7 Custom House Reach * SE16
148 E4 Cuthbert Street W2
156 B2 Cutlers Gardens Arcade E1
156 B2 Cutler Street EC3A
150 F1 Cynthia Street N1
151 H3 Cyrus Street EC1V

D

154 B4 Dacre Street SW1H
157 J2 Dakin Place E1
151 H3 Dallington Square EC1V
151 J3 Dallington Street EC1V
156 F2 Damien Street E1
156 D7 Damsel Court * SE16
150 E5 Dane Street WC1R
150 B7 Dansey Place W1D
155 H5 Dante Road SE11
153 G6 Danube Street SW3
152 F8 Danvers Street SW3
156 D1 Daplyn Street E1
150 A6 D'Arblay Street W1F
155 K8 Dartford Street SE17
154 B3 Dartmouth Street SW1H
155 L5 Darwin Street SE17
155 K7 Date Street SE17
156 D1 Davenant Street E1
148 F4 Daventry Street NW1
155 H3 Davidge Street SE1
149 J4 David Mews W1U
149 K7 Davies Mews W1K
149 K7 Davies Street W1K
155 L6 Dawes Street SE17
148 A7 Dawson Place W2
155 J5 Deacon Way SE17
157 H8 Deal Porters Way SE16
156 D1 Deal Street E1
154 C5 Dean Bradley Street SW1P
156 F3 Deancross Street E1
153 K1 Deanery Mews * W1K
153 K1 Deanery Street W1K
154 B4 Dean Farrar Street SW1H
154 C5 Dean Ryle Street SW1P
155 L6 Dean's Buildings SE17
151 J6 Dean's Court EC4V
149 L5 Dean's Mews * W1G
154 D4 Dean Stanley Street SW1P
150 B6 Dean Street W1F
154 C4 Deans Yard SW1P
154 C4 Dean Trench Street SW1P
155 M4 Decima Street SE1
157 J6 Deck Close SE16
157 L7 Defoe Road SE16
148 C5 Delamere Street W2
148 B4 Delamere Terrace W2
155 H7 De Laune Street SE17
148 B3 Delaware Road W9
156 F3 Dellow Street E1
154 A6 Dell's Mews * SW1V
155 H7 Delverton Road SE17
154 A6 Denbigh Place SW1V
154 A6 Denbigh Street SW1V
150 B7 Denman Street W1B
150 C6 Denmark Street WC2H
148 D2 Denning Close NW8
155 G6 Denny Crescent SE11
155 G6 Denny Street SE11
153 G5 Denyer Street SW3
154 D3 Derby Gate SW1A
153 K1 Derby Street W1J
149 L6 Dering Street W1S
152 B3 Derry Street W8
148 B4 Desborough Close W2
152 C3 De Vere Gardens W8
155 L4 Deverell Street SE1
152 C4 De Vere Mews W8
150 F7 Devereux Court WC2R
149 L4 Devonshire Close W1G
149 K4 Devonshire Mews South W1G
149 K4 Devonshire Mews West W1G
149 K4 Devonshire Place W1G
152 B5 Devonshire Place * W8
149 K4 Devonshire Place Mews W1U
156 A2 Devonshire Row EC2M
156 A2 Devonshire Square EC2M
149 K4 Devonshire Street W1G
148 D6 Devonshire Terrace W2
149 K5 De Walden Street W1G
150 B6 Diadem Court * W1D
149 L3 Diana Place NW1
156 D7 Dickens Estate SE16
151 H4 Dickens Mews EC1M
155 K4 Dickens Square SE1
157 H1 Diggon Street E1
153 H8 Dilke Street SW3
151 K2 Dingley Place EC1V
151 J2 Dingley Road EC1V
156 E4 Discovery Walk E1W
155 K3 Disney Place SE1
155 K2 Disney Street SE1
151 J7 Distaff Lane EC4V
154 F6 Distin Street SE11
156 C7 Dockhead SE1
157 J6 Dock Hill Avenue SE16
156 D8 Dockley Road SE16
156 D4 Dock Street E1
155 H7 Doddington Grove SE17
155 H8 Doddington Place SE17
155 G3 Dodson Street SE1
157 M2 Dod Street E14
155 H2 Dolben Street * SE1
154 F7 Dolland Street SE11
154 B7 Dolphin Square SW1V
150 E4 Dombey Street WC1N
151 J3 Domingo Street EC1V
151 L5 Dominion Street EC2M
150 F1 Donegal Street N1
157 J1 Dongola Road E1
153 G5 Donne Place SW3
154 F1 Doon Street SE1
157 L2 Dora Street E14
156 F2 Dorian Estate E1
150 B2 Doric Way NW1
151 G5 Dorrington Street EC1N
155 K2 Dorrit Street * SE1
149 H4 Dorset Close NW1
153 K3 Dorset Mews SW1X
151 G6 Dorset Rise EC4Y
149 H4 Dorset Square NW1
149 J5 Dorset Street W1U
150 E3 Doughty Mews WC1N
150 E3 Doughty Street WC1N
154 B6 Douglas Street SW1P
152 C4 Douro Place W8
156 E5 Douthwaite Square E1W
151 L6 Dove Court * EC2R
152 F7 Dovehouse Street SW3
152 C6 Dove Mews SW5
149 M8 Dover Street W1J
151 L7 Dowgate Hill EC4R
148 B4 Downfield Close W9
154 C2 Downing Street SW1A
153 K2 Down Street W1J
153 K2 Down Street Mews W1J
157 K6 Downtown Road SE16
155 J2 Doyce Street * SE1
153 J5 D'Oyley Street SW1X
155 J8 Draco Street SE17
154 E6 Dragon Road SE11
157 J6 Drake Close SE16
150 E5 Drake Street WC1N
155 J5 Draper Estate SE17
153 G5 Draycott Avenue SW3
153 H6 Draycott Place SW3
153 H5 Draycott Terrace SW3
152 A3 Drayson Mews W8
152 D7 Drayton Gardens SW10
156 C7 Druid Street SE1
150 B2 Drummond Crescent NW1
154 B7 Drummond Gate SW1V
156 E8 Drummond Road SE16
149 M3 Drummond Street NW1
156 C2 Drum Street E1
150 D6 Drury Lane WC1V
150 D6 Dryden Street WC2E
149 L5 Duchess Mews W1G
149 L5 Duchess Street W1B
155 G1 Duchy Street SE1
150 B6 Duck Lane W1F
148 D5 Dudley Street * W2
152 E7 Dudmaston Mews SW3
151 K3 Dufferin Avenue EC1Y
151 K4 Dufferin Street EC1Y
150 A7 Dufour's Place W1F
153 K3 Duke of Wellington Place W1J
153 H6 Duke of York Square SW3
150 A8 Duke of York Street SW1Y
152 A2 Dukes Lane W8
149 J6 Duke's Mews W1U
156 B3 Duke's Place EC3A
150 C2 Duke's Road WC1H
149 J6 Duke Street W1U
155 M1 Duke Street Hill SE1
150 A8 Duke Street St James's W1J
149 K7 Duke's Yard W1K
150 C8 Duncannon Street WC2N
151 H1 Duncan Terrace N1
156 F3 Dunch Street E1
156 E6 Dundee Street E1W
157 H2 Dunelm Street E1
156 C8 Dunlop Place SE16
149 H7 Dunraven Street W1K
149 K4 Dunstable Mews W1G
157 H1 Dunstan Houses E1
156 A3 Dunster Court EC3M

160 Dunsterville Way - Holford Street

155 L3 Dunsterville Way SE1
153 H3 Duplex Ride SW1X
150 D8 Durham House Street * WC2N
153 H7 Durham Place SW3
157 J1 Durham Row E1
154 E7 Durham Street SE11
148 A6 Durham Terrace W2
156 E1 Durward Street E1
149 H5 Durweston Mews * W1U
151 G5 Dyer's Buildings EC4A
150 C5 Dyott Street WC1B
151 M4 Dysart Street EC2A

E

151 H4 Eagle Court EC1M
152 D6 Eagle Place SW10
150 E5 Eagle Street WC1R
152 A7 Eardley Crescent SW5
150 C7 Earlham Street WC2H
152 B6 Earl's Court Gardens SW5
152 A5 Earl's Court Road SW5
152 A6 Earl's Court Square SW5
151 H2 Earlstoke Estate EC1V
151 H2 Earlstoke Street EC1V
151 M4 Earl Street EC2A
150 C6 Earnshaw Street WC1A
157 H2 East Arbour Street E1
148 D6 Eastbourne Mews W2
148 D6 Eastbourne Terrace W2
149 M6 Eastcastle Street W1W
151 M7 Eastcheap EC3M
157 K1 Eastfield Street E14
151 G6 East Harding Street EC4A
157 M3 East India Dock Road E14
156 F1 East Mount Street * E1
150 F3 Easton Street WC1X
151 J4 East Passage EC1A
151 H5 East Poultry Avenue EC1M
151 L2 East Road N1
156 C4 East Smithfield E1W
155 L6 East Street SE17
156 C3 East Tenter Street E1
153 J5 Eaton Close SW1W
153 J5 Eaton Gate SW1W
153 L4 Eaton Lane SW1W
153 J5 Eaton Mews North SW1X
153 K5 Eaton Mews South SW1W
153 J5 Eaton Mews West SW1W
153 J5 Eaton Place SW1X
153 K4 Eaton Row SW1W
153 K5 Eaton Square SW1W
153 J5 Eaton Terrace SW1W
153 J5 Eaton Terrace Mews SW1X
154 E8 Ebbisham Drive SW8
151 L2 Ebenezer Street N1
153 K6 Ebury Bridge SW1W
153 K7 Ebury Bridge Road SW1W
153 K5 Ebury Mews SW1W
153 K5 Ebury Mews East SW1W
153 K6 Ebury Square SW1W
153 L5 Ebury Street SW1W
153 K4 Eccleston Mews SW1X
153 L5 Eccleston Place SW1W
153 L6 Eccleston Square SW1V
153 L6 Eccleston Square Mews SW1V
153 K4 Eccleston Street SW1W
148 A3 Edbrooke Road W9
152 A4 Eden Close W8
152 A1 Edge Street W8
148 F5 Edgware Road W2
153 G3 Edinburgh Gate W2
157 J3 Edward Mann Close East * E1
157 J3 Edward Mann Close West * E1
149 L1 Edward Mews * NW1
149 J6 Edwards Mews W1H
152 F5 Egerton Crescent SW3
152 F5 Egerton Gardens SW3
153 G4 Egerton Gardens Mews SW3
153 G4 Egerton Place * SW3
153 G5 Egerton Terrace SW3
155 K5 Elba Place * SE17
152 B4 Eldon Road W8
151 L5 Eldon Street EC2M
155 J5 Elephant & Castle SE1
156 F6 Elephant Lane SE16
155 J5 Elephant Road SE17
157 H3 Elf Row E1W
157 K7 Elgar Street SE16
148 C2 Elgin Avenue W9
148 C2 Elgin Mews North W9
148 C2 Elgin Mews South W9
151 H1 Elia Mews N1
151 H1 Elia Street N1
155 M4 Elim Street SE1
153 L6 Elizabeth Bridge SW1W
148 D3 Elizabeth Close * W9
157 K4 Elizabeth Square SE16
153 K5 Elizabeth Street SW1W
156 D3 Ellen Street E1
155 H5 Elliott's Row SE11
153 J5 Ellis Street SW1X
152 E7 Elm Park Gardens SW3
152 D7 Elm Park Lane SW3
152 D8 Elm Park Road SW3
152 E7 Elm Place SW7
148 D7 Elms Mews W2
150 F4 Elm Street WC1X
148 E1 Elm Tree Close NW8
148 E2 Elm Tree Road NW8
148 B3 Elnathan Mews W9
157 J1 Elsa Street E1
148 A5 Elsie Lane Court W2
155 M6 Elsted Street SE17
152 D4 Elvaston Mews SW7
152 C4 Elvaston Place SW7
154 B5 Elverton Street SW1P
151 G5 Ely Place EC1N
153 G6 Elystan Place SW3
152 F6 Elystan Street SW3
153 H8 Embankment Gardens SW3
154 D1 Embankment Place WC2N
156 E7 Emba Street SE16
150 E4 Emerald Street WC1N
155 J1 Emerson Street SE1
154 A5 Emery Hill Street SW1P
155 G3 Emery Street SE1
152 C5 Emperor's Gate SW7
155 L3 Empire Square SE1
152 A7 Empress Place SW5
155 K8 Empress Street SE17
151 H3 Enclave Court EC1V
150 C6 Endell Street WC2H
150 B3 Endsleigh Gardens WC1H
150 B3 Endsleigh Place WC1H
150 B3 Endsleigh Street WC1H
149 G4 Enford Street W1H
156 C7 Enid Street SE1
152 F4 Ennismore Gardens SW7
152 F3 Ennismore Gardens Mews SW7
152 F3 Ennismore Mews SW7
152 F4 Ennismore Street SW7
156 D3 Ensign Street E1
152 D6 Ensor Mews SW7
151 L3 Epworth Street EC2A
154 C6 Erasmus Street SW1P
151 K4 Errol Street EC1Y
148 A3 Essendine Road W9
150 F7 Essex Court * WC2R
150 F7 Essex Street WC2R
154 B6 Esterbrooke Street SW1P
154 F6 Ethelred Estate SE11
155 K6 Ethel Street * SE17
151 K2 Europa Place EC1V
149 M3 Euston Centre NW1
149 M3 Euston Road NW1
150 B3 Euston Square NW1
150 A3 Euston Street NW1
156 D8 Eveline Lowe Estate SE16
152 D7 Evelyn Gardens SW10
151 L1 Evelyn Walk N1
150 A1 Eversholt Street NW1
149 M2 Everton Buildings NW1
155 J2 Ewer Street SE1
157 H1 Ewhurst Close E1
150 B8 Excel Court WC2H
156 A1 Exchange Arcade EC2M
150 D7 Exchange Court * WC2E
156 A1 Exchange Square * EC2A
150 D7 Exeter Street WC2E
152 E3 Exhibition Road SW7
151 G3 Exmouth Market EC1R
150 A2 Exmouth Mews * NW1
157 G2 Exmouth Street * E1
155 M6 Exon Street SE17
154 F2 Exton Street SE1
151 G4 Eyre Street Hill EC1R

F

151 L1 Fairbank Estate N1
156 D3 Fairclough Street E1
153 G4 Fairholt Street SW7
156 B6 Fair Street SE1
150 B6 Falconberg Court * W1D
155 J1 Falcon Close SE1
151 J1 Falcon Court N1
155 K4 Falmouth Road SE1
151 J4 Fann Street EC1M
151 M1 Fanshaw Street N1
150 B6 Fareham Street * W1F
152 A1 Farmer Street W8
152 A8 Farm Lane SW6
149 K8 Farm Street W1J
156 E7 Farncombe Street SE16
152 B7 Farnell Mews SW5
155 J1 Farnham Place SE1
154 E7 Farnham Royal SE11
157 M3 Farrance Street E14
152 C8 Farrier Walk SW10
151 G3 Farringdon Lane EC1R
151 H5 Farringdon Road EC1M
150 F3 Farringdon Road WC1X
151 H5 Farringdon Street EC1A
157 K5 Farrins Rents SE16
157 J7 Farrow Place SE16
156 C7 Farthing Alley SE1
156 F5 Farthing Fields E1W
156 C1 Fashion Street E1
155 H7 Faunce Street SE17
152 C8 Fawcett Street SW10
151 L3 Featherstone Street EC1Y
156 A3 Fenchurch Avenue EC3M
156 A3 Fenchurch Buildings EC3M
156 B3 Fenchurch Place * EC3M
151 M7 Fenchurch Street EC3M
156 B8 Fendall Street SE1
155 M2 Fenning Street SE1
150 F2 Fernsbury Street WC1X
151 G6 Fetter Lane EC4A
150 F5 Field Court WC1R
156 D2 Fieldgate Street E1
155 J7 Fielding Street SE17
150 E1 Field Street WC1X
152 B8 Finborough Road SW10
151 M6 Finch Lane EC3V
157 K8 Finland Street SE16
151 M5 Finsbury Avenue * EC2M
151 L5 Finsbury Circus EC2M
151 G3 Finsbury Estate EC1R
151 M4 Finsbury Market EC2A
151 L5 Finsbury Pavement EC2A
151 L4 Finsbury Square EC2A
151 L4 Finsbury Street EC1Y
153 G5 First Street SW3
157 K5 Fir Trees Close SE16
157 J6 Fishermans Drive SE16
150 E5 Fisher Street WC1B
148 E3 Fisherton Street NW8
151 M7 Fish Street Hill EC3R
154 F5 Fitzalan Street SE11
149 J6 Fitzhardinge Street W1H
149 L8 Fitzmaurice Place * W1J
149 M4 Fitzroy Mews W1W
149 M4 Fitzroy Square W1T
149 M3 Fitzroy Street NW1
150 A4 Fitzroy Street W1T
157 K3 Flamborough Street E14
157 K3 Flamborough Walk E14
156 D4 Flank Street E1
150 C2 Flaxman Terrace WC1H
151 H6 Fleet Place EC4M
150 E2 Fleet Square WC1X
151 G6 Fleet Street EC4A
150 F6 Fleet Street WC2R
155 H8 Fleming Road SE17
156 D3 Fletcher Street E1
155 L6 Flint Street SE17
150 C6 Flitcroft Street WC2H
156 D7 Flockton Street SE16
153 G7 Flood Street SW3
153 G8 Flood Walk SW3
150 D7 Floral Street WC2E
156 C1 Flower & Dean Walk E1
149 M5 Foley Street W1W
156 D3 Forbes Street E1
156 E2 Fordham Street E1
156 F2 Ford Square E1
151 L5 Fore Street EC2Y
148 C4 Formosa Street W9
149 G6 Forset Street W1H
155 H8 Forsyth Gardens SE17
156 B1 Fort Street * E1
151 K4 Fortune Street EC1Y
154 E3 Forum Magnum Square SE1
148 C8 Fosbury Mews W2
148 A4 Foscote Mews W9
151 J6 Foster Lane EC2V
149 M7 Foubert's Place W1B
150 A6 Foubert's Place W1F
152 E6 Foulis Terrace SW7
157 J5 Foundry Close SE16
150 A3 Foundry Mews NW1
156 E7 Fountain Green Square SE16
156 C1 Fournier Street E1
156 E5 Fowey Close E1W
151 J4 Fox and Knot Street * EC1M
148 E4 Frampton Street NW8
154 A5 Francis Street SW1P
152 E4 Frankland Road SW7
153 J7 Franklin's Row SW3
155 G3 Frazier Street SE1
156 D8 Frean Street SE16
149 G7 Frederick Close W2
155 H7 Frederick Road * SE17
151 K6 Frederick's Place * EC2R
157 J4 Frederick Square SE16
151 H1 Frederick's Row EC1V
150 E2 Frederick Street WC1X
153 J3 Frederic Mews * SW1X
155 M6 Freemantle Street SE17
155 H1 Friars Close * SE1
151 K7 Friday Street EC4V
151 H2 Friend Street EC1V
150 B6 Frith Street W1D
151 K6 Frobisher Crescent * EC2Y
156 C1 Frostic Walk E1
156 B1 Frying Pan Alley E1
156 E1 Fulbourne Street E1
157 F8 Fulford Street SE16
152 D8 Fulham Road SW10
151 L1 Fullwood's Mews * N1
148 C7 Fulton Mews W2
150 F5 Fulwood Place WC1R
151 G5 Furnival Street EC4A
151 J7 Fye Foot Lane EC4V
154 B5 Fynes Street SW1P

G

151 G8 Gabriel's Wharf SE1
156 B6 Gainsford Street SE1
155 K3 Gaitskell Way SE1
150 D5 Galen Place WC1A
157 H6 Galleon Close SE16
157 K2 Galsworthy Avenue E14
151 K2 Galway Street EC1V
155 H2 Gambia Street SE1
149 M7 Ganton Street W1B
149 J5 Garbutt Place * W1U
150 F7 Garden Court * WC2R
148 D1 Garden Road NW8
155 H4 Garden Row SE1
157 H1 Garden Street E1
154 B6 Garden Terrace SW1V
151 M3 Garden Walk EC2A
151 J7 Gardners Lane EC4V
151 J2 Gard Street EC1V
151 K7 Garlick Hill EC4V
151 G2 Garnault Mews EC1R
151 G2 Garnault Place EC1R
156 F4 Garnet Street E1W
151 K3 Garrett Street EC1Y
150 D7 Garrick Street WC2E
150 C7 Garrick Yard WC2N
148 A6 Garway Road W2
154 F7 Gasholder Place SE11
152 C5 Gaspar Close * SW5
152 B5 Gaspar Mews SW5
156 F8 Gataker Street * SE16
148 F3 Gateforth Street NW8
155 K1 Gatehouse Square SE1
153 G3 Gate Mews SW7
150 E5 Gate Street WC1V
155 K8 Gateway SE17
153 K7 Gatliff Road SW1W
155 J4 Gaunt Street SE1
155 M5 Gayfere Street * SE17
154 C4 Gayfere Street SW1P
155 H4 Gaywood Street SE1
155 H7 Gaza Street SE17
156 C7 Gedling Place SE1
149 K6 Gees Court W1U
151 J3 Gee Street EC1V
148 B4 George Lowe Court W2
155 H5 George Mathers Road * SE11
150 A2 George Mews NW1
156 D7 George Row SE16
149 H6 George Street W1H
151 L7 George Yard EC3V
149 K7 George Yard W1K
155 H4 Geraldine Street SE11
153 K5 Gerald Road SW1W
150 C7 Gerrard Place * W1D
150 B7 Gerrard Street W1D
155 G3 Gerridge Street SE1
154 E6 Gibson Road SE11
150 D5 Gilbert Place WC1A
155 G5 Gilbert Road SE11
149 K7 Gilbert Street W1K
149 L5 Gildea Street W1B
153 L5 Gillingham Mews SW1V
153 M5 Gillingham Row SW1V
153 M5 Gillingham Street SW1V
156 E8 Gillison Walk SE16
157 M3 Gill Street E14
148 D5 Gilpin Close W2
152 D7 Gilston Road SW10
151 H5 Giltspur Street EC1A
155 H4 Gladstone Street SE1
157 H4 Glamis Place E1W
157 G4 Glamis Road E1W
153 M7 Glasgow Terrace SW1V
155 H2 Glasshill Street SE1
157 H3 Glasshouse Fields E1W
150 A7 Glasshouse Street W1B
154 D7 Glasshouse Walk SE11
151 J4 Glasshouse Yard EC1A
157 G3 Glastonbury Place E1
152 F7 Glebe Place SW3
152 C6 Gledhow Gardens SW5
152 E5 Glendower Place SW7
149 H3 Glentworth Street NW1
157 J5 Globe Pond Road SE16
155 L3 Globe Street SE1
156 B4 Gloucester Court EC3R
148 C6 Gloucester Gardens W2
148 D6 Gloucester Mews W2
148 C6 Gloucester Mews West W2
149 H3 Gloucester Place NW1
149 H5 Gloucester Place Mews W1H
152 C4 Gloucester Road SW7
148 F7 Gloucester Square W2
153 M7 Gloucester Street SW1V
148 B6 Gloucester Terrace W2
152 A2 Gloucester Walk W8
151 G2 Gloucester Way EC1R
153 G5 Glynde Mews SW3
154 F7 Glyn Street SE11
153 G6 Godfrey Street SW3
155 K5 Goding Street SE11
151 J7 Godliman Street EC4V
150 F1 Godson Street N1
151 K1 Godwin Close N1
154 E1 Golden Jubilee Bridge SE1
151 K3 Golden Lane EC1Y
151 J4 Golden Lane Estate EC1Y
150 A7 Golden Square W1F
156 E3 Golding Street E1
151 K6 Goldsmith Street EC2V
157 G8 Gomm Road SE16
150 A5 Goodge Place W1T
150 A5 Goodge Street W1T
150 D2 Goodman's Stile E1
156 B3 Goodman's Yard EC3N
156 C8 Goodwin Close SE16
150 D8 Goodwins Court WC2N
151 C7 Gophir Lane * EC4R
152 A2 Gordon Place W8
150 B3 Gordon Square WC1H
150 B3 Gordon Street WC1H
152 D4 Gore Street SW7
156 B2 Goring Street EC3A
149 L5 Gosfield Street W1W
150 B6 Goslett Yard W1D
151 H2 Goswell Place EC1V
151 H2 Goswell Road EC1V
151 G6 Gough Square EC4A
150 F3 Gough Street WC1X
156 B2 Goulston Street E1
150 B5 Gower Mews WC1E
150 B3 Gower Place WC1H
150 B4 Gower Street WC1E
156 D2 Gower's Walk E1
151 M7 Gracechurch Street EC3V
154 D4 Grace's Alley E1
148 D1 Graces Mews * NW8
155 M3 Graduate Place SE1
149 M3 Grafton Mews W1T
150 B3 Grafton Place NW1
149 L8 Grafton Street W1J
150 A4 Grafton Way W1T
149 M4 Grafton Way W1W
151 J1 Graham Street N1
153 J6 Graham Terrace SW1W
149 M1 Granby Terrace NW1
151 H5 Grand Avenue EC1M
151 J1 Grand Junction Wharf * N1
148 A4 Grand Union Canal Walk W2
156 A8 Grange Road SE1
156 A8 Grange Walk SE1
156 B8 Grange Walk Mews SE1
156 B8 Grange Yard SE1
153 K2 Grantham Place W1J
148 B2 Grantully Road W9
149 J6 Granville Place W1H
148 A1 Granville Road NW6
150 F2 Granville Street WC1X
150 C6 Grape Street WC2H
154 E6 Graphite Square SE11
156 B2 Gravel Lane E1
150 D1 Gray's Inn Road N1
150 F5 Gray's Inn Square WC1R
155 G3 Gray Street SE1
149 K6 Gray's Yard * W1U
149 M6 Great Castle Street W1B
149 G4 Great Central Street NW1
150 B6 Great Chapel Street W1F
154 C3 Great College Street SW1P
149 H6 Great Cumberland Mews W1H
149 H6 Great Cumberland Place W1H
155 L4 Great Dover Street SE1
151 M3 Great Eastern Street EC2A
154 C3 Great George Street SW1H
155 J2 Great Guildford Street SE1
150 E4 Great James Street WC1N
149 M6 Great Marlborough Street W1F
155 L2 Great Maze Pond SE1
151 G6 Great New Street * EC4A
156 D1 Greatorex Street E1
150 D4 Great Ormond Street WC1N
150 F2 Great Percy Street WC1X
154 B4 Great Peter Street SW1P
149 M5 Great Portland Street W1W
150 A7 Great Pulteney Street W1F
150 E6 Great Queen Street WC2B
150 C5 Great Russell Street W1T
156 A2 Great St Helen's EC3A
151 K7 Great St Thomas Apostle EC4V
154 C1 Great Scotland Yard SW1A
154 C4 Great Smith Street SW1P
155 J3 Great Suffolk Street SE1
151 H4 Great Sutton Street EC1V
151 L6 Great Swan Alley EC2R
149 L4 Great Titchfield Street W1W
156 A4 Great Tower Street EC3R
151 K7 Great Trinity Lane EC4V
150 E5 Great Turnstile * WC1V
151 M5 Great Winchester Street EC2N
150 B7 Great Windmill Street W1F
150 B6 Greek Street W1D
157 J6 Greenacre Square SE16
151 H6 Green Arbour Court * EC4M
156 F5 Green Bank E1W
148 F1 Greenberry Street NW8
154 A5 Greencoat Place SW1P
154 A5 Greencoat Row SW1P
156 C2 Green Dragon Yard E1
156 D2 Greenfield Road E1
155 G3 Greenham Close SE1
151 H4 Greenhill's Rents * EC1M
150 B7 Green's Court W1F
149 J7 Green Street W1K
151 G2 Green Terrace EC1R
155 M4 Green Walk SE1
149 L4 Greenwell Street W1W
150 E3 Green Yard WC1X
155 G2 Greet Street SE1
152 B3 Gregory Place W8
155 J8 Greig Terrace SE17
157 L4 Grenade Street E14
148 F3 Grendon Street NW8
152 C5 Grenville Place SW7
150 D3 Grenville Street WC1N
151 J6 Gresham Street EC2V
150 B5 Gresse Street W1T
151 G5 Greville Street EC1N
154 B4 Greycoat Place SW1P
154 B5 Greycoat Street SW1P
156 B8 Grigg's Place SE1
154 F3 Grindal Street SE1
151 L6 Grocers' Hall Court * EC2R
153 K4 Groom Place SW1X
153 L8 Grosvenor Bridge SW1V
153 J5 Grosvenor Cottages SW1X
153 J3 Grosvenor Crescent SW1X
153 J3 Grosvenor Crescent Mews SW1X
153 L4 Grosvenor Gardens SW1W
153 L4 Grosvenor Gardens Mews East * SW1W
153 L4 Grosvenor Gardens Mews North SW1W
149 H8 Grosvenor Gate W2
149 L7 Grosvenor Hill W1K
153 K3 Grosvenor Place SW1X
153 L8 Grosvenor Road SW1V
149 J7 Grosvenor Square W1K
149 K7 Grosvenor Street W1K
155 J3 Grotto Court * SE1
149 J5 Grotto Passage W1U
153 G8 Grove Cottages SW3
148 D2 Grove End Road NW8
148 F2 Grove Gardens NW8
151 K6 Groveland Court EC4M
151 K6 Guildhall Buildings EC2V
151 K6 Guildhall Yard EC2V
153 M5 Guildhouse Street SW1V
150 E4 Guilford Place WC1N
150 E4 Guilford Street WC1N
156 A8 Guinness Square SE1
153 H6 Guinness Trust Estate SW3
157 L8 Gulliver Street SE16
156 B1 Gun Street E1
156 C2 Gunthorpe Street E1
157 J6 Gunwhale Close SE16
152 F6 Guthrie Street SW3
151 K6 Gutter Lane EC2V
155 L3 Guy Street SE1

H

151 M2 Haberdasher Place N1
151 L2 Haberdasher Street N1
156 F3 Hainton Close E1
156 F1 Halcrow Street * E1
156 C2 Half Moon Passage E1
153 L1 Half Moon Street W1J
152 A8 Halford Road SW6
153 J4 Halkin Arcade SW1X
153 J4 Halkin Mews * SW1X
153 J4 Halkin Place SW1X
153 J3 Halkin Street SW1X
149 L4 Hallam Mews W1B
149 L4 Hallam Street W1W
157 K1 Halley Street E14
148 C6 Hallfield Estate W2
148 D2 Hall Gate NW8
148 E4 Hall Place W2
148 D2 Hall Road NW8
151 H2 Hall Street EC1V
155 M6 Halpin Place SE17
153 G5 Halsey Street SW3
157 K7 Hamilton Close SE16
148 D2 Hamilton Close NW8
148 D2 Hamilton Gardens NW8
153 K2 Hamilton Place W1K
148 C1 Hamilton Terrace NW8
155 L3 Hamlet Way SE1
156 B4 Hammett Street EC3N
150 B1 Hampden Close NW1
149 H6 Hampden Gurney Street W1H
149 M2 Hampstead Road NW1
155 J6 Hampton Street SE17
150 B7 Ham Yard * W1D
156 D1 Hanbury Street E1
150 E5 Hand Court WC1V
150 D3 Handel Street WC1N
155 L3 Hankey Place SE1
150 D7 Hanover Place WC2E
149 L6 Hanover Square W1S
149 G7 Hanover Steps * W2
149 L7 Hanover Street W1S
149 G2 Hanover Terrace NW1
149 G2 Hanover Terrace Mews NW1
153 H3 Hans Crescent SW3
149 M4 Hanson Street W1W
153 H4 Hans Place SW1X
153 G4 Hans Road SW3
153 H4 Hans Street SW1X
150 B5 Hanway Place W1T
150 B6 Hanway Street W1T
148 F5 Harbet Road W2
149 G5 Harcourt Street NW1
152 C7 Harcourt Terrace SW10
155 J8 Harding Close SE17
157 H3 Hardinge Street E1
150 F2 Hardwicke Mews * WC1X
151 G2 Hardwick Street EC1R
155 M2 Hardwidge Street SE1
157 J6 Hardy Close SE16
151 G7 Hare Court * EC4Y
149 G4 Harewood Avenue NW1
149 L6 Harewood Place W1S
149 G4 Harewood Row NW1
154 E8 Harleyford Road SE11
154 F8 Harleyford Street SE11
152 D7 Harley Gardens SW10
149 K5 Harley Place W1G
149 K5 Harley Street W1G
155 G5 Harmsworth Mews SE1
155 H7 Harmsworth Street SE17
156 A4 Harp Cross Lane EC3R
155 K4 Harper Road SE1
150 E4 Harpur Street WC1N
153 H3 Harriet Street SW1X
153 H3 Harriet Walk SW1X
152 C6 Harrington Gardens SW7
152 D5 Harrington Road SW7
149 M1 Harrington Square NW1
149 M2 Harrington Street NW1
150 D2 Harrison Street WC1H
149 G6 Harrowby Street W1H
156 B2 Harrow Place E1
148 E5 Harrow Road Flyover W2
148 F4 Harrow Street * NW1
156 A3 Hart Street EC3R
153 G5 Hasker Street SW3
150 C2 Hastings Street WC1H
156 A7 Hatchers Mews SE1
155 G1 Hatfields SE1
148 B6 Hatherley Grove W2
154 A5 Hatherley Street SW1P
151 H4 Hat & Mitre Court EC1M
157 G6 Hatteraick Street SE16
151 G4 Hatton Garden EC1R
151 G4 Hatton Place EC1N
148 E4 Hatton Row * NW8
148 E4 Hatton Street NW8
151 G4 Hatton Wall EC1N
149 L7 Haunch of Venison Yard * W1K
157 L1 Havens Mews E3
157 H3 Havering Street E1
151 G1 Haverstock Place N1
151 J1 Haverstock Street N1
157 H6 Hawke Place SE16
156 E3 Hawksmoor Mews * E1
156 B3 Haydon Street EC3N
156 C3 Haydon Walk E1
149 G4 Hayes Place NW1
149 L8 Hay Hill W1J
155 H5 Hayles Street SE11
150 B8 Haymarket SW1Y
151 J4 Hayne Street EC1A
155 M1 Hays Lane SE1
153 K1 Hay's Mews W1J
151 H3 Hayward's Place * EC1R
153 K3 Headfort Place SW1X
157 H3 Head Street E1
155 M6 Hearn's Buildings SE17
150 E3 Heathcote Street WC1N
157 H3 Heckford Street E1W
149 M7 Heddon Street W1S
155 H5 Hedger Street SE11
155 J8 Heiron Street SE17
157 J4 Helena Square SE16
156 D5 Hellings Street E1W
153 K3 Helmet Row EC1V
157 L8 Helsinki Square SE16
155 L5 Hemp Walk SE17
148 E3 Henderson Drive NW8
156 B2 Heneage Lane EC3A
156 C1 Heneage Street E1
152 D8 Henniker Mews SW3
150 D3 Henrietta Mews WC1N
149 K6 Henrietta Place W1G
150 D7 Henrietta Street WC2E
156 D2 Henriques Street E1
155 L5 Henshaw Street SE17
155 G5 Heralds Place SE11
151 G4 Herbal Hill EC1R
153 H4 Herbert Crescent SW1X
150 D4 Herbrand Street WC1N
154 F4 Hercules Road SE1
148 A6 Hereford Mews W2
148 A7 Hereford Road W2
152 D6 Hereford Square SW7
150 F1 Hermes Street N1
148 E5 Hermitage Street W2
156 D5 Hermitage Wall E1W
151 H2 Hermit Street EC1V
154 C6 Herrick Street SW1P
153 K1 Hertford Street W1J
152 B6 Hesper Mews SW5
156 E3 Hessel Street E1
155 K5 Heygate Estate SE17
155 J5 Heygate Street SE17
154 B6 Hide Place SW1P
150 E5 High Holborn WC1V
151 J7 High Timber Street EC4V
149 G4 Highworth Street * NW1
152 A8 Hildyard Road SW6
155 L6 Hillery Close SE17
148 C7 Hill Gardens Craven * W2
156 F5 Hilliard's Court E1W
148 D1 Hill Road NW8
148 B1 Hillside Close NW6
149 M6 Hills Place W1F
153 K1 Hill Street W1J
151 G6 Hind Court EC4A
149 K6 Hinde Mews * W1U
149 K6 Hinde Street W1U
156 D4 Hindmarsh Close E1
153 K4 Hobart Place SW1W
156 D1 Hobsons Place E1
152 D8 Hobury Street SW10
151 L2 Hoffman Square * N1
148 D5 Hogan Mews W2
152 A6 Hogarth Place * SW5
152 B6 Hogarth Road SW5
156 F4 Hogshead Passage * E1W
153 J6 Holbein Mews SW1W
153 J6 Holbein Place SW1W
151 G5 Holborn EC1N
151 G5 Holborn Circus EC1N
150 E5 Holborn Place WC1V
151 G5 Holborn Viaduct EC1N
150 E2 Holford Mews * WC1X
150 F2 Holford Street WC1X

Holford Yard - Montpelier Street 161

150 F1 Holford Yard * N1
152 A3 Holland Place W8
152 A3 Holland Street W8
151 H8 Holland Street SE1
150 B6 Hollen Street W1F
149 L6 Holles Street W1G
152 D7 Holly Mews SW10
152 C8 Hollywood Mews SW10
152 C8 Hollywood Road SW10
155 G3 Holmes Terrace SE1
150 F4 Holsworthy Square WC1X
157 L6 Holyoake Court SE16
155 H5 Holyoak Road SE11
156 A6 Holyrood Street SE1
151 M4 Holywell Row EC2A
151 M1 Homefield Street * N1
150 G5 Homer Row NW1
149 G5 Homer Street NW1
151 J3 Honduras Street EC1V
156 D3 Hooper Street E1
156 C1 Hopetown Street * E1
150 C7 Hop Gardens WC2N
150 B7 Hopkins Street W1F
155 H1 Hoptons Gardens * SE1
151 H8 Hopton Street SE1
155 L8 Hopwood Road SE17
154 F5 Hornbeam Close SE11
152 A3 Hornton Place W8
152 A2 Hornton Street W8
157 J3 Horseferry Road E14
154 C5 Horseferry Road SW1P
154 D2 Horse Guards Avenue SW1A
154 C2 Horse Guards Road SW1A
156 B6 Horselydown Lane SE1
155 K8 Horsley Street SE17
155 K8 Horsman Street SE5
151 H5 Hosier Lane EC1A
157 G8 Hothfield Place SE16
154 F6 Hotspur Street SE11
150 E6 Houghton Street * WC2B
156 B2 Houndsditch EC3A
155 J6 Howell Walk SE17
154 A4 Howick Place SW1P
150 A4 Howland Mews East W1T
150 A4 Howland Street W1T
157 K7 Howland Way SE16
148 D4 Howley Place W2
151 M2 Hoxton Market N1
151 M2 Hoxton Square N1
157 M1 Huddart Street E3
151 K7 Huggin Hill EC4V
153 L6 Hugh Mews SW1V
154 B5 Hugh Place SW1P
153 L6 Hugh Street SW1V
156 C1 Huguenot Place E1
157 J6 Hull Close SE16
151 J2 Hull Street EC1V
155 K3 Hulme Place SE1
156 F2 Hungerford Street * E1
155 M4 Hunter Close SE1
150 D3 Hunter Street WC1N
150 B4 Huntley Street WC1E
156 D1 Hunton Street E1
155 M6 Huntsman Street SE17
149 G3 Huntsworth Mews NW1
151 G7 Hutton Street EC4Y
153 K2 Hyde Park Corner W1J
148 F6 Hyde Park Crescent W2
148 E7 Hyde Park Gardens W2
148 F7 Hyde Park Gardens Mews W2
152 C3 Hyde Park Gate W8
152 D3 Hyde Park Gate Mews * SW7
149 G7 Hyde Park Place W2
148 F7 Hyde Park Square W2
148 F7 Hyde Park Street W2

I

156 A4 Idol Lane EC3R
152 B8 Ifield Road SW10
148 B7 Ilchester Gardens W2
155 J6 Iliffe Street SE17
155 J6 Iliffe Yard SE17
152 E4 Imperial College Road SW7
156 B3 India Street EC3N
150 A7 Ingestre Place W1F
150 F2 Inglebert Street EC1R
156 F5 Inglefield Square * E1W
154 F5 Ingram Close SE11
149 J2 Inner Circle NW1
148 B6 Inver Court W2
152 A2 Inverness Gardens W8
148 B7 Inverness Mews W2
148 B7 Inverness Place W2
148 C7 Inverness Terrace W2
155 H1 Invicta Plaza SE1
155 L7 Inville Road SE17
151 K6 Ironmonger Lane EC2V
151 K2 Ironmonger Row EC1V
157 H6 Ironside Close SE16
150 C8 Irving Street WC2H
155 K3 Isaac Way SE1
155 H2 Isabella Street SE1
157 H6 Isambard Place SE16
157 L3 Island Row E14
152 A4 Iverna Court W8
152 A4 Iverna Gardens W8
153 G5 Ives Street SW3
149 H3 Ivor Place NW1
152 F6 Ixworth Place SW3

J

156 C6 Jacob Street SE1
149 J5 Jacob's Well Mews W1U
156 E7 Jamaica Road SE16
157 G2 Jamaica Street E1
152 A1 Jameson Street W8
150 D7 James Street WC2E
149 K6 James Street W1U
157 K1 Jamuna Close E14
156 E2 Jane Street E1
156 E7 Janeway Place SE16
156 E7 Janeway Street SE16
157 J4 Jardine Road E1W
152 D3 Jay Mews SW7
154 A1 Jermyn Street SW1Y
148 F3 Jerome Crescent NW8
156 B1 Jerome Street E1
151 H3 Jerusalem Passage EC1R
156 B3 Jewry Street EC3N
155 H2 Joan Street SE1
150 E4 Jockey's Fields WC1X
154 F3 Johanna Street * SE1
150 D8 John Adam Street WC2N
148 D5 John Aird Court W2
151 G7 John Carpenter Street EC4Y
156 D7 John Felton Road SE16
156 D4 John Fisher Street E1
157 J8 John Harrison Way SE16
154 C6 John Islip Street SW1P
155 L5 John Maurice Close SE17
156 E8 John McKenna Walk SE16
149 L6 John Prince's Street W1G
156 F5 John Rennie Walk E1W
156 D7 John Roll Way SE16
150 E4 John's Mews WC1N
151 G6 Johnson's Court EC4A
154 A7 Johnson's Place SW1V
157 G3 Johnson Street E1
156 F2 Johns Place E1
150 E4 John Street WC1N
151 J5 John Trundle Highwalk * EC2Y
155 L2 Joiner Street SE1
154 E6 Jonathan Street SE11
151 G2 Joseph Trotter Close EC1R
154 E2 Jubilee Gardens * SE1
153 G6 Jubilee Place SW3
156 G2 Jubilee Street E1
150 D2 Judd Street WC1H
148 F5 Junction Mews W2
148 F5 Junction Place * W2
157 G4 Juniper Street E1
152 F8 Justice Walk SW3
154 F5 Juxon Street SE11

K

157 H5 Katherine Close SE16
150 E6 Kean Street WC2B
157 J6 Keel Close SE16
150 E6 Keeley Street WC2B
155 L8 Keesey Street SE17
156 E8 Keeton's Road SE16
155 K4 Kell Street SE1
152 B4 Kelso Place W8
150 E6 Kemble Street WC2B
152 A7 Kempsford Gardens SW5
155 G6 Kempsford Road SE11
149 J5 Kendall Place W1U
149 G7 Kendal Steps * W2
149 G6 Kendal Street W2
152 E5 Kendrick Mews SW7
152 E6 Kendrick Place * SW7
155 L6 Kennedy Walk SE17
156 D5 Kennet Street E1W
151 K7 Kennett Wharf Lane EC4V
155 G6 Kenning Street SE16
155 G7 Kennings Way SE11
154 E8 Kennington Grove SE11
154 E7 Kennington Lane SE11
154 F8 Kennington Oval SE11
155 H8 Kennington Park Gardens SE11
155 G7 Kennington Park Place SE17
155 H6 Kennington Park Road SE11
155 G5 Kennington Road SE11
149 J5 Kenrick Place W1U
152 B3 Kensington Church Court W8
152 A1 Kensington Church Street W8
152 A3 Kensington Church Walk * W8
152 C3 Kensington Court W8
152 B4 Kensington Court Gardens * W8
152 B3 Kensington Court Mews * W8
152 B4 Kensington Court Place W8
148 B6 Kensington Gardens Square W2
152 C4 Kensington Gate SW7
152 D3 Kensington Gore SW7
152 A4 Kensington High Street W8
152 A1 Kensington Mall W8
152 B2 Kensington Palace * W8
152 B1 Kensington Palace Gardens W8
152 B3 Kensington Road W8
152 B3 Kensington Square W8
150 D3 Kenton Street WC1H
149 G3 Kent Passage NW1
149 G2 Kent Terrace NW1
153 G3 Kent Yard SW7
152 A6 Kenway Road SW5
150 C4 Keppel Street WC1E
156 C8 Keyse Road SE1
150 D1 Keystone Crescent N1
155 H4 Keyworth Street SE1
148 A1 Kilburn Park Road NW6
148 A6 Kildare Gardens W2
148 A6 Kildare Terrace W2
150 E1 Killick Street N1
157 H6 Kinburn Street SE16
156 E3 Kinder Street E1
154 C1 King Charles I Island WC2N
154 C3 King Charles Street SW1A
156 F5 King Charles Terrace * E1W
157 G3 King David Lane E1
156 E7 King Edward III Mews SE16
151 J6 King Edward Street EC1A
155 G4 King Edward Walk SE1
156 F4 King Henry Terrace * E1W
151 J5 Kinghorn Street EC1A
155 H3 King James Street SE1
157 J1 King John Street E1
155 M7 Kinglake Estate * SE17
155 M7 Kinglake Street SE17
150 A7 Kingly Court * W1B
149 M7 Kingly Street W1B
155 K6 King & Queen Street SE17
157 J5 King & Queen Wharf * SE16
151 L6 King's Arms Yard EC2R
155 H3 King's Bench Street SE1
151 G7 King's Bench Walk * EC4Y
151 H7 Kingscote Street EC4Y
155 J3 King's Court * SE1
150 D1 King's Cross Bridge * WC1X
150 E2 King's Cross Road WC1X
152 B4 Kingsley Mews * W8
156 F4 Kingsley Mews E1W
150 F4 King's Mews WC1N
155 K3 King's Place SE1
151 J2 King Square EC1V
151 G7 King's Reach * EC4Y
154 D1 Kings Reach SE1
153 K4 King's Road SW1W
153 M5 King's Scholars' Passage SW1P
156 F6 King Stairs Close SE16
151 K6 King Street EC2V
150 D7 King Street WC2E
154 A1 King Street SW1Y
150 E6 Kingsway WC2B
151 G3 Kingsway Place * EC1R
151 L8 King William Street EC4R
153 H3 Kinnerton Place North * SW1X
153 J3 Kinnerton Place South * SW1X
153 J3 Kinnerton Street SW1X
153 J3 Kinnerton Yard * SW1X
155 L3 Kipling Estate SE1
155 L3 Kipling Street SE1
156 F7 Kirby Estate SE16
155 M3 Kirby Grove SE1
151 G4 Kirby Street EC1N
152 B5 Knaresborough Place SW5
156 E6 Knighten Street E1W
151 J7 Knightrider Court EC4V
151 J7 Knightrider Street EC4V
153 H3 Knightsbridge SW1X
153 H3 Knightsbridge Green * SW1X
155 H6 Knights Walk SE11
149 H6 Knox Street W1H
152 A5 Kramer Mews SW5
152 C4 Kynance Mews W8
152 C4 Kynance Place W8

L

151 L4 Lackington Street EC2A
156 B6 Lafone Street SE1
157 J5 Lagado Mews SE16
151 J4 Lambert Jones Mews * EC2Y
154 D5 Lambeth Bridge SW1P
154 E5 Lambeth High Street SE1
151 J7 Lambeth Hill EC4V
154 E4 Lambeth Palace Road SE1
154 F4 Lambeth Road SE1
154 F5 Lambeth Walk SE11
150 E4 Lamb's Conduit Passage WC1X
150 E4 Lamb's Conduit Street WC1N
151 K4 Lamb's Passage EC1Y
156 B1 Lamb Street E1
156 A7 Lamb Walk SE1
155 H5 Lamlash Street SE11
152 E8 Lamont Road Passage SW10
148 D3 Lanark Place W9
148 C2 Lanark Road W9
149 L7 Lancashire Court W1K
148 D7 Lancaster Court W2
148 D8 Lancaster Gate W2
148 D7 Lancaster Mews W2
150 E8 Lancaster Place WC2E
155 H3 Lancaster Street SE1
148 E7 Lancaster Terrace W2
153 G3 Lancelot Place SW7
152 B3 Lancer Square W8
150 B2 Lancing Street NW1
153 H4 Landon Place SW1X
155 J8 Langdale Close SE17
156 E3 Langdale Street * E1
148 D1 Langford Place NW8
149 L5 Langham Place W1G
149 M5 Langham Street W1B
150 D7 Langley Court WC2E
154 D8 Langley Lane SW8
150 D7 Langley Street WC2H
151 L5 Langthorn Court * EC2R
150 E3 Langton Close WC1X
152 A7 Langtry Place SW6
155 L4 Lansdowne Place SE1
150 D3 Lansdowne Terrace WC1N
155 J3 Lant Street SE1
148 C5 Lapworth Court W2
155 K6 Larcom Street SE17
155 M6 Larissa Street * SE17
148 B3 Lauderdale Parade * W9
151 K5 Lauderdale Place * EC2Y
148 B3 Lauderdale Road W9
154 E7 Laud Street SE11
154 F3 Launcelot Street SE1
152 C4 Launceston Place W8
151 L7 Laurence Pountney Hill EC4R
151 L7 Laurence Pountney Lane EC4R
152 F8 Lavender Close SW3
157 K5 Lavender Road SE16
152 B6 Laverton Mews * SW5
152 B6 Laverton Place SW5
155 J2 Lavington Street SE1
154 D8 Lawn Lane SW8
151 K6 Lawrence Lane EC2V
152 F8 Lawrence Street SW3
155 L4 Law Street SE1
149 L3 Laxton Place NW1
150 F4 Laystall Street WC1X
150 D7 Lazenby Court * WC2E
156 A3 Leadenhall Place EC3M
151 M6 Leadenhall Street EC3V
154 F3 Leake Street SE1
151 G4 Leather Lane EC1R
155 M3 Leathermarket Court SE1
155 M3 Leathermarket Street SE1
157 H3 Leather Street E1W
152 E7 Lecky Street SW7
150 E2 Leeke Street WC1X
149 J7 Lees Place W1K
150 C7 Leicester Place * WC2H
150 C7 Leicester Square WC2H
150 B7 Leicester Street W1D
150 C5 Leigh Street WC1H
148 C6 Leinster Gardens W2
148 C7 Leinster Mews W2
148 C7 Leinster Place W2
148 A7 Leinster Square W2
148 C7 Leinster Terrace W2
156 C3 Leman Street E1
153 G5 Lennox Gardens SW1X
153 G5 Lennox Gardens Mews SW3
151 M3 Leonard Street EC2A
157 M1 Leopold Estate E3
157 M1 Leopold Street E3
155 M5 Leroy Street SE1
153 G8 Leverett Street SW3
151 J2 Lever Street EC1V
152 A5 Lexham Gardens W8
152 A5 Lexham Mews W8
150 A7 Lexington Street W1F
156 B2 Leyden Street E1
155 H3 Library Street SE1
149 M1 Lidlington Place NW1
157 J2 Lighterman Mews E1
154 E6 Lilac Place SE11
148 F3 Lilestone Street NW8
156 E5 Lilley Close E1W
152 A8 Lillie Yard SW6
154 A6 Lillington Gardens Estate SW1V
151 G4 Lily Place EC1N
151 H6 Limeburner Lane EC4M
156 D5 Lime Close E1W
157 M4 Limehouse * E14
157 M4 Limehouse Causeway E14
157 K1 Limehouse Fields Estate E1
157 K3 Limehouse Link E14
157 L3 Limehouse Link (Tunnel) E14
152 D8 Limerston Street SW10
151 M7 Lime Street EC3M
151 M7 Lime Street Passage * EC3V
150 E6 Lincoln's Inn Fields WC2A
153 H6 Lincoln Street SW3
148 A8 Linden Gardens W2
148 A8 Linden Mews W11
156 F1 Lindley Street E1
154 C7 Lindsay Square SW1V
151 J4 Lindsey Street EC1M
149 G3 Linhope Street NW1
156 C1 Links Yard E1
156 D8 Linsey Street SE16
150 B7 Lisle Street W1D
148 F4 Lisson Grove NW8
148 F4 Lisson Street NW8
150 C7 Litchfield Street WC2H
149 L3 Little Albany Street NW1
149 M6 Little Argyll Street * W1S
151 J5 Little Britain EC1A
153 K4 Little Chester Street SW1X
154 C4 Little Cloisters SW1P
154 C4 Little Deans Yard SW1P
155 K2 Little Dorrit Court SE1
149 L2 Little Edward Street * NW1
150 F7 Little Essex Street * WC2R
154 C3 Little George Street SW1P
149 M7 Little Marlborough Street * W1B
150 C7 Little Newport Street WC2H
151 G6 Little New Street EC4A
149 L6 Little Portland Street W1B
150 D5 Little Russell Street WC1A
153 M2 Little St James's Street SW1A
154 C4 Little Smith Street SW1P
149 M5 Little Titchfield Street W1W
151 K7 Little Trinity Lane EC4V
150 E5 Little Turnstile WC1V
155 K5 Liverpool Grove SE17
151 M5 Liverpool Street EC2M
151 K2 Lizard Street EC1V
156 D7 Llewellyn Street SE16
150 F2 Lloyd Baker Street WC1X
156 B3 Lloyd's Avenue EC3M
150 F2 Lloyd Square WC1X
151 G2 Lloyd's Row EC1R
150 F2 Lloyd Street WC1X
157 L2 Locksley Estate E14
157 L1 Locksley Street E14
156 E8 Lockwood Square SE16
155 L3 Lockyer Street SE1
148 F2 Lodge Road NW8
156 D7 Loftie Street SE16
156 C1 Lolesworth Close E1
154 F6 Lollard Street SE11
155 J2 Loman Street SE1
156 E1 Lomas Street E1
151 G6 Lombard Lane EC4Y
151 L7 Lombard Street EC3V
148 B7 Lombardy Place W2
151 L8 London Bridge EC4R
155 L1 London Bridge Street SE1
155 L1 London Bridge Walk * SE1
148 E6 London Mews W2
155 H4 London Road SE1
148 E6 London Street W2
156 A3 London Street * EC3M
151 L5 London Wall EC2Y
151 L5 London Wall Buildings EC2M
150 D7 Long Acre WC2E
149 L3 Longford Street NW1
151 J5 Long Lane EC1A
155 M3 Long Lane SE1
153 M6 Longmoore Street SW1V
155 H5 Longville Road SE11
156 B8 Long Walk SE1
150 E4 Long Yard WC1N
148 B4 Lord Hills Road W2
154 C4 Lord North Street SW1P
152 F8 Lordship Place SW3
148 F2 Lords View NW8
150 E1 Lorenzo Street WC1X
149 G2 Lorne Close NW8
155 J8 Lorrimore Road SE17
155 J8 Lorrimore Square SE17
151 L6 Lothbury EC2R
157 F1 Loughborough Street SE11
151 M7 Lovat Lane EC3M
151 K5 Love Lane EC2V
157 K7 Lovell Place SE16
157 K2 Lowell Street E14
153 K4 Lower Belgrave Street SW1W
153 L4 Lower Grosvenor Place SW1X
150 A7 Lower James Street * W1F
150 A7 Lower John Street W1F
154 F3 Lower Marsh SE1
157 G7 Lower Road SE16
153 J6 Lower Sloane Street SW1W
156 A4 Lower Thames Street EC3R
153 J4 Lowndes Close SW1X
149 M7 Lowndes Court * W1B
153 J4 Lowndes Place * SW1X
153 H3 Lowndes Square SW1X
153 J4 Lowndes Street SW1X
156 F4 Lowood Street E1
150 D2 Loxham Street * WC1H
152 F6 Lucan Place SW3
152 A1 Lucerne Mews * W8
156 D8 Lucey Road SE16
156 E8 Lucey Way SE16
151 H6 Ludgate Broadway * EC4V
151 H6 Ludgate Circus EC4M
151 H6 Ludgate Hill EC4M
151 H6 Ludgate Square * EC4V
151 J3 Ludlow Street * EC1V
151 M3 Luke Street EC2A
157 G3 Lukin Street E1
149 K6 Lumley Street W1K
153 L7 Lupus Street SW1V
148 E4 Luton Street NW8
149 J4 Luxborough Street W1U
153 J4 Lyall Mews SW1X
153 J5 Lyall Mews West * SW1X
153 J5 Lyall Street SW1X
153 L4 Lygon Place * SW1W
148 E3 Lyons Place NW8
155 L7 Lytham Street SE17

M

150 C2 Mabledon Place NW1
151 J2 Macclesfield Road EC1V
150 B7 Macclesfield Street * W1D
156 E5 Mace Close E1W
149 K4 Mac Farren Place NW1
148 F1 Mackennal Street NW8
150 D6 Macklin Street * WC2B
149 M2 Mackworth Street NW1
155 K7 Macleod Street SE17
155 H8 Maddock Way SE17
149 L7 Maddox Street W1K
153 G1 Magazine Gate * W2
156 A6 Magdalen Street SE1
154 F8 Magee Street SE11
157 G2 Magri Walk E1
156 C6 Maguire Street SE1
157 K6 Mahogany Close SE16
148 D4 Maida Avenue W2
148 B1 Maida Vale W9
150 D7 Maiden Lane WC2E
155 K1 Maiden Lane SE1
155 K2 Maidstone Buildings Mews SE1
156 E7 Major Road SE16
153 G5 Makins Street SW3
150 B4 Malet Street WC1E
152 A1 Mall Chambers * W8
152 E8 Mallord Street SW3
148 F3 Mallory Street NW8
151 L3 Mallow Street EC1V
151 H3 Malta Street EC1V
156 B7 Maltby Street SE1
156 B6 Maltings Place SE1
150 F7 Maltravers Street WC2R
149 J5 Manchester Mews W1U
149 J6 Manchester Square W1H
149 J5 Manchester Street W1U
155 L3 Manciple Street SE1
149 K6 Mandeville Place W1U
150 C6 Manette Street W1D
151 H2 Manningford Close * EC1V
156 C2 Manningtree Street E1
155 J7 Manor Place SE17
152 F7 Manresa Road SW3
156 C4 Mansell Street EC3N
149 L5 Mansfield Mews W1G
149 L5 Mansfield Street W1G
151 L7 Mansion House Place * EC4N
152 D5 Manson Mews SW7
152 D6 Manson Place SW7
157 J6 Maple Leaf Square SE16
150 A4 Maple Place W1T
156 F1 Maples Place E1
149 M4 Maple Street W1T
156 C5 Marble Quay E1W
150 D3 Marchmont Street WC1N
156 E8 Marden Square SE16
149 M6 Margaret Street W1W
152 F8 Margaretta Terrace SW3
150 F3 Margery Street WC1X
151 G8 Marigold Alley SE1
156 E7 Marigold Street SE16
156 D8 Marine Street SE16
153 K2 Market Mews W1J
149 M6 Market Place W1D
156 A7 Market Yard Mews SE1
153 G6 Markham Place * SW3
153 G6 Markham Square SW3
153 G6 Markham Street SW3
156 A4 Mark Lane EC3R
151 M3 Mark Street EC2A
155 J6 Marlborough Close SE17
149 M7 Marlborough Court * W1B
148 E7 Marlborough Gate W2
148 C1 Marlborough Place NW8
154 A2 Marlborough Road SW1A
152 F6 Marlborough Street SW3
152 A4 Marloes Road W8
157 H6 Marlow Way SE16
157 K2 Maroon Street E14
156 C8 Marshall's Place SE16
150 A7 Marshall Street W1F
155 K2 Marshalsea Road SE1
154 C5 Marsham Street SW1P
155 J7 Marsland Close SE17
151 L3 Martha's Buildings EC1V
156 F3 Martha Street E1
157 G3 Martineau Street E1
151 L7 Martin Lane EC4R
150 D6 Martlett Court WC2B
148 A4 Maryland Road W9
148 A3 Marylands Road W9
149 K5 Marylebone High Street W1U
149 K6 Marylebone Lane W1U
149 K5 Marylebone Mews W1G
150 A6 Marylebone Passage W1W
149 G4 Marylebone Road NW1
149 K5 Marylebone Street W1U
154 F6 Marylee Way SE11
149 L7 Mason's Arms Mews * W1S
151 L6 Mason's Avenue EC2V
151 H2 Mason's Place EC1V
155 M5 Mason Street SE17
151 J3 Masons Yard EC1V
154 A1 Masons Yard SW1Y
155 M6 Massinger Street SE17
157 J1 Master's Street E1
155 J7 Matara Mews SE17
150 C6 Mathews Yard * WC2H
155 H3 Mathieson Court SE1
157 J2 Matlock Street E14
154 B5 Maunsel Street SW1P
155 K2 Mayall Close SE1
153 L1 Mayfair Place W1J
156 F7 Mayflower Street SE16
156 F4 Maynards Quay E1W
150 C7 Mays Court WC2N
154 F4 McAuley Close SE1
155 J3 McCoid Way SE1
152 C5 McLeod's Mews SW7
155 H8 Meadcroft Road SE11
155 J5 Meadow Row SE1
155 G4 Mead Row SE1
150 B7 Meard Street W1F
150 E3 Mecklenburgh Place WC1N
150 E3 Mecklenburgh Square WC1N
150 E3 Mecklenburgh Street WC1N
154 B5 Medway Street SW1P
156 F5 Meeting House Alley * E1W
150 E7 Melbourne Place WC2B
149 G4 Melbury Terrace NW1
149 G4 Melcombe Place NW1
149 H4 Melcombe Street NW1
148 D2 Melina Place NW8
155 M2 Melior Place * SE1
155 M2 Melior Street SE1
152 A2 Melon Place * W8
150 B2 Melton Street NW1
151 J3 Memel Street EC1Y
154 F2 Mepham Street SE1
150 C7 Mercer Street WC2H
151 H2 Meredith Street EC1R
151 G2 Merlin Street WC1X
155 L2 Mermaid Court SE1
155 K4 Merrick Square SE1
152 A8 Merrington Road SW6
155 L7 Merrow Street SE17
155 L6 Merrow Walk SE17
149 G5 Mertoun Terrace * W1H
155 G7 Methley Street SE11
157 G5 Metropolitan Wharf * E1W
153 L4 Mews North SW1W
154 A7 Mews South SW1V
156 C5 Mews Street E1W
155 G2 Meymott Street SE1
156 D5 Miah Terrace * E1W
151 K1 Micawber Street N1
152 A8 Micklethwaite Road SW6
156 B1 Middlesex Street E1
151 J5 Middle Street EC1A
150 F6 Middle Temple Lane WC2R
149 M5 Middleton Buildings W1W
157 J6 Middleton Drive SE16
149 M5 Middleton Place W1W
155 M1 Middle Yard SE1
150 A4 Midford Place * W1T
150 D2 Midhope Street WC1H
150 C1 Midland Road NW1
157 J6 Midship Close SE16
152 D7 Milborne Grove SW10
155 H5 Milcote Street SE1
156 F1 Mile End Road E1
154 D8 Miles Street SW8
150 F7 Milford Lane WC2R
151 K6 Milk Street EC2V
157 G4 Milk Yard E1W
154 D5 Millbank SW1P
154 C6 Millbank Estate SW1P
151 J8 Millennium Bridge SE1
156 C6 Millennium Square SE1
155 G1 Miller Walk SE1
157 M4 Milligan Street E14
150 E4 Millman Mews * WC1N
150 E4 Millman Place WC1N
150 E3 Millman Street WC1N
157 L3 Mill Place E14
154 C1 Millshott Close SW1Y
156 B7 Millstream Road SE1
149 L7 Mill Street W1S
156 C7 Mill Street SE1
152 E8 Milman's Street SW10
153 G5 Milner Street SW3
151 G8 Milroy Walk SE1
151 L4 Milton Court EC2Y
151 K4 Milton Street EC2Y
155 G7 Milverton Street SE11
156 F1 Milward Street E1
156 A4 Mincing Lane EC3R
153 J5 Minera Mews SW1W
156 B3 Minories EC3N
156 A4 Minster Court * EC3M
155 J2 Mint Street SE1
156 F2 Miranda Close * E1
156 D3 Mitali Passage E1
151 J3 Mitchell Street EC1V
155 G3 Mitre Road SE1
156 B3 Mitre Square EC3A
156 B3 Mitre Street EC3A
157 M7 Moiety Road E14
149 G5 Molyneux Street W1H
154 C4 Monck Street SW1P
152 F3 Moncorvo Close SW7
155 G5 Monkton Street SE11
151 K5 Monkwell Square EC2Y
148 A6 Monmouth Place W2
148 A6 Monmouth Road W2
150 D6 Monmouth Street WC2H
155 L1 Montague Close SE1
150 C5 Montague Place WC1E
150 C4 Montague Street WC1B
151 J5 Montague Street EC1A
149 H5 Montagu Mansions W1U
149 H5 Montagu Mews North W1H
149 H6 Montagu Mews South W1H
149 H5 Montagu Mews West W1H
149 H5 Montagu Place W1H
149 H5 Montagu Row W1U
149 H5 Montagu Square W1H
149 H6 Montagu Street W1H
154 F8 Montford Place SE11
156 D1 Monthope Road E1
153 G4 Montpelier Mews SW7
153 G4 Montpelier Place SW7
157 G3 Montpelier Place E1
153 G3 Montpelier Square SW7
153 G3 Montpelier Street SW7

162 Montpelier Terrace - Rich Street

152 F3 Montpelier Terrace SW7
152 F3 Montpelier Walk SW7
150 E7 Montreal Place WC2B
153 K3 Montrose Place SW1X
151 M7 Monument Street EC3R
157 G4 Monza Street E1W
157 G7 Moodkee Street SE16
153 H5 Moore Street SW3
151 L5 Moorfields EC2M
151 L5 Moorfields Highwalk EC2Y
151 L6 Moorgate EC2R
151 L5 Moorgate Place * EC2R
151 L5 Moor Lane EC2Y
150 C7 Moor Street W1D
151 K2 Mora Street EC1V
157 H1 Morecambe Close E1
155 K6 Morecambe Street SE17
151 H2 Moreland Street EC1V
156 A5 More London Place SE1
156 A5 More London Riverside SE1
154 A6 Moreton Place SW1V
154 A7 Moreton Street SW1V
154 A6 Moreton Terrace SW1V
154 A7 Moreton Terrace Mews South SW1V
156 A5 Morgans Lane SE1
155 G3 Morley Street SE1
149 M1 Mornington Crescent NW1
149 L1 Mornington Place NW1
156 A7 Morocco Street SE1
153 M5 Morpeth Terrace SW1P
155 G7 Morrells Yard SE11
156 F3 Morris Street E1
148 A2 Morshead Road W9
149 L5 Mortimer Street W1B
152 B6 Morton Mews SW5
154 F4 Morton Place SE1
150 B5 Morwell Street W1T
148 B7 Moscow Place W2
148 A7 Moscow Road W2
156 D1 Moss Close E1
153 G5 Mossop Street SW3
153 J4 Motcomb Street SW1X
156 D2 Mountford Street E1
151 J3 Mount Mills EC1V
150 F4 Mount Pleasant WC1X
149 K8 Mount Row W1K
149 J8 Mount Street W1K
156 E1 Mount Terrace E1
149 J5 Moxon Street W1U
156 D2 Mulberry Street E1
152 E8 Mulberry Walk SW3
148 F4 Mulready Street NW8
151 K6 Mumford Court EC2V
151 M2 Mundy Street N1
149 L3 Munster Square NW1
155 K5 Munton Road SE17
154 F3 Murphy Street SE1
151 K1 Murray Grove N1
157 G2 Musbury Street E1
156 B4 Muscovy Street EC3N
150 D5 Museum Street WC1A
151 G2 Myddelton Passage EC1R
151 G2 Myddelton Square EC1R
151 G2 Myddelton Street EC1R
151 G1 Mylne Street EC1R
156 E2 Myrdle Street E1
151 M1 Myrtle Street N1
151 M1 Myrtle Walk N1

N

150 F2 Naoroji Street WC1X
151 K1 Napier Grove N1
157 K4 Narrow Street E14
149 L2 Nash Street NW1
149 M5 Nassau Street W1W
156 C2 Nathaniel Close E1
150 C6 Neal Street WC2H
150 C6 Neal Yard WC2H
155 M8 Neate Street SE5
153 M5 Neathouse Place SW1V
156 C7 Neckinger SE1
156 C8 Neckinger Estate SE16
156 C7 Neckinger Street SE1
157 H7 Needleman Street SE16
150 C6 Neils Yard * WC2H
148 A1 Nelson Close NW6
151 H1 Nelson Place N1
155 H2 Nelson Square SE1
156 F2 Nelson Street E1
151 H1 Nelson Terrace EC1V
157 G7 Neptune Street SE16
156 D4 Nesham Street E1W
154 B8 Ness Street SE16
152 D8 Netherton Grove SW10
149 M2 Netley Street NW1
152 A6 Nevern Place SW5
152 A6 Nevern Square SW5
152 E6 Neville Street SW7
152 E6 Neville Terrace * SW7
156 F1 Newark Street E1
149 L7 New Bond Street W1J
151 H6 New Bridge Street EC4M
151 M5 New Broad Street EC2M
150 A6 Newburgh Street W1F
149 M7 New Burlington Mews W1S
149 M7 New Burlington Place W1S
149 M7 New Burlington Street W1S
154 F7 Newburn Street SE11
151 J5 Newbury Street EC1A
151 H6 Newcastle Close EC4M
148 E5 Newcastle Place W2
151 G3 Newcastle Row EC1R
149 K5 New Cavendish Street W1U
151 J6 New Change EC4M
151 H2 New Charles Street EC1V
152 A1 Newcombe Street * W8
155 L2 Newcomen Street SE1
150 C6 New Compton Street * WC2H
150 F7 New Court * WC2R
148 F1 Newcourt Street NW8
157 G5 New Crane Place E1W
157 L3 Newell Street E14
151 G6 New Fetter Lane EC4A
151 H6 Newgate Street EC1A
155 J1 New Globe Walk SE1
156 B2 New Goulston Street E1
156 A7 Newham's Row SE1
155 H6 Newington Butts SE11
155 J4 Newington Causeway SE1
155 K5 New Kent Road SE1
157 G4 Newlands Quay E1W
156 B3 New London Street * EC3R
150 F5 Newman's Row WC2A
150 A5 Newman Street W1T
154 F4 Newnham Terrace SE1
151 M3 New North Place EC2A
151 L1 New North Road N1
150 E4 New North Street WC1N
150 D5 New Oxford Street WC1A
156 E7 New Place Square SE16
150 C7 Newport Court W1D
150 C7 Newport Place * W1D
154 E6 Newport Street SE11
149 H6 New Quebec Street W1H
156 E2 New Road E1
150 C7 New Row WC2N
154 D7 New Spring Gardens Walk * SE11
150 F6 New Square WC2A
156 A2 New Street EC2M
151 G6 New Street EC1A
151 G6 New Street Square EC4A
148 A6 Newton Road W2
150 D5 Newton Street WC2B
151 L5 New Union Street EC2Y
151 L7 Nicholas Lane EC4N
155 H2 Nicholson Street SE1
155 G5 Nightingale Mews SE11
152 D8 Nightingale Place SW10
151 J2 Nile Street N1
154 C8 Nine Elms Lane SW8
151 K6 Noble Street EC2V
150 A6 Noel Street W1F
157 L2 Norbiton Road E14
148 F6 Norfolk Crescent W2
148 E6 Norfolk Place W2
154 E5 Norfolk Row SE1
148 E6 Norfolk Square W2
148 E6 Norfolk Square Mews W2
151 J3 Norman Street EC1V
150 B8 Norris Street SW1Y
151 G3 Northampton Road EC1R
151 G3 Northampton Row * EC1R
151 H2 Northampton Square EC1V
149 J7 North Audley Street W1K
148 F2 North Bank NW8
151 H3 Northburgh Street EC1V
149 G7 North Carriage Drive W2
150 B4 North Crescent W1T
150 E1 Northdown Street N1
157 K4 Northey Street E14
150 A2 North Gower Street NW1
150 E4 Northington Street WC1N
150 F4 North Mews WC1N
149 G6 North Rise * W2
149 J7 North Row W1K
156 C3 North Tenter Street E1
152 F5 North Terrace SW3
156 B3 Northumberland Alley * EC3N
154 D1 Northumberland Avenue WC2N
148 A6 Northumberland Place W2
154 C1 Northumberland Street WC2N
148 E5 North Wharf Road W2
148 E3 Northwick Close NW8
148 D3 Northwick Terrace NW8
157 K7 Norway Gate SE16
157 L3 Norway Place E14
151 G5 Norwich Street EC4A
150 D6 Nottingham Court * WC2H
149 J4 Nottingham Place W1U
149 J4 Nottingham Street W1U
149 J4 Nottingham Terrace NW1
148 A8 Notting Hill Gate W8
148 D1 Nugent Terrace NW8
155 L6 Nursery Row SE17
149 G6 Nutford Place W2

O

155 G5 Oakden Street SE11
155 G4 Oakey Lane SE1
152 C8 Oakfield Street SW10
148 A3 Oakington Road W9
157 L3 Oak Lane E14
151 H1 Oakley Crescent * EC1V
153 G8 Oakley Gardens SW3
150 A1 Oakley Square NW1
152 F8 Oakley Street SW3
148 F2 Oak Tree Road NW8
151 K5 Oat Lane EC2V
152 A2 Observatory Gardens W8
152 E4 Observatory Road SW7
155 J6 Occupation Road SE17
157 J1 Ocean Estate E1
157 J1 Ocean Street E1
151 M5 Octagon Arcade * EC2M
157 L7 Odessa Street SE16
150 D6 Odhams Walk * WC2H
149 M4 Ogle Street W1W
151 H6 Old Bailey EC4M
153 J3 Old Barrack Yard SW1X
149 M8 Old Bond Street W1S
151 M5 Old Broad Street EC2M
152 A7 Old Brompton Road SW5
150 F6 Old Buildings WC2A
149 M7 Old Burlington Street W1S
149 J4 Oldbury Place W1U
156 C2 Old Castle Street E1
149 L6 Old Cavendish Street W1G
157 H2 Old Church Road E1
152 F8 Old Church Street SW3
150 B7 Old Compton Street W1D
152 B3 Old Court Place W8
151 J7 Old Fish Street Hill * EC4V
151 H6 Old Fleet Lane EC4M
150 D4 Old Gloucester Street WC1N
156 C7 Old Jamaica Road SE16
151 L6 Old Jewry * EC2R
152 A6 Old Manor Yard SW5
149 G5 Old Marylebone Road NW1
151 G6 Old Mitre Court * EC4Y
156 D1 Old Montague Street E1
150 E5 Old North Street * WC1X
154 E5 Old Paradise Street SE11
153 K2 Old Park Lane W1J
153 B4 Old Pye Street SW1P
149 H6 Old Quebec Street W1H
154 B3 Old Queen Street SW1H
151 H6 Old Seacoal Lane EC4M
150 F5 Old Square WC2A
151 K3 Old Street EC1V
157 G1 O'Leary Square E1
151 L3 Oliver's Yard EC1Y
155 J8 Olney Road SE17
155 K2 O'Meara Street SE1
150 D1 Omega Place N1
157 K8 Onega Gate SE16
152 A8 Ongar Road SW6
152 E5 Onslow Crescent SW7
152 E6 Onslow Gardens SW7
152 E6 Onslow Mews East SW7
152 E6 Onslow Mews West SW7
152 E6 Onslow Square SW7
151 G4 Onslow Street EC1M
155 J4 Ontario Street SE1
157 M4 Ontario Way E14
155 H6 Opal Street SE11
157 G8 Orange Place SE16
150 C8 Orange Street WC2H
156 D5 Orange Street E1W
152 F6 Oratory Lane * SW3
155 L6 Orb Street SE17
148 E4 Orchardson Street NW8
149 J6 Orchard Street W1H
150 E4 Orde Hall Street * WC1N
155 H5 Orient Street SE11
148 B8 Orme Court W2
148 B8 Orme Court Mews * W2
148 B8 Orme Lane W2
148 B8 Orme Square W2
148 B8 Orme Square Gate W8
150 D4 Ormond Close WC1N
153 H7 Ormonde Gate SW3
153 J6 Ormonde Place SW1W
154 A1 Ormond Yard SW1Y
148 C6 Orsett Mews W2
154 E6 Orsett Street SE11
148 C6 Orsett Terrace W2
156 D5 Orton Street E1W
154 B6 Osbert Street SW1P
156 C2 Osborn Street E1
149 L3 Osnaburgh Street NW1
149 L3 Osnaburgh Terrace NW1
148 A7 Ossington Close * W2
148 A7 Ossington Street W2
150 B1 Ossulston Street NW1
152 C5 Osten Mews SW7
155 H5 Oswin Street SE11
155 H6 Othello Close SE11
155 H8 Otto Street SE17
149 H3 Outer Circle NW1
156 A2 Outwich Street * EC3A
154 E7 Oval Way SE11
153 G4 Ovington Gardens SW3
153 G4 Ovington Mews SW3
153 G4 Ovington Square SW3
153 G5 Ovington Street SW3
151 H1 Owen's Row EC1V
151 G1 Owen Street EC1V
150 B8 Oxendon Street * W1D
151 L7 Oxford Court EC4N
148 F6 Oxford Square W2
149 J7 Oxford Street W1K
150 B6 Oxford Street W1F
157 G3 Oyster Row E1

P

156 F3 Pace Place E1
148 E5 Paddington Green W2
149 J5 Paddington Street W1U
157 L5 Pageant Crescent SE16
154 C5 Page Street SW1P
155 M5 Page's Walk SE1
151 H1 Paget Street EC1V
150 F3 Pakenham Street WC1X
152 B2 Palace Avenue W8
148 B8 Palace Court W2
152 A1 Palace Garden Mews W8
152 A1 Palace Gardens Terrace W8
148 A8 Palace Gardens Terrace W11
152 C3 Palace Gate W8
152 B2 Palace Green W8
153 M4 Palace Place SW1E
153 M4 Palace Street SW1E
149 G3 Palgrave Gardens NW1
154 B1 Pall Mall SW1Y
154 B1 Pall Mall East SW1Y
154 A1 Pall Mall Place SW1Y
154 B4 Palmer Street SW1H
151 K6 Pancras Lane EC4N
150 C1 Pancras Road NW1
150 B8 Panton Street SW1Y
156 E7 Paradise Street SE16
153 H8 Paradise Walk SW3
155 M5 Paragon Mews SE17
155 L4 Pardoner Street SE1
151 J3 Pardon Street EC1V
156 E2 Parfett Street E1
155 G1 Paris Garden SE1
156 F8 Park Approach SE16
153 G3 Park Close * SW7
149 L4 Park Crescent W1B
149 L4 Park Crescent Mews East W1B
149 K4 Park Crescent Mews West W1G
150 D6 Parker Mews * WC2B
156 C7 Parkers Row SE1
150 D6 Parker Street WC2B
149 H7 Park Lane W1H
149 J8 Park Lane W1J
153 M1 Park Place SW1A
148 D4 Park Place Villas W2
149 H3 Park Road NW1
149 K3 Park Square East NW1
149 K3 Park Square Mews NW1
149 K3 Park Square West NW1
149 G7 Park Steps * W2
149 J8 Park Street W1K
155 J1 Park Street SE1
152 D8 Park Walk SW10
149 G6 Park West W2
149 G6 Park West Place W2
156 B1 Parliament Court * E1
154 C3 Parliament Square SW1P
154 D2 Parliament Street SW1A
157 K2 Parnham Street E14
154 D8 Parry Street SW8
155 J7 Pasley Close SE17
153 J6 Passmore Street SW1W
155 H5 Pastor Street SE11
151 J6 Paternoster Row EC4M
151 J6 Paternoster Square EC4M
152 A4 Pater Street W8
157 L5 Pattina Walk SE16
151 M3 Paul Street EC2A
152 E8 Paultons Square SW3
152 E8 Paultons Street SW3
148 F2 Paveley Street NW8
153 H3 Pavilion Road SW1X
153 H4 Pavilion Street SW1X
153 L8 Paxton Terrace SW1V
153 J7 Peabody Avenue SW1V
153 L7 Peabody Close SW1V
151 G3 Peabody Estate * EC1R
155 G3 Peabody Estate * SE1
155 K1 Peabody Estate * SE1
151 K3 Peabody Estate * EC1Y
151 G4 Peabody Terrace * EC1R
155 J6 Peacock Street SE17
155 J6 Peacock Yard SE17
156 F5 Pearl Street E1W
155 G3 Pearman Street SE1
155 G3 Pear Place SE1
151 G3 Pear Tree Court EC1R
157 G4 Peartree Lane E1W
151 J3 Peartree Street EC1V
156 C1 Pecks Yard * E1
152 A2 Peel Passage * W8
151 K2 Peerless Street EC1V
154 F8 Pegasus Place SE11
152 F6 Pelham Crescent SW7
152 F5 Pelham Place SW7
152 F5 Pelham Street SW7
155 K8 Pelier Street SE17
157 M3 Pelling Street E14
151 G6 Pemberton Row EC4A
148 A8 Pembridge Gardens W2
148 A7 Pembridge Place W2
148 A7 Pembridge Square W2
153 J3 Pembroke Close SW1X
156 F5 Penang Street E1W
148 F5 Penfold Place W2
148 F4 Penfold Street NW8
152 B5 Pennant Mews W8
156 E4 Pennington Street E1W
155 J7 Penrose Grove SE17
155 J7 Penrose Street SE17
150 F1 Penton Grove N1
155 J7 Penton Place SE17
150 E2 Penton Rise WC1X
150 F1 Penton Street N1
150 F1 Pentonville Road N1
152 A7 Penywern Road SW5
155 J2 Pepper Street SE1
156 B4 Pepys Street EC3N
151 J2 Percival Street EC1V
150 B5 Percy Mews W1T
150 B5 Percy Street W1T
154 B4 Perkin's Rents SW1P
155 K1 Perkins Square SE1
156 E7 Perryn Road SE16
152 C4 Petersham Lane SW7
152 C4 Petersham Mews SW7
152 C4 Petersham Place SW7
151 J7 Peter's Hill EC4V
150 B7 Peter Street W1F
149 L3 Peto Place NW1
156 B2 Petticoat Lane E1
156 B2 Petticoat Square E1
156 B2 Petticoat Tower * E1
154 A3 Petty France SW1H
156 B4 Petty Wales EC3R
153 G8 Petyward SW3
155 L7 Phelp Street SE17
153 G8 Phene Street SW3
156 D3 Philchurch Place E1
151 M7 Philpot Lane EC3M
156 F2 Philpot Street E1
153 L5 Phipp's Mews SW1W
151 M3 Phipp Street EC2A
150 F3 Phoenix Place WC1X
150 B2 Phoenix Road NW1
150 C6 Phoenix Street WC2H
156 C7 Phoenix Wharf Road SE1
153 M1 Piccadilly W1J
153 M1 Piccadilly Arcade * W1J
150 B8 Piccadilly Circus W1J
151 J2 Pickard Street EC1V
154 A2 Pickering Place * SW1Y
151 J1 Pickfords Wharf * N1
155 J3 Pickwick Street SE1
149 K6 Picton Place W1H
156 E6 Pier Head E1W
157 M3 Pigott Street E14
155 L3 Pilgrimage Street SE1
151 H6 Pilgrim Street * EC4V
155 K6 Pilton Place SE17
153 K6 Pimlico Road SW1W
156 E3 Pinchin & Johnsons Yard E1
156 D3 Pinchin Street E1
151 M4 Pindar Street EC2A
148 B3 Pindock Mews W9
154 A4 Pine Apple Court * SW1E
157 M3 Pinefield Close E14
151 G3 Pine Street EC1R
151 M2 Pitfield Street N1
157 J3 Pitsea Place E1
157 J3 Pitsea Street E1
153 K2 Pitt's Head Mews W1K
152 A3 Pitt Street W8
157 L2 Pixley Street E14
155 L3 Plantain Place SE1
156 A3 Plantation Lane EC3M
151 L3 Platina Street EC2A
150 B1 Platt Street NW1
155 K2 Playhouse Court SE1
151 H7 Playhouse Yard EC4V
151 K2 Pleydell Estate EC1V
151 G6 Pleydell Street EC4Y
151 G6 Plough Place EC4A
156 C2 Plough Street * E1
157 K8 Plover Way SE16
156 D2 Plumbers Row E1
151 G5 Plumtree Court EC4A
148 F4 Plympton Place * NW8
148 F4 Plympton Street NW8
155 H3 Pocock Street SE1
150 A6 Poland Street W1F
149 L7 Pollen Street W1S
148 E3 Pollitt Drive NW8
155 G5 Polperro Mews SE11
150 B1 Polygon Road NW1
156 C2 Pomell Way E1
152 F6 Pond Place SW3
156 E3 Ponler Street E1
154 C6 Ponsonby Place SW1P
154 C6 Ponsonby Terrace SW1P
153 H4 Pont Street SW1X
153 G4 Pont Street Mews SW3
150 F4 Pooles Buildings WC1X
157 H6 Poolmans Street SE16
157 G3 Poonah Street E1
156 B7 Pope Street SE1
148 B7 Poplar Place W2
151 H6 Poppins Court EC4A
148 C7 Porchester Garden Mews * W2
148 B7 Porchester Gardens W2
148 C8 Porchester Gate * W2
149 G6 Porchester Place W2
148 B6 Porchester Road W2
148 B6 Porchester Square W2
148 B6 Porchester Square Mews W2
148 C7 Porchester Terrace W2
148 C6 Porchester Terrace North W2
155 L3 Porlock Street SE1
148 C8 Portchester Gate W2
149 H4 Porter Street W1U
155 K1 Porter Street SE1
156 F4 Porters Walk * E1W
148 D5 Porteus Road W2
150 A6 Portland Mews W1F
149 L5 Portland Place W1G
156 E5 Portland Square E1W
155 L7 Portland Street SE17
149 J6 Portman Close W1H
149 G4 Portman Gate NW8
149 J6 Portman Mews South W1H
149 J6 Portman Square W1H
149 J6 Portman Street W1H
149 H6 Portman Towers W1H
150 F4 Portpool Lane WC1X
149 G6 Portsea Mews W2
149 G6 Portsea Place W2
150 E6 Portsmouth Street WC2A
156 B3 Portsoken Street EC3N
150 E6 Portugal Street WC2A
155 M4 Potier Street SE1
156 B6 Potters Fields SE1
156 E7 Pottery Street SE16
151 L6 Poultry EC2R
150 D4 Powis Place WC1N
148 E6 Praed Mews W2
148 E6 Praed Street W2
154 E5 Pratt Walk SE11
156 C3 Prescot Street E1
156 E5 Presidents Drive E1W
151 J2 President Street * EC1V
155 M5 Preston Close SE1
151 K1 Prestwood Street * N1
155 H1 Price's Street SE1
150 F2 Prideaux Place WC1X
151 G7 Primrose Hill EC4Y
156 A1 Primrose Street EC2A
148 F1 Prince Albert Road NW8
152 D4 Prince Consort Road SW7
156 C1 Princelet Street E1
152 F3 Prince of Wales Gate SW7
149 M2 Prince of Wales Passage * NW1
152 C3 Prince of Wales Terrace W8
149 M2 Prince Regent Mews NW1
150 A8 Princes Arcade W1J
152 E4 Princes Gardens SW7
152 F3 Prince's Gate SW7
152 E3 Princes Gate Court SW7
152 E4 Princes Gate Mews SW7
148 A7 Prince's Mews W2
157 H5 Princes Riverside Road SE16
148 E4 Princess Louise Close W2
148 B7 Prince's Square W2
155 H4 Princess Street SE1
149 L6 Princes Street W1S
151 L6 Prince's Street EC2R
150 E5 Princeton Street WC1R
150 F5 Printers Inn Court EC4A
155 M4 Prioress Street SE1
151 H6 Priory Court * EC4V
152 D7 Priory Walk SW10
156 D8 Priter Road SE16
150 E5 Procter Street WC1R
157 G5 Prospect Place E1W
156 F7 Prospect Street SE16
149 J7 Providence Court W1K
155 M2 Providence Square SE1
151 L1 Provost Estate N1
151 L2 Provost Street EC1V
156 F5 Prusom Street E1W
151 M7 Pudding Lane EC3R
151 H7 Puddle Dock EC4V
156 C1 Puma Court E1
150 F7 Pump Court * EC4Y
156 D3 Pump House Mews E1
156 B7 Purbrook Street SE1
151 M1 Purcell Street N1

Q

150 A8 Quadrant Arcade W1B
150 F5 Quality Court EC4A
149 H6 Quebec Mews W1H
157 J7 Quebec Way SE16
149 L5 Queen Anne Mews W1G
154 B3 Queen Anne's Gate SW1H
149 K5 Queen Anne Street W1G
156 F4 Queen Anne Terrace * E1W
156 C6 Queen Elizabeth Street SE1
151 K7 Queenhithe EC4V
153 J2 Queen Mother Gate W2
152 D5 Queensberry Mews West * SW7
152 E5 Queensberry Place SW7
152 E5 Queensberry Way * SW7
148 C7 Queensborough Mews * W2
148 C7 Queensborough Passage W2
148 C7 Queensborough Studios W2
148 C7 Queensborough Terrace W2
152 E7 Queen's Elm Square SW3
148 C7 Queen's Gardens W2
152 D3 Queen's Gate SW7
152 D4 Queen's Gate Gardens SW7
152 D3 Queen's Gate Mews SW7
152 D4 Queen's Gate Place SW7
152 D5 Queen's Gate Place Mews SW7
152 D4 Queen's Gate Terrace SW7
148 B7 Queen's Mews W2
150 D4 Queen Square WC1N
155 K8 Queens Row SE17
151 K7 Queen Street EC4N
153 L1 Queen Street W1J
151 K8 Queen Street Place EC4R
148 B6 Queensway W2
150 A4 Queen's Yard W1T
151 J7 Queen Victoria Street EC4V
156 F4 Queen Victoria Terrace * E1W
151 H1 Quick Street N1
155 J2 Quilp Street SE1

R

152 A1 Rabbit Row * W8
157 K2 Raby Street E14
156 B8 Radcliffe Road SE1
155 G7 Radcot Street SE11
157 J6 Radley Court SE16
152 A5 Radley Mews W8
148 E6 Radnor Mews W2
148 F6 Radnor Place W2
151 K3 Radnor Street EC1V
153 G7 Radnor Walk SW3
155 L1 Railway Approach SE1
157 G6 Railway Avenue SE16
150 D1 Railway Street N1
156 F5 Raine Street E1W
148 F6 Rainsford Street W2
153 H7 Ralston Street SW3
149 M6 Ramillies Place W1F
149 M6 Ramillies Street W1F
156 E2 Rampart Street * E1
154 B6 Rampayne Street SW1V
154 E6 Randall Road SE11
154 E6 Randall Row SE11
148 C2 Randolph Avenue W9
148 C3 Randolph Crescent W9
148 B1 Randolph Gardens NW6
148 D4 Randolph Mews W9
148 C4 Randolph Road W9
153 K7 Ranelagh Grove SW1W
154 A7 Ranelagh Road SW1V
156 B3 Rangoon Street * EC3N
148 F4 Ranston Street NW8
153 G3 Raphael Street SW7
157 J3 Ratcliffe Cross Street E1
157 J3 Ratcliffe Lane E14
150 B4 Rathbone Place W1T
150 A5 Rathbone Street W1T
156 F1 Raven Row E1
155 G7 Ravensdon Street SE11
151 M3 Ravey Street EC2A
153 G5 Rawlings Street SW3
151 H2 Rawstorne Place * EC1V
151 H2 Rawstorne Street EC1V
151 G4 Ray Street EC1R
151 G4 Ray Street Bridge * EC1R
156 F5 Reardon Path E1W
156 F5 Reardon Street E1W
157 J1 Rectory Square E1
152 F8 Red Anchor Close * SW3
148 B6 Redan Place W2
153 G8 Redburn Street SW3
157 G4 Redcastle Close E1
152 B7 Redcliffe Close SW5
152 B7 Redcliffe Gardens SW10
152 C7 Redcliffe Mews SW10
152 C8 Redcliffe Place SW10
152 C7 Redcliffe Road SW10
152 C7 Redcliffe Square SW10
152 B8 Redcliffe Street SW10
155 K2 Redcross Way SE1
148 A7 Rede Place W2
153 G8 Redesdale Street SW3
152 A5 Redfield Lane SW5
149 L2 Redhill Street NW1
155 K8 Red Lion Close SE17
151 G6 Red Lion Court EC4A
155 K8 Red Lion Row SE17
150 E5 Red Lion Square WC1N
150 E5 Red Lion Street WC1R
153 K1 Red Lion Yard * W1K
157 H1 Redman's Road E1
156 D5 Redmead Lane * E1W
149 J7 Red Place W1K
157 K8 Redriff Road SE16
157 K6 Redwood Close SE16
152 E5 Reece Mews SW7
155 G6 Reedworth Street SE11
149 J8 Reeves Mews W1K
156 E1 Regal Close E1
151 M1 Regan Way N1
154 B5 Regency Place * SW1P
154 B5 Regency Street SW1P
152 E7 Regency Terrace * SW7
148 D1 Regents Mews NW8
150 D2 Regent Square WC1H
149 M7 Regent Street W1S
150 B8 Regent Street SW1Y
150 A3 Regnart Buildings NW1
153 G4 Relton Mews SW7
153 J6 Rembrandt Close SW1W
236 E5 Rembrandt Close E14
151 J1 Remington Street N1
150 E6 Remnant Street WC2B
157 G7 Renforth Street SE16
155 H5 Renfrew Road SE11
151 H8 Rennie Street SE1
155 M5 Rephidim Street SE1
157 K2 Repton Street E14
152 C3 Reston Place SW7
156 F4 Reunion Row E1W
157 K7 Reveley Square SE16
149 J8 Rex Place W1K
157 K1 Rhodeswell Road E3
149 M4 Richardson's Mews W1T
153 G5 Richard's Place SW3
156 E3 Richard Street E1
150 E4 Richbell Place WC1N
150 B6 Richmond Buildings W1F
150 B6 Richmond Mews W1F
154 D2 Richmond Terrace SW1A
157 M3 Rich Street E14

Rickett Street - Trevor Square 163

152 A8 Rickett Street SW6
150 B4 Ridgmount Gardens WC1E
150 B4 Ridgmount Street WC1E
149 M5 Riding House Street W1W
156 B7 Riley Road SE1
155 J2 Risborough Street SE1
157 G7 Risdon Street SE16
150 F1 Risinghill Street N1
151 G2 River Street EC1R
149 J6 Robert Adam Street W1H
148 D3 Robert Close W9
156 J6 Robert Dashwood Way SE17
153 J4 Roberts Mews * SW1X
151 G3 Robert's Place * EC1R
149 L2 Robert Street NW1
150 D8 Robert Street WC2N
153 G8 Robinson Street SW3
154 A5 Rochester Row SW1P
154 B5 Rochester Street SW1P
155 L1 Rochester Walk * SE1
155 J4 Rockingham Street SE1
151 H1 Rocliffe Street N1
156 D5 Roding Mews E1W
149 H5 Rodmarton Street W1U
155 K5 Rodney Place SE1
155 K5 Rodney Road SE17
150 E4 Roger Street WC1N
152 D6 Roland Gardens SW7
157 H1 Roland Mews E1
155 L7 Roland Way SE17
152 D6 Roland Way SW10
151 G6 Rolls Buildings EC4A
156 E2 Romford Street E1
150 B7 Romilly Street W1D
154 C5 Romney Street SW1P
151 M7 Rood Lane EC3M
157 K7 Ropemaker Road SE16
157 L4 Ropemaker's Fields E14
151 L4 Ropemaker Street EC2Y
156 B7 Roper Lane SE1
157 K8 Rope Street SE16
156 E2 Ropewalk Gardens * E1
152 D6 Rosary Gardens SW7
151 K3 Roscoe Street EC1Y
155 K1 Rose Alley SE1
150 F4 Rosebery Avenue EC1R
150 F3 Rosebery Court EC1R
156 C2 Rose Court E1
154 A1 Rose & Crown Yard * SW1Y
153 G6 Rosemoor Street SW3
150 C7 Rose Street WC2E
150 G3 Rosoman Place EC1R
151 G3 Rosoman Street EC1R
149 G4 Rossmore Close * NW8
149 G3 Rossmore Road NW8
155 H4 Rotary Street SE1
155 H2 Rotherham Walk * SE1
156 F6 Rotherhithe Street * SE16
155 M4 Rothsay Street SE1
155 G2 Roupell Street SE1
148 B4 Rowington Close W2
152 A8 Roxby Place SW6
149 M8 Royal Arcade W1S
153 H6 Royal Avenue SW3
151 L6 Royal Court EC3V
153 J7 Royal Hospital Road SW3
156 C4 Royal Mint Place E1
156 C4 Royal Mint Street EC3N
156 A7 Royal Oak Yard SE1
154 B1 Royal Opera Arcade * SW1Y
155 H8 Royal Road SE17
154 E4 Royal Street SE1
157 L4 Roy Square E14
154 D8 Rudolf Place SW8
148 A1 Rudolph Road NW6
151 M2 Rufus Street N1
150 E4 Rugby Street WC1N
157 M3 Rugg Street E14
156 F4 Rum Close E1W
157 G7 Rupack Street SE16
150 B7 Rupert Court W1D
150 B7 Rupert Street WC2H
155 H3 Rushworth Street SE1
154 A2 Russell Court SW1A
150 C4 Russell Square WC1E
150 D7 Russell Street WC2E
157 K6 Russia Dock Road SE16
151 K6 Russia Row EC2V
154 B5 Rutherford Street SW1P
152 F3 Rutland Court SW7
153 G3 Rutland Gardens SW7
152 F3 Rutland Gate SW7
152 F3 Rutland Gate Mews * SW7
152 F4 Rutland Mews South * SW7
151 J4 Rutland Place * EC1M
152 F4 Rutland Street SW7
155 H8 Rutley Close SE17
154 A1 Ryder Street SW1Y
153 H3 Rysbrack Street SW3

S

150 A8 Sackville Street W1J
151 G5 Saffron Hill EC1N
151 G4 Saffron Street EC1M
156 F3 Sage Street E1
150 E2 Sage Way WC1X
154 F5 Sail Street SE11
151 L3 St Agnes Well EC1Y
152 B4 St Albans Grove W8
148 E4 St Alban's Mews W2
150 B8 St Alban's Street SW1Y
151 K5 St Alphage Garden EC2Y
151 K5 St Alphage Highwalk EC2Y
151 H7 St Andrew's Hill EC4V
149 L3 St Andrew's Place NW1
151 G5 St Andrew Street EC1N
150 B6 St Annes Court W1F
157 L3 St Anne's Passage E14
157 M3 St Anne's Row E14
157 M3 St Anne Street E14
154 C4 St Ann's Street SW1P
149 K7 St Anselm's Place W1K
156 D5 St Anthony's Close E1W
153 K6 St Barnabas Street SW1W
156 B2 St Botolph Street EC3A
151 G6 St Bride Street EC4A
153 G5 St Catherines Mews SW3
150 D1 St Chad's Place WC1X
150 D2 St Chad's Street WC1H
149 K6 St Christopher's Place W1U
156 B3 St Clare Street EC3N
150 E6 St Clement's Lane WC2A
151 G4 St Cross Street EC1N
156 A4 St Dunstan's Hill * EC3R
151 M7 St Dunstan's Lane * EC3R
157 J7 St Elmos Road SE16
155 H3 St George's Circus SE1
153 M6 St George's Drive SW1V
156 D4 St George's Estate E1
149 G7 St George's Fields W2
151 M7 St George's Lane * EC3R
155 H4 St George's Road SE1
151 H6 St Georges's Court * EC4M
154 B7 St George's Square SW1V
154 B7 St George's Square Mews SW1V
149 L7 St George Street W1S
151 K5 St Giles Churchyard * EC2Y
150 C6 St Giles Circus W1D
150 C6 St Giles Court WC2H
150 C6 St Giles High Street WC2H
150 C6 St Giles Passage WC2H
150 F2 St Helena Street * WC1X
156 A2 St Helen's Place EC3N
154 A4 St James' Court * SW1E
154 A1 St James's Chambers * SW1Y
154 A4 St James's Court SW1E
149 M2 St James's Gardens * NW1
153 M1 St James's Place SW1A
156 D7 St James's Road SE16
154 B1 St James's Square SW1Y
153 M1 St James's Street SW1A
151 H3 St James Walk EC1R
151 H4 St John's Lane EC1M
151 H4 St John's Place EC1M
151 H4 St John's Square EC1M
151 H2 St John Street EC1V
152 B5 St Johns Villas W8
148 F1 St John's Wood High Street NW8
148 E3 St John's Wood Road NW8
156 C5 St Katharine's Way EC3N
153 H7 St Leonards Terrace SW3
153 G8 St Loo Avenue SW3
151 L3 St Luke's Estate EC1V
151 K3 St Lukes's Close EC1V
152 F6 St Luke's Street SW3
152 B4 St Margarets Lane W8
154 D3 St Margaret Street SW1P
156 C3 St Mark Street E1
150 C7 St Martin's Court WC2H
150 C7 St Martin's Lane WC2N
151 J6 St Martin's Le Grand EC1A
150 C8 St Martin's Place WC2H
150 C8 St Martin's Street * WC2H
151 M7 St Mary At Hill EC3R
156 A3 St Mary Axe EC3A
157 G6 St Marychurch Street SE16
156 C4 St Mary Graces Court * EC3N
155 G5 St Marys Gardens SE11
152 B4 St Marys Gate W8
148 D4 St Mary's Mansions W2
156 D2 St Mary's Path E1
152 B4 St Marys Place W8
148 E5 St Mary's Square W2
148 D4 St Mary's Terrace W2
155 G5 St Marys Walk SE11
154 B4 St Matthew Street SW1P
151 M6 St Michael's Alley EC3V
148 F6 St Michael's Street W2
151 L6 St Mildred's Court * EC2R
154 E7 St Oswald's Place SE11
154 C6 St Oswulf Street * SW1P
157 J5 St Paul's Avenue SE16
151 J6 St Paul's Church Yard EC4V
155 H7 St Pauls Terrace SE17
157 L1 St Paul's Way E14
148 B7 St Petersburgh Mews W2
148 B8 St Petersburgh Place W2
148 A3 St Peters Place W9
156 B7 St Saviour's Estate SE1
148 A5 St Stephen's Crescent * W2
148 A5 St Stephen's Gardens W2
148 A5 St Stephen's Mews W2
154 D3 St Stephen's Parade SW1A
152 C5 St Stephen's Walk SW7
151 L7 St Swithin's Lane EC4N
155 L2 St Thomas Street SE1
149 J5 St Vincent Street W1U
154 E6 Salamanca Place SE11
154 E6 Salamanca Street SE11
148 B7 Salem Road W2
148 F5 Sale Place W2
155 L5 Salisbury Close SE17
151 G6 Salisbury Court EC4Y
149 H4 Salisbury Place W1H
151 G6 Salisbury Square * EC4Y
148 F4 Salisbury Street NW8
157 K2 Salmon Lane E14
157 L2 Salmon Street E14
157 H5 Salter Road SE16
151 L7 Salters' Hall Court * EC4N
157 M4 Salter Street E14
155 L7 Saltwood Grove SE17
148 F4 Samford Street NW8
156 E5 Sampson Street E1W
154 F6 Sancroft Street SE11
155 K3 Sanctuary Street SE1
155 G2 Sandell Street SE1
155 L7 Sandford Row SE17
150 E5 Sandland Street WC1R
157 L6 Sandpiper Close SE16
150 C2 Sandwich Street WC1H
156 B1 Sandy's Row E1
151 H3 Sans Walk EC1R
154 F5 Saperton Walk SE11
150 E6 Sardinia Street WC2B
157 M4 Saunders Close * E14
154 F5 Saunders Street SE11
156 B3 Savage Gardens EC3N
149 M7 Savile Row W1S
150 D7 Savoy Court * WC2R
150 E7 Savoy Hill WC2R
150 D8 Savoy Place WC2N
150 E7 Savoy Row WC2R
150 E7 Savoy Steps * WC2R
150 E7 Savoy Street WC2R
150 E8 Savoy Way WC2R
155 J2 Sawyer Street SE1
150 A5 Scala Street W1T
156 E5 Scandrett Street E1W
156 C3 Scarborough Street E1
152 B4 Scarsdale Place * W8
152 A5 Scarsdale Villas W8
157 H3 Schoolhouse Lane E1
155 H2 Scoresby Street SE1
151 G3 Scotswood Street * EC1R
148 E2 Scott Ellis Gardens NW8
156 D7 Scott Lidgett Crescent SE16
155 J3 Scovell Crescent * SE1
155 J3 Scovell Road SE1
151 M3 Scrutton Street EC2A
150 D2 Seaford Street WC1H
157 L1 Seager Place E3
157 H2 Seagrave Close E1
152 A8 Seagrave Road SW6
155 L5 Searles Road SE1
155 G6 Seaton Close SE11
151 H2 Sebastian Street EC1V
154 F2 Secker Street SE1
155 M6 Sedan Way SE17
153 J5 Sedding Street SW1X
150 E3 Seddon Street WC1X
149 K6 Sedley Place W1K
156 B4 Seething Lane EC3N
151 H3 Sekforde Street EC1R
157 M1 Selsey Street E14
152 E7 Selwood Place SW7
152 E6 Selwood Terrace SW7
153 K6 Semley Place SW1W
148 B4 Senior Street W2
157 H2 Senrab Street E1
151 G6 Serjeant's Inn * EC4Y
150 F6 Serle Street WC2A
151 J7 Sermon Lane EC4V
153 H2 Serpentine Road W2
156 D2 Settles Street E1
150 C6 Seven Dials WC2H
156 C1 Seven Stars Yard E1
153 H3 Seville Street SW1X
148 A3 Sevington Street W9
151 J3 Seward Street EC1V
149 J6 Seymour Mews W1H
149 G5 Seymour Place W1H
149 G7 Seymour Street W2
152 C7 Seymour Walk SW10
156 C6 Shad Thames SE1
156 F3 Shadwell Gardens E1
157 G4 Shadwell Pierhead E1W
156 F3 Shadwell Place E1
150 C6 Shaftesbury Avenue WC2H
152 A5 Shaftesbury Mews * W8
151 J5 Shaftesbury Place * EC2Y
151 K1 Shaftesbury Street N1
153 H4 Shafto Mews SW1X
152 D8 Shalcomb Street SW10
156 A4 Shand Street SE1
155 H7 Sharsted Street SE17
150 B8 Shavers Place W1J
157 K2 Shaw Crescent E14
153 G7 Shawfield Street SW3
150 E6 Sheffield Street * WC2A
148 D5 Sheldon Square W2
157 M1 Shelmerdine Close E3
150 D6 Shelton Street * WC2H
151 K2 Shepherdess Place EC1V
151 K1 Shepherdess Walk N1
149 J7 Shepherds Place W1K
153 K2 Shepherd Street W1J
150 B6 Sheraton Street * W1F
151 L7 Sherborne Lane EC4N
156 F3 Sheridan Street E1
149 J4 Sherlock Mews W1U
149 G5 Sherwood Court W1H
150 A7 Sherwood Street W1D
149 G5 Shillibeer Place W1H
155 M3 Ship & Mermaid Row * SE1
151 M7 Ship Tavern Passage EC3V
157 K7 Shipwright Road SE16
155 M2 Shipwright Yard * SE1
148 A3 Shirland Road W9
151 G6 Shoe Lane EC4A
156 B1 Shoreditch High Street E1
156 C4 Shorter Street E1
150 D6 Shorts Gardens * WC2H
155 G2 Short Street SE1
157 L4 Shoulder of Mutton Alley E14
149 G5 Shouldham Street W1H
148 F4 Shroton Street NW1
150 D5 Sicilian Avenue * WC1A
149 H4 Siddons Lane NW1
154 F4 Sidford Place SE1
150 D3 Sidmouth Street WC1H
157 G2 Sidney Estate E1
151 H1 Sidney Grove EC1V
156 F2 Sidney Square E1
156 F2 Sidney Street E1
156 F1 Sidney Street Estate E1
151 L2 Silbury Street * N1
155 H3 Silex Street SE1
151 K4 Silk Street EC2Y
149 M1 Silverdale NW1
149 A7 Silver Place W1F
157 L5 Silver Walk SE16
155 K3 Silvester Street SE1
151 M3 Singer Street EC1V
152 E8 Sir Thomas More Estate SW3
151 K6 Sise Lane * EC4N
153 J6 Skinner Place * SW1W
151 K7 Skinners Lane EC4V
151 G3 Skinner Street EC1R
155 J8 Slade Walk SE17
150 C7 Slingsby Place WC2E
156 F8 Slippers Place SE16
153 G6 Sloane Avenue SW3
153 J6 Sloane Court East SW3
153 J7 Sloane Court West SW3
153 J6 Sloane Gardens SW1W
153 J6 Sloane Square SW1W
153 H3 Sloane Street SW1X
153 J5 Sloane Terrace SW1X
156 E2 Sly Street E1
148 D7 Smallbrook Mews W2
150 D6 Smart's Place WC1V
156 E5 Smeaton Street E1W
157 H5 Smith Close SE16
151 H5 Smithfield Street EC1A
150 B7 Smith's Court * W1D
154 C4 Smith Square SW1P
153 G7 Smith Street SW3
153 G7 Smith Terrace SW3
157 G1 Smithy Street E1
151 H5 Snow Hill EC1A
155 L2 Snowsfields SE1
150 B6 Soho Square W1D
150 B6 Soho Street W1D
156 F4 Solander Gardens E1
157 K7 Somerford Way SE16
150 B1 Somers Close * NW1
148 F6 Somers Crescent W2
156 B3 Somerset Street Little EC3N
155 L8 Sondes Street SE17
157 K4 Sophia Square SE16
155 L3 Southall Place SE1
150 D5 Southampton Place WC1A
150 D5 Southampton Row WC1B
150 D7 Southampton Street WC2E
149 K8 South Audley Street W1K
151 G8 South Bank SE1
152 C7 South Bolton Gardens SW10
153 H3 South Carriage Drive SW1X
152 F3 South Carriage Drive SW7
153 K5 South Eaton Place SW1W
152 B4 South End W8
152 B4 South End Row W8
151 E1 Southern Street N1
152 E5 South Kensington Station Arcade SW7
154 D8 South Lambeth Place SW8
154 D8 South Lambeth Road SW8
149 K7 South Molton Lane W1K
149 K6 South Molton Street W1K
152 E7 South Parade SW3
151 L5 South Place EC2M
151 L5 South Place Mews EC2M
149 G7 South Rise * W2
157 L8 South Sea Street SE16
150 F5 South Square WC1R
153 J1 South Street W1K
156 C3 South Tenter Street E1
152 F5 South Terrace SW7
155 K8 Southwark Bridge EC4R
155 J4 Southwark Bridge Road SE1
156 E7 Southwark Park Road SE16
155 H1 Southwark Street SE1
152 C5 Southwell Gardens SW7
148 E6 South Wharf Road W2
148 F6 Southwick Mews W2
148 F6 Southwick Place W2
148 F6 Southwick Street W2
148 F6 Southwick Yard * W2
156 F4 Sovereign Close E1W
157 K4 Sovereign Crescent SE16
151 G3 Spafield Street EC1R
151 G2 Spa Green Estate * EC1R
149 J5 Spanish Place * W1U
156 C8 Spa Road SE16
152 A6 Spear Mews SW5
155 L7 Spectrum Place SE17
156 C1 Spelman Street E1
157 L7 Spence Close SE16
154 A4 Spencer Place SW1P
151 H2 Spencer Street EC1V
154 A4 Spenser Street SW1E
157 J3 Spert Street E14
156 E5 Spirit Quay E1W
156 B1 Spital Square E1
156 C1 Spital Street E1
156 B1 Spital Yard * E1
153 G6 Sprimont Place SW3
154 C1 Spring Gardens SW1A
149 H5 Spring Mews * W1U
148 E6 Spring Street W2
156 D1 Spring Walk E1
155 L4 Spurgeon Street SE1
154 F3 Spur Road SE1
153 M3 Spur Road SW1A
148 E2 Squire Gardens NW8
154 F7 Stables Way SE11
150 D1 Stable Walk N1
154 A2 Stable Yard Road SW1A
150 C6 Stacey Street WC2H
153 H3 Stackhouse Street SW1X
153 M4 Stafford Place SW1E
149 M8 Stafford Street W1J
153 M4 Stag Place SW1E
155 M2 Stainer Street SE1
151 K6 Staining Lane EC2V
157 M2 Stainsby Place E14
148 F4 Stalbridge Street NW1
156 F8 Stalham Street SE16
155 G1 Stamford Street SE1
155 M6 Stanford Place SE1
152 B4 Stanford Road W8
154 B6 Stanford Street SW1P
157 J6 Stanhope Close SE16
152 D5 Stanhope Gardens SW7
149 G7 Stanhope Gate W2
153 K1 Stanhope Gate W1K
152 D5 Stanhope Mews East SW7
152 D6 Stanhope Mews South SW7
152 D5 Stanhope Mews West SW7
149 L2 Stanhope Parade NW1
149 G7 Stanhope Place W2
153 K2 Stanhope Row W1J
149 M2 Stanhope Street NW1
148 E7 Stanhope Terrace W2
150 C1 Stanley Passage NW1
155 G7 Stannary Place SE11
155 G8 Stannary Street SE11
156 C7 Stanworth Street SE1
150 F5 Staple Inn WC1V
157 K5 Staples Close SE16
155 L3 Staple Street SE1
150 A2 Starcross Street NW1
156 C4 Star Place E1W
148 F6 Star Street W2
150 F6 Star Yard WC2A
149 J4 Station Approach * NW1
149 L4 Station Arcade * W1W
151 H6 Stationers Hall Court * EC4M
157 J5 Stave Yard Road SE16
155 K6 Stead Street SE17
155 J6 Steedman Street SE17
151 K8 Steelyard Passage EC4R
157 K7 Steers Way SE16
150 B5 Stephen Mews W1T
150 A3 Stephenson Way NW1
150 B5 Stephen Street W1T
157 H3 Stepney Causeway E1
157 J1 Stepney Green E1
157 J1 Stepney High Street E1
156 E1 Stepney Way E1
153 G3 Sterling Street SW7
155 L3 Sterry Street SE1
156 E5 Stevedore Street E1W
156 B7 Stevens Street SE1
156 B1 Steward Street E1
152 F6 Stewarts Grove SW3
151 K7 Stew Lane EC4V
154 A5 Stillington Street SW1P
151 M1 St John's Estate N1
156 B6 St John's Estate SE1
150 C8 St Martin-in-the-Fields * WC2H
156 D5 Stockholm Way E1W
157 M3 Stocks Place E14
150 F5 Stone Buildings WC2A
151 H6 Stonecutter Street EC4A
152 B4 Stone Hall Gardens * W8
152 B4 Stone Hall Place * W8
156 A2 Stone House Court EC3A
155 J3 Stones End Street SE1
156 B2 Stoney Lane EC3A
155 K1 Stoney Street SE1
155 J7 Stopford Road * SE17
150 B5 Store Street WC1E
154 C3 Storeys Gate SW1H
156 E8 Storks Road SE16
154 E6 Stoughton Close SE11
149 G6 Stourcliffe Street W2
150 D8 Strand WC2R
149 K6 Stratford Place W1U
152 A5 Stratford Road W8
148 F7 Strathearn Place W2
153 L1 Stratton Street W1J
150 C5 Streatham Street WC1A
154 B4 Strutton Ground SW1P
156 B2 Strype Street E1
153 H3 Studio Place * SW1X
150 D6 Stukeley Street WC2B
155 J7 Sturgeon Road SE17
155 J3 Sturge Street SE1
151 K1 Sturt Street N1
156 D3 Stutfield Street E1
151 H1 Sudeley Street N1
155 J3 Sudrey Street SE1
151 L7 Suffolk Lane EC4R
150 C8 Suffolk Street SW1Y
155 G5 Sullivan Road SE11
157 G2 Summercourt Road E1
151 G4 Summers Street EC1R
152 E6 Sumner Place SW7
152 E6 Sumner Place Mews SW7
155 J1 Sumner Street SE1
148 A6 Sunderland Terrace W2
152 A5 Sunningdale Gardens W8
156 D8 Sun Passage SE16
151 M4 Sun Street EC2A
148 A4 Surrendale Place W9
155 M7 Surrey Grove SE17
157 H7 Surrey Quays Road SE16
155 H2 Surrey Row SE1
155 M6 Surrey Square SE17
150 F7 Surrey Street WC2R
157 J6 Surrey Water Road SE16
148 E7 Sussex Gardens W2
148 E7 Sussex Mews East * W2
148 E7 Sussex Mews West W2
148 E6 Sussex Place W2
149 H3 Sussex Place NW1
148 E7 Sussex Square W2
153 L7 Sussex Street SW1V
148 A4 Sutherland Avenue W9
153 L7 Sutherland Row SW1V
155 J7 Sutherland Square SE17
153 L7 Sutherland Street SW1V
155 K7 Sutherland Walk SE17
152 F6 Sutton Dwelling Estate SW3
151 H4 Sutton Lane EC1V
150 B6 Sutton Row W1D
157 G3 Sutton Street E1
148 F3 Swain Street NW8
149 L6 Swallow Place W1S
150 A8 Swallow Street W1S
151 L8 Swan Lane EC4R
156 A8 Swan Mead SE1
156 C4 Swan Passage E1
157 G6 Swan Road SE16
155 K3 Swan Street SE1
153 H8 Swan Walk SW3
156 E4 Swedenborg Gardens E1
157 K8 Sweden Gate SE16
156 C7 Sweeney Crescent SE1
150 E2 Swinton Place WC1X
150 E2 Swinton Street WC1X
151 J3 Sycamore Street EC1V
152 E6 Sydney Close SW7
152 E6 Sydney Mews SW7
152 F6 Sydney Place SW7
152 F6 Sydney Street SW3
151 M2 Symister Mews * N1
153 J6 Symons Street SW1W

T

155 L3 Tabard Garden Estate SE1
155 L4 Tabard Street SE1
151 L4 Tabernacle Street EC2A
154 A6 Tachbrook Street SW1V
151 M7 Talbot Court EC3V
148 A6 Talbot Road W2
148 E6 Talbot Square W2
155 L2 Talbot Yard SE1
151 G7 Tallis Street EC4Y
156 D5 Tamarind Yard E1W
150 D2 Tankerton Street WC1H
156 B7 Tanner Street SE1
155 G3 Tanswell Street * SE1
151 K1 Taplow Street N1
157 G3 Tarbert Walk E1
156 F3 Tarling Street E1
155 J4 Tarn Street SE1
149 G5 Tarrant Place W1H
155 J7 Tarver Road SE17
155 M6 Tatum Street SE17
149 G4 Taunton Mews NW1
149 G3 Taunton Place NW1
150 D7 Tavistock Court * WC2E
150 D3 Tavistock Place WC1H
150 C3 Tavistock Square WC1H
150 D7 Tavistock Street WC2E
150 B3 Taviton Street WC1H
155 G6 Tavy Close SE11
157 K6 Teak Close SE16
153 G7 Tedworth Gardens SW3
153 H7 Tedworth Square SW3
151 L6 Telegraph Street EC2R
156 D4 Telfords Yard E1W
153 M8 Telford Terrace SW1V
151 G7 Temple Avenue EC4Y
151 G7 Temple Gardens * EC4Y
151 G7 Temple Lane EC4Y
150 F7 Temple Place WC2R
152 A6 Templeton Place SW5
156 E5 Tench Street E1W
148 C7 Tenniel Close W2
155 L3 Tennis Street SE1
149 L6 Tenterden Street W1S
156 B1 Tenter Ground E1
153 L5 Terminus Place SW1V
152 B3 Thackeray Street W8
157 J6 Thame Road SE16
157 L8 Thames Path SE16
153 K8 Thames Path SW11
156 B4 Thames Path EC3N
154 B8 Thames Path SW8
154 D5 Thames Path SW1P
150 C2 Thanet Street WC1H
149 K5 Thayer Street W1U
151 M5 The Arcade * EC2M
150 D8 The Arches * WC2N
152 C7 The Boltons SW10
152 C1 The Broad Walk W8
151 H4 The Charterhouse * EC1M
155 G2 The Cut SE1
156 B8 The Grange SE1
157 J4 The Highway E1W
156 E4 The Highway E1
148 C1 The Lane NW8
152 C7 The Little Boltons SW10
154 B2 The Mall SW1A
150 D7 The Market WC2E
157 L3 The Mitre E14
151 K5 The Postern * EC2Y
148 F6 The Quadrangle W2
156 B5 The Queens Walk SE1
154 C3 The Sanctuary SW1P
152 E8 The Vale SW3
148 F6 The Water Gardens W2
155 G2 Theed Street SE1
150 E4 Theobald's Road WC1X
155 L5 Theobald Street SE1
151 J1 Theseus Walk N1
154 A4 Thirleby Road SW1P
152 D7 Thistle Grove SW10
155 H4 Thomas Doyle Street SE1
156 D4 Thomas More Square E1W
156 D4 Thomas More Street E1W
152 B4 Thomas Place W8
157 M2 Thomas Road E14
151 K1 Thoresby Street N1
154 B6 Thorndike Street * SW1V
154 D5 Thorney Street SW1P
148 A3 Thorngate Road W9
150 C4 Thornhaugh Street WC1H
149 H4 Thornton Place W1H
155 K2 Thrale Street SE1
156 C1 Thrawl Street E1
151 L6 Threadneedle Street EC2R
157 M4 Three Colt Street E14
149 K7 Three Kings Yard W1K
156 B6 Three Oak Lane SE1
151 L6 Throgmorton Avenue EC2N
151 L6 Throgmorton Street EC2R
155 J6 Thrush Street SE17
156 D8 Thurland Road SE16
152 F5 Thurloe Close SW7
152 F5 Thurloe Place SW7
152 E5 Thurloe Place Mews * SW7
152 F5 Thurloe Square SW7
152 E5 Thurloe Street SW7
155 M7 Thurlow Street SE17
155 M7 Thurlow Walk SE17
156 F3 Tillman Street E1
153 K1 Tilney Street W1K
156 F3 Timberland Road E1
157 J6 Timber Pond Road SE16
151 J3 Timber Street * EC1V
157 L1 Timothy Road E14
157 H1 Tinsley Road E1
155 G6 Tinworth Street SE11
155 L6 Tisdall Place SE17
148 F6 Titchborne Row W2
153 H7 Tite Street SW3
155 J4 Tiverton Street SE1
151 L6 Tokenhouse Yard EC2R
150 A3 Tolmer's Square NW1
157 L2 Tomlin's Terrace E14
151 H2 Tompion Street EC1V
150 D2 Tonbridge Street WC1H
151 F5 Took's Court EC4A
155 M2 Tooley Street SE1
151 G3 Topham Street * EC1R
148 A5 Torquay Street W2
151 G1 Torrens Street EC1V
150 B4 Torrington Place W1T
156 E5 Torrington Place E1W
150 B4 Torrington Square WC1E
154 B3 Tothill Street SW1H
157 J2 Tottan Terrace * E1
150 A4 Tottenham Court Road W1T
150 A5 Tottenham Mews * W1T
150 A5 Tottenham Street W1W
155 J3 Toulmin Street SE1
156 D8 Toussaint Walk SE16
156 C5 Tower Bridge EC3N
156 C5 Tower Bridge Approach EC3N
156 A8 Tower Bridge Road SE1
150 C7 Tower Court * WC2H
156 B4 Tower Hill EC3N
156 B4 Tower Hill Terrace EC3R
156 A4 Tower Place EC3R
151 K7 Tower Royal * EC4N
150 C7 Tower Street WC2H
155 L6 Townley Street SE17
155 M5 Townsend Street SE17
156 B1 Toynbee Street E1
157 J1 Trafalgar Gardens E1
150 C8 Trafalgar Square * WC2N
155 L7 Trafalgar Street SE17
148 F5 Transept Street NW1
156 E8 Tranton Road SE16
153 L1 Trebeck Street W1J
152 A6 Trebovir Road SW5
152 C7 Tregunter Road SW10
148 F3 Tresham Crescent NW8
155 H1 Treveris Street SE1
153 G3 Trevor Place SW7
153 G3 Trevor Square SW7

Index to place names

This index lists places appearing in the main-map section of the atlas in alphabetical order. The reference before each name gives the atlas page number and grid reference of the square in which the place appears. The map shows counties, unitary authorities and administrative areas, together with a list of the abbreviated name forms used in the index.

The top 100 places of tourist interest are indexed in red, airports in blue.

Scotland

Abers	**Aberdeenshire**
Ag & B	**Argyll & Bute**
Angus	**Angus**
Border	**Borders**
C Aber	**City of Aberdeen**
C Dund	**City of Dundee**
C Edin	**City of Edinburgh**
C Glas	**City of Glasgow**
Clacks	**Clackmannanshire (1)**
D & G	**Dumfries & Galloway**
E Ayrs	**East Ayrshire**
E Duns	**East Dunbartonshire (2)**
E Loth	**East Lothian**
E Rens	**East Renfrewshire (3)**
Falk	**Falkirk**
Fife	**Fife**
Highld	**Highland**
Inver	**Inverclyde (4)**
Mdloth	**Midlothian (5)**
Moray	**Moray**
N Ayrs	**North Ayrshire**
N Lans	**North Lanarkshire (6)**
Ork	**Orkney Islands**
P & K	**Perth & Kinross**
Rens	**Renfrewshire (7)**
S Ayrs	**South Ayrshire**
Shet	**Shetland Islands**
S Lans	**South Lanarkshire**
Stirlg	**Stirling**
W Duns	**West Dunbartonshire (8)**
W Isls	**Western Isles**
W Loth	**West Lothian**

Wales

Blae G	**Blaenau Gwent (9)**
Brdgnd	**Bridgend (10)**
Caerph	**Caerphilly (11)**
Cardif	**Cardiff**
Carmth	**Carmarthenshire**
Cerdgn	**Ceredigion**
Conwy	**Conwy**
Denbgs	**Denbighshire**
Flints	**Flintshire**
Gwynd	**Gwynedd**
IoA	**Isle of Anglesey**
Mons	**Monmouthshire**
Myr Td	**Merthyr Tydfil (12)**
Neath	**Neath Port Talbot (13)**
Newpt	**Newport (14)**
Pembks	**Pembrokeshire**
Powys	**Powys**
Rhondd	**Rhondda Cynon Taff (15)**
Swans	**Swansea**
Torfn	**Torfaen (16)**
V Glam	**Vale of Glamorgan (17)**
Wrexhm	**Wrexham**

Channel Islands & Isle of Man

Guern	**Guernsey**
Jersey	**Jersey**
IoM	**Isle of Man**

England

BaNES	**Bath & N E Somerset (18)**
Barns	**Barnsley (19)**
Beds	**Bedfordshire**
Birm	**Birmingham**
Bl w D	**Blackburn with Darwen (20)**
Bmouth	**Bournemouth**
Bolton	**Bolton (21)**
Bpool	**Blackpool**
Brad	**Bradford (22)**
Br & H	**Brighton and Hove (23)**
Br For	**Bracknell Forest (24)**
Bristl	**City of Bristol**
Bucks	**Buckinghamshire**
Bury	**Bury (25)**
C Derb	**City of Derby**
C KuH	**City of Kingston upon Hull**
C Leic	**City of Leicester**
C Nott	**City of Nottingham**
C Pete	**City of Peterborough**
C Plym	**City of Plymouth**
C Port	**City of Portsmouth**
C Sotn	**City of Southampton**
C Stke	**City of Stoke**
Calder	**Calderdale (26)**
Cambs	**Cambridgeshire**
Ches	**Cheshire**
Cnwll	**Cornwall**
Covtry	**Coventry**
Cumb	**Cumbria**
Darltn	**Darlington (27)**
Derbys	**Derbyshire**
Devon	**Devon**
Donc	**Doncaster (28)**
Dorset	**Dorset**
Dudley	**Dudley (29)**
Dur	**Durham**
E R Yk	**East Riding of Yorkshire**
E Susx	**East Sussex**

Essex	**Essex**
Gatesd	**Gateshead (30)**
Gloucs	**Gloucestershire**
Gt Lon	**Greater London**
Halton	**Halton (31)**
Hants	**Hampshire**
Hartpl	**Hartlepool (32)**
Herefs	**Herefordshire**
Herts	**Hertfordshire**
IoS	**Isles of Scilly**
IoW	**Isle of Wight**
Kent	**Kent**
Kirk	**Kirklees (33)**
Knows	**Knowsley (34)**
Lancs	**Lancashire**
Leeds	**Leeds**
Leics	**Leicestershire**
Lincs	**Lincolnshire**
Lpool	**Liverpool**
Luton	**Luton**
M Keyn	**Milton Keynes**
Manch	**Manchester**
Medway	**Medway**
Middsb	**Middlesbrough**
NE Lin	**North East Lincolnshire**
N Linc	**North Lincolnshire**
N Som	**North Somerset (35)**
N Tyne	**North Tyneside (36)**
N u Ty	**Newcastle upon Tyne**
N York	**North Yorkshire**
Nhants	**Northamptonshire**
Norfk	**Norfolk**
Notts	**Nottinghamshire**
Nthumb	**Northumberland**
Oldham	**Oldham (37)**
Oxon	**Oxfordshire**
Poole	**Poole**
R & Cl	**Redcar and Cleveland**
Readg	**Reading**
Rochdl	**Rochdale (38)**
Rothm	**Rotherham (39)**
Rutlnd	**Rutland**
S Glos	**South Gloucestershire (40)**
S on T	**Stockton-on-Tees (41)**
S Tyne	**South Tyneside (42)**
Salfd	**Salford (43)**
Sandw	**Sandwell (44)**
Sefton	**Sefton (45)**
Sheff	**Sheffield**
Shrops	**Shropshire**
Slough	**Slough (46)**
Solhll	**Solihull (47)**
Somset	**Somerset**
St Hel	**St Helens (48)**
Staffs	**Staffordshire**
Sthend	**Southend-on-Sea**
Stockp	**Stockport (49)**
Suffk	**Suffolk**
Sundld	**Sunderland**
Surrey	**Surrey**
Swindn	**Swindon**
Tamesd	**Tameside (50)**
Thurr	**Thurrock (51)**
Torbay	**Torbay**
Traffd	**Trafford (52)**
W & M	**Windsor & Maidenhead (53)**
W Berk	**West Berkshire**
W Susx	**West Sussex**
Wakefd	**Wakefield (54)**
Warrtn	**Warrington (55)**
Warwks	**Warwickshire**
Wigan	**Wigan (56)**
Wilts	**Wiltshire**
Wirral	**Wirral (57)**
Wokham	**Wokingham (58)**
Wolves	**Wolverhampton (59)**
Worcs	**Worcestershire**
Wrekin	**Telford and Wrekin (60)**
Wsall	**Walsall (61)**
York	**York**

166 Abbas Combe - Arleston

A

17 Q10 **Abbas Combe** Somset
39 N8 **Abberley** Worcs
39 N8 **Abberley Common** Worcs
34 G11 **Abberton** Essex
30 C4 **Abberton** Worcs
22 C2 **Abbess Roding** Essex
50 H4 **Abbeydale** Sheff
28 D3 **Abbey Dore** Herefs
50 C8 **Abbey Green** Staffs
87 P9 **Abbey St Bathans** Border
63 K10 **Abbeystead** Lancs
71 J5 **Abbey Town** Cumb
57 M4 **Abbey Village** Lancs
21 P7 **Abbey Wood** Gt Lon
80 E10 **Abbotrule** Border
14 G9 **Abbots Bickington** Devon
40 E3 **Abbots Bromley** Staffs
7 N6 **Abbotsbury** Dorset
92 G12 **Abbots Deuglie** P & K
14 H6 **Abbotsham** Devon
6 B8 **Abbotskerswell** Devon
20 H3 **Abbots Langley** Herts
17 M2 **Abbots Leigh** N Som
32 H5 **Abbotsley** Cambs
30 D3 **Abbots Morton** Worcs
32 H2 **Abbots Ripton** Cambs
30 E4 **Abbot's Salford** Warwks
9 N2 **Abbots Worthy** Hants
19 K11 **Abbotts Ann** Hants
8 E7 **Abbott Street** Dorset
39 L5 **Abdon** Shrops
36 G7 **Aberaeron** Cerdgn
27 L8 **Aberaman** Rhondd
47 N8 **Aberangell** Gwynd
99 J4 **Aberarder** Highld
92 H11 **Aberargie** P & K
36 H7 **Aberarth** Cerdgn
26 G10 **Aberavon** Neath
92 D10 **Abercairny** P & K
27 M7 **Abercanaid** Myr Td
27 P9 **Abercarn** Caerph
24 F3 **Abercastle** Pembks
47 N10 **Abercegir** Powys
98 D8 **Aberchalder Lodge** Highld
102 E5 **Aberchirder** Abers
26 H6 **Abercraf** Powys
26 H9 **Abercregan** Neath
27 L8 **Abercwmboi** Rhondd
36 D11 **Abercych** Pembks
27 M9 **Abercynon** Rhondd
92 G10 **Aberdalgie** P & K
27 L8 **Aberdare** Rhondd
46 C6 **Aberdaron** Gwynd
95 P1 **Aberdeen** C Aber
103 J11 **Aberdeen Airport** C Aber
86 E5 **Aberdour** Fife
26 G8 **Aberdulais** Neath
47 K11 **Aberdyfi** Gwynd
38 C11 **Aberedw** Powys
24 E3 **Abereiddy** Pembks
46 G4 **Abererch** Gwynd
27 M8 **Aberfan** Myr Td
92 C6 **Aberfeldy** P & K
54 E7 **Aberffraw** IoA
59 K6 **Aberford** Leeds
85 J3 **Aberfoyle** Stirlg
28 C6 **Abergavenny** Mons
55 P6 **Abergele** Conwy
26 D3 **Abergorlech** Carmth
37 P9 **Abergwesyn** Powys
25 Q5 **Abergwili** Carmth
27 J9 **Abergwynfi** Neath
55 J7 **Abergwyngregyn** Gwynd
47 L9 **Abergynolwyn** Gwynd
27 J11 **Aberkenfig** Brdgnd
87 J6 **Aberlady** E Loth
93 N5 **Aberlemno** Angus
47 M8 **Aberllefenni** Gwynd
27 N2 **Aberllynfi** Powys
101 K6 **Aberlour** Moray
38 D4 **Abermule** Powys
25 N4 **Abernant** Carmth
27 L7 **Aber-nant** Rhondd
92 H11 **Abernethy** P & K
93 J8 **Abernyte** P & K
36 D9 **Aberporth** Cerdgn
46 E6 **Abersoch** Gwynd
28 B7 **Abersychan** Torfn
16 D2 **Aberthin** V Glam
27 P7 **Abertillery** Blae G
27 N10 **Abertridwr** Caerph
48 B10 **Abertridwr** Powys
92 E11 **Aberuthven** P & K
37 J4 **Aberystwyth** Cerdgn
19 N2 **Abingdon** Oxon
10 H2 **Abinger** Surrey
10 H1 **Abinger Hammer** Surrey
32 A5 **Abington** Nhants
78 F4 **Abington** S Lans
33 K7 **Abington Pigotts** Cambs
41 Q3 **Ab Kettleby** Leics
30 E11 **Ablington** Gloucs
50 G5 **Abney** Derbys
95 J3 **Aboyne** Abers
57 L8 **Abram** Wigan
98 H2 **Abriachan** Highld
21 P4 **Abridge** Essex
85 N7 **Abronhill** N Lans
17 Q2 **Abson** S Glos
31 N5 **Abthorpe** Nhants
53 L7 **Aby** Lincs
59 N5 **Acaster Malbis** York
59 M6 **Acaster Selby** N York
57 N3 **Accrington** Lancs
88 F5 **Acha** Ag & B
83 L7 **Achahoish** Ag & B
92 G6 **Achalader** P & K
90 C9 **Achaleven** Ag & B
111 d2 **Acha Mor** W Isls
106 D9 **Achanalt** Highld
107 K7 **Achandunie** Highld
107 J3 **Achany** Highld
89 N3 **Acharacle** Highld
89 P6 **Acharn** Highld
92 B6 **Acharn** P & K
110 E7 **Achavanich** Highld
105 Q2 **Achduart** Highld
108 F7 **Achfary** Highld
96 C8 **A'Chill** Highld
105 Q1 **Achiltibuie** Highld
75 L8 **Achinhoan** Ag & B
97 N2 **Achintee** Highld
97 L2 **Achintraid** Highld
108 B10 **Achmelvich** Highld
97 M3 **Achmore** Highld
111 d2 **Achmore** W Isls
108 B8 **Achnacarnin** Highld
98 B10 **Achnacarry** Highld
96 H7 **Achnacloich** Highld
98 F5 **Achnaconeran** Highld
90 B7 **Achnacroish** Ag & B
89 K6 **Achnadrish Lodge** Ag & B
92 D8 **Achnafauld** P & K
107 L8 **Achnagarron** Highld
89 K3 **Achnaha** Highld
108 A11 **Achnahaird** Highld
109 K12 **Achnairn** Highld
90 B4 **Achnalea** Highld
83 L5 **Achnamara** Ag & B
106 C10 **Achnasheen** Highld
105 Q11 **Achnashellach Lodge** Highld
101 K8 **Achnastank** Moray
89 K3 **Achosnich** Highld
89 P6 **Achranich** Highld
110 B3 **Achreamie** Highld
90 F3 **Achriabhach** Highld
108 E5 **Achriesgill** Highld
109 M3 **Achtoty** Highld
42 E12 **Achurch** Nhants
107 L4 **Achvaich** Highld
110 G5 **Ackergill** Highld
66 C4 **Acklam** Middsb
60 D2 **Acklam** N York
39 P3 **Ackleton** Shrops
73 M1 **Acklington** Nthumb
59 K9 **Ackton** Wakefd
59 K10 **Ackworth Moor Top** Wakefd
45 N7 **Acle** Norfk
40 E10 **Acock's Green** Birm
23 P9 **Acol** Kent
72 G7 **Acomb** Nthumb
59 M4 **Acomb** York
28 F3 **Aconbury** Herefs
49 L5 **Acton** Ches
21 K7 **Acton** Gt Lon
49 P7 **Acton** Staffs
34 E7 **Acton** Suffk
39 Q8 **Acton** Worcs
39 M11 **Acton Beauchamp** Herefs
49 L1 **Acton Bridge** Ches
39 K2 **Acton Burnell** Shrops
39 M11 **Acton Green** Herefs
48 G5 **Acton Park** Wrexhm
39 L3 **Acton Round** Shrops
39 J4 **Acton Scott** Shrops
40 C4 **Acton Trussell** Staffs
18 B5 **Acton Turville** S Glos
49 N9 **Adbaston** Staffs
17 N11 **Adber** Dorset
51 N12 **Adbolton** Notts
31 L7 **Adderbury** Oxon
49 M7 **Adderley** Shrops
86 B9 **Addiewell** W Loth
58 E4 **Addingham** Brad
31 Q8 **Addington** Bucks
21 M9 **Addington** Gt Lon
22 D10 **Addington** Kent
21 M9 **Addiscombe** Gt Lon
20 G9 **Addlestone** Surrey
53 N9 **Addlethorpe** Lincs
20 H2 **Adeyfield** Herts
38 C2 **Adfa** Powys
38 H7 **Adforton** Herefs
23 N11 **Adisham** Kent
30 G8 **Adlestrop** Gloucs
60 E9 **Adlingfleet** E R Yk
57 L6 **Adlington** Lancs
40 D3 **Admaston** Staffs
49 L11 **Admaston** Wrekin
30 G5 **Admington** Warwks
36 E11 **Adpar** Cerdgn
16 H9 **Adsborough** Somset
16 G8 **Adscombe** Somset
31 Q7 **Adstock** Bucks
31 N4 **Adstone** Nhants
10 H5 **Adversane** W Susx
100 H8 **Advie** Highld
59 M11 **Adwick Le Street** Donc
51 L1 **Adwick upon Dearne** Donc
78 G10 **Ae** D & G
78 G10 **Ae Bridgend** D & G
26 H8 **Afan Forest Park** Neath
102 D7 **Affleck** Abers
8 B8 **Affpuddle** Dorset
98 B5 **Affric Lodge** Highld
48 D2 **Afon-wen** Flints
9 L9 **Afton** IoW
65 J9 **Agglethorpe** N York
56 H10 **Aigburth** Lpool
60 H5 **Aike** E R Yk
71 P6 **Aiketgate** Cumb
71 L5 **Aikton** Cumb
42 G9 **Ailsworth** C Pete
65 N10 **Ainderby Quernhow** N York
65 N8 **Ainderby Steeple** N York
35 J11 **Aingers Green** Essex
56 F6 **Ainsdale** Sefton
71 Q6 **Ainstable** Cumb
66 G6 **Ainthorpe** N York
86 D9 **Ainville** W Loth
83 L3 **Aird** Ag & B
68 E7 **Aird** D & G
111 e2 **Aird** W Isls
111 c3 **Aird a Mhulaidh** W Isls
111 c3 **Aird Asaig** W Isls
97 J2 **Aird Dhubh** Highld
90 D9 **Airdeny** Ag & B
89 L9 **Aird of Kinloch** Ag & B
96 H9 **Aird of Sleat** Highld
85 M9 **Airdrie** N Lans
85 N9 **Airdriehill** N Lans
90 D9 **Airds Bay** Ag & B
69 P5 **Airds of Kells** D & G
111 c2 **Aird Uig** W Isls
111 c3 **Airidh a bhruaich** W Isls
70 C4 **Airieland** D & G
93 K5 **Airlie** Angus
60 C8 **Airmyn** E R Yk
92 G8 **Airntully** P & K
97 K8 **Airor** Highld
85 Q5 **Airth** Falk
58 B3 **Airton** N York
42 E3 **Aisby** Lincs
52 C5 **Aisby** Lincs
5 N7 **Aish** Devon
6 A10 **Aish** Devon
16 G8 **Aisholt** Somset
65 M9 **Aiskew** N York
66 H9 **Aislaby** N York
67 J6 **Aislaby** N York
65 P5 **Aislaby** S on T
52 D7 **Aisthorpe** Lincs
111 k4 **Aith** Shet
81 K8 **Akeld** Nthumb
31 P6 **Akeley** Bucks
35 J7 **Akenham** Suffk
5 J6 **Albaston** Cnwll
48 G11 **Alberbury** Shrops
11 K6 **Albourne** W Susx
39 P2 **Albrighton** Shrops
49 J10 **Albrighton** Shrops
45 L11 **Alburgh** Norfk
33 M10 **Albury** Herts
10 G1 **Albury** Surrey
10 G2 **Albury Heath** Surrey
107 J10 **Alcaig** Highld
39 J5 **Alcaston** Shrops
30 E3 **Alcester** Warwks
11 P8 **Alciston** E Susx
32 H2 **Alconbury** Cambs
32 H2 **Alconbury Weston** Cambs
59 K2 **Aldborough** N York
45 K4 **Aldborough** Norfk
19 J5 **Aldbourne** Wilts
61 L6 **Aldbrough** E R Yk
65 L5 **Aldbrough St John** N York
20 F2 **Aldbury** Herts
63 J9 **Aldcliffe** Lancs
92 D3 **Aldclune** P & K
35 P5 **Aldeburgh** Suffk
45 P10 **Aldeby** Norfk
21 J4 **Aldenham** Herts
8 H2 **Alderbury** Wilts
45 J6 **Alderford** Norfk
8 G5 **Alderholt** Dorset
29 K10 **Alderley** Gloucs
57 Q12 **Alderley Edge** Ches
19 P7 **Aldermaston** W Berk
30 G4 **Alderminster** Warwks
20 D12 **Aldershot** Hants
30 D7 **Alderton** Gloucs
31 Q5 **Alderton** Nhants
35 M8 **Alderton** Suffk
18 C4 **Alderton** Wilts
50 H9 **Alderwasley** Derbys
58 H1 **Aldfield** N York
48 H4 **Aldford** Ches
42 E8 **Aldgate** Rutlnd
34 F10 **Aldham** Essex
34 H7 **Aldham** Suffk
10 E8 **Aldingbourne** W Susx
62 F7 **Aldingham** Cumb
13 K3 **Aldington** Kent
30 E5 **Aldington** Worcs
13 K3 **Aldington Corner** Kent
101 L9 **Aldivalloch** Moray
84 F5 **Aldochlay** Ag & B
33 M3 **Aldreth** Cambs
40 D7 **Aldridge** Wsall
35 P5 **Aldringham** Suffk
30 F11 **Aldsworth** Gloucs
101 M9 **Aldunie** Moray
50 G8 **Aldwark** Derbys
59 L2 **Aldwark** N York
10 E9 **Aldwick** W Susx
32 E1 **Aldwincle** Nhants
19 P5 **Aldworth** W Berk
84 G7 **Alexandria** W Duns
16 G8 **Aley** Somset
6 F4 **Alfington** Devon
10 G3 **Alfold** Surrey
10 G3 **Alfold Crossways** Surrey
102 D11 **Alford** Abers
53 M8 **Alford** Lincs
17 N9 **Alford** Somset
51 K9 **Alfreton** Derbys
39 N10 **Alfrick** Worcs
39 N10 **Alfrick Pound** Worcs
11 P9 **Alfriston** E Susx
43 J3 **Algarkirk** Lincs
17 P8 **Alhampton** Somset
60 F9 **Alkborough** N Linc
13 N2 **Alkham** Kent
50 F12 **Alkmonton** Derbys
5 Q9 **Allaleigh** Devon
94 B4 **Allanaquoich** Abers
85 P10 **Allanbank** N Lans
81 J4 **Allanton** Border
85 P10 **Allanton** N Lans
85 M11 **Allanton** S Lans
28 H7 **Allaston** Gloucs
9 M4 **Allbrook** Hants
18 F8 **All Cannings** Wilts
72 F9 **Allendale** Nthumb
40 F7 **Allen End** Warwks
72 F10 **Allenheads** Nthumb
33 M12 **Allen's Green** Herts
28 F2 **Allensmore** Herefs
41 J2 **Allenton** C Derb
15 N7 **Aller** Devon
17 K9 **Aller** Somset
70 H7 **Allerby** Cumb
6 E4 **Allercombe** Devon
16 B6 **Allerford** Somset
67 J10 **Allerston** N York
60 D5 **Allerthorpe** E R Yk
58 E7 **Allerton** Brad
107 M8 **Allerton** Highld
56 H10 **Allerton** Lpool
59 K8 **Allerton Bywater** Leeds
59 K3 **Allerton Mauleverer** N York
40 H10 **Allesley** Covtry
51 J11 **Allestree** C Derb
42 B9 **Allexton** Leics
50 C7 **Allgreave** Ches
22 G7 **Allhallows** Medway
105 M10 **Alligin Shuas** Highld
7 L4 **Allington** Dorset
42 C3 **Allington** Lincs
18 D5 **Allington** Wilts
18 F8 **Allington** Wilts
18 H11 **Allington** Wilts
62 H6 **Allithwaite** Cumb
85 P4 **Alloa** Clacks
70 H7 **Allonby** Cumb
76 F7 **Alloway** S Ayrs
17 K12 **Allowenshay** Somset
39 J3 **All Stretton** Shrops
90 G6 **Alltchaorunn** Highld
25 Q3 **Alltwalis** Carmth
26 G7 **Alltwen** Neath
36 H10 **Alltyblaca** Cerdgn
17 P12 **Allweston** Dorset
38 G11 **Almeley** Herefs
49 N8 **Almington** Staffs
92 F9 **Almondbank** P & K
58 F10 **Almondbury** Kirk
28 H11 **Almondsbury** S Glos
59 L2 **Alne** N York
107 L8 **Alness** Highld
81 L12 **Alnham** Nthumb
81 P11 **Alnmouth** Nthumb
81 P10 **Alnwick** Nthumb
21 J6 **Alperton** Gt Lon
34 E9 **Alphamstone** Essex
34 E6 **Alpheton** Suffk
6 C5 **Alphington** Devon
50 G7 **Alport** Derbys
49 L4 **Alpraham** Ches
34 H11 **Alresford** Essex
40 F5 **Alrewas** Staffs
49 P4 **Alsager** Ches
50 F9 **Alsop en le Dale** Derbys
72 D10 **Alston** Cumb
7 J3 **Alston** Devon
29 N3 **Alstone** Gloucs
50 F9 **Alstonefield** Staffs
17 K6 **Alston Sutton** Somset
15 M7 **Alswear** Devon
108 A12 **Altandhu** Highld
4 F4 **Altarnun** Cnwll
106 H3 **Altass** Highld
89 N8 **Altcreich** Ag & B
83 Q8 **Altgaltraig** Ag & B
22 H4 **Althorne** Essex
60 E11 **Althorpe** N Linc
110 B6 **Altnabreac Station** Highld
90 B9 **Altnacraig** Ag & B
109 K8 **Altnaharra** Highld
51 J7 **Alton** Derbys
10 B3 **Alton** Hants
50 E11 **Alton** Staffs
18 G8 **Alton Barnes** Wilts
7 Q3 **Alton Pancras** Dorset
18 G8 **Alton Priors** Wilts
50 E11 **Alton Towers** Staffs
57 P10 **Altrincham** Traffd
84 H3 **Altskeith Hotel** Stirlg
85 P4 **Alva** Clacks
49 J1 **Alvanley** Ches
41 K2 **Alvaston** C Derb
40 D11 **Alvechurch** Worcs
40 G6 **Alvecote** Warwks
8 E3 **Alvediston** Wilts
39 N5 **Alveley** Shrops
15 J7 **Alverdiscott** Devon
9 P7 **Alverstoke** Hants
9 P9 **Alverstone** IoW
58 H9 **Alverthorpe** Wakefd
42 B2 **Alverton** Notts
100 H3 **Alves** Moray
30 H12 **Alvescot** Oxon
28 H10 **Alveston** S Glos
30 G3 **Alveston** Warwks
53 K5 **Alvingham** Lincs
28 H8 **Alvington** Gloucs
42 G10 **Alwalton** C Pete
81 J11 **Alwinton** Nthumb
58 H6 **Alwoodley** Leeds
93 J6 **Alyth** P & K
51 J9 **Ambergate** Derbys
29 L8 **Amberley** Gloucs
10 G7 **Amberley** W Susx
81 Q12 **Amble** Nthumb
40 B9 **Amblecote** Dudley
58 E8 **Ambler Thorn** Brad
62 G2 **Ambleside** Cumb
24 H4 **Ambleston** Pembks
31 N9 **Ambrosden** Oxon
60 E10 **Amcotts** N Linc
20 F4 **Amersham** Bucks
20 F4 **Amersham Common** Bucks
20 F4 **Amersham Old Town** Bucks
20 F4 **Amersham on the Hill** Bucks
18 H11 **Amesbury** Wilts
111 c3 **Amhuinnsuidhe** W Isls
40 G6 **Amington** Staffs
78 G11 **Amisfield Town** D & G
54 F3 **Amlwch** IoA
26 E6 **Ammanford** Carmth
66 G11 **Amotherby** N York
9 L3 **Ampfield** Hants
66 E10 **Ampleforth** N York
18 F1 **Ampney Crucis** Gloucs
18 G1 **Ampney St Mary** Gloucs
18 F1 **Ampney St Peter** Gloucs
19 K11 **Amport** Hants
32 E8 **Ampthill** Beds
34 E3 **Ampton** Suffk
25 K7 **Amroth** Pembks
92 D8 **Amulree** P & K
21 J2 **Amwell** Herts
89 Q4 **Anaheilt** Highld
42 E2 **Ancaster** Lincs
81 L5 **Ancroft** Nthumb
80 E8 **Ancrum** Border
53 N8 **Anderby** Lincs
19 L10 **Andover** Hants
30 D9 **Andoversford** Gloucs
56 d2 **Andreas** IoM
21 M9 **Anerley** Gt Lon
56 G9 **Anfield** Lpool
2 E7 **Angarrack** Cnwll
39 L7 **Angelbank** Shrops
24 F8 **Angle** Pembks
54 F5 **Anglesey** IoA
10 H8 **Angmering** W Susx
59 M5 **Angram** N York
107 N7 **Ankerville** Highld
60 H8 **Anlaby** E R Yk
44 C4 **Anmer** Norfk
9 Q5 **Anmore** Hants
71 K3 **Annan** D & G
105 N10 **Annat** Highld
85 M8 **Annathill** N Lans
19 L11 **Anna Valley** Hants
76 G6 **Annbank** S Ayrs
30 F3 **Anne Hathaway's Cottage** Warwks
51 L9 **Annesley** Notts
51 L9 **Annesley Woodhouse** Notts
73 L9 **Annfield Plain** Dur
85 J8 **Anniesland** C Glas
56 G3 **Ansdell** Lancs
17 P9 **Ansford** Somset
40 H8 **Ansley** Warwks
40 G3 **Anslow** Staffs
40 G3 **Anslow Gate** Staffs
33 L9 **Anstey** Herts
41 M6 **Anstey** Leics
87 L2 **Anstruther** Fife
11 L5 **Ansty** W Susx
41 K10 **Ansty** Warwks
8 E3 **Ansty** Wilts
71 K4 **Anthorn** Cumb
45 L4 **Antingham** Norfk
111 c4 **An t-Ob** W Isls
43 J1 **Anton's Gowt** Lincs
5 J8 **Antony** Cnwll
57 M11 **Antrobus** Ches
52 G12 **Anwick** Lincs
69 N7 **Anwoth** D & G
21 N10 **Aperfield** Gt Lon
42 E10 **Apethorpe** Nhants
52 G8 **Apley** Lincs
51 J5 **Apperknowle** Derbys
29 M3 **Apperley** Gloucs
90 C7 **Appin** Ag & B
60 G10 **Appleby** N Linc
64 C4 **Appleby-in-Westmorland** Cumb
40 H5 **Appleby Magna** Leics
40 H6 **Appleby Parva** Leics
97 J2 **Applecross** Highld
14 H6 **Appledore** Devon
16 E12 **Appledore** Devon
13 J4 **Appledore** Kent
19 N3 **Appleford** Oxon
78 H11 **Applegarth Town** D & G
19 K10 **Appleshaw** Hants
57 K10 **Appleton** Halton
19 M1 **Appleton** Oxon
57 L11 **Appleton** Warrtn
66 G9 **Appleton-le-Moors** N York
66 G11 **Appleton-le-Street** N York
59 M6 **Appleton Roebuck** N York
57 M11 **Appleton Thorn** Warrtn
65 P6 **Appleton Wiske** N York
80 C10 **Appletreehall** Border
58 D3 **Appletreewick** N York
16 E10 **Appley** Somset
57 K7 **Appley Bridge** Lancs
9 P10 **Apse Heath** IoW
32 G9 **Apsley End** Beds
10 D9 **Apuldram** W Susx
107 N7 **Arabella** Highld
93 Q7 **Arbirlot** Angus
107 P6 **Arboll** Highld
20 C9 **Arborfield** Wokham
20 C9 **Arborfield Cross** Wokham
93 Q7 **Arbroath** Angus
95 N6 **Arbuthnott** Abers
25 Q8 **Archddu** Carmth
65 M4 **Archdeacon Newton** Darltn
84 G6 **Archencarroch** W Duns
101 J6 **Archiestown** Moray
49 P3 **Arclid Green** Ches
103 L7 **Ardallie** Abers
90 E10 **Ardanaiseig Hotel** Ag & B
97 L3 **Ardaneaskan** Highld
97 L2 **Ardarroch** Highld
74 F4 **Ardbeg** Ag & B
84 B9 **Ardbeg** Ag & B
84 C6 **Ardbeg** Ag & B
106 C5 **Ardcharnich** Highld
89 J11 **Ardchiavaig** Ag & B
83 P1 **Ardchonnel** Ag & B
85 K1 **Ardchullarie More** Stirlg
84 D4 **Arddarroch** Ag & B
98 A10 **Ardechive** Highld
76 E4 **Ardeer** N Ayrs
33 K10 **Ardeley** Herts
97 M4 **Ardelve** Highld
84 F6 **Arden** Ag & B
30 E4 **Ardens Grafton** Warwks
90 B10 **Ardentallen** Ag & B
84 D5 **Ardentinny** Ag & B
83 Q7 **Ardentraive** Ag & B
91 P8 **Ardeonaig Hotel** Stirlg
107 N10 **Ardersier** Highld
105 Q5 **Ardessie** Highld
83 M3 **Ardfern** Ag & B
107 K4 **Ardgay** Highld
90 D4 **Ardgour** Highld
84 D8 **Ardgowan** Inver
84 C7 **Ardhallow** Ag & B
111 c3 **Ardhasig** W Isls
105 L10 **Ardheslaig** Highld
106 C5 **Ardindrean** Highld
11 M4 **Ardingly** W Susx
19 M3 **Ardington** Oxon
83 P9 **Ardlamont** Ag & B
34 H10 **Ardleigh** Essex
34 H10 **Ardleigh Heath** Essex
93 J7 **Ardler** P & K
31 M8 **Ardley** Oxon
91 J12 **Ardlui** Ag & B
83 J5 **Ardlussa** Ag & B
90 E8 **Ardmaddy** Ag & B
106 B3 **Ardmair** Highld
84 B8 **Ardmaleish** Ag & B
75 J3 **Ardminish** Ag & B
89 P2 **Ardmolich** Highld
84 F7 **Ardmore** Ag & B
107 L5 **Ardmore** Highld
84 C7 **Ardnadam** Ag & B
106 H11 **Ardnagrask** Highld
97 M3 **Ardnarff** Highld
89 Q4 **Ardnastang** Highld
84 C2 **Ardno** Ag & B
98 B8 **Ardochy House** Highld
83 L10 **Ardpatrick** Ag & B
83 M6 **Ardrishaig** Ag & B
107 K7 **Ardross** Highld
76 D3 **Ardrossan** N Ayrs
58 H8 **Ardsley East** Leeds
89 L4 **Ardslignish** Highld
82 G11 **Ardtalla** Ag & B
89 M3 **Ardtoe** Highld
83 M2 **Arduaine** Ag & B
107 J9 **Ardullie** Highld
96 H8 **Ardvasar** Highld
91 P10 **Ardvorlich** P & K
111 c3 **Ardvourlie** W Isls
68 F9 **Ardwell** D & G
57 Q9 **Ardwick** Manch
39 P7 **Areley Kings** Worcs
89 N3 **Arevegaig** Highld
10 D3 **Arford** Hants
27 N8 **Argoed** Caerph
84 D3 **Argyll Forest Park** Ag & B
111 c3 **Aribruach** W Isls
88 H10 **Aridhglas** Ag & B
88 E5 **Arileod** Ag & B
88 F5 **Arinagour** Ag & B
90 B10 **Ariogan** Ag & B
97 J11 **Arisaig** Highld
97 J11 **Arisaig House** Highld
59 K2 **Arkendale** N York
33 M9 **Arkesden** Essex
63 L7 **Arkholme** Lancs
79 N10 **Arkleton** D & G
21 K4 **Arkley** Gt Lon
59 M11 **Arksey** Donc
51 K6 **Arkwright Town** Derbys
29 N4 **Arle** Gloucs
70 G10 **Arlecdon** Cumb
32 H9 **Arlesey** Beds
49 M12 **Arleston** Wrekin

Arley - Barlings 167

57 M11 **Arley** Ches
40 H8 **Arley** Warwks
29 J6 **Arlingham** Gloucs
15 K4 **Arlington** Devon
12 B8 **Arlington** E Susx
96 H8 **Armadale** Highld
109 N3 **Armadale** Highld
85 Q8 **Armadale** W Loth
71 J9 **Armaside** Cumb
71 Q6 **Armathwaite** Cumb
45 L8 **Arminghall** Norfk
40 E4 **Armitage** Staffs
58 H7 **Armley** Leeds
42 F11 **Armston** Nhants
59 N12 **Armthorpe** Donc
88 F4 **Arnabost** Ag & B
64 G12 **Arncliffe** N York
87 K2 **Arncroach** Fife
101 K6 **Arndilly House** Moray
8 E9 **Arne** Dorset
41 N8 **Arnesby** Leics
92 H12 **Arngask** P & K
97 L7 **Arnisdale** Highld
104 H11 **Arnish** Highld
86 G9 **Arniston** Mdloth
111 d1 **Arnol** W Isls
61 J6 **Arnold** E R Yk
51 N10 **Arnold** Notts
85 K4 **Arnprior** Stirlg
63 J6 **Arnside** Cumb
89 L7 **Aros** Ag & B
62 F6 **Arrad Foot** Cumb
60 H5 **Arram** E R Yk
75 P5 **Arran** N Ayrs
65 L8 **Arrathorne** N York
9 N9 **Arreton** IoW
105 L10 **Arrina** Highld
33 K6 **Arrington** Cambs
84 E3 **Arrochar** Ag & B
30 E3 **Arrow** Warwks
38 H1 **Arscott** Shrops
107 K11 **Artafallie** Highld
58 H5 **Arthington** Leeds
41 Q10 **Arthingworth** Nhants
103 K7 **Arthrath** Abers
103 L8 **Artrochie** Abers
12 C8 **Arundel** W Susx
70 H10 **Asby** Cumb
84 B9 **Ascog** Ag & B
20 E9 **Ascot** W & M
30 H9 **Ascott-under-Wychwood** Oxon
65 P11 **Asenby** N York
41 P4 **Asfordby** Leics
41 Q4 **Asfordby Hill** Leics
42 G2 **Asgarby** Lincs
53 K9 **Asgarby** Lincs
22 C9 **Ash** Kent
23 P10 **Ash** Kent
17 L11 **Ash** Somset
20 E12 **Ash** Surrey
19 P5 **Ashampstead** W Berk
35 J6 **Ashbocking** Suffk
35 K6 **Ashbocking Green** Suffk
50 F10 **Ashbourne** Derbys
16 E11 **Ashbrittle** Somset
5 P6 **Ashburton** Devon
15 J11 **Ashbury** Devon
19 J4 **Ashbury** Oxon
52 C2 **Ashby** N Linc
53 L9 **Ashby by Partney** Lincs
53 J4 **Ashby cum Fenby** NE Lin
52 F11 **Ashby de la Launde** Lincs
41 J4 **Ashby-de-la-Zouch** Leics
41 P5 **Ashby Folville** Leics
41 M9 **Ashby Magna** Leics
41 N9 **Ashby Parva** Leics
53 K8 **Ashby Puerorum** Lincs
31 M1 **Ashby St Ledgers** Nhants
45 M9 **Ashby St Mary** Norfk
29 N3 **Ashchurch** Gloucs
6 C6 **Ashcombe** Devon
17 J4 **Ashcombe** N Som
17 L8 **Ashcott** Somset
33 P8 **Ashdon** Essex
19 N10 **Ashe** Hants
23 J3 **Asheldham** Essex
34 C8 **Ashen** Essex
31 P10 **Ashendon** Bucks
20 F3 **Asheridge** Bucks
85 N3 **Ashfield** Stirlg
35 K4 **Ashfield** Suffk
35 L3 **Ashfield Green** Suffk
5 N9 **Ashford** Devon
15 J5 **Ashford** Devon
13 J2 **Ashford** Kent
20 H8 **Ashford** Surrey
39 K7 **Ashford Bowdler** Shrops
39 K7 **Ashford Carbonel** Shrops
19 P8 **Ashford Hill** Hants
50 G6 **Ashford in the Water** Derbys
77 N2 **Ashgill** S Lans
20 E12 **Ash Green** Surrey
41 J9 **Ash Green** Warwks
6 E1 **Ashill** Devon
44 E8 **Ashill** Norfk
17 J11 **Ashill** Somset
22 G5 **Ashingdon** Essex
73 M4 **Ashington** Nthumb
17 N11 **Ashington** Somset
11 J7 **Ashington** W Susx
79 P4 **Ashkirk** Border
29 L4 **Ashleworth** Gloucs
29 L4 **Ashleworth Quay** Gloucs
34 B5 **Ashley** Cambs
57 P11 **Ashley** Ches
15 L9 **Ashley** Devon
29 N9 **Ashley** Gloucs
9 J8 **Ashley** Hants
9 L2 **Ashley** Hants
13 P1 **Ashley** Kent
42 B11 **Ashley** Nhants
49 N7 **Ashley** Staffs
18 B7 **Ashley** Wilts
20 F3 **Ashley Green** Bucks
49 K7 **Ash Magna** Shrops
19 M8 **Ashmansworth** Hants
14 F8 **Ashmansworthy** Devon
15 N7 **Ash Mill** Devon
8 D4 **Ashmore** Dorset
19 N6 **Ashmore Green** W Berk
30 H3 **Ashorne** Warwks
51 J8 **Ashover** Derbys
40 H12 **Ashow** Warwks
49 L7 **Ash Parva** Shrops
28 H1 **Ashperton** Herefs
5 Q8 **Ashprington** Devon
16 F9 **Ash Priors** Somset
15 J9 **Ashreigney** Devon
34 G7 **Ash Street** Suffk
21 J10 **Ashtead** Surrey
6 D1 **Ash Thomas** Devon
49 J2 **Ashton** Ches
2 F9 **Ashton** Cnwll
6 B6 **Ashton** Devon
39 K8 **Ashton** Herefs
84 D7 **Ashton** Inver
31 Q4 **Ashton** Nhants
42 F11 **Ashton** Nhants
18 D8 **Ashton Common** Wilts
57 L8 **Ashton-in-Makerfield** Wigan
18 F2 **Ashton Keynes** Wilts
30 C6 **Ashton under Hill** Worcs
50 C2 **Ashton-under-Lyne** Tamesd
9 K5 **Ashurst** Hants
11 P3 **Ashurst** Kent
11 J6 **Ashurst** W Susx
11 N3 **Ashurstwood** W Susx
20 E11 **Ash Vale** Surrey
5 J2 **Ashwater** Devon
33 J8 **Ashwell** Herts
42 C7 **Ashwell** Rutlnd
33 J8 **Ashwell End** Herts
45 J9 **Ashwellthorpe** Norfk
17 P6 **Ashwick** Somset
44 B6 **Ashwicken** Norfk
62 E6 **Askam in Furness** Cumb
59 M10 **Askern** Donc
7 M4 **Askerswell** Dorset
20 D3 **Askett** Bucks
71 Q10 **Askham** Cumb
51 Q6 **Askham** Notts
59 M5 **Askham Bryan** York
59 M5 **Askham Richard** York
83 P5 **Asknish** Ag & B
64 G8 **Askrigg** N York
58 F5 **Askwith** N York
42 F4 **Aslackby** Lincs
45 J11 **Aslacton** Norfk
51 Q11 **Aslockton** Notts
71 J7 **Aspatria** Cumb
33 K10 **Aspenden** Herts
32 D9 **Aspley Guise** Beds
32 D9 **Aspley Heath** Beds
57 L7 **Aspull** Wigan
60 C8 **Asselby** E R Yk
34 F8 **Assington** Suffk
34 C6 **Assington Green** Suffk
49 Q3 **Astbury** Ches
31 P4 **Astcote** Nhants
53 J7 **Asterby** Lincs
38 G1 **Asterley** Shrops
38 H4 **Asterton** Shrops
30 H10 **Asthall** Oxon
30 H10 **Asthall Leigh** Oxon
107 M4 **Astle** Highld
49 K10 **Astley** Shrops
40 H9 **Astley** Warwks
57 M8 **Astley** Wigan
39 P8 **Astley** Worcs
39 N3 **Astley Abbots** Shrops
57 N6 **Astley Bridge** Bolton
39 P8 **Astley Cross** Worcs
49 L6 **Aston** Ches
57 K12 **Aston** Ches
50 F4 **Aston** Derbys
48 F3 **Aston** Flints
39 J7 **Aston** Herefs
33 J11 **Aston** Herts
31 J12 **Aston** Oxon
51 L4 **Aston** Rothm
39 P4 **Aston** Shrops
49 K9 **Aston** Shrops
40 B2 **Aston** Staffs
40 B3 **Aston** Staffs
49 N7 **Aston** Staffs
20 C6 **Aston** Wokham
49 L12 **Aston** Wrekin
32 C11 **Aston Abbotts** Bucks
39 L5 **Aston Botterell** Shrops
30 F3 **Aston Cantlow** Warwks
20 E2 **Aston Clinton** Bucks
29 J4 **Aston Crews** Herefs
33 J11 **Aston End** Herts
39 M4 **Aston-Eyre** Shrops
40 C12 **Aston Fields** Worcs
41 L8 **Aston Flamville** Leics
29 J4 **Aston Ingham** Herefs
31 L4 **Aston le Walls** Nhants
30 G7 **Aston Magna** Gloucs
39 K5 **Aston Munslow** Shrops
38 H6 **Aston on Clun** Shrops
38 G2 **Aston Pigott** Shrops
38 G2 **Aston Rogers** Shrops
20 B4 **Aston Rowant** Oxon
30 D6 **Aston Somerville** Worcs
30 F6 **Aston Subedge** Gloucs
19 P4 **Aston Tirrold** Oxon
41 K2 **Aston-upon-Trent** Derbys
19 P4 **Aston Upthorpe** Oxon
32 H8 **Astwick** Beds
32 D7 **Astwood** M Keyn
30 C2 **Astwood** Worcs
30 D2 **Astwood Bank** Worcs
42 F3 **Aswarby** Lincs
53 L9 **Aswardby** Lincs
39 K1 **Atcham** Shrops
8 B8 **Athelhampton** Dorset
35 K3 **Athelington** Suffk
17 J9 **Athelney** Somset
87 K6 **Athelstaneford** E Loth
15 K7 **Atherington** Devon
40 H7 **Atherstone** Warwks
30 G4 **Atherstone on Stour** Warwks
57 M8 **Atherton** Wigan
50 G10 **Atlow** Derbys
97 N3 **Attadale** Highld
52 E5 **Atterby** Lincs
51 J3 **Attercliffe** Sheff
41 J7 **Atterton** Leics
44 H10 **Attleborough** Norfk
41 J8 **Attleborough** Warwks
45 J6 **Attlebridge** Norfk
34 C6 **Attleton Green** Suffk
61 K4 **Atwick** E R Yk
18 C7 **Atworth** Wilts
52 D10 **Aubourn** Lincs
103 J8 **Auchedly** Abers
95 M6 **Auchenblae** Abers
85 N5 **Auchenbowie** Stirlg
70 D5 **Auchencairn** D & G
78 F11 **Auchencairn** D & G
75 Q6 **Auchencairn** N Ayrs
87 Q9 **Auchencrow** Border
86 F9 **Auchendinny** Mdloth
86 B10 **Auchengray** S Lans
101 M3 **Auchenhalrig** Moray
77 N3 **Auchenheath** S Lans
77 N11 **Auchenhessnane** D & G
83 P8 **Auchenlochan** Ag & B
76 F2 **Auchenmade** N Ayrs
68 G8 **Auchenmalg** D & G
76 F2 **Auchentiber** N Ayrs
85 J4 **Auchentroig** Stirlg
106 C6 **Auchindrean** Highld
102 E6 **Auchininna** Abers
77 J7 **Auchinleck** E Ayrs
85 L8 **Auchinloch** N Lans
85 M7 **Auchinstarry** N Lans
90 F2 **Auchintore** Highld
103 M7 **Auchiries** Abers
95 P3 **Auchlee** Abers
102 E9 **Auchleven** Abers
77 N4 **Auchlochan** S Lans
95 J2 **Auchlossan** Abers
91 M9 **Auchlyne** Stirlg
77 J5 **Auchmillan** E Ayrs
93 R6 **Auchmithie** Angus
86 E3 **Auchmuirbridge** Fife
94 H8 **Auchnacree** Angus
103 J7 **Auchnagatt** Abers
101 J9 **Auchnarrow** Moray
68 D7 **Auchnotteroch** D & G
101 L5 **Auchroisk** Moray
92 E12 **Auchterarder** P & K
98 E7 **Auchteraw** Highld
99 N5 **Auchterblair** Highld
105 M7 **Auchtercairn** Highld
86 E3 **Auchterderran** Fife
93 L8 **Auchterhouse** Angus
102 F7 **Auchterless** Abers
93 J12 **Auchtermuchty** Fife
106 H9 **Auchterneed** Highld
86 E4 **Auchtertool** Fife
97 L4 **Auchtertyre** Highld
91 N11 **Auchtubh** Stirlg
110 G3 **Auckengill** Highld
51 P1 **Auckley** Donc
50 B2 **Audenshaw** Tamesd
49 M6 **Audlem** Ches
49 P5 **Audley** Staffs
33 N8 **Audley End** Essex
33 N8 **Audley End** Essex
34 E6 **Audley End** Suffk
71 L7 **Aughertree** Cumb
60 C6 **Aughton** E R Yk
56 H7 **Aughton** Lancs
63 K8 **Aughton** Lancs
51 L4 **Aughton** Rothm
19 J9 **Aughton** Wilts
56 H7 **Aughton Park** Lancs
100 E4 **Auldearn** Highld
39 J10 **Aulden** Herefs
78 E10 **Auldgirth** D & G
77 K2 **Auldhouse** S Lans
97 N5 **Ault a' chruinn** Highld
105 N4 **Aultbea** Highld
105 L5 **Aultgrishin** Highld
106 F8 **Aultguish Inn** Highld
51 L7 **Ault Hucknall** Derbys
101 M3 **Aultmore** Moray
98 H4 **Aultnagoire** Highld
107 L6 **Aultnamain Inn** Highld
42 F3 **Aunsby** Lincs
28 G10 **Aust** S Glos
51 P2 **Austerfield** Donc
40 H6 **Austrey** Warwks
63 N8 **Austwick** N York
53 L7 **Authorpe** Lincs
18 G6 **Avebury** Wilts
22 C7 **Aveley** Thurr
29 M8 **Avening** Gloucs
51 Q9 **Averham** Notts
5 N10 **Aveton Gifford** Devon
99 N6 **Aviemore** Highld
19 L7 **Avington** W Berk
107 L10 **Avoch** Highld
8 G7 **Avon** Hants
85 Q8 **Avonbridge** Falk
31 K4 **Avon Dassett** Warwks
28 F12 **Avonmouth** Bristl
5 P8 **Avonwick** Devon
9 K3 **Awbridge** Hants
6 F3 **Awliscombe** Devon
29 J7 **Awre** Gloucs
51 L11 **Awsworth** Notts
17 L5 **Axbridge** Somset
19 Q11 **Axford** Hants
19 J6 **Axford** Wilts
6 H3 **Axminster** Devon
6 H5 **Axmouth** Devon
65 M3 **Aycliffe** Dur
72 H7 **Aydon** Nthumb
28 H8 **Aylburton** Gloucs
6 D4 **Aylesbeare** Devon
20 D1 **Aylesbury** Bucks
52 H3 **Aylesby** NE Lin
22 E10 **Aylesford** Kent
23 N11 **Aylesham** Kent
41 M7 **Aylestone** C Leic
45 K3 **Aylmerton** Norfk
45 K5 **Aylsham** Norfk
28 H2 **Aylton** Herefs
30 E9 **Aylworth** Gloucs
38 H8 **Aymestrey** Herefs
31 L7 **Aynho** Nhants
32 H12 **Ayot St Lawrence** Herts
76 F7 **Ayr** S Ayrs
64 H9 **Aysgarth** N York
16 E11 **Ayshford** Devon
62 H5 **Ayside** Cumb
42 C9 **Ayston** Rutlnd
22 C1 **Aythorpe Roding** Essex
81 J3 **Ayton** Border
65 M11 **Azerley** N York

B

6 C9 **Babbacombe** Torbay
33 L12 **Babbs Green** Herts
17 N9 **Babcary** Somset
17 Q6 **Babington** Somset
33 N6 **Babraham** Cambs
51 P5 **Babworth** Notts
111 h1 **Backaland** Ork
103 L5 **Backfolds** Abers
48 H2 **Backford** Ches
107 N3 **Backies** Highld
110 E5 **Backlass** Highld
97 J11 **Back of Keppoch** Highld
17 L3 **Backwell** N Som
45 J3 **Baconsthorpe** Norfk
28 D3 **Bacton** Herefs
45 M4 **Bacton** Norfk
34 H4 **Bacton** Suffk
57 Q4 **Bacup** Lancs
105 L7 **Badachro** Highld
18 H5 **Badbury** Swindn
31 M3 **Badby** Nhants
108 D7 **Badcall** Highld
108 E5 **Badcall** Highld
105 Q4 **Badcaul** Highld
40 G11 **Baddesley Clinton** Warwks
40 H7 **Baddesley Ensor** Warwks
108 C10 **Baddidarrach** Highld
86 D10 **Baddinsgill** Border
102 F7 **Badenscoth** Abers
101 L10 **Badenyon** Abers
39 N3 **Badger** Shrops
29 M5 **Badgeworth** Gloucs
17 K5 **Badgworth** Somset
97 K4 **Badicaul** Highld
35 M3 **Badingham** Suffk
23 J11 **Badlesmere** Kent
78 H5 **Badlieu** Border
110 F6 **Badlipster** Highld
105 P4 **Badluachrach** Highld
107 M4 **Badninish** Highld
105 Q4 **Badrallach** Highld
30 E5 **Badsey** Worcs
10 D1 **Badshot Lea** Surrey
59 L10 **Badsworth** Wakefd
34 G3 **Badwell Ash** Suffk
17 Q12 **Bagber** Dorset
66 C10 **Bagby** N York
53 K8 **Bag Enderby** Lincs
111 a7 **Bagh a Chaisteil** W Isls
111 a7 **Bagh a Tuath** W Isls
48 E1 **Bagillt** Flints
41 J11 **Baginton** Warwks
26 G9 **Baglan** Neath
48 H9 **Bagley** Shrops
17 L7 **Bagley** Somset
19 Q10 **Bagmore** Hants
50 B10 **Bagnall** Staffs
39 L7 **Bagot** Shrops
20 E10 **Bagshot** Surrey
29 J10 **Bagstone** S Glos
41 K6 **Bagworth** Leics
28 E4 **Bagwy Llydiart** Herefs
58 F6 **Baildon** Brad
58 F6 **Baildon Green** Brad
111 d2 **Baile Ailein** W Isls
111 b5 **Baile a Mhanaich** W Isls
88 G10 **Baile Mor** Ag & B
85 L9 **Baillieston** C Glas
64 G9 **Bainbridge** N York
102 D8 **Bainshole** Abers
42 F8 **Bainton** C Pete
60 G4 **Bainton** E R Yk
86 G2 **Baintown** Fife
80 E10 **Bairnkine** Border
50 G7 **Bakewell** Derbys
47 Q4 **Bala** Gwynd
111 d2 **Balallan** W Isls
98 F3 **Balbeg** Highld
92 H9 **Balbeggie** P & K
106 H12 **Balblair** Highld
107 L8 **Balblair** Highld
51 M1 **Balby** Donc
70 D5 **Balcary** D & G
98 G1 **Balchraggan** Highld
108 D4 **Balchreick** Highld
11 L4 **Balcombe** W Susx
87 M1 **Balcomie Links** Fife
65 N10 **Baldersby** N York
65 P11 **Baldersby St James** N York
57 L3 **Balderstone** Lancs
52 B12 **Balderton** Notts
93 M12 **Baldinnie** Fife
92 F11 **Baldinnies** P & K
33 J9 **Baldock** Herts
93 M8 **Baldovie** C Dund
56 d5 **Baldrine** IoM
12 F7 **Baldslow** E Susx
44 G3 **Bale** Norfk
93 K9 **Baledgarno** P & K
88 C7 **Balemartine** Ag & B
86 D8 **Balerno** C Edin
86 F2 **Balfarg** Fife
95 J8 **Balfield** Angus
111 h2 **Balfour** Ork
85 J5 **Balfron** Stirlg
102 E7 **Balgaveny** Abers
93 P5 **Balgavies** Angus
86 B4 **Balgonar** Fife
68 F9 **Balgowan** D & G
99 J9 **Balgowan** Highld
104 E8 **Balgown** Highld
68 D7 **Balgracie** D & G
93 M7 **Balgray** Angus
78 E4 **Balgray** S Lans
21 L8 **Balham** Gt Lon
93 J6 **Balhary** P & K
92 H8 **Balholmie** P & K
109 P3 **Baligill** Highld
93 K4 **Balintore** Angus
107 P7 **Balintore** Highld
107 M8 **Balintraid** Highld
111 b5 **Balivanich** W Isls
66 C10 **Balk** N York
93 K6 **Balkeerie** Angus
60 D8 **Balkholme** E R Yk
83 Q9 **Ballanlay** Ag & B
68 E3 **Ballantrae** S Ayrs
56 b6 **Ballasalla** IoM
94 F3 **Ballater** Abers
56 c3 **Ballaugh** IoM
107 M7 **Ballchraggan** Highld
87 J6 **Ballencrieff** E Loth
88 B7 **Ballevullin** Ag & B
50 G9 **Ballidon** Derbys
75 N5 **Balliekine** N Ayrs
84 B3 **Balliemore** Ag & B
68 G2 **Ballimorrie** S Ayrs
83 P6 **Ballimore** Ag & B
91 M11 **Ballimore** Stirlg
101 J7 **Ballindalloch** Moray
93 J9 **Ballindean** P & K
20 E3 **Ballinger Common** Bucks
28 G3 **Ballingham** Herefs
86 E3 **Ballingry** Fife
92 E5 **Ballinluig** P & K
93 M5 **Ballinshoe** Angus
92 G5 **Ballintuim** P & K
107 M11 **Balloch** Highld
85 M7 **Balloch** N Lans
92 C10 **Balloch** P & K
76 F11 **Balloch** S Ayrs
84 G6 **Balloch** W Duns
95 J3 **Ballogie** Abers
10 F5 **Balls Cross** W Susx
11 P3 **Balls Green** E Susx
89 J7 **Ballygown** Ag & B
82 E9 **Ballygrant** Ag & B
88 E5 **Ballyhaugh** Ag & B
84 E5 **Ballymenoch** Ag & B
69 P4 **Balmaclellan** D & G
69 P9 **Balmae** D & G
84 G5 **Balmaha** Stirlg
86 G1 **Balmalcolm** Fife
69 P9 **Balmangan** D & G
103 K10 **Balmedie** Abers
93 L10 **Balmerino** Fife
75 P6 **Balmichael** N Ayrs
94 D3 **Balmoral Castle Grounds** Abers
85 K8 **Balmore** E Duns
107 P6 **Balmuchy** Highld
93 P6 **Balmuir** Angus
86 E5 **Balmule** Fife
93 M10 **Balmullo** Fife
109 P12 **Balnacoil Lodge** Highld
105 P12 **Balnacra** Highld
94 E3 **Balnacroft** Abers
99 K2 **Balnafoich** Highld
92 E5 **Balnaguard** P & K
82 F3 **Balnahard** Ag & B
89 K9 **Balnahard** Ag & B
98 F3 **Balnain** Highld
108 G3 **Balnakeil** Highld
107 N8 **Balnapaling** Highld
59 N9 **Balne** N York
92 F8 **Balquharn** P & K
91 M11 **Balquhidder** Stirlg
40 G11 **Balsall Common** Solhll
40 E9 **Balsall Heath** Birm
31 K6 **Balscote** Oxon
33 P6 **Balsham** Cambs
111 m2 **Baltasound** Shet
69 K6 **Baltersan** D & G
17 M8 **Baltonsborough** Somset
94 B9 **Balvarran** P & K
89 Q11 **Balvicar** Ag & B
97 M6 **Balvraid** Highld
99 M3 **Balvraid** Highld
57 K4 **Bamber Bridge** Lancs
33 P11 **Bamber's Green** Essex
81 N7 **Bamburgh** Nthumb
81 N7 **Bamburgh Castle** Nthumb
93 J5 **Bamff** P & K
50 G4 **Bamford** Derbys
71 Q11 **Bampton** Cumb
16 C10 **Bampton** Devon
30 H12 **Bampton** Oxon
71 Q11 **Bampton Grange** Cumb
90 F2 **Banavie** Highld
31 L6 **Banbury** Oxon
26 C6 **Bancffosfelen** Carmth
95 L3 **Banchory** Abers
95 P2 **Banchory-Devenick** Abers
25 P6 **Bancycapel** Carmth
25 N5 **Bancyfelin** Carmth
93 J9 **Bandirran** P & K
102 F3 **Banff** Abers
54 H7 **Bangor** Gwynd
48 H6 **Bangor-is-y-coed** Wrexhm
14 D11 **Bangors** Cnwll
44 H11 **Banham** Norfk
9 K6 **Bank** Hants
70 G2 **Bankend** D & G
92 F8 **Bankfoot** P & K
77 K8 **Bankglen** E Ayrs
103 J12 **Bankhead** C Aber
86 B12 **Bankhead** S Lans
85 N7 **Banknock** Falk
56 H5 **Banks** Lancs
79 K11 **Bankshill** D & G
45 K4 **Banningham** Norfk
34 B11 **Bannister Green** Essex
85 N5 **Bannockburn** Stirlg
21 K10 **Banstead** Surrey
5 N10 **Bantham** Devon
85 M7 **Banton** N Lans
17 K4 **Banwell** N Som
22 H10 **Bapchild** Kent
18 E12 **Bapton** Wilts
111 d1 **Barabhas** W Isls
76 F5 **Barassie** S Ayrs
107 M7 **Barbaraville** Highld
76 G7 **Barbieston** S Ayrs
63 L6 **Barbon** Cumb
15 M3 **Barbrook** Devon
41 M12 **Barby** Nhants
90 D7 **Barcaldine** Ag & B
30 H6 **Barcheston** Warwks
11 N7 **Barcombe** E Susx
11 N6 **Barcombe Cross** E Susx
65 K8 **Barden** N York
12 C2 **Barden Park** Kent
33 Q9 **Bardfield End Green** Essex
34 B10 **Bardfield Saling** Essex
52 G9 **Bardney** Lincs
41 K5 **Bardon** Leics
72 E7 **Bardon Mill** Nthumb
85 K8 **Bardowie** E Duns
84 F8 **Bardrainney** Inver
62 F7 **Bardsea** Cumb
59 J5 **Bardsey** Leeds
34 F3 **Bardwell** Suffk
63 J8 **Bare** Lancs
38 H10 **Barewood** Herefs
69 J6 **Barfad** D & G
45 J8 **Barford** Norfk
30 H2 **Barford** Warwks
31 K7 **Barford St John** Oxon
8 F2 **Barford St Martin** Wilts
31 K7 **Barford St Michael** Oxon
23 N12 **Barfrestone** Kent
85 L9 **Bargeddie** N Lans
27 N8 **Bargoed** Caerph
69 J4 **Bargrennan** D & G
32 G2 **Barham** Cambs
23 N12 **Barham** Kent
35 J6 **Barham** Suffk
33 L4 **Bar Hill** Cambs
42 F7 **Barholm** Lincs
41 N5 **Barkby** Leics
41 N5 **Barkby Thorpe** Leics
41 R1 **Barkestone-le-Vale** Leics
20 C9 **Barkham** Wokham
21 N6 **Barking** Gt Lon
34 H6 **Barking** Suffk
21 N5 **Barkingside** Gt Lon
34 H6 **Barking Tye** Suffk
58 D9 **Barkisland** Calder
2 H5 **Barkla Shop** Cnwll
42 D2 **Barkston** Lincs
59 L7 **Barkston Ash** N York
33 L9 **Barkway** Herts
85 L9 **Barlanark** C Glas
50 B11 **Barlaston** Staffs
10 F6 **Barlavington** W Susx
51 L5 **Barlborough** Derbys
59 N7 **Barlby** N York
41 K6 **Barlestone** Leics
33 L8 **Barley** Herts
57 P1 **Barley** Lancs
42 C8 **Barleythorpe** Rutlnd
22 H5 **Barling** Essex
52 F8 **Barlings** Lincs

168 Barlochan - Bishopbriggs

70 D4 **Barlochan** D & G
51 J6 **Barlow** Derbys
73 K8 **Barlow** Gatesd
59 N8 **Barlow** N York
60 D4 **Barmby Moor** E R Yk
59 P8 **Barmby on the Marsh** E R Yk
75 M4 **Barmollack** Ag & B
47 K7 **Barmouth** Gwynd
65 N4 **Barmpton** Darltn
61 K3 **Barmston** E R Yk
83 Q4 **Barnacarry** Ag & B
42 F8 **Barnack** C Pete
65 J4 **Barnard Castle** Dur
31 K11 **Barnard Gate** Oxon
34 B7 **Barnardiston** Suffk
70 D4 **Barnbarroch** D & G
59 L12 **Barnburgh** Donc
45 P11 **Barnby** Suffk
59 N11 **Barnby Dun** Donc
52 C11 **Barnby in the Willows** Notts
51 P4 **Barnby Moor** Notts
68 E11 **Barncorkrie** D & G
21 K7 **Barnes** Gt Lon
12 D1 **Barnes Street** Kent
21 K4 **Barnet** Gt Lon
52 F2 **Barnetby le Wold** N Linc
44 G4 **Barney** Norfk
34 E2 **Barnham** Suffk
15 P6 **Barnham** W Susx
44 H8 **Barnham Broom** Norfk
93 R4 **Barnhead** Angus
93 N8 **Barnhill** C Dund
100 H4 **Barnhill** Moray
68 D5 **Barnhills** D & G
65 J5 **Barningham** Dur
34 F2 **Barningham** Suffk
52 H3 **Barnoldby le Beck** NE Lin
63 Q11 **Barnoldswick** Lancs
10 H5 **Barns Green** W Susx
59 J11 **Barnsley** Barns
30 E12 **Barnsley** Gloucs
15 K5 **Barnstaple** Devon
33 Q11 **Barnston** Essex
56 F11 **Barnston** Wirral
41 Q1 **Barnstone** Notts
40 D11 **Barnt Green** Worcs
86 E7 **Barnton** C Edin
49 L1 **Barnton** Ches
42 F12 **Barnwell All Saints** Nhants
42 F12 **Barnwell St Andrew** Nhants
29 M5 **Barnwood** Gloucs
76 E11 **Barr** S Ayrs
111 a6 **Barra Airport** W Isls
69 J8 **Barrachan** D & G
88 B7 **Barrapoll** Ag & B
72 G6 **Barrasford** Nthumb
84 H10 **Barrhead** E Rens
68 H3 **Barrhill** S Ayrs
33 L6 **Barrington** Cambs
17 K11 **Barrington** Somset
2 F7 **Barripper** Cnwll
84 F11 **Barrmill** N Ayrs
89 Q11 **Barrnacarry Bay** Ag & B
110 F2 **Barrock** Highld
29 M4 **Barrow** Gloucs
57 N2 **Barrow** Lancs
42 C7 **Barrow** Rutlnd
17 Q9 **Barrow** Somset
34 C4 **Barrow** Suffk
81 J11 **Barrow Burn** Nthumb
42 C3 **Barrowby** Lincs
42 D9 **Barrowden** Rutlnd
57 Q2 **Barrowford** Lancs
17 M3 **Barrow Gurney** N Som
60 H9 **Barrow Haven** N Linc
62 E8 **Barrow-in-Furness** Cumb
62 E8 **Barrow Island** Cumb
60 H9 **Barrow-upon-Humber** N Linc
41 M4 **Barrow upon Soar** Leics
41 J2 **Barrow upon Trent** Derbys
93 P8 **Barry** Angus
16 F3 **Barry** V Glam
16 F3 **Barry Island** V Glam
41 P5 **Barsby** Leics
45 N11 **Barsham** Suffk
40 G10 **Barston** Solhll
28 G1 **Bartestree** Herefs
102 H8 **Barthol Chapel** Abers
34 C11 **Bartholomew Green** Essex
49 N5 **Barthomley** Ches
9 K5 **Bartley** Hants
40 D10 **Bartley Green** Birm
33 P7 **Bartlow** Cambs
33 L5 **Barton** Cambs
49 J5 **Barton** Ches
30 E8 **Barton** Gloucs
56 G7 **Barton** Lancs
57 K2 **Barton** Lancs
65 M6 **Barton** N York
31 M11 **Barton** Oxon
6 C8 **Barton** Torbay
44 B8 **Barton Bendish** Norfk
29 L8 **Barton End** Gloucs
31 N7 **Barton Hartshorn** Bucks
41 M2 **Barton in Fabis** Notts
41 K6 **Barton in the Beans** Leics
32 F9 **Barton-le-Clay** Beds
66 G11 **Barton-le-Street** N York
60 C2 **Barton-le-Willows** N York
34 C3 **Barton Mills** Suffk
9 J8 **Barton-on-Sea** Hants
30 G7 **Barton-on-the-Heath** Warwks
17 M9 **Barton St David** Somset
32 C2 **Barton Seagrave** Nhants
19 M11 **Barton Stacey** Hants
15 L4 **Barton Town** Devon
45 M5 **Barton Turf** Norfk
40 F4 **Barton-under-Needwood** Staffs
60 H9 **Barton-upon-Humber** N Linc
60 H9 **Barton Waterside** N Linc
111 d1 **Barvas** W Isls
33 N2 **Barway** Cambs
41 K8 **Barwell** Leics
15 K10 **Barwick** Devon
17 M12 **Barwick** Somset
59 K6 **Barwick in Elmet** Leeds
48 H10 **Baschurch** Shrops
31 K2 **Bascote** Warwks
63 M12 **Bashall Eaves** Lancs
22 E5 **Basildon** Essex
19 Q9 **Basingstoke** Hants
50 G6 **Baslow** Derbys
17 J7 **Bason Bridge** Somset
28 C10 **Bassaleg** Newpt
80 E5 **Bassendean** Border
71 K8 **Bassenthwaite** Cumb
9 M4 **Bassett** C Sotn
33 K7 **Bassingbourn** Cambs
52 C10 **Bassingham** Lincs
42 D5 **Bassingthorpe** Lincs
33 K10 **Bassus Green** Herts
42 G7 **Baston** Lincs
45 N6 **Bastwick** Norfk
20 G5 **Batchworth** Herts
7 N3 **Batcombe** Dorset
17 Q8 **Batcombe** Somset
21 J1 **Batford** Herts
17 Q4 **Bath** BaNES
18 B7 **Bathampton** BaNES
16 E10 **Bathealton** Somset
18 B7 **Batheaston** BaNES
18 B7 **Bathford** BaNES
86 B8 **Bathgate** W Loth
51 Q8 **Bathley** Notts
4 G5 **Bathpool** Cnwll
16 H10 **Bathpool** Somset
35 L9 **Bath Side** Essex
85 Q9 **Bathville** W Loth
17 N6 **Bathway** Somset
58 G8 **Batley** Kirk
30 F7 **Batsford** Gloucs
66 E6 **Battersby** N York
21 L7 **Battersea** Gt Lon
34 G6 **Battisford Tye** Suffk
12 E7 **Battle** E Susx
27 L3 **Battle** Powys
93 M5 **Battledykes** Angus
52 H11 **Battle of Britain Memorial Flight** Lincs
22 F5 **Battlesbridge** Essex
16 C10 **Battleton** Somset
29 M1 **Baughton** Worcs
19 P8 **Baughurst** Hants
95 K4 **Baulds** Abers
19 K3 **Baulking** Oxon
52 H8 **Baumber** Lincs
30 D12 **Baunton** Gloucs
8 F2 **Baverstock** Wilts
45 J8 **Bawburgh** Norfk
44 H6 **Bawdeswell** Norfk
17 J8 **Bawdrip** Somset
35 M8 **Bawdsey** Suffk
51 P3 **Bawtry** Donc
57 P4 **Baxenden** Lancs
40 H7 **Baxterley** Warwks
104 C10 **Bay** Highld
111 e2 **Bayble** W Isls
9 N3 **Baybridge** Hants
62 F7 **Baycliff** Cumb
19 K5 **Baydon** Wilts
21 L2 **Bayford** Herts
17 Q9 **Bayford** Somset
111 a4 **Bayhead** W Isls
34 H6 **Baylham** Suffk
28 G4 **Baysham** Herefs
39 J1 **Bayston Hill** Shrops
34 C8 **Baythorne End** Essex
39 M7 **Bayton** Worcs
19 N1 **Bayworth** Oxon
31 Q6 **Beachampton** Bucks
44 C8 **Beachamwell** Norfk
12 C10 **Beachy Head** E Susx
6 G2 **Beacon** Devon
34 F10 **Beacon End** Essex
10 E3 **Beacon Hill** Surrey
20 C4 **Beacon's Bottom** Bucks
20 F5 **Beaconsfield** Bucks
66 F9 **Beadlam** N York
32 F8 **Beadlow** Beds
81 P8 **Beadnell** Nthumb
15 K8 **Beaford** Devon
59 M8 **Beal** N York
81 M6 **Beal** Nthumb
4 H5 **Bealsmill** Cnwll
7 L3 **Beaminster** Dorset
73 L9 **Beamish** Dur
58 E4 **Beamsley** N York
18 D7 **Beanacre** Wilts
81 M9 **Beanley** Nthumb
5 L4 **Beardon** Devon
6 D3 **Beare** Devon
11 J2 **Beare Green** Surrey
30 F3 **Bearley** Warwks
73 M11 **Bearpark** Dur
85 J8 **Bearsden** E Duns
22 F11 **Bearsted** Kent
49 N7 **Bearstone** Shrops
40 D9 **Bearwood** Birm
8 F7 **Bearwood** Poole
78 H8 **Beattock** D & G
22 C2 **Beauchamp Roding** Essex
27 N6 **Beaufort** Blae G
9 L7 **Beaulieu** Hants
9 L6 **Beaulieu House** Hants
107 J11 **Beauly** Highld
54 H6 **Beaumaris** IoA
71 M4 **Beaumont** Cumb
35 J10 **Beaumont** Essex
7 b2 **Beaumont** Jersey
40 G12 **Beausale** Warwks
9 P3 **Beauworth** Hants
14 H11 **Beaworthy** Devon
34 C10 **Beazley End** Essex
56 G11 **Bebington** Wirral
45 N11 **Beccles** Suffk
57 J4 **Becconsall** Lancs
39 N2 **Beckbury** Shrops
21 M9 **Beckenham** Gt Lon
52 G7 **Beckering** Lincs
62 B2 **Beckermet** Cumb
70 H5 **Beckfoot** Cumb
29 N2 **Beckford** Worcs
18 G7 **Beckhampton** Wilts
52 C11 **Beckingham** Lincs
51 R3 **Beckingham** Notts
18 B9 **Beckington** Somset
38 H6 **Beckjay** Shrops
12 G5 **Beckley** E Susx
31 M10 **Beckley** Oxon
34 B2 **Beck Row** Suffk
62 E6 **Beck Side** Cumb
21 N7 **Beckton** Gt Lon
58 H4 **Beckwithshaw** N York
21 P6 **Becontree** Gt Lon
65 M9 **Bedale** N York
8 C4 **Bedchester** Dorset
27 M10 **Beddau** Rhondd
54 H11 **Beddgelert** Gwynd
11 N8 **Beddingham** E Susx
21 L9 **Beddington** Gt Lon
21 L9 **Beddington Corner** Gt Lon
35 K4 **Bedfield** Suffk
32 F6 **Bedford** Beds
10 B8 **Bedhampton** Hants
35 K3 **Bedingfield** Suffk
35 K3 **Bedingfield Street** Suffk
58 H2 **Bedlam** N York
12 H2 **Bedlam Lane** Kent
73 M5 **Bedlington** Nthumb
27 M8 **Bedlinog** Myr Td
17 N2 **Bedminster** Bristl
17 N3 **Bedminster Down** Bristl
20 H3 **Bedmond** Herts
40 C4 **Bednall** Staffs
80 E10 **Bedrule** Border
38 G7 **Bedstone** Shrops
27 N10 **Bedwas** Caerph
27 N8 **Bedwellty** Caerph
41 J9 **Bedworth** Warwks
41 P6 **Beeby** Leics
10 B3 **Beech** Hants
49 Q7 **Beech** Staffs
20 B9 **Beech Hill** W Berk
18 G8 **Beechingstoke** Wilts
19 N5 **Beedon** W Berk
19 N5 **Beedon Hill** W Berk
61 J4 **Beeford** E R Yk
50 H7 **Beeley** Derbys
52 H3 **Beelsby** NE Lin
19 P7 **Beenham** W Berk
6 G5 **Beer** Devon
17 K9 **Beer** Somset
17 J11 **Beercrocombe** Somset
7 N1 **Beer Hackett** Dorset
5 Q11 **Beesands** Devon
53 M7 **Beesby** Lincs
5 Q11 **Beeson** Devon
32 G7 **Beeston** Beds
49 K4 **Beeston** Ches
58 H7 **Beeston** Leeds
44 E7 **Beeston** Norfk
51 M12 **Beeston** Notts
45 J2 **Beeston Regis** Norfk
70 E2 **Beeswing** D & G
63 J6 **Beetham** Cumb
6 H1 **Beetham** Somset
44 F6 **Beetley** Norfk
31 L10 **Begbroke** Oxon
25 K7 **Begelly** Pembks
38 E6 **Beguildy** Powys
45 N8 **Beighton** Norfk
51 K4 **Beighton** Sheff
50 H9 **Beighton Hill** Derbys
92 H11 **Bein Inn** P & K
84 F11 **Beith** N Ayrs
23 M11 **Bekesbourne** Kent
45 L6 **Belaugh** Norfk
40 B11 **Belbroughton** Worcs
8 B5 **Belchalwell** Dorset
8 B5 **Belchalwell Street** Dorset
34 D8 **Belchamp Otten** Essex
34 D8 **Belchamp St Paul** Essex
34 D8 **Belchamp Walter** Essex
53 J8 **Belchford** Lincs
81 M7 **Belford** Nthumb
41 N6 **Belgrave** C Leic
87 M6 **Belhaven** E Loth
103 K10 **Belhelvie** Abers
101 N9 **Belhinnie** Abers
101 L11 **Bellabeg** Abers
83 M5 **Bellanoch** Ag & B
93 J4 **Bellaty** Angus
58 B3 **Bell Busk** N York
53 L7 **Belleau** Lincs
40 C11 **Bell End** Worcs
65 K8 **Bellerby** N York
71 M4 **Belle Vue** Cumb
59 J9 **Belle Vue** Wakefd
78 D2 **Bellfield** S Lans
78 F5 **Bellfield** S Lans
20 F3 **Bellingdon** Bucks
72 F4 **Bellingham** Nthumb
75 K5 **Belloch** Ag & B
75 K6 **Bellochantuy** Ag & B
49 K6 **Bell o' th' Hill** Ches
85 M10 **Bellshill** N Lans
85 N10 **Bellside** N Lans
86 C8 **Bellsquarry** W Loth
12 C3 **Bells Yew Green** E Susx
17 N4 **Belluton** BaNES
107 K10 **Belmaduthy** Highld
57 M6 **Belmont** Bl w D
21 K10 **Belmont** Gt Lon
76 F7 **Belmont** S Ayrs
111 m2 **Belmont** Shet
101 M11 **Belnacraig** Abers
51 J10 **Belper** Derbys
51 J10 **Belper Lane End** Derbys
73 K5 **Belsay** Nthumb
80 D8 **Belses** Border
5 P8 **Belsford** Devon
20 G4 **Belsize** Herts
35 J8 **Belstead** Suffk
5 M2 **Belstone** Devon
57 N4 **Belthorn** Lancs
23 M9 **Beltinge** Kent
72 E7 **Beltingham** Nthumb
52 B3 **Beltoft** N Linc
41 K3 **Belton** Leics
42 D3 **Belton** Lincs
52 B3 **Belton** N Linc
45 P9 **Belton** Norfk
42 B9 **Belton** Rutlnd
21 P7 **Belvedere** Gt Lon
42 B4 **Belvoir** Leics
42 B4 **Belvoir Castle** Leics
9 Q9 **Bembridge** IoW
8 G2 **Bemerton** Wilts
67 P12 **Bempton** E R Yk
45 Q12 **Benacre** Suffk
111 b5 **Benbecula Airport** W Isls
77 M11 **Benbuie** D & G
90 C8 **Benderloch** Ag & B
12 F4 **Benenden** Kent
73 J9 **Benfieldside** Dur
21 L1 **Bengeo** Herts
30 D5 **Bengeworth** Worcs
35 N5 **Benhall Green** Suffk
35 M5 **Benhall Street** Suffk
95 N7 **Benholm** Abers
59 M3 **Beningbrough** N York
33 J11 **Benington** Herts
43 L2 **Benington** Lincs
54 G5 **Benllech** IoA
84 C6 **Benmore** Ag & B
4 G2 **Bennacott** Cnwll
75 Q8 **Bennan** N Ayrs
90 G3 **Ben Nevis** Highld
52 H7 **Benniworth** Lincs
12 E1 **Benover** Kent
58 F5 **Ben Rhydding** Brad
76 F3 **Benslie** N Ayrs
19 Q3 **Benson** Oxon
95 N2 **Benthoul** C Aber
59 M11 **Bentley** Donc
60 H7 **Bentley** E R Yk
10 C2 **Bentley** Hants
35 J8 **Bentley** Suffk
40 H8 **Bentley** Warwks
15 L5 **Benton** Devon
79 M10 **Bentpath** D & G
15 M5 **Bentwichen** Devon
19 Q11 **Bentworth** Hants
93 K8 **Benvie** Angus
7 M3 **Benville** Dorset
43 K11 **Benwick** Cambs
40 E12 **Beoley** Worcs
97 J10 **Beoraidbeg** Highld
10 D6 **Bepton** W Susx
33 M10 **Berden** Essex
24 E3 **Berea** Pembks
5 J6 **Bere Alston** Devon
5 K7 **Bere Ferrers** Devon
8 C8 **Bere Regis** Dorset
45 M9 **Bergh Apton** Norfk
19 P2 **Berinsfield** Oxon
29 J8 **Berkeley** Gloucs
20 F2 **Berkhamsted** Herts
18 B10 **Berkley** Somset
40 G10 **Berkswell** Solhll
21 M7 **Bermondsey** Gt Lon
97 L5 **Bernera** Highld
84 C5 **Bernice** Ag & B
104 E11 **Bernisdale** Highld
19 Q2 **Berrick Prior** Oxon
19 Q3 **Berrick Salome** Oxon
110 D10 **Berriedale** Highld
71 N9 **Berrier** Cumb
38 E2 **Berriew** Powys
39 K2 **Berrington** Shrops
39 L8 **Berrington** Worcs
39 L8 **Berrington Green** Worcs
16 H6 **Berrow** Somset
39 N9 **Berrow Green** Worcs
101 P3 **Berryhillock** Moray
101 P5 **Berryhillock** Moray
15 K3 **Berrynarbor** Devon
5 Q7 **Berry Pomeroy** Devon
48 F6 **Bersham** Wrexhm
11 P8 **Berwick** E Susx
18 G6 **Berwick Bassett** Wilts
73 L6 **Berwick Hill** Nthumb
18 F11 **Berwick St James** Wilts
8 D3 **Berwick St John** Wilts
8 D2 **Berwick St Leonard** Wilts
81 L4 **Berwick-upon-Tweed** Nthumb
42 B5 **Bescaby** Leics
56 H6 **Bescar** Lancs
30 B5 **Besford** Worcs
51 N1 **Bessacarr** Donc
19 M1 **Bessels Leigh** Oxon
61 K2 **Bessingby** E R Yk
45 J3 **Bessingham** Norfk
44 H10 **Besthorpe** Norfk
52 B9 **Besthorpe** Notts
51 M10 **Bestwood Village** Notts
60 H5 **Beswick** E R Yk
21 K12 **Betchworth** Surrey
34 H3 **Beth Chatto Garden** Essex
54 G8 **Bethel** Gwynd
54 E7 **Bethel** IoA
12 H3 **Bethersden** Kent
55 J8 **Bethesda** Gwynd
25 J5 **Bethesda** Pembks
26 F4 **Bethlehem** Carmth
21 M6 **Bethnal Green** Gt Lon
49 N6 **Betley** Staffs
22 C8 **Betsham** Kent
23 P11 **Betteshanger** Kent
7 K3 **Bettiscombe** Dorset
49 J8 **Bettisfield** Wrexhm
28 C10 **Bettws** Newpt
37 K9 **Bettws Bledrws** Cerdgn
38 D3 **Bettws Cedewain** Powys
36 E10 **Bettws Evan** Cerdgn
28 D7 **Bettws-Newydd** Mons
109 M4 **Bettyhill** Highld
27 J10 **Betws** Brdgnd
48 B6 **Betws Gwerfil Goch** Denbgs
55 L9 **Betws-y-Coed** Conwy
55 N6 **Betws-yn-Rhos** Conwy
36 E10 **Beulah** Cerdgn
37 Q9 **Beulah** Powys
51 P6 **Bevercotes** Notts
60 H6 **Beverley** E R Yk
29 M9 **Beverstone** Gloucs
71 Q1 **Bewcastle** Cumb
39 P7 **Bewdley** Worcs
58 F2 **Bewerley** N York
61 K4 **Bewholme** E R Yk
12 E8 **Bexhill** E Susx
21 P8 **Bexley** Gt Lon
21 P8 **Bexleyheath** Gt Lon
43 Q9 **Bexwell** Norfk
34 F4 **Beyton** Suffk
34 F4 **Beyton Green** Suffk
111 c2 **Bhaltos** W Isls
111 a7 **Bhatarsaigh** W Isls
30 E11 **Bibury** Gloucs
31 N9 **Bicester** Oxon
40 F10 **Bickenhill** Solhll
42 H3 **Bicker** Lincs
57 J7 **Bickerstaffe** Lancs
59 K4 **Bickerton** N York
40 B5 **Bickford** Staffs
5 Q6 **Bickington** Devon
15 J6 **Bickington** Devon
5 L7 **Bickleigh** Devon
6 C2 **Bickleigh** Devon
21 N9 **Bickley** Gt Lon
67 K8 **Bickley** N York
49 K6 **Bickley Moss** Ches
22 F3 **Bicknacre** Essex
16 F8 **Bicknoller** Somset
22 G10 **Bicknor** Kent
38 F5 **Bicton** Shrops
49 J11 **Bicton** Shrops
12 C2 **Bidborough** Kent
12 G3 **Biddenden** Kent
32 E6 **Biddenham** Beds
18 C6 **Biddestone** Wilts
17 K5 **Biddisham** Somset
31 N6 **Biddlesden** Bucks
50 B8 **Biddulph** Staffs
50 B8 **Biddulph Moor** Staffs
14 H6 **Bideford** Devon
30 E4 **Bidford-on-Avon** Warwks
60 D5 **Bielby** E R Yk
95 P2 **Bieldside** C Aber
9 N10 **Bierley** IoW
20 D1 **Bierton** Bucks
69 K9 **Big Balcraig** D & G
5 N10 **Bigbury** Devon
5 N10 **Bigbury-on-Sea** Devon
52 F3 **Bigby** Lincs
77 L10 **Big Carlae** D & G
78 G2 **Biggar** S Lans
50 F8 **Biggin** Derbys
50 H10 **Biggin** Derbys
59 M7 **Biggin** N York
21 N10 **Biggin Hill** Gt Lon
21 N10 **Biggin Hill Airport** Gt Lon
32 H7 **Biggleswade** Beds
79 M11 **Bigholms** D & G
109 Q3 **Bighouse** Highld
9 Q1 **Bighton** Hants
71 L5 **Biglands** Cumb
10 F7 **Bignor** W Susx
27 P7 **Big Pit Blaenavon** Torfn
70 G11 **Bigrigg** Cumb
105 L6 **Big Sand** Highld
111 k5 **Bigton** Shet
51 M11 **Bilborough** C Nott
16 D7 **Bilbrook** Somset
59 M5 **Bilbrough** N York
110 F5 **Bilbster** Highld
65 L3 **Bildershaw** Dur
34 G6 **Bildeston** Suffk
22 D5 **Billericay** Essex
41 Q7 **Billesdon** Leics
30 F3 **Billesley** Warwks
42 G4 **Billingborough** Lincs
57 K8 **Billinge** St Hel
35 J2 **Billingford** Norfk
44 G6 **Billingford** Norfk
66 C3 **Billingham** S on T
52 G11 **Billinghay** Lincs
59 K12 **Billingley** Barns
10 H5 **Billingshurst** W Susx
39 N5 **Billingsley** Shrops
32 D11 **Billington** Beds
57 N2 **Billington** Lancs
45 N7 **Billockby** Norfk
73 L12 **Billy Row** Dur
57 K2 **Bilsborrow** Lancs
53 M8 **Bilsby** Lincs
10 F9 **Bilsham** W Susx
13 K3 **Bilsington** Kent
51 N8 **Bilsthorpe** Notts
86 F8 **Bilston** Mdloth
40 C8 **Bilston** Wolves
41 J6 **Bilstone** Leics
61 K7 **Bilton** E R Yk
59 K3 **Bilton** N York
59 L4 **Bilton** N York
41 L11 **Bilton** Warwks
52 H5 **Binbrook** Lincs
7 P6 **Bincombe** Dorset
17 N6 **Binegar** Somset
20 D8 **Binfield** Br For
20 C7 **Binfield Heath** Oxon
72 H6 **Bingfield** Nthumb
51 P11 **Bingham** Notts
8 B7 **Bingham's Melcombe** Dorset
58 E6 **Bingley** Brad
44 G3 **Binham** Norfk
41 J10 **Binley** Covtry
19 M9 **Binley** Hants
41 K11 **Binley Woods** Warwks
8 C9 **Binnegar** Dorset
85 P8 **Binniehill** Falk
10 F2 **Binscombe** Surrey
9 P8 **Binstead** IoW
10 C2 **Binsted** Hants
10 F8 **Binsted** W Susx
30 F4 **Binton** Warwks
44 G5 **Bintree** Norfk
34 F11 **Birch** Essex
44 C4 **Bircham Newton** Norfk
44 C4 **Bircham Tofts** Norfk
33 N11 **Birchanger** Essex
40 E2 **Birch Cross** Staffs
39 J8 **Bircher** Herefs
34 F11 **Birch Green** Essex
27 N11 **Birchgrove** Cardif
26 F8 **Birchgrove** Swans
11 N4 **Birchgrove** W Susx
23 P9 **Birchington** Kent
40 H8 **Birchley Heath** Warwks
50 G8 **Birchover** Derbys
50 D4 **Birch Vale** Derbys
16 H12 **Birch Wood** Somset
57 M9 **Birchwood** Warrtn
51 N3 **Bircotes** Notts
34 B8 **Birdbrook** Essex
66 C11 **Birdforth** N York
10 D9 **Birdham** W Susx
31 K1 **Birdingbury** Warwks
29 N6 **Birdlip** Gloucs
60 E2 **Birdsall** N York
58 G11 **Birds Edge** Kirk
22 C2 **Birds Green** Essex
39 P5 **Birdsgreen** Shrops
7 K3 **Birdsmoorgate** Dorset
51 J1 **Birdwell** Barns
80 G6 **Birgham** Border
107 M4 **Birichin** Highld
65 N7 **Birkby** N York
56 G6 **Birkdale** Sefton
102 C3 **Birkenbog** Abers
56 G10 **Birkenhead** Wirral
102 F6 **Birkenhills** Abers
58 G8 **Birkenshaw** Kirk
94 F4 **Birkhall** Abers
93 L8 **Birkhill** Angus
79 K6 **Birkhill** D & G
59 M8 **Birkin** N York
39 J10 **Birley** Herefs
51 J3 **Birley Carr** Sheff
22 D10 **Birling** Kent
30 C5 **Birlingham** Worcs
40 E9 **Birmingham** Birm
40 F10 **Birmingham Airport** Solhll
92 F7 **Birnam** P & K
103 K8 **Birness** Abers
95 J3 **Birse** Abers
95 J3 **Birsemore** Abers
58 G8 **Birstall** Kirk
41 N5 **Birstall** Leics
58 G3 **Birstwith** N York
73 M9 **Birtley** Gatesd
38 G8 **Birtley** Herefs
72 F5 **Birtley** Nthumb
29 K2 **Birts Street** Worcs
42 C9 **Bisbrooke** Rutlnd
52 H6 **Biscathorpe** Lincs
20 D6 **Bisham** W & M
30 C4 **Bishampton** Worcs
15 M7 **Bish Mill** Devon
65 L2 **Bishop Auckland** Dur
52 E5 **Bishopbridge** Lincs
85 K8 **Bishopbriggs** E Duns

Bishop Burton - Bramshott 169

60 G6 Bishop Burton E R Yk
65 N2 Bishop Middleham Dur
101 J3 Bishopmill Moray
59 J2 Bishop Monkton N York
52 E5 Bishop Norton Lincs
23 M11 Bishopsbourne Kent
18 F7 Bishops Cannings Wilts
38 G4 Bishop's Castle Shrops
17 Q12 Bishop's Caundle Dorset
29 N4 Bishop's Cleeve Gloucs
39 M11 Bishop's Frome Herefs
33 Q12 Bishop's Green Essex
16 G10 Bishops Hull Somset
31 K3 Bishop's Itchington Warwks
16 G9 Bishops Lydeard Somset
29 L4 Bishop's Norton Gloucs
15 N7 Bishop's Nympton Devon
49 P9 Bishop's Offley Staffs
33 M11 Bishop's Stortford Herts
9 Q2 Bishop's Sutton Hants
30 H2 Bishop's Tachbrook Warwks
15 K6 Bishop's Tawton Devon
6 B7 Bishopsteignton Devon
9 M4 Bishopstoke Hants
26 D10 Bishopston Swans
20 C2 Bishopstone Bucks
11 P9 Bishopstone E Susx
38 H12 Bishopstone Herefs
23 N9 Bishopstone Kent
19 J4 Bishopstone Swindn
8 F3 Bishopstone Wilts
18 D11 Bishopstrow Wilts
17 N4 Bishop Sutton BaNES
9 P4 Bishop's Waltham Hants
6 H1 Bishopswood Somset
49 Q12 Bishop's Wood Staffs
17 N3 Bishopsworth Bristl
58 H2 Bishop Thornton N York
59 N5 Bishopthorpe York
65 P4 Bishopton Darltn
84 G8 Bishopton Rens
60 D3 Bishop Wilton E R Yk
28 D10 Bishton Newpt
40 D4 Bishton Staffs
29 M7 Bisley Gloucs
20 F10 Bisley Surrey
2 H7 Bissoe Cnwll
9 G7 Bisterne Hants
42 E4 Bitchfield Lincs
15 J4 Bittadon Devon
5 N8 Bittaford Devon
39 K6 Bitterley Shrops
9 M5 Bitterne C Sotn
41 M9 Bitteswell Leics
17 P3 Bitton S Glos
20 B6 Bix Oxon
111 k4 Bixter Shet
41 M7 Blaby Leics
80 H4 Blackadder Border
5 Q9 Blackawton Devon
6 E2 Blackborough Devon
43 Q7 Blackborough End Norfk
30 H12 Black Bourton Oxon
11 Q6 Blackboys E Susx
51 J10 Blackbrook Derbys
57 K9 Blackbrook St Hel
49 N7 Blackbrook Staffs
102 H11 Blackburn Abers
57 M4 Blackburn Bl w D
86 B8 Blackburn W Loth
73 L7 Black Callerton N u Ty
91 J5 Black Corries Lodge Highld
77 K9 Blackcraig E Ayrs
90 C8 Black Crofts Ag & B
103 K11 Blackdog Abers
15 N9 Black Dog Devon
7 K3 Blackdown Dorset
51 J1 Blacker Hill Barns
21 P8 Blackfen Gt Lon
9 M7 Blackfield Hants
85 P2 Blackford P & K
17 K6 Blackford Somset
17 P10 Blackford Somset
41 J4 Blackfordby Leics
86 E7 Blackhall C Edin
73 Q11 Blackhall Colliery Dur
79 N2 Blackhaugh Border
21 M7 Blackheath Gt Lon
51 N9 Blackheath Sandw
35 N2 Blackheath Suffk
10 G2 Blackheath Surrey
103 M4 Blackhill Abers
103 M6 Blackhill Abers
73 J9 Blackhill Dur
103 J6 Blackhill of Clackriach Abers
6 D4 Blackhorse Devon
78 G7 Blacklaw D & G
57 Q8 Blackley Manch
94 C9 Blacklunans P & K
28 F2 Blackmarstone Herefs
27 K10 Blackmill Brdgnd
10 C4 Blackmoor Hants
17 L4 Blackmoor N Som
58 E10 Blackmoorfoot Kirk
22 C3 Blackmore Essex
34 C9 Blackmore End Essex
86 C6 Blackness Falk
10 C2 Blacknest Hants
34 C11 Black Notley Essex
57 Q1 Blacko Lancs
26 E10 Black Pill Swans
56 F2 Blackpool Bpool
6 B12 Blackpool Devon
56 G3 Blackpool Airport Lancs
85 P9 Blackridge W Loth
57 L6 Blackrod Bolton
101 J7 Blacksboat Moray
70 G3 Blackshaw D & G
58 C8 Blackshaw Head Calder
57 N5 Blacksnape Bl w D
11 K6 Blackstone W Susx
45 Q11 Black Street Suffk
31 N9 Blackthorn Oxon
34 E4 Blackthorpe Suffk
60 E8 Blacktoft E R Yk
95 P2 Blacktop C Aber
14 H10 Black Torrington Devon
50 G10 Blackwall Derbys
2 H6 Blackwater Cnwll
20 D10 Blackwater Hants
9 N9 Blackwater IoW
16 H11 Blackwater Somset
75 N6 Blackwaterfoot N Ayrs
71 N5 Blackwell Cumb
50 E6 Blackwell Derbys
51 K8 Blackwell Derbys
30 G5 Blackwell Warwks
40 C11 Blackwell Worcs
27 N8 Blackwood Caerph
78 E10 Blackwood D & G
77 N3 Blackwood S Lans
48 H2 Blacon Ches
69 K8 Bladnoch D & G
31 K10 Bladon Oxon
36 D10 Blaenannerch Cerdgn
47 L3 Blaenau Ffestiniog Gwynd
27 Q7 Blaenavon Torfn
25 L2 Blaenffos Pembks
27 J9 Blaengarw Brdgnd
27 J7 Blaengwrach Neath
27 J9 Blaengwynfi Neath
37 K7 Blaenpennal Cerdgn
37 J5 Blaenplwyf Cerdgn
36 D10 Blaenporth Cerdgn
27 K8 Blaenrhondda Rhondd
25 L4 Blaenwaun Carmth
25 N4 Blaen-y-Coed Carmth
27 K8 Blaen-y-cwm Rhondd
17 M4 Blagdon N Som
16 G11 Blagdon Somset
6 B9 Blagdon Torbay
16 G11 Blagdon Hill Somset
90 E2 Blaich Highld
89 N3 Blain Highld
27 P7 Blaina Blae G
92 C3 Blair Atholl P & K
85 M3 Blair Drummond Stirlg
92 H6 Blairgowrie P & K
86 B5 Blairhall Fife
86 B3 Blairingone P & K
85 N4 Blairlogie Stirlg
84 D6 Blairmore Ag & B
108 D4 Blairmore Highld
101 J11 Blairnamarrow Moray
83 P8 Blair's Ferry Ag & B
29 J5 Blaisdon Gloucs
39 P6 Blakebrook Worcs
39 Q6 Blakedown Worcs
34 B11 Blake End Essex
49 K2 Blakemere Ches
28 D1 Blakemere Herefs
40 D7 Blakenall Heath Wsall
29 J7 Blakeney Gloucs
44 G2 Blakeney Norfk
49 N6 Blakenhall Ches
40 B7 Blakenhall Wolves
31 N4 Blakesley Nhants
72 H10 Blanchland Nthumb
8 C6 Blandford Forum Dorset
8 C6 Blandford St Mary Dorset
58 G4 Bland Hill N York
85 J7 Blanefield Stirlg
52 F10 Blankney Lincs
85 L10 Blantyre S Lans
90 F3 Blar a' Chaorainn Highld
98 H9 Blargie Highld
90 F3 Blarmachfoldach Highld
42 B10 Blaston Leics
42 D10 Blatherwycke Nhants
62 F5 Blawith Cumb
69 P3 Blawquhairn D & G
35 M5 Blaxhall Suffk
51 P2 Blaxton Donc
73 L8 Blaydon Gatesd
17 L7 Bleadney Somset
17 J5 Bleadon N Som
23 L10 Blean Kent
51 Q10 Bleasby Notts
63 L12 Bleasdale Lancs
93 M11 Blebocraigs Fife
38 E8 Bleddfa Powys
30 G9 Bledington Gloucs
20 C3 Bledlow Bucks
20 C4 Bledlow Ridge Bucks
87 J9 Blegbie E Loth
64 B2 Blencarn Cumb
71 K6 Blencogo Cumb
10 B7 Blendworth Hants
71 J7 Blennerhasset Cumb
31 L9 Bletchingdon Oxon
21 M12 Bletchingley Surrey
32 C9 Bletchley M Keyn
49 L8 Bletchley Shrops
25 J5 Bletherston Pembks
32 E5 Bletsoe Beds
19 N4 Blewbury Oxon
45 K4 Blickling Norfk
51 N9 Blidworth Notts
51 N9 Blidworth Bottoms Notts
71 J8 Blindcrake Cumb
11 M2 Blindley Heath Surrey
4 D5 Blisland Cnwll
8 H5 Blissford Hants
39 N7 Bliss Gate Worcs
31 Q4 Blisworth Nhants
40 E4 Blithbury Staffs
30 F7 Blockley Gloucs
45 M8 Blofield Norfk
45 M7 Blofield Heath Norfk
34 G2 Blo Norton Norfk
80 D8 Bloomfield Border
49 N8 Blore Staffs
50 F10 Blore Staffs
31 K7 Bloxham Oxon
52 F11 Bloxholm Lincs
40 D7 Bloxwich Wsall
8 C8 Bloxworth Dorset
58 F3 Blubberhouses N York
16 D7 Blue Anchor Somset
22 E10 Blue Bell Hill Kent
50 F4 Blue John Cavern Derbys
56 F8 Blundellsands Sefton
45 Q10 Blundeston Suffk
32 G6 Blunham Beds
18 G3 Blunsdon St Andrew Swindn
40 B11 Bluntington Worcs
33 K2 Bluntisham Cambs
52 D5 Blyborough Lincs
35 N2 Blyford Suffk
49 P11 Blymhill Staffs
51 N4 Blyth Notts
73 N5 Blyth Nthumb
86 D12 Blyth Bridge Border
35 P2 Blythburgh Suffk
80 D4 Blythe Border
52 C5 Blyton Lincs
93 P11 Boarhills Fife
9 P6 Boarhunt Hants
31 N10 Boarstall Bucks
107 J7 Boath Highld
99 P5 Boat of Garten Highld
22 H9 Bobbing Kent
39 P4 Bobbington Staffs
34 C11 Bocking Essex
34 C10 Bocking Churchstreet Essex
103 M6 Boddam Abers
111 k5 Boddam Shet
29 M4 Boddington Gloucs
54 D5 Bodedern IoA
55 Q6 Bodelwyddan Denbgs
39 K11 Bodenham Herefs
8 H3 Bodenham Wilts
39 K11 Bodenham Moor Herefs
54 E4 Bodewryd IoA
48 C2 Bodfari Denbgs
54 F6 Bodffordd IoA
46 E4 Bodfuan Gwynd
45 J3 Bodham Norfk
12 F5 Bodiam E Susx
12 F5 Bodiam Castle E Susx
31 L6 Bodicote Oxon
4 E9 Bodinnick Cnwll
12 D7 Bodle Street Green E Susx
3 N3 Bodmin Cnwll
4 F5 Bodmin Moor Cnwll
55 L7 Bodnant Garden Conwy
13 L2 Bodsham Green Kent
3 M4 Bodwen Cnwll
107 K11 Bogallan Highld
103 L8 Bogbrae Abers
76 G5 Bogend S Ayrs
87 J7 Boggs Holdings E Loth
86 F8 Boghall Mdloth
86 B8 Boghall W Loth
77 N3 Boghead S Lans
101 L3 Bogmoor Moray
95 K7 Bogmuir Abers
102 D6 Bogniebrae Abers
10 E9 Bognor Regis W Susx
99 N4 Bogroy Highld
69 P3 Bogue D & G
3 J8 Bohortha Cnwll
98 D11 Bohuntine Highld
65 L3 Bolam Dur
5 N11 Bolberry Devon
40 E8 Boldmere Birm
9 K7 Boldre Hants
65 J5 Boldron Dur
52 B6 Bole Notts
50 H9 Bolehill Derbys
16 C12 Bolham Devon
6 F1 Bolham Water Devon
2 H5 Bolingey Cnwll
50 C5 Bollington Ches
11 L5 Bolney W Susx
32 F5 Bolnhurst Beds
93 Q5 Bolshan Angus
51 L6 Bolsover Derbys
50 H2 Bolsterstone Sheff
66 C9 Boltby N York
101 M12 Boltenstone Abers
57 N7 Bolton Bolton
64 B3 Bolton Cumb
87 K8 Bolton E Loth
60 D4 Bolton E R Yk
81 M10 Bolton Nthumb
58 E4 Bolton Abbey N York
63 P11 Bolton by Bowland Lancs
71 P2 Boltonfellend Cumb
71 K7 Boltongate Cumb
63 J8 Bolton le Sands Lancs
71 K6 Bolton Low Houses Cumb
65 M7 Bolton-on-Swale N York
59 M6 Bolton Percy N York
51 L1 Bolton Upon Dearne Barns
4 E5 Bolventor Cnwll
49 J10 Bomere Heath Shrops
107 K4 Bonar Bridge Highld
90 D9 Bonawe Ag & B
60 G10 Bonby N Linc
25 L2 Boncath Pembks
80 D10 Bonchester Bridge Border
15 L10 Bondleigh Devon
63 J12 Bonds Lancs
86 B6 Bo'ness Falk
40 D5 Boney Hay Staffs
84 G7 Bonhill W Duns
39 P2 Boningale Shrops
80 E9 Bonjedward Border
85 P10 Bonkle N Lans
93 P7 Bonnington Angus
13 K3 Bonnington Kent
86 G2 Bonnybank Fife
85 N7 Bonnybridge Falk
102 H5 Bonnykelly Abers
86 G8 Bonnyrigg Mdloth
93 L7 Bonnyton Angus
50 H8 Bonsall Derbys
71 K2 Bonshaw Tower D & G
47 P10 Bont-Dolgadfan Powys
37 K7 Bontnewydd Cerdgn
54 G9 Bontnewydd Gwynd
48 C4 Bontuchel Denbgs
16 E2 Bonvilston V Glam
15 J5 Boode Devon
6 B11 Boohay Devon
20 D5 Booker Bucks
49 K9 Booley Shrops
80 D5 Boon Border
66 F4 Boosbeck R & Cl
34 E9 Boose's Green Essex
62 D3 Boot Cumb
58 D8 Booth Calder
60 C8 Booth E R Yk
52 E10 Boothby Graffoe Lincs
42 D4 Boothby Pagnell Lincs
57 N8 Boothstown Salfd
62 C5 Bootle Cumb
56 G9 Bootle Sefton
39 L8 Boraston Shrops
6 c1 Bordeaux Guern
22 G10 Borden Kent
72 B4 Border Forest Park
22 F2 Boreham Essex
18 D11 Boreham Wilts
12 D7 Boreham Street E Susx
21 J4 Borehamwood Herts
79 J10 Boreland D & G
104 B10 Boreraig Highld
111 a7 Borgh W Isls
111 d1 Borgh W Isls
109 M4 Borgie Highld
69 P9 Borgue D & G
110 D9 Borgue Highld
34 E7 Borley Essex
104 E7 Borneskitaig Highld
69 N9 Borness D & G
59 K2 Boroughbridge N York
22 C11 Borough Green Kent
41 K1 Borrowash Derbys
65 Q9 Borrowby N York
86 B6 Borrowstoun Falk
22 E9 Borstal Medway
37 K3 Borth Cerdgn
79 N6 Borthwickbrae Border
79 N6 Borthwickshiels Border
47 J4 Borth-y-Gest Gwynd
104 F11 Borve Highld
111 a7 Borve W Isls
111 c3 Borve W Isls
111 d1 Borve W Isls
63 K7 Borwick Lancs
39 M12 Bosbury Herefs
4 D3 Boscastle Cnwll
8 G8 Boscombe Bmouth
18 H11 Boscombe Wilts
10 D8 Bosham W Susx
24 G9 Bosherston Pembks
50 B7 Bosley Ches
3 K4 Bosoughan Cnwll
60 C3 Bossall N York
4 D3 Bossiney Cnwll
13 M1 Bossingham Kent
16 B6 Bossington Somset
49 M2 Bostock Green Ches
43 K2 Boston Lincs
59 K5 Boston Spa Leeds
3 L7 Boswinger Cnwll
2 B8 Botallack Cnwll
21 L4 Botany Bay Gt Lon
34 H2 Botesdale Suffk
73 M4 Bothal Nthumb
19 N5 Bothampstead W Berk
51 P6 Bothamsall Notts
71 K7 Bothel Cumb
7 L5 Bothenhampton Dorset
85 L10 Bothwell S Lans
20 F3 Botley Bucks
9 N5 Botley Hants
31 L11 Botley Oxon
31 Q8 Botolph Claydon Bucks
11 J8 Botolphs W Susx
42 B3 Bottesford Leics
52 C3 Bottesford N Linc
33 N5 Bottisham Cambs
93 L10 Bottomcraig Fife
58 B9 Bottoms Calder
5 J7 Botusfleming Cnwll
46 D5 Botwnnog Gwynd
11 P1 Bough Beech Kent
27 N2 Boughrood Powys
31 Q2 Boughton Nhants
44 B9 Boughton Norfk
51 P7 Boughton Notts
13 K1 Boughton Aluph Kent
22 F12 Boughton Green Kent
22 G12 Boughton Malherbe Kent
22 F12 Boughton Monchelsea Kent
23 K10 Boughton Street Kent
39 K5 Bouldon Shrops
81 Q10 Boulmer Nthumb
52 D9 Boultham Lincs
33 K5 Bourn Cambs
42 F6 Bourne Lincs
21 P5 Bournebridge Essex
40 D10 Bournebrook Birm
32 D7 Bourne End Beds
20 E6 Bourne End Bucks
20 G3 Bourne End Herts
8 G8 Bournemouth Bmouth
8 G7 Bournemouth Airport Dorset
22 H6 Bournes Green Sthend
40 C11 Bournheath Worcs
40 D10 Bournville Birm
8 B2 Bourton Dorset
19 J4 Bourton Oxon
39 L3 Bourton Shrops
18 F7 Bourton Wilts
41 K12 Bourton on Dunsmore Warwks
30 F7 Bourton-on-the-Hill Gloucs
30 F9 Bourton-on-the-Water Gloucs
88 G4 Bousd Ag & B
62 G5 Bouth Cumb
65 K12 Bouthwaite N York
91 M9 Bovain Stirlg
8 F4 Boveridge Dorset
5 Q5 Bovey Tracey Devon
20 G3 Bovingdon Herts
8 C9 Bovington Tank Museum Dorset
15 M10 Bow Devon
21 M6 Bow Gt Lon
111 h3 Bow Ork
32 C9 Bow Brickhill M Keyn
29 M7 Bowbridge Gloucs
73 N12 Bowburn Dur
9 M9 Bowcombe IoW
6 F5 Bowd Devon
80 D7 Bowden Border
18 D7 Bowden Hill Wilts
57 N10 Bowdon Traffd
110 E3 Bower Highld
8 F3 Bowerchalke Wilts
110 F3 Bowermadden Highld
49 P8 Bowers Staffs
22 E6 Bowers Gifford Essex
86 C4 Bowershall Fife
59 K8 Bower's Row Leeds
64 H5 Bowes Dur
63 J12 Bowgreave Lancs
70 G3 Bowhouse D & G
79 P2 Bowland Border
39 K10 Bowley Herefs
10 E3 Bowlhead Green Surrey
58 F7 Bowling Brad
84 G8 Bowling W Duns
62 F3 Bowmanstead Cumb
82 D10 Bowmore Ag & B
71 K3 Bowness-on-Solway Cumb
62 H3 Bowness-on-Windermere Cumb
93 K12 Bow of Fife Fife
93 N6 Bowriefauld Angus
81 L6 Bowsden Nthumb
37 K4 Bow Street Cerdgn
29 M8 Box Gloucs
18 C7 Box Wilts
34 F8 Boxford Suffk
19 M6 Boxford W Berk
10 E8 Boxgrove W Susx
22 F10 Boxley Kent
20 G3 Boxmoor Herts
34 G9 Boxted Essex
34 D6 Boxted Suffk
34 G9 Boxted Cross Essex
34 G9 Boxted Heath Essex
33 K4 Boxworth Cambs
23 N9 Boyden Gate Kent
40 F1 Boylestone Derbys
102 E3 Boyndie Abers
103 J3 Boyndlie Abers
61 K1 Boynton E R Yk
93 Q6 Boysack Angus
4 H2 Boyton Cnwll
35 N7 Boyton Suffk
18 D11 Boyton Wilts
22 D2 Boyton Cross Essex
34 C7 Boyton End Suffk
32 C5 Bozeat Nhants
13 L2 Brabourne Kent
13 L3 Brabourne Lees Kent
110 G2 Brabstermire Highld
96 D2 Bracadale Highld
42 F7 Braceborough Lincs
52 E9 Bracebridge Heath Lincs
52 D9 Bracebridge Low Fields Lincs
42 E3 Braceby Lincs
63 Q11 Bracewell Lancs
51 J8 Brackenfield Derbys
85 M8 Brackenhirst N Lans
98 B11 Brackletter Highld
31 N6 Brackley Nhants
20 E9 Bracknell Br For
85 N2 Braco P & K
101 P5 Bracobrae Moray
45 K9 Bracon Ash Norfk
97 K10 Bracora Highld
97 K10 Bracorina Highld
50 G9 Bradbourne Derbys
65 N2 Bradbury Dur
31 N5 Bradden Nhants
20 D4 Bradenham Bucks
18 E5 Bradenstoke Wilts
6 E2 Bradfield Devon
35 J9 Bradfield Essex
45 L4 Bradfield Norfk
50 H3 Bradfield Sheff
19 P6 Bradfield W Berk
34 E5 Bradfield Combust Suffk
49 M4 Bradfield Green Ches
35 J10 Bradfield Heath Essex
34 E5 Bradfield St Clare Suffk
34 E5 Bradfield St George Suffk
58 F7 Bradford Brad
14 G10 Bradford Devon
17 N12 Bradford Abbas Dorset
18 C8 Bradford Leigh Wilts
18 C8 Bradford-on-Avon Wilts
16 G10 Bradford-on-Tone Somset
7 P4 Bradford Peverell Dorset
15 K5 Bradiford Devon
9 Q9 Brading IoW
50 G10 Bradley Derbys
19 Q11 Bradley Hants
53 J3 Bradley NE Lin
49 Q11 Bradley Staffs
40 C8 Bradley Wolves
30 C2 Bradley Worcs
30 C2 Bradley Green Worcs
50 D11 Bradley in the Moors Staffs
28 H11 Bradley Stoke S Glos
41 N2 Bradmore Notts
6 D3 Bradninch Devon
50 D9 Bradnop Staffs
7 L4 Bradpole Dorset
58 E8 Bradshaw Calder
4 H4 Bradstone Devon
49 N3 Bradwall Green Ches
50 F5 Bradwell Derbys
34 D11 Bradwell Essex
32 B8 Bradwell M Keyn
45 Q8 Bradwell Norfk
23 J3 Bradwell-on-Sea Essex
23 J2 Bradwell Waterside Essex
14 F8 Bradworthy Devon
107 L9 Brae Highld
111 k3 Brae Shet
85 N7 Braeface Falk
95 L10 Braehead Angus
69 K8 Braehead D & G
77 Q2 Braehead S Lans
94 C4 Braemar Abers
106 D6 Braemore Highld
110 C9 Braemore Highld
98 D10 Brae Roy Lodge Highld
84 D7 Braeside Inver
93 K4 Braes of Coul Angus
101 M4 Braes of Enzie Moray
111 i1 Braeswick Ork
83 P2 Braevallich Ag & B
65 N4 Brafferton Darltn
66 B12 Brafferton N York
32 B5 Brafield-on-the-Green Nhants
111 d1 Bragar W Isls
33 J11 Bragbury End Herts
77 P2 Braidwood S Lans
50 G11 Brailsford Derbys
34 C11 Braintree Essex
35 J3 Braiseworth Suffk
9 L3 Braishfield Hants
71 K10 Braithwaite Cumb
51 M2 Braithwell Donc
11 J7 Bramber W Susx
41 K9 Bramcote Warwks
9 Q2 Bramdean Hants
45 L8 Bramerton Norfk
33 J12 Bramfield Herts
35 N3 Bramfield Suffk
35 J7 Bramford Suffk
50 B4 Bramhall Stockp
59 K5 Bramham Leeds
58 G5 Bramhope Leeds
19 Q8 Bramley Hants
58 G7 Bramley Leeds
51 L3 Bramley Rothm
10 G2 Bramley Surrey
19 Q8 Bramley Corner Hants
23 N11 Bramling Kent
6 C3 Brampford Speke Devon
32 H3 Brampton Cambs
64 C3 Brampton Cumb
71 Q4 Brampton Cumb
52 B7 Brampton Lincs
45 K5 Brampton Norfk
51 K1 Brampton Rothm
35 P1 Brampton Suffk
28 H4 Brampton Abbotts Herefs
42 B11 Brampton Ash Nhants
38 G7 Brampton Bryan Herefs
51 L4 Brampton-en-le-Morthen Rothm
40 D2 Bramshall Staffs
9 J4 Bramshaw Hants
10 D4 Bramshott Hants

170 Bramwell - Burnfoot

17 L9 Bramwell Somset
89 L3 Branault Highld
44 C2 Brancaster Norfk
44 D2 Brancaster Staithe Norfk
73 L12 Brancepeth Dur
100 G5 Branchill Moray
101 K2 Branderburgh Moray
61 J5 Brandesburton E R Yk
35 L5 Brandeston Suffk
45 J6 Brandiston Norfk
73 M11 Brandon Dur
42 C1 Brandon Lincs
44 D11 Brandon Suffk
41 K11 Brandon Warwks
44 H8 Brandon Parva Norfk
66 E11 Brandsby N York
52 E4 Brandy Wharf Lincs
33 Q10 Bran End Essex
8 F8 Branksome Poole
8 F8 Branksome Park Poole
19 M11 Bransbury Hants
52 C7 Bransby Lincs
6 G5 Branscombe Devon
39 P10 Bransford Worcs
8 H7 Bransgore Hants
61 J7 Bransholme C KuH
39 M7 Bransley Shrops
42 B4 Branston Leics
52 E9 Branston Lincs
40 G4 Branston Staffs
52 F9 Branston Booths Lincs
9 P10 Branstone IoW
52 D11 Brant Broughton Lincs
35 J9 Brantham Suffk
70 H9 Branthwaite Cumb
71 L7 Branthwaite Cumb
60 G8 Brantingham E R Yk
51 N1 Branton Donc
81 L10 Branton Nthumb
59 K2 Branton Green N York
81 J6 Branxton Nthumb
50 G9 Brassington Derbys
21 P11 Brasted Kent
21 P11 Brasted Chart Kent
95 L3 Brathens Abers
53 M9 Bratoft Lincs
52 D7 Brattleby Lincs
18 D9 Bratton Wilts
5 K2 Bratton Clovelly Devon
15 L5 Bratton Fleming Devon
17 P9 Bratton Seymour Somset
33 L10 Braughing Herts
31 M2 Braunston Nhants
42 B8 Braunston Rutlnd
41 M7 Braunstone Leics
14 H5 Braunton Devon
66 G11 Brawby N York
109 P3 Brawl Highld
20 E7 Bray W & M
41 Q9 Braybrooke Nhants
15 M5 Brayford Devon
4 H5 Bray Shop Cnwll
58 G4 Braythorn N York
59 N7 Brayton N York
20 E7 Braywick W & M
32 G11 Breachwood Green Herts
51 J11 Breadsall Derbys
29 J8 Breadstone Gloucs
2 F9 Breage Cnwll
106 H12 Breakachy Highld
106 H4 Brealangwell Lodge Highld
28 H7 Bream Gloucs
8 H4 Breamore Hants
16 H5 Brean Somset
111 b2 Breanais W Isls
58 H3 Brearton N York
111 c2 Breascleit W Isls
111 c2 Breasclete W Isls
41 L2 Breaston Derbys
26 C3 Brechfa Carmth
95 K9 Brechin Angus
44 F10 Breckles Norfk
78 D10 Breckonside D & G
27 L3 Brecon Powys
27 L4 Brecon Beacons National Park
50 B3 Bredbury Stockp
12 G6 Brede E Susx
39 L10 Bredenbury Herefs
35 L6 Bredfield Suffk
22 G10 Bredgar Kent
22 F10 Bredhurst Kent
29 N2 Bredon Worcs
29 M2 Bredon's Hardwick Worcs
29 N2 Bredon's Norton Worcs
38 G12 Bredwardine Herefs
41 K3 Breedon on the Hill Leics
85 Q10 Breich W Loth
57 N7 Breightmet Bolton
60 C7 Breighton E R Yk
28 F2 Breinton Herefs
18 E6 Bremhill Wilts
12 D2 Brenchley Kent
15 N3 Brendon Devon
83 M6 Brenfield Ag & B
111 b2 Brenish W Isls
34 F7 Brent Eleigh Suffk
21 J7 Brentford Gt Lon
42 B6 Brentingby Leics
17 J6 Brent Knoll Somset
5 N8 Brent Mill Devon
33 M10 Brent Pelham Herts
22 C5 Brentwood Essex
13 J5 Brenzett Kent
13 J4 Brenzett Green Kent
40 D4 Brereton Staffs
49 P3 Brereton Green Ches
34 H1 Bressingham Norfk
40 H3 Bretby Derbys
41 K11 Bretford Warwks
30 E5 Bretforton Worcs
57 J5 Bretherton Lancs
111 k4 Brettabister Shet
44 F12 Brettenham Norfk
34 F6 Brettenham Suffk
48 G3 Bretton Flints
40 B6 Brewood Staffs
8 B8 Briantspuddle Dorset
21 L2 Brickendon Herts
20 H3 Bricket Wood Herts
50 H5 Brick Houses Sheff
29 N1 Bricklehampton Worcs
56 e2 Bride IoM
71 J8 Bridekirk Cumb
5 L3 Bridestowe Devon
102 D7 Brideswell Abers
5 Q3 Bridford Devon
2 G6 Bridge Cnwll
23 M11 Bridge Kent
17 N10 Bridgehampton Somset
65 N12 Bridge Hewick N York
73 K9 Bridgehill Dur
9 P6 Bridgemary Hants
101 P7 Bridgend Abers
82 E9 Bridgend Ag & B
95 J8 Bridgend Angus
27 J11 Bridgend Brdgnd
78 H7 Bridgend D & G
5 L9 Bridgend Devon
93 L12 Bridgend Fife
101 M8 Bridgend Moray
92 G10 Bridgend P & K
86 C7 Bridgend W Loth
93 K5 Bridgend of Lintrathen Angus
102 D10 Bridge of Alford Abers
85 N4 Bridge of Allan Stirlg
100 H10 Bridge of Avon Moray
101 J7 Bridge of Avon Moray
91 N7 Bridge of Balgie P & K
94 C9 Bridge of Brewlands Angus
100 H10 Bridge of Brown Highld
92 H5 Bridge of Cally P & K
95 K3 Bridge of Canny Abers
93 J5 Bridge of Craigisla Angus
70 C4 Bridge of Dee D & G
103 K12 Bridge of Don C Aber
100 E7 Bridge of Dulsie Highld
95 K5 Bridge of Dye Abers
92 G11 Bridge of Earn P & K
91 M5 Bridge of Ericht P & K
95 L3 Bridge of Feugh Abers
110 B3 Bridge of Forss Highld
94 F3 Bridge of Gairn Abers
91 M5 Bridge of Gaur P & K
102 D5 Bridge of Marnoch Abers
91 J8 Bridge of Orchy Ag & B
92 D3 Bridge of Tilt P & K
101 M3 Bridge of Tynet Moray
111 j4 Bridge of Walls Shet
84 G9 Bridge of Weir Rens
14 E10 Bridgerule Devon
28 E1 Bridge Sollers Herefs
34 E6 Bridge Street Suffk
16 C9 Bridgetown Somset
49 J2 Bridge Trafford Ches
44 F11 Bridgham Norfk
39 N4 Bridgnorth Shrops
40 C6 Bridgtown Staffs
16 H8 Bridgwater Somset
61 K2 Bridlington E R Yk
7 L4 Bridport Dorset
28 G4 Bridstow Herefs
57 Q2 Brierfield Lancs
59 K11 Brierley Barns
28 H6 Brierley Gloucs
40 B9 Brierley Hill Dudley
52 E3 Brigg N Linc
45 M5 Briggate Norfk
67 J6 Briggswath N York
70 H9 Brigham Cumb
61 J4 Brigham E R Yk
58 F9 Brighouse Calder
9 M10 Brighstone IoW
31 K12 Brighthampton Oxon
15 K11 Brightley Devon
12 D6 Brightling E Susx
34 H12 Brightlingsea Essex
11 L8 Brighton Br & H
56 F8 Brighton le Sands Sefton
85 Q7 Brightons Falk
19 M5 Brightwalton W Berk
35 L7 Brightwell Suffk
19 Q2 Brightwell Baldwin Oxon
19 P3 Brightwell-cum-Sotwell Oxon
19 Q2 Brightwell Upperton Oxon
65 J5 Brignall Dur
85 J2 Brig o'Turk Stirlg
53 J3 Brigsley NE Lin
63 J4 Brigsteer Cumb
42 D11 Brigstock Nhants
31 P10 Brill Bucks
2 G9 Brill Cnwll
38 F11 Brilley Herefs
39 K8 Brimfield Herefs
39 K8 Brimfield Cross Herefs
51 K6 Brimington Derbys
5 Q5 Brimley Devon
29 N6 Brimpsfield Gloucs
19 P7 Brimpton W Berk
29 M8 Brimscombe Gloucs
56 F11 Brimstage Wirral
51 J4 Brincliffe Sheff
60 C7 Brind E R Yk
111 j4 Brindister Shet
57 L4 Brindle Lancs
49 P11 Brineton Staffs
42 B10 Bringhurst Leics
32 F2 Brington Cambs
44 G4 Briningham Norfk
53 L8 Brinkhill Lincs
33 Q6 Brinkley Cambs
41 K10 Brinklow Warwks
18 E4 Brinkworth Wilts
57 L5 Brinscall Lancs
51 L10 Brinsley Notts
51 K3 Brinsworth Rothm
44 G3 Brinton Norfk
111 h2 Brinyan Ork
44 F6 Brisley Norfk
17 N3 Brislington Bristl
12 H3 Brissenden Green Kent
17 N2 Bristol Bristl
17 M3 Bristol Airport N Som
17 N2 Bristol Zoo Bristl
44 H4 Briston Norfk
8 H2 Britford Wilts
27 N8 Brithdir Caerph
47 M7 Brithdir Gwynd
22 E11 British Legion Village Kent
26 G9 Briton Ferry Neath
19 R3 Britwell Salome Oxon
6 C10 Brixham Torbay
5 L9 Brixton Devon
21 L8 Brixton Gt Lon
18 C11 Brixton Deverill Wilts
41 Q12 Brixworth Nhants
30 H11 Brize Norton Oxon
30 H11 Brize Norton Airport Oxon
30 B1 Broad Alley Worcs
18 G3 Broad Blunsdon Swindn
50 C3 Broadbottom Tamesd
10 D8 Broadbridge W Susx
11 J4 Broadbridge Heath W Susx
30 F6 Broad Campden Gloucs
58 E9 Broad Carr Calder
8 F3 Broad Chalke Wilts
6 D4 Broadclyst Devon
84 F8 Broadfield Inver
96 H5 Broadford Highld
10 H6 Broadford Bridge W Susx
79 K6 Broadgairhill Border
34 E11 Broad Green Essex
39 P10 Broad Green Worcs
81 J4 Broadhaugh Border
24 F6 Broad Haven Pembks
57 N10 Broadheath Traffd
6 E2 Broadhembury Devon
5 Q7 Broadhempston Devon
18 G5 Broad Hinton Wilts
12 G6 Broadland Row E Susx
19 M8 Broad Laying Hants
101 M3 Broadley Moray
30 F5 Broad Marston Worcs
7 Q5 Broadmayne Dorset
25 J7 Broadmoor Pembks
7 L4 Broadoak Dorset
12 C5 Broad Oak E Susx
12 G6 Broad Oak E Susx
28 F5 Broad Oak Herefs
23 M10 Broad Oak Kent
57 K9 Broad Oak St Hel
22 E2 Broad's Green Essex
23 Q9 Broadstairs Kent
8 E8 Broadstone Poole
39 K4 Broadstone Shrops
12 G6 Broad Street E Susx
22 G11 Broad Street Kent
18 G5 Broad Town Wilts
39 N10 Broadwas Worcs
33 J11 Broadwater Herts
11 J8 Broadwater W Susx
39 Q6 Broadwaters Worcs
24 F6 Broadway Pembks
17 J11 Broadway Somset
30 E6 Broadway Worcs
28 G6 Broadwell Gloucs
30 G8 Broadwell Gloucs
30 G12 Broadwell Oxon
31 L2 Broadwell Warwks
7 L3 Broadwindsor Dorset
15 K10 Broadwood Kelly Devon
5 J3 Broadwoodwidger Devon
104 H12 Brochel Highld
39 P10 Brockamin Worcs
9 Q4 Brockbridge Hants
35 K2 Brockdish Norfk
9 K7 Brockenhurst Hants
78 D2 Brocketsbrae S Lans
35 J4 Brockford Street Suffk
31 N2 Brockhall Nhants
21 K12 Brockham Surrey
30 D9 Brockhampton Gloucs
10 B8 Brockhampton Hants
28 H3 Brockhampton Herefs
58 F11 Brockholes Kirk
61 K11 Brocklesby Lincs
17 L3 Brockley N Som
34 D3 Brockley Suffk
34 C7 Brockley Green Suffk
34 D6 Brockley Green Suffk
38 G2 Brockton Shrops
38 G5 Brockton Shrops
39 L4 Brockton Shrops
49 P8 Brockton Staffs
28 G8 Brockweir Gloucs
29 M5 Brockworth Gloucs
40 C4 Brocton Staffs
75 Q5 Brodick N Ayrs
100 F4 Brodie Moray
59 L11 Brodsworth Donc
104 F8 Brogaig Highld
18 D3 Brokenborough Wilts
50 B6 Broken Cross Ches
18 C9 Brokerswood Wilts
56 G11 Bromborough Wirral
35 J2 Brome Suffk
35 J2 Brome Street Suffk
35 M6 Bromeswell Suffk
71 J6 Bromfield Cumb
39 J6 Bromfield Shrops
32 E6 Bromham Beds
18 E7 Bromham Wilts
21 N9 Bromley Gt Lon
39 N3 Bromley Shrops
22 F9 Brompton Medway
65 P8 Brompton N York
67 K10 Brompton N York
65 L7 Brompton-on-Swale N York
16 E9 Brompton Ralph Somset
16 C9 Brompton Regis Somset
29 K3 Bromsberrow Gloucs
29 K3 Bromsberrow Heath Gloucs
40 C12 Bromsgrove Worcs
39 M10 Bromyard Herefs
37 K7 Bronant Cerdgn
36 E10 Brongest Cerdgn
49 J7 Bronington Wrexhm
27 N2 Bronllys Powys
25 P4 Bronwydd Carmth
48 F7 Bronygarth Shrops
9 J5 Brook Hants
9 L9 Brook IoW
13 K2 Brook Kent
10 E3 Brook Surrey
45 L9 Brooke Norfk
42 C8 Brooke Rutlnd
52 H4 Brookenby Lincs
84 G9 Brookfield Rens
17 P9 Brookhampton Somset
9 J5 Brook Hill Hants
63 K8 Brookhouse Lancs
51 L3 Brookhouse Rothm
49 P4 Brookhouse Green Ches
50 D3 Brookhouses Derbys
13 J5 Brookland Kent
57 P10 Brooklands Traffd
21 K3 Brookmans Park Herts
22 C5 Brook Street Essex
12 H4 Brook Street Kent
34 D7 Brook Street Suffk
29 L6 Brookthorpe Gloucs
20 F11 Brookwood Surrey
32 G8 Broom Beds
73 M11 Broom Dur
51 K3 Broom Rothm
30 E4 Broom Warwks
45 M10 Broome Norfk
38 H6 Broome Shrops
40 B10 Broome Worcs
57 N10 Broomedge Warrtn
22 E2 Broomfield Essex
22 G11 Broomfield Kent
23 M9 Broomfield Kent
16 G9 Broomfield Somset
60 F8 Broomfleet E R Yk
72 H8 Broomhaugh Nthumb
51 K1 Broom Hill Barns
59 K12 Broom Hill Notts
73 M1 Broomhill Nthumb
23 K10 Broom Street Kent
107 P2 Brora Highld
39 M2 Broseley Shrops
72 G12 Brotherlee Dur
59 L8 Brotherton N York
66 F4 Brotton R & Cl
110 B4 Broubster Highld
64 E5 Brough Cumb
60 F8 Brough E R Yk
110 E2 Brough Highld
52 B10 Brough Notts
111 m3 Brough Shet
49 K7 Broughall Shrops
111 m2 Brough Lodge Shet
64 E5 Brough Sowerby Cumb
78 H2 Broughton Border
33 J2 Broughton Cambs
48 G3 Broughton Flints
9 K2 Broughton Hants
57 K2 Broughton Lancs
32 C8 Broughton M Keyn
52 D2 Broughton N Linc
58 C4 Broughton N York
66 H11 Broughton N York
32 B2 Broughton Nhants
31 K6 Broughton Oxon
57 P8 Broughton Salfd
49 N8 Broughton Staffs
16 C3 Broughton V Glam
41 M8 Broughton Astley Leics
18 C7 Broughton Gifford Wilts
30 C2 Broughton Green Worcs
30 B3 Broughton Hackett Worcs
62 E5 Broughton-in-Furness Cumb
69 L9 Broughton Mains D & G
62 E4 Broughton Mills Cumb
70 H8 Broughton Moor Cumb
30 G12 Broughton Poggs Oxon
93 N9 Broughty Ferry C Dund
19 P11 Brown Candover Hants
50 B9 Brown Edge Staffs
102 H7 Brownhill Abers
93 P11 Brownhills Fife
40 D6 Brownhills Wsall
19 P8 Browninghill Green Hants
29 M8 Browns Hill Gloucs
5 N9 Brownston Devon
67 K8 Broxa N York
21 M3 Broxbourne Herts
87 N6 Broxburn E Loth
86 C7 Broxburn W Loth
33 P10 Broxted Essex
38 G10 Broxwood Herefs
110 G7 Bruan Highld
92 C3 Bruar P & K
107 Q5 Brucefield Highld
84 B10 Bruchag Ag & B
82 C10 Bruichladdich Ag & B
35 M4 Bruisyard Suffk
35 M4 Bruisyard Street Suffk
52 C2 Brumby N Linc
50 E8 Brund Staffs
45 M8 Brundall Norfk
35 L3 Brundish Suffk
35 L3 Brundish Street Suffk
73 M6 Brunswick Village N u Ty
58 D5 Brunthwaite Brad
41 N9 Bruntingthorpe Leics
93 K10 Brunton Fife
81 P8 Brunton Nthumb
19 J9 Brunton Wilts
16 C10 Brushford Somset
15 L9 Brushford Barton Devon
17 P8 Bruton Somset
30 B1 Bryan's Green Worcs
8 C6 Bryanston Dorset
71 K2 Brydekirk D & G
17 M11 Brympton Somset
26 D8 Bryn Carmth
26 H9 Bryn Neath
26 F6 Brynamman Carmth
25 J2 Brynberian Pembks
46 H3 Bryncir Gwynd
26 G8 Bryn-coch Neath
46 D5 Bryncroes Gwynd
47 K9 Bryncrug Gwynd
48 D6 Bryneglwys Denbgs
48 D1 Brynford Flints
57 L8 Bryn Gates Wigan
54 D6 Bryngwran IoA
28 D7 Bryngwyn Mons
38 E11 Bryngwyn Powys
24 H2 Bryn-Henllan Pembks
36 E9 Brynhoffnant Cerdgn
27 P6 Brynmawr Blae G
46 D5 Bryn-mawr Gwynd
27 J10 Brynmenyn Brdgnd
26 E9 Brynmill Swans
27 L11 Brynna Rhondd
54 H8 Brynrefail Gwynd
27 L11 Brynsadler Rhondd
48 C5 Bryn Saith Marchog Denbgs
54 F7 Brynsiencyn IoA
55 M6 Bryn-y-Maen Conwy
96 E5 Bualintur Highld
41 J11 Bubbenhall Warwks
60 C7 Bubwith E R Yk
84 H5 Buchanan Smithy Stirlg
103 M6 Buchanhaven Abers
92 D9 Buchanty P & K
85 M3 Buchany Stirlg
85 J4 Buchlyvie Stirlg
71 M6 Buckabank Cumb
32 H4 Buckden Cambs
64 G11 Buckden N York
45 M8 Buckenham Norfk
6 F3 Buckerell Devon
5 P6 Buckfast Devon
5 P7 Buckfastleigh Devon
86 G3 Buckhaven Fife
28 F5 Buckholt Mons
17 R10 Buckhorn Weston Dorset
21 N5 Buckhurst Hill Essex
101 M3 Buckie Moray
31 P7 Buckingham Bucks
20 E2 Buckland Bucks
5 N10 Buckland Devon
30 E7 Buckland Gloucs
33 K9 Buckland Herts
13 P2 Buckland Kent
19 K2 Buckland Oxon
21 K12 Buckland Surrey
14 G7 Buckland Brewer Devon
20 E3 Buckland Common Bucks
17 R6 Buckland Dinham Somset
14 H9 Buckland Filleigh Devon
5 P5 Buckland in the Moor Devon
5 K6 Buckland Monachorum Devon
7 P2 Buckland Newton Dorset
7 P6 Buckland Ripers Dorset
16 H12 Buckland St Mary Somset
5 P10 Buckland-Tout-Saints Devon
19 P6 Bucklebury W Berk
9 L7 Bucklers Hard Hants
35 L8 Bucklesham Suffk
48 F3 Buckley Flints
57 N11 Bucklow Hill Ches
42 C5 Buckminster Leics
50 B10 Bucknall C Stke
52 G9 Bucknall Lincs
31 M8 Bucknell Oxon
38 G7 Bucknell Shrops
101 M3 Buckpool Moray
103 J12 Bucksburn C Aber
14 F7 Buck's Cross Devon
10 H4 Bucks Green W Susx
10 D2 Bucks Horn Oak Hants
14 F7 Buck's Mills Devon
67 P11 Buckton E R Yk
81 M6 Buckton Nthumb
32 G2 Buckworth Cambs
51 N6 Budby Notts
93 N8 Buddon Angus
14 E10 Budd's Titson Cnwll
14 D10 Bude Cnwll
4 H8 Budge's Shop Cnwll
6 E6 Budleigh Salterton Devon
2 H9 Budock Water Cnwll
49 M6 Buerton Ches
31 P3 Bugbrooke Nhants
3 M4 Bugle Cnwll
8 B3 Bugley Dorset
60 D3 Bugthorpe E R Yk
39 L2 Buildwas Shrops
38 B11 Builth Wells Powys
8 G2 Bulbridge Wilts
110 B3 Buldoo Highld
18 H11 Bulford Wilts
49 K5 Bulkeley Ches
41 K9 Bulkington Warwks
18 D8 Bulkington Wilts
14 G8 Bulkworthy Devon
20 E9 Bullbrook Br For
19 M11 Bullington Hants
52 F7 Bullington Lincs
34 D8 Bulmer Essex
60 C1 Bulmer N York
34 D8 Bulmer Tye Essex
22 D6 Bulphan Thurr
103 J6 Bulwark Abers
51 M11 Bulwell C Nott
42 D10 Bulwick Nhants
21 N3 Bumble's Green Essex
97 J11 Bunacaimb Highld
98 B10 Bunarkaig Highld
49 K4 Bunbury Ches
107 K12 Bunchrew Highld
97 M4 Bundalloch Highld
89 J11 Bunessan Ag & B
45 M11 Bungay Suffk
82 F8 Bunnahabhain Ag & B
41 N2 Bunny Notts
98 E3 Buntait Highld
33 K10 Buntingford Herts
45 J10 Bunwell Norfk
45 J10 Bunwell Street Norfk
41 K8 Burbage Leics
19 J8 Burbage Wilts
20 D7 Burchett's Green W & M
8 F2 Burcombe Wilts
32 C11 Burcott Bucks
34 E9 Bures Essex
30 G10 Burford Oxon
39 L8 Burford Shrops
89 J7 Burg Ag & B
10 C4 Burgates Hants
11 L6 Burgess Hill W Susx
35 K6 Burgh Suffk
71 M4 Burgh by Sands Cumb
45 P8 Burgh Castle Norfk
19 M8 Burghclere Hants
100 H2 Burghead Moray
19 Q7 Burghfield W Berk
19 Q7 Burghfield Common W Berk
21 K10 Burgh Heath Surrey
39 J12 Burghill Herefs
53 N9 Burgh le Marsh Lincs
45 K5 Burgh next Aylsham Norfk
52 H6 Burgh on Bain Lincs
45 P7 Burgh St Margaret Norfk
45 P10 Burgh St Peter Norfk
59 M10 Burghwallis Donc
22 E10 Burham Kent
10 C6 Buriton Hants
49 L5 Burland Ches
3 M2 Burlawn Cnwll
29 M8 Burleigh Gloucs
16 E11 Burlescombe Devon
8 B8 Burleston Dorset
8 H6 Burley Hants
42 C7 Burley Rutlnd
49 L7 Burleydam Ches
39 L11 Burley Gate Herefs
58 F5 Burley in Wharfedale Brad
8 H6 Burley Street Hants
58 F5 Burley Wood Head Brad
49 J9 Burlton Shrops
13 L4 Burmarsh Kent
30 H6 Burmington Warwks
59 N8 Burn N York
57 Q9 Burnage Manch
40 H2 Burnaston Derbys
85 P10 Burnbrae N Lans
60 E5 Burnby E R Yk
63 J3 Burneside Cumb
65 N9 Burneston N York
17 P3 Burnett BaNES
79 N6 Burnfoot Border
80 C10 Burnfoot Border

Clodock - Crawford 173

28 C4 Clodock Herefs
103 K6 Clola Abers
32 F8 Clophill Beds
32 F1 Clopton Nhants
35 K6 Clopton Suffk
35 K6 Clopton Corner Suffk
6 c1 Clos du Valle Guern
78 E9 Closeburn D & G
78 E9 Closeburnmill D & G
7 N2 Closworth Somset
33 J9 Clothall Herts
49 K3 Clotton Ches
58 B9 Clough Foot Calder
58 E9 Clough Head Calder
67 L8 Cloughton N York
111 k4 Clousta Shet
94 F7 Clova Angus
14 F7 Clovelly Devon
79 P2 Clovenfords Border
90 D4 Clovulin Highld
57 P4 Clow Bridge Lancs
51 L6 Clowne Derbys
39 N7 Clows Top Worcs
97 Q7 Cluanie Inn Highld
97 Q7 Cluanie Lodge Highld
69 J7 Clugston D & G
38 F6 Clun Shrops
100 D6 Clunas Highld
38 G6 Clunbury Shrops
25 K5 Clunderwen Carmth
99 L4 Clune Highld
98 B10 Clunes Highld
38 H6 Clungunford Shrops
102 E5 Clunie Abers
92 G6 Clunie P & K
38 G6 Clunton Shrops
86 F3 Cluny Fife
17 N4 Clutton BaNES
49 J5 Clutton Ches
17 P4 Clutton Hill BaNES
27 P6 Clydach Mons
26 F8 Clydach Swans
27 K9 Clydach Vale Rhondd
84 H8 Clydebank W Duns
18 F5 Clyffe Pypard Wilts
84 D6 Clynder Ag & B
26 H8 Clyne Neath
54 E10 Clynnog-fawr Gwynd
38 E12 Clyro Powys
6 D4 Clyst Honiton Devon
6 D3 Clyst Hydon Devon
6 D5 Clyst St George Devon
6 D3 Clyst St Lawrence Devon
6 C5 Clyst St Mary Devon
111 d2 Cnoc W Isls
37 L5 Cnwch Coch Cerdgn
4 G5 Coad's Green Cnwll
78 D2 Coalburn S Lans
73 K8 Coalburns Gatesd
29 K8 Coaley Gloucs
22 F4 Coalhill Essex
29 J11 Coalpit Heath S Glos
39 M2 Coalport Wrekin
85 Q4 Coalsnaughton Clacks
86 G3 Coaltown of Balgonie Fife
86 G3 Coaltown of Wemyss Fife
41 K5 Coalville Leics
72 C8 Coanwood Nthumb
17 L11 Coat Somset
85 M9 Coatbridge N Lans
85 M9 Coatdyke N Lans
18 H4 Coate Swindn
18 F8 Coate Wilts
43 K9 Coates Cambs
29 N8 Coates Gloucs
52 C6 Coates Lincs
10 F6 Coates W Susx
15 K6 Cobbaton Devon
29 N5 Coberley Gloucs
22 D9 Cobham Kent
20 H10 Cobham Surrey
39 J9 Cobnash Herefs
6 b1 Cobo Guern
103 J3 Coburby Abers
33 J6 Cockayne Hatley Beds
101 K12 Cock Bridge Abers
87 P7 Cockburnspath Border
22 F3 Cock Clarks Essex
86 H7 Cockenzie and Port Seton E Loth
63 J10 Cockerham Lancs
71 J9 Cockermouth Cumb
32 G11 Cockernhoe Green Herts
26 E9 Cockett Swans
65 K3 Cockfield Dur
34 E6 Cockfield Suffk
21 L4 Cockfosters Gt Lon
34 B11 Cock Green Essex
10 E6 Cocking W Susx
10 E6 Cocking Causeway W Susx
6 B9 Cockington Torbay
17 L6 Cocklake Somset
73 L3 Cockle Park Nthumb
44 D8 Cockley Cley Norfk
12 G6 Cock Marling E Susx
20 C7 Cockpole Green Wokham
48 H9 Cockshutt Shrops
44 G2 Cockthorpe Norfk
6 D6 Cockwood Devon
50 D5 Cockyard Derbys
35 J6 Coddenham Suffk
29 J1 Coddington Herefs
52 B11 Coddington Notts
18 E11 Codford St Mary Wilts
18 E11 Codford St Peter Wilts
32 H11 Codicote Herts
10 G6 Codmore Hill W Susx
51 K10 Codnor Derbys
29 K11 Codrington S Glos
39 Q2 Codsall Staffs
39 Q2 Codsall Wood Staffs
54 F5 Coedana IoA
48 F5 Coedpoeth Wrexhm
48 F4 Coed Talon Flints
28 D8 Coed-y-paen Mons
6 B8 Coffinswell Devon
6 C6 Cofton Devon
40 D11 Cofton Hackett Worcs
16 G2 Cogan V Glam
32 B5 Cogenhoe Nhants
34 E11 Coggeshall Essex
99 K5 Coignafearn Highld
94 E3 Coilacriech Abers
85 K2 Coilantogle Stirlg
96 D3 Coillore Highld
98 E7 Coiltry Highld
27 K11 Coity Brdgnd
111 d2 Col W Isls
107 J1 Colaboll Highld
3 K4 Colan Cnwll
6 E5 Colaton Raleigh Devon
104 B11 Colbost Highld
65 L7 Colburn N York
64 C4 Colby Cumb
56 b6 Colby IoM
34 G10 Colchester Essex
19 N6 Cold Ash W Berk
41 P11 Cold Ashby Nhants
17 Q2 Cold Ashton S Glos
30 F9 Cold Aston Gloucs
109 L4 Coldbackie Highld
32 D6 Cold Brayfield M Keyn
11 M8 Coldean Br & H
5 Q5 Coldeast Devon
58 C8 Colden Calder
9 N3 Colden Common Hants
35 P5 Coldfair Green Suffk
52 E6 Cold Hanworth Lincs
11 J2 Coldharbour Surrey
31 P4 Cold Higham Nhants
81 J2 Coldingham Border
66 D10 Cold Kirby N York
49 Q8 Coldmeece Staffs
22 G4 Cold Norton Essex
42 B7 Cold Overton Leics
13 P1 Coldred Kent
15 M10 Coldridge Devon
80 H6 Coldstream Border
10 G6 Coldwaltham W Susx
28 E2 Coldwell Herefs
103 K7 Coldwells Abers
17 P9 Cole Somset
38 G5 Colebatch Shrops
6 D2 Colebrook Devon
15 N11 Colebrooke Devon
52 D10 Coleby Lincs
60 F9 Coleby N Linc
15 N11 Coleford Devon
28 G6 Coleford Gloucs
17 P6 Coleford Somset
16 F8 Coleford Water Somset
45 K11 Colegate End Norfk
47 F8 Colehill Dorset
11 N4 Coleman's Hatch E Susx
48 H8 Colemere Shrops
10 B4 Colemore Hants
92 G9 Colenden P & K
18 B6 Colerne Wilts
30 D10 Colesbourne Gloucs
20 F4 Coleshill Bucks
19 J3 Coleshill Oxon
40 G9 Coleshill Warwks
17 N5 Coley BaNES
11 K4 Colgate W Susx
87 J2 Colinsburgh Fife
86 E8 Colinton C Edin
83 Q7 Colintraive Ag & B
44 F5 Colkirk Norfk
93 J8 Collace P & K
111 k3 Collafirth Shet
5 P11 Collaton Devon
6 B10 Collaton St Mary Torbay
100 H3 College of Roseisle Moray
20 D10 College Town Br For
93 K11 Collessie Fife
21 P5 Collier Row Gt Lon
33 L11 Collier's End Herts
12 E2 Collier Street Kent
103 L9 Collieston Abers
70 G1 Collin D & G
19 J9 Collingbourne Ducis Wilts
19 J9 Collingbourne Kingston Wilts
59 K5 Collingham Leeds
52 B10 Collingham Notts
39 M9 Collington Herefs
31 Q3 Collingtree Nhants
57 K9 Collins Green Warrtn
93 Q6 Colliston Angus
6 E2 Colliton Devon
42 E9 Collyweston Nhants
68 F2 Colmonell S Ayrs
32 F5 Colmworth Beds
20 G7 Colnbrook Slough
33 L2 Colne Cambs
58 B6 Colne Lancs
34 E10 Colne Engaine Essex
45 K8 Colney Norfk
21 K3 Colney Heath Herts
30 E11 Coln Rogers Gloucs
30 F12 Coln St Aldwyns Gloucs
30 E11 Coln St Dennis Gloucs
102 E8 Colpy Abers
79 M1 Colquhar Border
63 D5 Colsterworth Lincs
41 P2 Colston Bassett Notts
100 H3 Coltfield Moray
45 L6 Coltishall Norfk
62 G5 Colton Cumb
59 J7 Colton Leeds
59 M5 Colton N York
44 H7 Colton Norfk
40 D4 Colton Staffs
12 D2 Colt's Hill Kent
70 E5 Colvend D & G
29 K1 Colwall Herefs
72 G6 Colwell Nthumb
40 D4 Colwich Staffs
16 C2 Colwinston V Glam
10 E9 Colworth W Susx
55 M6 Colwyn Bay Conwy
6 H4 Colyford Devon
6 H4 Colyton Devon
31 K10 Combe Oxon
19 L8 Combe W Berk
18 B8 Combe Down BaNES
6 A9 Combe Fishacre Devon
16 F9 Combe Florey Somset
17 Q4 Combe Hay BaNES
6 B8 Combeinteignhead Devon
15 K3 Combe Martin Devon
6 F3 Combe Raleigh Devon
57 M12 Comberbach Ches
40 F6 Comberford Staffs
33 L5 Comberton Cambs
39 J8 Comberton Herefs
7 J1 Combe St Nicholas Somset
30 H4 Combrook Warwks
50 D5 Combs Derbys
34 H5 Combs Suffk
34 H5 Combs Ford Suffk
16 H7 Combwich Somset
95 L1 Comers Abers
39 Q8 Comhampton Worcs
25 K5 Commercial Pembks
47 N10 Commins Coch Powys
66 F5 Commondale N York
70 G10 Common End Cumb
4 F6 Common Moor Cnwll
50 C3 Compstall Stockp
69 P8 Compstonend D & G
6 B9 Compton Devon
9 M3 Compton Hants
39 P5 Compton Staffs
10 F1 Compton Surrey
19 N5 Compton W Berk
10 C7 Compton W Susx
18 G9 Compton Wilts
8 C4 Compton Abbas Dorset
30 D10 Compton Abdale Gloucs
18 F6 Compton Bassett Wilts
19 J4 Compton Beauchamp Oxon
17 K5 Compton Bishop Somset
8 F2 Compton Chamberlayne Wilts
17 P4 Compton Dando BaNES
17 L9 Compton Dundon Somset
17 K11 Compton Durville Somset
28 G11 Compton Greenfield S Glos
17 M5 Compton Martin BaNES
17 P10 Compton Pauncefoot Somset
7 N4 Compton Valence Dorset
86 B4 Comrie Fife
92 B10 Comrie P & K
90 E3 Conaglen House Highld
97 M4 Conchra Highld
92 G6 Concraigie P & K
29 N2 Conderton Worcs
30 F8 Condicote Gloucs
85 M8 Condorrat N Lans
39 J2 Condover Shrops
29 L5 Coney Hill Gloucs
10 H5 Coneyhurst Common W Susx
66 G12 Coneysthorpe N York
34 F2 Coney Weston Suffk
4 G5 Congdon's Shop Cnwll
41 J6 Congerstone Leics
44 B5 Congham Norfk
49 Q3 Congleton Ches
17 L4 Congresbury N Som
70 G2 Conheath D & G
100 F5 Conicavel Moray
52 H11 Coningsby Lincs
33 K4 Conington Cambs
42 H11 Conington Cambs
51 L2 Conisbrough Donc
53 L4 Conisholme Lincs
62 F3 Coniston Cumb
61 K7 Coniston E R Yk
58 B3 Coniston Cold N York
58 C1 Conistone N York
48 F2 Connah's Quay Flints
90 C9 Connel Ag & B
77 K8 Connel Park E Ayrs
2 E7 Connor Downs Cnwll
107 J10 Conon Bridge Highld
58 C5 Cononley N York
50 C10 Consall Staffs
73 K10 Consett Dur
65 L8 Constable Burton N York
2 G9 Constantine Cnwll
3 K2 Constantine Bay Cnwll
106 G10 Contin Highld
55 L6 Conwy Conwy
34 E3 Conyer's Green Suffk
12 E8 Cooden E Susx
14 G10 Cookbury Devon
20 E6 Cookham W & M
20 D6 Cookham Dean W & M
20 E6 Cookham Rise W & M
30 D3 Cookhill Worcs
35 M2 Cookley Suffk
39 Q6 Cookley Worcs
20 B5 Cookley Green Oxon
95 P4 Cookney Abers
35 K11 Cook's Green Essex
34 G6 Cooks Green Suffk
22 D3 Cooksmill Green Essex
10 H5 Coolham W Susx
22 F8 Cooling Medway
6 C7 Coombe Devon
6 E4 Coombe Devon
29 K9 Coombe Gloucs
9 Q4 Coombe Hants
8 G3 Coombe Bissett Wilts
6 B8 Coombe Cellars Devon
16 D9 Coombe End Somset
29 M4 Coombe Hill Gloucs
8 C9 Coombe Keynes Dorset
6 C9 Coombe Pafford Torbay
11 J8 Coombes W Susx
38 G9 Coombes-Moor Herefs
21 P3 Coopersale Common Essex
35 J8 Copdock Suffk
34 F11 Copford Green Essex
59 J2 Copgrove N York
111 k3 Copister Shet
32 F7 Cople Beds
65 J3 Copley Dur
59 M5 Copmanthorpe York
49 P9 Copmere End Staffs
56 H2 Copp Lancs
14 D11 Coppathorne Cnwll
40 B4 Coppenhall Staffs
2 E8 Copperhouse Cnwll
32 G2 Coppingford Cambs
15 N10 Copplestone Devon
57 K6 Coppull Lancs
11 J5 Copsale W Susx
57 M3 Copster Green Lancs
41 L9 Copston Magna Warwks
23 P10 Cop Street Kent
65 N12 Copt Hewick N York
11 L3 Copthorne W Susx
41 L5 Copt Oak Leics
9 K5 Copythorne Hants
22 C6 Corbets Tey Gt Lon
7 a2 Corbiere Jersey
72 H7 Corbridge Nthumb
42 C11 Corby Nhants
42 E5 Corby Glen Lincs
75 Q6 Cordon N Ayrs
39 L7 Coreley Shrops
16 G11 Corfe Somset
8 E10 Corfe Castle Dorset
8 E8 Corfe Mullen Dorset
39 J5 Corfton Shrops
94 E1 Corgarff Abers
9 Q4 Corhampton Hants
40 H9 Corley Warwks
40 H9 Corley Ash Warwks
94 E8 Cormuir Angus
34 E8 Cornard Tye Suffk
65 N1 Cornforth Dur
102 D4 Cornhill Abers
81 J6 Cornhill-on-Tweed Nthumb
58 B8 Cornholme Calder
88 C7 Cornoigmore Ag & B
73 K11 Cornsay Dur
73 L11 Cornsay Colliery Dur
107 J10 Corntown Highld
27 J12 Corntown V Glam
30 H8 Cornwell Oxon
5 M8 Cornwood Devon
5 Q8 Cornworthy Devon
90 F2 Corpach Highld
45 J4 Corpusty Norfk
94 H2 Corrachree Abers
90 D4 Corran Highld
97 M7 Corran Highld
79 K10 Corrie D & G
75 Q4 Corrie N Ayrs
75 P7 Corriecravie N Ayrs
75 Q5 Corriegills N Ayrs
98 C9 Corriegour Lodge Hotel Highld
106 F9 Corriemoille Highld
98 E3 Corrimony Highld
52 C5 Corringham Lincs
22 E6 Corringham Thurr
47 M9 Corris Gwynd
47 M9 Corris Uchaf Gwynd
84 D3 Corrow Ag & B
96 H5 Corry Highld
15 L11 Corscombe Devon
7 M2 Corscombe Dorset
29 K3 Corse Gloucs
29 L3 Corse Lawn Gloucs
18 C6 Corsham Wilts
102 F12 Corsindae Abers
18 C10 Corsley Wilts
18 B10 Corsley Heath Wilts
78 C12 Corsock D & G
17 Q3 Corston BaNES
18 D4 Corston Wilts
86 E7 Corstorphine C Edin
94 F9 Cortachy Angus
45 Q10 Corton Suffk
18 D11 Corton Wilts
17 P10 Corton Denham Somset
90 E3 Coruanan Lodge Highld
48 C6 Corwen Denbgs
5 K4 Coryton Devon
22 E6 Coryton Thurr
41 M8 Cosby Leics
40 C8 Coseley Dudley
32 B8 Cosgrove Nhants
9 Q6 Cosham C Port
24 H7 Cosheston Pembks
92 B6 Coshieville P & K
51 L11 Cossall Notts
41 N5 Cossington Leics
17 J7 Cossington Somset
45 K7 Costessey Norfk
41 M3 Costock Notts
42 B6 Coston Leics
44 H8 Coston Norfk
19 L1 Cote Oxon
49 L3 Cotebrook Ches
71 P5 Cotehill Cumb
41 M4 Cotes Leics
41 M10 Cotesbach Leics
16 G9 Cotford St Luke Somset
41 N1 Cotgrave Notts
102 H11 Cothal Abers
42 B1 Cotham Notts
64 H4 Cotherstone Dur
19 M2 Cothill Oxon
6 G3 Cotleigh Devon
51 L11 Cotmanhay Derbys
33 L5 Coton Cambs
41 P12 Coton Nhants
49 P10 Coton Staffs
49 Q10 Coton Clanford Staffs
49 J11 Coton Hill Shrops
40 G4 Coton in the Elms Derbys
30 C11 Cotswolds
5 Q7 Cott Devon
57 J3 Cottam Lancs
52 B7 Cottam Notts
33 M4 Cottenham Cambs
33 K10 Cottered Herts
42 F11 Cotterstock Nhants
41 P11 Cottesbrooke Nhants
42 C7 Cottesmore Rutlnd
60 H7 Cottingham E R Yk
42 B11 Cottingham Nhants
58 E6 Cottingley Brad
31 N7 Cottisford Oxon
34 H4 Cotton Suffk
101 P9 Cottown Abers
102 G11 Cottown Abers
102 H7 Cottown of Gight Abers
5 J7 Cotts Devon
30 E3 Coughton Warwks
83 K9 Coulaghailtro Ag & B
97 N1 Coulags Highld
94 H2 Coull Abers
84 D5 Coulport Ag & B
21 L10 Coulsdon Gt Lon
18 D9 Coulston Wilts
78 G3 Coulter S Lans
66 E11 Coulton N York
93 L10 Coultra Fife
39 K2 Cound Shrops
65 M2 Coundon Dur
64 G9 Countersett N York
6 C5 Countess Wear Devon
41 N8 Countesthorpe Leics
15 M3 Countisbury Devon
93 J7 Coupar Angus P & K
81 K7 Coupland Nthumb
75 M3 Cour Ag & B
78 H10 Courance D & G
97 J9 Courteachan Highld
31 Q4 Courteenhall Nhants
26 D4 Court Henry Carmth
23 K5 Courtsend Essex
16 G8 Courtway Somset
86 H8 Cousland Mdloth
12 D4 Cousley Wood E Susx
84 D6 Cove Ag & B
87 P7 Cove Border
16 C11 Cove Devon
20 D11 Cove Hants
105 M4 Cove Highld
95 Q2 Cove Bay C Aber
35 Q1 Covehithe Suffk
40 B6 Coven Staffs
33 M1 Coveney Cambs
53 K5 Covenham St Bartholomew Lincs
53 K5 Covenham St Mary Lincs
41 J10 Coventry Covtry
41 J11 Coventry Airport Warwks
2 H11 Coverack Cnwll
2 G9 Coverack Bridges Cnwll
65 K9 Coverham N York
32 F3 Covington Cambs
78 F2 Covington S Lans
63 L7 Cowan Bridge Lancs
12 C7 Cowbeech E Susx
43 J6 Cowbit Lincs
16 D2 Cowbridge V Glam
11 P3 Cowden Kent
86 D4 Cowdenbeath Fife
50 H10 Cowers Lane Derbys
9 N8 Cowes IoW
66 C9 Cowesby N York
11 K5 Cowfold W Susx
28 H9 Cowhill S Glos
30 E5 Cow Honeybourne Worcs
85 P5 Cowie Stirlg
6 B4 Cowley Devon
29 N6 Cowley Gloucs
20 G7 Cowley Gt Lon
31 M12 Cowley Oxon
57 L5 Cowling Lancs
58 C5 Cowling N York
65 M9 Cowling N York
34 B6 Cowlinge Suffk
73 N5 Cowpen Nthumb
10 B7 Cowplain Hants
72 F11 Cowshill Dur
17 L4 Cowslip Green N Som
59 K4 Cowthorpe N York
49 M7 Coxbank Ches
51 J11 Coxbench Derbys
14 C11 Coxford Cnwll
44 E4 Coxford Norfk
22 E12 Coxheath Kent
65 N1 Coxhoe Dur
17 M7 Coxley Somset
17 M7 Coxley Wick Somset
22 C4 Coxtie Green Essex
66 D11 Coxwold N York
27 K11 Coychurch Brdgnd
76 G7 Coylton S Ayrs
99 N6 Coylumbridge Highld
27 J10 Coytrahen Brdgnd
30 D2 Crabbs Cross Worcs
11 K5 Crabtree W Susx
64 C3 Crackenthorpe Cumb
14 C11 Crackington Haven Cnwll
49 N12 Crackleybank Shrops
58 C3 Cracoe N York
6 E1 Craddock Devon
40 C9 Cradley Dudley
39 N11 Cradley Herefs
40 C9 Cradley Heath Sandw
27 L3 Cradoc Powys
4 H9 Crafthole Cnwll
32 C11 Crafton Bucks
100 F9 Craggan Highld
58 D9 Cragg Vale Calder
73 L10 Craghead Dur
27 J4 Crai Powys
101 P4 Craibstone Moray
93 N6 Craichie Angus
95 L10 Craig Angus
105 Q11 Craig Highld
77 K8 Craigbank E Ayrs
86 F10 Craigburn Border
79 M10 Craigcleuch D & G
102 H8 Craigdam Abers
83 M2 Craigdhu Ag & B
102 F11 Craigearn Abers
101 K6 Craigellachie Moray
92 G10 Craigend P & K
84 H8 Craigend Rens
84 E6 Craigendoran Ag & B
69 J6 Craighlaw D & G
82 G9 Craighouse Ag & B
92 G7 Craigie P & K
76 G5 Craigie S Ayrs
103 J3 Craigiefold Abers
70 C4 Craigley D & G
26 G7 Craig Llangiwg Neath
86 E7 Craiglockhart C Edin
101 L4 Craiglug Moray
86 G7 Craigmillar C Edin
78 C10 Craigneston D & G
85 N10 Craigneuk N Lans
85 N9 Craigneuk N Lans
89 P8 Craignure Ag & B
95 L8 Craigo Angus
93 L12 Craigrothie Fife
91 M11 Craigruie Stirlg
93 N7 Craigton Angus
95 N2 Craigton C Aber
84 H11 Craigton E Rens
93 K5 Craigton of Airlie Angus
87 L1 Crail Fife
80 F8 Crailing Border
51 Q2 Craiselound N Linc
65 M9 Crakehall N York
60 C2 Crambe N York
73 M5 Cramlington Nthumb
86 E7 Cramond C Edin
86 E7 Cramond Bridge C Edin
49 N2 Cranage Ches
49 P8 Cranberry Staffs
8 F5 Cranborne Dorset
12 F3 Cranbrook Kent
32 D8 Cranfield Beds
20 H7 Cranford Gt Lon
32 D2 Cranford St Andrew Nhants
32 D2 Cranford St John Nhants
29 M6 Cranham Gloucs
57 J8 Crank St Hel
10 G3 Cranleigh Surrey
17 P7 Cranmore Somset
41 Q8 Cranoe Leics
35 M4 Cransford Suffk
87 N9 Cranshaws Border
2 H4 Crantock Cnwll
52 E12 Cranwell Lincs
44 C10 Cranwich Norfk
44 G8 Cranworth Norfk
83 M2 Craobh Haven Ag & B
83 Q4 Crarae Ag & B
109 J10 Crask Inn Highld
98 F1 Crask of Aigas Highld
81 Q9 Craster Nthumb
35 M2 Cratfield Suffk
95 M3 Crathes Abers
95 M3 Crathes Castle Abers
94 E3 Crathie Abers
98 H9 Crathie Highld
66 B6 Crathorne N York
38 H5 Craven Arms Shrops
73 K8 Crawcrook Gatesd
78 F5 Crawford S Lans

Digby - East Hendred 175

52 F11 Digby Lincs
104 F8 Digg Highld
58 D11 Diggle Oldham
57 J7 Digmoor Lancs
36 H9 Dihewyd Cerdgn
45 M5 Dilham Norfk
50 C11 Dilhorne Staffs
32 G4 Dillington Cambs
72 H8 Dilston Nthumb
18 C10 Dilton Wilts
18 C10 Dilton Marsh Wilts
38 H10 Dilwyn Herefs
46 E4 Dinas Gwynd
24 H2 Dinas Pembks
87 P8 Dinas-Mawddwy Gwynd
16 F2 Dinas Powys V Glam
17 N7 Dinder Somset
28 G2 Dinedor Herefs
28 E6 Dingestow Mons
56 G10 Dingle Lpool
41 Q9 Dingley Nhants
107 J9 Dingwall Highld
94 H3 Dinnet Abers
73 L6 Dinnington N u Ty
51 M4 Dinnington Rothm
17 K12 Dinnington Somset
54 H8 Dinorwic Gwynd
31 Q11 Dinton Bucks
8 E2 Dinton Wilts
78 H10 Dinwoodie D & G
14 F8 Dinworthy Devon
16 G10 Dipford Somset
75 M5 Dippen Ag & B
75 Q7 Dippen N Ayrs
5 J4 Dippertown Devon
101 L4 Dipple Moray
76 D10 Dipple S Ayrs
5 P8 Diptford Devon
73 K9 Dipton Dur
87 K5 Dirleton E Loth
72 F10 Dirt Pot Nthumb
41 L3 Diseworth Leics
65 P11 Dishforth N York
50 C4 Disley Ches
35 J1 Diss Norfk
70 G10 Distington Cumb
8 G2 Ditchampton Wilts
81 N9 Ditchburn Nthumb
17 P8 Ditcheat Somset
45 M11 Ditchingham Norfk
11 M7 Ditchling E Susx
49 J11 Ditherington Shrops
18 B6 Ditteridge Wilts
6 B10 Dittisham Devon
57 J10 Ditton Halton
22 E10 Ditton Kent
33 Q5 Ditton Green Cambs
39 L4 Ditton Priors Shrops
29 N3 Dixton Gloucs
28 F6 Dixton Mons
58 C11 Dobcross Oldham
4 F7 Dobwalls Cnwll
5 Q3 Doccombe Devon
99 J2 Dochgarroch Highld
63 L7 Docker Lancs
44 C3 Docking Norfk
39 K10 Docklow Herefs
71 N10 Dockray Cumb
22 C4 Doddinghurst Essex
43 L11 Doddington Cambs
22 H11 Doddington Kent
52 C9 Doddington Lincs
81 L7 Doddington Nthumb
39 L6 Doddington Shrops
6 B5 Doddiscombsleigh Devon
49 L6 Dodd's Green Ches
31 N3 Dodford Nhants
40 C11 Dodford Worcs
29 K11 Dodington S Glos
16 G7 Dodington Somset
48 G4 Dodleston Ches
84 H11 Dodside E Rens
40 D1 Dod's Leigh Staffs
58 H12 Dodworth Barns
52 H11 Dogdyke Lincs
20 C11 Dogmersfield Hants
48 C11 Dolanog Powys
46 H3 Dolbenmaen Gwynd
47 P10 Dolfach Powys
38 C5 Dolfor Powys
55 L7 Dolgarrog Conwy
47 M7 Dolgellau Gwynd
107 P2 Doll Highld
85 Q4 Dollar Clacks
85 Q4 Dollarfield Clacks
48 E2 Dolphin Flints
63 K10 Dolphinholme Lancs
85 L11 Dolphinton S Lans
15 K9 Dolton Devon
55 N6 Dolwen Conwy
55 K10 Dolwyddelan Conwy
48 F10 Domgay Powys
59 M12 Doncaster Donc
8 D3 Donhead St Andrew Wilts
8 D3 Donhead St Mary Wilts
86 E5 Donibristle Fife
16 E7 Doniford Somset
42 H3 Donington Lincs
52 H7 Donington on Bain Lincs
40 H5 Donisthorpe Leics
30 F8 Donnington Gloucs
39 L1 Donnington Shrops
19 M7 Donnington W Berk
10 D9 Donnington W Susx
49 N11 Donnington Wrekin
17 J12 Donyatt Somset
76 F7 Doonfoot S Ayrs
76 F7 Doonholm S Ayrs
100 G11 Dorback Lodge Highld
7 Q5 Dorchester Dorset
19 P2 Dorchester Oxon
40 H7 Dordon Warwks
50 H5 Dore Sheff
98 H3 Dores Highld
21 J12 Dorking Surrey
11 N2 Dormans Land Surrey
28 G2 Dormington Herefs
30 C3 Dormston Worcs
20 E7 Dorney Bucks
97 M5 Dornie Highld
107 N4 Dornoch Highld
71 K3 Dornock D & G
110 C5 Dorrery Highld
40 F11 Dorridge Solhll
52 F11 Dorrington Lincs
39 J2 Dorrington Shrops
49 N7 Dorrington Shrops
30 F4 Dorsington Warwks
28 C1 Dorstone Herefs
31 P10 Dorton Bucks
56 d6 Douglas IoM
78 D3 Douglas S Lans
93 M8 Douglas and Angus C Dund
78 D3 Douglas Castle S Lans
84 D3 Douglas Pier Ag & B
93 M6 Douglastown Angus
78 E2 Douglas Water S Lans
78 D3 Douglas West S Lans
17 P7 Doulting Somset
111 g2 Dounby Ork
106 G3 Doune Highld
85 M3 Doune Stirlg
76 D11 Dounepark S Ayrs
107 J4 Dounie Highld
5 L6 Dousland Devon
50 E5 Dove Holes Derbys
70 H8 Dovenby Cumb
13 P2 Dover Kent
13 P2 Dover Castle Kent
35 L9 Dovercourt Essex
39 Q8 Doverdale Worcs
40 E1 Doveridge Derbys
11 K1 Doversgreen Surrey
92 E6 Dowally P & K
30 D9 Dowdeswell Gloucs
27 M7 Dowlais Myr Td
15 K9 Dowland Devon
7 K1 Dowlish Wake Somset
18 G2 Down Ampney Gloucs
4 G9 Downderry Cnwll
21 N10 Downe Gt Lon
29 L8 Downend Gloucs
28 H12 Downend S Glos
93 L8 Downfield C Dund
4 G6 Downgate Cnwll
4 H5 Downgate Cnwll
22 E4 Downham Essex
21 M8 Downham Gt Lon
63 P12 Downham Lancs
43 P9 Downham Market Norfk
29 M4 Down Hatherley Gloucs
17 N10 Downhead Somset
17 Q7 Downhead Somset
92 G9 Downhill P & K
65 K7 Downholme N York
95 Q3 Downies Abers
20 D4 Downley Bucks
15 M10 Down St Mary Devon
20 H10 Downside Surrey
5 K9 Down Thomas Devon
9 J8 Downton Hants
8 H3 Downton Wilts
38 H7 Downton on the Rock Herefs
42 G4 Dowsby Lincs
17 Q2 Doynton S Glos
27 P10 Draethen Caerph
77 N3 Draffan S Lans
51 P3 Drakeholes Notts
76 E2 Drakemyre N Ayrs
30 B4 Drakes Broughton Worcs
58 D4 Draughton N York
41 Q11 Draughton Nhants
59 P8 Drax N York
41 K12 Draycote Warwks
41 K2 Draycott Derbys
30 F7 Draycott Gloucs
17 L6 Draycott Somset
40 F2 Draycott in the Clay Staffs
50 C11 Draycott in the Moors Staffs
9 R6 Drayton C Port
42 B10 Drayton Leics
45 K7 Drayton Norfk
19 N2 Drayton Oxon
31 K6 Drayton Oxon
17 K10 Drayton Somset
40 B11 Drayton Worcs
40 G7 Drayton Bassett Staffs
20 E2 Drayton Beauchamp Bucks
40 G7 Drayton Manor Park Staffs
32 B10 Drayton Parslow Bucks
19 P2 Drayton St Leonard Oxon
24 G6 Dreen Hill Pembks
25 N2 Drefach Carmth
26 D6 Drefach Carmth
36 H10 Drefach Cerdgn
76 F4 Dreghorn N Ayrs
13 N2 Drellingore Kent
87 K6 Drem E Loth
5 P3 Drewsteignton Devon
53 L8 Driby Lincs
60 H3 Driffield E R Yk
18 F2 Driffield Gloucs
2 C9 Drift Cnwll
62 C3 Drigg Cumb
58 G8 Drighlington Leeds
89 L5 Drimnin Highld
7 K2 Drimpton Dorset
90 C1 Drimsallie Highld
59 N4 Dringhouses York
34 F5 Drinkstone Suffk
34 F5 Drinkstone Green Suffk
40 D3 Drointon Staffs
30 B2 Droitwich Worcs
92 H11 Dron P & K
51 J5 Dronfield Derbys
76 H7 Drongan E Ayrs
93 L8 Dronley Angus
7 Q2 Droop Dorset
9 Q4 Droxford Hants
50 B2 Droylsden Tamesd
48 B6 Druid Denbgs
24 F5 Druidston Pembks
90 F7 Druimachoish Highld
90 E3 Druimarbin Highld
83 L8 Druimdrishaig Ag & B
97 J11 Druimindarroch Highld
83 P7 Drum Ag & B
86 C3 Drum P & K
78 E2 Drumalbin S Lans
108 C8 Drumbeg Highld
102 D7 Drumblade Abers
68 E9 Drumbreddon D & G
97 K4 Drumbuie Highld
71 L4 Drumburgh Cumb
70 E5 Drumburn D & G
85 J8 Drumchapel C Glas
91 Q5 Drumchastle P & K
77 L4 Drumclog S Lans
87 J3 Drumeldrie Fife
79 J3 Drumelzier Border
97 J6 Drumfearn Highld
95 M3 Drumfrennie Abers
93 M5 Drumgley Angus
99 L8 Drumguish Highld
101 J8 Drumin Moray
77 J10 Drumjohn D & G
68 H4 Drumlamford S Ayrs
95 K2 Drumlasie Abers
71 L5 Drumleaning Cumb
75 K8 Drumlemble Ag & B
95 N6 Drumlithie Abers
69 K9 Drummoddie D & G
68 F10 Drummore D & G
101 M6 Drummuir Moray
98 G3 Drumnadrochit Highld
68 F11 Drumnaglaur D & G
102 C5 Drumnagorrach Moray
78 E11 Drumpark D & G
106 C2 Drumrunie Lodge Highld
76 E8 Drumshang S Ayrs
104 F11 Drumuie Highld
99 P5 Drumuillie Highld
85 L3 Drumvaich Stirlg
86 D1 Drunzie P & K
64 C5 Drybeck Cumb
101 N3 Drybridge Moray
76 F4 Drybridge N Ayrs
28 H5 Drybrook Gloucs
80 D7 Dryburgh Border
42 G7 Dry Doddington Lincs
33 L4 Dry Drayton Cambs
2 F8 Drym Cnwll
84 H5 Drymen Stirlg
103 J6 Drymuir Abers
96 E4 Drynoch Highld
102 G3 Dubford Abers
108 G11 Duchally Highld
31 J11 Ducklington Oxon
33 M9 Duddenhoe End Essex
86 F7 Duddingston C Edin
42 E9 Duddington Nhants
16 H11 Duddlestone Somset
39 M5 Duddlewick Shrops
81 K6 Duddo Nthumb
49 K3 Duddon Ches
48 G7 Dudleston Shrops
40 C9 Dudley Dudley
73 M6 Dudley N Tyne
40 C8 Dudley Port Sandw
8 F7 Dudsbury Dorset
51 J11 Duffield Derbys
26 H9 Duffryn Neath
101 L7 Dufftown Moray
101 J2 Duffus Moray
64 C3 Dufton Cumb
60 F2 Duggleby N York
97 L4 Duirinish Highld
97 J7 Duisdalemore Highld
90 D2 Duisky Highld
34 H8 Duke Street Suffk
50 C2 Dukinfield Tamesd
17 N7 Dulcote Somset
6 E2 Dulford Devon
92 B6 Dull P & K
85 M7 Dullatur N Lans
33 Q5 Dullingham Cambs
33 Q5 Dullingham Ley Cambs
99 P4 Dulnain Bridge Highld
32 G5 Duloe Beds
4 F8 Duloe Cnwll
16 C9 Dulverton Somset
21 M8 Dulwich Gt Lon
84 G7 Dumbarton W Duns
30 D7 Dumbleton Gloucs
70 F1 Dumfries D & G
85 J6 Dumgoyne Stirlg
19 P10 Dummer Hants
23 Q9 Dumpton Kent
95 L9 Dun Angus
91 Q5 Dunalastair P & K
84 C8 Dunan Ag & B
96 G4 Dunan Highld
91 L5 Dunan P & K
75 K10 Dunaverty Ag & B
17 J7 Dunball Somset
87 M6 Dunbar E Loth
110 D9 Dunbeath Highld
90 B9 Dunbeg Ag & B
85 N3 Dunblane Stirlg
93 K11 Dunbog Fife
107 J10 Duncanston Highld
102 D9 Duncanstone Abers
6 B5 Dunchideock Devon
41 L12 Dunchurch Warwks
78 F11 Duncow D & G
86 D1 Duncrievie P & K
10 F6 Duncton W Susx
93 M9 Dundee C Dund
93 L9 Dundee Airport C Dund
17 L9 Dundon Somset
76 F5 Dundonald S Ayrs
106 B5 Dundonnell Highld
71 K5 Dundraw Cumb
98 D6 Dundreggan Highld
70 C6 Dundrennan D & G
17 N3 Dundry N Som
102 G12 Dunecht Abers
86 C5 Dunfermline Fife
18 G2 Dunfield Gloucs
77 L4 Dungavel S Lans
13 L6 Dungeness Kent
52 B8 Dunham Notts
49 J2 Dunham-on-the-Hill Ches
39 Q8 Dunhampton Worcs
57 N10 Dunham Town Traffd
57 N10 Dunham Woodhouses Traffd
52 E7 Dunholme Lincs
93 P12 Dunino Fife
85 N6 Dunipace Falk
92 F7 Dunkeld P & K
17 Q4 Dunkerton BaNES
6 F2 Dunkeswell Devon
58 H5 Dunkeswick N York
23 L10 Dunkirk Kent
18 B4 Dunkirk S Glos
22 C11 Dunk's Green Kent
95 K8 Dunlappie Angus
39 P8 Dunley Worcs
76 G2 Dunlop E Ayrs
98 H5 Dunmaglass Highld
85 P5 Dunmore Falk
110 E2 Dunnet Highld
93 N6 Dunnichen Angus
92 F11 Dunning P & K
61 K4 Dunnington E R Yk
30 E4 Dunnington Warwks
59 P4 Dunnington York
57 P4 Dunnockshaw Lancs
84 C7 Dunoon Ag & B
100 F5 Dunphail Moray
68 F7 Dunragit D & G
80 G4 Duns Border
42 F5 Dunsby Lincs
78 E11 Dunscore D & G
59 P11 Dunscroft Donc
66 E4 Dunsdale R & Cl
20 B7 Dunsden Green Oxon
14 F9 Dunsdon Devon
10 G3 Dunsfold Surrey
5 Q3 Dunsford Devon
93 J12 Dunshalt Fife
103 K5 Dunshillock Abers
51 L8 Dunsill Notts
67 J5 Dunsley N York
39 Q5 Dunsley Staffs
20 D3 Dunsmore Bucks
63 M11 Dunsop Bridge Lancs
32 E11 Dunstable Beds
40 F4 Dunstall Staffs
81 Q9 Dunstan Nthumb
16 D7 Dunster Somset
31 L8 Duns Tew Oxon
73 M8 Dunston Gatesd
52 F10 Dunston Lincs
45 K9 Dunston Norfk
40 B4 Dunston Staffs
5 M9 Dunstone Devon
5 P5 Dunstone Devon
59 N11 Dunsville Donc
61 J7 Dunswell E R Yk
86 C11 Dunsyre S Lans
4 H4 Dunterton Devon
29 N7 Duntisbourne Abbots Gloucs
29 P7 Duntisbourne Rouse Gloucs
7 Q2 Duntish Dorset
84 H8 Duntocher W Duns
33 J7 Dunton Beds
32 B11 Dunton Bucks
44 E4 Dunton Norfk
41 M8 Dunton Bassett Leics
21 P11 Dunton Green Kent
104 F7 Duntulm Highld
76 E8 Dunure S Ayrs
26 D9 Dunvant Swans
104 C11 Dunvegan Highld
35 P3 Dunwich Suffk
2 H9 Durgan Cnwll
73 M11 Durham Dur
73 M11 Durham Cathedral Dur
65 P5 Durham Tees Valley Airport S on T
78 E8 Durisdeer D & G
78 E7 Durisdeermill D & G
16 H8 Durleigh Somset
9 N4 Durley Hants
19 J7 Durley Wilts
9 N4 Durley Street Hants
23 P10 Durlock Kent
23 P9 Durlock Kent
108 G3 Durness Highld
102 F9 Durno Abers
90 D5 Duror Highld
83 P2 Durran Ag & B
10 H8 Durrington W Susx
18 H10 Durrington Wilts
95 M3 Durris Abers
29 K8 Dursley Gloucs
29 J5 Dursley Cross Gloucs
16 H9 Durston Somset
8 C6 Durweston Dorset
31 Q2 Duston Nhants
99 P4 Duthil Highld
57 L11 Dutton Ches
33 M7 Duxford Cambs
19 L2 Duxford Oxon
33 M7 Duxford Aircraft Museum Cambs
55 K6 Dwygyfylchi Conwy
54 F8 Dwyran IoA
103 J11 Dyce C Aber
47 J6 Dyffryn Ardudwy Gwynd
27 J6 Dyffryn Cellwen Neath
42 F5 Dyke Lincs
100 F4 Dyke Moray
93 J5 Dykehead Angus
94 F9 Dykehead Angus
85 P10 Dykehead N Lans
85 K4 Dykehead Stirlg
95 L8 Dykelands Abers
93 J4 Dykends Angus
102 F6 Dykeside Abers
13 L4 Dymchurch Kent
29 J3 Dymock Gloucs
17 Q2 Dyrham S Glos
86 G4 Dysart Fife
56 C11 Dyserth Denbgs

E

62 H12 Eagland Hill Lancs
52 C9 Eagle Lincs
65 Q5 Eaglescliffe S on T
70 H9 Eaglesfield Cumb
71 K1 Eaglesfield D & G
85 J11 Eaglesham E Rens
57 N6 Eagley Bolton
51 P8 Eakring Notts
60 D10 Ealand N Linc
21 J7 Ealing Gt Lon
72 C9 Eals Nthumb
71 Q9 Eamont Bridge Cumb
58 B5 Earby Lancs
39 N4 Eardington Shrops
38 H9 Eardisland Herefs
38 F11 Eardisley Herefs
48 G9 Eardiston Shrops
39 M8 Eardiston Worcs
33 L2 Earith Cambs
57 L9 Earlestown St Hel
20 C8 Earley Wokham
104 E9 Earlish Highld
32 C4 Earls Barton Nhants
34 E10 Earls Colne Essex
30 C3 Earls Common Worcs
29 M1 Earl's Croome Worcs
40 H10 Earlsdon Covtry
87 J3 Earlsferry Fife
21 K8 Earlsfield Gt Lon
102 H8 Earlsford Abers
58 H9 Earlsheaton Kirk
41 L7 Earl Shilton Leics
35 K4 Earl Soham Suffk
50 E7 Earl Sterndale Derbys
80 D6 Earlston Border
76 G4 Earlston E Ayrs
21 L12 Earlswood Surrey
40 E11 Earlswood Warwks
10 D10 Earnley W Susx
73 N6 Earsdon N Tyne
73 L3 Earsdon Nthumb
45 M11 Earsham Norfk
10 F8 Eartham W Susx
66 E6 Easby N York
89 P11 Easdale Ag & B
10 E5 Easebourne W Susx
41 L10 Easenhall Warwks
10 F2 Eashing Surrey
31 P11 Easington Bucks
73 P11 Easington Dur
61 P9 Easington E R Yk
66 G4 Easington R & Cl
73 Q11 Easington Colliery Dur
66 D12 Easingwold N York
93 L6 Eassie and Nevay Angus
16 D3 East Aberthaw V Glam
5 P9 East Allington Devon
15 P6 East Anstey Devon
9 P9 East Ashey IoW
10 D8 East Ashling W Susx
67 L9 East Ayton N York
52 G7 East Barkwith Lincs
22 E11 East Barming Kent
66 H5 East Barnby N York
21 L4 East Barnet Gt Lon
87 N7 East Barns E Loth
44 F4 East Barsham Norfk
45 J3 East Beckham Norfk
20 H8 East Bedfont Gt Lon
34 H9 East Bergholt Suffk
44 F6 East Bilney Norfk
11 P9 East Blatchington E Susx
73 P8 East Boldon S Tyne
9 L7 East Boldre Hants
65 N5 Eastbourne Darltn
12 C9 Eastbourne E Susx
44 F8 East Bradenham Norfk
17 J6 East Brent Somset
35 P4 Eastbridge Suffk
51 P11 East Bridgford Notts
15 L6 East Buckland Devon
6 E6 East Budleigh Devon
58 D5 Eastburn Brad
20 H5 Eastbury Herts
19 K5 Eastbury W Berk
52 B3 East Butterwick N Linc
58 D4 Eastby N York
86 C8 East Calder W Loth
45 K9 East Carleton Norfk
58 G5 East Carlton Leeds
42 B11 East Carlton Nhants
8 B10 East Chaldon (Chaldon Herring) Dorset
19 L3 East Challow Oxon
5 P10 East Charleton Devon
7 M2 East Chelborough Dorset
11 M7 East Chiltington E Susx
17 L12 East Chinnock Somset
18 G9 East Chisenbury Wilts
23 J8 Eastchurch Kent
20 G11 East Clandon Surrey
31 Q8 East Claydon Bucks
7 M1 East Coker Somset
29 M7 Eastcombe Gloucs
16 F9 East Combe Somset
17 N7 East Compton Somset
6 B10 East Cornworthy Devon
20 H6 Eastcote Gt Lon
31 P4 Eastcote Nhants
40 G10 Eastcote Solhll
18 F9 Eastcott Wilts
60 C6 East Cottingwith E R Yk
19 J8 Eastcourt Wilts
29 N9 Eastcourt Wilts
9 N8 East Cowes IoW
59 P9 East Cowick E R Yk
65 N6 East Cowton N York
17 P7 East Cranmore Somset
8 D10 East Creech Dorset
12 C9 East Dean E Susx
28 H5 East Dean Gloucs
9 J3 East Dean Hants
10 E7 East Dean W Susx
15 K4 East Down Devon
51 Q6 East Drayton Notts
21 M8 East Dulwich Gt Lon
17 N3 East Dundry N Som
60 H8 East Ella C KuH
22 H5 Eastend Essex
9 L7 East End Hants
19 M8 East End Hants
12 G3 East End Kent
31 K10 East End Oxon
78 F2 Eastend S Lans
17 P6 East End Somset
94 E3 Easter Balmoral Abers
28 G11 Easter Compton S Glos
107 M11 Easter Dalziel Highld
10 F8 Eastergate W Susx
85 L9 Easterhouse C Glas
86 F9 Easter Howgate Mdloth
107 J10 Easter Kinkell Highld
98 H1 Easter Moniack Highld
40 H10 Eastern Green Covtry
95 N2 Easter Ord Abers
87 L2 Easter Pitkierie Fife
111 k4 Easter Skeld Shet
80 G7 Easter Softlaw Border
107 L10 Easter Suddie Highld
18 F9 Easterton Wilts
18 H9 East Everleigh Wilts
22 E11 East Farleigh Kent
41 Q9 East Farndon Nhants
52 B4 East Ferry Lincs
85 P9 Eastfield N Lans
67 M10 Eastfield N York
87 K6 East Fortune E Loth
19 L5 East Garston W Berk
72 G12 Eastgate Dur
45 J5 Eastgate Norfk
41 N5 East Goscote Leics
19 J8 East Grafton Wilts
9 J2 East Grimstead Wilts
11 N3 East Grinstead W Susx
12 H6 East Guldeford E Susx
31 P1 East Haddon Nhants
19 N3 East Hagbourne Oxon
61 K9 East Halton N Linc
21 N6 East Ham Gt Lon
20 D9 Easthampstead Br For
38 H9 Easthampton Herefs
19 M3 East Hanney Oxon
22 F3 East Hanningfield Essex
59 L9 East Hardwick Wakefd
44 G11 East Harling Norfk
65 Q7 East Harlsey N York
8 G2 East Harnham Wilts
17 N5 East Harptree BaNES
65 Q4 East Hartburn S on T
10 C6 East Harting W Susx
8 D2 East Hatch Wilts
33 J6 East Hatley Cambs
65 L8 East Hauxwell N York
93 P8 East Haven Angus
42 H2 East Heckington Lincs
73 K11 East Hedleyhope Dur
110 B11 East Helmsdale Highld
19 M3 East Hendred Oxon

Farnell - Garlinge Green 177

93 Q5 Farnell Angus
8 E4 Farnham Dorset
33 M10 Farnham Essex
59 J3 Farnham N York
35 M5 Farnham Suffk
10 D1 Farnham Surrey
20 F6 Farnham Common Bucks
20 F6 Farnham Royal Bucks
22 B9 Farningham Kent
58 G7 Farnley Leeds
58 G5 Farnley N York
58 F10 Farnley Tyas Kirk
51 P9 Farnsfield Notts
57 N7 Farnworth Bolton
57 K10 Farnworth Halton
29 N7 Far Oakridge Gloucs
99 K3 Farr Highld
99 M8 Farr Highld
109 M3 Farr Highld
98 H5 Farraline Highld
6 D5 Farringdon Devon
17 P5 Farrington Gurney BaNES
62 H3 Far Sawrey Cumb
31 M6 Farthinghoe Nhants
31 N3 Farthingstone Nhants
53 J8 Far Thorpe Lincs
58 F9 Fartown Kirk
58 G7 Fartown Leeds
6 G4 Farway Street Devon
90 D6 Fasnacloich Ag & B
98 D4 Fasnakyle Highld
90 D1 Fassfern Highld
73 N9 Fatfield Sundld
85 Q10 Fauldhouse W Loth
34 D12 Faulkbourne Essex
17 Q5 Faulkland Somset
49 L8 Fauls Shrops
23 K10 Faversham Kent
66 B11 Fawdington N York
73 M7 Fawdon N u Ty
81 L10 Fawdon Nthumb
22 C9 Fawkham Green Kent
31 J10 Fawler Oxon
20 C6 Fawley Bucks
9 M6 Fawley Hants
19 L5 Fawley W Berk
60 E8 Faxfleet E R Yk
11 K4 Faygate W Susx
56 G9 Fazakerley Lpool
40 G7 Fazeley Staffs
65 L10 Fearby N York
107 N7 Fearn Highld
91 Q7 Fearnan P & K
105 L9 Fearnbeg Highld
105 K9 Fearnmore Highld
83 P7 Fearnoch Ag & B
40 C6 Featherstone Staffs
59 K9 Featherstone Wakefd
30 D2 Feckenham Worcs
34 E11 Feering Essex
64 H7 Feetham N York
11 M3 Felbridge Surrey
45 K3 Felbrigg Norfk
11 M2 Felcourt Surrey
25 N2 Felindre Carmth
26 D5 Felindre Carmth
38 D6 Felindre Powys
26 E8 Felindre Swans
36 B11 Felindre Farchog Pembks
26 C4 Felin gwm Isaf Carmth
26 C4 Felin gwm Uchaf Carmth
66 C9 Felixkirk N York
35 L9 Felixstowe Suffk
73 M8 Felling Gatesd
32 E5 Felmersham Beds
45 L4 Felmingham Norfk
10 F9 Felpham W Susx
34 F5 Felsham Suffk
34 B11 Felsted Essex
20 H8 Feltham Gt Lon
20 H8 Felthamhill Surrey
45 J6 Felthorpe Norfk
39 L11 Felton Herefs
17 M3 Felton N Som
73 L2 Felton Nthumb
48 H11 Felton Butler Shrops
44 B11 Feltwell Norfk
57 P2 Fence Lancs
51 K4 Fence Rothm
65 M8 Fencote N York
31 M10 Fencott Oxon
53 M10 Fendike Corner Lincs
33 M5 Fen Ditton Cambs
33 K3 Fen Drayton Cambs
57 M4 Feniscowles Bl w D
6 F3 Feniton Devon
39 P5 Fenn Green Shrops
22 F8 Fenn Street Medway
50 F10 Fenny Bentley Derbys
6 F3 Fenny Bridges Devon
31 K4 Fenny Compton Warwks
41 J7 Fenny Drayton Leics
33 K3 Fenstanton Cambs
44 G10 Fen Street Norfk
50 B11 Fenton C Stke
33 K2 Fenton Cambs
71 Q4 Fenton Cumb
52 B8 Fenton Lincs
52 C12 Fenton Lincs
52 B6 Fenton Notts
81 K7 Fenton Nthumb
87 K6 Fenton Barns E Loth
59 N10 Fenwick Donc
76 H3 Fenwick E Ayrs
73 J6 Fenwick Nthumb
81 M6 Fenwick Nthumb
3 J7 Feock Cnwll
82 F8 Feolin Ferry Ag & B
76 F3 Fergushill N Ayrs
104 B11 Feriniquarrie Highld
94 H9 Fern Angus
27 L9 Ferndale Rhondd
8 F7 Ferndown Dorset
100 E6 Ferness Highld
19 K3 Fernham Oxon
39 Q9 Fernhill Heath Worcs
10 E4 Fernhurst W Susx
93 K11 Fernie Fife
85 M11 Ferniegair S Lans
96 D3 Fernilea Highld
50 D5 Fernilee Derbys
52 B12 Fernwood Notts
59 J3 Ferrensby N York
97 J7 Ferrindonald Highld
10 H9 Ferring W Susx
93 M9 Ferryden Angus
65 M2 Ferryhill Dur
107 M5 Ferry Point Highld
25 N6 Ferryside Carmth
107 M5 Ferrytown Highld
44 H12 Fersfield Norfk
91 K2 Fersit Highld
99 M8 Feshiebridge Highld
21 J11 Fetcham Surrey
103 K5 Fetterangus Abers
95 K7 Fettercairn Abers
58 G4 Fewston N York
26 E5 Ffairfach Carmth
37 M7 Ffair Rhos Cerdgn
47 L3 Ffestiniog Gwynd
47 K3 Ffestiniog Railway Gwynd
26 D7 Fforest Carmth
26 E9 Fforest Fach Swans
36 F10 Ffostrasol Cerdgn
48 F4 Ffrith Flints
56 D11 Ffynnongroyw Flints
108 H9 Fiag Lodge Highld
21 M10 Fickleshole Surrey
29 N3 Fiddington Gloucs
16 G7 Fiddington Somset
8 B5 Fiddleford Dorset
3 J5 Fiddlers Green Cnwll
40 D2 Field Staffs
62 H6 Field Broughton Cumb
44 G3 Field Dalling Norfk
41 L5 Field Head Leics
8 B3 Fifehead Magdalen Dorset
8 B5 Fifehead Neville Dorset
8 B5 Fifehead St Quintin Dorset
101 M5 Fife Keith Moray
30 G9 Fifield Oxon
20 E7 Fifield W & M
18 H10 Figheldean Wilts
45 P7 Filby Norfk
67 N10 Filey N York
32 C7 Filgrave M Keyn
30 G12 Filkins Oxon
15 L6 Filleigh Devon
15 M9 Filleigh Devon
52 D6 Fillingham Lincs
40 H9 Fillongley Warwks
28 H11 Filton S Glos
60 F3 Fimber E R Yk
93 N4 Finavon Angus
44 B8 Fincham Norfk
20 C10 Finchampstead Wokham
83 N3 Fincharn Ag & B
10 B7 Finchdean Hants
34 B9 Finchingfield Essex
21 L5 Finchley Gt Lon
40 H2 Findern Derbys
100 G3 Findhorn Moray
99 M4 Findhorn Bridge Highld
101 N2 Findochty Moray
92 E10 Findo Gask P & K
95 Q3 Findon Abers
10 H8 Findon W Susx
107 K9 Findon Mains Highld
95 K2 Findrack House Abers
32 D3 Finedon Nhants
35 K3 Fingal Street Suffk
92 H10 Fingask P & K
20 C5 Fingest Bucks
65 L9 Finghall N York
77 M7 Fingland D & G
23 P11 Finglesham Kent
34 G11 Fingringhoe Essex
91 N9 Finlarig Stirlg
31 N7 Finmere Oxon
91 M5 Finnart P & K
34 H3 Finningham Suffk
51 P2 Finningley Donc
111 c4 Finsbay W Isls
40 C12 Finstall Worcs
62 G5 Finsthwaite Cumb
31 J10 Finstock Oxon
111 h2 Finstown Ork
102 G4 Fintry Abers
85 K5 Fintry Stirlg
95 K4 Finzean Abers
88 G10 Fionnphort Ag & B
111 c4 Fionnsbhagh W Isls
63 L4 Firbank Cumb
51 M3 Firbeck Rothm
60 C2 Firby N York
65 M9 Firby N York
53 M10 Firsby Lincs
65 K1 Fir Tree Dur
9 P8 Fishbourne IoW
10 D8 Fishbourne W Susx
10 D8 Fishbourne Roman Palace W Susx
65 P2 Fishburn Dur
85 P4 Fishcross Clacks
102 E8 Fisherford Abers
86 G7 Fisherrow E Loth
9 N4 Fisher's Pond Hants
107 M11 Fisherton Highld
76 E7 Fisherton S Ayrs
18 E11 Fisherton de la Mere Wilts
24 G2 Fishguard Pembks
59 P10 Fishlake Donc
89 N7 Fishnish Pier Ag & B
17 P2 Fishponds Bristl
43 K2 Fishtoft Lincs
43 K1 Fishtoft Drove Lincs
96 D3 Fiskavaig Highld
52 F8 Fiskerton Lincs
51 Q9 Fiskerton Notts
18 G10 Fittleton Wilts
10 G6 Fittleworth W Susx
49 J11 Fitz Shrops
16 F9 Fitzhead Somset
59 K10 Fitzwilliam Wakefd
11 P5 Five Ash Down E Susx
12 B5 Five Ashes E Susx
17 J10 Fivehead Somset
4 F4 Fivelanes Cnwll
12 D2 Five Oak Green Kent
7 c2 Five Oaks Jersey
10 H4 Five Oaks W Susx
20 E5 Flackwell Heath Bucks
30 C5 Fladbury Worcs
111 k4 Fladdabister Shet
50 F7 Flagg Derbys
67 Q12 Flamborough E R Yk
67 Q12 Flamborough Head E R Yk
66 H10 Flamingo Land Theme Park N York
20 H1 Flamstead Herts
10 F9 Flansham W Susx
58 H9 Flanshaw Wakefd
58 C3 Flasby N York
50 D7 Flash Staffs
104 D10 Flashader Highld
20 G4 Flaunden Herts
42 B2 Flawborough Notts
59 L2 Flawith N York
17 M3 Flax Bourton N Som
59 K3 Flaxby N York
29 J6 Flaxley Gloucs
16 F8 Flaxpool Somset
59 P2 Flaxton N York
41 P8 Fleckney Leics
31 L2 Flecknoe Warwks
52 B8 Fledborough Notts
7 P6 Fleet Dorset
20 D11 Fleet Hants
43 L5 Fleet Lincs
43 L5 Fleet Hargate Lincs
62 G11 Fleetwood Lancs
16 D3 Flemingston V Glam
85 L10 Flemington S Lans
34 D3 Flempton Suffk
71 K7 Fletchertown Cumb
11 N5 Fletching E Susx
14 D10 Flexbury Cnwll
20 E12 Flexford Surrey
70 G8 Flimby Cumb
12 E4 Flimwell E Susx
48 E2 Flint Flints
51 Q10 Flintham Notts
61 L7 Flinton E R Yk
44 C5 Flitcham Norfk
32 F9 Flitton Beds
32 E9 Flitwick Beds
60 E10 Flixborough N Linc
60 E10 Flixborough Stather N Linc
67 M10 Flixton N York
45 M11 Flixton Suffk
57 N9 Flixton Traffd
58 G10 Flockton Kirk
58 G10 Flockton Green Kirk
104 F7 Flodigarry Highld
62 G7 Flookburgh Cumb
45 K10 Flordon Norfk
31 N3 Flore Nhants
34 H7 Flowton Suffk
3 J8 Flushing Cnwll
6 E4 Fluxton Devon
30 C3 Flyford Flavell Worcs
22 E6 Fobbing Thurr
101 L4 Fochabers Moray
60 E9 Fockerby N Linc
17 N9 Foddington Somset
48 B12 Foel Powys
60 D6 Foggathorpe E R Yk
80 G4 Fogo Border
101 K4 Fogwatt Moray
108 D6 Foindle Highld
94 C8 Folda Angus
50 D12 Fole Staffs
41 J10 Foleshill Covtry
17 P12 Folke Dorset
13 N3 Folkestone Kent
42 F4 Folkingham Lincs
12 C8 Folkington E Susx
42 G11 Folksworth Cambs
67 M10 Folkton N York
102 F8 Folla Rule Abers
59 J4 Follifoot N York
15 K11 Folly Gate Devon
8 D2 Fonthill Bishop Wilts
8 D2 Fonthill Gifford Wilts
8 C4 Fontmell Magna Dorset
8 C5 Fontmell Parva Dorset
10 F8 Fontwell W Susx
50 F5 Foolow Derbys
101 M11 Forbestown Abers
65 L5 Forcett N York
83 N3 Ford Ag & B
31 Q11 Ford Bucks
51 K5 Ford Derbys
5 Q11 Ford Devon
14 G7 Ford Devon
30 E8 Ford Gloucs
81 K6 Ford Nthumb
16 E9 Ford Somset
50 E9 Ford Staffs
10 F8 Ford W Susx
18 C6 Ford Wilts
11 Q3 Fordcombe Kent
86 D5 Fordell Fife
38 E2 Forden Powys
34 B12 Ford End Essex
5 Q6 Forder Green Devon
33 Q3 Fordham Cambs
34 F10 Fordham Essex
43 P9 Fordham Norfk
8 G5 Fordingbridge Hants
67 M11 Fordon E R Yk
95 M6 Fordoun Abers
34 F10 Fordstreet Essex
16 F11 Ford Street Somset
23 M10 Fordwich Kent
102 D3 Fordyce Abers
40 B3 Forebridge Staffs
41 J3 Foremark Derbys
6 b2 Forest Guern
63 P11 Forest Becks Lancs
50 C6 Forest Chapel Ches
21 N6 Forest Gate Gt Lon
10 H2 Forest Green Surrey
73 M6 Forest Hall N Tyne
21 M8 Forest Hill Gt Lon
31 N11 Forest Hill Oxon
59 J3 Forest Lane Head N York
90 H7 Forest Lodge Ag & B
85 Q4 Forest Mill Clacks
28 H6 Forest of Dean Gloucs
11 N3 Forest Row E Susx
10 C7 Forestside W Susx
93 M5 Forfar Angus
92 G11 Forgandenny P & K
28 C9 Forge Hammer Torfn
101 M4 Forgie Moray
101 M5 Forgieside Moray
102 D6 Forgue Abers
56 F7 Formby Sefton
45 J10 Forncett End Norfk
45 J10 Forncett St Mary Norfk
45 J10 Forncett St Peter Norfk
34 D4 Fornham All Saints Suffk
34 E4 Fornham St Martin Suffk
100 E5 Fornighty Highld
100 F4 Forres Moray
50 C11 Forsbrook Staffs
110 E8 Forse Highld
110 E8 Forse House Highld
109 Q7 Forsinard Highld
98 E7 Fort Augustus Highld
92 F11 Forteviot P & K
85 Q11 Forth S Lans
29 M3 Forthampton Gloucs
91 Q6 Fortingall P & K
19 M11 Forton Hants
63 J11 Forton Lancs
48 H11 Forton Shrops
7 J2 Forton Somset
49 N10 Forton Staffs
102 E6 Fortrie Abers
107 M10 Fortrose Highld
7 P7 Fortuneswell Dorset
90 F2 Fort William Highld
21 M4 Forty Hill Gt Lon
19 K8 Fosbury Wilts
30 G9 Foscot Oxon
43 K4 Fosdyke Lincs
92 B4 Foss P & K
30 E11 Fossebridge Gloucs
21 P2 Foster Street Essex
40 F2 Foston Derbys
41 N8 Foston Leics
42 C2 Foston Lincs
59 P2 Foston N York
61 J3 Foston on the Wolds E R Yk
53 K5 Fotherby Lincs
42 F10 Fotheringhay Nhants
81 K3 Foulden Border
44 C9 Foulden Norfk
40 G8 Foul End Warwks
58 B6 Foulridge Lancs
44 G5 Foulsham Norfk
87 J11 Fountainhall Border
34 G3 Four Ashes Suffk
48 F10 Four Crosses Powys
11 P1 Four Elms Kent
16 G8 Four Forks Somset
43 M6 Four Gotes Cambs
2 G7 Four Lanes Cnwll
9 R1 Four Marks Hants
54 C6 Four Mile Bridge IoA
40 G10 Four Oaks Solhll
107 N4 Fourpenny Highld
25 Q7 Four Roads Carmth
72 F7 Fourstones Nthumb
12 F4 Four Throws Kent
8 E2 Fovant Wilts
103 K9 Foveran Abers
4 D9 Fowey Cnwll
12 E2 Fowlhall Kent
93 K8 Fowlis Angus
92 D10 Fowlis Wester P & K
33 L7 Fowlmere Cambs
28 G3 Fownhope Herefs
84 H10 Foxbar Rens
17 Q5 Foxcote Somset
56 b5 Foxdale IoM
34 D7 Foxearth Essex
62 E5 Foxfield Cumb
3 L5 Foxhole Cnwll
67 L11 Foxholes N York
44 H6 Foxley Norfk
50 D10 Foxt Staffs
33 L7 Foxton Cambs
41 P9 Foxton Leics
65 Q8 Foxton N York
39 L6 Foxwood Shrops
28 H3 Foy Herefs
98 G5 Foyers Highld
100 D5 Foynesfield Highld
3 K4 Fraddon Cnwll
40 F5 Fradley Staffs
40 C2 Fradswell Staffs
61 K2 Fraisthorpe E R Yk
11 P6 Framfield E Susx
45 L9 Framingham Earl Norfk
45 L9 Framingham Pigot Norfk
35 L4 Framlingham Suffk
7 P4 Frampton Dorset
43 K3 Frampton Lincs
29 J11 Frampton Cotterell S Glos
29 N8 Frampton Mansell Gloucs
29 K7 Frampton on Severn Gloucs
35 K5 Framsden Suffk
73 M11 Framwellgate Moor Dur
57 L2 Frances Green Lancs
39 P6 Franche Worcs
56 E10 Frankby Wirral
40 C10 Frankley Worcs
41 K12 Frankton Warwks
12 C3 Frant E Susx
103 K2 Fraserburgh Abers
34 H11 Frating Essex
34 H11 Frating Green Essex
9 Q7 Fratton C Port
5 J9 Freathy Cnwll
33 Q3 Freckenham Suffk
56 H3 Freckleton Lancs
42 B6 Freeby Leics
19 N10 Freefolk Hants
31 K10 Freeland Oxon
45 N8 Freethorpe Norfk
45 N8 Freethorpe Common Norfk
43 L2 Freiston Lincs
15 J6 Fremington Devon
65 J7 Fremington N York
28 H12 Frenchay S Glos
92 C4 Frenich P & K
10 D2 Frensham Surrey
56 F7 Freshfield Sefton
18 B8 Freshford Wilts
9 K9 Freshwater IoW
35 L2 Fressingfield Suffk
35 J8 Freston Suffk
110 G3 Freswick Highld
29 K6 Fretherne Gloucs
45 L6 Frettenham Norfk
86 F2 Freuchie Fife
24 G6 Freystrop Pembks
40 D8 Friar Park Sandw
43 M8 Friday Bridge Cambs
35 N5 Friday Street Suffk
60 E3 Fridaythorpe E R Yk
21 L5 Friern Barnet Gt Lon
88 F5 Friesland Bay Ag & B
52 F6 Friesthorpe Lincs
42 D1 Frieston Lincs
20 C5 Frieth Bucks
19 M2 Frilford Oxon
19 P6 Frilsham W Berk
20 E10 Frimley Surrey
22 E9 Frindsbury Medway
44 C3 Fring Norfk
31 N8 Fringford Oxon
22 H11 Frinsted Kent
35 K11 Frinton-on-Sea Essex
93 Q6 Friockheim Angus
41 P4 Frisby on the Wreake Leics
53 M11 Friskney Lincs
12 B9 Friston E Susx
35 N5 Friston Suffk
51 J9 Fritchley Derbys
9 J5 Fritham Hants
14 H8 Frithelstock Devon
14 H8 Frithelstock Stone Devon
53 K12 Frithville Lincs
12 F2 Frittenden Kent
5 Q10 Frittiscombe Devon
45 K10 Fritton Norfk
45 P9 Fritton Norfk
31 M8 Fritwell Oxon
58 F7 Frizinghall Brad
70 G11 Frizington Cumb
29 K8 Frocester Gloucs
39 K2 Frodesley Shrops
57 K12 Frodsham Ches
80 G8 Frogden Border
33 L7 Frog End Cambs
50 G5 Froggatt Derbys
50 D10 Froghall Staffs
5 P10 Frogmore Devon
42 G7 Frognall Lincs
39 P8 Frog Pool Worcs
4 H6 Frogwell Cnwll
41 L8 Frolesworth Leics
18 B10 Frome Somset
7 N3 Frome St Quintin Dorset
39 M11 Fromes Hill Herefs
48 F7 Froncysyllte Denbgs
47 P4 Fron-goch Gwynd
48 F7 Fron Isaf Wrexhm
72 H12 Frosterley Dur
19 K7 Froxfield Wilts
10 B5 Froxfield Green Hants
9 M4 Fryern Hill Hants
22 D4 Fryerning Essex
89 M7 Fuinary Highld
52 D12 Fulbeck Lincs
33 N5 Fulbourn Cambs
30 H10 Fulbrook Oxon
9 M2 Fulflood Hants
16 G9 Fulford Somset
50 C12 Fulford Staffs
59 N4 Fulford York
21 K8 Fulham Gt Lon
11 K7 Fulking W Susx
76 F4 Fullarton N Ayrs
34 C12 Fuller Street Essex
19 L11 Fullerton Hants
53 J8 Fulletby Lincs
30 H5 Fullready Warwks
60 D3 Full Sutton E R Yk
76 G2 Fullwood E Ayrs
20 F6 Fulmer Bucks
44 G4 Fulmodeston Norfk
52 F7 Fulnetby Lincs
43 J5 Fulney Lincs
53 K4 Fulstow Lincs
31 J9 Fulwell Oxon
73 P8 Fulwell Sundld
57 K3 Fulwood Lancs
50 H4 Fulwood Sheff
45 J10 Fundenhall Norfk
10 C8 Funtington W Susx
92 B9 Funtullich P & K
6 H2 Furley Devon
83 Q3 Furnace Ag & B
26 C8 Furnace Carmth
50 D4 Furness Vale Derbys
33 L10 Furneux Pelham Herts
9 K4 Furzley Hants
22 C3 Fyfield Essex
19 K10 Fyfield Hants
19 M2 Fyfield Oxon
18 G7 Fyfield Wilts
18 H8 Fyfield Wilts
67 K6 Fylingthorpe N York
10 D5 Fyning W Susx
102 G7 Fyvie Abers

G

76 H2 Gabroc Hill E Ayrs
41 P5 Gaddesby Leics
20 G2 Gaddesden Row Herts
76 G6 Gadgirth S Ayrs
28 E9 Gaer-llwyd Mons
54 F7 Gaerwen IoA
76 F4 Gailes N Ayrs
40 B5 Gailey Staffs
65 L4 Gainford Dur
52 B5 Gainsborough Lincs
34 C9 Gainsford End Essex
105 M7 Gairloch Highld
98 B11 Gairlochy Highld
86 D3 Gairneybridge P & K
58 F6 Gaisby Brad
71 N6 Gaitsgill Cumb
80 C7 Galashiels Border
63 J10 Galgate Lancs
17 P9 Galhampton Somset
90 B10 Gallanach Ag & B
86 G4 Gallatown Fife
22 E3 Galleywood Essex
98 H10 Gallovie Highld
69 L3 Galloway Forest Park
93 M7 Gallowfauld Angus
92 H8 Gallowhill P & K
97 L5 Galltair Highld
5 N11 Galmpton Devon
6 B10 Galmpton Torbay
65 M11 Galphay N York
76 H4 Galston E Ayrs
8 B9 Galton Dorset
72 B11 Gamblesby Cumb
33 J6 Gamlingay Cambs
32 H6 Gamlingay Great Heath Cambs
102 G3 Gamrie Abers
51 N12 Gamston Notts
51 P5 Gamston Notts
90 B9 Ganavan Bay Ag & B
47 M6 Ganllwyd Gwynd
95 K7 Gannachy Angus
61 K7 Ganstead E R Yk
66 F12 Ganthorpe N York
67 L11 Ganton N York
101 L5 Garbity Moray
34 G1 Garboldisham Norfk
101 L12 Garchory Abers
20 D9 Gardeners Green Wokham
102 G3 Gardenstown Abers
50 H2 Garden Village Sheff
111 k4 Garderhouse Shet
18 B11 Gare Hill Somset
84 D5 Garelochhead Ag & B
19 M2 Garford Oxon
59 K7 Garforth Leeds
58 B4 Gargrave N York
85 M4 Gargunnock Stirlg
45 K12 Garlic Street Norfk
69 L9 Garlieston D & G
23 P9 Garlinge Kent
23 L11 Garlinge Green Kent

178 Garlogie - Great Stoke

95 M2 Garlogie Abers
102 G5 Garmond Abers
101 L3 Garmouth Moray
39 L2 Garmston Shrops
46 H3 Garn-Dolbenmaen Gwynd
85 L8 Garnkirk N Lans
111 e2 Garrabost W Isls
77 J7 Garrallan E Ayrs
2 G10 Garras Cnwll
47 K3 Garreg Gwynd
72 D11 Garrigill Cumb
69 N3 Garroch D & G
68 F10 Garrochtrie D & G
84 B11 Garrochty Ag & B
104 G9 Garros Highld
64 E8 Garsdale Head Cumb
18 E4 Garsdon Wilts
40 C1 Garshall Green Staffs
31 M12 Garsington Oxon
63 J12 Garstang Lancs
20 H4 Garston Herts
56 H11 Garston Lpool
82 E10 Gartachossan Ag & B
85 L9 Gartcosh N Lans
37 Q10 Garth Powys
48 F7 Garth Wrexhm
85 L9 Garthamlock C Glas
38 E3 Garthmyl Powys
42 B6 Garthorpe Leics
60 E9 Garthorpe N Linc
37 K4 Garth Penrhyncoch Cerdgn
63 K3 Garth Row Cumb
102 C8 Gartly Abers
85 J4 Gartmore Stirlg
85 N9 Gartness N Lans
84 H5 Gartness Stirlg
84 G6 Gartocharn W Duns
61 M7 Garton E R Yk
60 G3 Garton-on-the-Wolds E R Yk
110 B11 Gartymore Highld
87 L7 Garvald E Loth
90 D2 Garvan Highld
82 E5 Garvard Ag & B
106 G9 Garve Highld
44 G8 Garvestone Norfk
84 E8 Garvock Inver
28 E4 Garway Herefs
28 F4 Garway Common Herefs
111 d2 Garyvard W Isls
8 B2 Gasper Wilts
18 C7 Gastard Wilts
34 F1 Gasthorpe Norfk
33 N12 Gaston Green Essex
9 N9 Gatcombe IoW
52 B7 Gate Burton Lincs
59 M8 Gateforth N York
76 G4 Gatehead E Ayrs
59 P3 Gate Helmsley N York
72 E3 Gatehouse Nthumb
69 N7 Gatehouse of Fleet D & G
44 F5 Gateley Norfk
65 N9 Gatenby N York
80 G9 Gateshaw Border
73 M8 Gateshead Gatesd
93 M6 Gateside Angus
84 H10 Gateside E Rens
86 E1 Gateside Fife
84 F11 Gateside N Ayrs
78 E8 Gateslack D & G
57 Q10 Gatley Stockp
80 D7 Gattonside Border
11 L2 Gatwick Airport W Susx
41 P7 Gaulby Leics
93 L10 Gauldry Fife
93 J5 Gauldswell P & K
52 H8 Gautby Lincs
80 G4 Gavinton Border
31 P7 Gawcott Bucks
50 B6 Gawsworth Ches
63 M5 Gawthrop Cumb
62 F5 Gawthwaite Cumb
31 J4 Gaydon Warwks
32 C7 Gayhurst M Keyn
64 F9 Gayle N York
65 K6 Gayles N York
31 P4 Gayton Nhants
44 C6 Gayton Norfk
40 C2 Gayton Staffs
53 L6 Gayton le Marsh Lincs
44 C6 Gayton Thorpe Norfk
43 Q6 Gaywood Norfk
34 C4 Gazeley Suffk
111 d2 Gearraidh Bhaird W Isls
104 C9 Geary Highld
34 F5 Gedding Suffk
13 N2 Geddinge Kent
42 C12 Geddington Nhants
51 N11 Gedling Notts
43 L5 Gedney Lincs
43 L5 Gedney Broadgate Lincs
43 M4 Gedney Drove End Lincs
43 L5 Gedney Dyke Lincs
43 K7 Gedney Hill Lincs
42 E8 Geeston Rutlnd
45 N10 Geldeston Norfk
48 D3 Gellifor Denbgs
27 N9 Gelligaer Caerph
47 L4 Gellilydan Gwynd
26 G7 Gellinudd Neath
92 G7 Gellyburn P & K
25 M4 Gellywen Carmth
70 C4 Gelston D & G
42 C2 Gelston Lincs
61 J3 Gembling E R Yk
40 D5 Gentleshaw Staffs
79 L9 Georgefield D & G
20 F7 George Green Bucks
14 H4 Georgeham Devon
15 M7 George Nympton Devon
111 h2 Georth Ork
5 J2 Germansweek Devon
3 K8 Gerrans Cnwll
20 G6 Gerrards Cross Bucks
66 G5 Gerrick R & Cl
34 D8 Gestingthorpe Essex
48 E11 Geuffordd Powys
21 Q5 Gidea Park Gt Lon
85 J10 Giffnock E Rens
87 K8 Gifford E Loth
93 K12 Giffordtown Fife
63 P9 Giggleswick N York
60 E8 Gilberdyke E R Yk
87 J8 Gilchriston E Loth
70 H7 Gilcrux Cumb
58 G8 Gildersome Leeds
51 M4 Gildingwells Rothm
73 N11 Gilesgate Moor Dur
16 D3 Gileston V Glam
27 N8 Gilfach Caerph
27 K10 Gilfach Goch Brdgnd
36 G8 Gilfachrheda Cerdgn
70 G10 Gilgarran Cumb
66 F9 Gillamoor N York
104 C9 Gillen Highld
79 J9 Gillesbie D & G
66 E11 Gilling East N York
8 B3 Gillingham Dorset
22 F9 Gillingham Medway
45 N10 Gillingham Norfk
65 L6 Gilling West N York
110 E4 Gillock Highld
110 G2 Gills Highld
79 M5 Gilmanscleuch Border
86 F8 Gilmerton C Edin
92 D10 Gilmerton P & K
64 H5 Gilmonby Dur
41 M9 Gilmorton Leics
72 B7 Gilsland Cumb
87 J10 Gilston Border
21 N2 Gilston Herts
27 Q6 Gilwern Mons
45 L3 Gimingham Norfk
34 H4 Gipping Suffk
53 J12 Gipsey Bridge Lincs
76 F3 Girdle Toll N Ayrs
111 k4 Girlsta Shet
65 N6 Girsby N York
69 N8 Girthon D & G
33 L4 Girton Cambs
52 B9 Girton Notts
76 D10 Girvan S Ayrs
63 P11 Gisburn Lancs
45 Q11 Gisleham Suffk
34 H3 Gislingham Suffk
45 J11 Gissing Norfk
6 F3 Gittisham Devon
38 E10 Gladestry Powys
87 J7 Gladsmuir E Loth
26 F8 Glais Swans
66 H6 Glaisdale N York
93 L6 Glamis Angus
26 F6 Glanaman Carmth
44 H2 Glandford Norfk
25 L3 Glandwr Pembks
47 L11 Glandyfi Cerdgn
27 J10 Glanllynfi Brdgnd
81 M10 Glanton Nthumb
7 P2 Glanvilles Wootton Dorset
56 D11 Glan-y-don Flints
42 E11 Glapthorn Nhants
51 L7 Glapwell Derbys
27 P2 Glasbury Powys
38 D10 Glascwm Powys
55 N10 Glasfryn Conwy
85 K9 Glasgow C Glas
84 H9 Glasgow Airport Rens
85 J9 Glasgow Science Centre C Glas
54 H7 Glasinfryn Gwynd
97 J9 Glasnacardoch Bay Highld
96 G7 Glasnakille Highld
69 K10 Glasserton D & G
77 M2 Glassford S Lans
29 J5 Glasshouse Gloucs
58 F2 Glasshouses N York
71 L4 Glasson Cumb
63 J10 Glasson Lancs
72 B12 Glassonby Cumb
93 Q5 Glasterlaw Angus
42 C9 Glaston Rutlnd
17 M8 Glastonbury Somset
42 G11 Glatton Cambs
57 M9 Glazebrook Warrtn
57 M9 Glazebury Warrtn
39 N5 Glazeley Shrops
62 F7 Gleaston Cumb
98 G5 Glebe Highld
58 H6 Gledhow Leeds
69 P8 Gledpark D & G
48 F7 Gledrid Shrops
34 D7 Glemsford Suffk
101 K7 Glenallachie Moray
97 J10 Glenancross Highld
89 L7 Glenaros House Ag & B
56 d3 Glen Auldyn IoM
75 K5 Glenbarr Ag & B
102 D4 Glenbarry Abers
89 M4 Glenbeg Highld
100 F9 Glenbeg Highld
95 M6 Glenbervie Abers
85 M8 Glenboig N Lans
89 M4 Glenborrodale Highld
84 B4 Glenbranter Ag & B
78 H5 Glenbreck Border
96 E5 Glenbrittle House Highld
77 M5 Glenbuck E Ayrs
94 F8 Glencally Angus
70 G2 Glencaple D & G
105 R11 Glencarron Lodge Highld
92 H10 Glencarse P & K
90 F6 Glenceitlein Highld
94 C5 Glen Clunie Lodge Abers
90 F5 Glencoe Highld
78 H3 Glencothe Border
86 E4 Glencraig Fife
78 C10 Glencrosh D & G
104 B11 Glendale Highld
83 Q6 Glendaruel Ag & B
86 B2 Glendevon P & K
98 E7 Glendoe Lodge Highld
93 J10 Glendoick P & K
93 K11 Glenduckie Fife
85 Q2 Gleneagles P & K
85 Q2 Gleneagles Hotel P & K
74 D3 Glenegedale Ag & B
97 L6 Glenelg Highld
100 F6 Glenerney Moray
92 G12 Glenfarg P & K
99 M9 Glenfeshie Lodge Highld
41 M6 Glenfield Leics
97 M12 Glenfinnan Highld
98 C10 Glenfintaig Lodge Highld
92 H11 Glenfoot P & K
90 H12 Glenfyne Lodge Ag & B
84 F11 Glengarnock N Ayrs
110 C3 Glengolly Highld
89 K5 Glengorm Castle Ag & B
96 E1 Glengrasco Highld
78 H3 Glenholm Border
69 N2 Glenhoul D & G
94 D9 Glenisla Angus
84 C7 Glenkin Ag & B
101 N11 Glenkindie Abers
101 J9 Glenlivet Moray
70 C3 Glenlochar D & G
86 E2 Glenlomond P & K
68 G7 Glenluce D & G
84 B5 Glenmassen Ag & B
85 M9 Glenmavis N Lans
56 b5 Glen Maye IoM
96 E2 Glenmore Highld
99 P7 Glenmore Lodge Highld
90 F2 Glen Nevis House Highld
85 P4 Glenochil Clacks
41 M7 Glen Parva Leics
94 G9 Glenquiech Angus
83 M8 Glenralloch Ag & B
71 N11 Glenridding Cumb
86 F3 Glenrothes Fife
94 E6 Glenshee P & K
98 H9 Glenshero Lodge Highld
84 B7 Glenstriven Ag & B
52 E5 Glentham Lincs
99 L9 Glentromie Lodge Highld
69 K3 Glen Trool Lodge D & G
69 J4 Glentrool Village D & G
99 K9 Glentruim House Highld
52 D6 Glentworth Lincs
89 N2 Glenuig Highld
90 E6 Glenure Ag & B
96 F2 Glenvarragill Highld
68 G5 Glenwhilly D & G
78 D4 Glespin S Lans
28 G4 Glewstone Herefs
42 G8 Glinton C Pete
41 Q8 Glooston Leics
50 D3 Glossop Derbys
81 Q12 Gloster Hill Nthumb
29 L5 Gloucester Gloucs
29 M5 Gloucestershire Airport Gloucs
58 D5 Glusburn N York
110 B8 Glutt Lodge Highld
3 K3 Gluvian Cnwll
31 K9 Glympton Oxon
36 E10 Glynarthen Cerdgn
48 E7 Glyn Ceiriog Wrexhm
27 J8 Glyncorrwg Neath
11 P8 Glynde E Susx
48 D7 Glyndyfrdwy Denbgs
27 J7 Glynneath Neath
26 H5 Glyntawe Powys
25 N2 Glynteg Carmth
49 P10 Gnosall Staffs
49 P10 Gnosall Heath Staffs
41 Q7 Goadby Leics
41 R3 Goadby Marwood Leics
18 F5 Goatacre Wilts
83 Q3 Goatfield Ag & B
17 P11 Goathill Dorset
67 J7 Goathland N York
16 H8 Goathurst Somset
48 F8 Gobowen Shrops
10 F2 Godalming Surrey
12 G3 Goddard's Green Kent
33 J3 Godmanchester Cambs
7 P4 Godmanstone Dorset
23 K12 Godmersham Kent
17 L7 Godney Somset
2 F9 Godolphin Cross Cnwll
26 G7 Godre'r-graig Neath
9 N10 Godshill IoW
21 M11 Godstone Surrey
28 C7 Goetre Mons
21 M3 Goff's Oak Herts
28 B6 Gofilon Mons
86 E7 Gogar C Edin
37 L4 Goginan Cerdgn
46 H3 Golan Gwynd
4 D8 Golant Cnwll
4 H6 Golberdon Cnwll
57 L8 Golborne Wigan
58 E10 Golcar Kirk
28 D11 Goldcliff Newpt
12 D1 Golden Green Kent
9 L2 Golden Pot Hants
21 K6 Golders Green Gt Lon
22 H2 Goldhanger Essex
32 F6 Goldington Beds
59 K3 Goldsborough N York
67 J5 Goldsborough N York
2 E9 Goldsithney Cnwll
20 F10 Goldsworth Park Surrey
59 L12 Goldthorpe Barns
14 G7 Goldworthy Devon
107 N10 Gollanfield Highld
107 N3 Golspie Highld
8 H1 Gomeldon Wilts
10 H1 Gomshall Surrey
51 P10 Gonalston Notts
111 k3 Gonfirth Shet
22 D2 Good Easter Essex
44 C9 Gooderstone Norfk
15 K5 Goodleigh Devon
60 F5 Goodmanham E R Yk
21 P6 Goodmayes Gt Lon
23 K10 Goodnestone Kent
23 N11 Goodnestone Kent
28 G5 Goodrich Herefs
28 G5 Goodrich Castle Herefs
6 B10 Goodrington Torbay
57 P4 Goodshaw Fold Lancs
24 G2 Goodwick Pembks
19 L11 Goodworth Clatford Hants
60 C9 Goole E R Yk
30 D3 Goom's Hill Worcs
2 G6 Goonbell Cnwll
2 H5 Goonhavern Cnwll
2 G6 Goonvrea Cnwll
95 M5 Goosecruives Abers
5 N2 Gooseford Devon
35 J10 Goose Green Essex
35 J10 Goose Green Essex
17 P2 Goose Green S Glos
19 L3 Goosey Oxon
57 K2 Goosnargh Lancs
49 P2 Goostrey Ches
80 E5 Gordon Border
79 L4 Gordon Arms Hotel Border
102 D4 Gordonstown Abers
102 F7 Gordonstown Abers
86 G9 Gorebridge Mdloth
43 L7 Gorefield Cambs
18 G8 Gores Wilts
7 c2 Gorey Jersey
19 P5 Goring Oxon
10 H9 Goring-by-Sea W Susx
45 Q8 Gorleston on Sea Norfk
102 F4 Gorrachie Abers
3 M7 Gorran Cnwll
3 M7 Gorran Haven Cnwll
56 D12 Gorsedd Flints
18 H4 Gorse Hill Swindn
26 D8 Gorseinon Swans
36 H9 Gorsgoch Cerdgn
26 D6 Gorslas Carmth
29 J4 Gorsley Gloucs
29 J4 Gorsley Common Herefs
106 F9 Gorstan Highld
48 G3 Gorstella Ches
40 E2 Gorsty Hill Staffs
89 P9 Gorten Ag & B
98 G5 Gorthleck Highld
50 B2 Gorton Manch
35 J5 Gosbeck Suffk
43 J4 Gosberton Lincs
34 D10 Gosfield Essex
62 C2 Gosforth Cumb
73 M7 Gosforth N u Ty
40 B8 Gospel End Staffs
9 Q7 Gosport Hants
29 K8 Gossington Gloucs
41 M2 Gotham Notts
29 N3 Gotherington Gloucs
16 H9 Gotton Somset
12 E3 Goudhurst Kent
53 J7 Goulceby Lincs
102 G7 Gourdas Abers
93 L8 Gourdie C Dund
95 N7 Gourdon Abers
84 D7 Gourock Inver
85 J9 Govan C Glas
5 P10 Goveton Devon
59 N9 Gowdall E R Yk
106 H10 Gower Highld
26 C10 Gower Swans
26 D9 Gowerton Swans
86 C5 Gowkhall Fife
61 K5 Goxhill E R Yk
61 J9 Goxhill N Linc
111 d3 Grabhair W Isls
10 E6 Graffham W Susx
32 G3 Grafham Cambs
10 G2 Grafham Surrey
59 K2 Grafton N York
19 J1 Grafton Oxon
48 H10 Grafton Shrops
29 N2 Grafton Worcs
30 C3 Grafton Flyford Worcs
31 Q5 Grafton Regis Nhants
32 D2 Grafton Underwood Nhants
12 G1 Grafty Green Kent
55 L7 Graig Conwy
48 D5 Graig-fechan Denbgs
22 H7 Grain Medway
53 J4 Grainsby Lincs
53 L4 Grainthorpe Lincs
3 L6 Grampound Cnwll
3 K5 Grampound Road Cnwll
111 b5 Gramsdal W Isls
111 b5 Gramsdale W Isls
31 Q8 Granborough Bucks
41 Q1 Granby Notts
31 L2 Grandborough Warwks
7 c2 Grand Chemins Jersey
6 b1 Grandes Rocques Guern
41 K3 Grand Prix Collection Donington Leics
92 D5 Grandtully P & K
71 L11 Grange Cumb
22 F9 Grange Medway
93 K10 Grange P & K
101 N4 Grange Crossroads Moray
100 G3 Grange Hall Moray
78 F1 Grangehall S Lans
21 N5 Grange Hill Essex
50 G8 Grangemill Derbys
58 G10 Grange Moor Kirk
85 Q6 Grangemouth Falk
93 J11 Grange of Lindores Fife
62 H6 Grange-over-Sands Cumb
86 B6 Grangepans Falk
66 D4 Grangetown R & Cl
73 P9 Grangetown Sundld
73 M9 Grange Villa Dur
61 J3 Gransmoor E R Yk
24 F2 Granston Pembks
33 M6 Grantchester Cambs
42 D3 Grantham Lincs
86 F6 Granton C Edin
100 F9 Grantown-on-Spey Highld
87 P8 Grantshouse Border
52 F3 Grasby Lincs
62 G1 Grasmere Cumb
58 C12 Grasscroft Oldham
56 H10 Grassendale Lpool
58 D2 Grassington N York
51 K7 Grassmoor Derbys
52 B9 Grassthorpe Notts
19 J11 Grateley Hants
33 J4 Graveley Cambs
32 H10 Graveley Herts
23 K10 Graveney Kent
22 D8 Gravesend Kent
111 d3 Gravir W Isls
52 D4 Grayingham Lincs
63 L3 Grayrigg Cumb
22 C7 Grays Thurr
10 E3 Grayshott Hants
10 E3 Grayswood Surrey
51 K2 Greasbrough Rothm
56 F10 Greasby Wirral
51 L10 Greasley Notts
33 N7 Great Abington Cambs
32 D2 Great Addington Nhants
30 E3 Great Alne Warwks
56 G7 Great Altcar Lancs
21 M2 Great Amwell Herts
64 C5 Great Asby Cumb
34 G4 Great Ashfield Suffk
66 D5 Great Ayton N York
22 E3 Great Baddow Essex
18 B4 Great Badminton S Glos
34 B10 Great Bardfield Essex
32 G6 Great Barford Beds
40 D8 Great Barr Sandw
30 G10 Great Barrington Gloucs
49 J2 Great Barrow Ches
34 E4 Great Barton Suffk
66 G10 Great Barugh N York
72 H5 Great Bavington Nthumb
35 K7 Great Bealings Suffk
19 J7 Great Bedwyn Wilts
35 J11 Great Bentley Essex
32 B4 Great Billing Nhants
44 C4 Great Bircham Norfk
35 J6 Great Blakenham Suffk
71 P8 Great Blencow Cumb
49 M10 Great Bolas Wrekin
21 J11 Great Bookham Surrey
2 C8 Great Bosullow Cnwll
31 L5 Great Bourton Oxon
41 Q9 Great Bowden Leics
34 B6 Great Bradley Suffk
22 G1 Great Braxted Essex
34 G6 Great Bricett Suffk
32 C10 Great Brickhill Bucks
40 B3 Great Bridgeford Staffs
31 P2 Great Brington Nhants
34 H10 Great Bromley Essex
70 H8 Great Broughton Cumb
66 D6 Great Broughton N York
57 M12 Great Budworth Ches
65 N4 Great Burdon Darltn
22 D5 Great Burstead Essex
66 D6 Great Busby N York
53 L6 Great Carlton Lincs
42 E8 Great Casterton Rutlnd
18 C7 Great Chalfield Wilts
13 J2 Great Chart Kent
49 P11 Great Chatwell Staffs
33 N8 Great Chesterford Essex
18 E9 Great Cheverell Wilts
33 L8 Great Chishill Cambs
35 K12 Great Clacton Essex
70 G9 Great Clifton Cumb
61 L11 Great Coates NE Lin
29 N1 Great Comberton Worcs
71 P5 Great Corby Cumb
34 E8 Great Cornard Suffk
61 L6 Great Cowden E R Yk
19 J3 Great Coxwell Oxon
32 B2 Great Cransley Nhants
44 E9 Great Cressingham Norfk
71 L10 Great Crosthwaite Cumb
50 F12 Great Cubley Derbys
41 Q5 Great Dalby Leics
32 C4 Great Doddington Nhants
44 E7 Great Dunham Norfk
33 Q11 Great Dunmow Essex
18 G12 Great Durnford Wilts
33 P10 Great Easton Essex
42 C10 Great Easton Leics
56 H2 Great Eccleston Lancs
44 G10 Great Ellingham Norfk
17 Q6 Great Elm Somset
5 Q8 Great Englebourne Devon
31 N3 Great Everdon Nhants
33 K6 Great Eversden Cambs
34 G5 Great Finborough Suffk
42 F7 Greatford Lincs
44 E7 Great Fransham Norfk
20 G2 Great Gaddesden Herts
50 D11 Greatgate Staffs
42 G12 Great Gidding Cambs
60 E4 Great Givendale E R Yk
35 M4 Great Glemham Suffk
41 P7 Great Glen Leics
42 C3 Great Gonerby Lincs
33 J5 Great Gransden Cambs
33 J7 Great Green Cambs
34 F5 Great Green Suffk
66 G11 Great Habton N York
42 G2 Great Hale Lincs
33 N11 Great Hallingbury Essex
10 C4 Greatham Hants
66 C3 Greatham Hartpl
10 G6 Greatham W Susx
20 D3 Great Hampden Bucks
32 C3 Great Harrowden Nhants
57 N3 Great Harwood Lancs
19 Q1 Great Haseley Oxon
61 K5 Great Hatfield E R Yk
40 D3 Great Haywood Staffs
59 N9 Great Heck N York
34 E8 Great Henny Essex
18 D8 Great Hinton Wilts
44 F10 Great Hockham Norfk
35 K11 Great Holland Essex
34 F9 Great Horkesley Essex
33 L10 Great Hormead Herts
58 F7 Great Horton Brad
31 Q7 Great Horwood Bucks
59 K11 Great Houghton Barns
32 B5 Great Houghton Nhants
50 F5 Great Hucklow Derbys
61 J3 Great Kelk E R Yk
20 D3 Great Kimble Bucks
20 E4 Great Kingshill Bucks
62 F2 Great Langdale Cumb
65 N8 Great Langton N York
34 C12 Great Leighs Essex
52 G2 Great Limber Lincs
32 C8 Great Linford M Keyn
34 E3 Great Livermere Suffk
50 G6 Great Longstone Derbys
73 N10 Great Lumley Dur
39 P11 Great Malvern Worcs
34 D9 Great Maplestead Essex
56 G2 Great Marton Bpool
44 D5 Great Massingham Norfk
19 Q1 Great Milton Oxon
20 E3 Great Missenden Bucks
57 N2 Great Mitton Lancs
23 Q12 Great Mongeham Kent
45 J11 Great Moulton Norfk
64 D5 Great Musgrave Cumb
48 H10 Great Ness Shrops
28 D6 Great Oak Mons
35 K10 Great Oakley Essex
42 C11 Great Oakley Nhants
32 G10 Great Offley Herts
64 C4 Great Ormside Cumb
71 M5 Great Orton Cumb
59 K2 Great Ouseburn N York
41 Q10 Great Oxendon Nhants
22 D3 Great Oxney Green Essex
32 H4 Great Paxton Cambs
56 H3 Great Plumpton Lancs
45 L7 Great Plumstead Norfk
42 D4 Great Ponton Lincs
59 K8 Great Preston Leeds
33 J1 Great Raveley Cambs
30 G10 Great Rissington Gloucs
31 J7 Great Rollright Oxon
44 F5 Great Ryburgh Norfk
81 L10 Great Ryle Nthumb
39 J2 Great Ryton Shrops
34 B10 Great Saling Essex
71 Q8 Great Salkeld Cumb
33 Q9 Great Sampford Essex
48 G2 Great Saughall Ches
19 L6 Great Shefford W Berk
33 M6 Great Shelford Cambs
65 N6 Great Smeaton N York
44 F4 Great Snoring Norfk
18 E4 Great Somerford Wilts
49 N9 Great Soudley Shrops
65 N3 Great Stainton Darltn
22 H5 Great Stambridge Essex
32 G4 Great Staughton Cambs
53 M9 Great Steeping Lincs
28 H11 Great Stoke S Glos

Greatstone-on-Sea - Hathersage 179

13 L5 Greatstone-on-Sea Kent
71 Q10 Great Strickland Cumb
32 H2 Great Stukeley Cambs
52 H7 Great Sturton Lincs
72 G6 Great Swinburne Nthumb
31 K8 Great Tew Oxon
34 E10 Great Tey Essex
15 J8 Great Torrington Devon
72 H2 Great Tosson Nthumb
22 G2 Great Totham Essex
22 G2 Great Totham Essex
62 F7 Great Urswick Cumb
22 H6 Great Wakering Essex
34 E7 Great Waldingfield Suffk
44 F3 Great Walsingham Norfk
22 E2 Great Waltham Essex
22 C5 Great Warley Essex
29 N2 Great Washbourne Gloucs
5 P3 Great Weeke Devon
42 D11 Great Weldon Nhants
34 H8 Great Wenham Suffk
72 H6 Great Whittington Nthumb
23 J1 Great Wigborough Essex
33 N5 Great Wilbraham Cambs
8 F1 Great Wishford Wilts
29 M6 Great Witcombe Gloucs
39 N8 Great Witley Worcs
30 G7 Great Wolford Warwks
31 M6 Greatworth Nhants
34 B7 Great Wratting Suffk
32 H10 Great Wymondley Herts
40 C6 Great Wyrley Staffs
45 Q8 Great Yarmouth Norfk
34 C8 Great Yeldham Essex
85 Q10 Greenburn W Loth
33 K11 Green End Herts
33 K9 Green End Herts
84 D5 Greenfield Ag & B
32 F9 Greenfield Beds
56 E12 Greenfield Flints
99 B8 Greenfield Highld
58 C12 Greenfield Oldham
21 J7 Greenford Gt Lon
85 N8 Greengairs N Lans
58 G6 Greengates Brad
56 H2 Greenhalgh Lancs
16 E11 Greenham Somset
59 L3 Green Hammerton N York
72 E4 Greenhaugh Nthumb
72 C7 Greenhead Nthumb
40 C5 Green Heath Staffs
78 H11 Greenhill D & G
85 N7 Greenhill Falk
23 M9 Greenhill Kent
78 F3 Greenhill S Lans
22 C8 Greenhithe Kent
77 J4 Greenholm E Ayrs
80 D9 Greenhouse Border
58 E2 Greenhow Hill N York
110 E3 Greenland Highld
51 K3 Greenland Sheff
80 F5 Greenlaw Border
70 G1 Greenlea D & G
85 N2 Greenloaning P & K
57 P6 Greenmount Bury
84 E7 Greenock Inver
62 G6 Greenodd Cumb
17 N6 Green Ore Somset
63 J2 Green Quarter Cumb
86 B12 Greenshields S Lans
73 K8 Greenside Gatesd
58 F10 Greenside Kirk
31 P4 Greens Norton Nhants
34 G10 Greenstead Essex
34 D10 Greenstead Green Essex
21 J4 Green Street Herts
33 M11 Green Street Herts
22 C8 Green Street Green Kent
33 M11 Green Tye Herts
17 J10 Greenway Somset
21 M7 Greenwich Gt Lon
30 D7 Greet Gloucs
39 L7 Greete Shrops
53 K8 Greetham Lincs
42 D7 Greetham Rutlnd
58 E9 Greetland Calder
17 K8 Greinton Somset
56 b6 Grenaby IoM
32 C5 Grendon Nhants
40 H7 Grendon Warwks
31 P9 Grendon Underwood Bucks
51 J3 Grenoside Sheff
111 c3 Greosabhagh W Isls
48 G5 Gresford Wrexhm
45 J3 Gresham Norfk
104 D10 Greshornish House Hotel Highld
44 F7 Gressenhall Norfk
44 F6 Gressenhall Green Norfk
63 K8 Gressingham Lancs
65 J5 Greta Bridge Dur
71 M3 Gretna D & G
71 M2 Gretna Green D & G
30 D7 Gretton Gloucs
42 C10 Gretton Nhants
39 K3 Gretton Shrops
65 M11 Grewelthorpe N York
78 H10 Greyrigg D & G
20 B6 Greys Green Oxon
70 H9 Greysouthen Cumb
71 P8 Greystoke Cumb
93 P7 Greystone Angus
20 B12 Greywell Hants
41 J9 Griff Warwks
28 C8 Griffithstown Torfn
57 L6 Grimeford Village Lancs
51 J3 Grimesthorpe Sheff
59 K11 Grimethorpe Barns
39 Q9 Grimley Worcs
76 F8 Grimmet S Ayrs
53 L6 Grimoldby Lincs
48 G9 Grimpo Shrops
57 L3 Grimsargh Lancs
61 M11 Grimsby NE Lin
31 P4 Grimscote Nhants
14 E10 Grimscott Cnwll
111 d2 Grimshader W Isls
42 F5 Grimsthorpe Lincs
41 P3 Grimston Leics
44 C5 Grimston Norfk
7 P4 Grimstone Dorset
34 F3 Grimstone End Suffk
67 N12 Grindale E R Yk
50 G5 Grindleford Derbys
63 N11 Grindleton Lancs
49 K7 Grindley Brook Shrops
50 F5 Grindlow Derbys
50 E9 Grindon Staffs
73 P9 Grindon Sundld
51 Q3 Gringley on the Hill Notts
71 M4 Grinsdale Cumb
49 K10 Grinshill Shrops
65 J7 Grinton N York
111 d2 Griomaisiader W Isls
111 b5 Griomsaigh W Isls
88 F5 Grishipoll Ag & B
67 M10 Gristhorpe N York
44 F9 Griston Norfk
111 h2 Gritley Ork
18 F4 Grittenham Wilts
18 C5 Grittleton Wilts
62 E5 Grizebeck Cumb
62 G4 Grizedale Cumb
41 M6 Groby Leics
55 Q8 Groes Conwy
27 M11 Groes-faen Rhondd
27 N10 Groes-Wen Caerph
111 a5 Grogarry W Isls
75 M4 Grogport Ag & B
111 a5 Groigearraidh W Isls
56 C11 Gronant Flints
11 Q3 Groombridge E Susx
111 c3 Grosebay W Isls
28 E4 Grosmont Mons
67 J6 Grosmont N York
34 F8 Groton Suffk
7 c2 Grouville Jersey
51 Q5 Grove Notts
19 L3 Grove Oxon
22 F11 Grove Green Kent
21 N8 Grove Park Gt Lon
26 D8 Grovesend Swans
105 P4 Gruinard Highld
82 D9 Gruinart Ag & B
96 D4 Grula Highld
89 L8 Gruline Ag & B
35 K6 Grundisburgh Suffk
111 j4 Gruting Shet
90 F7 Gualachulain Highld
93 M11 Guardbridge Fife
39 P11 Guarlford Worcs
92 E6 Guay P & K
6 b2 Guernsey Airport Guern
12 G7 Guestling Green E Susx
12 G6 Guestling Thorn E Susx
44 H5 Guestwick Norfk
57 N4 Guide Bl w D
73 M4 Guide Post Nthumb
33 J7 Guilden Morden Cambs
49 J2 Guilden Sutton Ches
20 F12 Guildford Surrey
92 G8 Guildtown P & K
41 P11 Guilsborough Nhants
48 E12 Guilsfield Powys
76 F8 Guiltreehill S Ayrs
15 J5 Guineaford Devon
66 E4 Guisborough R & Cl
58 G6 Guiseley Leeds
44 G5 Guist Norfk
30 E8 Guiting Power Gloucs
87 J5 Gullane E Loth
2 D9 Gulval Cnwll
5 K5 Gulworthy Devon
25 J8 Gumfreston Pembks
41 P9 Gumley Leics
52 D9 Gunby Lincs
42 D6 Gunby Lincs
9 Q2 Gundleton Hants
12 C7 Gun Hill E Susx
15 L5 Gunn Devon
64 G7 Gunnerside N York
72 G6 Gunnerton Nthumb
60 E11 Gunness N Linc
5 J6 Gunnislake Cnwll
111 k4 Gunnista Shet
52 B4 Gunthorpe N Linc
44 G3 Gunthorpe Norfk
51 P11 Gunthorpe Notts
2 F10 Gunwalloe Cnwll
9 N8 Gurnard IoW
17 N6 Gurney Slade Somset
26 G7 Gurnos Powys
8 E5 Gussage All Saints Dorset
8 E5 Gussage St Andrew Dorset
8 E5 Gussage St Michael Dorset
13 P2 Guston Kent
111 k2 Gutcher Shet
93 P5 Guthrie Angus
43 L8 Guyhirn Cambs
81 P12 Guyzance Nthumb
56 C11 Gwaenysgor Flints
54 E6 Gwalchmai IoA
26 F6 Gwaun-Cae-Gurwen Carmth
2 G9 Gweek Cnwll
38 C12 Gwenddwr Powys
2 H7 Gwennap Cnwll
48 E3 Gwernaffield Flints
28 E8 Gwernesney Mons
26 D3 Gwernogle Carmth
48 E3 Gwernymynydd Flints
56 C11 Gwespyr Flints
2 E8 Gwinear Cnwll
2 E7 Gwithian Cnwll
48 C6 Gwyddelwern Denbgs
26 C2 Gwyddgrug Carmth
55 N8 Gwytherin Conwy

H

38 H2 Habberley Shrops
39 P6 Habberley Worcs
57 P3 Habergham Lancs
53 N9 Habertoft Lincs
61 K10 Habrough NE Lin
42 F5 Hacconby Lincs
42 E3 Haceby Lincs
35 M5 Hacheston Suffk
21 L9 Hackbridge Gt Lon
51 K4 Hackenthorpe Sheff
44 H9 Hackford Norfk
65 M8 Hackforth N York
111 h2 Hackland Ork
32 B6 Hackleton Nhants
23 Q11 Hacklinge Kent
67 L9 Hackness N York
21 M6 Hackney Gt Lon
52 E7 Hackthorn Lincs
71 Q10 Hackthorpe Cumb
80 G7 Hadden Border
20 B2 Haddenham Bucks
33 M2 Haddenham Cambs
87 K7 Haddington E Loth
52 D10 Haddington Lincs
45 P10 Haddiscoe Norfk
102 H7 Haddo Abers
42 G10 Haddon Cambs
50 D2 Hadfield Derbys
33 M11 Hadham Ford Herts
22 F6 Hadleigh Essex
34 G8 Hadleigh Suffk
39 Q8 Hadley Worcs
40 F4 Hadley End Staffs
21 L4 Hadley Wood Gt Lon
22 D12 Hadlow Kent
11 Q5 Hadlow Down E Susx
49 K10 Hadnall Shrops
33 N7 Hadstock Essex
30 B2 Hadzor Worcs
111 k4 Haggersta Shet
81 L5 Haggerston Nthumb
85 N7 Haggs Falk
28 G1 Hagley Herefs
40 B10 Hagley Worcs
53 K9 Hagworthingham Lincs
62 B1 Haile Cumb
31 J10 Hailey Oxon
12 C8 Hailsham E Susx
32 G4 Hail Weston Cambs
21 P5 Hainault Gt Lon
45 K6 Hainford Norfk
52 H6 Hainton Lincs
61 J2 Haisthorpe E R Yk
24 F7 Hakin Pembks
51 P9 Halam Notts
86 D5 Halbeath Fife
6 D1 Halberton Devon
110 E4 Halcro Highld
63 J6 Hale Cumb
57 J11 Hale Halton
8 H4 Hale Hants
10 D1 Hale Surrey
57 P10 Hale Traffd
12 B7 Hale Green E Susx
45 N10 Hales Norfk
49 N8 Hales Staffs
40 C10 Halesowen Dudley
23 M10 Hales Place Kent
22 D12 Hale Street Kent
35 N2 Halesworth Suffk
57 J10 Halewood Knows
5 Q5 Halford Devon
30 H5 Halford Warwks
39 P4 Halfpenny Green Staffs
48 G12 Halfway House Shrops
22 H8 Halfway Houses Kent
58 E8 Halifax Calder
110 D4 Halkirk Highld
48 E2 Halkyn Flints
84 G11 Hall E Rens
11 P6 Halland E Susx
42 B10 Hallaton Leics
17 P5 Hallatrow BaNES
72 B8 Hallbankgate Cumb
62 E3 Hall Dunnerdale Cumb
28 G11 Hallen S Glos
73 N11 Hallgarth Dur
85 P7 Hall Glen Falk
40 E10 Hall Green Birm
104 C9 Hallin Highld
22 E10 Halling Medway
53 K6 Hallington Lincs
72 H6 Hallington Nthumb
57 M6 Halliwell Bolton
51 P9 Halloughton Notts
39 P9 Hallow Worcs
5 Q11 Hallsands Devon
33 J10 Hall's Green Herts
79 K2 Hallyne Border
29 J8 Halmore Gloucs
10 E8 Halnaker W Susx
56 G6 Halsall Lancs
31 M6 Halse Nhants
16 F9 Halse Somset
2 D7 Halsetown Cnwll
61 M8 Halsham E R Yk
34 D10 Halstead Essex
21 P10 Halstead Kent
41 Q6 Halstead Leics
7 M2 Halstock Dorset
16 F8 Halsway Somset
53 J10 Haltham Lincs
20 E2 Halton Bucks
63 J8 Halton Lancs
59 J7 Halton Leeds
72 H7 Halton Nthumb
48 F7 Halton Wrexhm
58 D4 Halton East N York
64 F11 Halton Gill N York
53 L9 Halton Holegate Lincs
72 C8 Halton Lea Gate Nthumb
72 H7 Halton Shields Nthumb
63 Q10 Halton West N York
72 D7 Haltwhistle Nthumb
45 N8 Halvergate Norfk
5 Q9 Halwell Devon
14 H11 Halwill Devon
14 H11 Halwill Junction Devon
6 H3 Ham Devon
29 J8 Ham Gloucs
21 J8 Ham Gt Lon
23 P11 Ham Kent
16 H10 Ham Somset
19 K8 Ham Wilts
20 C6 Hambleden Bucks
9 Q4 Hambledon Hants
10 F3 Hambledon Surrey
9 N6 Hamble-le-Rice Hants
56 G1 Hambleton Lancs
59 M7 Hambleton N York
17 K10 Hambridge Somset
10 C8 Hambrook W Susx
53 K9 Hameringham Lincs
32 G2 Hamerton Cambs
30 D2 Ham Green Worcs
85 M11 Hamilton S Lans
7 N2 Hamlet Dorset
21 K7 Hammersmith Gt Lon
40 E6 Hammerwich Staffs
8 B5 Hammoon Dorset
111 k4 Hamnavoe Shet
12 C9 Hampden Park E Susx
30 E10 Hampnett Gloucs
59 L11 Hampole Donc
8 F7 Hampreston Dorset
21 L6 Hampstead Gt Lon
19 N5 Hampstead Norrey's W Berk
58 H3 Hampsthwaite N York
42 G10 Hampton C Pete
21 J9 Hampton Gt Lon
23 M9 Hampton Kent
39 N5 Hampton Shrops
18 H3 Hampton Swindn
30 D5 Hampton Worcs
28 G2 Hampton Bishop Herefs
21 J9 Hampton Court Palace & Gardens Gt Lon
49 J5 Hampton Heath Ches
40 G10 Hampton in Arden Solhll
30 B2 Hampton Lovett Worcs
30 G3 Hampton Lucy Warwks
30 H2 Hampton Magna Warwks
31 L10 Hampton Poyle Oxon
21 J9 Hampton Wick Gt Lon
9 J4 Hamptworth Wilts
11 N7 Hamsey E Susx
40 E4 Hamstall Ridware Staffs
19 M7 Hamstead Marshall W Berk
65 K2 Hamsterley Dur
73 K9 Hamsterley Dur
13 J4 Hamstreet Kent
17 M8 Ham Street Somset
8 E8 Hamworthy Poole
40 F2 Hanbury Staffs
30 C2 Hanbury Worcs
49 Q7 Hanchurch Staffs
6 E4 Hand and Pen Devon
48 H3 Handbridge Ches
11 L4 Handcross W Susx
57 Q11 Handforth Ches
49 J4 Handley Ches
51 J8 Handley Derbys
40 D9 Handsworth Birm
51 K4 Handsworth Sheff
58 G9 Hanging Heaton Kirk
41 Q11 Hanging Houghton Nhants
18 F12 Hanging Langford Wilts
11 L8 Hangleton Br & H
17 P2 Hanham S Glos
49 M6 Hankelow Ches
29 N9 Hankerton Wilts
50 B10 Hanley C Stke
50 B10 Hanley C Stke
39 Q12 Hanley Castle Worcs
39 M8 Hanley Child Worcs
39 P12 Hanley Swan Worcs
39 M8 Hanley William Worcs
58 B2 Hanlith N York
49 J7 Hanmer Wrexhm
15 K6 Hannaford Devon
19 N9 Hannington Hants
32 B3 Hannington Nhants
18 H3 Hannington Swindn
18 H2 Hannington Wick Swindn
32 B7 Hanslope M Keyn
42 F5 Hanthorpe Lincs
21 J7 Hanwell Gt Lon
31 K5 Hanwell Oxon
49 J12 Hanwood Shrops
20 H8 Hanworth Gt Lon
45 K3 Hanworth Norfk
78 E3 Happendon S Lans
45 N4 Happisburgh Norfk
45 N4 Happisburgh Common Norfk
49 J1 Hapsford Ches
57 P3 Hapton Lancs
45 K10 Hapton Norfk
5 Q8 Harberton Devon
5 Q8 Harbertonford Devon
23 L10 Harbledown Kent
40 D10 Harborne Birm
41 L10 Harborough Magna Warwks
81 K12 Harbottle Nthumb
5 P7 Harbourneford Devon
31 J3 Harbury Warwks
41 Q2 Harby Leics
52 C8 Harby Notts
6 B6 Harcombe Devon
6 F5 Harcombe Devon
7 J4 Harcombe Bottom Devon
58 E6 Harden Brad
40 D7 Harden Wsall
95 N2 Hardgate Abers
70 D3 Hardgate D & G
84 H8 Hardgate W Duns
10 G6 Hardham W Susx
44 H8 Hardingham Norfk
31 Q3 Hardingstone Nhants
17 Q5 Hardington Somset
7 M1 Hardington Mandeville Somset
7 M2 Hardington Marsh Somset
7 M1 Hardington Moor Somset
14 E7 Hardisworthy Devon
9 M6 Hardley Hants
45 N9 Hardley Street Norfk
64 F8 Hardraw N York
51 K8 Hardstoft Derbys
9 Q7 Hardway Hants
17 Q8 Hardway Somset
32 B11 Hardwick Bucks
33 L5 Hardwick Cambs
32 C3 Hardwick Nhants
45 K11 Hardwick Norfk
31 J11 Hardwick Oxon
31 M7 Hardwick Oxon
29 L6 Hardwicke Gloucs
29 M4 Hardwicke Gloucs
34 F11 Hardy's Green Essex
53 K9 Hareby Lincs
58 E7 Hare Croft Brad
20 G5 Harefield Gt Lon
34 H10 Hare Green Essex
20 C7 Hare Hatch Wokham
40 F1 Harehill Derbys
59 J7 Harehills Leeds
80 C9 Harelaw Border
79 N12 Harelaw D & G
29 L6 Harescombe Gloucs
29 L6 Haresfield Gloucs
9 M2 Harestock Hants
21 N2 Hare Street Essex
33 L10 Hare Street Herts
58 H5 Harewood Leeds
28 F4 Harewood End Herefs
5 M8 Harford Devon
49 J3 Hargrave Ches
32 E3 Hargrave Nhants
34 C5 Hargrave Green Suffk
35 K9 Harkstead Suffk
40 G5 Harlaston Staffs
42 C4 Harlaxton Lincs
47 J5 Harlech Gwynd
49 J11 Harlescott Shrops
21 K6 Harlesden Gt Lon
51 L5 Harlesthorpe Derbys
5 Q10 Harleston Devon
45 L12 Harleston Norfk
34 G5 Harleston Suffk
31 P2 Harlestone Nhants
57 Q2 Harle Syke Lancs
51 J2 Harley Rothm
39 L2 Harley Shrops
32 E10 Harlington Beds
51 L1 Harlington Donc
20 H7 Harlington Gt Lon
96 C2 Harlosh Highld
21 N2 Harlow Essex
73 J7 Harlow Hill Nthumb
60 C6 Harlthorpe E R Yk
33 L6 Harlton Cambs
3 K1 Harlyn Cnwll
8 E10 Harman's Cross Dorset
65 K9 Harmby N York
33 J12 Harmer Green Herts
49 J10 Harmer Hill Shrops
52 D10 Harmston Lincs
39 K2 Harnage Shrops
18 F1 Harnhill Gloucs
21 Q5 Harold Hill Gt Lon
24 F6 Haroldston West Pembks
111 m2 Haroldswick Shet
22 B5 Harold Wood Gt Lon
66 F10 Harome N York
21 J1 Harpenden Herts
6 E5 Harpford Devon
61 J2 Harpham E R Yk
44 D5 Harpley Norfk
39 M9 Harpley Worcs
31 P2 Harpole Nhants
110 D5 Harpsdale Highld
52 D5 Harpswell Lincs
57 Q8 Harpurhey Manch
71 N5 Harraby Cumb
15 K6 Harracott Devon
97 J5 Harrapool Highld
92 E9 Harrietfield P & K
22 G11 Harrietsham Kent
21 L6 Harringay Gt Lon
70 G9 Harrington Cumb
53 L8 Harrington Lincs
41 Q10 Harrington Nhants
42 D10 Harringworth Nhants
58 H3 Harrogate N York
32 D5 Harrold Beds
21 J6 Harrow Gt Lon
5 J6 Harrowbarrow Cnwll
34 E6 Harrow Green Suffk
21 J6 Harrow on the Hill Gt Lon
21 J5 Harrow Weald Gt Lon
33 L6 Harston Cambs
42 B4 Harston Leics
60 E6 Harswell E R Yk
66 C1 Hart Hartpl
73 J4 Hartburn Nthumb
34 D6 Hartest Suffk
11 P3 Hartfield E Susx
33 J3 Hartford Cambs
49 L2 Hartford Ches
20 C10 Hartfordbridge Hants
34 B12 Hartford End Essex
65 L6 Hartforth N York
8 C4 Hartgrove Dorset
49 J4 Harthill Ches
85 Q9 Harthill N Lans
51 L5 Harthill Rothm
50 F8 Hartington Derbys
14 E7 Hartland Devon
14 D7 Hartland Quay Devon
39 Q7 Hartlebury Worcs
66 C2 Hartlepool Hartpl
64 E6 Hartley Cumb
12 F3 Hartley Kent
22 C9 Hartley Kent
20 B10 Hartley Wespall Hants
20 C11 Hartley Wintney Hants
22 G9 Hartlip Kent
60 C2 Harton N York
73 P7 Harton S Tyne
29 L4 Hartpury Gloucs
58 F9 Hartshead Kirk
49 Q6 Hartshill C Stke
41 J8 Hartshill Warwks
41 J4 Hartshorne Derbys
81 K10 Hartside Nthumb
32 B6 Hartwell Nhants
58 G2 Hartwith N York
85 P10 Hartwood N Lans
79 N4 Hartwoodmyre Border
22 D10 Harvel Kent
30 D4 Harvington Worcs
39 Q7 Harvington Worcs
51 P3 Harwell Notts
19 N3 Harwell Oxon
35 L9 Harwich Essex
67 L8 Harwood Dale N York
51 N3 Harworth Notts
40 C10 Hasbury Dudley
10 G3 Hascombe Surrey
41 P11 Haselbech Nhants
7 L1 Haselbury Plucknett Somset
30 G1 Haseley Warwks
30 E3 Haselor Warwks
29 L4 Hasfield Gloucs
56 G7 Haskayne Lancs
35 L6 Hasketon Suffk
10 E4 Haslemere Surrey
57 P4 Haslingden Lancs
33 L6 Haslingfield Cambs
49 N4 Haslington Ches
45 N8 Hassingham Norfk
11 L7 Hassocks W Susx
50 G6 Hassop Derbys
110 G5 Haster Highld
13 L2 Hastingleigh Kent
12 G7 Hastings E Susx
21 P2 Hastingwood Essex
20 E2 Hastoe Herts
73 P11 Haswell Dur
73 P11 Haswell Plough Dur
17 J11 Hatch Beauchamp Somset
21 J5 Hatch End Gt Lon
49 K2 Hatchmere Ches
52 H4 Hatcliffe NE Lin
59 P11 Hatfield Donc
39 L9 Hatfield Herefs
21 K2 Hatfield Herts
33 N12 Hatfield Broad Oak Essex
21 Q1 Hatfield Heath Essex
22 F2 Hatfield Peverel Essex
59 P11 Hatfield Woodhouse Donc
19 K2 Hatford Oxon
19 K10 Hatherden Hants
15 J10 Hatherleigh Devon
41 L3 Hathern Leics
30 F11 Hatherop Gloucs
50 G5 Hathersage Derbys

180 Hathersage Booths - Holbury

50 G5 **Hathersage Booths** Derbys
49 M6 **Hatherton** Ches
40 C5 **Hatherton** Staffs
33 J6 **Hatley St George** Cambs
5 J7 **Hatt** Cnwll
50 C2 **Hattersley** Tamesd
103 L7 **Hatton** Abers
93 N7 **Hatton** Angus
40 G2 **Hatton** Derbys
20 H8 **Hatton** Gt Lon
52 H7 **Hatton** Lincs
39 J4 **Hatton** Shrops
57 L11 **Hatton** Warrtn
30 G1 **Hatton** Warwks
102 H11 **Hatton of Fintray** Abers
76 H6 **Haugh** E Ayrs
53 K7 **Haugham** Lincs
85 K7 **Haughhead** E Duns
34 G4 **Haughley** Suffk
34 G4 **Haughley Green** Suffk
101 M7 **Haugh of Glass** Moray
70 D3 **Haugh of Urr** D & G
39 N1 **Haughton** Shrops
48 H9 **Haughton** Shrops
49 Q10 **Haughton** Staffs
65 N4 **Haughton le Skerne** Darltn
49 L4 **Haughton Moss** Ches
33 K11 **Haultwick** Herts
40 G5 **Haunton** Staffs
33 M6 **Hauxton** Cambs
10 B8 **Havant** Hants
9 P8 **Havenstreet** IoW
59 K10 **Havercroft** Wakefd
24 G6 **Haverfordwest** Pembks
33 Q7 **Haverhill** Suffk
62 D6 **Haverigg** Cumb
21 P5 **Havering-atte-Bower** Gt Lon
32 B8 **Haversham** M Keyn
62 G5 **Haverthwaite** Cumb
17 L4 **Havyat** N Som
48 G3 **Hawarden** Flints
34 D11 **Hawbush Green** Essex
36 F10 **Hawen** Cerdgn
64 F9 **Hawes** N York
45 L9 **Hawe's Green** Norfk
39 Q9 **Hawford** Worcs
80 C10 **Hawick** Border
7 J3 **Hawkchurch** Devon
34 D6 **Hawkedon** Suffk
18 C9 **Hawkeridge** Wilts
18 B4 **Hawkesbury** S Glos
18 B4 **Hawkesbury Upton** S Glos
12 F4 **Hawkhurst** Kent
13 N3 **Hawkinge** Kent
10 C4 **Hawkley** Hants
15 P6 **Hawkridge** Somset
62 G3 **Hawkshead** Cumb
62 G3 **Hawkshead Hill** Cumb
78 D2 **Hawksland** S Lans
33 Q9 **Hawkspur Green** Essex
49 L9 **Hawkstone** Shrops
64 G12 **Hawkswick** N York
58 F6 **Hawksworth** Leeds
51 Q11 **Hawksworth** Notts
22 G5 **Hawkwell** Essex
20 D10 **Hawley** Hants
30 E9 **Hawling** Gloucs
66 D9 **Hawnby** N York
58 D6 **Haworth** Brad
34 E5 **Hawstead** Suffk
73 P10 **Hawthorn** Dur
52 H11 **Hawthorn Hill** Lincs
52 B12 **Hawton** Notts
59 N3 **Haxby** York
51 Q2 **Haxey** N Linc
57 K9 **Haydock** St Hel
72 F7 **Haydon Bridge** Nthumb
18 G4 **Haydon Wick** Swindn
20 H7 **Hayes** Gt Lon
21 N9 **Hayes** Gt Lon
20 H7 **Hayes End** Gt Lon
90 E10 **Hayfield** Ag & B
50 D4 **Hayfield** Derbys
93 N7 **Hayhillock** Angus
2 E8 **Hayle** Cnwll
40 C10 **Hayley Green** Dudley
10 B9 **Hayling Island** Hants
5 P3 **Hayne** Devon
16 C11 **Hayne** Devon
32 F8 **Haynes (Church End)** Beds
32 F8 **Haynes (Northwood End)** Beds
32 F8 **Haynes (Silver End)** Beds
32 F8 **Haynes (West End)** Beds
27 P1 **Hay-on-Wye** Powys
24 F4 **Hayscastle** Pembks
24 F4 **Hayscastle Cross** Pembks
33 L10 **Hay Street** Herts
70 H7 **Hayton** Cumb
71 Q4 **Hayton** Cumb
60 E5 **Hayton** E R Yk
51 Q4 **Hayton** Notts
5 P5 **Haytor Vale** Devon
14 G8 **Haytown** Devon
11 M5 **Haywards Heath** W Susx
59 N10 **Haywood** Donc
77 P3 **Hazelbank** S Lans
7 Q2 **Hazelbury Bryan** Dorset
22 G3 **Hazeleigh** Essex
50 B4 **Hazel Grove** Stockp
93 L10 **Hazelton Walls** Fife
51 J10 **Hazelwood** Derbys
20 E4 **Hazlemere** Bucks
73 M6 **Hazlerigg** N u Ty
30 E9 **Hazleton** Gloucs
44 B3 **Heacham** Norfk
9 N2 **Headbourne Worthy** Hants
12 G2 **Headcorn** Kent
58 H7 **Headingley** Leeds
31 M11 **Headington** Oxon
65 L4 **Headlam** Dur
85 Q10 **Headlesscross** N Lans
30 D2 **Headless Cross** Worcs
10 D3 **Headley** Hants
19 N8 **Headley** Hants
21 K11 **Headley** Surrey
10 D3 **Headley Down** Hants
51 Q5 **Headon** Notts
77 M2 **Heads** S Lans
71 P5 **Heads Nook** Cumb
51 J10 **Heage** Derbys
59 L5 **Healaugh** N York
64 H7 **Healaugh** N York
57 Q10 **Heald Green** Stockp
16 H11 **Heale** Somset
17 K10 **Heale** Somset
65 L10 **Healey** N York
73 J10 **Healeyfield** Dur
61 L11 **Healing** NE Lin
2 C9 **Heamoor** Cnwll
51 K10 **Heanor** Derbys
15 J5 **Heanton Punchardon** Devon
52 C6 **Heapham** Lincs
15 M6 **Heasley Mill** Devon
96 H6 **Heast** Highld
51 K7 **Heath** Derbys
59 J9 **Heath** Wakefd
32 D10 **Heath and Reach** Beds
50 F8 **Heathcote** Derbys
10 D1 **Heath End** Surrey
41 K5 **Heather** Leics
12 C6 **Heathfield** E Susx
16 F10 **Heathfield** Somset
40 E12 **Heath Green** Worcs
78 G11 **Heath Hall** D & G
40 D5 **Heath Hayes & Wimblebury** Staffs
49 N11 **Heath Hill** Shrops
20 H8 **Heathrow Airport** Gt Lon
39 P4 **Heathton** Shrops
40 B7 **Heath Town** Wolves
40 E3 **Heatley** Staffs
57 N10 **Heatley** Warrtn
58 F7 **Heaton** Brad
73 M7 **Heaton** N u Ty
50 C8 **Heaton** Staffs
56 H6 **Heaton's Bridge** Lancs
22 C10 **Heaverham** Kent
6 C4 **Heavitree** Devon
73 N7 **Hebburn** S Tyne
58 D2 **Hebden** N York
58 C8 **Hebden Bridge** Calder
33 K11 **Hebing End** Herts
25 L4 **Hebron** Carmth
73 L3 **Hebron** Nthumb
20 B10 **Heckfield** Hants
35 K2 **Heckfield Green** Suffk
34 F11 **Heckfordbridge** Essex
42 G2 **Heckington** Lincs
58 G9 **Heckmondwike** Kirk
18 E7 **Heddington** Wilts
73 K7 **Heddon-on-the-Wall** Nthumb
45 M10 **Hedenham** Norfk
9 N5 **Hedge End** Hants
20 F6 **Hedgerley** Bucks
17 J9 **Hedging** Somset
73 J8 **Hedley on the Hill** Nthumb
40 D5 **Hednesford** Staffs
61 K8 **Hedon** E R Yk
20 E6 **Hedsor** Bucks
111 k4 **Heglibister** Shet
65 M3 **Heighington** Darltn
52 E9 **Heighington** Lincs
39 N7 **Heightington** Worcs
80 F7 **Heiton** Border
6 D3 **Hele** Devon
15 J3 **Hele** Devon
16 G10 **Hele** Somset
84 E6 **Helensburgh** Ag & B
76 G5 **Helenton** S Ayrs
2 H9 **Helford** Cnwll
2 H9 **Helford Passage** Cnwll
44 E5 **Helhoughton** Norfk
33 Q8 **Helions Bumpstead** Essex
3 N2 **Helland** Cnwll
4 G3 **Hellescott** Cnwll
45 K7 **Hellesdon** Norfk
31 M3 **Hellidon** Nhants
63 Q10 **Hellifield** N York
12 C7 **Hellingly** E Susx
73 L2 **Helm** Nthumb
31 N5 **Helmdon** Nhants
58 E10 **Helme** Kirk
35 K5 **Helmingham** Suffk
110 B11 **Helmsdale** Highld
57 P5 **Helmshore** Lancs
66 E10 **Helmsley** N York
59 K1 **Helperby** N York
67 K12 **Helperthorpe** N York
42 G3 **Helpringham** Lincs
42 G8 **Helpston** C Pete
49 J1 **Helsby** Ches
2 F9 **Helston** Cnwll
4 D4 **Helstone** Cnwll
71 Q10 **Helton** Cumb
20 G2 **Hemel Hempstead** Herts
5 L8 **Hemerdon** Devon
59 P7 **Hemingbrough** N York
53 J8 **Hemingby** Lincs
33 J3 **Hemingford Abbots** Cambs
33 J3 **Hemingford Grey** Cambs
35 J6 **Hemingstone** Suffk
41 L2 **Hemington** Leics
42 F12 **Hemington** Nhants
17 Q5 **Hemington** Somset
35 L8 **Hemley** Suffk
66 C5 **Hemlington** Middsb
45 L10 **Hempnall** Norfk
45 L10 **Hempnall Green** Norfk
100 H3 **Hempriggs** Moray
33 Q8 **Hempstead** Essex
44 H3 **Hempstead** Norfk
45 N5 **Hempstead** Norfk
44 E4 **Hempton** Norfk
31 K7 **Hempton** Oxon
45 P6 **Hemsby** Norfk
52 D5 **Hemswell** Lincs
52 D5 **Hemswell Cliff** Lincs
59 K10 **Hemsworth** Wakefd
16 F12 **Hemyock** Devon
80 G7 **Hendersyde Park** Border
21 K5 **Hendon** Gt Lon
73 P9 **Hendon** Sundld
26 D7 **Hendy** Carmth
11 K6 **Henfield** W Susx
27 N9 **Hengoed** Caerph
38 E10 **Hengoed** Powys
34 D3 **Hengrave** Suffk
33 N10 **Henham** Essex
38 D1 **Heniarth** Powys
16 H10 **Henlade** Somset
7 Q2 **Henley** Dorset
17 L9 **Henley** Somset
35 J6 **Henley** Suffk
10 E5 **Henley** W Susx
30 F2 **Henley-in-Arden** Warwks
20 C6 **Henley-on-Thames** Oxon
12 E7 **Henley's Down** E Susx
36 F11 **Henllan** Cerdgn
55 Q7 **Henllan** Denbgs
28 B9 **Henllys** Torfn
32 H8 **Henlow** Beds
5 Q4 **Hennock** Devon
34 E8 **Henny Street** Essex
55 L6 **Henryd** Conwy
24 H4 **Henry's Moat (Castell Hendre)** Pembks
59 N9 **Hensall** N York
72 D7 **Henshaw** Nthumb
70 G11 **Hensingham** Cumb
45 P11 **Henstead** Suffk
9 N3 **Hensting** Hants
17 Q11 **Henstridge** Somset
17 Q11 **Henstridge Ash** Somset
20 C3 **Henton** Oxon
17 L7 **Henton** Somset
39 Q10 **Henwick** Worcs
4 G5 **Henwood** Cnwll
27 K11 **Heol-y-Cyw** Brdgnd
72 H1 **Hepple** Nthumb
73 L4 **Hepscott** Nthumb
58 C8 **Heptonstall** Calder
58 F11 **Hepworth** Kirk
34 G2 **Hepworth** Suffk
24 F7 **Herbrandston** Pembks
28 F2 **Hereford** Herefs
23 Q9 **Hereson** Kent
104 E8 **Heribusta** Highld
86 H10 **Heriot** Border
86 E8 **Hermiston** C Edin
79 P9 **Hermitage** Border
7 P2 **Hermitage** Dorset
19 N6 **Hermitage** W Berk
25 N3 **Hermon** Carmth
25 L3 **Hermon** Pembks
23 M9 **Herne** Kent
23 M9 **Herne Bay** Kent
21 L8 **Herne Hill** Gt Lon
22 D11 **Herne Pound** Kent
15 K6 **Herner** Devon
23 K10 **Hernhill** Kent
4 F7 **Herodsfoot** Cnwll
68 F3 **Heronsford** S Ayrs
19 Q10 **Herriard** Hants
45 P9 **Herringfleet** Suffk
34 C3 **Herringswell** Suffk
51 K3 **Herringthorpe** Rothm
73 N9 **Herrington** Sundld
23 M10 **Hersden** Kent
20 H9 **Hersham** Surrey
12 D7 **Herstmonceux** E Susx
111 h3 **Herston** Ork
21 M2 **Hertford** Herts
21 M2 **Hertford Heath** Herts
21 L2 **Hertingfordbury** Herts
57 J4 **Hesketh Bank** Lancs
57 L1 **Hesketh Lane** Lancs
71 M7 **Hesket Newmarket** Cumb
73 Q12 **Hesleden** Dur
59 N4 **Heslington** York
59 M4 **Hessay** York
4 G8 **Hessenford** Cnwll
34 F4 **Hessett** Suffk
60 H8 **Hessle** E R Yk
59 K10 **Hessle** Wakefd
63 J8 **Hest Bank** Lancs
20 H7 **Heston** Gt Lon
111 g2 **Hestwall** Ork
56 F11 **Heswall** Wirral
31 N8 **Hethe** Oxon
45 J8 **Hethersett** Norfk
71 P3 **Hethersgill** Cumb
81 J8 **Hethpool** Nthumb
73 M12 **Hett** Dur
58 C3 **Hetton** N York
73 N10 **Hetton-le-Hole** Sundld
73 J6 **Heugh** Nthumb
101 M11 **Heughhead** Abers
87 Q9 **Heugh Head** Border
35 M3 **Heveningham** Suffk
11 P2 **Hever** Kent
63 J5 **Heversham** Cumb
45 K6 **Hevingham** Norfk
3 L6 **Hewas Water** Cnwll
28 G8 **Hewelsfield** Gloucs
7 K2 **Hewish** Somset
7 J3 **Hewood** Dorset
72 G7 **Hexham** Nthumb
21 P8 **Hextable** Kent
51 M1 **Hexthorpe** Donc
32 F10 **Hexton** Herts
4 H4 **Hexworthy** Cnwll
5 N6 **Hexworthy** Devon
22 D4 **Heybridge** Essex
22 G2 **Heybridge** Essex
5 K9 **Heybrook Bay** Devon
33 M8 **Heydon** Cambs
45 J5 **Heydon** Norfk
42 E3 **Heydour** Lincs
88 B7 **Heylipoll** Ag & B
111 j3 **Heylor** Shet
62 H9 **Heysham** Lancs
10 E6 **Heyshott** W Susx
18 D11 **Heytesbury** Wilts
31 J8 **Heythrop** Oxon
57 Q6 **Heywood** Rochdl
18 C9 **Heywood** Wilts
52 D3 **Hibaldstow** N Linc
59 L12 **Hickleton** Donc
45 N5 **Hickling** Norfk
41 P2 **Hickling** Notts
45 N5 **Hickling Green** Norfk
11 L6 **Hickstead** W Susx
30 F5 **Hidcote Bartrim** Gloucs
30 F6 **Hidcote Boyce** Gloucs
59 K9 **High Ackworth** Wakefd
58 H11 **Higham** Barns
51 K8 **Higham** Derbys
12 C1 **Higham** Kent
22 E8 **Higham** Kent
57 P2 **Higham** Lancs
34 C4 **Higham** Suffk
34 G9 **Higham** Suffk
73 K6 **Higham Dykes** Nthumb
32 D3 **Higham Ferrers** Nhants
32 F9 **Higham Gobion** Beds
21 M5 **Higham Hill** Gt Lon
41 J8 **Higham on the Hill** Leics
14 H10 **Highampton** Devon
21 M5 **Highams Park** Gt Lon
68 E9 **High Ardwell** D & G
78 E10 **High Auldgirth** D & G
71 Q7 **High Bankhill** Cumb
21 N4 **High Beach** Essex
63 M8 **High Bentham** N York
15 K7 **High Bickington** Devon
63 L6 **High Biggins** Cumb
85 L10 **High Blantyre** S Lans
85 N7 **High Bonnybridge** Falk
15 M5 **High Bray** Devon
17 J6 **Highbridge** Somset
11 M4 **Highbrook** W Susx
12 C2 **High Brooms** Kent
58 F10 **Highburton** Kirk
21 L6 **Highbury** Gt Lon
17 Q6 **Highbury** Somset
63 L6 **High Casterton** Cumb
60 C4 **High Catton** E R Yk
19 M8 **Highclere** Hants
8 H8 **Highcliffe** Dorset
65 M5 **High Coniscliffe** Darltn
71 P4 **High Crosby** Cumb
76 G3 **High Cross** E Ayrs
10 B5 **High Cross** Hants
33 K11 **High Cross** Herts
30 G1 **High Cross** Warwks
68 F11 **High Drummore** D & G
22 C1 **High Easter** Essex
65 L10 **High Ellington** N York
8 B6 **Higher Ansty** Dorset
57 J3 **Higher Bartle** Lancs
7 Q4 **Higher Bockhampton** Dorset
6 C10 **Higher Brixham** Torbay
49 L11 **High Ercall** Wrekin
7 K2 **Higher Chillington** Somset
57 M8 **Higher Folds** Wigan
6 C8 **Higher Gabwell** Devon
62 H9 **Higher Heysham** Lancs
57 N9 **Higher Irlam** Salfd
48 G4 **Higher Kinnerton** Flints
15 K5 **Higher Muddiford** Devon
57 K3 **Higher Penwortham** Lancs
3 J6 **Higher Town** Cnwll
3 M4 **Higher Town** Cnwll
2 c1 **Higher Town** IoS
57 L4 **Higher Walton** Lancs
57 L10 **Higher Walton** Warrtn
6 H2 **Higher Wambrook** Somset
7 Q4 **Higher Waterston** Dorset
57 L4 **Higher Wheelton** Lancs
57 L11 **Higher Whitley** Ches
7 N3 **Higher Wraxhall** Dorset
49 J6 **Higher Wych** Ches
65 L2 **High Etherley** Dur
73 K8 **Highfield** Gatesd
76 E2 **Highfield** N Ayrs
34 C10 **High Garrett** Essex
21 L6 **Highgate** Gt Lon
65 M12 **High Grantley** N York
45 J11 **High Green** Norfk
45 J8 **High Green** Norfk
51 J2 **High Green** Sheff
39 Q11 **High Green** Worcs
12 H3 **High Halden** Kent
22 F8 **High Halstow** Medway
17 K9 **High Ham** Somset
58 H3 **High Harrogate** N York
49 L9 **High Hatton** Shrops
73 M1 **High Hauxley** Nthumb
67 K6 **High Hawsker** N York
71 P6 **High Hesket** Cumb
58 H11 **High Hoyland** Barns
11 P5 **High Hurstwood** E Susx
60 D1 **High Hutton** N York
71 K7 **High Ireby** Cumb
66 D10 **High Kilburn** N York
65 K3 **High Lands** Dur
99 M7 **Highland Wildlife Park** Highld
51 K4 **Highlane** Derbys
50 C4 **High Lane** Stockp
2 E8 **High Lanes** Cnwll
29 K4 **Highleadon** Gloucs
57 M11 **High Legh** Ches
10 D9 **Highleigh** W Susx
66 C5 **High Leven** S on T
39 N5 **Highley** Shrops
17 P5 **High Littleton** BaNES
71 J9 **High Lorton** Cumb
52 B9 **High Marnham** Notts
51 L1 **High Melton** Donc
73 J8 **High Mickley** Nthumb
20 B6 **Highmoor** Oxon
20 B6 **Highmoor Cross** Oxon
29 K5 **Highnam** Gloucs
73 P9 **High Newport** Sundld
62 H5 **High Newton** Cumb
62 F4 **High Nibthwaite** Cumb
49 P9 **High Offley** Staffs
22 C3 **High Ongar** Essex
49 P11 **High Onn** Staffs
34 G11 **High Park Corner** Essex
76 H9 **High Pennyvenie** E Ayrs
33 P12 **High Roding** Essex
10 H8 **High Salvington** W Susx
73 K8 **High Spen** Gatesd
22 H10 **Highstead** Kent
3 L5 **High Street** Cnwll
23 L10 **Highstreet** Kent
35 P6 **High Street** Suffk
10 F3 **Highstreet Green** Surrey
78 H11 **Hightae** D & G
56 F7 **Hightown** Sefton
34 F5 **Hightown Green** Suffk
53 J9 **High Toynton** Lincs
81 L11 **High Trewhitt** Nthumb
73 M9 **High Urpeth** Dur
86 B5 **High Valleyfield** Fife
6 B8 **Highweek** Devon
21 K5 **Highwood Hill** Gt Lon
18 H3 **Highworth** Swindn
62 G3 **High Wray** Cumb
21 P1 **High Wych** Herts
20 D5 **High Wycombe** Bucks
44 D9 **Hilborough** Norfk
18 G8 **Hilcott** Wilts
12 C1 **Hildenborough** Kent
12 C1 **Hilden Park** Kent
33 N7 **Hildersham** Cambs
40 C1 **Hilderstone** Staffs
61 K2 **Hilderthorpe** E R Yk
7 P2 **Hilfield** Dorset
43 P9 **Hilgay** Norfk
28 H9 **Hill** S Glos
31 L2 **Hill** Warwks
59 L8 **Hillam** N York
10 C5 **Hill Brow** Hants
8 E7 **Hillbutts** Dorset
49 P7 **Hill Chorlton** Staffs
50 H10 **Hillcliffane** Derbys
16 F10 **Hill Common** Somset
43 K1 **Hill Dyke** Lincs
86 C3 **Hill End** Fife
86 D5 **Hillend** Fife
29 M2 **Hill End** Gloucs
86 F8 **Hillend** Mdloth
85 N9 **Hillend** N Lans
31 P8 **Hillesden** Bucks
29 K10 **Hillesley** Gloucs
16 F10 **Hillfarrance** Somset
22 G10 **Hill Green** Kent
9 P6 **Hill Head** Hants
78 F2 **Hillhead** S Lans
103 M6 **Hillhead of Cocklaw** Abers
110 D3 **Hilliclay** Highld
20 H6 **Hillingdon** Gt Lon
85 J9 **Hillington** C Glas
44 C5 **Hillington** Norfk
41 M11 **Hillmorton** Warwks
86 D4 **Hill of Beath** Fife
107 N6 **Hill of Fearn** Highld
93 L12 **Hill of Tarvit Mansion House** Fife
70 C3 **Hillowton** D & G
40 E4 **Hill Ridware** Staffs
95 Q3 **Hillside** Abers
95 L9 **Hillside** Angus
58 F10 **Hill Side** Kirk
51 L6 **Hills Town** Derbys
9 K4 **Hillstreet** Hants
111 j3 **Hillswick** Shet
59 J10 **Hill Top** Wakefd
5 L4 **Hilltown** Devon
86 G8 **Hilltown** Mdloth
111 k5 **Hillwell** Shet
18 E6 **Hilmarton** Wilts
18 C8 **Hilperton** Wilts
9 Q6 **Hilsea** C Port
61 M7 **Hilston** E R Yk
81 J4 **Hilton** Border
33 J4 **Hilton** Cambs
64 D4 **Hilton** Cumb
40 G2 **Hilton** Derbys
8 B6 **Hilton** Dorset
65 L3 **Hilton** Dur
107 P7 **Hilton** Highld
66 C5 **Hilton** S on T
39 P3 **Hilton** Shrops
30 C3 **Himbleton** Worcs
39 Q4 **Himley** Staffs
63 K5 **Hincaster** Cumb
21 J9 **Hinchley Wood** Surrey
41 K8 **Hinckley** Leics
34 G2 **Hinderclay** Suffk
66 H4 **Hinderwell** N York
10 E3 **Hindhead** Surrey
57 L7 **Hindley** Wigan
39 Q9 **Hindlip** Worcs
44 G4 **Hindolveston** Norfk
8 D2 **Hindon** Wilts
44 G3 **Hindringham** Norfk
44 G9 **Hingham** Norfk
49 M9 **Hinstock** Shrops
34 H7 **Hintlesham** Suffk
28 D2 **Hinton** Herefs
17 Q2 **Hinton** S Glos
38 H1 **Hinton** Shrops
9 P2 **Hinton Ampner** Hants
17 N5 **Hinton Blewett** BaNES
18 B8 **Hinton Charterhouse** BaNES
31 M6 **Hinton-in-the-Hedges** Nhants
8 E6 **Hinton Martell** Dorset
30 D6 **Hinton on the Green** Worcs
19 J4 **Hinton Parva** Swindn
7 K1 **Hinton St George** Somset
8 B4 **Hinton St Mary** Dorset
19 L2 **Hinton Waldrist** Oxon
40 F6 **Hints** Staffs
32 D5 **Hinwick** Beds
13 K2 **Hinxhill** Kent
33 M7 **Hinxton** Cambs
32 H8 **Hinxworth** Herts
58 E8 **Hipperholme** Calder
65 L7 **Hipswell** N York
95 M2 **Hirn** Abers
48 B10 **Hirnant** Powys
73 M4 **Hirst** Nthumb
59 N8 **Hirst Courtney** N York
27 K7 **Hirwaun** Rhondd
15 J7 **Hiscott** Devon
33 M4 **Histon** Cambs
34 G6 **Hitcham** Suffk
34 G6 **Hitcham Causeway** Suffk
34 G6 **Hitcham Street** Suffk
32 H10 **Hitchin** Herts
21 M8 **Hither Green** Gt Lon
5 P2 **Hittisleigh** Devon
60 E7 **Hive** E R Yk
40 D3 **Hixon** Staffs
23 N10 **Hoaden** Kent
40 F3 **Hoar Cross** Staffs
28 G3 **Hoarwithy** Herefs
23 M9 **Hoath** Kent
38 F6 **Hobarris** Shrops
80 D11 **Hobkirk** Border
73 L9 **Hobson** Dur
41 P4 **Hoby** Leics
44 H7 **Hockering** Norfk
51 Q9 **Hockerton** Notts
22 G5 **Hockley** Essex
40 F11 **Hockley Heath** Solhll
32 D10 **Hockliffe** Beds
44 C11 **Hockwold cum Wilton** Norfk
16 D11 **Hockworthy** Devon
21 M2 **Hoddesdon** Herts
57 N4 **Hoddlesden** Bl w D
71 J2 **Hoddom Cross** D & G
71 J2 **Hoddom Mains** D & G
24 H8 **Hodgeston** Pembks
49 L9 **Hodnet** Shrops
22 D10 **Hodsall Street** Kent
51 N4 **Hodsock** Notts
18 H5 **Hodson** Swindn
51 M5 **Hodthorpe** Derbys
44 G6 **Hoe** Norfk
23 K11 **Hogben's Hill** Kent
32 B10 **Hoggeston** Bucks
40 G8 **Hoggrill's End** Warwks
57 L4 **Hoghton** Lancs
50 G10 **Hognaston** Derbys
53 N8 **Hogsthorpe** Lincs
43 K5 **Holbeach** Lincs
43 K5 **Holbeach Bank** Lincs
43 K5 **Holbeach Clough** Lincs
43 K7 **Holbeach Drove** Lincs
43 L5 **Holbeach Hurn** Lincs
43 K6 **Holbeach St Johns** Lincs
43 L4 **Holbeach St Mark's** Lincs
43 L4 **Holbeach St Matthew** Lincs
51 M6 **Holbeck** Notts
30 D3 **Holberrow Green** Worcs
5 M9 **Holbeton** Devon
21 L7 **Holborn** Gt Lon
51 J11 **Holbrook** Derbys
35 J9 **Holbrook** Suffk
9 M6 **Holbury** Hants

Holcombe - Inverurie 181

6 C7 Holcombe Devon
17 P6 Holcombe Somset
16 E11 Holcombe Rogus Devon
32 B3 Holcot Nhants
63 P11 Holden Lancs
31 P1 Holdenby Nhants
33 Q10 Holder's Green Essex
39 K4 Holdgate Shrops
42 F1 Holdingham Lincs
7 J3 Holditch Dorset
14 H10 Hole Devon
16 F7 Holford Somset
59 N4 Holgate York
62 G6 Holker Cumb
44 E2 Holkham Norfk
44 E2 Holkham Hall Norfk
14 G10 Hollacombe Devon
52 H12 Holland Fen Lincs
35 K12 Holland-on-Sea Essex
111 i1 Hollandstoun Ork
71 L2 Hollee D & G
35 M7 Hollesley Suffk
6 B9 Hollicombe Torbay
22 G11 Hollingbourne Kent
11 L8 Hollingbury Br & H
32 C10 Hollingdon Bucks
50 G11 Hollington Derbys
50 D11 Hollington Staffs
50 D2 Hollingworth Tamesd
50 E7 Hollinsclough Staffs
51 J4 Hollins End Sheff
57 M10 Hollins Green Warrtn
15 L9 Hollocombe Devon
51 J9 Holloway Derbys
21 L6 Holloway Gt Lon
41 P11 Hollowell Nhants
49 J2 Hollowmoor Heath Ches
79 N12 Hollows D & G
27 N7 Hollybush Caerph
76 G8 Hollybush E Ayrs
29 K2 Hollybush Herefs
29 M1 Holly Green Worcs
62 N8 Hollym E R Yk
58 E11 Holmbridge Kirk
10 H2 Holmbury St Mary Surrey
3 M5 Holmbush Cnwll
40 B3 Holmcroft Staffs
42 H11 Holme Cambs
63 K6 Holme Cumb
58 E11 Holme Kirk
65 P10 Holme N York
52 B10 Holme Notts
57 Q3 Holme Chapel Lancs
59 M6 Holme Green N York
44 E8 Holme Hale Norfk
28 G2 Holme Lacy Herefs
38 G10 Holme Marsh Herefs
44 B2 Holme next the Sea Norfk
60 G5 Holme on the Wolds E R Yk
51 N11 Holme Pierrepont Notts
28 F1 Holmer Herefs
20 E4 Holmer Green Bucks
70 H6 Holme St Cuthbert Cumb
49 N3 Holmes Chapel Ches
50 H5 Holmesfield Derbys
56 H5 Holmeswood Lancs
21 L12 Holmethorpe Surrey
60 D6 Holme upon Spalding Moor E R Yk
51 K7 Holmewood Derbys
58 F11 Holmfirth Kirk
77 J7 Holmhead E Ayrs
61 N9 Holmpton E R Yk
62 C3 Holmrook Cumb
73 L10 Holmside Dur
5 N6 Holne Devon
7 P2 Holnest Dorset
16 C6 Holnicote Somset
14 F10 Holsworthy Devon
14 G9 Holsworthy Beacon Devon
8 F6 Holt Dorset
44 H3 Holt Norfk
18 C8 Holt Wilts
39 P9 Holt Worcs
48 H5 Holt Wrexhm
59 P4 Holtby York
40 E12 Holt End Worcs
39 P9 Holt Heath Worcs
31 N11 Holton Oxon
17 P10 Holton Somset
35 N2 Holton Suffk
52 G7 Holton cum Beckering Lincs
53 J3 Holton le Clay Lincs
52 F4 Holton le Moor Lincs
34 H8 Holton St Mary Suffk
7 Q1 Holwell Dorset
32 G9 Holwell Herts
41 Q3 Holwell Leics
30 G11 Holwell Oxon
64 G3 Holwick Dur
10 B2 Holybourne Hants
54 C5 Holyhead IoA
54 C5 Holy Island IoA
81 N6 Holy Island Nthumb
51 J7 Holymoorside Derbys
20 E7 Holyport W & M
72 G1 Holystone Nthumb
85 M10 Holytown N Lans
32 E12 Holywell Beds
33 K3 Holywell Cambs
2 H4 Holywell Cnwll
7 N2 Holywell Dorset
48 E1 Holywell Flints
58 E9 Holywell Green Calder
16 F11 Holywell Lake Somset
34 B2 Holywell Row Suffk
78 F11 Holywood D & G
78 F11 Holywood Village D & G
39 L2 Homer Shrops
56 G8 Homer Green Sefton
45 L11 Homersfield Suffk
8 G3 Homington Wilts
30 E5 Honeybourne Worcs
15 L10 Honeychurch Devon
18 G8 Honeystreet Wilts
34 F9 Honey Tye Suffk
40 G11 Honiley Warwks
45 M5 Honing Norfk
44 H7 Honingham Norfk
42 D2 Honington Lincs
34 E2 Honington Suffk
30 H5 Honington Warwks
6 F3 Honiton Devon
58 F10 Honley Kirk
5 K9 Hooe C Plym
12 E7 Hooe E Susx
57 N11 Hoo Green Ches
56 G2 Hoohill Bpool
60 D8 Hook E R Yk
21 J9 Hook Gt Lon
20 B11 Hook Hants
24 G6 Hook Pembks
18 F4 Hook Wilts
7 M3 Hooke Dorset
12 D3 Hook Green Kent
22 C8 Hook Green Kent
31 J7 Hook Norton Oxon
15 P11 Hookway Devon
21 L11 Hooley Surrey
22 F8 Hoo St Werburgh Medway
51 M3 Hooton Levitt Rothm
59 L11 Hooton Pagnell Donc
51 L2 Hooton Roberts Rothm
50 F4 Hope Derbys
5 N11 Hope Devon
48 F4 Hope Flints
39 L7 Hope Shrops
50 E9 Hope Staffs
39 J4 Hope Bowdler Shrops
79 L5 Hopehouse Border
100 H2 Hopeman Moray
28 H5 Hope Mansell Herefs
38 H5 Hopesay Shrops
39 K10 Hope under Dinmore Herefs
59 N3 Hopgrove York
59 K3 Hopperton N York
39 P4 Hopstone Shrops
50 H9 Hopton Derbys
40 C3 Hopton Staffs
34 G2 Hopton Suffk
39 K6 Hopton Cangeford Shrops
38 G6 Hopton Castle Shrops
38 H6 Hoptonheath Shrops
45 Q9 Hopton on Sea Norfk
39 M6 Hopton Wafers Shrops
40 F6 Hopwas Staffs
40 D11 Hopwood Worcs
12 C6 Horam E Susx
42 G3 Horbling Lincs
58 H9 Horbury Wakefd
73 Q11 Horden Dur
9 J8 Hordle Hants
48 H8 Hordley Shrops
17 N2 Horfield Bristl
35 K3 Horham Suffk
34 G10 Horkesley Heath Essex
60 G9 Horkstow N Linc
31 K5 Horley Oxon
11 L2 Horley Surrey
17 N9 Hornblotton Green Somset
63 L8 Hornby Lancs
65 L8 Hornby N York
65 P6 Hornby N York
53 J9 Horncastle Lincs
21 Q6 Hornchurch Gt Lon
81 K4 Horncliffe Nthumb
81 J4 Horndean Border
10 B7 Horndean Hants
5 L4 Horndon Devon
22 D6 Horndon on the Hill Thurr
11 M2 Horne Surrey
16 B7 Horner Somset
45 M6 Horning Norfk
42 B10 Horninghold Leics
40 G3 Horninglow Staffs
33 M4 Horningsea Cambs
18 B11 Horningsham Wilts
44 F5 Horningtoft Norfk
14 G7 Horns Cross Devon
61 K5 Hornsea E R Yk
21 L5 Hornsey Gt Lon
31 K5 Hornton Oxon
111 k2 Horra Shet
5 K6 Horrabridge Devon
5 P5 Horridge Devon
34 D4 Horringer Suffk
63 N12 Horrocksford Lancs
5 J5 Horsebridge Devon
12 C7 Horsebridge E Susx
9 L2 Horsebridge Hants
38 G2 Horsebridge Shrops
33 P7 Horseheath Cambs
65 J10 Horsehouse N York
20 F10 Horsell Surrey
49 J7 Horseman's Green Wrexhm
45 P5 Horsey Norfk
17 J8 Horsey Somset
45 K6 Horsford Norfk
58 G6 Horsforth Leeds
11 J4 Horsham W Susx
39 N9 Horsham Worcs
45 K7 Horsham St Faith Norfk
52 H9 Horsington Lincs
17 Q10 Horsington Somset
51 J11 Horsley Derbys
29 L8 Horsley Gloucs
72 F2 Horsley Nthumb
73 J7 Horsley Nthumb
35 J10 Horsleycross Street Essex
80 C9 Horsleyhill Border
51 K11 Horsley Woodhouse Derbys
12 E2 Horsmonden Kent
31 M12 Horspath Oxon
45 L6 Horstead Norfk
11 M5 Horsted Keynes W Susx
32 D11 Horton Bucks
8 F6 Horton Dorset
63 Q11 Horton Lancs
32 B6 Horton Nhants
18 A4 Horton S Glos
17 J12 Horton Somset
50 C8 Horton Staffs
26 C10 Horton Swans
20 G8 Horton W & M
18 F7 Horton Wilts
49 M11 Horton Wrekin
31 N10 Horton-cum-Studley Oxon
49 J5 Horton Green Ches
64 E12 Horton in Ribblesdale N York
22 C9 Horton Kirby Kent
57 M6 Horwich Bolton
15 J6 Horwood Devon
79 N6 Hoscote Border
41 Q2 Hose Leics
92 C10 Hosh P & K
111 K5 Hoswick Shet
60 F7 Hotham E R Yk
13 J2 Hothfield Kent
41 M3 Hoton Leics
72 E4 Hott Nthumb
49 N5 Hough Ches
42 C2 Hougham Lincs
57 J10 Hough Green Halton
42 D2 Hough-on-the-Hill Lincs
33 J3 Houghton Cambs
9 K2 Houghton Hants
24 H7 Houghton Pembks
10 G7 Houghton W Susx
32 F8 Houghton Conquest Beds
12 H5 Houghton Green E Susx
73 N10 Houghton-le-Spring Sundld
41 P6 Houghton on the Hill Leics
32 E11 Houghton Regis Beds
44 F3 Houghton St Giles Norfk
20 B10 Hound Green Hants
80 E5 Houndslow Border
87 Q9 Houndwood Border
21 J8 Hounslow Gt Lon
33 Q12 Hounslow Green Essex
100 D4 Househill Highld
58 G10 Houses Hill Kirk
72 E7 Housesteads Roman Fort Nthumb
103 J9 Housieside Abers
84 G9 Houston Rens
110 D8 Houstry Highld
111 g2 Houton Ork
11 L8 Hove Br & H
51 P10 Hoveringham Notts
45 M6 Hoveton Norfk
66 F11 Hovingham N York
28 H3 How Caple Herefs
60 D8 Howden E R Yk
65 L2 Howden-le-Wear Dur
110 F4 Howe Highld
65 P10 Howe N York
45 L9 Howe Norfk
22 E3 Howe Green Essex
22 G3 Howegreen Essex
42 G2 Howell Lincs
102 G6 Howe of Teuchar Abers
71 K3 Howes D & G
22 E1 Howe Street Essex
34 B9 Howe Street Essex
27 Q3 Howey Powys
70 G10 Howgate Cumb
86 F10 Howgate Mdloth
81 Q10 Howick Nthumb
65 J3 Howle Dur
49 M10 Howle Wrekin
28 H5 Howle Hill Herefs
33 P9 Howlett End Essex
6 H2 Howley Somset
71 Q4 How Mill Cumb
111 a5 Howmore W Isls
80 G9 Hownam Border
52 E3 Howsham N Linc
60 C2 Howsham N York
81 J7 Howtel Nthumb
84 G10 Howwood Rens
35 K2 Hoxne Suffk
56 E10 Hoylake Wirral
51 J1 Hoyland Nether Barns
58 H12 Hoyland Swaine Barns
24 F7 Hubberston Pembks
58 H5 Huby N York
59 M2 Huby N York
29 M5 Hucclecote Gloucs
22 G10 Hucking Kent
51 M10 Hucknall Notts
58 F10 Huddersfield Kirk
30 C3 Huddington Worcs
65 K7 Hudswell N York
60 F3 Huggate E R Yk
20 D4 Hughenden Valley Bucks
39 K3 Hughley Shrops
2 c2 Hugh Town IoS
15 J9 Huish Devon
18 G7 Huish Wilts
16 E9 Huish Champflower Somset
17 L10 Huish Episcopi Somset
32 C12 Hulcott Bucks
6 D6 Hulham Devon
50 G10 Hulland Derbys
50 G10 Hulland Ward Derbys
18 D4 Hullavington Wilts
22 F4 Hullbridge Essex
57 Q9 Hulme Manch
50 C10 Hulme Staffs
57 L9 Hulme Warrtn
50 E8 Hulme End Staffs
49 Q3 Hulme Walfield Ches
9 J9 Hulverstone IoW
45 P11 Hulver Street Suffk
61 J11 Humberside Airport N Linc
53 K3 Humberston NE Lin
41 N6 Humberstone C Leic
87 J9 Humbie E Loth
61 L7 Humbleton E R Yk
42 E4 Humby Lincs
80 F6 Hume Border
72 G6 Humshaugh Nthumb
110 G2 Huna Highld
41 M7 Huncote Leics
80 E9 Hundalee Border
64 H4 Hunderthwaite Dur
53 L9 Hundleby Lincs
24 G8 Hundleton Pembks
34 C7 Hundon Suffk
56 H4 Hundred End Lancs
38 C10 Hundred House Powys
41 P6 Hungarton Leics
16 E7 Hungerford Somset
19 K7 Hungerford W Berk
19 L6 Hungerford Newtown W Berk
28 E2 Hungerstone Herefs
67 N11 Hunmanby N York
31 J1 Hunningham Warwks
31 Q3 Hunsbury Hill Nhants
21 N1 Hunsdon Herts
59 K4 Hunsingore N York
58 H7 Hunslet Leeds
64 B1 Hunsonby Cumb
43 Q3 Hunstanton Norfk
72 G10 Hunstanworth Dur
49 M6 Hunsterson Ches
34 F3 Hunston Suffk
10 D9 Hunston W Susx
17 P4 Hunstrete BaNES
58 F8 Hunsworth Kirk
84 C7 Hunter's Quay Ag & B
17 J10 Huntham Somset
94 H7 Hunthill Lodge Angus
33 J3 Huntingdon Cambs
35 M2 Huntingfield Suffk
48 H3 Huntington Ches
87 J7 Huntington E Loth
38 F10 Huntington Herefs
40 C5 Huntington Staffs
59 N3 Huntington York
29 J5 Huntley Gloucs
102 C7 Huntly Abers
19 N11 Hunton Hants
22 E12 Hunton Kent
65 L8 Hunton N York
16 C7 Huntscott Somset
16 D11 Huntsham Devon
15 J7 Huntshaw Devon
17 J7 Huntspill Somset
16 H9 Huntstile Somset
17 J8 Huntworth Somset
65 L2 Hunwick Dur
44 H3 Hunworth Norfk
8 H1 Hurdcott Wilts
50 B6 Hurdsfield Ches
20 D6 Hurley W & M
40 G8 Hurley Warwks
40 G7 Hurley Common Warwks
76 H4 Hurlford E Ayrs
8 G7 Hurn Dorset
9 M3 Hursley Hants
20 C8 Hurst Wokham
19 M10 Hurstbourne Priors Hants
19 L9 Hurstbourne Tarrant Hants
12 E5 Hurst Green E Susx
34 H12 Hurst Green Essex
57 M2 Hurst Green Lancs
21 N12 Hurst Green Surrey
11 L6 Hurstpierpoint W Susx
57 Q3 Hurstwood Lancs
111 h2 Hurtiso Ork
65 N5 Hurworth-on-Tees Darltn
65 N5 Hurworth Place Darltn
41 N10 Husbands Bosworth Leics
32 D9 Husborne Crawley Beds
66 D11 Husthwaite N York
51 L8 Huthwaite Notts
53 N8 Huttoft Lincs
81 J4 Hutton Border
60 H4 Hutton E R Yk
22 D4 Hutton Essex
57 J4 Hutton Lancs
17 J4 Hutton N Som
65 N7 Hutton Bonville N York
67 L10 Hutton Buscel N York
65 N11 Hutton Conyers N York
60 H4 Hutton Cranswick E R Yk
71 P7 Hutton End Cumb
65 Q1 Hutton Henry Dur
66 G9 Hutton-le-Hole N York
66 E5 Hutton Lowcross R & Cl
65 K5 Hutton Magna Dur
63 K6 Hutton Roof Cumb
71 M8 Hutton Roof Cumb
66 C6 Hutton Rudby N York
66 C11 Hutton Sessay N York
59 L4 Hutton Wandesley N York
6 C4 Huxham Devon
49 K3 Huxley Ches
57 J10 Huyton Knows
62 C4 Hycemoor Cumb
50 C2 Hyde Tamesd
20 E4 Hyde Heath Bucks
40 B4 Hyde Lea Staffs
78 E1 Hyndford Bridge S Lans
88 C8 Hynish Ag & B
38 F4 Hyssington Powys
9 M6 Hythe Hants
13 M3 Hythe Kent
20 G8 Hythe End W & M

I

8 B6 Ibberton Dorset
50 G9 Ible Derbys
8 H5 Ibsley Hants
41 K5 Ibstock Leics
20 C5 Ibstone Bucks
19 L9 Ibthorpe Hants
67 J6 Iburndale N York
19 P9 Ibworth Hants
44 D10 Ickburgh Norfk
20 H6 Ickenham Gt Lon
31 N11 Ickford Bucks
23 N10 Ickham Kent
32 H9 Ickleford Herts
12 G6 Icklesham E Susx
33 M7 Ickleton Cambs
34 C3 Icklingham Suffk
58 C5 Ickornshaw N York
32 G7 Ickwell Green Beds
34 D4 Ickworth Suffk
30 G9 Icomb Gloucs
30 G9 Idbury Oxon
15 K9 Iddesleigh Devon
6 B5 Ide Devon
6 B7 Ideford Devon
21 P11 Ide Hill Kent
12 H5 Iden E Susx
12 E3 Iden Green Kent
12 F4 Iden Green Kent
58 F6 Idle Brad
3 J6 Idless Cnwll
30 H5 Idlicote Warwks
18 H12 Idmiston Wilts
25 P6 Idole Carmth
50 H10 Idridgehay Derbys
104 E9 Idrigill Highld
19 J4 Idstone Oxon
31 M12 Iffley Oxon
11 K3 Ifield W Susx
8 G8 Iford Bmouth
11 N8 Iford E Susx
28 F10 Ifton Mons
49 L7 Ightfield Shrops
22 C11 Ightham Kent
35 N5 Iken Suffk
50 F10 Ilam Staffs
17 M10 Ilchester Somset
81 L9 Ilderton Nthumb
21 N6 Ilford Gt Lon
17 K11 Ilford Somset
15 J3 Ilfracombe Devon
51 L11 Ilkeston Derbys
45 N11 Ilketshall St Andrew Suffk
45 M11 Ilketshall St Margaret Suffk
58 E5 Ilkley Brad
4 G5 Illand Cnwll
40 C10 Illey Dudley
2 G7 Illogan Cnwll
41 P7 Illston on the Hill Leics
20 C3 Ilmer Bucks
30 G5 Ilmington Warwks
17 J12 Ilminster Somset
5 Q5 Ilsington Devon
26 D10 Ilston Swans
65 L11 Ilton N York
17 J11 Ilton Somset
75 N4 Imachar N Ayrs
61 K10 Immingham NE Lin
61 K10 Immingham Dock NE Lin
33 M4 Impington Cambs
57 J12 Ince Ches
56 G8 Ince Blundell Sefton
57 L7 Ince-in-Makerfield Wigan
106 G8 Inchbae Lodge Hotel Highld
95 K8 Inchbare Angus
101 L4 Inchberry Moray
105 Q9 Incheril Highld
84 H8 Inchinnan Rens
98 B8 Inchlaggan Highld
93 J9 Inchmichael P & K
98 E6 Inchnacardoch Hotel Highld
108 E10 Inchnadamph Highld
93 K9 Inchture P & K
98 C2 Inchvuilt Highld
92 H10 Inchyra P & K
3 K4 Indian Queens Cnwll
22 D4 Ingatestone Essex
58 G11 Ingbirchworth Barns
40 C3 Ingestre Staffs
52 D6 Ingham Lincs
45 N5 Ingham Norfk
34 E3 Ingham Suffk
45 N5 Ingham Corner Norfk
41 J3 Ingleby Derbys
66 C7 Ingleby Arncliffe N York
66 C5 Ingleby Barwick S on T
66 E6 Ingleby Greenhow N York
15 K10 Ingleigh Green Devon
17 Q4 Inglesbatch BaNES
18 H2 Inglesham Swindn
70 F3 Ingleston D & G
65 L4 Ingleton Dur
63 M7 Ingleton N York
57 K2 Inglewhite Lancs
73 J6 Ingoe Nthumb
57 K3 Ingol Lancs
44 B4 Ingoldisthorpe Norfk
53 N9 Ingoldmells Lincs
42 E4 Ingoldsby Lincs
81 L10 Ingram Nthumb
22 D5 Ingrave Essex
58 D6 Ingrow Brad
63 J3 Ings Cumb
28 G10 Ingst S Glos
42 E8 Ingthorpe Rutlnd
45 K4 Ingworth Norfk
30 D3 Inkberrow Worcs
103 J7 Inkhorn Abers
19 L7 Inkpen W Berk
110 F2 Inkstack Highld
84 C8 Innellan Ag & B
79 M2 Innerleithen Border
86 H3 Innerleven Fife
68 E6 Innermessan D & G
87 N7 Innerwick E Loth
101 K3 Innesmill Moray
102 E9 Insch Abers
99 M8 Insh Highld
57 J2 Inskip Lancs
14 H6 Instow Devon
51 K4 Intake Sheff
94 D4 Inver Abers
107 P6 Inver Highld
92 F7 Inver P & K
97 K12 Inverailort Highld
105 M10 Inveralligin Highld
103 L3 Inverallochy Abers
107 J3 Inveran Highld
84 B2 Inveraray Ag & B
96 G3 Inverarish Highld
93 M6 Inverarity Angus
91 J11 Inverarnan Stirlg
105 M5 Inverasdale Highld
85 Q7 Inveravon Falk
90 D9 Inverawe Ag & B
84 F4 Inverbeg Ag & B
95 N7 Inverbervie Abers
102 E3 Inver-boyndie Abers
106 C5 Inverbroom Highld
90 D7 Invercreran House Hotel Ag & B
99 N6 Inverdruie Highld
86 G7 Inveresk E Loth
90 D8 Inveresragan Ag & B
105 M6 Inverewe Garden Highld
94 B4 Inverey Abers
98 G4 Inverfarigaig Highld
90 C7 Inverfolla Ag & B
98 D8 Invergarry Highld
91 Q10 Invergeldie P & K
98 C10 Invergloy Highld
107 L8 Invergordon Highld
93 L9 Invergowrie P & K
97 K8 Inverguseran Highld
91 P5 Inverhadden P & K
91 K10 Inverherive Hotel Stirlg
97 K9 Inverie Highld
90 D11 Inverinan Ag & B
97 N5 Inverinate Highld
93 R6 Inverkeilor Angus
86 D5 Inverkeithing Fife
102 E6 Inverkeithny Abers
84 D8 Inverkip Inver
108 B10 Inverkirkaig Highld
106 C5 Inverlael Highld
98 D11 Inverlair Highld
83 N2 Inverliever Lodge Ag & B
90 G10 Inverlochy Ag & B
94 G6 Invermark Angus
101 M7 Invermarkie Abers
98 F5 Invermoriston Highld
107 L12 Inverness Highld
107 M11 Inverness Dalcross Airport Highld
84 C4 Invernoaden Ag & B
90 H7 Inveroran Hotel Ag & B
93 M4 Inverquharity Angus
103 L6 Inverquhomery Abers
98 C11 Inverroy Highld
90 C4 Inversanda Highld
97 N6 Invershiel Highld
107 J3 Invershin Highld
110 F8 Invershore Highld
84 F2 Inversnaid Hotel Stirlg
103 M6 Inverugie Abers
84 F2 Inveruglas Ag & B
99 M8 Inveruglass Highld
102 G10 Inverurie Abers

182 Inwardleigh - Kirkby Malham

15 K11 Inwardleigh Devon
34 E12 Inworth Essex
111 a5 Iochdar W Isls
88 G10 Iona Ag & B
10 D5 Iping W Susx
5 Q7 Ipplepen Devon
19 Q4 Ipsden Oxon
50 D10 Ipstones Staffs
35 J7 Ipswich Suffk
56 F11 Irby Wirral
53 M10 Irby in the Marsh Lincs
52 H3 Irby upon Humber NE Lin
32 D4 Irchester Nhants
71 K7 Ireby Cumb
63 M7 Ireby Lancs
62 E6 Ireleth Cumb
72 F12 Ireshopeburn Dur
50 H10 Ireton Wood Derbys
57 N9 Irlam Salfd
42 E5 Irnham Lincs
29 J11 Iron Acton S Glos
39 M2 Ironbridge Wrekin
39 M2 Iron Bridge Museum Wrekin
69 P4 Ironmacannie D & G
51 K9 Ironville Derbys
45 M6 Irstead Norfk
71 P4 Irthington Cumb
32 D3 Irthlingborough Nhants
67 L10 Irton N York
76 F4 Irvine N Ayrs
76 E4 Irvine Maritime Centre N Ayrs
110 A3 Isauld Highld
111 k2 Isbister Shet
111 m3 Isbister Shet
11 N6 Isfield E Susx
32 C3 Isham Nhants
10 C2 Isington Hants
74 D3 Islay Airport Ag & B
17 J11 Isle Abbotts Somset
17 K11 Isle Brewers Somset
33 Q2 Isleham Cambs
21 M7 Isle of Dogs Gt Lon
56 b7 Isle of Man Ronaldsway Airport IoM
8 E10 Isle of Purbeck Dorset
23 J9 Isle of Sheppey Kent
69 L10 Isle of Whithorn D & G
9 N9 Isle of Wight IoW
97 J7 Isleornsay Highld
2 c2 Isles of Scilly St Mary's Airport IoS
70 F2 Islesteps D & G
21 J8 Isleworth Gt Lon
41 K3 Isley Walton Leics
111 b2 Islibhig W Isls
21 L6 Islington Gt Lon
32 E2 Islip Nhants
31 M10 Islip Oxon
111 b2 Islivig W Isls
49 L11 Isombridge Wrekin
9 N2 Itchen Abbas Hants
9 P2 Itchen Stoke Hants
11 J4 Itchingfield W Susx
45 J4 Itteringham Norfk
15 L11 Itton Devon
28 F9 Itton Mons
71 N6 Ivegill Cumb
20 G7 Iver Bucks
20 G6 Iver Heath Bucks
73 K10 Iveston Dur
32 D12 Ivinghoe Bucks
32 D12 Ivinghoe Aston Bucks
39 J10 Ivington Herefs
39 J10 Ivington Green Herefs
5 M8 Ivybridge Devon
13 K5 Ivychurch Kent
22 C11 Ivy Hatch Kent
22 H9 Iwade Kent
8 C5 Iwerne Courtney or Shroton Dorset
8 C5 Iwerne Minster Dorset
34 F3 Ixworth Suffk
34 F3 Ixworth Thorpe Suffk

J

6 D4 Jack-in-the-Green Devon
85 K11 Jackton S Lans
4 F2 Jacobstow Cnwll
15 K10 Jacobstowe Devon
25 J8 Jameston Pembks
106 H10 Jamestown Highld
84 G6 Jamestown W Duns
110 E8 Janetstown Highld
110 G5 Janets-town Highld
78 H10 Jardine Hall D & G
73 N7 Jarrow S Tyne
34 C10 Jasper's Green Essex
85 P7 Jawcraig Falk
23 M1 Jaywick Essex
80 E9 Jedburgh Border
25 J7 Jeffreyston Pembks
107 M8 Jemimaville Highld
6 c2 Jerbourg Guern
7 a2 Jersey Airport Jersey
73 M7 Jesmond N u Ty
12 C9 Jevington E Susx
20 C1 Jockey End Herts
71 N8 Johnby Cumb
56 H11 John Lennon Airport Lpool
110 H2 John o' Groats Highld
95 N8 Johnshaven Abers
24 G6 Johnston Pembks
79 L8 Johnstone D & G
84 G9 Johnstone Rens
78 H9 Johnstonebridge D & G
25 P5 Johnstown Carmth
48 F6 Johnstown Wrexhm
86 G7 Joppa C Edin
37 J7 Joppa Cerdgn
76 G7 Joppa S Ayrs
24 G3 Jordanston Pembks
21 P8 Joyden's Wood Kent
72 G8 Juniper Nthumb
86 E8 Juniper Green C Edin
56 c2 Jurby IoM

K

64 E5 Kaber Cumb
86 B11 Kaimend S Lans
83 P8 Kames Ag & B
77 L6 Kames E Ayrs
3 J7 Kea Cnwll
60 E10 Keadby N Linc
53 K10 Keal Cotes Lincs
57 N7 Kearsley Bolton
72 H6 Kearsley Nthumb
13 P2 Kearsney Kent
63 L6 Kearstwick Cumb
34 B7 Kedington Suffk
50 H11 Kedleston Derbys
61 K11 Keelby Lincs
49 P6 Keele Staffs
58 E7 Keelham Brad
24 F5 Keeston Pembks
18 D8 Keevil Wilts
41 L3 Kegworth Leics
2 F7 Kehelland Cnwll
102 D10 Keig Abers
58 D6 Keighley Brad
85 P4 Keilarsbrae Clacks
92 E9 Keillour P & K
94 C4 Keiloch Abers
82 G8 Keils Ag & B
17 M9 Keinton Mandeville Somset
78 E9 Keir Mill D & G
64 D3 Keisley Cumb
110 G4 Keiss Highld
101 N5 Keith Moray
93 J7 Keithick P & K
95 K8 Keithock Angus
106 H10 Keithtown Highld
58 B5 Kelbrook Lancs
84 D10 Kelburn N Ayrs
42 E2 Kelby Lincs
64 F7 Keld N York
59 N6 Kelfield N York
51 Q9 Kelham Notts
71 J2 Kelhead D & G
56 H3 Kellamergh Lancs
93 M8 Kellas Angus
101 J5 Kellas Moray
5 Q11 Kellaton Devon
44 H2 Kelling Norfk
59 M8 Kellington N York
73 N12 Kelloe Dur
77 M8 Kelloholm D & G
5 J4 Kelly Devon
41 Q10 Kelmarsh Nhants
19 J2 Kelmscott Oxon
35 N4 Kelsale Suffk
49 K2 Kelsall Ches
33 K9 Kelshall Herts
71 K5 Kelsick Cumb
80 G7 Kelso Border
51 J7 Kelstedge Derbys
53 J5 Kelstern Lincs
17 Q3 Kelston BaNES
92 B6 Keltneyburn P & K
70 G2 Kelton D & G
86 D4 Kelty Fife
34 E11 Kelvedon Essex
22 C4 Kelvedon Hatch Essex
2 B9 Kelynack Cnwll
93 M11 Kemback Fife
39 N2 Kemberton Shrops
29 P8 Kemble Gloucs
29 N2 Kemerton Worcs
28 D7 Kemeys Commander Mons
102 F11 Kemnay Abers
29 J3 Kempley Gloucs
29 J3 Kempley Green Gloucs
39 Q11 Kempsey Worcs
18 H2 Kempsford Gloucs
19 P10 Kempshott Hants
32 E7 Kempston Beds
38 G5 Kempton Shrops
11 M8 Kemp Town Br & H
22 B10 Kemsing Kent
13 J4 Kenardington Kent
38 H12 Kenchester Herefs
30 G12 Kencot Oxon
63 K4 Kendal Cumb
26 H11 Kenfig Brdgnd
40 H12 Kenilworth Warwks
21 L10 Kenley Gt Lon
39 K3 Kenley Shrops
105 L10 Kenmore Highld
92 B6 Kenmore P & K
6 C6 Kenn Devon
17 K3 Kenn N Som
83 M9 Kennacraig Ag & B
15 P10 Kennerleigh Devon
56 H8 Kennessee Green Sefton
85 Q5 Kennet Clacks
102 C9 Kennethmont Abers
34 B3 Kennett Cambs
6 C5 Kennford Devon
44 G11 Kenninghall Norfk
13 K2 Kennington Kent
19 N1 Kennington Oxon
86 G2 Kennoway Fife
17 J11 Kenny Somset
33 Q2 Kennyhill Suffk
60 D2 Kennythorpe N York
88 C7 Kenovay Ag & B
104 F11 Kensaleyre Highld
21 K7 Kensington Gt Lon
32 E12 Kensworth Common Beds
90 D5 Kentallen Highld
28 E4 Kentchurch Herefs
34 B4 Kentford Suffk
23 P9 Kent International Airport Kent
6 E2 Kentisbeare Devon
15 L4 Kentisbury Devon
21 L6 Kentish Town Gt Lon
63 J2 Kentmere Cumb
6 C6 Kenton Devon
21 J6 Kenton Gt Lon
73 L7 Kenton N u Ty
35 K4 Kenton Suffk
89 N3 Kentra Highld
29 K4 Kent's Green Gloucs
9 K3 Kent's Oak Hants
3 J6 Kenwyn Cnwll
108 G3 Keoldale Highld
97 M5 Keppoch Highld
66 C8 Kepwick N York
40 H10 Keresley Covtry
2 C9 Kerris Cnwll
38 D4 Kerry Powys
84 B10 Kerrycroy Ag & B
51 Q8 Kersall Notts
6 E6 Kersbrook Devon
34 G7 Kersey Suffk
111 d2 Kershader W Isls
6 E2 Kerswell Devon
39 Q11 Kerswell Green Worcs
35 K7 Kesgrave Suffk
45 Q11 Kessingland Suffk
3 L6 Kestle Cnwll
3 J4 Kestle Mill Cnwll
21 N9 Keston Gt Lon
71 L10 Keswick Cumb
45 K8 Keswick Norfk
53 L8 Ketsby Lincs
32 C2 Kettering Nhants
45 J9 Ketteringham Norfk
93 J7 Kettins P & K
34 F6 Kettlebaston Suffk
86 G2 Kettlebridge Fife
40 G6 Kettlebrook Staffs
35 L5 Kettleburgh Suffk
79 J12 Kettleholm D & G
50 C5 Kettleshulme Ches
58 G3 Kettlesing N York
58 G3 Kettlesing Bottom N York
44 F4 Kettlestone Norfk
52 C8 Kettlethorpe Lincs
111 i1 Kettletoft Ork
64 H11 Kettlewell N York
42 E8 Ketton Rutlnd
21 J7 Kew Gt Lon
21 J7 Kew Gardens Gt Lon
17 J4 Kewstoke N Som
52 C6 Kexby Lincs
60 C4 Kexby York
50 B7 Key Green Ches
41 P6 Keyham Leics
9 K8 Keyhaven Hants
61 L8 Keyingham E R Yk
11 L7 Keymer W Susx
17 P3 Keynsham BaNES
32 F4 Keysoe Beds
32 F5 Keysoe Row Beds
32 F2 Keyston Cambs
41 N2 Keyworth Notts
73 M9 Kibblesworth Gatesd
41 P8 Kibworth Beauchamp Leics
41 P8 Kibworth Harcourt Leics
21 N7 Kidbrooke Gt Lon
39 Q6 Kidderminster Worcs
31 L10 Kidlington Oxon
20 B7 Kidmore End Oxon
69 L10 Kidsdale D & G
49 Q5 Kidsgrove Staffs
25 P7 Kidwelly Carmth
90 C8 Kiel Crofts Ag & B
72 B3 Kielder Nthumb
82 F8 Kiells Ag & B
84 G9 Kilbarchan Rens
97 J8 Kilbeg Highld
83 K9 Kilberry Ag & B
84 E11 Kilbirnie N Ayrs
83 L7 Kilbride Ag & B
83 Q9 Kilbride Ag & B
90 B10 Kilbride Ag & B
100 G4 Kilbuiack Moray
51 J10 Kilburn Derbys
21 K6 Kilburn Gt Lon
66 D10 Kilburn N York
41 N8 Kilby Leics
83 M10 Kilchamaig Ag & B
82 E4 Kilchattan Ag & B
84 B11 Kilchattan Ag & B
89 Q8 Kilcheran Ag & B
89 K4 Kilchoan Highld
82 C9 Kilchoman Ag & B
90 E10 Kilchrenan Ag & B
87 J2 Kilconquhar Fife
29 J4 Kilcot Gloucs
107 J11 Kilcoy Highld
84 D6 Kilcreggan Ag & B
66 E5 Kildale N York
75 L8 Kildalloig Ag & B
107 M7 Kildary Highld
83 Q9 Kildavaig Ag & B
83 Q9 Kildavanan Ag & B
109 Q10 Kildonan Highld
75 Q8 Kildonan N Ayrs
109 Q10 Kildonan Lodge Highld
96 F11 Kildonnan Highld
68 E7 Kildrochet House D & G
101 N10 Kildrummy Abers
58 D5 Kildwick N York
83 P7 Kilfinan Ag & B
98 C9 Kilfinnan Highld
25 K7 Kilgetty Pembks
76 E10 Kilgrammie S Ayrs
28 F8 Kilgwrrwg Common Mons
60 H2 Kilham E R Yk
88 B7 Kilkenneth Ag & B
75 K7 Kilkenzie Ag & B
75 L8 Kilkerran Ag & B
14 E9 Kilkhampton Cnwll
51 L5 Killamarsh Derbys
26 E9 Killay Swans
85 J6 Killearn Stirlg
107 L10 Killen Highld
65 L4 Killerby Darltn
6 D3 Killerton Devon
91 M5 Killichonan P & K
89 L7 Killiechronan Ag & B
92 D3 Killiecrankie P & K
97 N4 Killilan Highld
91 N9 Killin Stirlg
58 H3 Killinghall N York
63 L5 Killington Cumb
73 M6 Killingworth N Tyne
87 J12 Killochyett Border
84 F8 Kilmacolm Inver
85 K2 Kilmahog Stirlg
83 L4 Kilmahumaig Ag & B
104 F7 Kilmaluag Highld
93 L10 Kilmany Fife
76 G4 Kilmarnock E Ayrs
83 M3 Kilmartin Ag & B
76 G3 Kilmaurs E Ayrs
83 M1 Kilmelford Ag & B
17 Q6 Kilmersdon Somset
9 P3 Kilmeston Hants
75 K7 Kilmichael Ag & B
83 N4 Kilmichael Glassary Ag & B
83 L6 Kilmichael of Inverlussa Ag & B
6 H4 Kilmington Devon
18 B12 Kilmington Wilts
8 B1 Kilmington Common Wilts
8 B1 Kilmington Street Wilts
106 H12 Kilmorack Highld
90 B10 Kilmore Ag & B
97 J8 Kilmore Highld
83 K7 Kilmory Ag & B
89 L3 Kilmory Highld
75 P7 Kilmory N Ayrs
104 C11 Kilmuir Highld
104 E8 Kilmuir Highld
107 L11 Kilmuir Highld
107 M7 Kilmuir Highld
84 C6 Kilmun Ag & B
82 D8 Kilnave Ag & B
77 P2 Kilncadzow S Lans
12 E3 Kilndown Kent
89 Q11 Kilninver Ag & B
73 J9 Kiln Pit Hill Nthumb
61 P10 Kilnsea E R Yk
58 C1 Kilnsey N York
60 G4 Kilnwick E R Yk
82 E4 Kiloran Ag & B
75 N7 Kilpatrick N Ayrs
28 E3 Kilpeck Herefs
60 D8 Kilpin E R Yk
87 L2 Kilrenny Fife
41 M12 Kilsby Nhants
93 J9 Kilspindie P & K
68 F10 Kilstay D & G
85 M7 Kilsyth N Lans
98 G2 Kiltarlity Highld
66 F4 Kilton R & Cl
66 F4 Kilton Thorpe R & Cl
104 E8 Kilvaxter Highld
16 F7 Kilve Somset
42 B2 Kilvington Notts
76 E3 Kilwinning N Ayrs
44 H8 Kimberley Norfk
51 L11 Kimberley Notts
51 K3 Kimberworth Rothm
73 M10 Kimblesworth Dur
32 F4 Kimbolton Cambs
39 K9 Kimbolton Herefs
41 N9 Kimcote Leics
8 D10 Kimmeridge Dorset
19 J10 Kimpton Hants
32 H11 Kimpton Herts
109 Q8 Kinbrace Highld
85 N3 Kinbuck Stirlg
93 N11 Kincaple Fife
85 Q5 Kincardine Fife
107 K5 Kincardine Highld
95 K3 Kincardine O'Neil Abers
92 H7 Kinclaven P & K
95 Q2 Kincorth C Aber
100 F3 Kincorth House Moray
99 M7 Kincraig Highld
92 E6 Kincraigie P & K
92 E6 Kindallachan P & K
75 J2 Kinerarach Ag & B
30 E8 Kineton Gloucs
31 J4 Kineton Warwks
92 H10 Kinfauns P & K
76 F4 Kinfold S Ayrs
84 B10 Kingarth Ag & B
47 M9 King Arthur's Labyrinth Gwynd
95 P3 Kingcausie Abers
28 E7 Kingcoed Mons
52 F5 Kingerby Lincs
14 E10 Kingford Devon
30 H8 Kingham Oxon
70 F2 Kingholm Quay D & G
86 F5 Kinghorn Fife
86 E3 Kinglassie Fife
93 L5 Kingoldrum Angus
93 L9 Kingoodie P & K
5 J9 Kingsand Cnwll
93 Q12 Kingsbarns Fife
5 P10 Kingsbridge Devon
16 D8 Kingsbridge Somset
40 E4 King's Bromley Staffs
104 E10 Kingsburgh Highld
21 J5 Kingsbury Gt Lon
40 G8 Kingsbury Warwks
17 L11 Kingsbury Episcopi Somset
28 G3 Kings Caple Herefs
19 N8 Kingsclere Hants
42 E10 King's Cliffe Nhants
29 L9 Kingscote Gloucs
15 J8 Kingscott Devon
30 E3 King's Coughton Warwks
75 Q6 Kingscross N Ayrs
17 M10 Kingsdon Somset
13 Q1 Kingsdown Kent
18 H3 Kingsdown Swindn
18 B7 Kingsdown Wilts
86 D4 Kingseat Fife
20 C3 Kingsey Bucks
11 J3 Kingsfold W Susx
95 P1 Kingsford C Aber
76 H2 Kingsford E Ayrs
23 Q8 Kingsgate Kent
34 F4 Kingshall Street Suffk
15 K5 Kingsheanton Devon
40 E10 King's Heath Birm
22 D11 Kings Hill Kent
40 C8 King's Hill Wsall
90 H5 Kings House Hotel Highld
91 N11 Kingshouse Hotel Stirlg
6 B8 Kingskerswell Devon
86 G1 Kingskettle Fife
39 J9 Kingsland Herefs
54 C5 Kingsland IoA
20 H3 Kings Langley Herts
49 K1 Kingsley Ches
10 C3 Kingsley Hants
50 D10 Kingsley Staffs
10 E4 Kingsley Green W Susx
31 Q2 Kingsley Park Nhants
43 P6 King's Lynn Norfk
64 B4 Kings Meaburn Cumb
6 b2 King's Mills Guern
93 N6 Kingsmuir Angus
79 L2 Kings Muir Border
87 K1 Kingsmuir Fife
41 L11 Kings Newnham Warwks
13 J3 Kingsnorth Kent
40 D10 King's Norton Birm
41 P7 King's Norton Leics
15 M8 King's Nympton Devon
38 H11 King's Pyon Herefs
33 J2 Kings Ripton Cambs
9 L2 King's Somborne Hants
7 Q1 King's Stag Dorset
29 L7 King's Stanley Gloucs
31 L6 King's Sutton Nhants
40 E8 Kingstanding Birm
6 B8 Kingsteignton Devon
28 F3 Kingsthorne Herefs
31 Q2 Kingsthorpe Nhants
33 K6 Kingston Cambs
4 H5 Kingston Cnwll
5 M10 Kingston Devon
7 Q2 Kingston Dorset
8 E10 Kingston Dorset
87 K6 Kingston E Loth
9 N10 Kingston IoW
23 M12 Kingston Kent
19 L2 Kingston Bagpuize Oxon
20 B4 Kingston Blount Oxon
18 C12 Kingston Deverill Wilts
28 E2 Kingstone Herefs
17 K12 Kingstone Somset
40 D2 Kingstone Staffs
19 K4 Kingston Lisle Oxon
11 N8 Kingston near Lewes E Susx
41 L2 Kingston on Soar Notts
101 L3 Kingston on Spey Moray
7 N5 Kingston Russell Dorset
16 G9 Kingston St Mary Somset
17 K3 Kingston Seymour N Som
61 J8 Kingston upon Hull C KuH
21 J9 Kingston upon Thames Gt Lon
32 G11 King's Walden Herts
6 B11 Kingswear Devon
95 P1 Kingswells C Aber
28 G12 Kings Weston Bristl
40 B9 Kingswinford Dudley
31 P9 Kingswood Bucks
29 K9 Kingswood Gloucs
17 P2 Kingswood S Glos
16 F8 Kingswood Somset
21 K11 Kingswood Surrey
40 F12 Kingswood Warwks
39 Q2 Kingswood Common Staffs
9 N2 Kings Worthy Hants
52 G8 Kingthorpe Lincs
38 F10 Kington Herefs
28 H10 Kington S Glos
30 C3 Kington Worcs
18 D5 Kington Langley Wilts
8 B3 Kington Magna Dorset
18 D5 Kington St Michael Wilts
99 L8 Kingussie Highld
17 M9 Kingweston Somset
103 J8 Kinharrachie Abers
70 F3 Kinharvie D & G
92 D11 Kinkell Bridge P & K
103 L7 Kinknockie Abers
86 E8 Kinleith C Edin
39 N6 Kinlet Shrops
96 E9 Kinloch Highld
108 G8 Kinloch Highld
109 K5 Kinloch Highld
92 H6 Kinloch P & K
93 J6 Kinloch P & K
84 H3 Kinlochard Stirlg
108 E4 Kinlochbervie Highld
90 D1 Kinlocheil Highld
105 Q9 Kinlochewe Highld
97 N8 Kinloch Hourn Highld
98 G10 Kinlochlaggan Highld
90 G4 Kinlochleven Highld
89 P2 Kinlochmoidart Highld
97 K11 Kinlochnanuagh Highld
91 P5 Kinloch Rannoch P & K
100 G3 Kinloss Moray
55 P5 Kinmel Bay Conwy
102 H10 Kinmuck Abers
103 J10 Kinmundy Abers
74 D4 Kinnabus Ag & B
103 K6 Kinnadie Abers
92 E4 Kinnaird P & K
93 Q4 Kinnaird Castle Angus
101 J2 Kinneddar Moray
95 N6 Kinneff Abers
78 G8 Kinnelhead D & G
93 Q5 Kinnell Angus
48 G10 Kinnerley Shrops
38 G11 Kinnersley Herefs
39 Q12 Kinnersley Worcs
38 E9 Kinnerton Powys
86 E2 Kinnesswood P & K
65 J3 Kinninvie Dur
93 L5 Kinnordy Angus
41 P2 Kinoulton Notts
86 D2 Kinross P & K
92 H8 Kinrossie P & K
38 G8 Kinsham Herefs
29 N2 Kinsham Worcs
59 K10 Kinsley Wakefd
8 F7 Kinson Bmouth
97 P6 Kintail Highld
19 L7 Kintbury W Berk
100 F4 Kintessack Moray
92 G11 Kintillo P & K
38 H7 Kinton Herefs
48 G10 Kinton Shrops
102 G11 Kintore Abers
74 F3 Kintour Ag & B
88 H10 Kintra Ag & B
83 M3 Kintraw Ag & B
75 L5 Kintyre Ag & B
99 N5 Kinveachy Highld
39 Q5 Kinver Staffs
59 K7 Kippax Leeds
85 L4 Kippen Stirlg
70 D5 Kippford or Scaur D & G
12 D3 Kipping's Cross Kent
111 h2 Kirbister Ork
45 L8 Kirby Bedon Norfk
41 Q4 Kirby Bellars Leics
45 N10 Kirby Cane Norfk
35 K11 Kirby Cross Essex
41 M6 Kirby Fields Leics
60 F1 Kirby Grindalythe N York
59 K1 Kirby Hill N York
65 K6 Kirby Hill N York
66 C9 Kirby Knowle N York
35 K11 Kirby le Soken Essex
66 H10 Kirby Misperton N York
41 M6 Kirby Muxloe Leics
45 N10 Kirby Row Norfk
65 P8 Kirby Sigston N York
60 D3 Kirby Underdale E R Yk
65 P9 Kirby Wiske N York
10 G5 Kirdford W Susx
110 F4 Kirk Highld
111 k4 Kirkabister Shet
69 N9 Kirkandrews D & G
71 M4 Kirkandrews upon Eden Cumb
71 L4 Kirkbampton Cumb
70 F4 Kirkbean D & G
59 N10 Kirk Bramwith Donc
71 K4 Kirkbride Cumb
93 N7 Kirkbuddo Angus
79 L2 Kirkburn Border
60 G3 Kirkburn E R Yk
58 G10 Kirkburton Kirk
56 H8 Kirkby Knows
52 F5 Kirkby Lincs
66 D6 Kirkby N York
65 M8 Kirkby Fleetham N York
52 F11 Kirkby Green Lincs
51 L9 Kirkby in Ashfield Notts
62 E6 Kirkby-in-Furness Cumb
42 F2 Kirkby la Thorpe Lincs
63 L6 Kirkby Lonsdale Cumb
58 B3 Kirkby Malham N York

Kirkby Mallory - Leven 183

41 L7 **Kirkby Mallory** Leics
65 M11 **Kirkby Malzeard** N York
66 F9 **Kirkbymoorside** N York
53 J10 **Kirkby on Bain** Lincs
59 J4 **Kirkby Overblow** N York
64 E6 **Kirkby Stephen** Cumb
64 B3 **Kirkby Thore** Cumb
42 F5 **Kirkby Underwood** Lincs
59 L6 **Kirkby Wharf** N York
86 F4 **Kirkcaldy** Fife
71 Q2 **Kirkcambeck** Cumb
69 P8 **Kirkchrist** D & G
68 D5 **Kirkcolm** D & G
77 M8 **Kirkconnel** D & G
69 P7 **Kirkconnell** D & G
70 F2 **Kirkconnell** D & G
69 J7 **Kirkcowan** D & G
69 P8 **Kirkcudbright** D & G
56 G9 **Kirkdale** Lpool
59 K4 **Kirk Deighton** N York
60 H8 **Kirk Ella** E R Yk
77 P3 **Kirkfieldbank** S Lans
70 E3 **Kirkgunzeon** D & G
51 L11 **Kirk Hallam** Derbys
56 H3 **Kirkham** Lancs
60 C2 **Kirkham** N York
58 H9 **Kirkhamgate** Wakefd
59 L3 **Kirk Hammerton** N York
72 H4 **Kirkharle** Nthumb
72 C10 **Kirkhaugh** Nthumb
58 F9 **Kirkheaton** Kirk
72 H5 **Kirkheaton** Nthumb
107 J12 **Kirkhill** Highld
78 F7 **Kirkhope** S Lans
96 G6 **Kirkibost** Highld
93 K6 **Kirkinch** P & K
69 K8 **Kirkinner** D & G
85 L8 **Kirkintilloch** E Duns
50 H10 **Kirk Ireton** Derbys
70 H11 **Kirkland** Cumb
77 M8 **Kirkland** D & G
78 D10 **Kirkland** D & G
78 G10 **Kirkland** D & G
50 H11 **Kirk Langley** Derbys
66 E3 **Kirkleatham** R & Cl
66 B5 **Kirklevington** S on T
45 Q10 **Kirkley** Suffk
65 N10 **Kirklington** N York
51 P8 **Kirklington** Notts
71 N3 **Kirklinton** Cumb
86 D7 **Kirkliston** C Edin
69 L7 **Kirkmabreck** D & G
68 F10 **Kirkmaiden** D & G
65 M2 **Kirk Merrington** Dur
56 c4 **Kirk Michael** IoM
94 B9 **Kirkmichael** P & K
76 F9 **Kirkmichael** S Ayrs
77 N3 **Kirkmuirhill** S Lans
81 J8 **Kirknewton** Nthumb
86 D8 **Kirknewton** W Loth
101 P8 **Kirkney** Abers
85 P9 **Kirk of Shotts** N Lans
71 Q7 **Kirkoswald** Cumb
76 D9 **Kirkoswald** S Ayrs
78 E10 **Kirkpatrick** D & G
70 C2 **Kirkpatrick Durham** D & G
71 L2 **Kirkpatrick-Fleming** D & G
59 N11 **Kirk Sandall** Donc
62 D6 **Kirksanton** Cumb
59 M10 **Kirk Smeaton** N York
58 H7 **Kirkstall** Leeds
52 H10 **Kirkstead** Lincs
102 C8 **Kirkstile** Abers
79 M10 **Kirkstile** D & G
110 G2 **Kirkstyle** Highld
59 J9 **Kirkthorpe** Wakefd
102 E9 **Kirkton** Abers
102 H6 **Kirkton** Abers
78 F11 **Kirkton** D & G
93 L10 **Kirkton** Fife
97 L4 **Kirkton** Highld
97 N2 **Kirkton** Highld
92 E11 **Kirkton** P & K
79 K2 **Kirkton Manor** Border
93 K5 **Kirkton of Airlie** Angus
93 L7 **Kirkton of Auchterhouse** Angus
107 N11 **Kirkton of Barevan** Highld
92 H8 **Kirkton of Collace** P & K
101 M11 **Kirkton of Glenbuchat** Abers
103 K8 **Kirkton of Logie Buchan** Abers
95 J8 **Kirkton of Menmuir** Angus
93 N7 **Kirkton of Monikie** Angus
102 F8 **Kirkton of Rayne** Abers
95 N1 **Kirkton of Skene** Abers
93 L8 **Kirkton of Strathmartine** Angus
93 M7 **Kirkton of Tealing** Angus
102 D11 **Kirkton of Tough** Abers
103 K3 **Kirktown** Abers
103 M5 **Kirktown** Abers
102 E4 **Kirktown of Alvah** Abers
102 G9 **Kirktown of Bourtie** Abers
95 N5 **Kirktown of Fetteresso** Abers
101 L7 **Kirktown of Mortlach** Moray
103 L9 **Kirktown of Slains** Abers
86 D12 **Kirkurd** Border
111 h2 **Kirkwall** Ork
111 h2 **Kirkwall Airport** Ork
72 H4 **Kirkwhelpington** Nthumb
80 H8 **Kirk Yetholm** Border
61 J11 **Kirmington** N Linc
52 H5 **Kirmond le Mire** Lincs
84 C7 **Kirn** Ag & B
93 L5 **Kirriemuir** Angus
45 L10 **Kirstead Green** Norfk
71 K2 **Kirtlebridge** D & G
34 B5 **Kirtling** Cambs
34 B5 **Kirtling Green** Cambs
31 L9 **Kirtlington** Oxon
109 N3 **Kirtomy** Highld
43 K3 **Kirton** Lincs
51 P7 **Kirton** Notts
35 L8 **Kirton** Suffk
84 G7 **Kirtonhill** W Duns
52 D4 **Kirton in Lindsey** N Linc
69 K8 **Kirwaugh** D & G
97 L2 **Kishorn** Highld
31 P3 **Kislingbury** Nhants
16 E10 **Kittisford** Somset
95 Q1 **Kittybrewster** C Aber
28 F3 **Kivernoll** Herefs
51 L4 **Kiveton Park** Rothm
52 B6 **Knaith** Lincs
8 B3 **Knap Corner** Dorset
20 F10 **Knaphill** Surrey
17 J10 **Knapp** Somset
67 J11 **Knapton** N York
45 M4 **Knapton** Norfk
59 M4 **Knapton** York
33 K4 **Knapwell** Cambs
59 J3 **Knaresborough** N York
72 C9 **Knarsdale** Nthumb
103 J6 **Knaven** Abers
66 B9 **Knayton** N York
33 J11 **Knebworth** Herts
60 C8 **Knedlington** E R Yk
51 P7 **Kneesall** Notts
33 K7 **Kneesworth** Cambs
51 P10 **Kneeton** Notts
26 C10 **Knelston** Swans
50 B12 **Knenhall** Staffs
31 K4 **Knightcote** Warwks
49 P9 **Knightley** Staffs
41 N7 **Knighton** C Leic
7 N1 **Knighton** Dorset
38 F7 **Knighton** Powys
16 G7 **Knighton** Somset
49 N7 **Knighton** Staffs
49 N9 **Knighton** Staffs
39 L7 **Knighton on Teme** Worcs
39 N10 **Knightwick** Worcs
38 F9 **Knill** Herefs
42 B4 **Knipton** Leics
50 G10 **Kniveton** Derbys
64 C3 **Knock** Cumb
97 J7 **Knock** Highld
102 C5 **Knock** Moray
111 d2 **Knock** W Isls
110 D9 **Knockally** Highld
106 D1 **Knockan** Highld
101 J7 **Knockando** Moray
98 H1 **Knockbain** Highld
107 K10 **Knockbain** Highld
84 D9 **Knock Castle** N Ayrs
110 D4 **Knockdee** Highld
18 C3 **Knockdown** Wilts
76 E11 **Knockeen** S Ayrs
75 Q7 **Knockenkelly** N Ayrs
76 G4 **Knockentiber** E Ayrs
21 P10 **Knockholt** Kent
21 P10 **Knockholt Pound** Kent
48 G10 **Knockin** Shrops
76 G4 **Knockinlaw** E Ayrs
68 C6 **Knocknain** D & G
69 N3 **Knocksheen** D & G
70 C2 **Knockvennie Smithy** D & G
35 N4 **Knodishall** Suffk
17 L10 **Knole** Somset
57 P11 **Knolls Green** Ches
48 H7 **Knolton** Wrexhm
18 D11 **Knook** Wilts
42 B8 **Knossington** Leics
62 G11 **Knott End-on-Sea** Lancs
32 E4 **Knotting** Beds
32 E4 **Knotting Green** Beds
59 L9 **Knottingley** Wakefd
56 H9 **Knotty Ash** Lpool
39 L7 **Knowbury** Shrops
69 J5 **Knowe** D & G
69 N2 **Knowehead** D & G
76 E8 **Knoweside** S Ayrs
17 N3 **Knowle** Bristl
6 D2 **Knowle** Devon
6 E6 **Knowle** Devon
15 J5 **Knowle** Devon
15 N10 **Knowle** Devon
39 L7 **Knowle** Shrops
40 F11 **Knowle** Solhll
16 C7 **Knowle** Somset
71 N4 **Knowlefield** Cumb
57 L2 **Knowle Green** Lancs
7 J1 **Knowle St Giles** Somset
20 D7 **Knowl Hill** W & M
56 H9 **Knowsley** Knows
57 J9 **Knowsley Safari Park** Knows
15 P7 **Knowstone** Devon
12 F2 **Knox Bridge** Kent
38 F7 **Knucklas** Powys
32 D4 **Knuston** Nhants
57 N12 **Knutsford** Ches
58 D9 **Krumlin** Calder
2 G11 **Kuggar** Cnwll
97 K4 **Kyleakin** Highld
97 K4 **Kyle of Lochalsh** Highld
97 L5 **Kylerhea** Highld
108 E8 **Kylesku** Highld
97 L10 **Kylesmorar** Highld
111 c3 **Kyles Scalpay** W Isls
108 E8 **Kylestrome** Highld
49 M11 **Kynnersley** Wrekin
39 L8 **Kyrewood** Worcs

L

111 d2 **Lacasaigh** W Isls
111 d2 **Lacasdal** W Isls
52 H3 **Laceby** NE Lin
20 D4 **Lacey Green** Bucks
49 N2 **Lach Dennis** Ches
34 D3 **Lackford** Suffk
34 D3 **Lackford Green** Suffk
18 D7 **Lacock** Wilts
31 K3 **Ladbroke** Warwks
12 E1 **Laddingford** Kent
3 K5 **Ladock** Cnwll
111 i1 **Lady** Ork
93 K12 **Ladybank** Fife
78 F4 **Ladygill** S Lans
62 E5 **Lady Hall** Cumb
81 J5 **Ladykirk** Border
40 D9 **Ladywood** Birm
39 Q9 **Ladywood** Worcs
6 c1 **La Fontenelle** Guern
78 E10 **Lag** D & G
89 N4 **Laga** Highld
74 F4 **Lagavulin** Ag & B
75 P7 **Lagg** N Ayrs
98 D9 **Laggan** Highld
99 J9 **Laggan** Highld
7 a1 **La Greve de Lecq** Jersey
108 H4 **Laid** Highld
105 N4 **Laide** Highld
96 F11 **Laig** Highld
76 H2 **Laigh Clunch** E Ayrs
76 H3 **Laigh Fenwick** E Ayrs
77 K7 **Laigh Glenmuir** E Ayrs
85 M11 **Laighstonehall** S Lans
22 D5 **Laindon** Essex
107 J2 **Lairg** Highld
58 F7 **Laisterdyke** Brad
9 P10 **Lake** IoW
8 E8 **Lake** Poole
18 G11 **Lake** Wilts
62 E1 **Lake District National Park** Cumb
44 B12 **Lakenheath** Suffk
43 N10 **Lakesend** Norfk
27 J11 **Laleston** Brdgnd
86 E10 **Lamancha** Border
34 E9 **Lamarsh** Essex
45 L5 **Lamas** Norfk
80 G5 **Lambden** Border
12 D3 **Lamberhurst** Kent
12 D3 **Lamberhurst Down** Kent
81 K3 **Lamberton** Border
21 L7 **Lambeth** Gt Lon
34 B6 **Lambfair Green** Suffk
51 N10 **Lambley** Notts
72 C8 **Lambley** Nthumb
19 K5 **Lambourn** W Berk
21 P5 **Lambourne End** Essex
11 K3 **Lambs Green** W Susx
5 K5 **Lamerton** Devon
73 M8 **Lamesley** Gatesd
78 F3 **Lamington** S Lans
75 Q6 **Lamlash** N Ayrs
71 N8 **Lamonby** Cumb
2 C10 **Lamorna** Cnwll
3 K7 **Lamorran** Cnwll
37 J10 **Lampeter** Cerdgn
25 K6 **Lampeter Velfrey** Pembks
24 H8 **Lamphey** Pembks
70 H10 **Lamplugh** Cumb
41 Q11 **Lamport** Nhants
17 P8 **Lamyatt** Somset
77 P3 **Lanark** S Lans
63 J9 **Lancaster** Lancs
73 L10 **Lanchester** Dur
11 J8 **Lancing** W Susx
6 c1 **L'Ancresse** Guern
33 M4 **Landbeach** Cambs
14 H7 **Landcross** Devon
95 M2 **Landerberry** Abers
9 J4 **Landford** Wilts
110 E8 **Land-hallow** Highld
26 C9 **Landimore** Swans
15 K6 **Landkey** Devon
15 K6 **Landkey Town** Devon
26 F9 **Landore** Swans
4 H7 **Landrake** Cnwll
5 Q6 **Landscove** Devon
2 A10 **Land's End** Cnwll
2 B9 **Land's End Airport** Cnwll
5 J7 **Landulph** Cnwll
3 J4 **Lane** Cnwll
4 F4 **Laneast** Cnwll
20 D5 **Lane End** Bucks
18 B10 **Lane End** Wilts
40 G1 **Lane Ends** Derbys
62 C4 **Lane End Waberthwaite** Cumb
52 B8 **Laneham** Notts
65 K5 **Lane Head** Dur
72 F11 **Lanehead** Dur
16 H10 **Langaller** Somset
41 Q1 **Langar** Notts
84 F8 **Langbank** Rens
58 E4 **Langbar** N York
63 P8 **Langcliffe** N York
67 K8 **Langdale End** N York
9 M6 **Langdown** Hants
86 G2 **Langdyke** Fife
34 G11 **Langenhoe** Essex
32 H8 **Langford** Beds
6 D3 **Langford** Devon
22 G2 **Langford** Essex
52 B10 **Langford** Notts
30 G12 **Langford** Oxon
16 F10 **Langford Budville** Somset
34 G9 **Langham** Essex
44 G2 **Langham** Norfk
42 B7 **Langham** Rutlnd
34 F3 **Langham** Suffk
57 N3 **Langho** Lancs
79 M11 **Langholm** D & G
80 C7 **Langlee** Border
9 M7 **Langley** Hants
32 H11 **Langley** Herts
22 F11 **Langley** Kent
72 E8 **Langley** Nthumb
20 G7 **Langley** Slough
16 E9 **Langley** Somset
10 D4 **Langley** W Susx
30 F2 **Langley** Warwks
18 D6 **Langley Burrell** Wilts
34 E11 **Langley Green** Essex
16 E9 **Langley Marsh** Somset
73 L11 **Langley Park** Dur
45 N9 **Langley Street** Norfk
33 M9 **Langley Upper Green** Essex
12 D9 **Langney** E Susx
51 N4 **Langold** Notts
4 G3 **Langore** Cnwll
17 K10 **Langport** Somset
43 J1 **Langrick** Lincs
17 Q3 **Langridge** BaNES
71 J6 **Langrigg** Cumb
10 B5 **Langrish** Hants
50 G2 **Langsett** Barns
92 B11 **Langside** P & K
10 B8 **Langstone** Hants
65 M8 **Langthorne** N York
59 K1 **Langthorpe** N York
64 H7 **Langthwaite** N York
60 H2 **Langtoft** E R Yk
42 G7 **Langtoft** Lincs
65 L4 **Langton** Dur
52 H9 **Langton** Lincs
53 L9 **Langton** Lincs
60 D2 **Langton** N York
52 G7 **Langton by Wragby** Lincs
12 B3 **Langton Green** Kent
7 N6 **Langton Herring** Dorset
8 E10 **Langton Matravers** Dorset
14 H8 **Langtree** Devon
71 R8 **Langwathby** Cumb
110 D10 **Langwell House** Highld
52 F8 **Langworth** Lincs
3 N3 **Lanhydrock House & Gardens** Cnwll
3 M3 **Lanivet** Cnwll
3 N1 **Lank** Cnwll
3 N4 **Lanlivery** Cnwll
2 G7 **Lanner** Cnwll
4 E8 **Lanreath** Cnwll
4 E9 **Lansallos** Cnwll
4 D4 **Lanteglos** Cnwll
4 E9 **Lanteglos Highway** Cnwll
80 E9 **Lanton** Border
81 K7 **Lanton** Nthumb
15 M9 **Lapford** Devon
74 E4 **Laphroaig** Ag & B
49 Q11 **Lapley** Staffs
40 F12 **Lapworth** Warwks
89 N6 **Larachbeg** Highld
85 P6 **Larbert** Falk
102 D8 **Largie** Abers
83 P6 **Largiemore** Ag & B
87 J1 **Largoward** Fife
84 D10 **Largs** N Ayrs
75 Q7 **Largybeg** N Ayrs
75 Q7 **Largymore** N Ayrs
84 D7 **Larkfield** Inver
22 E10 **Larkfield** Kent
77 M2 **Larkhall** S Lans
18 G11 **Larkhill** Wilts
44 G11 **Larling** Norfk
7 c2 **La Rocque** Jersey
64 H4 **Lartington** Dur
10 A2 **Lasham** Hants
50 B9 **Lask Edge** Staffs
86 D4 **Lassodie** Fife
86 G8 **Lasswade** Mdloth
66 G9 **Lastingham** N York
22 G4 **Latchingdon** Essex
5 J5 **Latchley** Cnwll
32 C7 **Lathbury** M Keyn
110 E8 **Latheron** Highld
110 E8 **Latheronwheel** Highld
87 J1 **Lathones** Fife
20 G4 **Latimer** Bucks
29 J10 **Latteridge** S Glos
17 Q10 **Lattiford** Somset
18 G2 **Latton** Wilts
80 C5 **Lauder** Border
25 M6 **Laugharne** Carmth
52 B8 **Laughterton** Lincs
11 P7 **Laughton** E Susx
41 P9 **Laughton** Leics
42 F4 **Laughton** Lincs
52 B4 **Laughton** Lincs
51 M4 **Laughton-en-le-Morthen** Rothm
14 E10 **Launcells** Cnwll
4 H4 **Launceston** Cnwll
31 N9 **Launton** Oxon
95 L7 **Laurencekirk** Abers
69 P6 **Laurieston** D & G
85 Q7 **Laurieston** Falk
32 D6 **Lavendon** M Keyn
34 F7 **Lavenham** Suffk
16 G3 **Lavernock** V Glam
71 P3 **Laversdale** Cumb
8 H2 **Laverstock** Wilts
19 N10 **Laverstoke** Hants
30 E7 **Laverton** Gloucs
65 M11 **Laverton** N York
18 B9 **Laverton** Somset
6 b2 **La Villette** Guern
48 G4 **Lavister** Wrexhm
85 N11 **Law** S Lans
91 Q8 **Lawers** P & K
34 H9 **Lawford** Essex
16 F8 **Lawford** Somset
92 G9 **Lawgrove** P & K
85 N11 **Law Hill** S Lans
4 H4 **Lawhitton** Cnwll
63 P8 **Lawkland** N York
24 H7 **Lawrenny** Pembks
34 E6 **Lawshall** Suffk
111 d2 **Laxay** W Isls
111 d2 **Laxdale** W Isls
56 d4 **Laxey** IoM
35 L3 **Laxfield** Suffk
108 E6 **Laxford Bridge** Highld
111 K3 **Laxo** Shet
60 D8 **Laxton** E R Yk
42 D10 **Laxton** Nhants
51 Q7 **Laxton** Notts
58 D6 **Laycock** Brad
34 F12 **Layer Breton** Essex
34 F11 **Layer-de-la-Haye** Essex
34 F12 **Layer Marney** Essex
34 G8 **Layham** Suffk
7 K2 **Laymore** Dorset
60 D6 **Laytham** E R Yk
71 K4 **Laythes** Cumb
71 Q7 **Lazonby** Cumb
51 J8 **Lea** Derbys
28 H4 **Lea** Herefs
52 B6 **Lea** Lincs
38 G4 **Lea** Shrops
18 E4 **Lea** Wilts
107 K12 **Leachkin** Highld
86 F10 **Leadburn** Border
52 D11 **Leadenham** Lincs
22 C1 **Leaden Roding** Essex
73 K9 **Leadgate** Dur
78 E6 **Leadhills** S Lans
30 H10 **Leafield** Oxon
32 F11 **Leagrave** Luton
53 L11 **Leake Common Side** Lincs
66 G6 **Lealholm** N York
104 G9 **Lealt** Highld
40 G8 **Lea Marston** Warwks
31 K1 **Leamington Hastings** Warwks
30 H2 **Leamington Spa** Warwks
12 C7 **Leap Cross** E Susx
63 J5 **Leasgill** Cumb
42 F1 **Leasingham** Lincs
65 M2 **Leasingthorne** Dur
21 J11 **Leatherhead** Surrey
58 G5 **Leathley** N York
49 J10 **Leaton** Shrops
23 J11 **Leaveland** Kent
34 F8 **Leavenheath** Suffk
60 D2 **Leavening** N York
21 N10 **Leaves Green** Gt Lon
67 M10 **Lebberston** N York
6 b2 **Le Bourg** Guern
18 H2 **Lechlade on Thames** Gloucs
82 D8 **Lecht Gruinart** Ag & B
63 M6 **Leck** Lancs
91 Q8 **Leckbuie** P & K
19 L12 **Leckford** Hants
31 Q6 **Leckhampstead** Bucks
19 M5 **Leckhampstead** W Berk
19 M5 **Leckhampstead Thicket** W Berk
29 N5 **Leckhampton** Gloucs
106 C4 **Leckmelm** Highld
60 H5 **Leconfield** E R Yk
90 C8 **Ledaig** Ag & B
32 C11 **Ledburn** Bucks
29 J2 **Ledbury** Herefs
38 H11 **Ledgemoor** Herefs
108 E12 **Ledmore Junction** Highld
59 L8 **Ledsham** Leeds
59 K8 **Ledston** Leeds
31 K8 **Ledwell** Oxon
14 H3 **Lee** Devon
21 M8 **Lee** Gt Lon
39 J3 **Leebotwood** Shrops
49 K9 **Lee Brockhurst** Shrops
62 E8 **Leece** Cumb
22 E6 **Lee Chapel** Essex
20 E3 **Lee Clump** Bucks
22 G11 **Leeds** Kent
58 H7 **Leeds** Leeds
58 G6 **Leeds Bradford Airport** Leeds
22 G11 **Leeds Castle** Kent
2 E8 **Leedstown** Cnwll
50 C9 **Leek** Staffs
30 H1 **Leek Wootton** Warwks
5 M8 **Lee Mill** Devon
65 N9 **Leeming** N York
65 M9 **Leeming Bar** N York
9 P7 **Lee-on-the-Solent** Hants
50 H12 **Lees** Derbys
58 C12 **Lees** Oldham
50 H12 **Lees Green** Derbys
42 B7 **Leesthorpe** Leics
48 F4 **Leeswood** Flints
93 J10 **Leetown** P & K
49 M2 **Leftwich** Ches
53 L6 **Legbourne** Lincs
80 D5 **Legerwood** Border
20 F8 **Legoland** W & M
52 G6 **Legsby** Lincs
41 N6 **Leicester** C Leic
41 M6 **Leicester Forest East** Leics
7 N2 **Leigh** Dorset
29 M4 **Leigh** Gloucs
12 B2 **Leigh** Kent
11 K1 **Leigh** Surrey
57 M8 **Leigh** Wigan
18 F3 **Leigh** Wilts
39 P10 **Leigh** Worcs
22 F6 **Leigh Beck** Essex
18 C5 **Leigh Delamere** Wilts
12 H4 **Leigh Green** Kent
77 K2 **Leigh Knoweglass** S Lans
22 G6 **Leigh-on-Sea** Sthend
8 F7 **Leigh Park** Dorset
39 P11 **Leigh Sinton** Worcs
40 D7 **Leighswood** Wsall
29 L9 **Leighterton** Gloucs
38 E2 **Leighton** Powys
39 L2 **Leighton** Shrops
32 G2 **Leighton Bromswold** Cambs
32 D10 **Leighton Buzzard** Beds
17 Q6 **Leigh upon Mendip** Somset
17 N2 **Leigh Woods** N Som
39 J8 **Leinthall Earls** Herefs
38 H8 **Leinthall Starkes** Herefs
38 H7 **Leintwardine** Herefs
41 M9 **Leire** Leics
35 P4 **Leiston** Suffk
93 J6 **Leitfie** P & K
86 F7 **Leith** C Edin
80 G5 **Leitholm** Border
2 E8 **Lelant** Cnwll
61 L7 **Lelley** E R Yk
80 G7 **Lempitlaw** Border
111 d3 **Lemreway** W Isls
21 K2 **Lemsford** Herts
30 D5 **Lenchwick** Worcs
68 F2 **Lendalfoot** S Ayrs
85 J2 **Lendrick** Stirlg
103 M7 **Lendrum Terrace** Abers
22 H11 **Lenham** Kent
22 H12 **Lenham Heath** Kent
98 G4 **Lenie** Highld
80 H6 **Lennel** Border
69 N8 **Lennox Plunton** D & G
85 K7 **Lennoxtown** E Duns
51 M11 **Lenton** C Nott
42 E4 **Lenton** Lincs
44 H6 **Lenwade** Norfk
85 L8 **Lenzie** E Duns
102 C12 **Leochel-Cushnie** Abers
39 J9 **Leominster** Herefs
29 L7 **Leonard Stanley** Gloucs
104 B11 **Lephin** Highld
60 D2 **Leppington** N York
58 G10 **Lepton** Kirk
6 a2 **L'Eree** Guern
4 E8 **Lerryn** Cnwll
111 k4 **Lerwick** Shet
81 P10 **Lesbury** Nthumb
102 D9 **Leslie** Abers
86 F2 **Leslie** Fife
78 D2 **Lesmahagow** S Lans
4 E3 **Lesnewth** Cnwll
6 c1 **Les Quartiers** Guern
7 a2 **Les Quennevais** Jersey
45 N5 **Lessingham** Norfk
71 K5 **Lessonhall** Cumb
68 D6 **Leswalt** D & G
7 a1 **L'Etacq** Jersey
21 J4 **Letchmore Heath** Herts
32 H9 **Letchworth Garden City** Herts
19 L4 **Letcombe Bassett** Oxon
19 L4 **Letcombe Regis** Oxon
93 P6 **Letham** Angus
80 F11 **Letham** Border
85 P6 **Letham** Falk
93 K11 **Letham** Fife
93 Q6 **Letham Grange** Angus
92 G7 **Lethendy** P & K
102 D10 **Lethenty** Abers
102 H7 **Lethenty** Abers
35 L5 **Letheringham** Suffk
44 H3 **Letheringsett** Norfk
105 P7 **Letterewe** Highld
97 M5 **Letterfearn** Highld
98 C10 **Letterfinlay Lodge Hotel** Highld
97 K10 **Lettermorar** Highld
106 C5 **Letters** Highld
78 E5 **Lettershaw** S Lans
24 G3 **Letterston** Pembks
99 Q5 **Lettoch** Highld
100 H8 **Lettoch** Highld
38 G11 **Letton** Herefs
21 L2 **Letty Green** Herts
51 M4 **Letwell** Rothm
93 M10 **Leuchars** Fife
111 d3 **Leumrabhagh** W Isls
111 d2 **Leurbost** W Isls
40 B4 **Levedale** Staffs
61 J5 **Leven** E R Yk

Milton-under-Wychwood - New Forest 187

30 H9 Milton-under-Wychwood Oxon
16 F10 Milverton Somset
30 H2 Milverton Warwks
40 C2 Milwich Staffs
83 P4 Minard Ag & B
29 M8 Minchinhampton Gloucs
16 C6 Minehead Somset
48 F5 Minera Wrexhm
18 F3 Minety Wilts
47 J4 Minffordd Gwynd
89 N3 Mingarrypark Highld
53 K10 Miningsby Lincs
4 G6 Minions Cnwll
76 F8 Minishant S Ayrs
47 P8 Minllyn Gwynd
69 K6 Minnigaff D & G
102 G4 Minnonie Abers
59 K2 Minskip N York
9 K5 Minstead Hants
10 D6 Minsted W Susx
23 J8 Minster Kent
23 P9 Minster Kent
38 G2 Minsterley Shrops
30 H10 Minster Lovell Oxon
29 K5 Minsterworth Gloucs
7 P2 Minterne Magna Dorset
52 H8 Minting Lincs
103 K6 Mintlaw Abers
80 D9 Minto Border
38 H4 Minton Shrops
70 F11 Mirehouse Cumb
58 G9 Mirfield Kirk
29 N7 Miserden Gloucs
27 L11 Miskin Rhondd
51 P2 Misson Notts
41 M10 Misterton Leics
51 Q2 Misterton Notts
7 L2 Misterton Somset
35 J9 Mistley Essex
21 L9 Mitcham Gt Lon
29 J5 Mitcheldean Gloucs
3 J5 Mitchell Cnwll
78 F9 Mitchellslacks D & G
28 F6 Mitchel Troy Mons
73 L4 Mitford Nthumb
2 H5 Mithian Cnwll
31 N7 Mixbury Oxon
57 P11 Mobberley Ches
50 D11 Mobberley Staffs
38 C4 Mochdre Powys
69 J9 Mochrum D & G
12 E1 Mockbeggar Kent
70 H10 Mockerkin Cumb
5 N9 Modbury Devon
50 B12 Moddershall Staffs
54 G4 Moelfre IoA
48 E9 Moelfre Powys
78 H7 Moffat D & G
32 G6 Mogerhanger Beds
40 H4 Moira Leics
23 K11 Molash Kent
96 E7 Mol-chlach Highld
48 E3 Mold Flints
58 F10 Moldgreen Kirk
33 P10 Molehill Green Essex
60 H6 Molescroft E R Yk
32 F2 Molesworth Cambs
15 N6 Molland Devon
48 H2 Mollington Ches
31 K5 Mollington Oxon
85 M8 Mollinsburn N Lans
95 M6 Mondynes Abers
35 L5 Monewden Suffk
92 F9 Moneydie P & K
78 C10 Moniaive D & G
93 N8 Monifieth Angus
93 N7 Monikie Angus
93 K11 Monimail Fife
21 K4 Monken Hadley Gt Lon
59 L8 Monk Fryston N York
39 L12 Monkhide Herefs
71 M4 Monkhill Cumb
39 L4 Monkhopton Shrops
39 J10 Monkland Herefs
14 H7 Monkleigh Devon
16 C3 Monknash V Glam
15 K10 Monkokehampton Devon
73 N6 Monkseaton N Tyne
34 F7 Monks Eleigh Suffk
11 K5 Monk's Gate W Susx
49 Q1 Monks Heath Ches
19 Q9 Monk Sherborne Hants
13 L3 Monks Horton Kent
16 E8 Monksilver Somset
41 L10 Monks Kirby Warwks
35 K4 Monk Soham Suffk
20 D3 Monks Risborough Bucks
53 M9 Monksthorpe Lincs
33 P10 Monk Street Essex
28 D8 Monkswood Mons
6 G3 Monkton Devon
23 P9 Monkton Kent
76 F6 Monkton S Ayrs
73 N8 Monkton S Tyne
18 B8 Monkton Combe BaNES
18 C12 Monkton Deverill Wilts
18 B7 Monkton Farleigh Wilts
16 H10 Monkton Heathfield Somset
7 J4 Monkton Wyld Dorset
73 P8 Monkwearmouth Sundld
9 Q2 Monkwood Hants
40 B7 Monmore Green Wolves
28 F6 Monmouth Mons
38 G12 Monnington on Wye Herefs
69 J10 Monreith D & G
17 M11 Montacute Somset
48 H11 Montford Shrops
48 H11 Montford Bridge Shrops
102 D10 Montgarrie Abers
77 J6 Montgarswood E Ayrs
38 E3 Montgomery Powys
95 L9 Montrose Angus
6 b2 Mont Saint Guern
19 K11 Monxton Hants
50 F7 Monyash Derbys
102 F11 Monymusk Abers
92 C9 Monzie P & K
85 L8 Moodiesburn N Lans
93 L11 Moonzie Fife
58 H6 Moor Allerton Leeds
53 J10 Moorby Lincs
8 E6 Moor Crichel Dorset
8 G8 Moordown Bmouth
57 L11 Moore Halton
58 D8 Moor End Calder
59 P10 Moorends Donc
51 L10 Moorgreen Notts
58 F6 Moorhead Brad
71 M4 Moorhouse Cumb
51 Q7 Moorhouse Notts
21 N11 Moorhouse Bank Surrey
17 K8 Moorlinch Somset
59 L3 Moor Monkton N York
66 F5 Moorsholm R & Cl
8 B4 Moorside Dorset
4 F7 Moorswater Cnwll
59 L11 Moorthorpe Wakefd
58 H6 Moortown Leeds
52 F4 Moortown Lincs
107 M5 Morangie Highld
97 J10 Morar Highld
42 G10 Morborne Cambs
15 N10 Morchard Bishop Devon
7 K4 Morcombelake Dorset
42 D9 Morcott RutInd
48 F9 Morda Shrops
8 D8 Morden Dorset
21 K9 Morden Gt Lon
28 G2 Mordiford Herefs
65 N3 Mordon Dur
38 G4 More Shrops
16 C10 Morebath Devon
80 G8 Morebattle Border
62 H8 Morecambe Lancs
18 G4 Moredon Swindn
106 B4 Morefield Highld
13 N3 Morehall Kent
5 P9 Moreleigh Devon
91 N8 Morenish P & K
9 N3 Morestead Hants
8 B9 Moreton Dorset
21 Q3 Moreton Essex
39 J8 Moreton Herefs
20 B3 Moreton Oxon
56 F10 Moreton Wirral
49 K10 Moreton Corbet Shrops
5 P3 Moretonhampstead Devon
30 G7 Moreton-in-Marsh Gloucs
39 L11 Moreton Jeffries Herefs
30 H3 Moreton Morrell Warwks
39 J11 Moreton on Lugg Herefs
31 M4 Moreton Pinkney Nhants
49 L8 Moreton Say Shrops
29 K6 Moreton Valence Gloucs
46 E4 Morfa Nefyn Gwynd
87 K7 Morham E Loth
64 B3 Morland Cumb
57 P11 Morley Ches
51 K11 Morley Derbys
58 H8 Morley Leeds
57 P11 Morley Green Ches
44 H9 Morley St Botolph Norfk
86 F7 Morningside C Edin
85 N11 Morningside N Lans
45 K10 Morningthorpe Norfk
73 L4 Morpeth Nthumb
95 L8 Morphie Abers
40 E4 Morrey Staffs
26 F8 Morriston Swans
44 G2 Morston Norfk
14 H3 Mortehoe Devon
51 L3 Morthen Rothm
19 Q7 Mortimer W Berk
19 Q7 Mortimer West End Hants
21 K8 Mortlake Gt Lon
71 N5 Morton Cumb
51 K8 Morton Derbys
42 F5 Morton Lincs
52 B5 Morton Lincs
51 Q9 Morton Notts
48 F9 Morton Shrops
65 N8 Morton-on-Swale N York
45 J6 Morton on the Hill Norfk
2 B8 Morvah Cnwll
4 G8 Morval Cnwll
97 N5 Morvich Highld
39 M4 Morville Shrops
5 J6 Morwellham Quay Devon
14 D8 Morwenstow Cnwll
51 K5 Mosborough Sheff
76 H4 Moscow E Ayrs
40 E10 Moseley Birm
40 C7 Moseley Wolves
39 P9 Moseley Worcs
88 B7 Moss Ag & B
59 N10 Moss Donc
101 N10 Mossat Abers
111 k3 Mossbank Shet
57 K8 Moss Bank St Hel
70 G9 Mossbay Cumb
76 G6 Mossblown S Ayrs
80 F10 Mossburnford Border
69 P5 Mossdale D & G
76 H9 Mossdale E Ayrs
62 H12 Moss Edge Lancs
85 M10 Mossend N Lans
50 C1 Mossley Tamesd
79 N8 Mosspaul Hotel Border
100 D4 Moss-side Highld
101 L4 Mosstodloch Moray
69 M8 Mossyard D & G
57 K6 Mossy Lea Lancs
7 L2 Mosterton Dorset
57 Q8 Moston Manch
56 D11 Mostyn Flints
8 C3 Motcombe Dorset
5 M10 Mothecombe Devon
71 N9 Motherby Cumb
85 M10 Motherwell N Lans
21 K9 Motspur Park Gt Lon
21 N8 Mottingham Gt Lon
9 K3 Mottisfont Hants
9 L10 Mottistone IoW
50 C2 Mottram in Longdendale Tamesd
57 Q12 Mottram St Andrew Ches
49 J2 Mouldsworth Ches
92 E4 Moulin P & K
11 M8 Moulsecoomb Br & H
19 P4 Moulsford Oxon
32 C8 Moulsoe M Keyn
107 K7 Moultavie Highld
49 M2 Moulton Ches
43 K5 Moulton Lincs
65 M6 Moulton N York
32 B4 Moulton Nhants
34 B4 Moulton Suffk
16 E3 Moulton V Glam
43 J6 Moulton Chapel Lincs
45 N8 Moulton St Mary Norfk
43 K5 Moulton Seas End Lincs
4 E6 Mount Cnwll
58 E7 Mountain Brad
27 L8 Mountain Ash Rhondd
86 D11 Mountain Cross Border
2 G7 Mount Ambrose Cnwll
34 E9 Mount Bures Essex
12 E6 Mountfield E Susx
107 J9 Mountgerald House Highld
2 G6 Mount Hawke Cnwll
3 K4 Mountjoy Cnwll
86 F10 Mount Lothian Mdloth
22 D4 Mountnessing Essex
28 F9 Mounton Mons
51 J10 Mount Pleasant Derbys
34 C7 Mount Pleasant Suffk
41 M5 Mountsorrel Leics
58 D8 Mount Tabor Calder
10 F2 Mousehill Surrey
2 C9 Mousehole Cnwll
70 H2 Mouswald D & G
80 H9 Mowhaugh Border
41 N9 Mowsley Leics
98 F11 Moy Highld
99 L3 Moy Highld
97 M6 Moye Highld
36 B10 Moylgrove Pembks
75 K4 Muasdale Ag & B
95 P4 Muchalls Abers
28 F3 Much Birch Herefs
39 L11 Much Cowarne Herefs
28 F3 Much Dewchurch Herefs
17 K10 Muchelney Somset
17 L10 Muchelney Ham Somset
33 L11 Much Hadham Herts
57 J4 Much Hoole Lancs
4 F8 Muchlarnick Cnwll
28 H3 Much Marcle Herefs
39 L3 Much Wenlock Shrops
44 H2 Muckleburgh Collection Norfk
49 N7 Mucklestone Staffs
53 L7 Muckton Lincs
15 K5 Muddiford Devon
12 B7 Muddles Green E Susx
8 H8 Mudeford Dorset
17 N11 Mudford Somset
17 M11 Mudford Sock Somset
85 J7 Mugdock Stirlg
96 E2 Mugeary Highld
50 H11 Mugginton Derbys
102 F5 Muirden Abers
93 P8 Muirdrum Angus
102 F5 Muiresk Abers
93 L8 Muirhead Angus
86 F2 Muirhead Fife
85 L8 Muirhead N Lans
77 L6 Muirkirk E Ayrs
85 M6 Muirmill Stirlg
102 D11 Muir of Fowlis Abers
101 J4 Muir of Miltonduff Moray
107 J11 Muir of Ord Highld
92 F8 Muir of Thorn P & K
98 A11 Muirshearlich Highld
103 K7 Muirtack Abers
85 Q1 Muirton P & K
106 H10 Muirton Mains Highld
92 H7 Muirton of Ardblair P & K
64 G7 Muker N York
45 K9 Mulbarton Norfk
101 L5 Mulben Moray
89 M8 Mull Ag & B
2 G11 Mullion Cnwll
2 F11 Mullion Cove Cnwll
53 N8 Mumby Lincs
39 M10 Munderfield Row Herefs
39 M11 Munderfield Stocks Herefs
45 M3 Mundesley Norfk
44 D10 Mundford Norfk
45 M9 Mundham Norfk
22 G3 Mundon Hill Essex
71 M9 Mungrisdale Cumb
107 K10 Munlochy Highld
76 E2 Munnoch N Ayrs
29 J1 Munsley Herefs
39 K5 Munslow Shrops
5 N3 Murchington Devon
31 N10 Murcott Oxon
110 D3 Murkle Highld
97 P10 Murlaggan Highld
93 N8 Murroes Angus
43 L8 Murrow Cambs
32 B10 Mursley Bucks
93 N4 Murthill Angus
92 G7 Murthly P & K
64 D3 Murton Cumb
73 P10 Murton Dur
81 K5 Murton Nthumb
59 P4 Murton York
6 H4 Musbury Devon
86 G7 Musselburgh E Loth
42 B3 Muston Leics
67 N10 Muston N York
21 L5 Muswell Hill Gt Lon
69 P8 Mutehill D & G
45 P11 Mutford Suffk
92 C11 Muthill P & K
110 D5 Mybster Highld
26 G3 Myddfai Carmth
49 J10 Myddle Shrops
36 G9 Mydroilyn Cerdgn
3 J8 Mylor Cnwll
3 J8 Mylor Bridge Cnwll
25 K3 Mynachlog ddu Pembks
38 H4 Myndtown Shrops
28 F9 Mynydd-bach Mons
26 E8 Mynydd-bach Swans
95 M3 Myrebird Abers
72 B2 Myredykes Border
20 E11 Mytchett Surrey
58 C8 Mytholm Calder
58 D8 Mytholmroyd Calder
59 K2 Myton-on-Swale N York

N

105 M6 Naast Highld
111 c3 Na Buirgh W Isls
59 N5 Naburn York
23 M11 Nackington Kent
35 K8 Nacton Suffk
60 H3 Nafferton E R Yk
16 G9 Nailsbourne Somset
17 L3 Nailsea N Som
41 K6 Nailstone Leics
29 L8 Nailsworth Gloucs
100 D4 Nairn Highld
48 D2 Nannerch Flints
41 L4 Nanpantan Leics
3 L5 Nanpean Cnwll
3 M3 Nanstallon Cnwll
36 F8 Nanternis Cerdgn
26 C5 Nantgaredig Carmth
55 Q8 Nantglyn Denbgs
38 B8 Nantmel Powys
47 K3 Nantmor Gwynd
54 H9 Nant Peris Gwynd
49 M5 Nantwich Ches
27 P6 Nantyglo Blae G
27 K9 Nant-y-moel Brdgnd
20 D4 Naphill Bucks
31 L2 Napton on the Hill Warwks
25 J6 Narberth Pembks
41 M7 Narborough Leics
44 C7 Narborough Norfk
54 F10 Nasareth Gwynd
41 P10 Naseby Nhants
32 B9 Nash Bucks
28 D11 Nash Newpt
39 L7 Nash Shrops
19 R10 Nash's Green Hants
42 F10 Nassington Nhants
64 E6 Nateby Cumb
63 J12 Nateby Lancs
41 N6 National Space Science Centre C Leic
63 K4 Natland Cumb
34 G7 Naughton Suffk
30 E9 Naunton Gloucs
29 M2 Naunton Worcs
30 C4 Naunton Beauchamp Worcs
52 E10 Navenby Lincs
21 Q4 Navestock Essex
22 C4 Navestock Side Essex
110 B11 Navidale House Hotel Highld
107 N8 Navity Highld
66 F9 Nawton N York
34 F9 Nayland Suffk
21 N3 Nazeing Essex
111 k4 Neap Shet
50 E10 Near Cotton Staffs
62 G3 Near Sawrey Cumb
21 K6 Neasden Gt Lon
65 N5 Neasham Darltn
26 G8 Neath Neath
10 C3 Neatham Hants
45 M6 Neatishead Norfk
37 J7 Nebo Cerdgn
55 M9 Nebo Conwy
54 F10 Nebo Gwynd
54 F4 Nebo IoA
44 E8 Necton Norfk
108 C8 Nedd Highld
34 G7 Nedging Suffk
34 G6 Nedging Tye Suffk
35 K1 Needham Norfk
34 H6 Needham Market Suffk
33 K3 Needingworth Cambs
39 M6 Neen Savage Shrops
39 M7 Neen Sollars Shrops
39 M5 Neenton Shrops
46 E4 Nefyn Gwynd
84 H10 Neilston E Rens
27 M9 Nelson Caerph
57 Q2 Nelson Lancs
77 P3 Nemphlar S Lans
17 M4 Nempnett Thrubwell BaNES
72 E11 Nenthead Cumb
80 F6 Nenthorn Border
48 E4 Nercwys Flints
82 C11 Nereabolls Ag & B
85 L10 Nerston S Lans
81 K7 Nesbit Nthumb
58 E4 Nesfield N York
48 F1 Ness Botanic Gardens Ches
48 H10 Nesscliffe Shrops
56 F12 Neston Ches
18 C7 Neston Wilts
39 L4 Netchwood Shrops
49 Q1 Nether Alderley Ches
18 G10 Netheravon Wilts
80 D5 Nether Blainslie Border
102 G4 Netherbrae Abers
41 P3 Nether Broughton Leics
77 N2 Netherburn S Lans
7 L3 Netherbury Dorset
59 J5 Netherby N York
7 P3 Nether Cerne Dorset
79 J10 Nethercleuch D & G
17 N11 Nether Compton Dorset
102 H10 Nether Crimond Abers
101 M3 Nether Dallachy Moray
28 G8 Netherend Gloucs
6 C3 Nether Exe Devon
12 E6 Netherfield E Susx
12 E6 Netherfield Road E Susx
78 F6 Nether Fingland S Lans
8 G2 Netherhampton Wilts
93 L7 Nether Handwick Angus
51 K2 Nether Haugh Rothm
7 K2 Netherhay Dorset
51 Q5 Nether Headon Notts
51 J10 Nether Heage Derbys
31 P3 Nether Heyford Nhants
78 G6 Nether Howcleugh S Lans
63 J8 Nether Kellet Lancs
103 L6 Nether Kinmundy Abers
51 M6 Nether Langwith Notts
70 C6 Netherlaw D & G
95 P4 Netherley Abers
78 G10 Nethermill D & G
51 J7 Nether Moor Derbys
103 J6 Nethermuir Abers
21 L11 Netherne-on-the-Hill Surrey
58 F9 Netheroyd Hill Kirk
50 G5 Nether Padley Derbys
85 J11 Netherplace E Rens
59 M4 Nether Poppleton York
40 H5 Netherseal Derbys
66 C8 Nether Silton N York
16 G8 Nether Stowey Somset
58 F11 Netherthong Kirk
93 P4 Netherton Angus
6 B8 Netherton Devon
40 C9 Netherton Dudley
58 F10 Netherton Kirk
85 N11 Netherton N Lans
81 K11 Netherton Nthumb
92 H5 Netherton P & K
39 N5 Netherton Shrops
85 J7 Netherton Stirlg
58 H10 Netherton Wakefd
62 B1 Nethertown Cumb
110 G1 Nethertown Highld
40 E4 Nethertown Staffs
86 D12 Netherurd Border
19 K12 Nether Wallop Hants
62 D2 Nether Wasdale Cumb
30 G9 Nether Westcote Gloucs
40 G8 Nether Whitacre Warwks
78 D5 Nether Whitecleuch S Lans
31 Q10 Nether Winchendon Bucks
73 K3 Netherwitton Nthumb
99 Q5 Nethy Bridge Highld
9 M6 Netley Hants
9 K5 Netley Marsh Hants
20 B6 Nettlebed Oxon
17 P6 Nettlebridge Somset
7 M4 Nettlecombe Dorset
20 G2 Nettleden Herts
52 E8 Nettleham Lincs
22 D11 Nettlestead Kent
22 D12 Nettlestead Green Kent
9 Q8 Nettlestone IoW
73 M10 Nettlesworth Dur
52 G4 Nettleton Lincs
18 B5 Nettleton Wilts
18 G12 Netton Wilts
36 B11 Nevern Pembks
42 B10 Nevill Holt Leics
70 F3 New Abbey D & G
103 J3 New Aberdour Abers
21 M10 New Addington Gt Lon
58 G5 Newall Leeds
9 P2 New Alresford Hants
93 J6 New Alyth P & K
111 i1 Newark Ork
52 B11 Newark-on-Trent Notts
85 N10 Newarthill N Lans
22 C9 New Ash Green Kent
52 B11 New Balderton Notts
22 C9 New Barn Kent
21 L4 New Barnet Gt Lon
86 G8 Newbattle Mdloth
81 M9 New Bewick Nthumb
71 J3 Newbie D & G
64 B2 Newbiggin Cumb
71 P9 Newbiggin Cumb
71 Q6 Newbiggin Cumb
64 G3 Newbiggin Dur
64 H9 Newbiggin N York
73 N4 Newbiggin-by-the-Sea Nthumb
93 K7 Newbigging Angus
93 M8 Newbigging Angus
93 N8 Newbigging Angus
86 B11 Newbigging S Lans
63 N2 Newbiggin-on-Lune Cumb
41 L11 New Bilton Warwks
51 J6 Newbold Derbys
41 L11 Newbold on Avon Warwks
30 G5 Newbold on Stour Warwks
30 H3 Newbold Pacey Warwks
41 K6 Newbold Verdon Leics
53 K11 New Bolingbroke Lincs
42 H8 Newborough C Pete
54 F8 Newborough IoA
40 F3 Newborough Staffs
52 D8 New Boultham Lincs
35 L8 Newbourne Suffk
32 B8 New Bradwell M Keyn
51 J6 New Brampton Derbys
73 M11 New Brancepeth Dur
86 D7 Newbridge C Edin
27 P8 Newbridge Caerph
2 C9 Newbridge Cnwll
78 F11 Newbridge D & G
9 K4 Newbridge Hants
9 M9 Newbridge IoW
29 L2 Newbridge Green Worcs
38 B9 Newbridge on Wye Powys
56 F9 New Brighton Wirral
72 F7 Newbrough Nthumb
44 H11 New Buckenham Norfk
15 N10 Newbuildings Devon
103 K4 Newburgh Abers
103 K9 Newburgh Abers
93 J11 Newburgh Fife
57 J6 Newburgh Lancs
66 D11 Newburgh Priory N York
73 L7 Newburn N u Ty
17 Q6 Newbury Somset
19 M7 Newbury W Berk
21 N6 Newbury Park Gt Lon
64 B4 Newby Cumb
63 P11 Newby Lancs
63 N8 Newby N York
66 C5 Newby N York
62 G5 Newby Bridge Cumb
71 P4 Newby East Cumb
102 H5 New Byth Abers
71 M5 Newby West Cumb
65 P9 Newby Wiske N York
28 E5 Newcastle Mons
38 F5 Newcastle Shrops
73 L6 Newcastle Airport Nthumb
36 E11 Newcastle Emlyn Carmth
79 P10 Newcastleton Border
49 Q6 Newcastle-under-Lyme Staffs
73 M7 Newcastle upon Tyne N u Ty
36 D11 Newchapel Pembks
11 M2 Newchapel Surrey
9 P9 Newchurch IoW
13 K4 Newchurch Kent
28 E8 Newchurch Mons
38 E11 Newchurch Powys
40 F3 Newchurch Staffs
45 K7 New Costessey Norfk
86 G7 Newcraighall C Edin
59 K10 New Crofton Wakefd
21 M7 New Cross Gt Lon
17 K11 New Cross Somset
77 K8 New Cumnock E Ayrs
103 J6 New Deer Abers
20 G6 New Denham Bucks
11 K2 Newdigate Surrey
31 Q2 New Duston Nhants
59 N3 New Earswick York
51 M2 New Edlington Donc
101 J3 New Elgin Moray
61 K6 New Ellerby E R Yk
20 E8 Newell Green Br For
21 N8 New Eltham Gt Lon
30 D3 New End Worcs
12 G5 Newenden Kent
42 H9 New England C Pete
29 J4 Newent Gloucs
65 L2 Newfield Dur
107 N7 Newfield Highld
42 H9 New Fletton C Pete
9 K6 New Forest Hants

188 Newgale - Old

24 E4 Newgale Pembks
69 P4 New Galloway D & G
21 L3 Newgate Street Herts
87 J1 New Gilston Fife
2 b1 New Grimsby IoS
49 L6 Newhall Ches
73 N5 New Hartley Nthumb
86 F7 Newhaven C Edin
11 N9 Newhaven E Susx
20 G10 New Haw Surrey
61 J9 New Holland N Linc
67 J5 Newholm N York
51 L7 New Houghton Derbys
44 D5 New Houghton Norfk
85 N10 Newhouse N Lans
63 K4 New Hutton Cumb
11 N6 Newick E Susx
13 M3 Newington Kent
22 G9 Newington Kent
19 Q2 Newington Oxon
26 C2 New Inn Carmth
28 C8 New Inn Torfn
38 F6 New Invention Shrops
78 E1 New Lanark S Lans
60 H7 Newland C KuH
28 G6 Newland Gloucs
59 P8 Newland N York
15 P5 Newland Somset
39 P11 Newland Worcs
86 H9 Newlandrig Mdloth
79 Q9 Newlands Border
73 J9 Newlands Nthumb
101 L5 Newlands of Dundurcas Moray
79 M11 New Langholm D & G
53 L11 New Leake Lincs
103 K4 New Leeds Abers
59 J11 New Lodge Barns
57 K4 New Longton Lancs
68 G6 New Luce D & G
2 C9 Newlyn Cnwll
3 J5 Newlyn East Cnwll
103 J10 Newmachar Abers
85 N10 Newmains N Lans
21 K9 New Malden Gt Lon
34 E7 Newman's Green Suffk
33 Q4 Newmarket Suffk
111 d2 Newmarket W Isls
66 E4 New Marske R & Cl
31 M11 New Marston Oxon
95 N5 New Mill Abers
79 P6 Newmill Border
2 C8 New Mill Cnwll
58 F11 New Mill Kirk
101 N5 Newmill Moray
59 J10 Newmillerdam Wakefd
94 G9 Newmill of Inshewan Angus
86 E8 Newmills C Edin
3 K5 New Mills Cnwll
50 D4 New Mills Derbys
86 B5 Newmills Fife
28 F7 Newmills Mons
38 C2 New Mills Powys
92 G9 Newmiln P & K
77 J4 Newmilns E Ayrs
9 J8 New Milton Hants
35 J9 New Mistley Essex
25 J4 New Moat Pembks
22 D3 Newney Green Essex
29 J6 Newnham Gloucs
20 B11 Newnham Hants
33 J8 Newnham Herts
23 J11 Newnham Kent
31 M3 Newnham Nhants
39 M8 Newnham Worcs
51 P7 New Ollerton Notts
103 J4 New Pitsligo Abers
4 H3 Newport Cnwll
15 K6 Newport Devon
60 E7 Newport E R Yk
33 N9 Newport Essex
29 J8 Newport Gloucs
110 D10 Newport Highld
9 N9 Newport IoW
28 C10 Newport Newpt
25 J2 Newport Pembks
49 N10 Newport Wrekin
93 M9 Newport-on-Tay Fife
32 C7 Newport Pagnell M Keyn
76 F6 New Prestwick S Ayrs
36 F8 New Quay Cerdgn
3 J4 Newquay Cnwll
3 K3 Newquay Airport Cnwll
45 L7 New Rackheath Norfk
38 E9 New Radnor Powys
73 J8 New Ridley Nthumb
13 K5 New Romney Kent
51 N2 New Rossington Donc
85 P4 New Sauchie Clacks
102 F8 Newseat Abers
57 K2 Newsham Lancs
65 K5 Newsham N York
65 P9 Newsham N York
73 N5 Newsham Nthumb
59 J9 New Sharlston Wakefd
60 C8 Newsholme E R Yk
73 P9 New Silksworth Sundld
58 F10 Newsome Kirk
42 D3 New Somerby Lincs
80 D7 Newstead Border
51 L9 Newstead Notts
81 N8 Newstead Nthumb
85 M10 New Stevenston N Lans
101 N6 Newtack Moray
59 L7 Newthorpe N York
51 L10 Newthorpe Notts
83 Q4 Newton Ag & B
32 H7 Newton Beds
80 E9 Newton Border
26 H12 Newton Brdgnd
33 M6 Newton Cambs
43 M7 Newton Cambs
48 H2 Newton Ches
49 J4 Newton Ches
62 E7 Newton Cumb
51 K8 Newton Derbys
28 D3 Newton Herefs
39 K10 Newton Herefs
107 J11 Newton Highld
107 M11 Newton Highld
107 M8 Newton Highld
63 M11 Newton Lancs
42 F3 Newton Lincs
86 G8 Newton Mdloth
100 H3 Newton Moray
101 L3 Newton Moray
42 C12 Newton Nhants
44 D7 Newton Norfk
51 P11 Newton Notts
73 J7 Newton Nthumb
78 F3 Newton S Lans
85 L10 Newton S Lans
16 F8 Newton Somset
40 D3 Newton Staffs
34 F8 Newton Suffk
86 C6 Newton W Loth
41 M10 Newton Warwks
6 B8 Newton Abbot Devon
71 K5 Newton Arlosh Cumb
65 M3 Newton Aycliffe Dur
66 C3 Newton Bewley Hartpl
32 D6 Newton Blossomville M Keyn
32 E4 Newton Bromswold Nhants
41 J6 Newton Burgoland Leics
81 P8 Newton-by-the-Sea Nthumb
52 F6 Newton by Toft Lincs
4 H7 Newton Ferrers Cnwll
5 L9 Newton Ferrers Devon
111 b4 Newton Ferry W Isls
45 K9 Newton Flotman Norfk
102 D8 Newtongarry Croft Abers
86 G8 Newtongrange Mdloth
41 N7 Newton Harcourt Leics
57 Q8 Newton Heath Manch
95 P4 Newtonhill Abers
59 L5 Newton Kyme N York
65 L9 Newton-le-Willows N York
57 L9 Newton-le-Willows St Hel
86 G9 Newtonloan Mdloth
32 C9 Newton Longville Bucks
85 J11 Newton Mearns E Rens
95 K8 Newtonmill Angus
99 K8 Newtonmore Highld
65 M5 Newton Morrell N York
92 H12 Newton of Balcanquhal P & K
87 K2 Newton of Balcormo Fife
59 L3 Newton on Ouse N York
66 H9 Newton-on-Rawcliffe N York
81 N12 Newton-on-the-Moor Nthumb
52 B8 Newton on Trent Lincs
6 E5 Newton Poppleford Devon
31 N7 Newton Purcell Oxon
40 H6 Newton Regis Warwks
71 P8 Newton Reigny Cumb
110 G6 Newton Row Highld
15 Q11 Newton St Cyres Devon
45 K6 Newton St Faith Norfk
17 Q3 Newton St Loe BaNES
14 G9 Newton St Petrock Devon
40 H3 Newton Solney Derbys
19 M11 Newton Stacey Hants
69 K6 Newton Stewart D & G
19 J11 Newton Tony Wilts
15 J6 Newton Tracey Devon
66 D5 Newton under Roseberry R & Cl
60 C4 Newton upon Derwent E R Yk
10 B4 Newton Valence Hants
78 H9 Newton Wamphray D & G
57 J3 Newton with Scales Lancs
49 L6 Newtown Ches
70 H6 Newtown Cumb
71 P3 Newtown Cumb
77 N8 Newtown D & G
6 E3 Newtown Devon
15 N7 Newtown Devon
8 D4 New Town Dorset
8 E4 New Town Dorset
11 P6 New Town E Susx
29 J8 Newtown Gloucs
9 Q5 Newtown Hants
29 J2 Newtown Herefs
39 L12 Newtown Herefs
98 E7 Newtown Highld
9 M8 Newtown IoW
73 J1 Newtown Nthumb
81 L8 Newtown Nthumb
8 F8 Newtown Poole
38 C4 Newtown Powys
48 H10 Newtown Shrops
49 J8 Newtown Shrops
6 H1 Newtown Somset
50 B8 Newtown Staffs
57 K7 Newtown Wigan
39 Q10 Newtown Worcs
41 M5 Newtown Linford Leics
84 F10 Newtown of Beltrees Rens
80 D7 Newtown St Boswells Border
27 N7 New Tredegar Caerph
77 N4 New Trows S Lans
93 K7 Newtyle Angus
43 M8 New Walsoken Cambs
53 J3 New Waltham NE Lin
87 J7 New Winton E Loth
83 P2 Newyork Ag & B
53 J11 New York Lincs
24 G7 Neyland Pembks
16 E11 Nicholashayne Devon
26 C10 Nicholaston Swans
58 H3 Nidd N York
95 Q2 Nigg C Aber
107 N7 Nigg Highld
16 B10 Nightcott Somset
72 E9 Ninebanks Nthumb
18 G4 Nine Elms Swindn
39 L8 Nineveh Worcs
12 E7 Ninfield E Susx
9 L9 Ningwood IoW
80 F8 Nisbet Border
80 H4 Nisbet Hill Border
9 N11 Niton IoW
85 J10 Nitshill C Glas
52 F10 Nocton Lincs
31 M10 Noke Oxon
24 F5 Nolton Pembks
24 F5 Nolton Haven Pembks
49 K6 No Man's Heath Ches
40 H6 No Man's Heath Warwks
15 P9 Nomansland Devon
9 J4 Nomansland Wilts
49 J9 Noneley Shrops
23 N11 Nonington Kent
63 K6 Nook Cumb
21 K9 Norbiton Gt Lon
49 K6 Norbury Ches
50 F11 Norbury Derbys
21 L9 Norbury Gt Lon
38 G4 Norbury Shrops
49 P10 Norbury Staffs
39 Q8 Norchard Worcs
43 N9 Nordelph Norfk
39 M3 Nordley Shrops
45 P8 Norfolk Broads Norfk
81 J5 Norham Nthumb
58 E9 Norland Town Calder
49 K2 Norley Ches
9 L7 Norleywood Hants
52 E6 Normanby Lincs
60 F10 Normanby N Linc
66 G10 Normanby N York
66 D4 Normanby R & Cl
52 G5 Normanby le Wold Lincs
20 E11 Normandy Surrey
6 E3 Norman's Green Devon
41 J2 Normanton C Derb
42 B2 Normanton Leics
42 D2 Normanton Lincs
51 P9 Normanton Notts
59 J9 Normanton Wakefd
41 J5 Normanton le Heath Leics
41 L3 Normanton on Soar Notts
41 N2 Normanton on the Wolds Notts
52 B9 Normanton on Trent Notts
32 D11 Northall Bucks
65 P8 Northallerton N York
9 M5 Northam C Sotn
14 H6 Northam Devon
31 Q2 Northampton Nhants
39 Q8 Northampton Worcs
51 M4 North Anston Rothm
20 E9 North Ascot Br For
31 L8 North Aston Oxon
21 L3 Northaw Herts
6 H1 Northay Somset
9 L4 North Baddesley Hants
90 E4 North Ballachulish Highld
17 N9 North Barrow Somset
44 F3 North Barsham Norfk
22 F5 North Benfleet Essex
10 E9 North Bersted W Susx
87 K5 North Berwick E Loth
9 P5 North Boarhunt Hants
42 G8 Northborough C Pete
23 P11 Northbourne Kent
5 P4 North Bovey Devon
18 C9 North Bradley Wilts
5 K4 North Brentor Devon
17 Q8 North Brewham Somset
19 N11 Northbrook Hants
14 H4 North Buckland Devon
45 N7 North Burlingham Norfk
17 P10 North Cadbury Somset
52 D7 North Carlton Lincs
51 N4 North Carlton Notts
60 F7 North Cave E R Yk
30 D11 North Cerney Gloucs
11 N6 North Chailey E Susx
10 F4 Northchapel W Susx
8 H4 North Charford Hants
81 N9 North Charlton Nthumb
21 K9 North Cheam Gt Lon
17 Q10 North Cheriton Somset
7 K4 North Chideock Dorset
20 F2 Northchurch Herts
60 E6 North Cliffe E R Yk
52 B8 North Clifton Notts
53 L5 North Cockerington Lincs
90 C9 North Connel Ag & B
26 H11 North Cornelly Brdgnd
90 B6 North Corry Highld
53 K4 North Cotes Lincs
4 H2 Northcott Devon
19 N2 Northcourt Oxon
45 P11 North Cove Suffk
65 M6 North Cowton N York
32 D7 North Crawley M Keyn
44 E3 North Creake Norfk
17 J10 North Curry Somset
60 F4 North Dalton E R Yk
59 K4 North Deighton N York
23 Q8 Northdown Kent
22 H11 North Downs
59 P6 North Duffield N York
104 F7 North Duntulm Highld
13 M2 North Elham Kent
44 G6 North Elmham Norfk
59 L10 North Elmsall Wakefd
9 Q7 North End C Port
33 Q11 North End Essex
8 G4 North End Hants
32 D3 North End Nhants
10 F8 North End W Susx
31 K4 Northend Warwks
57 P10 Northenden Manch
105 L6 North Erradale Highld
41 N6 North Evington C Leic
22 G4 North Fambridge Essex
60 G8 North Ferriby E R Yk
40 D10 Northfield Birm
103 J12 Northfield C Aber
60 H8 Northfield E R Yk
42 E8 Northfields Lincs
22 D8 Northfleet Kent
61 J4 North Frodingham E R Yk
8 H5 North Gorley Hants
35 M4 North Green Suffk
52 E8 North Greetwell Lincs
60 E1 North Grimston N York
10 B9 North Hayling Hants
4 G5 North Hill Cnwll
20 H6 North Hillingdon Gt Lon
31 L11 North Hinksey Oxon
11 J1 North Holmwood Surrey
5 P8 North Huish Devon
52 D9 North Hykeham Lincs
12 G5 Northiam E Susx
32 G7 Northill Beds
19 P12 Northington Hants
52 F3 North Kelsey Lincs
107 L11 North Kessock Highld
61 K10 North Killingholme N Linc
65 Q9 North Kilvington N York
41 N10 North Kilworth Leics
52 G11 North Kyme Lincs
67 Q12 North Landing E R Yk
53 K11 Northlands Lincs
30 E10 Northleach Gloucs
20 D2 North Lee Bucks
6 G4 Northleigh Devon
15 K5 Northleigh Devon
31 K10 North Leigh Oxon
52 B7 North Leverton with Habblesthorpe Notts
15 J11 Northlew Devon
30 E5 North Littleton Worcs
44 G12 North Lopham Norfk
42 D9 North Luffenham Rutlnd
10 D6 North Marden W Susx
31 Q9 North Marston Bucks
86 G9 North Middleton Mdloth
68 E8 North Milmain D & G
15 M6 North Molton Devon
31 K12 Northmoor Oxon
19 P3 North Moreton Oxon
93 L5 Northmuir Angus
10 E9 North Mundham W Susx
52 B10 North Muskham Notts
60 F6 North Newbald E R Yk
31 K6 North Newington Oxon
18 G8 North Newnton Wilts
17 J9 North Newton Somset
10 B8 Northney Hants
29 K9 North Nibley Gloucs
21 J6 Northolt Gt Lon
48 E2 Northop Flints
48 F2 Northop Hall Flints
66 D4 North Ormesby Middsb
53 J5 North Ormsby Lincs
42 H3 Northorpe Lincs
52 C4 Northorpe Lincs
65 P9 North Otterington N York
52 F5 North Owersby Lincs
58 E8 Northowram Calder
7 L2 North Perrott Somset
16 H9 North Petherton Somset
4 G3 North Petherwin Cnwll
44 E8 North Pickenham Norfk
30 C3 North Piddle Worcs
5 Q11 North Pool Devon
7 M3 North Poorton Dorset
8 D9 Northport Dorset
86 D6 North Queensferry Fife
15 N5 North Radworthy Devon
42 E2 North Rauceby Lincs
45 L3 Northrepps Norfk
53 L6 North Reston Lincs
58 H4 North Rigton N York
50 B7 North Rode Ches
111 i1 North Ronaldsay Airport Ork
43 Q6 North Runcton Norfk
52 C9 North Scarle Lincs
90 C7 North Shian Ag & B
73 N7 North Shields N Tyne
22 H6 North Shoebury Sthend
56 F2 North Shore Bpool
43 J9 North Side C Pete
53 L4 North Somercotes Lincs
65 M11 North Stainley N York
22 C7 North Stifford Thurr
17 Q3 North Stoke BaNES
19 Q4 North Stoke Oxon
10 G7 North Stoke W Susx
23 K10 North Street Kent
19 Q6 North Street W Berk
81 P7 North Sunderland Nthumb
14 F11 North Tamerton Cnwll
15 L10 North Tawton Devon
85 M5 North Third Stirlg
53 J4 North Thoresby Lincs
111 b3 Northton W Isls
15 J9 North Town Devon
17 N7 North Town Somset
20 E7 North Town W & M
44 G7 North Tuddenham Norfk
72 F1 Northumberland National Park Nthumb
45 L4 North Walsham Norfk
19 P10 North Waltham Hants
20 B12 North Warnborough Hants
16 F9 Northway Somset
21 P3 North Weald Bassett Essex
51 Q4 North Wheatley Notts
49 M2 Northwich Ches
39 Q9 Northwick Worcs
17 N5 North Widcombe BaNES
52 G6 North Willingham Lincs
51 K7 North Wingfield Derbys
42 D6 North Witham Lincs
44 C10 Northwold Norfk
20 H5 Northwood Gt Lon
9 N8 Northwood IoW
49 J8 Northwood Shrops
29 J5 Northwood Green Gloucs
17 P12 North Wootton Dorset
43 Q5 North Wootton Norfk
17 N7 North Wootton Somset
18 B6 North Wraxall Wilts
66 G7 North York Moors National Park
59 M10 Norton Donc
11 P9 Norton E Susx
29 M4 Norton Gloucs
66 H12 Norton N York
31 N2 Norton Nhants
51 M6 Norton Notts
38 F8 Norton Powys
66 C3 Norton S on T
39 N3 Norton Shrops
34 F4 Norton Suffk
10 E8 Norton W Susx
18 C4 Norton Wilts
30 D5 Norton Worcs
39 Q11 Norton Worcs
18 D11 Norton Bavant Wilts
49 Q9 Norton Bridge Staffs
40 D6 Norton Canes Staffs
38 H11 Norton Canon Herefs
52 C10 Norton Disney Lincs
16 G10 Norton Fitzwarren Somset
9 K9 Norton Green IoW
17 N4 Norton Hawkfield BaNES
22 C3 Norton Heath Essex
49 N7 Norton in Hales Shrops
41 J6 Norton-Juxta-Twycross Leics
65 P12 Norton-le-Clay N York
30 G2 Norton Lindsey Warwks
34 F4 Norton Little Green Suffk
17 N3 Norton Malreward BaNES
18 B9 Norton St Philip Somset
45 N9 Norton Subcourse Norfk
17 L11 Norton sub Hamdon Somset
38 G11 Norton Wood Herefs
51 Q8 Norwell Notts
51 Q8 Norwell Woodhouse Notts
45 K8 Norwich Norfk
45 K7 Norwich Airport Norfk
45 K8 Norwich Cathedral Norfk
111 m2 Norwick Shet
85 P4 Norwood Clacks
21 J7 Norwood Green Gt Lon
11 K2 Norwood Hill Surrey
41 Q7 Noseley Leics
5 L10 Noss Mayo Devon
65 M10 Nosterfield N York
97 M4 Nostie Highld
30 E9 Notgrove Gloucs
26 H12 Nottage Brdgnd
5 J7 Notter Cnwll
51 M11 Nottingham C Nott
41 K3 Nottingham East Midlands Airport Leics
59 J10 Notton Wakefd
18 D6 Notton Wilts
39 P8 Noutard's Green Worcs
48 H12 Nox Shrops
19 Q4 Nuffield Oxon
60 E5 Nunburnholme E R Yk
41 J8 Nuneaton Warwks
19 P2 Nuneham Courtenay Oxon
21 M8 Nunhead Gt Lon
61 K4 Nunkeeling E R Yk
59 L3 Nun Monkton N York
17 Q7 Nunney Somset
66 F10 Nunnington N York
53 J2 Nunsthorpe NE Lin
66 D5 Nunthorpe Middsb
59 N4 Nunthorpe York
66 D5 Nunthorpe Village Middsb
8 H3 Nunton Wilts
65 N11 Nunwick N York
9 L4 Nursling Hants
10 C8 Nutbourne W Susx
10 H6 Nutbourne W Susx
21 L12 Nutfield Surrey
51 M11 Nuthall Notts
33 L9 Nuthampstead Herts
11 J5 Nuthurst W Susx
11 N5 Nutley E Susx
110 G3 Nybster Highld
10 E9 Nyetimber W Susx
10 C6 Nyewood W Susx
15 M9 Nymet Rowland Devon
15 M11 Nymet Tracey Devon
29 L8 Nympsfield Gloucs
10 E8 Nyton W Susx

O

41 N7 Oadby Leics
22 G10 Oad Street Kent
50 D11 Oakamoor Staffs
86 C8 Oakbank W Loth
15 J11 Oak Cross Devon
27 P8 Oakdale Caerph
16 F10 Oake Somset
39 Q2 Oaken Staffs
63 K11 Oakenclough Lancs
49 M12 Oakengates Wrekin
73 L12 Oakenshaw Dur
58 F8 Oakenshaw Kirk
50 H8 Oaker Side Derbys
36 G8 Oakford Cerdgn
16 C11 Oakford Devon
42 C8 Oakham Rutlnd
10 C3 Oakhanger Hants
17 P6 Oakhill Somset
33 L4 Oakington Cambs
29 K5 Oakle Street Gloucs
32 E6 Oakley Beds
31 N10 Oakley Bucks
86 B4 Oakley Fife
19 P9 Oakley Hants
35 J2 Oakley Suffk
29 M7 Oakridge Gloucs
29 P9 Oaksey Wilts
40 H5 Oakthorpe Leics
51 J12 Oakwood C Derb
11 J3 Oakwoodhill Surrey
58 D6 Oakworth Brad
23 J10 Oare Kent
15 N3 Oare Somset
18 H7 Oare Wilts
42 E3 Oasby Lincs
17 K10 Oath Somset
93 N4 Oathlaw Angus
20 H9 Oatlands Park Surrey
90 B9 Oban Ag & B
38 G6 Obley Shrops
92 F8 Obney P & K
17 P11 Oborne Dorset
35 J3 Occold Suffk
110 F8 Occumster Highld
76 H7 Ochiltree E Ayrs
41 K1 Ockbrook Derbys
20 H11 Ockham Surrey
89 L3 Ockle Highld
11 J3 Ockley Surrey
39 L11 Ocle Pychard Herefs
17 M11 Odcombe Somset
17 Q4 Odd Down BaNES
30 B3 Oddingley Worcs
30 G8 Oddington Gloucs
31 M10 Oddington Oxon
32 D5 Odell Beds
20 C12 Odiham Hants
58 F8 Odsal Brad
33 J8 Odsey Cambs
8 G3 Odstock Wilts
41 K6 Odstone Leics
31 J2 Offchurch Warwks
30 D5 Offenham Worcs
50 B3 Offerton Stockp
11 N7 Offham E Susx
22 D11 Offham Kent
10 G8 Offham W Susx
32 H4 Offord Cluny Cambs
32 H4 Offord Darcy Cambs
34 H6 Offton Suffk
6 G3 Offwell Devon
18 H6 Ogbourne Maizey Wilts
18 H6 Ogbourne St Andrew Wilts
18 H6 Ogbourne St George Wilts
73 K5 Ogle Nthumb
56 H11 Oglet Lpool
16 B2 Ogmore V Glam
16 B2 Ogmore-by-Sea V Glam
27 K10 Ogmore Vale Brdgnd
8 B5 Okeford Fitzpaine Dorset
5 M2 Okehampton Devon
32 B3 Old Nhants

Old Aberdeen - Philiphaugh 189

95 Q1 Old Aberdeen C Aber
9 P1 Old Alresford Hants
108 C8 Oldany Highld
77 M11 Old Auchenbrack D & G
51 M11 Old Basford C Nott
19 Q9 Old Basing Hants
44 F6 Old Beetley Norfk
30 E2 Oldberrow Warwks
81 M9 Old Bewick Nthumb
53 K9 Old Bolingbroke Lincs
58 G5 Old Bramhope Leeds
51 J6 Old Brampton Derbys
70 C3 Old Bridge of Urr D & G
44 H10 Old Buckenham Norfk
19 M8 Old Burghclere Hants
40 C9 Oldbury Sandw
39 N4 Oldbury Shrops
40 H8 Oldbury Warwks
28 H9 Oldbury-on-Severn S Glos
18 B3 Oldbury on the Hill Gloucs
66 D9 Old Byland N York
51 N1 Old Cantley Donc
28 C4 Oldcastle Mons
53 J2 Old Clee NE Lin
16 E7 Old Cleeve Somset
51 N7 Old Clipstone Notts
51 N3 Oldcotes Notts
76 D10 Old Dailly S Ayrs
41 P3 Old Dalby Leics
103 K6 Old Deer Abers
51 M2 Old Edlington Donc
61 K6 Old Ellerby E R Yk
35 M9 Old Felixstowe Suffk
39 Q8 Oldfield Worcs
42 H10 Old Fletton C Pete
18 B10 Oldford Somset
28 G5 Old Forge Herefs
2 b1 Old Grimsby IoS
33 L11 Old Hall Green Herts
58 B12 Oldham Oldham
87 N7 Oldhamstocks E Loth
21 P2 Old Harlow Essex
44 B2 Old Hunstanton Norfk
33 J2 Old Hurst Cambs
63 K5 Old Hutton Cumb
3 J7 Old Kea Cnwll
84 H8 Old Kilpatrick W Duns
32 H11 Old Knebworth Herts
17 P2 Oldland S Glos
57 M2 Old Langho Lancs
53 L12 Old Leake Lincs
66 H11 Old Malton N York
102 H9 Oldmeldrum Abers
59 K7 Old Micklefield Leeds
4 H5 Oldmill Cnwll
30 H1 Old Milverton Warwks
17 J5 Oldmixon N Som
34 H4 Old Newton Suffk
38 F9 Old Radnor Powys
102 E9 Old Rayne Abers
13 K5 Old Romney Kent
11 K8 Old Shoreham W Susx
108 D4 Oldshoremore Highld
29 K11 Old Sodbury S Glos
42 D4 Old Somerby Lincs
66 D10 Oldstead N York
31 Q6 Old Stratford Nhants
40 B10 Old Swinford Dudley
66 B10 Old Thirsk N York
63 L5 Old Town Cumb
12 C9 Old Town E Susx
2 c2 Old Town IoS
57 P9 Old Trafford Traffd
71 P4 Oldwall Cumb
26 C9 Oldwalls Swans
32 G7 Old Warden Beds
32 F2 Old Weston Cambs
110 G6 Old Wick Highld
20 F8 Old Windsor W & M
23 K11 Old Wives Lees Kent
20 G11 Old Woking Surrey
40 E4 Olive Green Staffs
78 H4 Oliver Border
9 M2 Oliver's Battery Hants
111 k3 Ollaberry Shet
96 F3 Ollach Highld
57 P12 Ollerton Ches
51 P7 Ollerton Notts
49 M9 Ollerton Shrops
32 C6 Olney M Keyn
110 E3 Olrig House Highld
40 F10 Olton Solhll
28 H10 Olveston S Glos
39 Q8 Ombersley Worcs
51 P7 Ompton Notts
56 d5 Onchan IoM
50 D9 Onecote Staffs
39 J6 Onibury Shrops
90 E4 Onich Highld
26 H6 Onllwyn Neath
49 N6 Onneley Staffs
20 F12 Onslow Village Surrey
49 L1 Onston Ches
105 L7 Opinan Highld
101 L4 Orbliston Moray
96 B2 Orbost Highld
53 M9 Orby Lincs
16 H10 Orchard Portman Somset
18 F10 Orcheston Wilts
28 F4 Orcop Herefs
28 F4 Orcop Hill Herefs
102 E4 Ord Abers
102 E12 Ordhead Abers
94 G2 Ordie Abers
101 L4 Ordiequish Moray
72 G8 Ordley Nthumb
51 P5 Ordsall Notts
12 G7 Ore E Susx
35 N6 Orford Suffk
57 L10 Orford Warrtn
8 D8 Organford Dorset
13 J3 Orlestone Kent
39 J8 Orleton Herefs
39 M8 Orleton Worcs
32 C3 Orlingbury Nhants
66 D4 Ormesby R & Cl
45 P7 Ormesby St Margaret Norfk
45 P7 Ormesby St Michael Norfk
105 M4 Ormiscaig Highld
86 H8 Ormiston E Loth
89 K4 Ormsaigmore Highld
83 L8 Ormsary Ag & B
56 H7 Ormskirk Lancs
82 E5 Oronsay Ag & B
111 h2 Orphir Ork
21 P9 Orpington Gt Lon
56 G9 Orrell Sefton
57 K7 Orrell Wigan
70 C6 Orroland D & G
22 D7 Orsett Thurr
49 P11 Orslow Staffs
51 Q11 Orston Notts
63 L1 Orton Cumb
32 B2 Orton Nhants
39 Q3 Orton Staffs
42 G10 Orton Longueville C Pete
40 H6 Orton-on-the-Hill Leics
42 G10 Orton Waterville C Pete
33 K6 Orwell Cambs
57 M3 Osbaldeston Lancs
59 N4 Osbaldwick York
41 K6 Osbaston Leics
48 G10 Osbaston Shrops
9 N8 Osborne House IoW
42 F3 Osbournby Lincs
49 J3 Oscroft Ches
96 C2 Ose Highld
41 K4 Osgathorpe Leics
52 F5 Osgodby Lincs
59 N7 Osgodby N York
67 M9 Osgodby N York
96 G3 Oskaig Highld
89 K8 Oskamull Ag & B
50 G11 Osmaston Derbys
7 Q6 Osmington Dorset
7 Q6 Osmington Mills Dorset
59 J7 Osmondthorpe Leeds
66 C7 Osmotherley N York
31 L11 Osney Oxon
23 J10 Ospringe Kent
58 H9 Ossett Wakefd
51 Q7 Ossington Notts
21 J7 Osterley Gt Lon
66 E10 Oswaldkirk N York
57 N4 Oswaldtwistle Lancs
48 F9 Oswestry Shrops
21 Q10 Otford Kent
22 F11 Otham Kent
17 K9 Othery Somset
58 G5 Otley Leeds
35 K5 Otley Suffk
9 M3 Otterbourne Hants
63 Q9 Otterburn N York
72 F3 Otterburn Nthumb
83 P6 Otter Ferry Ag & B
4 E3 Otterham Cnwll
16 H7 Otterhampton Somset
111 b4 Otternish W Isls
20 G9 Ottershaw Surrey
111 K3 Otterswick Shet
6 E6 Otterton Devon
5 J5 Ottery Devon
6 E4 Ottery St Mary Devon
13 M2 Ottinge Kent
61 M8 Ottringham E R Yk
71 J7 Oughterside Cumb
50 H3 Oughtibridge Sheff
57 M10 Oughtrington Warrtn
66 D11 Oulston N York
71 K5 Oulton Cumb
45 J4 Oulton Norfk
40 B1 Oulton Staffs
45 Q10 Oulton Suffk
45 Q10 Oulton Broad Suffk
45 J5 Oulton Street Norfk
42 E11 Oundle Nhants
39 Q4 Ounsdale Staffs
64 B1 Ousby Cumb
34 C5 Ousden Suffk
60 E9 Ousefleet E R Yk
73 M9 Ouston Dur
62 G3 Outgate Cumb
64 E7 Outhgill Cumb
30 E2 Outhill Warwks
58 E9 Outlane Kirk
56 H1 Out Rawcliffe Lancs
43 N8 Outwell Norfk
11 L2 Outwood Surrey
49 P11 Outwoods Staffs
59 J8 Ouzlewell Green Leeds
33 L3 Over Cambs
29 N2 Overbury Worcs
7 Q6 Overcombe Dorset
17 N11 Over Compton Dorset
50 G7 Over Haddon Derbys
63 K8 Over Kellet Lancs
31 K9 Over Kiddington Oxon
17 L8 Overleigh Somset
30 H8 Over Norton Oxon
49 P1 Over Peover Ches
56 H12 Overpool Ches
108 H10 Overscaig Hotel Highld
40 H4 Overseal Derbys
66 C8 Over Silton N York
23 K11 Oversland Kent
32 B4 Overstone Nhants
16 G8 Over Stowey Somset
45 L3 Overstrand Norfk
17 L11 Over Stratton Somset
31 L6 Overthorpe Nhants
102 H11 Overton C Aber
19 N10 Overton Hants
62 H9 Overton Lancs
59 M3 Overton N York
39 J7 Overton Shrops
26 B10 Overton Swans
58 H10 Overton Wakefd
48 G7 Overton Wrexhm
63 L7 Overtown Lancs
85 N11 Overtown N Lans
19 K11 Over Wallop Hants
40 G8 Over Whitacre Warwks
31 K8 Over Worton Oxon
32 A11 Oving Bucks
10 E8 Oving W Susx
11 M8 Ovingdean Br & H
73 J7 Ovingham Nthumb
65 K5 Ovington Dur
34 C8 Ovington Essex
9 P2 Ovington Hants
44 F9 Ovington Norfk
73 J7 Ovington Nthumb
9 K4 Ower Hants
8 B9 Owermoigne Dorset
51 J3 Owlerton Sheff
20 D10 Owlsmoor Br For
20 C3 Owlswick Bucks
52 E6 Owmby Lincs
52 F3 Owmby Lincs
9 N3 Owslebury Hants
59 M11 Owston Donc
41 Q6 Owston Leics
52 B4 Owston Ferry N Linc
61 M7 Owstwick E R Yk
61 N8 Owthorne E R Yk
41 P2 Owthorpe Notts
44 C9 Oxborough Norfk
7 L4 Oxbridge Dorset
53 K7 Oxcombe Lincs
33 Q10 Oxen End Essex
63 K4 Oxenholme Cumb
58 D7 Oxenhope Brad
62 G5 Oxen Park Cumb
17 L7 Oxenpill Somset
29 N3 Oxenton Gloucs
19 K8 Oxenwood Wilts
31 L11 Oxford Oxon
20 H4 Oxhey Herts
30 H5 Oxhill Warwks
40 B7 Oxley Wolves
22 H1 Oxley Green Essex
43 M11 Oxlode Cambs
80 F9 Oxnam Border
45 K5 Oxnead Norfk
21 J10 Oxshott Surrey
50 H1 Oxspring Barns
21 M11 Oxted Surrey
80 C4 Oxton Border
59 L5 Oxton N York
51 N9 Oxton Notts
26 C10 Oxwich Swans
26 C10 Oxwich Green Swans
106 F3 Oykel Bridge Hotel Highld
102 E9 Oyne Abers
26 E10 Oystermouth Swans

P

111 e2 Pabail W Isls
41 J5 Packington Leics
93 M5 Padanaram Angus
31 Q7 Padbury Bucks
21 L7 Paddington Gt Lon
13 M3 Paddlesworth Kent
22 D10 Paddlesworth Kent
12 D2 Paddock Wood Kent
57 P3 Padiham Lancs
58 F3 Padside N York
3 K1 Padstow Cnwll
19 Q7 Padworth W Berk
10 E9 Pagham W Susx
22 H5 Paglesham Essex
6 B10 Paignton Torbay
41 L10 Pailton Warwks
38 D11 Painscastle Powys
73 J8 Painshawfield Nthumb
60 E3 Painsthorpe E R Yk
29 M6 Painswick Gloucs
23 J10 Painter's Forstal Kent
84 H9 Paisley Rens
45 Q11 Pakefield Suffk
34 F4 Pakenham Suffk
20 E7 Paley Street W & M
40 D7 Palfrey Wsall
35 J2 Palgrave Suffk
8 B8 Pallington Dorset
76 H7 Palmerston E Ayrs
70 D4 Palnackie D & G
69 L6 Palnure D & G
51 L7 Palterton Derbys
19 Q8 Pamber End Hants
19 Q8 Pamber Green Hants
19 Q8 Pamber Heath Hants
29 N3 Pamington Gloucs
8 E7 Pamphill Dorset
33 N7 Pampisford Cambs
93 P8 Panbride Angus
14 F10 Pancrasweek Devon
28 D4 Pandy Mons
55 M8 Pandy Tudur Conwy
34 C10 Panfield Essex
19 Q5 Pangbourne W Berk
11 L7 Pangdean W Susx
58 H4 Pannal N York
58 H4 Pannal Ash N York
94 G3 Pannanich Wells Hotel Abers
48 F10 Pant Shrops
48 D1 Pantasaph Flints
27 K11 Pant-ffrwyth Brdgnd
46 H2 Pant Glas Gwynd
47 M10 Pantglas Powys
52 H7 Panton Lincs
37 R6 Pant-y-dwr Powys
48 E3 Pant-y-mwyn Flints
45 M7 Panxworth Norfk
111 h1 Papa Westray Airport Ork
70 H8 Papcastle Cumb
110 H5 Papigoe Highld
87 L7 Papple E Loth
51 M9 Papplewick Notts
33 J4 Papworth Everard Cambs
33 J4 Papworth St Agnes Cambs
3 N5 Par Cnwll
57 J6 Parbold Lancs
17 N8 Parbrook Somset
47 P5 Parc Gwynd
28 E9 Parc Seymour Newpt
70 H9 Pardshaw Cumb
35 M5 Parham Suffk
95 N3 Park Abers
78 E10 Park D & G
72 C8 Park Nthumb
20 B6 Park Corner Oxon
28 H7 Parkend Gloucs
12 C1 Parkers Green Kent
13 J3 Park Farm Kent
56 F12 Parkgate Ches
78 G10 Parkgate D & G
9 N6 Park Gate Hants
58 F6 Park Gate Leeds
11 K2 Parkgate Surrey
84 H8 Parkhall W Duns
14 G7 Parkham Devon
103 J11 Parkhill House Abers
26 D10 Parkmill Swans
21 K7 Park Royal Gt Lon
73 Q10 Parkside Dur
85 N10 Parkside N Lans
8 F8 Parkstone Poole
21 J3 Park Street Herts
21 N2 Parndon Essex
15 J3 Parracombe Devon
43 L8 Parson Drove Cambs
34 G10 Parson's Heath Essex
85 J9 Partick C Glas
57 N9 Partington Traffd
53 L9 Partney Lincs
70 F10 Parton Cumb
11 J6 Partridge Green W Susx
50 F9 Parwich Derbys
32 A8 Passenham Nhants
45 M4 Paston Norfk
11 L8 Patcham Br & H
10 H8 Patching W Susx
28 H11 Patchway S Glos
58 F2 Pateley Bridge N York
86 F4 Pathhead Fife
86 H9 Pathhead Mdloth
92 G12 Path of Condie P & K
76 G8 Patna E Ayrs
18 F8 Patney Wilts
56 b5 Patrick IoM
65 L8 Patrick Brompton N York
57 N8 Patricroft Salfd
61 M9 Patrington E R Yk
61 M9 Patrington Haven E R Yk
23 M11 Patrixbourne Kent
71 N11 Patterdale Cumb
39 P3 Pattingham Staffs
31 P4 Pattishall Nhants
34 D10 Pattiswick Green Essex
2 C9 Paul Cnwll
31 Q5 Paulerspury Nhants
61 K8 Paull E R Yk
8 G2 Paul's Dene Wilts
17 P5 Paulton BaNES
73 K2 Pauperhaugh Nthumb
32 E5 Pavenham Beds
16 H7 Pawlett Somset
30 F6 Paxford Gloucs
81 K4 Paxton Border
6 E3 Payhembury Devon
63 P10 Paythorne Lancs
11 N9 Peacehaven E Susx
50 F3 Peak District National Park
50 E5 Peak Forest Derbys
42 G8 Peakirk C Pete
89 P1 Peanmeanach Highld
17 Q5 Peasedown St John BaNES
44 H6 Peaseland Green Norfk
19 M5 Peasemore W Berk
35 M3 Peasenhall Suffk
11 L4 Pease Pottage W Susx
10 H2 Peaslake Surrey
57 K9 Peasley Cross St Hel
12 H5 Peasmarsh E Susx
103 J3 Peathill Abers
87 J1 Peat Inn Fife
41 N8 Peatling Magna Leics
41 N9 Peatling Parva Leics
34 E9 Pebmarsh Essex
30 F5 Pebworth Worcs
58 C8 Pecket Well Calder
49 K4 Peckforton Ches
21 M8 Peckham Gt Lon
41 L7 Peckleton Leics
13 L3 Pedlinge Kent
40 B10 Pedmore Dudley
17 K8 Pedwell Somset
79 L2 Peebles Border
56 b4 Peel IoM
13 M3 Peene Kent
32 G9 Pegsdon Beds
73 M4 Pegswood Nthumb
23 Q9 Pegwell Kent
96 G3 Peinchorran Highld
104 F10 Peinlich Highld
34 G12 Peldon Essex
40 D6 Pelsall Wsall
73 M9 Pelton Dur
4 F8 Pelynt Cnwll
26 D8 Pemberton Carmth
57 K7 Pemberton Wigan
25 P8 Pembrey Carmth
38 H9 Pembridge Herefs
24 H8 Pembroke Pembks
24 G7 Pembroke Dock Pembks
24 E5 Pembrokeshire Coast National Park Pembks
12 D2 Pembury Kent
28 F6 Penallt Mons
25 K8 Penally Pembks
28 G3 Penalt Herefs
16 G2 Penarth V Glam
37 L4 Pen-bont Rhydybeddau Cerdgn
36 E9 Penbryn Cerdgn
25 Q2 Pencader Carmth
87 J8 Pencaitland E Loth
54 D6 Pencarnisiog IoA
37 J10 Pencarreg Carmth
27 M4 Pencelli Powys
26 D9 Penclawdd Swans
27 K11 Pencoed Brdgnd
39 L10 Pencombe Herefs
28 G5 Pencraig Herefs
48 B9 Pencraig Powys
2 B8 Pendeen Cnwll
27 K7 Penderyn Rhondd
25 L7 Pendine Carmth
57 P8 Pendlebury Salfd
57 N2 Pendleton Lancs
29 K3 Pendock Worcs
4 C4 Pendoggett Cnwll
7 M1 Pendomer Somset
16 E2 Pendoylan V Glam
47 M10 Penegoes Powys
25 J4 Pen-ffordd Pembks
27 N8 Pengam Caerph
27 P12 Pengam Cardif
21 M8 Penge Gt Lon
4 D4 Pengelly Cnwll
3 M6 Pengrugla Cnwll
2 H5 Penhallow Cnwll
2 G8 Penhalvean Cnwll
18 H3 Penhill Swindn
28 E10 Penhow Newpt
86 F9 Penicuik Mdloth
96 F2 Penifiler Highld
75 L7 Peninver Ag & B
50 G1 Penistone Barns
76 D10 Penkill S Ayrs
40 B5 Penkridge Staffs
14 D11 Penlean Cnwll
48 H7 Penley Wrexhm
16 C2 Penllyn V Glam
55 L10 Penmachno Conwy
27 P8 Penmaen Caerph
26 D10 Penmaen Swans
55 K6 Penmaenmawr Conwy
47 L7 Penmaenpool Gwynd
16 E3 Penmark V Glam
47 J3 Penmorfa Gwynd
54 G6 Penmynydd IoA
20 E5 Penn Bucks
47 L10 Pennal Gwynd
102 H3 Pennan Abers
47 P10 Pennant Powys
38 G3 Pennerley Shrops
58 C7 Pennines
62 F6 Pennington Cumb
27 M4 Penorth Powys
20 E4 Penn Street Bucks
62 F5 Penny Bridge Cumb
89 L10 Pennycross Ag & B
89 L10 Pennyghael Ag & B
76 E8 Pennyglen S Ayrs
15 P9 Pennymoor Devon
36 D10 Penparc Cerdgn
28 C7 Penperlleni Mons
4 E8 Penpoll Cnwll
2 F7 Penponds Cnwll
78 D9 Penpont D & G
36 D11 Pen-rhiw Pembks
27 M8 Penrhiwceiber Rhondd
26 G6 Pen Rhiwfawr Neath
36 F11 Penrhiwllan Cerdgn
36 F10 Penrhiw-pal Cerdgn
46 F5 Penrhos Gwynd
28 E5 Penrhos Mons
55 M5 Penrhyn Bay Conwy
54 H7 Penrhyn Castle Gwynd
47 K4 Penrhyndeudraeth Gwynd
26 C10 Penrice Swans
75 N4 Penrioch N Ayrs
71 Q9 Penrith Cumb
3 K2 Penrose Cnwll
71 N9 Penruddock Cumb
2 H8 Penryn Cnwll
25 P5 Pensarn Carmth
55 P6 Pensarn Conwy
39 N8 Pensax Worcs
17 R9 Penselwood Somset
17 N4 Pensford BaNES
30 C5 Pensham Worcs
73 N9 Penshaw Sundld
11 Q2 Penshurst Kent
4 G6 Pensilva Cnwll
3 M6 Pentewan Cnwll
54 H8 Pentir Gwynd
2 H4 Pentire Cnwll
34 D7 Pentlow Essex
44 C7 Pentney Norfk
79 P12 Pentonbridge Cumb
19 K10 Penton Mewsey Hants
54 G6 Pentraeth IoA
27 K9 Pentre Rhondd
48 G11 Pentre Shrops
27 M7 Pentrebach Myr Td
27 J3 Pentre-bach Powys
54 F7 Pentre Berw IoA
48 D5 Pentre-celyn Denbgs
47 P9 Pentre-celyn Powys
26 F9 Pentre-chwyth Swans
25 P2 Pentre-cwrt Carmth
48 E6 Pentredwr Denbgs
47 J4 Pentrefelin Gwynd
55 M10 Pentrefoelas Conwy
36 F9 Pentregat Cerdgn
26 E5 Pentre-Gwenlais Carmth
38 G6 Pentre Hodrey Shrops
48 C3 Pentre Llanrhaeadr Denbgs
16 C2 Pentre Meyrick V Glam
55 M8 Pentre-tafarn-y-fedw Conwy
51 J9 Pentrich Derbys
8 F4 Pentridge Hill Dorset
28 F7 Pen-twyn Mons
27 P9 Pentwynmaur Caerph
27 M11 Pentyrch Cardif
3 M5 Penwithick Cnwll
26 E4 Penybanc Carmth
38 C8 Penybont Powys
48 E10 Pen-y-bont Powys
48 C9 Pen-y-bont-fawr Powys
36 C11 Pen-y-bryn Pembks
48 F6 Penycae Wrexhm
28 E7 Pen-y-clawdd Mons
27 M10 Pen-y-coedcae Rhondd
24 E4 Pen-y-cwn Pembks
48 D2 Pen-y-felin Flints
48 F3 Penyffordd Flints
48 C10 Pen-y-Garnedd Powys
46 C5 Pen-y-graig Gwynd
27 L10 Penygraig Rhondd
26 D6 Penygroes Carmth
54 F10 Penygroes Gwynd
54 F4 Penysarn IoA
48 E5 Pen-y-stryt Denbgs
27 K7 Penywaun Rhondd
2 D9 Penzance Cnwll
2 D9 Penzance Heliport Cnwll
30 C4 Peopleton Worcs
49 L9 Peplow Shrops
76 F4 Perceton N Ayrs
103 K3 Percyhorner Abers
19 J10 Perham Down Wilts
16 C7 Periton Somset
21 J6 Perivale Gt Lon
6 D5 Perkins Village Devon
51 N6 Perlethorpe Notts
2 H7 Perranarworthal Cnwll
2 H5 Perranporth Cnwll
2 D9 Perranuthnoe Cnwll
2 H7 Perranwell Cnwll
2 H5 Perranzabuloe Cnwll
40 E8 Perry Barr Birm
18 E3 Perry Green Wilts
49 P9 Pershall Staffs
30 C5 Pershore Worcs
32 F4 Pertenhall Beds
92 G10 Perth P & K
48 G8 Perthy Shrops
28 H2 Perton Herefs
39 Q3 Perton Staffs
42 H9 Peterborough C Pete
28 D2 Peterchurch Herefs
95 N2 Peterculter C Aber
103 M6 Peterhead Abers
73 Q11 Peterlee Dur
10 C5 Petersfield Hants
32 G11 Peter's Green Herts
21 J8 Petersham Gt Lon
14 H9 Peters Marland Devon
28 B11 Peterstone Wentlooge Newpt
16 E2 Peterston-super-Ely V Glam
28 G4 Peterstow Herefs
5 K5 Peter Tavy Devon
23 L12 Petham Kent
4 G3 Petherwin Gate Cnwll
15 J9 Petrockstow Devon
12 G7 Pett E Susx
35 J5 Pettaugh Suffk
93 M7 Petterden Angus
78 F1 Pettinain S Lans
35 L6 Pettistree Suffk
16 D10 Petton Devon
21 N9 Petts Wood Gt Lon
86 F5 Pettycur Fife
103 J9 Pettymuk Abers
10 F6 Petworth W Susx
12 D8 Pevensey E Susx
18 H8 Pewsey Wilts
30 C3 Phepson Worcs
14 E7 Philham Devon
79 N4 Philiphaugh Border

Ratcliffe on the Wreake - St Briavels 191

41 N5 Ratcliffe on the Wreake Leics
103 K3 Rathen Abers
93 L10 Rathillet Fife
63 P9 Rathmell N York
86 D7 Ratho C Edin
86 D7 Ratho Station C Edin
101 N3 Rathven Moray
31 J5 Ratley Warwks
23 N11 Ratling Kent
38 H3 Ratlinghope Shrops
110 F2 Rattar Highld
5 P7 Rattery Devon
34 F5 Rattlesden Suffk
12 C9 Ratton Village E Susx
92 H6 Rattray P & K
32 E3 Raunds Nhants
51 L2 Ravenfield Rothm
62 C3 Ravenglass Cumb
45 N10 Raveningham Norfk
67 L7 Ravenscar N York
32 F6 Ravensden Beds
51 M9 Ravenshead Notts
58 G9 Ravensthorpe Kirk
41 P12 Ravensthorpe Nhants
41 K5 Ravenstone Leics
32 C6 Ravenstone M Keyn
63 N2 Ravenstonedale Cumb
77 Q3 Ravenstruther S Lans
65 K6 Ravensworth N York
59 P9 Rawcliffe E R Yk
59 M4 Rawcliffe York
58 G6 Rawdon Leeds
22 H10 Rawling Street Kent
51 K2 Rawmarsh Rothm
22 F5 Rawreth Essex
6 G2 Rawridge Devon
57 P4 Rawtenstall Lancs
34 H8 Raydon Suffk
22 F5 Rayleigh Essex
34 C11 Rayne Essex
21 K9 Raynes Park Gt Lon
33 P4 Reach Cambs
57 P2 Read Lancs
20 B8 Reading Readg
12 H4 Reading Street Kent
23 Q9 Reading Street Kent
64 B4 Reagill Cumb
107 M4 Rearquhar Highld
41 P5 Rearsby Leics
110 A3 Reay Highld
23 N9 Reculver Kent
16 E11 Red Ball Devon
25 J7 Redberth Pembks
20 H2 Redbourn Herts
52 D4 Redbourne N Linc
28 G6 Redbrook Gloucs
49 K7 Redbrook Wrexhm
12 H3 Redbrook Street Kent
100 E6 Redburn Highld
66 E3 Redcar R & Cl
70 D3 Redcastle D & G
107 J11 Redcastle Highld
85 Q7 Redding Falk
85 Q7 Reddingmuirhead Falk
30 D1 Redditch Worcs
34 D5 Rede Suffk
45 L12 Redenhall Norfk
72 F5 Redesmouth Nthumb
95 M7 Redford Abers
93 P6 Redford Angus
10 D5 Redford W Susx
79 M6 Redfordgreen Border
92 G9 Redgorton P & K
34 H2 Redgrave Suffk
95 M2 Redhill Abers
8 G8 Red Hill Bmouth
33 J9 Redhill Herts
17 M4 Redhill N Som
21 L12 Redhill Surrey
30 F3 Red Hill Warwks
45 N12 Redisham Suffk
17 N2 Redland Bristl
111 h2 Redland Ork
35 K3 Redlingfield Suffk
35 K3 Redlingfield Green Suffk
34 B3 Red Lodge Suffk
17 Q9 Redlynch Somset
8 H3 Redlynch Wilts
39 N8 Redmarley Worcs
29 K3 Redmarley D'Abitot Gloucs
65 P4 Redmarshall S on T
42 B3 Redmile Leics
65 J8 Redmire N York
95 M6 Redmyre Abers
48 G9 Rednal Shrops
80 D7 Redpath Border
105 K8 Redpoint Highld
25 L6 Red Roses Carmth
73 M2 Red Row Nthumb
2 G7 Redruth Cnwll
92 H8 Redstone P & K
54 G5 Red Wharf Bay IoA
28 E11 Redwick Newpt
28 G10 Redwick S Glos
65 M3 Redworth Darltn
33 K9 Reed Herts
45 N9 Reedham Norfk
60 D9 Reedness E R Yk
52 E8 Reepham Lincs
44 H5 Reepham Norfk
65 J7 Reeth N York
40 H11 Reeves Green Solhll
108 A11 Reiff Highld
21 K12 Reigate Surrey
67 N11 Reighton N York
103 J10 Reisque Abers
110 G5 Reiss Highld
2 E8 Relubbus Cnwll
100 F5 Relugas Moray
20 C6 Remenham Wokham
20 C6 Remenham Hill Wokham
41 M3 Rempstone Notts
30 D11 Rendcomb Gloucs
35 M4 Rendham Suffk
35 M6 Rendlesham Suffk
84 H9 Renfrew Rens
32 F6 Renhold Beds
51 K5 Renishaw Derbys
81 P9 Rennington Nthumb
84 G7 Renton W Duns
72 B11 Renwick Cumb
45 N6 Repps Norfk
40 H3 Repton Derbys
107 L12 Resaurie Highld
3 L7 Rescassa Cnwll
89 P4 Resipole Highld
2 F7 Reskadinnick Cnwll
107 L8 Resolis Highld
26 H8 Resolven Neath
84 D2 Rest and be thankful Ag & B
87 R9 Reston Border
93 N5 Reswallie Angus
51 P5 Retford Notts
22 F4 Rettendon Essex
53 J10 Revesby Lincs
6 C3 Rewe Devon
9 M8 Rew Street IoW
35 P2 Reydon Suffk
44 G8 Reymerston Norfk
25 J7 Reynalton Pembks
26 C10 Reynoldston Swans
4 H5 Rezare Cnwll
37 M11 Rhandirmwyn Carmth
37 Q7 Rhayader Powys
106 H11 Rheindown Highld
48 E2 Rhes-y-cae Flints
48 C4 Rhewl Denbgs
48 D6 Rhewl Denbgs
108 C10 Rhicarn Highld
108 E5 Rhiconich Highld
107 L7 Rhicullen Highld
27 K7 Rhigos Rhondd
105 Q4 Rhireavach Highld
107 N3 Rhives Highld
27 N11 Rhiwbina Cardif
28 B10 Rhiwderyn Newpt
54 H8 Rhiwlas Gwynd
12 D2 Rhoden Green Kent
13 M2 Rhodes Minnis Kent
24 D4 Rhodiad-y-brenin Pembks
70 C4 Rhonehouse D & G
16 E3 Rhoose V Glam
25 P2 Rhos Carmth
26 G8 Rhos Neath
54 E4 Rhosbeirio IoA
54 C6 Rhoscolyn IoA
24 F8 Rhoscrowther Pembks
48 E2 Rhosesmor Flints
38 E11 Rhosgoch Powys
36 C11 Rhoshill Pembks
46 C5 Rhoshirwaun Gwynd
47 J9 Rhoslefain Gwynd
48 F6 Rhosllanerchrugog Wrexhm
54 F6 Rhosmeirch IoA
54 D7 Rhosneigr IoA
55 M5 Rhos-on-Sea Conwy
25 P10 Rhossili Swans
54 G9 Rhostryfan Gwynd
48 F6 Rhostyllen Wrexhm
54 F4 Rhosybol IoA
47 Q4 Rhos-y-gwaliau Gwynd
48 F7 Rhosymedre Wrexhm
84 E6 Rhu Ag & B
48 C1 Rhuallt Denbgs
83 Q8 Rhubodach Ag & B
55 Q6 Rhuddlan Denbgs
75 K3 Rhunahaorine Ag & B
47 K3 Rhyd Gwynd
25 Q4 Rhydargaeau Carmth
26 D2 Rhydcymerau Carmth
54 H10 Rhyd-Ddu Gwynd
36 F10 Rhydlewis Cerdgn
36 G10 Rhydowen Cerdgn
47 P4 Rhyd-uchaf Gwynd
46 E4 Rhyd-y-clafdy Gwynd
55 N6 Rhyd-y-foel Conwy
26 F7 Rhydyfro Neath
54 H8 Rhyd-y-groes Gwynd
37 K4 Rhyd-y pennau Cerdgn
55 Q5 Rhyl Denbgs
27 N7 Rhymney Caerph
92 H10 Rhynd P & K
101 P9 Rhynie Abers
107 P6 Rhynie Highld
39 P7 Ribbesford Worcs
57 K3 Ribbleton Lancs
57 M2 Ribchester Lancs
52 H3 Riby Lincs
59 N6 Riccall N York
79 Q9 Riccarton Border
76 G4 Riccarton E Ayrs
39 J8 Richards Castle Herefs
21 J8 Richmond Gt Lon
65 L7 Richmond N York
51 K4 Richmond Sheff
40 B4 Rickerscote Staffs
17 L4 Rickford N Som
5 P11 Rickham Devon
34 H2 Rickinghall Suffk
33 N10 Rickling Green Essex
20 G5 Rickmansworth Herts
80 C8 Riddell Border
15 K8 Riddlecombe Devon
58 E5 Riddlesden Brad
8 D9 Ridge Dorset
21 K4 Ridge Herts
8 D2 Ridge Wilts
17 M4 Ridgehill N Som
40 H8 Ridge Lane Warwks
51 K5 Ridgeway Derbys
34 C8 Ridgewell Essex
11 P6 Ridgewood E Susx
32 D9 Ridgmont Beds
72 H8 Riding Mill Nthumb
45 M4 Ridlington Norfk
42 C9 Ridlington Rutlnd
72 G4 Ridsdale Nthumb
66 E9 Rievaulx N York
66 E9 Rievaulx Abbey N York
71 L3 Rigg D & G
85 M8 Riggend N Lans
100 D5 Righoul Highld
53 L8 Rigsby Lincs
78 E2 Rigside S Lans
57 L4 Riley Green Lancs
4 G5 Rilla Mill Cnwll
67 J11 Rillington N York
63 P11 Rimington Lancs
17 N10 Rimpton Somset
61 M8 Rimswell E R Yk
24 H4 Rinaston Pembks
39 N3 Rindleford Shrops
69 Q7 Ringford D & G
45 J7 Ringland Norfk
11 N7 Ringmer E Susx
5 N10 Ringmore Devon
6 C8 Ringmore Devon
101 K6 Ringorm Moray
45 N11 Ringsfield Suffk
45 N11 Ringsfield Corner Suffk
20 F1 Ringshall Herts
34 G6 Ringshall Suffk
34 H6 Ringshall Stocks Suffk
32 E2 Ringstead Nhants
44 B3 Ringstead Norfk
8 H6 Ringwood Hants
13 Q1 Ringwould Kent
11 P7 Ripe E Susx
51 K10 Ripley Derbys
8 H7 Ripley Hants
58 H3 Ripley N York
20 G11 Ripley Surrey
9 Q3 Riplington Hants
65 N12 Ripon N York
42 F5 Rippingale Lincs
23 Q12 Ripple Kent
29 M2 Ripple Worcs
58 D9 Ripponden Calder
74 D4 Risabus Ag & B
39 K10 Risbury Herefs
34 D4 Risby Suffk
27 P9 Risca Caerph
61 K6 Rise E R Yk
42 H4 Risegate Lincs
32 F4 Riseley Beds
20 B10 Riseley Wokham
35 J3 Rishangles Suffk
57 N3 Rishton Lancs
58 D9 Rishworth Calder
41 L1 Risley Derbys
57 M9 Risley Warrtn
58 G1 Risplith N York
13 P2 River Kent
10 F5 River W Susx
107 J10 Riverford Highld
21 P11 Riverhead Kent
57 L6 Rivington Lancs
31 Q4 Roade Nhants
77 P2 Roadmeetings S Lans
77 K7 Roadside E Ayrs
110 D4 Roadside Highld
16 D8 Roadwater Somset
96 C2 Roag Highld
76 E9 Roan of Craigoch S Ayrs
27 P12 Roath Cardif
79 N6 Roberton Border
78 F3 Roberton S Lans
12 E5 Robertsbridge E Susx
58 G9 Roberttown Kirk
25 J5 Robeston Wathen Pembks
71 L2 Robgill Tower D & G
51 P2 Robin Hood Doncaster Sheffield Airport Donc
67 K6 Robin Hood's Bay N York
5 K7 Roborough Devon
15 K8 Roborough Devon
56 H10 Roby Knows
50 E11 Rocester Staffs
24 F5 Roch Pembks
58 B10 Rochdale Rochdl
3 L4 Roche Cnwll
22 E9 Rochester Medway
72 E2 Rochester Nthumb
22 G5 Rochford Essex
39 L8 Rochford Worcs
3 L1 Rock Cnwll
81 P9 Rock Nthumb
39 N7 Rock Worcs
6 D4 Rockbeare Devon
8 G4 Rockbourne Hants
71 M4 Rockcliffe Cumb
70 D5 Rockcliffe D & G
6 C9 Rockend Torbay
56 G10 Rock Ferry Wirral
107 Q6 Rockfield Highld
28 F6 Rockfield Mons
15 N3 Rockford Devon
28 H9 Rockhampton S Glos
38 F6 Rockhill Shrops
42 C10 Rockingham Nhants
44 G10 Rockland All Saints Norfk
45 M8 Rockland St Mary Norfk
44 G9 Rockland St Peter Norfk
51 Q6 Rockley Notts
18 H6 Rockley Wilts
84 D5 Rockville Ag & B
20 C6 Rockwell End Bucks
29 L7 Rodborough Gloucs
18 G4 Rodbourne Swindn
18 D4 Rodbourne Wilts
7 N6 Rodden Dorset
18 B9 Rode Somset
49 P4 Rode Heath Ches
111 c4 Rodel W Isls
49 L11 Roden Wrekin
16 D8 Rodhuish Somset
49 L11 Rodington Wrekin
49 L11 Rodington Heath Wrekin
29 K6 Rodley Gloucs
29 N8 Rodmarton Gloucs
11 N8 Rodmell E Susx
22 H10 Rodmersham Kent
22 H10 Rodmersham Green Kent
17 L6 Rodney Stoke Somset
50 G11 Rodsley Derbys
59 J2 Roecliffe N York
21 K2 Roe Green Herts
33 K9 Roe Green Herts
21 K8 Roehampton Gt Lon
11 K4 Roffey W Susx
107 M2 Rogart Highld
10 D5 Rogate W Susx
28 C10 Rogerstone Newpt
111 c4 Roghadal W Isls
28 E10 Rogiet Mons
19 Q3 Roke Oxon
73 P8 Roker Sundld
45 P7 Rollesby Norfk
41 Q7 Rolleston Leics
51 Q9 Rolleston Notts
40 G3 Rolleston Staffs
61 L5 Rolston E R Yk
12 G4 Rolvenden Kent
12 G4 Rolvenden Layne Kent
64 H3 Romaldkirk Dur
17 Q3 Roman Baths & Pump Room BaNES
65 P8 Romanby N York
86 D11 Romanno Bridge Border
15 M7 Romansleigh Devon
104 E10 Romesdal Highld
8 F5 Romford Dorset
21 P5 Romford Gt Lon
50 C3 Romiley Stockp
9 L3 Romsey Hants
39 P5 Romsley Shrops
40 C10 Romsley Worcs
83 L11 Ronachan Ag & B
72 G11 Rookhope Dur
9 N9 Rookley IoW
17 K5 Rooks Bridge Somset
16 E9 Rooks Nest Somset
65 L9 Rookwith N York
61 M7 Roos E R Yk
32 F5 Roothams Green Beds
9 Q2 Ropley Hants
9 Q2 Ropley Dean Hants
42 E4 Ropsley Lincs
103 L5 Rora Abers
38 F3 Rorrington Shrops
101 M5 Rosarie Moray
2 H5 Rose Cnwll
15 N7 Rose Ash Devon
77 N2 Rosebank S Lans
25 J3 Rosebush Pembks
66 G8 Rosedale Abbey N York
34 E10 Rose Green Essex
34 F7 Rose Green Suffk
34 F8 Rose Green Suffk
10 E9 Rose Green W Susx
106 H2 Rosehall Highld
103 J2 Rosehearty Abers
57 P3 Rose Hill Lancs
100 H2 Roseisle Moray
12 C9 Roselands E Susx
24 G7 Rosemarket Pembks
107 M10 Rosemarkie Highld
16 F12 Rosemary Lane Devon
92 H7 Rosemount P & K
3 L3 Rosenannon Cnwll
86 F9 Rosewell Mdloth
65 Q3 Roseworth S on T
71 Q11 Rosgill Cumb
96 C1 Roskhill Highld
71 M6 Rosley Cumb
86 F9 Roslin Mdloth
40 G4 Rosliston Derbys
84 E6 Rosneath Ag & B
69 P9 Ross D & G
48 G4 Rossett Wrexhm
58 H4 Rossett Green N York
51 N2 Rossington Donc
84 G8 Rossland Rens
28 H4 Ross-on-Wye Herefs
110 F7 Roster Highld
57 N11 Rostherne Ches
71 L11 Rosthwaite Cumb
50 F11 Roston Derbys
86 D5 Rosyth Fife
73 J1 Rothbury Nthumb
41 P4 Rotherby Leics
12 B4 Rotherfield E Susx
20 B7 Rotherfield Greys Oxon
20 B7 Rotherfield Peppard Oxon
51 K3 Rotherham Rothm
31 Q3 Rothersthorpe Nhants
20 B11 Rotherwick Hants
101 K5 Rothes Moray
84 B9 Rothesay Ag & B
102 G7 Rothiebrisbane Abers
102 D5 Rothiemay Moray
99 P7 Rothiemurchus Lodge Highld
102 F7 Rothienorman Abers
41 N5 Rothley Leics
102 F8 Rothmaise Abers
59 J8 Rothwell Leeds
52 G4 Rothwell Lincs
32 B1 Rothwell Nhants
94 F7 Rottal Lodge Angus
11 M9 Rottingdean Br & H
70 F11 Rottington Cumb
78 G12 Roucan D & G
44 D6 Rougham Norfk
34 E4 Rougham Green Suffk
23 L10 Rough Common Kent
101 L11 Roughpark Abers
53 J9 Roughton Lincs
45 K3 Roughton Norfk
39 N4 Roughton Shrops
22 C1 Roundbush Green Essex
7 K2 Roundham Somset
59 J6 Roundhay Leeds
18 E7 Roundway Wilts
93 L5 Roundyhill Angus
6 H5 Rousdon Devon
31 L8 Rousham Oxon
30 D4 Rous Lench Worcs
84 D10 Routenburn N Ayrs
61 J6 Routh E R Yk
63 J4 Row Cumb
79 N12 Rowanburn D & G
84 F4 Rowardennan Hotel Stirlg
84 F4 Rowardennan Lodge Stirlg
50 D3 Rowarth Derbys
17 L5 Rowberrow Somset
18 E8 Rowde Wilts
55 L7 Rowen Conwy
72 C8 Rowfoot Nthumb
34 G11 Rowhedge Essex
40 G12 Rowington Warwks
50 G6 Rowland Derbys
10 B7 Rowland's Castle Hants
73 L8 Rowland's Gill Gatesd
10 D2 Rowledge Surrey
73 J10 Rowley Dur
60 G7 Rowley E R Yk
41 J10 Rowley Green Covtry
40 C9 Rowley Regis Sandw
28 D4 Rowlstone Herefs
10 G2 Rowly Surrey
9 P7 Rowner Hants
40 D12 Rowney Green Worcs
9 L4 Rownhams Hants
70 H10 Rowrah Cumb
32 C12 Rowsham Bucks
50 G7 Rowsley Derbys
52 F11 Rowston Lincs
49 J3 Rowton Ches
49 L10 Rowton Wrekin
80 F7 Roxburgh Border
60 F10 Roxby N Linc
32 G6 Roxton Beds
22 D2 Roxwell Essex
98 C11 Roy Bridge Highld
21 N2 Roydon Essex
34 H1 Roydon Norfk
44 B5 Roydon Norfk
21 N2 Roydon Hamlet Essex
59 J11 Royston Barns
33 K8 Royston Herts
58 B11 Royton Oldham
7 c1 Rozel Jersey
48 F6 Ruabon Wrexhm
88 D6 Ruaig Ag & B
3 K7 Ruan Lanihorne Cnwll
2 G11 Ruan Major Cnwll
2 G11 Ruan Minor Cnwll
28 H5 Ruardean Gloucs
28 H5 Ruardean Hill Gloucs
28 H5 Ruardean Woodside Gloucs
40 C11 Rubery Birm
111 b6 Rubha Ban W Isls
28 E2 Ruckhall Herefs
13 K4 Ruckinge Kent
39 K3 Ruckley Shrops
66 C6 Rudby N York
73 K7 Rudchester Nthumb
41 M2 Ruddington Notts
18 C9 Rudge Somset
28 H10 Rudgeway S Glos
10 H4 Rudgwick W Susx
49 M2 Rudheath Ches
22 G3 Rudley Green Essex
18 C6 Rudloe Wilts
27 P10 Rudry Caerph
61 J1 Rudston E R Yk
50 C8 Rudyard Staffs
80 E9 Ruecastle Border
57 J6 Rufford Lancs
59 M4 Rufforth York
41 L11 Rugby Warwks
40 D4 Rugeley Staffs
16 H10 Ruishton Somset
20 H6 Ruislip Gt Lon
101 M5 Rumbach Moray
86 B3 Rumbling Bridge P & K
35 M1 Rumburgh Suffk
3 K2 Rumford Cnwll
85 Q7 Rumford Falk
27 P11 Rumney Cardif
57 K11 Runcorn Halton
10 E9 Runcton W Susx
43 P8 Runcton Holme Norfk
10 D1 Runfold Surrey
44 H8 Runhall Norfk
45 P7 Runham Norfk
16 F10 Runnington Somset
66 H4 Runswick N York
94 E8 Runtaleave Angus
22 F5 Runwell Essex
20 C8 Ruscombe Wokham
28 H2 Rushall Herefs
45 K12 Rushall Norfk
18 G9 Rushall Wilts
34 E5 Rushbrooke Suffk
39 K4 Rushbury Shrops
33 K9 Rushden Herts
32 D4 Rushden Nhants
34 F1 Rushford Norfk
23 M1 Rush Green Essex
21 P6 Rush Green Gt Lon
12 D6 Rushlake Green E Susx
45 P11 Rushmere Suffk
10 E3 Rushmoor Surrey
40 B12 Rushock Worcs
57 Q9 Rusholme Manch
49 L3 Rushton Ches
42 B12 Rushton Nhants
50 C8 Rushton Spencer Staffs
39 P10 Rushwick Worcs
65 M2 Rushyford Dur
85 K3 Ruskie Stirlg
52 F12 Ruskington Lincs
62 G5 Rusland Cumb
11 K3 Rusper W Susx
29 J6 Ruspidge Gloucs
20 B5 Russell's Water Oxon
11 K3 Russ Hill Surrey
12 C3 Rusthall Kent
10 G9 Rustington W Susx
67 K10 Ruston N York
60 H2 Ruston Parva E R Yk
67 J5 Ruswarp N York
80 E7 Rutherford Border
85 K10 Rutherglen S Lans
3 M3 Ruthernbridge Cnwll
48 D4 Ruthin Denbgs
95 Q2 Ruthrieston C Aber
101 P6 Ruthven Abers
93 K6 Ruthven Angus
99 L8 Ruthven Highld
93 K6 Ruthven House Angus
3 K4 Ruthvoes Cnwll
70 H3 Ruthwell D & G
48 H10 Ruyton-XI-Towns Shrops
72 H6 Ryal Nthumb
7 K4 Ryall Dorset
29 M1 Ryall Worcs
22 D10 Ryarsh Kent
62 G2 Rydal Cumb
9 P8 Ryde IoW
12 H6 Rye E Susx
12 H5 Rye Foreign E Susx
29 K2 Rye Street Worcs
42 E7 Ryhall Rutlnd
59 J10 Ryhill Wakefd
73 P9 Ryhope Sundld
52 E7 Ryland Lincs
41 M1 Rylands Notts
58 C3 Rylstone N York
7 N1 Ryme Intrinseca Dorset
59 M6 Ryther N York
73 K7 Ryton Gatesd
39 N2 Ryton Shrops
41 J11 Ryton-on-Dunsmore Warwks

S

57 P2 Sabden Lancs
33 K11 Sacombe Herts
73 M10 Sacriston Dur
65 N4 Sadberge Darltn
75 L6 Saddell Ag & B
41 P8 Saddington Leics
43 P7 Saddle Bow Norfk
11 L7 Saddlescombe W Susx
33 N8 Saffron Walden Essex
25 J7 Sageston Pembks
44 E9 Saham Hills Norfk
44 E9 Saham Toney Norfk
49 J3 Saighton Ches
81 J1 St Abbs Border
87 M9 St Agnes Border
2 G5 St Agnes Cnwll
21 J2 St Albans Herts
3 J5 St Allen Cnwll
6 b2 St Andrew Guern
93 N11 St Andrews Fife
93 N11 St Andrew's Botanic Gardens Fife
16 F2 St Andrew's Major V Glam
7 L4 St Andrews Well Dorset
56 G3 St Anne's Lancs
78 H9 St Ann's D & G
5 J6 St Ann's Chapel Cnwll
5 N10 St Ann's Chapel Devon
2 H10 St Anthony Cnwll
12 D9 St Anthony's Hill E Susx
28 F9 St Arvans Mons
48 B1 St Asaph Denbgs
16 D3 St Athan V Glam
7 b2 St Aubin Jersey
3 M5 St Austell Cnwll
70 F12 St Bees Cumb
3 N5 St Blazey Cnwll
80 D7 St Boswells Border
7 a2 St Brelade Jersey
7 a2 St Brelade's Bay Jersey
3 L2 St Breock Cnwll
4 D5 St Breward Cnwll
28 G7 St Briavels Gloucs

U